ALEXANDER OF MACEDON

356–323 B.C.

A HISTORICAL BIOGRAPHY

PETER GREEN

UNIVERSITY OF CALIFORNIA PRESS

Berkeley   Los Angeles   Oxford

Original version published as *Alexander the Great* by Weidenfeld & Nicolson, 1970.
This edition, revised and enlarged, first published in Pelican Books, 1974.

University of California Press
Berkeley and Los Angeles, California

University of California Press, Ltd.
Oxford, England

© 1991 by
Peter Green
First California Paperback Printing 1992

Library of Congress Cataloging-in-Publication Data

Green, Peter, 1924–
    Alexander of Macedon, 356–323 B.C. : a historical biography /
Peter Green.
        p.   cm.—(Hellenistic culture and society : 11)
    Reprint. Originally published: Harmondsworth : Penguin, 1974.
    Includes bibliographical references and index.
    ISBN 0-520-07165-4 (cloth). — ISBN 0-520-07166-2 (paper)
        1. Alexander, the Great, 356–323 B.C.   2. Greece—History—
Macedonian Expansion, 359–323 B.C.   3. Generals—Greece—Biography.
4. Greece—Kings and rulers—Biography   I. Title. II. Series.
DF234.G68   1991
938'.07'092—dc20   91–7292
[B]   CIP

Printed in the United States of America

9   8   7   6   5   4   3   2   1

Set in Monotype Baskerville.

For Ernst Badian

il miglior fabbro

— ποῦ εἶναι ὁ Μεγαλέξανδρος;
— ὁ Μεγαλέξανδρος ζεῖ καὶ βασιλεύει
— Where is Great Alexander?
— Great Alexander lives and reigns

> – Medieval Greek proverb

Ἡδέως ἂν πρὸς ὀλίγον ἀνεβίουν, ὦ Ὀνεσίκριτε, ἀποθανὼν ὡς μάθοιμι ὅπως ταῦτα οἱ ἄνθρωποι τότε ἀναγιγνώσκουν. εἰ δὲ νῦν αὐτὰ ἐπαινοῦσι καὶ ἀσπάζονται, μὴ θαυμάσῃς· οἴονται γὰρ οὐ μικρῷ τινι τῷ δελέατι τούτῳ ἀνασπάσειν ἕκαστος τὴν παρ'ἡμῶν εὔνοιαν.

I should be glad, Onesicritus, to come back to life for a little while after my death to discover how men read these present events then. If now they praise and welcome them do not be surprised; they think, every one of them, that this is a fine bait to catch my goodwill.

> – Alexander the Great, quoted by Lucian in
> c. 40 of his essay *How to Write History*

Contents

Preface to the 1991 Reprint

It is now over twenty-two years since I packed up my working notes and basic texts—Arrian, Plutarch, Diodorus, Quintus Curtius Rufus, Justin—and retreated to the then little-known Greek island of Astypálaia to hammer out the first draft of *Alexander of Macedon*. I had immersed myself in Alexander scholarship, English, American, French, German, Italian, modern Greek (Alexander as patriotic ikon, not least under the Colonels, deserves a separate monograph), till I felt near drowning-point. I needed to get away, clear my head, re-establish a sense of perspective and try to see Alexander plain, free from that distracting chorus of conflicting ideological claims. It was, of course, a vain endeavor. Propaganda (some of it self-generated) surrounded the King all his life, and mythification took over the moment he was dead—had, indeed, been developing at an alarming rate during the last few years of his life.

Nevertheless, the circumstances in which I first articulated my narrative left their mark on the book, just as not dissimilar restrictions did on A.H.M. Jones's brilliant and idiosyncratic study of Sparta (1967). In particular, I was forced to focus my attention, far more closely than I might otherwise have done, on the surviving sources *as they stood* (even the earliest, Diodorus, being some three centuries after the events he described), rather than embarking on a complicated exercise in historiographical *Quellenforschung* designed to extrapolate and evaluate those earlier authors on which our extant tradition drew.

As a working method, this had advantages as well as drawbacks. It meant, among other things, that judgments were frequently based on common sense rather than on scholarly argument or consensus; but I did not think then, nor looking back, do I think today, that this was necessarily a bad thing. The scholarship in which I had been immersed —above all, the powerful minimalist arguments then being advanced by Ernst Badian—could not fail (as subsequent reviewers pointed out) to leave its mark on me; and, living in Greece, I was more conscious than most of the exciting turn Macedonian studies were taking. But to a great extent *Alexander of Macedon* remained a solitary exercise in textually based historiography, reinforced by the kind of familiarity with Greek landscape, climate, and *mores* that only long residence can bring. These essential characteristics were not fundamentally altered by the very considerable revisions I undertook, between 1971 and 1973, prior to the publication of the present text: revisions carried out in a university department, with full access to academic literature, and designed to provide the scaffolding of scholarly backing and debate that my original draft had very often bypassed.

The result was an interesting hybrid, which, for several reasons unconnected with literature or history (copyright tangles, disagreements among publishers), saw the light of day only as a fat paperback in the U.K., and thereafter— since this one edition went out of print comparatively soon —existed for some years in a kind of ghostly academic limbo, kept just clear of the iniquity of oblivion by a few scholars who were kind enough to find merit in my investigation, and went on referring to it and recommending it to their students. Unfortunately, running down copies became an increasingly hard business. During the last sixteen years or so the idea of a reprint was raised more than once, but only now has the idea finally been brought to fruition, at a point when, some might argue, it is effectively too late.

Because of the long time-lapse, and the progress of Alexander scholarship since 1974, my thoughts have turned increasingly during the last year or two to the idea of a fairly radically revised second edition; and the University of California Press has now agreed to publish such a text when I have prepared it. The task is an extensive one, and will in all likelihood—granted my other responsibilities—take three or four years to complete.

Much has been accomplished, in many fields, of which I need to take cognizance. The history of Macedonia (to take the most obvious example) has been advanced to a remarkable degree by the labours of Borza, Cawkwell, Errington, Griffith, Hammond, Walbank, and the famous (if still ambiguous) archaeological discoveries made by Andronikos in the Great Tumulus of Vergina (now known to be ancient Aegae, as Hammond had already predicted). New study of Persian and other Oriental archives by scholars such as Heleen Sancisi-Weerdenburg, Susan Sherwin-White and Amélie Kuhrt has shed fresh light on Alexander's Eastern relations and imperial administration. Inscriptions have been reexamined, coin-issues studied, topography revised; the whole vast problem of military logistics has been put on a fresh footing by my one-time student Don Engels. Any revision will need to take this rich harvest, and more, into account, and I fully intend to do so.

Yet I also think a strong case can be made for reissuing the 1974 edition—never actually published in the U.S.A.— to meet (better late than never) a steady, on-going demand, in colleges and universities above all, while the revised and updated text is in process of preparation. It is of course true that my study as it stands lacks the extra dimension that nearly two decades of fruitful new scholarship (including, incredible though this may sound, the first critical commentary on Arrian ever written) both can and should provide. The usual small but irritating crop of misprints and verbal or factual slips (e.g., "Lyceum" for "Academy" on p. 53 and "headquarters" for "headwaters" on p. 405) still survives to provide satisfying pabulum for particularist critics.

But a recent re-reading of the entire text—accompanied by the kind of fierce and by no means always friendly scrutiny that a seminar of ambitious graduate students can be relied on to provide—reassured me in unexpected ways. Here and there, it is true (e.g., in the matter of Philotas: conspiracy *by* or *against?*), I have been forced to rethink the issue. Some puzzles (e.g., the first flight of Harpalus) are as baffling as ever. In one major instance, my Appendix on the battle of the Granicus, new studies have convinced me that I was flat wrong. But overall I have found no arguments to convince me that my basic analysis in 1968 of Alexander's character, genius, or motivation was mistaken, and a great deal to support the conclusions—unpalatable to believers in Macedonian rulers as pillars of *Völkerrecht* and government by law no less than to adventure-struck romantic idealists still clinging wistfully to Tarn's vision of the Brotherhood of Man—that were forced upon me by close study of the ancient sources. It is not without significance, besides, that the Greek island where I embarked on my solitary task happened to be one used by the Colonels as a dumping-ground for royalist officers and thinkers with minds of their own. *Sois mon frère ou je te tue* was a revolutionary joke that I saw being worked out in my daily life at the same time as I was watching Alexander play it against the Thebans, the Greeks of Asia Minor, the defenders of Tyre or Sangala. Looking back, I can see clearly that contemporary events helped in shaping my judgment, just as Syme's verdict on Augustus, conceived during the Twenties at the American Academy in Rome, could not fail to be influenced by the activities of Mussolini's fascists.

There is a tendency among academics to decry this kind of adventitious personal experience as disruptive of objective and dispassionate historiography. I disagree. Thucydides and Polybius knew very well that to write history one must be, however marginally, involved in it. Gibbon saw that the captain of the Hampshire grenadiers had not been useless to the historian of the Roman empire. The Colonels, as it happened, promoted Alexander as a great Greek hero, especially to army recruits: the Greeks of the fourth century B.C., to whom Alexander was a half-Macedonian, half-Epirote barbarian conqueror, would have found this metamorphosis as ironic as I did.

Furthermore, a decade spent investigating the Hellenistic age, not least the imperial habits of Alexander's successors (Diadochoi), the hard-bitten marshals to whom fell the division of the spoils, has sharply reinforced my conviction that Alexander himself was not only the most brilliant (and ambitious) field-commander in history, but also supremely indifferent to all those administrative excellences and idealistic yearnings foisted upon him by later generations, especially those who found the conqueror, *tout court*, a little hard upon their liberal sensibilities. I am pretty sure that my revised second edition will not substantially alter this verdict. After all, in the broadest sense (however we may quibble over details) the *facts* of Alexander's life are not really in dispute. It is, ultimately, our interpretation of them that matters. On that basis I am very happy to see the present text, with all its faults, given a fresh lease of life.

The University of Texas at Austin   Peter Green
October 1990

Preface and Acknowledgements

THE genesis of this book perhaps calls for a word of explanation. I had long been interested in Alexander when, six years ago, Weidenfeld & Nicolson invited me to write a short biography of him. The research I undertook for this task led me into a more extensive treatment of the subject than either I or my publishers had anticipated. My original draft proved far too long; I reduced it, removed the documentation, and produced a second version. This in turn was cut and edited, on a massive scale, to achieve the text finally published in 1970 as *Alexander the Great*. For the present work I have returned to my original first draft as a basis for revision, and my final text is between three and four times the length of the earlier published version. The core of the original concept survives in the broad arrangement by chapters; but the text has been so thoroughly revised and expanded that it would take a philosopher to determine whether the two books are in any sense one and the same work. Nor, indeed, have I simply reissued my first draft and restored that draft's documentation. At countless points I have revised my opinions (sometimes as a result of cogent criticism, both public and private, sometimes after reading new books and articles published since 1968–9) and incorporated such revisions in the final text as here presented.

I am greatly indebted to my fellow-workers in the field of Alexander studies: this time I am happy to be able to acknowledge the many and varied benefits I have derived from their scholarly publications, *privatim et seriatim*, in my notes and references. Once again, however, I cannot forbear to mention the name, *honoris causa*, of Professor Ernst Badian, the universally acknowledged *doyen* of researchers in this field, and among the most distinguished of living ancient historians, who has, as always, given most generously of his time and unrivalled knowledge whenever I have called upon him for advice. On any occasion that I find myself differing from his views it is always with a sense of profound temerity. Thus it is no mere polite formula to emphasize that neither he nor any other scholar mentioned here should be held responsible for the views expressed in these pages, much less for the book's many and inevitable shortcomings. Its dedication – imperfections and all – is a less than adequate *quid pro quo* for many kindnesses and much illumination.

The researching and writing of this final draft were carried out during my year of residence in the University of Texas as Visiting Professor of Classics for 1971–2, in conditions as nearly ideal as any scholar is likely to find this side of Paradise. My grateful thanks go to all those colleagues in the Department of Classics who did so much, and in so many ways, to make my stay a happy one. During the autumn of 1971 I conducted a graduate seminar in Alexander studies from which, it is safe to say, I learnt at least as much as my students did; I am grateful to them for many highly perceptive suggestions, some of which have found their way, with due acknowledgement, into my text. The Librarian of the Battle Collection, Mrs Anne Vanderhoof, has given me unstinted help – far beyond the call of duty – not only during this particular project, but over every aspect of my research work.

Lastly, I would like to express my thanks to Professor Eugene N. Borza, who not only reviewed my original short text far more kindly than it deserved, but also, by inviting me to address the Annual Conference of American Ancient Historians, ensured, indirectly, that my Appendix on 'Propaganda at the Granicus' got at least some of its faults and errors removed before publication. Here, once again, I am deeply indebted to Professor Badian, whose searching criticisms of the original paper (first made on the occasion of its delivery, and afterwards augmented by discussion and correspondence) proved him, as so often, the ideal critic: sympathetic, imaginative, but totally impervious to non-sense.

The translation of Arrian used here (often with variations of my own) is that by the late Aubrey de Selincourt (Penguin Classics), now once more available in a revised edition, with new introduction and notes, by that excellent scholar Dr J. R. Hamilton. Diodorus is quoted (again with occasional modifications) in the Loeb version by the late Professor C. Bradford Welles (published by Heinemann); Plutarch's *Life* of Alexander is, similarly, the Loeb version, by Bernadotte Perrin (Heinemann). The quotation from Euripides' *Andromache* on p. 364 is translated by Mr John Frederick Nims in the *Complete Greek Tragedies* series published by the University of Chicago Press; that from his *Bacchae*, on p. 377, is translated by Professor William Arrowsmith, in the same series.

Department of Classics,   PETER GREEN
The University of Texas at Austin,
March 1972

List of Maps and Battle Plans

Key to Abbreviations

[] indicates alternative forms of abbreviation

Acta Class.:	*Acta Classica.* Proceedings of the Classical Association of South Africa. Cape Town, Balkema.
Aelian:	Claudius Aelianus (*c.* A.D. 170–235). *VH: Varia Historia* *HA: Historia Animalium*
Aeschin.:	Aeschines, Athenian orator (*c.* 397–*c.* 322 B.C.) *De Fals. Leg.*: *De Falsa Legatione* *In Ctesiph.*: *In Ctesiphontem*
AHR:	*American Historical Review.* New York, Macmillan.
AJA:	*American Journal of Archaeology.* Princeton, 231 McCormick Hall.
AJPh:	*American Journal of Philology.* Baltimore, Johns Hopkins Press.
AM:	*Ancient Macedonia.* Papers read at the First International Symposium held in Thessaloniki, 26–9 August 1968. Ed. Basil Laourdas and Ch.Makaronas. Institute for Balkan Studies, Thessaloniki, 1970.
Andoc.:	Andocides, Athenian orator (*c.* 440–*c.* 390 B.C.).
Ann. Serv. Ant. Egypt.:	*Annales du Service des Antiquités d'Egypte.* Cairo, Impr. de l'Inst. Français d'Archéol. Orientale.
ANSMusN:	*The American Numismatic Society Museum Notes.* New York, Broadway between 155th and 156th Streets.
A[nt]. C[l].:	*L'Antiquité Classique.* Louvain, Vlamingenstraat 83.
A[nth]. P[al].:	*Anthologia Palatina, Planudea.*
Ant. Kunst.:	*Antike Kunst.* Hrsg. von der Vereinigung der Freunde antiker Kunst in Basel. Olten, Urs Graf-Verlag.

Appian: Appianos of Alexandria, Greek historian (first–second century A.D.).
BC: *Bella Civilia*
Syr: *Syriaké* [*Syrian Wars*]

Aristoph.:   Aristophanes, Athenian comic playwright (?445–?385 B.C.).
Thesmoph.: *Thesmophoriazusae.*

Arist.:   Aristotle of Stagira, Greek philosopher (384–322 B.C.).
Eth. Eud.: *Ethica Eudemia* [*Eudemian Ethics*].
Pol.: *Politica* [*Politics*].
Rhet.: *Rhetorica.*

Arrian: Aulus (or Lucius) Flavius Arrianus Xenophon, Greek historian (second century A.D.).

Athen.:   Athenaeus of Naucratis (*fl. c.* A.D. 200).

Athenaeum: *Athenaeum.* Studi periodici di Letteratura e Storia dell 'Antichità. Pavia, Università.

Aul. Gell.:   Aulus Gellius, Roman author (*c.* A.D. 130–*c.* 180).
NA: *Noctes Atticae.*

Badian, *Stud. Ehrenb.*:   *Ancient Society and Institutions.* Studies presented to Victor Ehrenberg on his 75th birthday. Ed. E. Badian. Oxford, 1966.

Badian, *Stud. GRHist.*:   E. Badian, *Studies in Greek and Roman History.* Oxford, 1964.

Bellinger: A. R. Bellinger, *Essays on the Coinage of Alexander the Great* (Numismatic Studies 11). New York, 1963.

Beloch, *GG* :   K. J. Beloch, *Griechische Geschichte.* 2nd edn. Vols. III i–ii, IV i. Leipzig–Berlin, 1922–5.

Berve, *APG*:   H. Berve, *Das Alexanderreich auf prosopographischer Grundlage.* 2 vols. Munich, 1926.

Bickerman, *Chronology* :   E. J. Bickerman, *Chronology of the Ancient World.* London, 1968.

Bieber, [*Portraits*]:   M. Bieber, *Alexander the Great in Greek and Roman Art.* Chicago, 1964.

B MusB: *Bulletin* of the Museum of Fine Arts, Boston.

Bonner Jahrb.:   *Bonner Jahrbücher des Rheinischen Landesmuseums in Bonn und des Vereins von Altertumsfreunden im Rheinlande.*

Bull. Class. Lett. Acad. R. Belg.:   *Bulletin de la Classe des Lettres de l'Académie Royal de Belgique.* Brussels.

B[*ull*]. *C*[*orr*]. *H*[*ell*].:   *Bulletin de Correspondance Hellénique.* Paris.

Bull. Inst. Egypt.:   *Bulletin de l'Institut Egyptien.* Cairo.

Bull. Inst. Franç. d'Arch.
Orient.:
    Bulletin de *l'Institut français d'Archéologie Orientale.* Cairo.

B[ull]. V[er.] A[nt.] B[eschaving]:
    Bulletin van de Vereeniging tot Bevordering der Kennis van de Antieke Beschaving. Leiden, Brill.

Burn, [*AG*]:
    A. R. Burn, *Alexander the Great and the Hellenistic World.* 2nd rev. edn, New York, 1962.

CAH:
    The *Cambridge Ancient History.* Cambridge, 1923–39.

Cary, *GB*:
    M. Cary, *The Geographic Background of Greek and Roman History.* Oxford, 1949.

Cic[ero]:
    Marcus Tullius Cicero, Roman scholar and orator (106–43 B.C.).
    Pro Arch.: *Pro Archia*
    Tusc. Disp.: *Tusculanae Disputationes*

Classical Folia:
    Classical Folia. Studies in the Christian perpetuation of the Classics. New York.

Clem. Alex.:
    Clement of Alexandria (Titus Flavius Clemens Alexandrinus) (*c.* A.D. 150–*c.* 215)
    Protrept.: *Protrepticus*

Comp. Rend. Acad. Inscr.:
    Comptes rendus de l'Académie des Inscriptions et Belles-Lettres. Paris.

CPh:
    Classical Philology. Chicago, University of Chicago Press.

CQ:
    Classical Quarterly. Oxford University Press.

CW:
    The Classical World. Bethlehem, Pa.

Deinarch.:
    Deinarchus, Greek orator (*c.* 360–*c.* 290 B.C.).
    In Demosth.: *In Demosthenem*
    In Philocl.: *In Philoclem*

Demades:
    Demades, Athenian politician (*fl.* 350–319 B.C.).
    Twelve Years: Ὑπὲρ τῆς δωδεκετείας', attributed to Demades but almost certainly not by him.

Demetr.:
    Demetrius, Greek literary critic (late Hellenistic or Roman period).
    De Eloc.: *De Elocutione* [*On Style*]

Demosth.:
    Demosthenes, Athenian orator (384–322 B.C.).
    C. Aristocr.: *Contra Aristocratem*
    Chers.: *De Chersoneso*
    De Cor.: *De Corona*
    Halonn.: *De Halonneso*
    In Leptin.: *In Leptinem*
    Olynth.: *Olynthiaca*
    Phil.: *Philippica*

Dio Chrys.:	Dio Cocceianus or Chrysostomus, Greek orator and philosopher (*c.* A.D. 40–*c.* 115).
Diod.:	Diodorus Siculus of Agyrium, Greek historian (first century B.C.).
D[*iog.*] L[*aert.*]:	Diogenes Laertius, Greek biographer (? third century A.D.).
Dion. Hal.:	Dionysius of Halicarnassus, Greek rhetorician and antiquarian (first century B.C.–first century A.D.).
	De Comp. Verb.: *De Compositione Verborum*
Diss. Abstracts:	*Dissertation Abstracts. A guide to Dissertations and Monographs available in microfilm.* Ann Arbor, Michigan.
Eddy:	S. K. Eddy, *The King is Dead. Studies in the Near Eastern Resistance to Hellenism, 334–331* B.C. Lincoln, Nebraska, 1961.
Eur.:	Euripides, Athenian tragic playwright (*c.* 485–406 B.C.).
	Androm.: *Andromache*
	Hipp.: *Hippolytus*
	IA: *Iphigeneia at Aulis*
Eustath.:	Eustathius, Metropolitan of Thessalonica (d. *c.* A.D. 1194).
Festschr.:	*Festschrift.*
FGrH:	F. Jacoby, *Fragmente der griechischen Historiker,* 1923– Leiden, Brill.
fl.:	*floruit.*
Front.:	Sextus Julius Frontinus, Roman consul and technical writer (*c.* A.D. 30–104).
	Strat.: *Strategemata*
Fuller:	J. F. C. Fuller, *The Generalship of Alexander the Great.* London, 1958.
F[*orsch.*] *und* F[*ortschr.*]	*Forschungen und Fortschritte.* Berlin, Akademie-Verlag.
Geogr. Journ.:	The *Geographical Journal.* London, Geographic Society.
GR:	*Greece and Rome.* Oxford, Clarendon Press.
GRByS:	*Greek, Roman and Byzantine Studies.* Durham, N.C., Duke University.
Grote, *HG*:	G. Grote, *A History of Greece.* Rev. edn, 12 vols. London, 1888.
Hamilton, *PA*:	J. R. Hamilton, *Plutarch: Alexander.* A Commentary. Oxford, 1968.
Hammond, *HG*:	N. G. L. Hammond, *A History of Greece.* 2nd edn. Oxford, 1967.

Hammond, *Epirus*:	N. G. L. Hammond, *Epirus. The geography, the ancient remains, the history and topography of Epirus and adjacent areas.* Oxford, 1967.
Harv. Theol. Rev.:	*Harvard Theological Review.* Cambridge, Mass., Harvard University Press.
Harv. Stud. [Class. Phil.]:	*Harvard Studies in Classical Philology.* Cambridge, Mass. Harvard University Press.
Hdt:	Herodotus of Halicarnassus, Greek historian (*c.* 485–*c.* 425 B.C.).
Head-Hill-Walker, *Guide*:	*A Guide to the Principal Coins of the Greeks from circ. 700 B.C. to A.D. 270.* Based on the work of B. V. Head, rev. G. F. Hill, John Walker. London, British Museum, 1959.
Hellenica.:	Ἑλληνικά. Φιλολ., ἱστορ. καὶ λαογρ. Περιοδικὸν Σύγγραμμα τῆς Εταιρείας Μακεδονικῶν Σπουδῶν. Thessalonica.
Hermes:	Hermes. Zeitschrift für klassische Philologie. Wiesbaden.
Hesperia:	*Hesperia.* Journal of the American School of Classical Studies at Athens. Athens American School.
Historia:	*Historia.* Wiesbaden.
Hist. Rel.:	*History of Religions.* Chicago, University of Chicago Press.
Hist. Today:	*History Today.* A monthly magazine. London, Bracken House.
Hist. Zeitschr.:	*Historische Zeitschrift.* Munich, Oldenbourg.
Hogarth:	D. G. Hogarth, *Philip and Alexander of Macedon.* New York, 1897.
Homer, *Il.*:	Homer, The *Iliad.*
Homer, *Od.*:	Homer, The *Odyssey.*
Horace:	Quintus Horatius Flaccus, Roman poet (65–8 B.C.).
	Epp.: *Epistulae*
	AP: *Ars Poetica*
Hypereides:	Hypereides, Athenian orator (389–322 B.C.).
	Eux.: *pro Euxenippo*
IG:	*Inscriptiones Graecae*, 1873–
	ii^2: *Editio minor* of vols. ii and iii, ed. J. Kirchner, 1913–35.
Inform. Hist.:	*L'Information Historique*, Paris.
Isocr.:	Isocrates, Athenian orator and pamphleteer (436–338 B.C.).
	Epist.: *Epistulae* [Letters]

Jahr. Oest. Arch. Inst.:

JBerlM:
JHS:
JNG:

Josephus:

Journ. Austral.
Univ. Lang. Assoc.:
Jul. Val.:

Justin:

Klio:

Lucian:

Lycurg.:

Lydus:

MAO:

MDAI(A):

MDAI(R):

Milns:

Ep. Phil.: *Epistulae Philippo* [Letters I and II to Philip]
Panath.: *Panathenaicus*
Paneg.: *Panegyricus*
Phil.: *Philippus*
Jahreshefte des Oesterreichischen Archäologischen Instituts. Vienna.
Jahrbuch der Berliner Museen. Berlin.
Journal of Hellenic Studies. London.
Jahrbuch für Numismatik und Geldgeschichte. Kallmünz.
Flavius Josephus, Romanized Jewish historian (first century A.D.).
Ant. Jud.: *Antiquitates Judaicae*
Journal of the Australasian Universities Languages Association.
Julius Valerius Alexander Polemius, Latin author (third–fourth century A.D.).
Marcus Junianus Justinus, Latin epitomator (? third century A.D.).
Klio. Beiträge zur alten Geschichte. Berlin, Akademie-Verlag.
Lucianus of Samosata, Aramaic-Greek writer (*c*. A.D. 120–*c*. 180).
Cal.: *Calumniae non temere credendum*
Quom. Hist. Conscr.: *Quomodo historia conscribenda sit*
Rhet. Praec.: *Rhetorum Praeceptor*
Lycurgus, Athenian statesman and orator (*c*. 390–*c*. 325/4 B.C.).
In Leocr.: *In Leocratem*
Ioannes Laurentius Lydus, Greek writer (sixth century, A.D.).
De Mens.: *De Mensibus*
Minor Attic Orators. Vol. I: Antiphon, Andocides, ed. K. J. Maidment, London, 1941. Vol. II: Lycurgus, Demades, Dinarchus, Hyperides, ed. J. O. Burtt, London, 1954 (Loeb).
Mitteilungen des Deutschen Archäologischen Institut (Athen. Abt.), Berlin.
Mitteilungen des Deutschen Archäologischen Institut (Röm. Abt.), Berlin.
R. D. Milns, *Alexander the Great*, London, 1968.

MP: *Alexander the Great: the main problems.* Ed. G. T. Griffith. Cambridge, 1966.

Nat. Geogr. Mag.:   *National Geographic Magazine.* New York.

Nouv. Clio: *La Nouvelle Clio.* Brussels.

ns: New Series.

Olmstead: A. T. Olmstead, *A History of the Persian Empire*, Chicago, 1948.

Opus [cula] Arch[aeologica]:   *Opuscula Archaeologica*, Lund.

Orac. Sib.:   *Oracula Sibyllina.*

Parke: H. W. Parke, *Greek Mercenaries*, Oxford, 1933.

PP: *La Parola del Passato.* Rivista di Studi antichi. Naples.

Paus.:   Pausanias of (?) Lydia, Greek travel-writer (second century A.D.).

Philostratus: Flavius Philostratus, Greek writer (second–third century A.D.).

     Vit. Apoll. Tyan.: *Vita Apollonii Tyanae*

     Vit. Soph.: *Vitae Sophistarum*

Phoenix: *The Phoenix.* The Journal of the Classical Association of Canada. Toronto, University of Toronto Press.

Plato: Plato, Athenian philosopher (*c.* 429–347 B.C.).

     Gorg.: *Gorgias*

     Protag.: *Protagoras*

     Rep.: *Respublica [Republic]*

     Symp.: *Symposium*

Pliny: Gaius Plinius Secundus [Pliny the Elder], Roman scholar and antiquarian (A.D. 23/4–79).

     HN: *Historia Naturalis*

Plut.:   (?) Mestrius Plutarchus of Chaeronea, Greek scholar and biographer (*c* 46 B.C.–*c.* A.D. 120).

     Moral.: *Moralia*

     Vit. Par.: *Vitae Parallelae*

         Ages.: *Agesilaus*

         Alex.: *Alexander*

         Artax.: *Artaxerxes*

         Cam.: *Camillus*

         Demosth.: *Demosthenes*

         Eum.: *Eumenes*

         Lys.: *Lysander*

	Pelop.: *Pelopidas*
	Per.: *Pericles*
	Phoc.: *Phocion*
	Pyrrh.: *Pyrrhus*
Polyaenus:	Polyaenus, Macedonian rhetorician (second century A.D.).
	Strat.: *Strategemata*
Polyb.:	Polybius, Greek statesman and historian (?203–?120 B.C).
P. Oxyrh.:	*Oxyrhynchus Papyri*, ed. B. P. Grenfell and A. S. Hunt. London, 1898–
Proc. Afr. Class. Assoc.:	*Proceedings of the African Classical Association.* Salisbury, S. Rhodesia.
Proc. Brit. Acad.:	*Proceedings of the British Academy.* Oxford University Press.
Proc. Camb. Phil. Soc.:	*Proceedings of the Cambridge Philological Society.* Cambridge University Press.
Ps–[Arist.], *Oecon.*:	Pseudo-Aristotle, *Oeconomicus.*
Ps–Call[isth.]:	Pseudo-Callisthenes, title given to anonymous author of the 'Alexander-Romance'.
PWK [*RE*]:	*Real-Encyclopädie der classischen Altertumswissenschaft.* Ed. A. Pauly, Georg Wissowa, W. Kroll, K. Mittelhaus, K. Ziegler. Stuttgart [1839], 1893–.
Quintil.:	Marcus Fabius Quintilianus, Roman rhetorician (*c.* A.D. 30–*c.* 100).
	Inst. Orat.: *Institutio Oratoria*
QC:	Quintus Curtius Rufus, Roman Alexander-historian (first century A.D.).
RA:	*Revue Archéologique.* Paris.
Radet, *AG*:	G. Radet, *Alexandre le Grand.* 2nd edn. Paris, 1950.
REA:	*Revue des Etudes Anciennes.* Bordeaux.
REG:	*Revue des Etudes Grecques.* Paris.
Rev. Bibl.:	*Revue Biblique.* Paris.
Rev. Phil.:	*Revue de Philologie.* Paris.
RFIC:	*Rivista di Filologia e di Istruzione Classica.* Turin.
Rhein. Mus.:	*Rheinisches Museum.* Frankfurt.
Riv. Fil.:	*Rivista di Filosofia.* Turin.
Riv. Stor. Ital.:	*Rivista Storica Italiana.* Naples.
Robinson, *HA*:	C. A. Robinson (ed.), *The History of Alexander the Great*, vol. I [Brown University Studies XVI], Providence, R.I. (1953).
Saeculum:	*Saeculum. Jahrbuch für Universalgeschichte.* Freiburg.

Sallust:	Gaius Sallustius Crispus, Roman historian (?86–35 B.C.).
	Bell. Iug.: *Bellum Iugurthinum* [Jugurtha].
schol.:	scholium, scholiast.
SE:	*Studi Etruschi*. Florence.
SEG:	*Supplementum Epigraphicum Graecum*. Leyden, 1923–71.
Seltman, *GC²*:	C. Seltman, *Greek Coins*. 2nd edn. London, 1955.
Seneca:	Lucius Annaeus Seneca, Roman philosopher and moralist (4 B.C.–A.D. 65).
	De Benef.: *De Beneficiis*.
Sext. Emp.:	Sextus Empiricus, Greek doctor and philosopher (? first–second century A.D.).
	Adv. Math.: *Adversus Mathematicos*
	Adv. Gramm.: *Adversus Grammaticos* [= Bk I of *Adv. Math.*]
SIG³:	W. Dittenberger, *Sylloge Inscriptionum Graecarum*, 3rd edn, Leipzig, 1915–24.
Sitzungsb. d. preuss. Akad.:	*Sitzungsberichte der preussischen Akademie der Wissenschaften, Philos.–hist. klasse.*
Snodgrass:	A. M. Snodgrass, *Arms and Armour of the Greeks*, New York, 1967.
Snyder:	J. W. Snyder, *Alexander the Great*, New York, 1966.
Stark, *AP*:	Freya Stark, *Alexander's Path*, London, 1958.
Stud. Class. e Orient.:	*Studi Classici e Orientali*. Pisa.
Symb. Osl.:	*Symbolae Osloenses*. Oslo.
TAPhA:	*Transactions and Proceedings of the American Philological Association*. Cleveland, Ohio.
Tarn, [*AG*]:	W. W. Tarn, *Alexander the Great*. 2 vols., Cambridge, 1948.
Temenos:	*Temenos*. Studies in comparative religion presented by scholars in Denmark, Finland, Norway and Sweden. Helsinki.
Theophr.:	Theophrastus, Greek philosopher and scientist (c 370–288/5 B.C.).
	HP: *Historia Plantarum*
Thuc.:	Thucydides, Greek historian (c. 460–c. 400 B.C.).
Tod, II:	M. N. Tod, *Greek Historical Inscriptions*, vol. II: From 403 to 323 B.C. Oxford, 1948.
Val. Max.:	Valerius Maximus, Roman historian (first century A.D.).

Vell. Pat.:	Velleius Paterculus, Roman historian (first century B.C.–first century A.D.).
Vet. Test.:	*Vetus Testamentum*. Leiden, Brill.
Virgil, *Aen.*:	P. Vergilius Maro, 70–19 B.C., The *Aeneid*.
Wilcken–[Borza]:	U. Wilcken, *Alexander the Great*. Trs G. C. Richards. New edn with introduction, notes and bibliography by E. N. Borza. New York, 1967.
Xen.:	Xenophon, Athenian soldier and historian (428/7–*c*. 354 B.C.).
	Anab.: *Anabasis*
	Hell.: *Hellenica*
Yale Class. Stud.:	*Yale Classical Studies*. New Haven, Yale University Press.
Zeitschr. f. Alttest. Wiss.:	*Zeitschrift für die Alttestamentliche Wissenschaft*. Berlin.

Table of Dates

Siege of Tyre begun.

? June: second peace-offer by Darius refused.

29 July: fall of Tyre.

September–October: Gaza captured.

14 November (?): Alexander crowned as Pharaoh at Memphis.

331 Early spring: visit to the Oracle of Ammon at Siwah.

? 7–8 April: foundation of Alexandria.

Alexander returns to Tyre.

July–August: Alexander reaches Thapsacus on Euphrates; Darius moves his main forces from Babylon.

18 September: Alexander crosses the Tigris.

Darius' final peace-offer rejected.

30 September or 1 October: Battle of Gaugamela.

Macedonians advance from Arbela on Babylon, which falls in mid-October.

Revolt of Agis defeated at Megalopolis.

Early December: Alexander occupies Susa unopposed.

331/0 Alexander forces Susian Gates.

330 ? January: Alexander reaches and sacks Persepolis.

? May: burning of temples etc. in Persepolis.

Early June: Alexander sets out for Ecbatana.

Darius retreats towards Bactria.

Greek allies dismissed at Ecbatana; Parmenio left behind there, with Harpalus as treasurer.

Pursuit of Darius renewed, via Caspian Gates.

July (after 15th): Darius found murdered near Hecatompylus.

Bessus establishes himself as 'Great King' in Bactria.

March for Hyrcania begins (July–August).

Late August: march to Drangiana (Lake Seistan).

The 'conspiracy of Philotas'.

March through Arachosia to Parapamisidae.

329 March–April: Alexander crosses Hindu Kush by Khawak pass.

April–May: Alexander advancing to Bactria; Bessus retreats across the Oxus.

June: Alexander reaches and crosses the Oxus; veterans and Thessalian volunteers dismissed.

Surrender of Bessus.

Alexander advances to Maracanda (Samarkand).

Revolt of Spitamenes, annihilation of Macedonian detachment.

329/8 Alexander takes up winter quarters at Zariaspa. Execution of Bessus.

328 Campaign against Spitamenes.
Autumn: murder of Cleitus the Black.

328/7 Defeat and death of Spitamenes.

327 Spring: capture of the Soghdian Rock.
Alexander's marriage to Roxane.
Recruitment of 30,000 Persian 'Successors'.
The 'Pages' Conspiracy' and Callisthenes' end.
Early summer: Alexander recrosses Hindu Kush by Kushan pass: the invasion of India begins.

327/6 Alexander reaches Nysa (Jelalabad); the 'Dionysus episode'.
Capture of Aornos (Pir-Sar).

326 Advance to Taxila.
Battle of the Hydaspes (Jhelum) against the rajah Porus.
Death of Bucephalas.
? July: mutiny at the Hyphasis (Beas).
Return to the Jhelum; reinforcements from Greece.
Early November: fleet and army move down-river.

326/5 Campaign against Brahmin cities; Alexander seriously wounded.

325 Revolt in Bactria: 3,000 mercenaries loose in Asia.
Alexander reaches Patala, builds harbour and dockyards.
? September: Alexander's march through Gedrosian Desert.
Defection of Harpalus from Asia Minor to Greece.
The satrapal purge begins (December).
Nearchus and the fleet reach Harmozia, link up with Alexander at Salmous (Gulashkird).
Arrival of Craterus from Drangiana.

324 January: Nearchus and fleet sent on to Susa.
The episode of Cyrus' tomb.
Alexander returns to Persepolis.
Move to Susa, long halt there (February–March).
Spring: arrival of 30,000 trained Persian 'Successors'.
The Susa mass-marriages.
March: the Exiles' Decree and the Deification Decree.
Craterus appointed to succeed Antipater as regent, and convoy troops home.

Alexander moves from Susa to Ecbatana.

Death of Hephaestion.

323 Assassination of Harpalus in Crete.

Alexander's campaign against the Cossaeans and return to Babylon (spring).

Alexander explores Pallacopas Canal; his boat-trip through the marshes.

Arrival of Antipater's son Cassander to negotiate with Alexander.

29/30 May: Alexander falls ill after a party, and dies on 10/11 June.

[1]

Philip of Macedon

THE story of Alexander the Great is inexorably bound up
with that of his father, King Philip II, and with his country,
Macedonia. Philip was a most remarkable and dominating
figure in his own right; while Macedonia, as has recently
been observed,[1] 'was the first large territorial state with an
effectively centralized political, military and administrative
structure to come into being on the continent of Europe'.
Unless we understand this, and them, Alexander's career
must remain for us no more than the progress of a comet,
flaring in unparalleled majesty across the sky: a marvel, but
incomprehensible. Genius Alexander had, and in full
measure; yet even genius remains to a surprising extent the
product of its environment. What Alexander was, Philip
and Macedonia in great part made him, and it is with them
that we must begin.

On an early September day in the year 356 B.C.[2] a courier
rode out of Pella, Macedonia's new royal capital, bearing
dispatches for the king. He headed south-east, across the
plain, past Lake Yanitza (known then as Borboros, or Mud,
a godsend for superior Greek punsters: *borboros-barbaros*,
uncouth primitivism in a nutshell), with Ossa and Olympus
gleaming white on the far horizon, as Xerxes had seen them
when he camped by Homer's 'wide-flowing Axius' at the
head of his invading host. The courier's destination was
Potidaea, a city of the Chalcidic peninsula, where the
Macedonian army now lay; and he did not waste any time
on his journey. Philip, son of Amyntas, since 359 B.C. ruler
over a dubiously united Macedonia,[3] was not a man who
took kindly to delay or inefficiency in his servants. At present,
however, having recently forced the surrender of Potidaea –

for over a century a bone of contention between various Greek powers, Athens included, and a most valuable addition to his steadily expanding domains – he was liable to be in a benevolent mood, and very probably drunk as well.

If the courier had not known Philip by sight, he might have been hard put to it to pick him out from among his fellow-nobles and staff officers. The king wore the same purple cloak and broad-brimmed hat that formed the regular attire of a Macedonian aristocrat. He affected no royal insignia of any sort, was addressed by his name, without honorifics, and indeed never described himself as 'king' on any official document.[4] Here, as so often in Macedonia, Mycenaean parallels apply:[5] Philip was an overlord among equals, the *wanax* maintaining a precarious authority over his turbulent barons. Perhaps he felt, too, that his position, especially in the faction-torn feudal court of Pella, was better not too closely defined. Rivals for the throne had spread a rumour that he and his two brothers – both kings before him, both violently killed – were impostors;[6] accusations of bastardy formed a stock weapon in the Macedonian power-game.

Philip was now twenty-seven years old: a strong, sensual, heavily bearded man much addicted to drink, women, and (when the fancy took him) boys. Normally of a jovial disposition, he had even more reason for cheerfulness after studying the dispatches which the courier brought him. His most reliable general, Parmenio, had won a decisive victory over a combined force of Illyrians and Paeonians – powerful tribes on the Macedonian marches, occupying districts roughly equivalent to modern Albania and Serbia. In the Olympic Games, which had just ended, his entry for the horse-race had carried off first prize. Best of all, on about 20 July[7] his wife Myrtale – better known to us by her adopted name of Olympias – had given birth to a son: his name (two previous Argead monarchs had already borne it) was Alexander.

After he had finished reading, Philip is said to have

begged Fortune to do him some small disservice, to offset such overwhelming favours.[8] Perhaps he recalled the cautionary tale of Polycrates, tyrant of Samos, who received a letter from the Egyptian Pharaoh Amasis expressing anxiety at his excessive good fortune. 'I have never yet heard of a man,' Amasis declared, 'who after an unbroken run of luck was not finally brought to complete ruin.' He advised Polycrates to throw away the object he valued most; Polycrates tossed an emerald ring into the sea, but got it back a week later in the belly of a fish.[9] Amasis promptly broke off their alliance, and Polycrates ended up impaled by a Persian satrap. It is, therefore, curious – though by no means out of character – that of the three events listed in that memorable dispatch, the only one we know Philip to have publicly commemorated is his victory at Olympia. The Macedonian royal mint put out a new issue of silver coins: their obverse displayed the head of Zeus, their reverse a large and spirited horse, whose diminutive naked jockey was shown crowned with the wreath of victory and waving a palm-branch.[10]

What was it that gave these three particular events such extreme, almost symbolic significance for him? To understand the king's reaction it is necessary to look back for a moment, at the chequered history and archaic customs of Macedonia before his accession.

First – and perhaps most important of all – the country was divided, both geographically and ethnically, into two quite distinct regions: lowlands and highlands.[11] The case of Scotland provides close and illuminating parallels. Lower Macedonia comprised the flat, fertile plain round the Thermaic Gulf. This plain is watered by two great rivers, the Axius (Vardár) and the Haliacmon (Vistritza), and ringed by hills on all sides except towards the east, where the first natural frontier is provided by a third river, the Strymon (Struma). Lower Macedonia was the old central kingdom, founded by semi-legendary cattle barons who knew good pasturage when they saw it, and ruled over by the royal dynasty of the Argeads, to which Philip himself belonged. About 700 B.C. this noble clan had migrated eastward from Orestis in the Pindus mountains, looking for arable land. They first occupied Pieria, the coastal plain running northward from Mt Olympus, and afterwards extended their conquests to include the alluvial plain of Bottiaea – Homer's Emathia – lying west of the Thermaic Gulf. During this process of expansion they also captured the picturesque fortress town of Edessa, on the north-west frontier. The district was so rich in orchards and vineyards that people called it the 'Gardens of Midas'. Edessa also had considerable strategic value, lying as it did above the pass which carried the trans-Balkan trunk road – later the Roman Via Egnatia – through to Illyria and the West.[12] Near Edessa the Argeads established their first capital, Aegae. Even after the seat of government was transferred to Pella, down in the plain, Aegae remained the sacred burial-ground of the Macedonian kings, and all important royal ceremonies were conducted there.[13]

Upper Macedonia and Paeonia formed a single geo-graphical unit: a high horseshoe of upland plateaux and grazing-land, encircling the plain from south to north-east, and itself backed – except, again, towards the Strymon – by mountain ranges. Passes across these mountains are few, the best-known being the Vale of Tempe by Mt Olympus, and that followed by the Via Egnatia. Thus Macedonia as a whole tended to remain in isolation from the rest of the Balkan peninsula; like Sparta, it preserved institutions (such as kingship and baronial feudalism) which had lapsed else-where. The highlands lay mostly to the west and south-west of the central plain, and were divided into three originally autonomous kingdoms: Elimiotis in the south, Orestis and Lyncestis to the west and north-west, the latter by Lake Lychnitis. The northern frontier of Lyncestis marched with Paeonia, and all three cantons shared frontiers with Illyria and Epirus. Indeed, in many ways their inhabitants were more akin to Illyrians or Paeonians or Thracians than they were to their own lowland cousins. The men of Lower Macedonia worshipped Greek gods; the royal family claimed descent from Heracles. But the highlanders were much addicted to Thracian deities, Sabazius, the Clodones and Mimallones, whose wild orgiastic cult-practices closely resembled those portrayed by Euripides in the *Bacchae*. They were, indeed, partly of Illyrian stock, and they intermarried with Thracians or Epirots rather more often than they did with Macedonians of the plain.

Originally, too, the three cantons had been independent kingdoms, each with its own ambitious and well-connected royal house. Efforts to preserve that independence – or to reassert it – naturally drove them into alliances with the Epirots, Paeonians or Illyrians. The sovereigns of Lower Macedonia were equally determined to annex these 'out-kingdoms', whether by conquest, political persuasion, or dynastic inter-marriage.[14] Lyncestis was ruled by descendants of the Bacchiad dynasty, who had moved on to Macedonia after their expulsion from Corinth in 657 B.C.[15] Excavations at Trebenishte have revealed a wealth of gold masks and tomb furniture of the period between 650 and 600;[16] these were powerful princes in the true Homeric tradition, like the kings of Cyprus. The Molossian dynasty of Epirus, on the marches of Orestis and Elimiotis, claimed descent from Achilles, through his grandson Pyrrhus – a fact destined to have immeasurable influence on the young Alexander, whose mother Olympias was of Molossian stock.

The Argeads themselves, as we have seen, headed their pedigree with Heracles, and could thus (since Heracles was the son of Zeus) style themselves 'Zeus-born' like any Mycenaean dynast: both Zeus and Heracles appear regularly on Philip's coinage. It is clear, however, that there were other clans whose claim to the throne of a united Macedonia could at least be urged with some plausibility. From the Argead viewpoint no real advance was possible until Upper Macedonia had been brought under some sort of central control. Paradoxically (but for obvious enough reasons) the nearer this aim came to fulfilment, the greater the danger of a palace *coup d'état* by some desperate out-kingdom prince determined to keep his crown at all costs.

At least as early as the fifth century B.C. the Argeads were claiming 'traditional' suzerainty over Upper Macedonia – again, on quasi-Homeric lines. The overlordship much resembled that of Agamemnon over his fellow-kings: each canton gave just as much allegiance to the Argead throne as any individual monarch could exact. The out-kingdoms were quite liable to connive at Illyrian or Paeonian invasions, if not to give them active backing. Add to this the endless intrigue – often ending in bloody murder and usurpation – which took place at the Argead court, and we begin to see why Macedonia, before Philip's time, played so insignificant a part in Greek history. The country was frankly primitive, preserving customs and institutions which might have made even a Spartan raise his eyebrows. To achieve formal purification of the army, a dog was cut in two by a priest, and the troops then marched between the severed halves. Various ritual war-dances, mimetic in nature, have an unmistakably Zulu air about them for the modern reader.

The attitude of city-state Greeks to this sub-Homeric enclave was one of genial and sophisticated contempt. They regarded Macedonians in general as semi-savages, uncouth of speech and dialect, retrograde in their political institutions, negligible as fighters, and habitual oath-breakers, who dressed in bear-pelts and were much given to deep and swinish potations, tempered with regular bouts of assassination and incest. In a more benevolent mood, Athenians would watch the attempts of the Argead court to Hellenize itself with the patronizing indulgence of some blue-blooded duke called upon to entertain a colonial sugar-baron. No one had forgotten that Alexander I, known ironically as 'the Philhellene', had been debarred from the Olympic

Games until he manufactured a pedigree connecting the
Argeads with the ancient Argive kings.[17]

Nor was Macedonia's record in the Persian and Peloponnesian Wars liable to improve her standing with patriotic
city-state Greeks. Alexander I had collaborated wholeheartedly with the Persians, marrying his sister to a Persian
satrap, and accompanying Xerxes' army as a kind of liaison
officer – though he was not above hedging his bets discreetly when a Greek victory seemed possible.[18] After
Plataea, he turned on the retreating Persians and carved up
a large body of them at Nine Ways (Ennea Hodoi) on the
lower Strymon. From the spoils he then set up a gold
statue of himself at Delphi, to emphasize his having (even
at the eleventh hour) fought on the right side, against the
Barbarian.[19] As though to add insult to injury, he profited
by the Persian retreat to subjugate the tribes of the Pindus
in the west and the Thracian Bistonae and Crestonians in
the east, thus almost quadrupling his royal territory. From
silver mines on the Lower Strymon he now drew revenues
amounting to one silver talent daily. He began to strike
coins in his own name, the first Macedonian monarch to do
so. These were sizeable achievements, but not of the sort
to win him popularity among the Greek states. His successors presented an even shadier picture. His son Perdiccas II
switched his allegiance so many times during the Peloponnesian War that one modern scholar thoughtfully provides
a tabulated chart to show which side he was on at any
given point.[20] What, Athenian democrats must have said,
could you do with a man like *that*? Not to mention the un-
speakable Archelaus, Perdiccas' illegitimate son, who
reached the throne by murdering his uncle, cousin and
half-brother, proceeded to marry his father's widow, and
was finally murdered himself as a result of his lurid homosexual intrigues.[21]

Yet it is, precisely, the careers of Perdiccas and Archelaus
which hint at Macedonia's true potential. Perdiccas' remarkable tergiversations were mostly due to his possessing,

in abundance, a basic raw material which both sides needed
desperately: good Macedonian fir for shipbuilding and oars.
Upper Macedonia has a continental rather than a Mediterranean climate, and its mountains still show traces of the
thick primeval forests which covered them in antiquity.
Perdiccas was at pains to establish a treaty of alliance and
friendship with Athens (Thuc. 1.57.2), though this was an
agreement which both sides honoured in the breach rather
than the observance. If the Macedonian king showed himself a slippery customer, it was not for lack of harassment on
Athens' part. The foundation of Amphipolis in 437 and the
acquisition of Methone three years later enabled the
Athenians to put direct pressure on Macedonia; by 413 they
were prohibiting Perdiccas from exporting timber without
specific permission from Athens (who held the monopoly).[22] However, it was Perdiccas who got the best of the
exchange in the long run, playing Sparta and Athens off
against each other with cool cynicism, selling timber to both
sides, making and tearing up monopoly treaties like so much
confetti. He also contrived to keep Macedonia from any
serious involvement during the Peloponnesian War, thus
preventing that ruinous drainage of manpower which so
weakened both main combatants. It was surely Perdiccas'
example that Philip had in mind when he said: 'Cheat boys
with knucklebones, but men with oaths.'[23]

It is hard to see what else Perdiccas could have done;
Macedonia during his reign was still so weak and disunited
that effective resistance, let alone any kind of expansion,
was out of the question. At least he managed to safeguard
the country's natural resources – in the circumstances no
mean achievement. But it was Archelaus who, with realistic
insight, first formulated the basic problems which had to be
dealt with before Macedonia could become any kind of
force in Greek affairs, and who seriously applied himself to
solving them. Alexander I had, of course, pointed the way,
and not merely in the field of territorial expansion. He
worked hard to get Macedonia accepted as a member of

the Hellenic family (mainly by establishing a fictitious link between the Argead dynasty and Argos), and encouraged Greeks to domicile themselves on Macedonian soil, a policy which both Perdiccas and Archelaus followed. In particular, he offered attractive patronage to such distinguished artists as Pindar and Bacchylides.[24] His general policy was clear enough: extend the frontiers while polishing up Macedonia's cultural image abroad.

When Archelaus came to the throne, in 413/12, Athens was no longer an immediate danger: the failure of the Sicilian Expedition had seen to that. When her rulers now approached the Macedonian king it was as petitioners, desperate for ship-timber: a decree honouring Archelaus as 'proxenos and benefactor', together with evidence supplied by that shifty Athenian politician Andocides, suggests that (in 407/6) they attained their desired end.[25] But it was still vital to safeguard the country against constant incursions by ambitious neighbours. This meant both strengthening the army, and achieving some kind of permanent unification between Upper and Lower Macedonia. Alexander I had already systematized the old institution of the 'Companions' (*hetairoi*), landed gentry who served the king, into formal cavalry units, the famous Companion Cavalry. It also seems probable that it was he who first created an equivalent infantry body, the Foot Companions or *pezetairoi*, making large grants of land in the freshly conquered territories to Companions of every degree, and thus ensuring stability for his new frontiers. Also, as Edson points out,[26] 'by means of these grants he would increase the prestige of the kingship and the loyalty of the Macedonians to himself and to the Argead house'. Archelaus seems to have improved the supply of arms, horses, and other military equipment; he also built a network of roads and fortified posts, which served the double purpose of improving communications and letting him keep a firmer hand on his unruly vassals.[27] Whether by force or diplomacy, he established so secure an entente with the out-kingdoms that

by the end of his reign (400/399) he was ready to acquire
a little *Lebensraum* at the expense of Thessaly and the
Chalcidic League.

He also saw, very clearly, that a great deal more Hellenization – a programme, in fact, of conscious cultural propaganda – was essential before more advanced Greek states
would begin to treat Macedonia on equal terms. He
established a special Macedonian festival at Dium in
Pieria, dedicated to the Nine Muses, and boldly entitled
'Olympian'. Like its namesake, it offered both athletic and
musical contests. Like so many tyrants in antiquity, he set
himself up as an enlightened patron of literature, science,
and the arts. The famous painter Zeuxis was commissioned
to decorate his palace. Amongst various other distinguished
figures who took up residence in Macedonia were the tragic
poet Agathon and the now octogenarian Euripides: seldom
can patronage have been more memorably rewarded than
by that terrifying final explosion of genius, the *Bacchae*.
The luxury and dissipation of Archelaus' court were notorious; but few men had the strength of mind to refuse an
invitation there. (Agathon, indeed, if Aristophanes' picture
of his effeminate habits is remotely near the truth, must
have felt more than at home in Archelaus' company.) One
of the few exceptions, characteristically enough, was
Socrates, who remarked that he would rather not accept
favours he could never repay.[28]

But after Archelaus was murdered, the whole edifice he
had laboured to build up collapsed overnight, to be followed
by forty years of the worst anarchy and intrigue Macedonia
had ever experienced. His claim to the throne, dynastically,
was weak at best, and his heir was a child. The out-kingdom
princes saw their chance, and took it. For this they can
hardly be blamed. The glimpse of the future which Archelaus had given them was far from enticing. They had no
intention of being reduced to the status of provincial vassal
barons if they could help it; and most of them viewed the
late king's Hellenization policy with fierce distaste. Warriors

who wore cords round their waists until they had killed a
man in battle, who could not even sit at meat with their
fellows until they had speared a wild boar single-handed,
who drank from cattle-horns like Vikings – such men
were not the stuff of which a cultural renaissance is
made.[29]

We may doubt, then, whether Archelaus' support for the
arts made any impression beyond his immediate entourage.
Most Macedonian nobles preferred the more manly plea-
sures of hunting, carousing, and casual fornication.
Sodomy – with young boys or, at a pinch, with each other –
they also much enjoyed; but they had no intention of
letting it be contaminated with decadent Platonic notions ✳
of spiritual uplift.[30] The simultaneous presence in Alexander's headquarters of tough Macedonian officers and
Greek civilian intellectuals was to produce untold tension and
hostility (see below, pp. 163, 372 ff.). All the same, Archelaus' failure to establish a lasting settlement was not entirely
due to baronial intransigence. National income – or the
lack of it – must also be taken into account. Timber-
export and mining rights brought in a fair return, but
hardly enough to subsidize military stockpiling, lavish
hand-outs to visiting celebrities, and road-construction on a
nation-wide scale. It seems at least possible that Archelaus
had begun to alienate crown land in return for immediate
cash subsidies – a practice which Alexander later revived
before the launching of his expedition (see below, pp. 155–6).
The out-kingdom barons in particular would jump at such
an opportunity: whatever Archelaus demanded was cheap
in return for a 'gift-fief' in Lower Macedonia.

Granted these circumstances, it may not be without
significance that the 'guardian' of Archelaus' young son
Orestes was a prince of Lyncestis, Aeropus. Until 396 they
ruled conjointly. Then Aeropus, having secured his own
position, did away with Orestes and ruled alone. Two years
later he died: since his grandson was of age, it may even
have been from natural causes. His son Pausanias succeeded

him, but was promptly assassinated by the legitimate Argead claimant, Alexander I's grandson Amyntas.

In 394 Amyntas was nearer sixty than fifty; he had already made one unsuccessful bid for power, some three decades earlier, against his wily old uncle Perdiccas. Even now he found it a hard business claiming his inheritance. The House of Lyncestis, having once got its hands on the Macedonian crown, did not mean to relinquish it without a struggle. The Lyncestian barons, led by Pausanias' son, called in an Illyrian army to help them and drove Amyntas out of Macedonia again. But in 392, with Thessalian support, he made his comeback – this time for good.[31] His reign lasted until 370: precariously enough, but the main wonder is that he survived so long. In his old age he sired three legitimate sons – a very necessary precaution, since he already had three bastards with designs on the throne. The youngest of these late-born heirs was Philip, Alexander's father, born in 383/2, when Amyntas was well over sixty-five. It is not hard to see how the rumour arose that all three of them were illegitimate.

For the old king the price of survival was constant and open humiliation. At first he managed to stave off the Illyrians by paying them heavy annual tribute. This did not stop them intriguing with the rebellious out-kingdom barons, who wanted nothing better than a *coup d'état* that would put the House of Lyncestis back into power. From 384 onwards, indeed, Illyria exercised *de facto* sovereignty over the western marches of Lyncestis itself – a strategically vital region between Lake Lychnidus (Okhrida) and the Tcherna River. Amyntas could still count on the support of Elymiotis, the remaining out-kingdom: its chieftain, Derdas, was his personal friend. But he dared not risk a full-scale civil war. Nor had he any firmer a hold over Macedonia's ill-defined eastern frontier. Before his forcible expulsion in 394/3, he had ceded a valuable strip of border territory to Olynthus, the most powerful maritime city in the Chalcidic peninsula – presumably as a *quid pro quo* for promised military aid, which in the event came too late, if at all. When he finally established himself on the throne he claimed this land back, on the grounds that he had merely left it in trust with the Olynthians till his restoration. They blandly ignored his protests, and made still further encroachments.

Nothing more clearly reveals Macedonia's weakness during this period than the off-hand treatment which Amyntas received from powers such as Athens or Sparta: unwisely, since the raids of wild tribesmen from the north, Triballi and others, was as prejudicial to Greek as to Macedonian interests. To Athens Macedonia was simply a useful buffer-state in her complex dealings with Chalcidice and Thrace, a pawn in the end-game which aimed, ultimately, at secure control of the Black Sea grain-route through the Bosporus. When Sparta was persuaded to send an expedition against Olynthus, it was not out of regard for Amyntas, but because the Chalcidic League (of which Olynthus was the head) represented a growing threat in the Thraceward regions. Olynthus surrendered in 379; the Chalcidic League was – temporarily – broken up; and the Spartans doubtless went home congratulating themselves on having done a statesmanlike job of work. In fact their action constituted one of the most disastrous errors of judgement imaginable. Forty years later they – along with every other city-state, not least Athens and Thebes – realized the truth: that they had fatally weakened the one power-group which might conceivably have checkmated Macedonia's meteoric rise to power before it was well begun. Knowledge, as so often, came too late.

Yet it would have taken more than Delphic prescience to have foreseen, in 379, just what the future held. Amyntas, everyone agreed, was a joke, like most of his predecessors. Trimmers, traitors, drunks, murderers, vacillating money-grubbers, cowardly and inefficient despots – the Argead dynasty had not won much respect from Greek public opinion, and Amyntas in this respect did little to improve

matters. He touted indiscriminately for alliances, approaching, at various times, everyone from the Thebans to that
remarkable *condottiere* Jason of Pherae. In his efforts to
please Athens (and to protect his own crumbling authority)
he had even gone so far as to adopt an Athenian general,
Iphicrates, as his son. He, and Macedonia, could clearly be
discounted.

On top of all this, the usual palace intrigues continued to
flourish. The king's-wife, Eurydice, had taken a lover, a
Macedonian nobleman named Ptolemy, from Alorus. With
enviable *sang-froid* she married off Ptolemy to her own
daughter – in order, presumably, to have an unchallengeable
reason for keeping him around the house. After a while she
got careless, and Amyntas actually caught her in bed with
his son-in-law. Unwisely, he did nothing – as usual. He was
much attached to his daughter, and anxious to avoid any
scandal that might cause her distress.[32] Ptolemy, however,
showed little gratitude for this forbearance. Like most
Macedonian aristocrats, his ambition was only equalled by
his unscrupulousness. To enjoy the queen's person was, for
him, simply a foretaste of the headier delights conferred by
royal authority. Compared to him, Rizzio and Darnley
were sentimental amateurs; but then Eurydice, one suspects,
could have taught Mary a thing or two as well.

This fascinating pair now decided to murder Amyntas,
and set up Ptolemy as King of Macedonia in his stead: an
act of pure usurpation rather than a bid on behalf of one
of the out-kingdoms, since Alorus lay in Bottiaea, and thus
formed part of Lower Macedonia. (The tradition that
Ptolemy was in fact Amyntas' son[33] clearly represents
dynastic propaganda on his behalf.) Here, however, they
reckoned without Eurydice's daughter, whose Grizelda-like
submissiveness clearly drew the line at parricide, and who
lost no time in warning her father what was afoot. However,
any social embarrassment the situation might have caused
at court was obviated by Amyntas promptly dying, perhaps of shock. After all, he was close on eighty.

If Ptolemy had hoped to occupy this conveniently vacant throne without trouble, he was disappointed. The king's eldest legitimate son, Alexander II, at once established his claim to the succession. However, he was unwise enough to get himself involved in a war between the rival dynasts of Thessaly, and during his absence Ptolemy made a spirited bid at usurping his crown. He met with enough opposition for the case to be decided by arbitration. The eminent Theban statesman Pelopidas gave his verdict in favour of Alexander, and Ptolemy retired gracefully – at least until Pelopidas was safely out of the country. Then, resourceful as ever, he had the young king assassinated during a Macedonian folk-dancing exhibition, married Eurydice (what became of her daughter history does not relate), and assumed the office of regent on behalf of Perdiccas, Alexander's brother, who was next in line for the throne, but still a minor. Realizing that such a move was open to misconstruction by political cynics abroad, he proceeded to negotiate an alliance with the Thebans, who had just smashed the myth of Spartan military supremacy in a pitched battle at Leuctra (371), and were rapidly emerging as the most powerful state in Greece.

As a proof of his sincerity, he also dispatched to Thebes a highly distinguished group of hostages: perhaps he was glad to have some of them safely out of the way – especially Amyntas' only other legitimate son, the young Philip, at this time fifteen years old.[34] Ptolemy can hardly have foreseen the consequences of his action. For Philip, while in Thebes, stayed with Pammenes, who was not only a skilled general himself, but a close friend of Epaminondas, the ✳ victor of Leuctra, and perhaps the finest strategist Greece produced before Alexander. Philip's whole military career (and that of Alexander after him) was incalculably influenced by the lessons the great Theban commander taught him. He learnt the importance of professional training in drill and tactics, of close cooperation between cavalry and infantry, of meticulous staff planning combined with speed in attack. By watching the manoeuvres of the Sacred Band, Thebes' crack infantry regiment, he came to appreciate the potential of a permanent *corps d'élite* – so much so that thirty years later he and his formidable son were at pains to wipe out this famous military unit almost to the last man. Above all, he learnt one cardinal principle: that 'the quickest and most economical way of winning a military decision is to defeat an enemy not at his weakest but at his strongest point'.[35]

Philip's training for power was proceeding along useful if unorthodox lines. His experience as a member of the Macedonian royal household had given him an understandably cynical view of human nature: in this world murder, adultery and usurpation were commonplace, as liable to be practised by one's own mother as by anyone else. In later life Philip took it as axiomatic that all diplomacy was based on self-interest, and every man had his price: events seldom proved him wrong. In Thebes he saw, too, the besetting weaknesses of a democratic city-state – constant party intrigue, lack of a strong executive power, the inability to force quick decisions, the unpredictable vagaries of the assembly at voting-time, the system of annual elections which made any serious long-term planning almost impossible, the amateur *ad hoc* military levies (though here Thebes was better off than, say, Athens). For the first time he began to understand how Macedonia's outdated institutions, so despised by the rest of Greece, might prove a source of strength when dealing with such opponents. Throughout his life he gained his greatest advances by exploiting human cupidity and democratic incompetence – most often at the same time.

The King of Macedonia was, with certain caveats, the supreme authority over his people: in a very literal sense he could make that famous Bourbon boast '*L'état c'est moi.*' Much has been made of the tradition that the king could not execute a free citizen on a charge of high treason (i.e. attempted murder or usurpation directed against himself), but must appear before the Macedonian assembly in the guise of a plaintiff.[36] But there are so many instances on record of monarchs who put leading Macedonians to death without consulting the assembly at all that the rule, if it ever existed, would seem to have been something of a dead letter. The Macedonian assembly did, it is true, confirm each king's succession (usurpers might get away with it if they won public approval) and could, in theory at least, depose him by vote; they also heard capital charges. Apart from this, however, and a requirement that he observe the 'traditional laws', the king's power was absolute. He 'owned all land, held supreme command in war, was judge, priest, and treasurer, and could delegate his powers during absence abroad'.[37] His status much resembled that of a Mycenaean *wanax*, ruling over a tribally orientated society.

Macedonian noblemen were the ancient equivalent of feudal barons; as a general rule they held their lands in fee from the king, and owed him personal service, together with their retainers, in return. It was from these tribal aristocrats that the king selected his Companions, or *hetairoi*, who acted both as a peacetime council, and as a general staff when Macedonia was at war. (Again, Homer provides a close parallel, in the example of Achilles and his Myrmidons.) They also furnished Gentlemen of the Body-guard (*somatophylakes*), who appear to have been eight in number,[38] and who attended the king at all times, not merely in battle. They were on terms of frank and easy familiarity with him, wearing the same dress and addressing him as an equal. Macedonian royal absolutism certainly did not lack the common touch.

Like that other feudally organized horse-breeding state, Thessaly, Macedonia possessed a fine heavy cavalry arm. We find these troopers giving an excellent account of themselves against the Thracians in 429; a squadron from Elimiotis distinguished itself during the Olynthian campaign of 382/1. The nucleus of this Macedonian cavalry was provided by the Companions themselves, who originally did duty as a royal mounted escort. They wore helmets and

cuirasses; Thucydides describes them as 'excellent horsemen' and says that 'no one could stand up to them'. But
– as one scholar has recently reminded us – it would be a
mistake to think of them as resembling medieval knights, or
even Napoleonic dragoons. Their horses were small and
unshod, little more than sturdy ponies, though they had
begun to breed heavier mounts from bloodstock captured
during the Persian Wars. They used neither saddle nor
stirrups, as we can see from the Sidon sarcophagus; and this
meant that the lance-charge of the Middle Ages was unknown to them. Instead, they carried a short stabbing-spear,
the *xyston*, some six feet long, with which they were adept
at spiking their opponents through the face during close-
quarters combat.[39]

As regards infantry, however, Macedonia – at least
before Philip's reforms – was lamentably weak. This tends
to be an occupational defect of any aristocratic feudal state,
and Macedonia, like Persia, was no exception to the rule.
(One reason why the Achaemenid empire fell to Alexander
was that he and his father between them had solved the
infantry problem, whereas the Great King had not.)
Originally this arm consisted of mere tribal levies, peasants
and shepherds following the cavalry in an unruly mass.
During most of the fifth century they remained negligible,
though under Archelaus there was some effort to train and
organize them. But economic progress slowly produced a
yeoman middle class, even in Macedonia; and a middle
class, throughout Greece, was synonymous with the emergence of a heavy infantry force, however inadequate.

It was, as we have seen, Alexander I[40] who formally
established a regular body of *pezetairoi*, or 'Foot Companions', perhaps *inter alia* as a counterweight against the
pretensions of his more than usually turbulent barons. The
name implies not merely organization but also – perhaps as
important – social acceptance. These 'Foot Companions'
became a permanent addition to the Macedonian military
establishment; but it took Philip to see their true potential,

and forge them into one of the most formidable fighting units the world has ever seen – the legendary Macedonian phalanx. Its members were as highly trained and drilled as Roman legionaries; for their main weapon they had the terrible *sarissa*, a spear some 13–14 feet long, heavily tapered from butt to tip, and much resembling a medieval Swiss pike. To handle such a weapon effectively required parade-ground dressing and discipline; but once that discipline had been acquired, the phalanx enjoyed a vast initial advantage in battle. Since a normal infantry thrusting spear was only half the length of the *sarissa*, the Macedonians could always rely on making their first strike before the enemy got to grips with them.[41]

From Thebes the young Philip waited on events at home, in the intervals of studying military tactics and being lectured by his tutor, a Pythagorean. (It would be hard, on the face of it, to find a less likely convert than Philip of Macedon to the philosophy which advocated vegetarianism, pacifism, and total abstinence.) Opposition to Ptolemy's rule was considerable; but most of it, once again, came from the House of Lyncestis, which now backed yet another Pausanias – perhaps the last claimant's nephew – in a near-successful bid for the throne. Eurydice made a highly emotional appeal to Iphicrates, the Athenian general whom her late husband had adopted. No Athenian ever passed up the chance of getting his political foot in someone else's door; so Iphicrates (with the tacit backing of his government) drove out Pausanias, and with due filial restraint made no reference to Eurydice's marital peccadilloes.

No one paid much attention to young Perdiccas, and this, as things turned out, was a mistake. Perdiccas might, like Archelaus, have a weakness for literature and philosophy; but he was not on that account a person to trifle with. He waited three years, until he attained his majority (there was to be no excuse for foisting another regent on him) and then had Ptolemy executed (365/4). What his mother had to say about this, or how he dealt with her after her lover's removal, our sources do not relate; but we never hear of her again. Perdiccas now settled down to rule Macedonia in his own right; and one of his first acts as king was to arrange for Philip's release, or escape, from Thebes. His mentor and *éminence grise* was a philosopher named Euphraeus, who came to Macedonia on Plato's recommendation. He is described as being of common origin and very slanderous in his conversation; moreover, as Carystius tells us, 'he was so pedantic in his selection of the king's associates that nobody could share in the common mess if he did not know how to practise geometry or philosophy'.[42] But he gave Perdiccas one excellent piece of advice, which was to appoint Philip governor of a district, and let him recruit and train troops there.

Philip at once began to put the lessons of Epaminondas into practice. Discipline and organization were completely overhauled. Macedonian troops, infantry of the levy, suddenly found themselves learning tactical manoeuvres and complex close-order drill. Philip sent them on thirty-five mile route-marches with full pack and provisions, and then (when they were too tired to protest) subjected them to morale-boosting lectures. Aristocratic cavalrymen and footslogging peasants found themselves involved in extended joint exercises: it is a moot point which of them (to begin with at least) were the more disconcerted by the experience. Certainly Philip showed himself no respecter of persons. One officer who ventured to take a bath in camp was stripped of his command; a young sprig of the nobility who broke ranks to get a drink was publicly flogged.[43] Hitherto only mercenaries had attained such a level of efficiency. Now, slowly but surely, Philip began to train a nucleus of professional soldiers who were still, at the same time, Macedonia's free national levy. It was a momentous innovation.

Meanwhile Perdiccas, who possessed all his father's political pliability, and a good deal more drive, arranged a fresh alliance with Athens. He might be building up an army, but he was still very short on ships and naval expertise, and Athens had both in full measure. The Athenian with whom he had to deal was a genial *condottiere* named Timotheus, a friend of Iphicrates. For a time all went well. Timotheus campaigned in the Thracian Chersonese, now the Gallipoli Peninsula (Athens, as usual, was anxious about her grain-route through the Dardanelles), and, with Macedonian assistance, captured several vital Chalcidic towns, including Potidaea. But Timotheus was, after all, an Athenian, and had an Athenian policy to carry out. He now, very coolly, snapped up two of Perdiccas' own best southern ports, Methone and Pydna, and then turned his attention to the vital frontier city of Amphipolis, on the Strymon, where Macedonia maintained a garrison. No one could now fail to recognize that Athens' real object was the recovery of her lost fifth-century maritime empire. Perdiccas promptly switched what troops he could spare to the city's defence; by 362 the *entente cordiale* had gone up in smoke. A year later, nothing daunted, Athens concluded an 'eternal alliance' with Thessaly instead, and – more ominously – began to extend a helping hand to the out-kingdom barons.[44]

Those who condemn Philip's subsequent policy of aggression (particularly against Athens: modern scholars seldom get morally worked up about the Chalcidic peninsula) sometimes forget Athens' own record of freebooting grab-as-grab-can in north-east Greece. One must not believe everything one reads in Demosthenes.[45] The Athenians themselves had an enviable facility for swallowing their own propaganda: Aeschines not only blamed Perdiccas for failing to help Athens capture Amphipolis, but actually gave Athens credit for remaining friendly despite the wrong done her.[46] The only difference between Philip and Athens, politically speaking, lay in their relative success. Philip turned out a better general, a subtler diplomat, and a larger personality than any Athenian with whom he had to deal; but so far as political morality went there was not a penny to choose between them.

By 359 Perdiccas felt strong enough to try conclusions with Illyria. The situation on his western frontier was, obviously, intolerable. Lyncestis had more or less seceded from Macedonian control; despite the humiliating annual tribute which he paid, Perdiccas had no guarantee that at any time he would not be swept off his throne by an Illyrian-backed *coup*. He mustered a large army, left Philip behind as regent during his absence, and marched westward. Days later a dusty and panic-stricken messenger came back with disastrous news: Perdiccas had been defeated and killed in a great battle against the Illyrians, and some 4,000 Macedonians lay dead on the battlefield with him.[47] Philip of Macedon had come into his inheritance at last; but it would be hard to imagine a reign which began under less hopeful auspices.

Few political experts of the day, in Athens or anywhere else, can have given the new king much more than six months, even at the shortest odds. The western frontier was wide open, and a large proportion of Philip's newly-trained troops were dead. The Illyrians, under their king, Bardylis, were preparing for a mass invasion. The Paeonians had already begun swarming down from the north to pillage Macedonian territory. At home things were no better. On Perdiccas' death no fewer than five would-be usurpers (not counting Philip himself) had thrown their coronets into the ring: they form an interesting group. Pausanias of Lyncestis we have met already: for this, his second attempt, he had secured Thracian backing. Argaeus was Athens' candidate. He had already snatched power briefly once, in the 390s, and was now assembling a sizeable force at Methone. In return for the Athenians' support he had promised – if successful – to cede them Amphipolis. Lastly, there were Philip's three illegitimate half-brothers, Archelaus, Arrhidaeus, and Menelaus. They, presumably, hoped to win the direct support of the Macedonian people; the old *canard* about Philip's origins began to circulate once more.

Philip coolly assessed this impossible situation, rather in

the manner of Marshal Foch, and then struck, with lethal speed and efficiency. First, he arrested and executed Archelaus: the other two brothers managed to escape, but fled the country and sought refuge in Olynthus (see below, p. 45). Next, Philip bribed the King of Thrace not only to withdraw his backing from Pausanias, but also (two birds neatly with one stone) to arrange for the pretender's assassination. He then sent off an embassy to Paeonia, and, says Diodorus, 'by corrupting some with gifts and persuading others by generous promises he made an agreement with them to maintain peace for the present'.[48] All this was accomplished in a matter of weeks, or less.

Philip was now at leisure to deal with the one remaining pretender, Argaeus, who in addition to his mercenaries had at Methone no fewer than 3,000 Athenian hoplites, under their own general. Philip promptly pulled his garrison out of Amphipolis, declared it a free city, and made a secret deal with Athens whereby it would be restored to her in exchange for Pydna. Argaeus, somewhat bewildered, found himself advancing on Aegae, the old capital, with only his mercenaries to back him. Making the best of a bad job, he called on the citizens to 'welcome him back and become the founders of his kingship'. The citizens politely ignored him; by now they had taken Philip's measure. Argaeus had no option but to turn about and trail back to Methone. Philip, who had been watching this little comedy with cynical amusement, intercepted the pretender en route and forced him into ignominious surrender. All Athenians among the mercenaries were carefully weeded out and sent home, with compensation. The last thing Philip wanted, now or at any time, was Athens' open hostility.[49]

The Illyrians, seeing that this new ruler of Macedonia was a far tougher proposition than any of his predecessors, postponed their invasion. Having thus stalled or eliminated all opposition between summer and autumn, Philip spent the winter of 359/8 putting through a crash military training programme. In the early spring came news that the King of Paeonia had just died. Here was too good a chance to miss. Before the barbarian monarch's successor could establish himself, Philip swept over the northern passes, defeated the Paeonians in a pitched battle, and forced them to acknowledge Macedonian overlordship. Attack is the best defence: Philip knew that at this psychological moment he had a unique chance to smash the Illyrian threat once and for all. But it was a tremendous gamble. He mobilized every able-bodied fighting man in the kingdom; when he marched westward into Lyncestis he had 600 horse and no less than 10,000 infantrymen behind him. Bardylis, in some alarm, offered terms, but only on the basis of the status quo; he refused to give up any of the territory he had won. Philip rejected his offer: not, in all likelihood, without some qualms, since the Illyrians who fought Perdiccas gave no quarter and took no ransom, and were unlikely to change their policy when confronted by his brother.[50] The two armies finally met in the plain near Monastir, by Lake Okhrida.[51]

The most interesting thing about this crucial battle is that here, for the first time, we see Philip applying the tactical lessons of Epaminondas, as Alexander was to apply them after him. There was little to choose between Illyrians and Macedonians numerically; what told were superior strategy and training. The Illyrians, seeing themselves in danger of being outflanked by Philip's cavalry, formed up in a hollow square. Philip himself led the infantry, holding back his centre and left, deploying his line in the oblique echelon that was Epaminondas' speciality. As he had anticipated, the Illyrian right wing stretched and slewed round to force an engagement. Philip waited until the inevitable, fatal gap appeared in the left of the square, and then sent in his right-wing cavalry, flank and rear. They drove a great wedge through the gap, and the Macedonian phalanx followed in their wake. A long and desperate struggle ensued. But at last the square broke, and 7,000 Illyrians – three-quarters of Bardylis' entire force – were slaughtered before the fugitives reached the safety of the hills. Here, *mutatis mutandis*, we have precisely the tactics which produced victory for Philip or Alexander at Chaeronea, the Granicus, and Issus – the oblique advance, with centre and left deliberately echeloned back so that they formed, as it were, a pivot for the knock-out charge delivered by the cavalry from the right; the careful manoeuvring to create a gap in the enemy line; Epaminondas' principle of economy of force coupled with overwhelming strength at the decisive point.[52]

Now, at last, Philip was in a position to dictate terms, and did so with some relish. Bardylis, grumbling, but knowing when he was beaten, abandoned all his territorial gains in western Macedonia. The immediate threat to Philip's western frontier was now removed, and the danger of out-kingdom disloyalty correspondingly reduced. The next time there was campaigning to be done against the Illyrians, in 356, it was, as we have seen, Parmenio whom Philip delegated for the task.[53] During the rest of his reign Philip continued to campaign on the Illyrian marches, especially during the periods 355–1 and 346–2, but now with ever-increasing confidence, strengthening the frontier line by ejecting potentially hostile tribesmen, and in the end bringing many of the Illyrian clans under his direct rule.[54] Almost more important for Philip personally was the fact that this crushing defeat of Bardylis at once enhanced his own prestige out of all recognition. His brother's defeat and death had been more than amply avenged; he found himself something of a national hero. There was no further question, now, of his position being challenged. Indeed, he very soon emerged as one of the most popular monarchs ever to rule over Macedonia, a tribute to his vigorous personality no less than his exceptional skill as a commander in the field. For a young man of twenty-three it was no mean achievement.

Among other concessions which Philip obtained from

Bardylis was the hand in marriage of his daughter Audata. Feudal societies such as Macedonia, Thrace and Illyria (unlike the more developed Greek city-states) operated on a tribal system of kinship and reciprocal obligations. For them dynastic marriage, as an instrument of political self-insurance, stood second only to dynastic murder. Those with whom one had acquired a formal family relationship were that degree less likely to conspire against one; and a chieftain's daughter could always, at a pinch, be used as a high-level hostage. Philip, of all people, was unlikely to ignore so promising a diplomatic weapon. During his comparatively short life he took no fewer than five wives.

Philip's general attitude to sex, women and marriage has been seriously confused by most scholars from Plutarch onwards. Middle-class romantic respectability (Plutarch on the conjugal–domestic ideal is almost as mawkish as Coventry Patmore) makes very heavy weather of fourth-century Macedonian *mores*: this applies to drinking habits no less than to sex. Macedonian society knew nothing of conjugal romance, and only insisted on conjugal fidelity in wives to guard against the appearance of unsuspected cuckoos in the dynastic nest. Like any tribal leader, Philip took wives to breed sons, secure the succession, run his household, and cement alliances. His marriages, therefore, must be sharply distinguished from his innumerable *amours*, which did not affect his marital relationships in any way (though they might have similarly quasi-diplomatic objectives on occasion). The idea that any man should restrict his sexual activities to the marriage-bed, much less cultivate a relationship with his wife in the modern sense, would have struck a Macedonian as both pointless and grotesque. Macedonian wives were not, therefore, given to fits of romantic jealousy if their husbands chose to take mistresses or cultivate the company of young boys. What roused Olympias to fury, as we shall see, was any threat to her own royal position, or her first-born son's status as heir to the throne.

It was a standing joke in antiquity that Philip 'always married a new wife with each campaign he undertook'.[55] This should be regarded as a tribute to his political acumen rather than his concupiscence. The idea of marrying one's mistress, which drove Dr Crippen to murder, is a bourgeois notion little older than the present century. Philip's attitude to marriage, in fact, much resembles that of the Austrian Habsburgs: as an instrument of diplomacy it came cheaper than war. 'The complicated history of his matrimonial affairs,' it has been well said, 'mirrors the progress of his political expansion.'[56]

However, Philip's liaison with this Illyrian princess brought him only temporary security abroad, and did little to stabilize his position at home. Audata died, probably in childbirth (spring 357) leaving Philip with a daughter, Cynane (or Cynna), rather than the male heir for whom he must have prayed. He now, predictably, sought a wife nearer home, from the princely clan of Elimiotis, most consistently loyal among the out-kingdoms. Phila was a princess in her own right, Derdas' daughter – and, incidentally, the aunt of Alexander's imperial treasurer, Harpalus (see Genealogical Chart, and below, p. 101). It was, on the face of it, an ideal match. But ill-fortune seemed to attend all Philip's early ventures into matrimony. Phila, too, died not long after her wedding. By the high summer of 357 Philip was once more looking for a suitable wife.

Meanwhile he had been busy in other fields. During the winter of 358/7 Alexander of Pherae was assassinated, and his relatives embarked upon such a reign of terror that some rival Thessalian aristocrats, the Aleuadae, invited Philip to come and suppress them (the murder had been carried out by Alexander's own wife in concert with her brothers). Philip, always on the look-out for a political entrée in neighbouring states, duly obliged. The Thessalians were grateful; Philip exercised all his considerable charm. (He had certainly achieved more than Isocrates, who merely sent the conspirators an open letter advocating moderation.)

It was now that he acquired as his mistress a dancing-girl named Philinna, from Larissa, the home of the Aleuadae, 'wishing,' as Satyrus tells us, 'to put in a claim to the Thessalian nation as his own besides others'. Legitimate inheritance in the Macedonian royal house depended on paternity alone, and Philinna's son Arrhidaeus afterwards found neither bastardy nor half-wittedness impediments to his succession.[57]

Nothing, however, gives so clear a foretaste of Philip's diplomatic in-fighting techniques as his record over Amphipolis. When he bargained this vital port away to Athens (see above, p. 22) he had not the slightest intention of keeping his word; he was merely, as so often, buying time. Amphipolis, lying as it did on the Strymon, at the frontiers of Thrace and Macedonia, had enormous commercial and strategic importance. It provided a port for the shipping of Macedonian timber; more important still, it gave access to the rich mining area round Mt Pangaeus. The Athenian general Thucydides had been exiled for losing Amphipolis during the Peloponnesian War (a fact to which we indirectly owe his *History*) and Athens had been trying, unsuccessfully, to get it back ever since.

In the spring of 357 Philip picked a quarrel with the Amphipolitan government (where Greeks were concerned it was never hard to engineer a *casus belli*) and laid their city under siege. They promptly appealed to Athens. But the Athenians had a famine on their hands, and were too busy bargaining for grain-supplies from Thrace and the Black Sea to consider campaigning on the Strymon.[58] Besides, they still believed – with that special naivety which sometimes afflicts the politically corrupt – that Philip intended to honour his underhand agreement with them. Why should they go and fight against Macedonians at Amphipolis when it was on Athens' behalf that the assault was being made? And once Amphipolis was theirs, they argued, Philip could whistle for Pydna. It never, seemingly, entered their heads that Philip might pull precisely the same trick on them.

Amphipolis fell that autumn. Philip, far from making Athens a present of his new acquisition, confirmed its independence – thus winning a grateful ally, and much credit for honest dealing among the cities of north-east Greece. The Athenians, morally outraged by this neat finesse – they wanted allies in the north-east themselves – declared war on Macedonia.[59] But what with the grain-shortage and a revolt of their own allies in the Aegean, there was little enough they could do – exactly as Philip had calculated. Adding insult to injury, he now marched on Pydna and recovered it for himself. The sheer gullibility of Athenian statesmen at this time is only equalled by Philip's willingness to exploit it. When the Olynthians, somewhat alarmed by Philip's activities, applied to Athens for an alliance, they were politely choked off. Philip, it was thought, would still, somehow, honour his promises. The Olynthians, who were hardheaded realists (as their wealth indicates) thereupon went back home and made a treaty with Philip instead, on behalf of the Chalcidic League. One clause of this document stipulated that Philip should, on Olynthus' behalf, recover Potidaea – 'a city', says Diodorus, 'which the Olynthians had set their heart on possessing'.[60] This time Philip kept his word: he needed a free hand in the Thraceward regions. However, after reducing Potidaea, he carefully sent the Athenian garrison back home. There was no harm in hedging one's bets.

Philip's third and by far his most famous wife was, once again, a foreigner, from the royal Molossian house of Epirus. Illyria might be secure for the moment, but an alliance with her southern neighbour and rival offered decided advantages. The reigning prince, Arybbas, had two nieces. The elder, Troas, he had, economically, married himself; but her sister Myrtale (or Olympias, as we know her) was still available, and Arybbas promptly – almost too promptly – gave his consent to the match. Plutarch asserts that Philip and Olympias had already met some four or five years previously, during their initiation into the Mysteries on Samothrace, and had fallen in love at first sight. The story could just be true, though Plutarch's matrimonial idealism leaves him a suspect witness in such matters, and Olympias can have been barely past puberty at the supposed time of her initiation. In any case, Philip had not shown himself in any desperate hurry to follow matters up. Two previous wives and at least one mistress hardly conjure up the image of a pining lover.

At all events, in the autumn of 357 Philip married his Epirot princess, and for the first time in his life found he had taken on rather more than he could handle. Olympias, though not yet eighteen, had already emerged as a forceful, not to say eccentric, personality. She was, among other things, passionately devoted to the orgiastic rites of Dionysus, and her Maenadic frenzies can scarcely have been conducive to peaceful domestic life. One of her more *outré* habits (unless, as has been suggested, it had a ritual origin) was keeping an assortment of large tame snakes as pets. To employ these creatures on religious occasions could raise no objections; but their intermittent appearance in Olympias' bed must have been a hazard calculated to put even the toughest bridegroom off his stroke. Our sources, furthermore, while admitting Olympias' beauty, describe her variously as sullen, jealous, bloody-minded, arrogant, headstrong and meddlesome. To these attributes we may add towering political ambition and a literally murderous temper. She was determined to be queen in something more than name: this did not endear her to the Macedonian barons, and was later to involve Philip in the most serious crisis of his career. But for the moment his main concern was to sire an heir, and he lost no time in getting Olympias with child.[61]

So far, both as strategist and diplomat, Philip had scarcely put a foot wrong. Nevertheless, there was still one vital element lacking to his plans for expansion, and that was a large and regular source of income. Philip, like his son, was no natural economist; both of them had the pirate's mentality when it came to finance. For them credit meant, quite simply, enough gold and silver in the vaults to stave off an immediate crisis: the Treasury was equated with treasure. Furthermore, they knew only two ways of acquiring these precious metals: to dig them out of the ground, or to steal them off anyone weaker than themselves. Neither Philip nor Alexander ever understood what a balance of trade meant – a failing which left their Hellenistic successors with some severe economic headaches.

The nearest and best source of both gold and silver was the region round Mt Pangaeus, east of the Strymon. Technically this lay in Thracian territory, and Philip had no wish, as yet, to be branded as an aggressor. However, the stronghold of Crenides provided him with just the excuse he needed. This town, north-east of Pangaeus, had been colonized by Thasos. Its occupants (perhaps in response to a broad hint) appealed to Philip for help against Thracian aggression. Philip occupied Crenides in the spring of 356, renamed it Philippi, sent a large body of settlers there, and put his mining engineers to work. Before long precious metals, gold above all, began to pour into the Macedonian treasury. Philip's annual income was now increased by 1,000 talents, or 300,000 gold pieces – as much as fifth-century Athens had extracted from her whole great maritime empire. He at once began to coin on an extensive scale, issuing gold staters (which he called 'Philips', perhaps in conscious emulation of their Persian equivalent, the 'Daric') and silver *sigloi*, or shekels. This surplus was quickly mopped up by the needs of Philip's near-professional army, and – perhaps an almost greater drain – by the lavish bribes which he was for ever handing out to foreign politicians. He himself afterwards boasted that 'it was far more by the use of gold than of arms that he had enlarged his kingdom', and his prodigal expenditure was a by-word throughout Greece.[62]

So, on that late summer day in 356 B.C., Philip of Macedon sat and read the dispatches from Pella, and called on Fate to grant him some small setback to offset so unbroken a line of successes. In less than four years he had transformed Macedonia from a backward and primitive kingdom to one of the most powerful states in the Greek world. The threat to his frontiers was, if not removed, at least substantially diminished. The country had a secure and indeed princely national income, not to mention a legitimate heir to the throne. A formidable new army was being trained, while the out-kingdoms were beginning to show some grudging respect for Argead sovereignty. Lastly, his victory at Olympia would, Philip hoped, form the prelude to social acceptance by the Greek city-states – above all, by Athens.

Philip's relations with Athens were always somewhat ambivalent. He despised her chattering, venal demagogues, with their empty rhetoric and sordid petty intrigues. He found the whole ramshackle democratic system mildly ridiculous. 'The Athenians,' he once remarked, 'manage to dig up ten generals* every year; I only ever discovered one in my life – Parmenio.'[63] Yet he did not underestimate his opponents. He knew that venality often goes hand in hand with genuine patriotism – as the example of Themistocles so strikingly demonstrates – and that even a democracy can, on occasion, act with speed and decision. He had some very practical motives for avoiding a head-on clash, not least the formidable Athenian fleet: Macedonia had never been a maritime nation. But he was also impressed, despite himself, by Athens' near-legendary past, The charismatic mystique of the city that had broken the Great King's ambitions at Marathon and Salamis, that had produced Aeschylus and Pericles and Plato, could not fail to leave its mark on him. His contempt was always mingled with a kind of wide-eyed colonial admiration.

Now, at last, he was ready to embark on that astonishing

---

*The annually elected Board of Generals [*strategoi*] was in effect a kind of civil and military cabinet.

career of expansion and conquest which only ended with
his premature death. He had been well-trained for the task
ahead of him. His eye for a man's or a city's weakest spot
was unerring. He made rival factions his allies by playing
them off one against the other. The idea of seasonal campaigning and citizen-levies he regarded with contempt. For
Philip there was no close season in war, and victory went
to the side that had trained the hardest. He himself exercised unbroken and near-absolute control over Macedonia's
affairs, civil no less than military. This, as Demosthenes for
one realized, gave him an enormous advantage over any
elected democracy when it came to the planning and execution of long-term projects. His parents' example, indeed the
whole pattern of Macedonian baronial intrigue, left him
with a genial contempt for all human pretensions to virtue
or idealism. (No city, he said, was impregnable if it had a
postern-gate big enough to admit an ass laden with gold.)
His country's long history of humiliation and impotence
showed him the ultimate goal at which he must aim. Every
personal or national slight would be wiped out, each
sneering allusion to barbarism, cowardice or incompetence
paid for in full.

At the same time, Sparta's shocking record as an imperial
power (404–371) had taught Philip one extremely important lesson. Naked *Machtpolitik* created, in the long run,
more problems than it solved.[64] Conciliation always paid
off better, even if it conceded no advantage except the
semblance of self-respect. The pill of aggression must be
gilded with appeals to principle and professions of honest
dealing. Here we have yet another of Philip's policies which
was afterwards taken over and carried to its logical extreme
by his more famous son. The shifty Athenian demagogues
who lied and shuffled would find that they had met a more
charmingly persuasive liar than themselves. The hotheads
who prated of patriotism and liberty would see both cut
down to size by troops trained on deeds rather than rhetoric.
It was the triumph, ultimately, of authoritarian efficiency

[2]

The Gardens of Midas

ON the night of Alexander's birth, tradition alleged, the temple of Artemis was burnt down. The local Persian Magi interpreted this as an omen of further disasters to come. They 'ran about beating their faces and crying aloud that woe and great calamity for Asia had that day been born', a firebrand that was destined to destroy the entire East. The night before her wedding, similarly, Olympias dreamed she was penetrated by a thunderbolt, so that fire gushed out of her womb, spreading far and wide before it was extinguished. A month or two later Philip also had a dream: he was sealing up his wife's vagina, and the wax bore the stamped device of a lion. Some of the palace seers took this to mean that Philip should keep a closer watch on his wife. But Aristander of Telmessus – who afterwards accompanied Alexander to Asia (see below, p. 168) – had a more acceptable explanation: Olympias was pregnant, and with a spirited, lion-like son. One did not, he told Philip, put a seal on an empty jar.

It was also rumoured that the king (perhaps taking the other diviners' advice more seriously than he would admit) had one day peered through a crack in his bedroom door and seen Olympias embracing a snake. The obvious explanation, that this was merely one of her Maenadic pets, did not occur to him. Convinced that she was either an enchantress or the *inamorata* of some god in disguise, he began to avoid conjugal relations with her. So perturbed was he, indeed, that he took his troubles to the Delphic Oracle, and got a very specific response. From henceforth, he was told, he must pay special reverence to Zeus-Ammon, the Hellenized Egyptian deity whose shrine and oracle were at the Siwah oasis, on the borders of Libya. He would also

lose that eye with which he had seen 'the god, in the form
of a serpent, sharing the couch of his wife'. For once Delphi
could hardly be accused of ambivalence.[1]

Legends such as these always tended to accumulate round
the birth and childhood of any famous character in antiquity. It was a *sine qua non* that the first should be accompanied by portents, and the second abound in episodes
suggestive of future greatness. If this background material
did not exist, it was manufactured. Few people, then as
now, possessed that special insight which detects tomorrow's
leader in today's schoolboy, and a world without adequate
records or archives was even readier to be wise after the
event. There were always contemporaries of the great man
anxious to prove that they recognized his greatness from
the very first, and jealous rivals eager to pay off old scores.
For such witnesses truth was an infinitely flexible commodity.

In Alexander's case the unscrupulous propaganda, both
favourable and hostile, began very early, before he had
even become king. Almost everyone who wrote about him
from personal acquaintance – and many who did not[2] – had
some sort of axe to grind. The anecdotes quoted above
illustrate this point only too well. Each of them, it is clear,
was invented, and for some very specific purpose: to attack
or defend Olympias, to impugn or uphold the legitimacy
of her son's birth, to give Alexander's conquests, and his
supposed divine relationship to Zeus-Ammon, the retro-
spective endorsement of Fate. The snake story, of course,
was a double-edged weapon: it could be used to hint at
either divine or else all too human bastardy. The most
tell-tale detail is the 'prediction' about Philip's eye, which
was actually shot out at the siege of Methone in 354, two
years after Alexander's birth. This incident provided, long
afterwards, the starting-point for a false oracle designed to
confirm Alexander's assumptions of godhead. The temple
of Artemis at Ephesus was, in fact, burnt down about this
time; but the prophecy of a firebrand which would destroy

Asia sounds suspiciously like Persian propaganda, put out when the invasion had already taken place.[3]

The truth of the matter is that we have surprisingly little direct evidence about Alexander's childhood from any source, and what does exist is of very limited historical value.[4] He is generally represented as a precocious *enfant terrible*, and this is likely enough. Macedonian court life, with its quarrels and intrigues, its drunken feasts and coarse sexual escapades, was not calculated to encourage innocence in the young. Precocity is just what we might expect from a clever boy brought up in such an environment. It also suggests that special knowingness so often found among the children of public figures, who become accustomed – almost before they can walk – to the company of politicians, artists, ambassadors or generals, imitating their turns of phrase and their conversational gambits with uncomprehending accuracy. When Alexander was only seven, it is said, he entertained a group of Persian envoys during Philip's absence on campaign. (They had come with the Great King's pardon and recall for three rebels who had found refuge with Philip: Menapis the Egyptian, the satrap Artabazus, and the Greek mercenary captain Memnon of Rhodes.) After the usual exchange of courtesies, Alexander proceeded to grill his guests like any intelligence officer. Not for him wide-eyed questions about such marvels as the Hanging Gardens, or the Persian royal regalia, or the Great King's golden vine, with its clusters of jewels. What *he* wanted to know – or so we are asked to believe – were such things as the size and morale of the Persian army, the length of the journey to Susa, and the condition of the roads that led there.

This anecdote has obviously been touched up for propaganda purposes; but it could just contain an element of truth. The envoys, Plutarch says, were much impressed. Whether they told him what he wanted to know is another matter; but Artabazus and Memnon, at least, are unlikely to have forgotten the incident if it in fact took place. By a

curious quirk of fate, the first afterwards became one of
Alexander's own Eastern satraps (see below, p. 353), while
the second was his most formidable opponent in Asia
Minor (see pp. 170 ff.). Memnon, unlike his Persian em-
ployers, never made the mistake of underestimating
Alexander. It is an intriguing thought that this brilliant
commander may have remembered, and taken warning
from, the alarming inquisitiveness of a seven-year-old
child.[5] On the other hand, his visit can have left him in no
doubt as to the aggressive intentions of the child's father.
After an almost unbroken string of successes, in Thrace,
Thessaly and elsewhere, Philip had now turned his attention to the Chalcidic peninsula. The reason he could not
entertain Persia's envoys in person was that he happened,
at the time, to be besieging Olynthus. Another reminder of
his ubiquitous interests was a good-looking twelve-year-old,
Alexander's namesake from Epirus, now permanently resident at the Macedonian court. This boy was Olympias' young
brother; Philip had brought him back, after a whirlwind punitive expedition, as hostage, minion, and – if his uncle
Arybbas, Philip's father-in-law, showed any further signs of
independence or opposition – as prospective King of Epirus.[6]

Philip's expansionist progress up to 349 is graphically
described by Demosthenes, in the first of his speeches
urging support for the beleaguered Olynthians: 'Has any
man amongst you,' he asks his Athenian audience, 'watched
Philip's progress, observed his rise from weakness to
strength? First he seizes Amphipolis, next Pydna, then
Potidaea. After that it is Methone's turn. Next he invades
Thessaly ... and then goes off to Thrace, deposing various
chieftains and appointing his own nominees in their place.
A short interval, while he is sick, and then, the minute he
recovers, off he goes to invest Olynthus. All this quite
apart from minor campaigns against Illyria and Paeonia
and King Arybbas, to name but a few.'[7] It is all uncomfortably like Churchill or Vansittart recapitulating
Hitler's activities before the Munich Agreement.

The composition of Philip's court also caused widespread comment, and with good reason. He had augmented the original Macedonian Companions with distinguished mercenary officers drawn from every part of Greece. Amongst them were Demaratus of Corinth, and two brothers from Mytilene, Erigyius and Laomedon: all three subsequently served under Alexander. This professional officer-corps numbered about 800, and its members were allocated lands from Philip's frontier conquests: Erigyius and Laomedon, for instance, had estates near Amphipolis. Hostile Greek propaganda drew a lurid picture of these men's morals and social habits. 'Philip's court in Macedonia,' wrote Theopompus, 'was the gathering-place of all the most debauched and brazen-faced characters in Greece or abroad, who were there styled the King's Companions.' They were, he went on, carefully selected for their prowess at drinking, gambling, or sexual debauchery. 'Some of them used to shave their bodies and make them smooth although they were men, and others actually practised lewdness with each other though bearded ... Nearly every man in the Greek or barbarian world of a lecherous, loathsome, or ruffianly character flocked to Macedonia.'

Demosthenes, while cataloguing much the same faults, admitted (what it would have been hard to deny) that the Companions had a reputation as 'admirable soldiers, well grounded in the science of war'. In a surviving fragment of Mnesimachus' propaganda play, *Philip*, one of them speaks for himself:

> Have you any idea
> What we're like to fight against? Our sort make their dinner
> Off honed-up swords, and swallow blazing torches
> For a savoury snack. Then, by way of dessert,
> They bring us, not nuts, but broken arrow-heads
> And splintered spear-shafts. For pillows we make do
> With our shields and breastplates; arrows and slings lie strewn
> Under our feet, and we wreathe our brows with catapults.

Allowing for obvious exaggeration, the general atmosphere was probably much as these sources describe it. Mercenaries

– and Macedonians – were never renowned in antiquity for the austereness of their lives.[8]

This, then, was the society in which the young Alexander grew up: a loud, clamorous male world of rough professional soldiers, who rode or drank or fought or fornicated with the same rude energy and enthusiasm. Though Olympias spoilt her son outrageously, she never set herself to diminish his masculine self-confidence: as we shall see, the reverse seems to have been true. Nor, on the evidence available, did she systematically poison his mind against his father from childhood: this often-repeated story is a modern psychological myth. The split between Philip and Olympias did not take place until 338, when Alexander had turned eighteen, and was in any case primarily due to dynastic politics. Until then they seem to have cooperated amicably enough over their son's upbringing, and indeed to have devoted much thought and care to it.[9]

There can be no doubt, however, that Alexander idolized Olympias. Tarn claims that 'he never cared for any woman except his terrible mother',[10] a verdict which it would be hard to refute. His relationship with Philip, which has received less attention, was rather more complex, an ambivalent blend of genuine admiration and underlying competitiveness. If imitation be the sincerest form of flattery, then Alexander's attitude to his father fell little short of hero-worship. But the rivalry was there too: *odi et amo*, the perennial love – hate relationship. The son followed in his father's footsteps not only to emulate, but also to excel. As a boy he identified himself closely with Achilles, from whom, through the Aeacids, his mother's house claimed descent. On his father's side he could trace his ancestry back to Heracles. It is a great mistake to underestimate the seriousness with which such genealogies were regarded by the ancient world. Heroic myth was, for Greeks and Macedonians alike, a living reality, invoked time and again by politicians or pamphleteers.[11] The fact that sophisticated statesmen sometimes used such myths in cynical justification of their policies merely confirms this. What they were exploiting was near-universal faith: otherwise no one would have listened to them.

Alexander's favourite line in the *Iliad* shows his declared ambition, to be 'at the same time a good king and a strong spear-fighter'. Yet he must surely have remembered Achilles' other, perhaps more characteristic aim – 'ever to strive to be best, and outstanding above all others'. As Philip's dazzling career proceeded, with victory succeeding victory, Alexander used to complain to his friends that his father was anticipating him in everything – 'and for me,' he said, 'he will leave no great or brilliant achievement to be displayed to the world with your aid.' 'But,' his friends objected, 'he is acquiring all this for you.' Alexander replied: 'What use are possessions to me if I achieve nothing?'[12]

History tells us something of Alexander's teachers, but remains almost wholly silent as to what they taught him. His nurse's name was Lanice; her brother Cleitus, known as 'the Black', saved Alexander's life at the Granicus, and was afterwards murdered by him during a drunken quarrel in Samarkand (see below, pp. 178 and 361 ff.). His first tutor was a kinsman of Olympias, a stern and crabbed old disciplinarian called Leonidas, who (like his Spartan namesake) placed great emphasis on feats of physical endurance. Alexander used to say that Leonidas' idea of breakfast was a long night-march – and of supper, a light breakfast. Though the boy chafed under this discipline at the time – Philip said that he was amenable to argument, but not to compulsion – Leonidas' training left its mark on him. His personal powers of endurance, his forced marches through deserts and over mountains became legendary. He never forgot his old bear of a tutor; we find him telling Queen Ada of Caria, with a kind of rueful pride, how Leonidas 'used to come and open my chests of bedding and clothes, to see that my mother did not hide there for me some luxury or superfluity'. At this level, clearly, the doting Olympias was kept firmly in her place.

But there is one anecdote about Alexander and Leonidas which has never had quite the attention it deserves. Once, when the young prince was offering sacrifice, with would-be royal lavishness he scooped up two whole fistfuls of incense to cast on the altar-fire. This brought down a stinging rebuke on his head from his tutor. 'When you've conquered the spice-bearing regions,' Leonidas said, with that elaborate sarcasm characteristic of schoolmasters the world over, 'you can throw away all the incense you like. Till then, don't waste it.' Years later, Alexander captured Gaza, the main spice-entrepôt for the whole Middle East. As always, he sent presents home to his mother and sister. But this time there was one for Leonidas as well. A consignment of no less than *eighteen tons* of frankincense and myrrh was delivered to the old man (enough to make him rich beyond his wildest dreams on the resale price), 'in remembrance of the hope with which that teacher had inspired his boyhood' – together with an admonition to cease being parsimonious towards the gods.[13]

There is something terrifying about this story: the minor slight that rankled for perhaps fifteen years, the crushing generosity, the elaborate and unanswerable *réplique*. But it affords us a most valuable insight into Alexander's character. Anyone who ever did him a disservice, however trivial, lived to regret it in the end. He never forgot, seldom forgave: 'Vengeance is mine, I will repay, saith the Lord.' His implacability was only equalled by his patience. He would nurse a grudge for a decade or more, waiting for the propitious moment; and when that moment came, he struck.

Alexander's second tutor, Lysimachus of Acarnania, was a very different character: a shrewd if uncultured old lickspittle who earned himself some easy popularity by encouraging his royal pupil's fantasies. He used to call Alexander Achilles, Philip Peleus, and himself Phoenix (the name of Achilles' elderly mentor in the *Iliad*). The boy was taught music – he showed a remarkable aptitude for playing the lyre – and reading and writing. Experts instructed him in the arts of sword-play, archery, and javelin-throwing. Like all well-born Macedonian children, he could ride a horse almost before he could walk. But he never, it seems, learnt how to swim; and throughout his life he retained a marked distaste for the sea.

His precocious horsemanship, indeed, gave rise to one of the most famous surviving anecdotes about him. When he was not more than eight or nine – perhaps in 347, on the occasion of Philip's 'Olympian' Games at Dium – a Thessalian horsebreeder, Philoneicus, brought the king a pedigree stallion, which he offered to sell him for the vast sum of thirteen talents. (Modern equivalents are misleading: this sum, in the fourth century B.C., would have lasted one man as a living wage for about a hundred years.) The stallion was black, except for a white blaze on its forehead, and branded with an ox-head, the mark of Philoneicus' ranch: hence his name, Bucephalas. To command such a price, Bucephalas must have been in his prime – that is, about seven years old.[14]

The story as told by Plutarch abounds in circumstantial detail and dramatic immediacy. Philip, together with his friends and attendants, went down to the open plain to try the horse out. Alexander followed. The king's grooms soon found that Bucephalas was quite unmanageable. They could neither coax nor mount him; he reared and plunged, seemingly deaf to all words of command. Philip lost patience, and told Philoneicus to take his horse away. This was too much for Alexander. 'What a horse they're losing!' he exclaimed. 'And all because they haven't the skill or courage to master him!' The boy's distress was genuine and obvious; and his father, alert as always, had caught his muttered comment.

'Oh,' he said, eyeing his eight-year-old son, 'so you think you know more about managing horses than your elders, do you?'

'Well, I could certainly deal with *this* horse better than they've done.'

Philip's one eye twinkled in his seamed and bearded face. 'All right, then. Suppose you try, and fail, what forfeit will you pay for your presumption?'

'The price of the horse,' Alexander said boldly. A ripple of laughter ran through the group round the king.

'Done,' said his father.

Alexander ran across to Bucephalas, took his bridle, and turned him towards the sun. One thing he had noticed was that the horse started and shied at his own shadow fluttering in front of him. He stood there for a little, stroking and patting the great stallion, calming him down, taking the measure of his spirit. Then he threw off his cloak and vaulted lightly on to Bucephalas' back, with that dynamic agility which was so characteristic of him as a grown man. At first he held the stallion on a tight rein; then, at last, he gave him his head, and the powerful steed went thundering away over the plain. Philip and those round him were 'speechless with anxiety', Plutarch tells us; but Alexander soon wheeled around and came cantering back to them. There was cheering from the crowd. Philip, half-proud, half-resentful, said jokingly: 'You'll have to find another kingdom; Macedonia isn't going to be big enough for you.' Tears in his eyes, he kissed his son. But it was Demaratus of Corinth who brought matters to a triumphant conclusion by buying Bucephalas himself, and giving him to Alexander as a present. Boy and horse became inseparable. Bucephalas carried Alexander into almost every major battle he fought. He died at the ripe old age of thirty, soon after his master's last great victory, over the Indian rajah Porus (Paurava) on the Jhelum River (see below, pp. 389 ff.).[15]

I have quoted this anecdote at length partly because it is one of the very few significant exchanges on record between Alexander and his father. The truth is that they seldom met. Philip spent most of his time away on campaign, and when he did return to Pella he was fully occupied with diplomatic work – not to mention the uproarious state banquets laid on for visiting ambassadors. Surprisingly enough, Alexander seems to have participated in these junketings from a very early age – which may account for his addiction to them later. Aeschines, one of the ten Athenian envoys at Pella in 346, reported that the ten-year-old prince entertained them on the lyre after dinner, and also gave some sort of recitation packed with pointed personal allusions. It may have been on this occasion that Philip asked his son whether he was not ashamed to play so well, the point being (as Plutarch emphasizes) that 'for a king it is surely enough if he can find time to hear others play'.[16] Whatever else one can say about Alexander's upbringing, he certainly learnt the facts of life young.

In August 348 Olynthus fell to Philip's siege-engineers, and his two surviving half-brothers were captured and executed. The Athenians, who had dithered in the assembly and sent reinforcements too late to save the city, made a great huff-and-puff about treachery. Aeschines denounced Philip's cruelty and ambition, but when he tried to raise a coalition of Greek states against Macedonia, the result was a total fiasco. Athens salved her conscience by admitting Olynthian refugees, and after long negotiations finally sent a peace-embassy to Pella in March 346.[17] The way Philip handled these wretched envoys forms one of the more hilarious, if regrettable, chapters in the history of diplomacy. Their leader, Philocrates, was his paid agent. Most of the rest he managed to bribe during their visit. Demosthenes proved obdurate, so Philip played him off against his fellow-delegates – an all too easy task. When peace was voted, on the basis of the territorial status quo, Athens' signatories were kept kicking their heels in Pella while Philip captured a large slice of Thrace. Then, at last, he ratified the agreement.[18]

The Athenian assembly was somehow bamboozled into

thinking that Thebes would be neutralized, Oropus recovered, and Euboea horse-traded for Amphipolis, all
without any effort on their part. They soon learnt better.
The repercussions and recriminations that resulted from
this affair kept the Athenian courts busy for years. Charges
and counter-charges of bribery and corruption were hurled
to and fro like so many custard pies in a farce: most of them
contained an uncomfortable amount of truth. Like all
people who have been made complete fools of, those
responsible nearly burst themselves trying to shift the blame
elsewhere. Philocrates was impeached, and fled the country.
Demosthenes prosecuted Aeschines, who scraped an acquittal by one bare vote. A splendid amount of political
dirty linen was washed in public, the chief beneficiary, of
course, being Philip himself. By thus discrediting Athens'
leaders, who had been made to look not only underhanded
but also inept, he considerably strengthened his bargaining
position with rival states such as Thebes. The divide-and-
rule policy had once again paid handsome dividends.[19]

Meanwhile Philip had been consolidating his position in
other quarters. One golden opportunity for him was the
so-called 'Sacred War'. The citizens of Phocis, feeling
(reasonably enough) that since Delphi lay in their territory
they were entitled to control the shrine, had taken it over
by force, and all efforts to dislodge them had failed. Phocis,
it is true, was one of the smallest states in Greece; but this
hardly mattered, since Apollo's accumulated offerings
could support a large mercenary army more or less *ad
infinitum*. The Amphictyonic council, an interstate religious
body responsible for administering Delphi, appealed to
Philip for help.

The king responded with alacrity, and small wonder. He
could, at one and the same time, pose as the champion of
religious orthodoxy, win himself international prestige, and
have a perfect excuse for moving troops down into central
Greece. Nor would the political support of the oracle itself
come amiss during the next few years: Delphi, despite its

somewhat chequered history, still carried immense authority and prestige. By late summer 346 Philip had smashed the last remnants of Phocian resistance, and brought his troops as far south as Thermopylae. His reward was the presidency of that year's Pythian Games, and Phocis' two seats on the Amphictyonic council.[20]

Philip was now unquestionably the most powerful ruler in Greece. Perhaps as early as 352[21] he had been appointed Archon of Thessaly for life; he now proceeded to organize the country into four tetrarchies, so that it became, to all intents and purposes, a Macedonian out-kingdom. While in Thessaly for this purpose (344) he acquired another mistress, Nicesipolis. Rumours reached Olympias that this woman was using magic spells and potions on the king (Thessalian witches had a notorious reputation throughout antiquity). The queen sent for Nicesipolis, and found her not only beautiful, but also witty and well-bred. 'Away with these slanders!' Olympias is said to have exclaimed. 'You are your own best magic, my dear.' The two women seem, rather improbably, to have struck up a lasting friendship. When Nicesipolis died, Olympias brought up her daughter by Philip, Thessalonice, who afterwards married Antipater's son Cassander. The episode goes a long way to dispel that modern romantic legend which portrays Olympias as a jealous monogamist. Fierce and murderous she could undoubtedly be; but her morals were those of the clan, and dominated by kinship loyalties. So long as her own and her son's status remained undisturbed, Philip was welcome to as many mistresses as he liked. Indeed, the offspring of such liaisons were entitled to a recognized position within the royal household.[22]

It was now, in the autumn of 346, that the veteran Athenian pamphleteer Isocrates published his *Address to Philip*, calling for a Panhellenic crusade against Persia, under Philip's leadership. The idea of such a crusade was by no means new. Gorgias had propounded it at the Olympic

Festival in 408. Lysias brought it up again in 384 – and with good reason. Three years earlier Sparta had forced the Greek states into a humiliating settlement with Persia known as the Peace of Antalcidas. The Hellenic cities of Asia Minor were ceded to the Great King, and the descendants of men who had fought at Salamis or Thermopylae acknowledged his overlordship, his right to arbitrate in Greek disputes, his guardianship of each state's 'autonomy'.[23] As might be expected, this gave rise to a good deal of wild talk about launching a joint campaign to end so humiliating a state of affairs, and to free the Ionian cities from Persian control.[24] But the first serious rational attempt to expound such a programme was Isocrates' own *Panegyricus* (380), a high-minded monograph which envisaged Athens leading the crusade against barbarian Asia, with a penitent and regenerate Sparta at her side.

Its actual effects were somewhat different. The Athenians found it a splendid justification for attempting to recover their old Aegean sea-empire, and the original plan disappeared in a welter of internecine feuding and bloody-minded intrigue. Isocrates regretfully wrote off Athens as a potential leader for his crusade, and composed an admonitory little tract about irresponsible aggression and the bitter fruits of imperialism.[25] But he never abandoned the project, which he regarded as 'the only war that is better than peace: more like a sacred mission than a military expedition'. About 356 he put the idea up to young Archidamus, the future King of Sparta; he had even toyed with the idea of approaching that formidable tyrant Dionysius of Syracuse.[26] This shows very clearly in what direction his ideas were moving. Athens might be the fountain-head of civilization, liberty and democracy; that did not necessarily make her an effective leader, least of all when the cooperation of other Greek cities was essential. The emergence of Philip must have seemed the answer to all Isocrates' prayers. What a crusade needed was a strong leader.

Despite the great difference in tone between the *Pane-*

gyricus and the *Address to Philip* (the intervening years had rubbed Isocrates' idealism perilously thin) several of the main arguments are identical. There is the same emphasis on Persian cowardice, effeminacy, and military incompetence. Both pamphlets dilate on the fabulously rich pickings to be had, for little effort, by an invading army: what an intolerable situation, when barbarians were more prosperous than Greeks! Both, too, stress the fact that a crusade of this kind would absorb the dangerously large number of landless and unemployed mercenaries now loose in Greece, a legacy of endless wars and factions. Both, above all, recommend common action, against a common foe, as the best possible antidote to those interminable interstate feuds which continued to tear Greece apart, rendering her incapable of any concerted action. 'It is much more glorious,' Isocrates asserted, 'to fight against the king for his empire than to contend against each other for the hegemony.' He, like most of his contemporaries, regarded the Persians as 'both natural enemies and hereditary foes': the crusade was to be at once ethnic, cultural, and religious.[27]

The *Address to Philip*, on the other hand, was designed for a specific audience, and contains certain new features. The glorification of free institutions is discreetly dropped; instead we get a set-piece on the advantages of one-man rule. There are extended parallels with the war conducted by Heracles against Troy, for the general good of mankind: Heracles, of course, was held to be Philip's direct ancestor, and is described as such. 'It is your privilege,' Isocrates wrote, working up for his peroration, 'as one who has been blessed with untrammelled freedom, to consider all Hellas your fatherland' – rhetorical hyperbole which Philip, in the event, took somewhat more literally than had been intended.[28] Indeed, taken as a whole the *Address to Philip* must have caused its recipient considerable sardonic amusement.

To begin with, its ethnic conceit was only equalled by its naivety. As everyone knew, Isocrates had only turned to the strong man of Macedonia after canvassing every possible alternative. The flattery was too palpable, the political *volte-face* too gross. Moreover, it appeared that Philip was to lead this crusade for entirely altruistic motives – was to act, in fact, as the unpaid military leader of a free Greek confederacy, and get nothing for his pains except a little booty and the good opinion of the Greek world. It never seems to have struck Isocrates that Philip might have ideas of his own on the subject. However, the king was by no means ungrateful. It was pleasant – and advantageous – to have his Heraclid descent upheld by so venerable an Athenian pundit. Furthermore, the scheme the pundit advocated was an eminently practical one, and many of his detailed suggestions were subsequently carried out.[29] And though Philip did not give a fig for Panhellenism as an idea, he at once saw how it could be turned into highly effective camouflage (a notion which his son subsequently took over ready-made). Isocrates had, unwittingly, supplied him with the propaganda-line he needed. From now on he merely had to clothe his Macedonian ambitions in a suitably Panhellenic dress.

But Philip was not the only interested party who read Isocrates' *Address*; it clearly came to the attention of the Great King himself. When the complete text reached Susa, late in 346, it must have caused considerable alarm. Many rebels and exiles from Persia already saw the powerful young King of Macedonia as their future leader in a crusade against the Achaemenid regime; and Philip, who had given refuge to some of them at Pella, did nothing to discourage such a notion. The possibility that he might act on so tempting a programme could by no means be ruled out.[30] Persia at the time was under the rule of Artaxerxes III Ochus, variously described as 'the last of the great rulers of the ancient Near East' and 'the most blood-thirsty of all Achaemenid monarchs' – not necessarily incompatible statements. The harsh regime he introduced had driven some of his subjects to revolt, and many more to seek asylum abroad. One of Artaxerxes' first acts on accession had been to kill off all his relatives, without distinction of age or sex. He then ordered his satraps in Asia Minor to disband their mercenaries. It was one of these satraps, Artabazus, who ended up at Philip's court (see above, p. 37), after an abortive attempt at rebellion for which he had contrived to secure some support from Athens.

The rebellion fizzled out; the Great King soon bullied Athens into withdrawing her support; and at this point Isocrates began, for a while, to get cold feet about his crusade. These Persians were no longer the cowardly and effeminate cut-out figures of Greek propaganda: they had suddenly turned hostile in earnest. Artaxerxes Ochus was not, it appeared, a man to trifle with (his letters to the Athenian government left little doubt on *that* score). Rumours filled the air. Ochus had ambitions to be a second Xerxes, and reconquer Greece. Twelve thousand camels were padding down the Royal Road from Susa, laden with gold for the purchase of Greek mercenaries. The Athenian demagogues had a field-day.

In Egypt, too, Artaxerxes acted with disconcerting speed and decisiveness. For some time now this vital province had been lost to Persia, and governed by a rebel nationalist regime. In 345, less than twelve months after the publication of the *Address*, a Persian army marched from Babylon to the Phoenician coast, and captured Sidon. In 344/3 a general assembly was dispatched to the Greek states, appealing for help in the Great King's forthcoming campaign against Egypt. This was a neat move on Artaxerxes' part. Philip, of course, supported – and was known to support – the Egyptian rebels. Thus Greek reaction to this embassy should, within limits, reveal just how far each city's traditional hostility to Persia had been eclipsed by its more immediate fear of Macedonian expansion. In the event Thebes and Argos offered assistance, while Athens and Sparta abstained. The line-up was now clear enough. At this point the Athenians – acting, for once, on the dictates of reason rather than emotion – passed a decree calling upon Philip to make common cause with them against Persia. But Philip had no intention of being hustled into premature action. Before he invaded Asia he had to be sure of Greece – and one of the main unknown quantities in Greece was Athens herself. The appeal went unanswered.

Any lingering doubts Philip might have had were removed by the events of the next few months. Artaxerxes had weighed up his chances to a nicety. His troops – strongly reinforced now by Greek mercenaries – smashed their way south through the Negev into Egypt. By late autumn all resistance was broken. Nectanebo, the native Pharaonic pretender, fled the country (to reappear later, in legend, as Alexander's putative father). Phoenicia and Egypt were once more in Persian hands, and the latter was quickly reorganized as an imperial province. At some time during these operations Artaxerxes sent envoys to Philip and negotiated a non-aggression pact, on terms extremely favourable to the Great King.[31] His main condition of alliance was very simple: Macedonia must withdraw her backing from all rebels who owed Artaxerxes allegiance. Now Philip had not only harboured any anti-Achaemenid rebel who sought his protection; he had also given private backing, for his own ends, to various would-be independent local rulers in Asia Minor itself. Some of these deals he had kept secret. Others – such as his support for the rebellious local kings of Cyprus – were public knowledge.

Philip was nothing if not a realist; he now cut his losses and repudiated his secret agreements – those, at least, of which the Persians had already been apprised. The Persian – Macedonian alliance went through, and the Cypriot revolt collapsed. Once again, at a slightly stiffer price than usual, Philip had bought himself precious time. He also (taking a calculated risk) kept up his private understanding with Hermeias, the eunuch and ex-slave who ruled over Atarneus in the southern Troad, opposite Mytilene, and whose territory offered a most promising bridgehead for any future invasion.[32] Just how long this link could be preserved, however, was another matter. Already Hermeias had come under some suspicion. He controlled too much of the Troad, he was acting too independently, he possessed a formidable army of mercenaries. Sooner or later the Great King must surely close in on him. When that moment came, there was one member of his family whom Philip would much prefer to have safe at Pella – not merely for his own sake (he was a brilliant man) but also on account of the special knowledge he had concerning Philip's invasion plans.

This was the son of old Amyntas' court physician, a boyhood friend some three years older than Philip himself (who in 343 had just turned forty). He had been one of Plato's most distinguished pupils, and just before the master's death, in 348/7, there was a strong likelihood of his being nominated to succeed him as head of the Academy. In the event, however, the dying Plato chose his own nephew, Speusippus: a bitter disappointment. About the same time his home-town was sacked and burnt by Macedonian troops, busy mopping up pockets of resistance in the Chalcidic peninsula. As a Macedonian dependant himself he was by no means popular in Athens, either; and now there was nothing to keep him there any longer.

He therefore emigrated, together with his friend Xenocrates, the future head of the Lyceum. They took up residence at Hermeias' court, and promptly set about the task – so dear to Greek philosophers, so *outré* by modern standards – of transforming this ex-slave and ex-banker into the ideal philosopher-king. The little group got on famously: treaties with neighbouring cities were made in the name of 'Hermeias and the Companions'. In due course Hermeias' zealous mentor married his patron's niece; unkind rumour claimed that he had previously been involved with Hermeias himself. Quite apart from his scientific and philosophical activities, he was also acting as a confidential political agent, a link-man between Hermeias and Philip.*[33] His personal appearance was foppish, not to say eccentric. He was balding, spindle-shanked, and had small eyes. Perhaps in an effort to compensate for these disadvantages, he wore dandified clothes, cut and curled his hair in an affected manner, and spoke with a lisp. Numerous rings sparkled on his fingers: the overall effect must have been rather like the young Disraeli at his worst.[34] His name was Aristotle.

He had realized, sooner than most people, that Arta-xerxes' new, dynamic policy might well mean trouble for Hermeias. In 345/4, with canny foresight, he moved across the straits to Mytilene, perhaps at the invitation of a young local botanist named Theophrastus, who had come to Atarneus to hear him lecture. For a couple of years Aristotle remained on the island, teaching, researching, and keeping an eye on Persian activities in the Troad. It was here, during the winter of 343/2, that Philip's invitation reached him. Would he – in return for a suitably high honorarium – agree to come back to Macedonia, and act as personal tutor to Alexander? The boy was thirteen now, and needed a first-class teacher to supervise his studies. He was, Philip indicated delicately, proving a trifle unmanageable. As an extra inducement, Philip promised to restore Aristotle's birthplace, Stagira, and to recall 'those of its citizens who were in exile or slavery'.[35] This was to be no ordinary tutorship; it would carry very special personal and political responsibilities.

The philosopher's decision was never in doubt.

Alexander had grown into a boy of rather below average

---

* It has recently been argued, by Chroust, that he in fact left Athens as early as 348, before Plato's death, and because of anti-Macedonian feeling rather than through frustrated philosophical ambitions; further, that his subsequent residence with Hermeias, and on Mytilene, was dictated not so much by scientific curiosity as by Philip's political requirements. While the political element should not be minimized, this seems a needlessly extreme position.

height, but very muscular and compact of body. He was
already (like his hero Achilles) a remarkably fast runner.
His hair, blond and tousled, is traditionally said to have
resembled a lion's mane, and he had that high complexion
which fair-skinned people so often display. His eyes were
odd, one being grey-blue and the other dark brown. His
teeth were sharply pointed – 'like little pegs', says the
Alexander-Romance, an uncharacteristically realistic touch
which carries instant conviction. He had a somewhat high-
pitched voice, which tended to harshness when he was
excited. His gait was fast and nervous, a habit he had picked
up from old Leonidas; and he carried his head bent slightly
upwards and to the left – whether because of some physical
defect, or through mere affectation, cannot now be determined. There is something almost girlish about his earliest
portraits (cf. below, p. 66), a hint of leashed hysteria
behind the melting charm. Aristotle, one feels, probably
had a testing time.[36]

Philip decided, wisely, that what with political intrigues
and the omnipresent influence of Olympias, Pella was no
place for the young prince at this stage in his career. Higher
education demanded rural solitude. He therefore assigned
to Aristotle the so-called Precinct of the Nymphs at Mieza,
a village in the eastern foothills of the Bermius range, north
of Beroea (Verria). This precinct probably formed part of
the famous Gardens of Midas (see above, p. 4), which
covered the modern Verria–Naoussa–Vodena area: a district of fine vineyards and orchards (Naoussa still produces an excellent red wine much akin to Burgundy).[37] As
late as Plutarch's day, in the first century A.D., visitors were
still shown the stone benches and shady avenues where
Aristotle had conducted his lessons. Nor was Alexander
Aristotle's only pupil; and again, this shows good sense on
Philip's part. A select group of the young prince's contemporaries joined him at Mieza. They included his lifelong
friend Hephaestion; Cassander, son of Antipater, and
Ptolemy, son of Lagus, both themselves future kings; and

Marsyas of Pella, who afterwards wrote a treatise, now lost, on *The Education of Alexander*.[38]

Philip, we are told, enjoined his son to study hard, and to pay close attention to all Aristotle taught him – 'so that,' he said, 'you may not do a great many things of the sort that I am sorry to have done'. At this point Alexander, somewhat pertly, took Philip to task 'because he was having children by other women beside his wife'. Having *children*, be it noted, not merely *relations*: this alone should suffice to dispel the modern notion that Alexander was playing an adolescent Hamlet to Philip's Claudius. What in fact we observe here is an entirely natural anxiety about the succession. After all, Philip had had trouble enough with *his* illegitimate half-brothers (see above, pp. 22 ff.); why should he, Alexander, be made to go through the whole weary business over again? The king's reply, too, shows that he knew very well what lay at the root of the matter. In answer to his son's criticisms he said: 'Well then, *if you have many competitors for the kingdom* [my italics], prove yourself honourable and good, so that you may obtain the kingdom not because of me, but because of yourself.'[39]

This story does much to discredit that quasi-Freudian element which some modern scholars[40] have professed to discover in the relationship between Alexander and Olympias. The truth is less romantic, but of considerable significance for future events. Even at this age Alexander's one overriding obsession (and, if it comes to that, his mother's) was with his future status as king. If he had any kind of Oedipus complex it came a very poor second to the burning dynastic ambition which Olympias so sedulously fostered in him: those who insist on his psychological motivation would do better to take Adler as their mentor than Freud.

When it was suggested to him that he was a fast enough sprinter to enter for the Olympic Games, he replied that he would only run if he had kings as his competitors:[41] a revealing remark, and one which agrees well with what we know of his adult character. While pursuing Darius through Asia, he heard that Aristotle had published, as a treatise, the more esoteric material on metaphysics which had hitherto been reserved for verbal discussion with a few select pupils – and had, therefore, formed part of the course at Mieza. The king, though occupied with far more pressing matters, still found time to dash off a short and furious note of complaint to his former teacher. 'In what,' he asked, 'shall I surpass other men if those doctrines wherein I have been trained are to be all men's common property?' Aristotle replied, soothingly, that the treatise would mean nothing to those who had not taken part in his classes, and was, in fact, only published as an *aide-mémoire* for the initiated[42] – a somewhat lame *réplique*, by no means calculated to soothe that inflamed and ultra-royal ego.

Ever to strive to be best: the Homeric ideal forms a recurrent leitmotiv, dominating every branch of Alexander's multifarious activities. Nor indeed (if Book III of the *Politics* bears any relation to the views expounded at Mieza) were Aristotle's political opinions likely to lessen the crown prince's opinion of himself. As a good Greek philosopher, one might have thought, Aristotle was liable to find his royal pupil's status and ambitions more than mildly embarrassing. The whole trend of current political theory, liberal and authoritarian alike, was towards some form of republicanism. The *Politics* suggests how he contrived to circumvent this difficulty. While deploring monarchy in general as an institution, he nevertheless allowed one justification for it, and one alone: outstanding personal *areté* (achievement, Renaissance *virtù*). The choice of this peculiarly Homeric criterion was, surely, no accident. Such an individual, 'a very god among men', no more amenable than Zeus himself to the rule of his fellows, and above legal sanctions since he embodied the law, could only, said Aristotle, become a king; there was no other course open to him.

Yet even so, only in one case was monarchy *right* (that is, morally justified): 'when the *areté* of the king or of his family is so preeminent that it outclasses the *areté* of *all* the citizens put together'. It would have been tactless, to say the least, had Philip's employee not made it clear that the Argead royal house fell squarely into this category. Such a doctrine may not have encouraged Alexander to claim divinity in after years (even this has been seriously suggested) but it certainly did nothing to diminish his royal self-assurance.[43] Nor was Aristotle slow to find intellectual arguments in support of Alexander's passionate longing to win glory at the expense of the Barbarian. Indeed, his attitude to Persia was uncompromisingly ethnocentric. He believed slavery to be a natural institution, and equally that all 'barbarians' (i.e. non-Greeks) were slaves by nature. It was therefore right and fitting for Greeks to rule over barbarians, but not for barbarians to rule over Greeks. Like many intellectuals with a racialist axe to grind, Aristotle found support for his thesis in facts drawn from geopolitics or 'natural law'. Greek superiority had to be proved demonstrably innate, a gift of nature. In one celebrated fragment he counsels Alexander to be 'a hegemon [leader] to the Greeks and a despot to the barbarians, to look after the former as after friends and relatives, and to deal with the latter as with beasts or plants'.[44]

There were good personal reasons for him to feel as he did. In 341 Hermeias' private dealings with Philip became known at Susa. The Great King sent Mentor, his Greek mercenary general, to deal with the philosopher–eunuch of Atarneus. Mentor tricked Hermeias into attending a conference, and promptly placed him under arrest. In Athens, Demosthenes gloated rather unpleasantly over the top-secret Macedonian plans Hermeias was bound to reveal under torture. But he misjudged his man. Mutilated, impaled, and dying, Hermeias nevertheless managed to get one final message out to his former friends. He had done nothing, he said, unworthy of a scholar and a gentleman. Philip's secrets went to the grave with him, and Aristotle, from his comfortable retreat in Mieza, wrote a glowing ode to his memory.[45]

It is most often assumed that Alexander was fundamentally at odds with his tutor's xenophobia: that already the embryo world-conqueror looked to wider political horizons than those of the *polis*. One scholar even goes so far as to claim that 'the meeting of genius with genius . . . remained without a deeper meaning and without effect.'[46] But even supposing Alexander later adopted, in some form or other, a policy of racial fusion – in itself a highly debatable point – there is no reason to suppose he did not wholeheartedly share Aristotle's views to begin with. Even his most idealistic champion concedes as much. 'The primary reason why Alexander invaded Persia,' says Tarn, 'was, no doubt, that he never thought of *not* doing it; it was his inheritance.'[47]

Besides, he had the whole body of Greek civilized opinion behind him. Euripides held that it was proper (*eikos*) for 'barbarians' to be subject to Greeks. Plato and Isocrates both thought of all non-Hellenes as natural enemies who could be enslaved or exterminated at will. Aristotle himself regarded a war against barbarians as essentially just.[48] Such theories may well be dismissed as grotesque; but they are no more grotesque than de Gobineau's concept of the Aryan superman. And grotesque or not, they have the power to compel belief, and thus to affect men's lives in the most fundamental way. When Hitler exterminated the European Jews, he based his actions, precisely, on the belief that certain categories of mankind could be dismissed as subhuman – that is, like Aristotle, he equated them with beasts or plants.

For Aristotle, however, the brute or vegetable nature of barbarians had a special quality, which must have struck a responsive chord in his pupil. 'No one,' he wrote, 'would value existence for the pleasure of eating alone, or that of sex . . . unless he were utterly servile' (i.e. slave or barbarian). To such a person, on the other hand, it would make no difference whether he were beast or man. The key example he cites is the Assyrian voluptuary Sardanapalus (Assurbanipal): barbarians, it is clear, are to be despised above all *because they live exclusively through and for the senses*.[49] The purely hedonistic life, in fact, was something which Aristotle taught his pupil to regard as beneath contempt. Such a doctrine must have had a strong appeal for Alexander, who always placed a premium on self-control and self-denial (at least during the earlier stages of his career), and whose enthusiastic, impressionable nature reveals a strong hero-worshipping streak. (It made no odds to him whether his hero was mythical or contemporary: he may have modelled himself on Achilles, but he was equally ready to adopt the quick-stepping gait of his old tutor Leonidas.) The Alexander who ate so sparingly, who gave away the spoils of war with such contemptuous generosity, keeping little for himself, and who said he was never more conscious of his own mortality than 'during the time he lay with a woman or slept'[50] – this, surely, was a man whose debt to Aristotle's teaching and influence was fundamental. For good or ill, the years at Mieza left a permanent mark on him.

Aristotle's advice on the respective treatment of Greeks and barbarians is, of course, capable of a more mundane interpretation: that in order to get the best out of those whom one intends to exploit, one must humour them far enough to win their cooperation. Greeks required to be treated as equals, to have their sense of independence – however illusory – fostered with the greatest care. Asiatics, on the other hand, would only respond to, or respect, a show of rigorous authoritarianism – the Victorian district officer's creed. Whether Aristotle intended this lesson or not, it was one that Alexander learnt all too well. As we shall see, he applied it to every individual or group with whom he subsequently came in contact.

He also absorbed a great deal of his tutor's own omnivorous scientific curiosity, and the sharply empirical cast of mind that went with it. Once, on being asked, as a schoolroom test, what he would do in certain circumstances, he replied that he could not tell until the circumstances arose – an answer which must surely have won Aristotle's approval. Like his great predecessor Hippocrates, Aristotle believed that experiment and observation formed the only proper basis for scientific advance, an axiom on which modern science still largely rests. When Alexander launched his Asiatic invasion, he took with him a whole host of zoologists, botanists and surveyors; the material and information they collected laid the foundations for several epoch-making scientific works, including Aristotle's own *Historia Animalium*. Again, there can be little doubt as to the source of this unprecedented undertaking.

In addition, Alexander developed a strong interest in medicine and biology – two more of Aristotle's own favourite subjects. Throughout his life he was, Plutarch says, 'not only fond of the theory of medicine, but actually came to the aid of his friends when they were sick, and prescribed for them certain treatments and regimens'.[51] Perhaps what benefited him most in this scientific training was the observant flexibility of mind it produced, the ability to deal with any problem as it arose, on its own merits and without preconceptions. Here, indeed, we touch on his most characteristic quality as a field-commander.

At a more formal level, the course of studies he followed was that prescribed by Plato and current among all Academics of the day. He read and discussed poetry, above all Homer: we have already seen how great an enthusiasm he had for the *Iliad*. He was given a grounding in geometry, astronomy, and rhetoric – particularly in that branch of rhetoric known as eristics, which meant arguing a point from either side with equal facility. Alexander developed a great taste for eristics: this was one sphere in which Aristotle's training had disastrous consequences later, and it is not hard to see why. To ordinary unsophisticated Macedonians, 'a man ready to speak pro and con was clearly a false person who proved that he was a good liar'.[52] Old

Isocrates, understandably piqued that Alexander's education had not been entrusted to himself, or at least to a member of his own rhetorical school, regarded the entire Academic discipline as worse than useless. We have a letter he wrote Alexander about 342, warning the young prince, in veiled diplomatic language, against these hair-splitting sophists who will never teach him how to cope with the harsh realities of politics. A prince's part, he implies, is not to persuade, but to command: Alexander should avoid eristics. This, as things turned out, was a shrewd piece of advice, even if given for *parti pris* motives. Needless to say, it was ignored.[53]

Alexander's sojourn in the Gardens of Midas lasted for three years, during which time relations between Macedonia and the Greek states, Athens in particular, grew steadily worse. While the young prince and his tutor paced the shady walks of Mieza, Philip had more immediate and practical affairs to deal with. He spent most of 342 in Thrace, where his frontiers were weakest, planting military colonies along the Hebrus Valley. The colonists were the scum of Macedonia – jailbirds, unemployed mercenaries, troublemakers of every sort. One such settlement acquired the nickname of Poneropolis, or 'Thugsville': Philip, it is clear, was economically solving two problems at once. It was now, too, that (in accordance with his usual dynastic policy: see above, p. 27) he married his fourth wife – Meda, the daughter of a Thracian prince name Cothelas. She brought him a handsome dowry and a valuable alliance. Olympias, as far as we know, raised no objections.[54]

Demosthenes had no illusions about Philip's ultimate goal. The king, he said, was not wintering 'in that purgatory for the sake of the rye and millet of the Thracian store-pits', but as part of a long-term scheme for taking over 'the Athenian harbours and dockyards and war-galleys and silver-mines'.[55] This prospect was alarming enough to make the Athenians send out a *condottiere* called Diopeithes to the

Thracian Chersonese (Gallipoli Peninsula), with the task of 'safeguarding Athenian interests' there – a classic euphemism. Diopeithes took some so-called 'colonists' with him, who seem to have been the same sort of riff-raff as Philip was establishing along the Hebrus. He himself was little more than a government-sponsored pirate, who lived by extorting protection money. Isocrates, made somewhat nervous by these aggressive tactics, sent an open letter to Philip, suggesting a Macedonian – Athenian entente, and renewing his proposals for a joint expedition against Persia.[56]

Philip sent a formal protest about Diopeithes' activities, which was debated in the Athenian assembly. At the same time he began gathering a large army in Thrace, with reinforcements from Thessaly and Macedonia. Demosthenes made two fighting speeches against Diopeithes' recall, emphasizing the urgency of not letting Philip get the upper hand in the Dardanelles or the Bosporus. He also pointed out what an advantage Macedonia's standing army enjoyed over the conscript levies of a democratic city-state. Philip's men were far better trained; Philip himself 'makes no difference between summer and winter and has no season set apart for inaction'; Athens might not be at war with Philip, but Philip was already at war with Athens.[57] Demosthenes also saw, more clearly than anyone, just how Philip could apply pressure to Athens most effectively. Already the Macedonian was 'laying down warships and building docks', nor could there be much doubt as to their purpose. If Philip captured Byzantium, Athenian grain-supplies would be seriously imperilled. Years later, when recapitulating Philip's career, Demosthenes put the matter in a nutshell: 'Observing that we consume more imported corn than any other nation, he proposed to get control of the carrying trade in corn.' Behind all the complex political manoeuvres of the years between 342 and 338 looms the ever-present – and highly effective – threat of economic blackmail.[58]

Demosthenes' positive recommendations were uncompromising. Diopeithes must be recalled. More important, an embassy should be sent to Susa: the time had come for a *rapprochement* with the Great King. The Greek states must sink their differences and form a new Panhellenic League. In particular, Byzantium must be persuaded to renew her ancient friendship with Athens.[59] These recommendations were, for the most part, carried out. Byzantium and Abydos joined the Athenian alliance. Diopeithes remained in his command, and a league of Greek states was formed against Macedonia. When Philip expelled Olympias' uncle Arybbas from the throne of Epirus, and replaced him with young Alexander the Molossian, Athens pointedly offered Arybbas political asylum. The naval building programme was stepped up. Friendly towns in the Thracian Chersonese were voted special honours by the Athenian assembly, and in March 340 Demosthenes was voted a gold crown, which he received at the Greater Dionysia.[60]

Most important of all, a secret embassy was dispatched from Athens to Susa, with highly successful results. The Great King was at last persuaded to make an open declaration of hostility to Macedonia. The psychological effect of this move on the city-states must have been considerable. He also provided the envoys with a lavish contingency fund, for the express purpose of bribing Greek politicians to stir up war against Philip (Demosthenes alone was later accused of pocketing no less than 3,000 gold darics from this source). Philip, finding himself up against the most serious crisis of his career, acted with characteristic promptness and vigour.[61] As a test case, he called on Byzantium and Perinthus (a key port in the Propontis) to honour their agreements with Macedonia by supporting him in his campaign against Diopeithes. Both were still – nominally at least – his allies; and both refused point-blank. Philip, without further argument, mobilized his new fleet, bent on whipping these recalcitrant allies back into line before the rot could spread. Since he meant to command this expedition in person, he summoned the sixteen-year-old Alexander home to Pella, where he formally appointed him Regent of Macedonia and Master of the Royal Seal, with the experienced Antipater as his adviser.

⌈3⌋

From a View to a Death

ALEXANDER'S schooldays were over. From now on the young crown prince was to be trained in a harder school, and with greater responsibilities, than even Isocrates would have dared to prescribe. This may well have been a deliberate 'hardening' policy on Philip's part. Both he and Olympias (according to Theophrastus)[1] were worried by, among other things, the boy's lack of heterosexual interests. They feared he might be turning out a girlish invert (*gynnis*), and even went so far as to procure a beautiful Thessalian courtesan named Callixeina to help develop his manly nature. Olympias herself, we are told, frequently begged him to have intercourse with this woman – which does not suggest any great enthusiasm on his part; but then, what son would take kindly to a maternally selected mistress?

On the other hand, there was nothing effeminate about Alexander's conduct as regent. No sooner had Philip left on his Byzantine campaign (sailing, in the first instance, against Perinthus) than rebellion broke out among the Maedi, a powerful and warlike tribe on the borders of Thrace and Paeonia. Alexander took a flying expedition up north, defeated the rebels, captured their city, and turned it into a Macedonian military outpost. This new settlement he renamed Alexandropolis, in imitation of Philip's similar outpost, Philippopolis. Where his father was concerned, Alexander never lacked the competitive spirit. It is often argued that to have named a *polis*, a civic foundation, after himself would have been open *lèse-majesté*, tantamount to an act of rebellion. On the other hand he was regent, and the possession of the Great Seal reveals the extent of his powers. Besides, with a mere military colony he may have been technically within his rights. But even so his act was a danger-signal which Philip surely recognized. Alexander's appetite for royal power, long fostered by Olympias, would not long content itself with a temporary regency; and Philip himself was still a vigorous man in the prime of life. Sooner or later there was bound to be trouble between them.[2]

But for the moment they remained on close and friendly terms. During his absence abroad Philip kept up a regular correspondence with the young regent, and such fragments from his letters as have survived are as full of solid parental

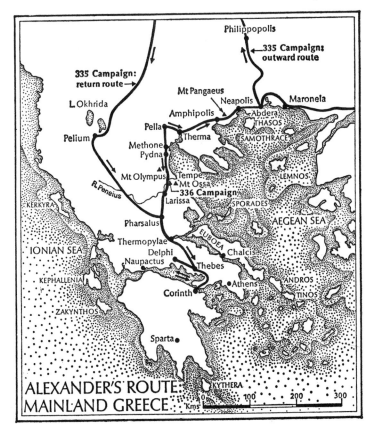

advice as those of Lord Chesterfield. Alexander must cultivate friends among the Macedonian nobility while he
could (few of the boy's close friends seem, in fact, to have
belonged to the higher aristocracy, a significant pointer:
perhaps his half-Epirot blood was responsible). As crown
prince he was also in a position to win favour with the
masses, since he could, like Shakespeare's Prince Hal, still
afford to be easy-going. For a reigning monarch it was quite
another matter. 'He also advised him,' says Plutarch, 'that,
among the men of influence in the cities, he should make
friends of both the good and the bad, and that later he
should use the former and abuse the latter.' But a report that
Alexander had been trying to secure the allegiance of
certain Macedonians by bribes brought down a stinging
rebuke on the young regent's head. Since Philip was a
past master at the art of bribery himself, his comment is
worth noting: 'What on earth,' he inquired, 'gave you the
deluded idea that you would ever make faithful friends out
of those whose affections you had bought?'[3]

Philip's campaign, meanwhile, was not going at all well.
He had been forced to raise the siege of Perinthus after
three months. His seizure of 230 Athenian merchantmen
provoked some acrimonious diplomatic exchanges, which
culminated in Athens declaring war on Macedonia. In the
late autumn he switched his attack against Byzantium; but
the city was strongly held (Athens had sent a naval contingent to help in its defence), and his final assault was betrayed
by inopportunely barking dogs. Once again he had to pull
out, and it was only by a somewhat desperate ruse that he
extricated his fleet from the Black Sea. By now he was in a
decidedly awkward position. Athenian privateers were
harassing his shipping and supplies. Persia had declared
against him, and this might well impress a city like Thebes,
which could cut his land-communications to the south.
The last straw was a disastrous raid which he conducted into
the Thracian Dobrudja (spring 339). On his way home he

was ambushed and defeated by the Triballi, a hairy and primitive tribe which had provided Aristophanes with some of his best music-hall jokes. He lost all his booty, and received a nasty spear-thrust through one thigh, which left him permanently lame (see below, p. 89).[5]

By the summer of 339 – though his opponents never seem fully to have appreciated this – Philip's position was highly critical. For years he had successfully played the divide-and-rule game with the Greek states; now there was an all-too-real danger of *their* combining against him. He had looked forward to leading a Persian invasion under the flag of Panhellenism, with Athens, Thebes, and Sparta, cowed or cooperative, marching at his side. Now it seemed more likely that the boot would be on the other foot: the Greeks had done a deal with Artaxerxes, and if Philip did not move fast it would be they who invaded his territory, not he theirs. In the event, he moved faster than anyone could have predicted.

While the Macedonian army was actually on the march south into central Greece, Philip still kept up a smoke-screen of diplomatic blarney to lull the Greeks' suspicions. His ambassadors went ahead of him to Athens and Thebes, carrying letters that cleverly played on the traditional enmity between these two powerful city-states: a last-minute *détente* between them was something he had every intention of avoiding if he could. Even at this late stage in the game he still seems to have hoped for a peaceful settlement, especially with Athens. His admiration for the 'violet-crowned city' was genuine enough; but there were other more practical factors influencing him. The sooner he came to grips with Artaxerxes, clearly, the better. But to cross the Dardanelles before he had all Greece secure behind him would be political and military suicide. An Athenian alliance would bring him great prestige; it might also swing a number of undecided states into line at the same time. Nor had Philip any intention of wasting precious months battering away at the immensely powerful

naval defences of Piraeus.[6] If Athens would not come over of
her own free will, an Athenian army must be brought to
battle and defeated by land, for all the world to see. Somehow or other Philip must provoke the Athenians and their
allies into fighting on *his* terms – not at sea, where they
enjoyed every advantage, but against the superbly trained
infantrymen of the Macedonian phalanx. By one of Fate's
more bitter ironies, it was Demosthenes who finally gave
him what he wanted.

Late one September evening, a horrified Athenian
assembly heard the news that Philip, far from marching
on south-west to Amphissa (his declared objective), had
turned east at Cytinium in Doris – as momentous a decision
in its way as Caesar's crossing of the Rubicon – and
occupied Elatea, a key-point on the main road through to
Thebes and Attica. Demosthenes now emerged as the
patriotic hero of the hour, the impassioned champion of
Athenian liberty. Hitherto, he informed his fellow-citizens
with withering sarcasm, they had been 'lucky enough to
enjoy the fruits of that factitious humanity in which
[Philip] clothed himself with an eye to the future'. But now
they could no longer rely on his calculated forbearance. By
sheer vehemence and conviction the great orator brought
about what Philip had most feared – a defensive coalition
between Athens and Thebes. Isocrates, still holding out for
alliance with Philip, found himself dismissed as a mere
senile *collabo*.[8]

An Athenian army marched into Boeotia, and the two
new allies promptly set about fortifying the north-west
passes. A force of 10,000 mercenaries was also sent westward
towards Amphissa. If Philip captured Naupactus, he could
cross the Corinthian Gulf at its narrowest point, link up
with his Peloponnesian allies, and march on Athens by
way of the Isthmus. These dispositions blocked both his
possible lines of advance. During the winter of 339/8 Philip
made no move, and the Athenians congratulated themselves
on their foresight. In March 338 Demosthenes was once

more awarded a gold crown at the Greater Dionysia for distinguished public service. Patriotism, unfortunately, does not of itself guarantee strategic common sense. Demosthenes has often been condemned for destroying Athenian freedom when Isocrates' policy could have preserved it; but his real and fatal error was to implement a military policy which played straight into Philip's hands.

Despite Themistocles' strategy at Salamis, despite the endless costly lessons of the Peloponnesian War, Athenian statesmen were still, in moments of national crisis, bedazzled by the conservative legend of the Marathonian hoplite. They neglected the fact that for over a century Athens had ceased to be a land-power, and that her once-formidable citizen-hoplites were now largely replaced by mercenaries. Athens' real strength and expertise lay in her still-formidable navy. At this period she had over 300 triremes available for active service. Athenian operations in the Hellespont, and during the siege of Byzantium, had shown just how vulnerable Philip was at sea. If, immediately after the occupation of Elatea, Athens had mobilized her naval reserves and sent a strong fleet north to the Thermaic Gulf, Philip would almost certainly have pulled his army out of central Greece. Yet here was Demosthenes, with what can only be termed self-destructive bravado, proposing to block his advance by land. Nothing could have suited the king's plans better.[9]

Now his only remaining task was to lure the Greek forces out of their defensive positions and force an engagement. Once this had been done, Macedonia's formidable cavalry and the trained regiments of the phalanx would do the rest. In the event everything proved absurdly easy. Philip arranged for a bogus dispatch to be captured by the task-force guarding Amphissa. This informed them that the king was withdrawing his army to deal with an uprising in Thrace. Thinking the enemy had gone, the Greek mercenaries became careless. Philip launched a night-attack in strength, and annihilated them.[10] His column swept through Amphissa and Delphi, thus turning the flank of the troops holding north-west Boeotia, and debouched in the plain a little way south of them, near Lebadea.

The Greeks did the only thing possible in the circumstances: they abandoned the passes, and established a shorter line of defence at Chaeronea, between the Cephisus River and the citadel. This put them in a very strong position. To west, east and south they were protected by mountains. In the south they had the further advantage of controlling the Kérata pass to Lebadea, so that Philip could not force them into a reversed-front engagement. Their communications were excellent: as things stood they could, with luck, hold the Macedonians till winter. If Philip bypassed them and marched on Attica, they were in his rear. His only chance was to make a direct frontal assault on their lines from the north, with what – despite later Greek propaganda claims – was in fact a somewhat smaller force. In cavalry they were about equally matched, with 2,000 on either side; but the Greeks had mustered some 35,000 infantry to Philip's 30,000, and the latter probably represented the full field strength of the Macedonian army. On the other hand, Philip had the advantage of experience and professionalism. Athens' best generals were now dead, and her present commander-in-chief, Chares, something of a mediocrity.[11]

Nevertheless, Philip was sufficiently impressed to make one last attempt at negotiating a peaceful settlement with Athens and Thebes. The Athenian commander Phocion, back from a minor and ineffectual naval sortie to the North Aegean, recommended accepting his proposals; but Demosthenes, tireless and adamant, blocked all attempts to reach a solution through diplomatic channels. The Delphic Oracle made gloomy pronouncements; these he brushed aside as mere propaganda, asserting – what may well have been true – that the Pythia had become no more than Philip's paid mouthpiece. The king, seeing that diplomacy would get him nowhere, now prepared for a final show-down. He captured

Naupactus, as the Athenians had anticipated, left a small holding force at Delphi, and deployed the rest of his troops across the plain north of Chaeronea. It was here, on 4 August 338, that the two armies met, in one of the most decisive encounters of all Greek history.[12]

The battle took place at dawn. On the allied right wing were the Boeotians, some 12,000 strong, led by the famous Theban Sacred Band, which in 371 had broken Sparta's hitherto invincible army at Leuctra. On the left wing were stationed Athens' 10,000 hoplites. The centre was made up from the remaining allied contingents, with a stiffening of 5,000 mercenaries. On the extreme left, a screen of light-

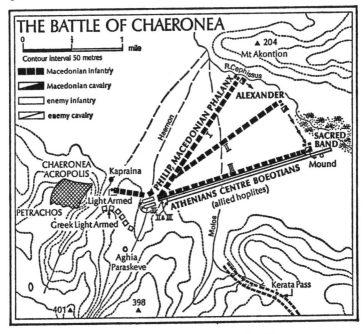

THE BATTLE OF CHAERONEA

Contour interval 50 metres

■■■ Macedonian infantry
◢ Macedonian cavalry
☐ enemy infantry
◿ enemy cavalry

Phase I
Macedonians advance; Greeks stationary.

Phase II
Philip retreats, his centre and left advancing; Athenians, Centre and Boeotians advance to left front, but Sacred Band stands firm.

Phase III
Alexander charges, the centres engage, and Philip drives the Athenian wing up the Haemon valley.

armed troops linked the main force with the citadel. The cavalry was held in reserve. The Greek commanders had drawn up their line of battle slantwise across the plain, from west-south-west to east-north-east. If Philip's attack ran into trouble, a left-wing advance by the Athenians could press him back across open country to the river – a pivotal movement not unlike the closing of a fan. If, on the other hand, he succeeded in breaking through, they would still be able to retreat in good order over the Kérata pass to Lebadea. It was an ingenious plan, and under better commanders – or against a less brilliant and professional opponent – it might well have succeeded.

Philip knew that any serious opposition he got would come from the Thebans. Since they had been technically allied to him when they threw in their lot with Athens, they had the most to fear at his hands in the event of a defeat. Philip was a man who gave traitors very short shrift. Furthermore, their troops were experienced veterans, as well trained as his own: Philip knew, better than anyone, just how much Macedonian discipline owed to Theban methods (see above, pp. 15-16). The Athenians, on the other hand, were citizen-volunteers, without any real combat experience. It had been well over twenty years since Athens had put an army into the field, and then only for a month's campaigning. Philip saw that his main objective must, inevitably, be the annihilation of the Sacred Band. He also realized that Athenian impetuosity and lack of discipline could materially help him to achieve this end.[13]

His tactical dispositions were made accordingly. He himself commanded the right wing, at the head of his Guards Brigade, the Hypaspists, with a strong light-armed force to protect his flank. In the centre he placed the regiments of the phalanx. The command of the heavy cavalry on the extreme left wing, opposite the Sacred Band, went to Alexander – an extraordinarily responsible appointment for a boy of eighteen, since it was he who had to deliver the knock-out blow that would, if successful, clinch Philip's victory. (Over four hundred years later Plutarch, himself a native of Chaeronea, was shown a tree by the Cephisus still known as 'Alexander's Oak', under which, it was said, he had pitched his tent on the night before the battle.) This battle-plan was, in essence, a replica of that which Philip had employed against the Illyrians at Lake Okhrida (see above, pp. 24-6).

When battle was joined, Philip's right wing slightly outflanked the Athenian left, while his own centre and left were echeloned back at an angle from the Greek line – 'refused' is the technical military term. Thus when he and the Guards Brigade engaged the Athenians, the rest of the Macedonian army was still advancing. More important still, these tactics produced an inevitable – and probably unconscious – drift to the left among the Athenians, followed by the allied and mercenary troops of the Greek centre. At the first onset the Athenians – as Philip had probably anticipated – launched a wildly enthusiastic charge. Their general Stratocles, seeing the Guards Brigade give way, completely lost his head, and began shouting: 'Come on, let's drive them back to Macedonia!'

But Philip's withdrawal (as Stratocles should have seen) was anything but disorderly. Step by well-drilled step the Guards Brigade moved back, still facing to their front, a hedgehog bristle of *sarissas* holding the pursuit at bay. On rushed the Athenians, yelling and cheering, the Greek centre stretching ever more perilously as they pressed forward. Presently two things happened for which Philip had been waiting. The Macedonians backed up on to rising ground by the banks of a small stream, the Haemus (Blood River); and that fatal gap at last opened between the Greek centre and the Theban brigades on their right. Superior discipline, ironically, had sealed the fate of the Sacred Band. They held their formation; the troops in the centre did not. Into the gap thus opened, at the head of Macedonia's finest cavalry division, thundered the young crown prince (the only recorded occasion on which he held a left-flank position), while a second mounted brigade attacked the Sacred Band from the flank. Very soon the Thebans were completely surrounded. At the same time Philip, away on the right, halted his retreat, and launched a downhill counter-charge – 'not', as Diodorus says, 'conceding credit for the victory even to Alexander' (see below, pp. 91-2, 361).

The Athenians had become badly disorganized during their advance, and now they were to pay the price for Stratocles' amateurish hot-headedness. The Macedonians drove them headlong into the foothills, killed a thousand of them, and took twice that number prisoner. The remainder managed to get away over the Kérata pass. Among the fugitives was Demosthenes. 'As he was running away,' Plutarch tells us, 'a bramble-bush caught his cloak, where-upon he turned round and said "Take me alive!"' Even a defeat has its moments of incidental comedy. But for the most part this rout was a grim enough business. What the cavalry had begun, the phalanx completed. They poured through the broken lines in Alexander's wake, and engaged the Greek centre front and flank simultaneously. After a last desperate struggle the entire allied army broke and fled – with the exception of the Sacred Band. Like Leonidas' Spartans at Thermopylae, these 300 Thebans fought and died where they stood, as though on parade, amid piles of corpses. Only forty-six of them were taken alive. The re-maining 254 were buried on the site of their last heroic stand. There they lie to this day, in seven soldierly rows, as the excavator's spade revealed them; and close by their common grave the Lion of Chaeronea still stands guard, weathered and brooding, over that melancholy plain.[14]

When the battle was over, Philip called off his cavalry pursuit, raised a victory trophy, made sacrifice to the gods, and decorated a number of his officers and men for con-spicuous gallantry. (We do not know whether Alexander was included among them; he certainly deserved to be.) In due course there followed a great celebratory banquet, at which the king, with characteristic Macedonian abandon, drank a quite inordinate amount of strong wine. Garlanded and tipsy, he then went out on a post-prandial tour of the battlefield, his senior officers accompanying him. He laughed raucously – and perhaps in nervous relief – over the piles of enemy dead, disparaging their valour, and hurling coarse insults at them. (Some say, on the other hand, that he wept over the annihilation of the Sacred Band: that, too, would be in character.) He took childish pleasure in repeating, over and over again, the official preamble to Demosthenes' motions in the Athenian assembly, which accidentally formed a catchy metrical jingle: '*Demosthenes, Demosthenes' son, Paeonian, proposes –*' The future of Greece lay, at long last, in Philip's strong and capable hands. But he knew, better than anyone, how close-run a fight Chaeronea had been.

In this exhausted and exultant mood he was even pre-pared to dismiss the Greek herald who presently arrived from Lebadea, asking permission to remove and bury the bodies of the allied dead. But one of his prisoners, the Athenian orator Demades, sobered him up sharply. 'King Philip,' he said, 'Fortune has cast you as Agamemnon; but you seem determined to act the part of Thersites.' The flattery implicit in this censure had its effect. Yet it remains a tribute to Philip's character that he at once shrugged off his drunkenness – more than one anecdote suggests his ability to do this at need – and expressed warm admiration for the man who had dared to criticize him so boldly. In-deed, he afterwards released Demades from captivity, and henceforth treated him as an honoured guest.[15]

There was, however, a sound practical reason for Philip's apparently quixotic behaviour. He may – as we shall see – have found Demades a congenial boon-companion; but he also needed an Athenian of good standing to present his peace terms before the assembly: someone, for choice, who would sincerely urge their acceptance, and report the King of Macedonia as a civilized, generous victor. Athens could still cause Philip a great deal of trouble, and he knew it. Indeed, the following day the battle news reached Chaeronea that the Athenians were arming their slaves and resident aliens, and making ready to defend their city to the death. We are told – and there is no reason to disbelieve such a report – that Philip was thoroughly alarmed by this reaction. The Athenian fleet remained intact; so did the harbour and arsenals of Piraeus. Unless Philip breached those monumental defences, the Athenians could maintain supplies and communications by sea more or less indefinitely.

In the circumstances, however complete his triumph at Chaeronea, there was every reason for the king to show himself conciliatory. The last thing he wanted at this point was a repetition of his prolonged and abortive assault on Byzantium, for which he certainly had not the time, and perhaps not the resources either. Besides, from now on he would be mainly concerned with building up a Panhellenic expeditionary force for the invasion of Asia. There was little sense in destroying Athenian installations and warships – or, indeed, any chance of Athenian goodwill – when he would soon need both these valuable commodities for himself.[16]

Demades is a fascinating character: one of those quirky and colourful rogues who crowd the margins of fourth-century Greek history, yet seldom get the attention they deserve from historians. His anti-Macedonian enemies described him as vulgar, treacherous, and corrupt. Plutarch says he was the 'shipwreck of his country', a phrase in all likelihood borrowed from some fourth-century pamphlet or speech. He made no secret of his venality. When he heard a playwright boast of having earned a talent by giving recitations, Demades remarked: 'That's nothing; I was once paid ten by the king to keep quiet.' Pot-bellied and gluttonous, he spent money as fast as he made it; Antipater said of him, in his old age, that he was 'nothing but tongue and stomach'. The tongue, however, wagged to some effect. No one could deny his abilities as an off-the-cuff orator, or his gift for memorable invective – Demosthenes he once described as 'a little man made up of syllables and a tongue'. When he got back to Athens with the king's peace terms he found the city, he said, 'like an old woman dragging her sandals and swallowing soothing drinks', and his words to the assembly were brutally frank: 'It is with peace, not argument, that we must counter the Macedonian phalanx; for argument lacks power to take effect when urged by men whose strength is less than their desire.'[17]

Philip had timed his psychological *volte-face* well. Reaction against the war-party in Athens had already begun to make itself felt, and the terms which Demades now read out before an astonished assembly were better than anyone had dared to hope. The Athenian dead – or rather their ashes, it still being the hot season – would, after all, be given up. All 2,000 prisoners would be released without ransom. Philip guaranteed not to send Macedonian troops across the frontiers of Attica, or Macedonian warships into Piraeus. Athens was to keep a nucleus of Aegean islands, including Delos and Samos. She also received Oropus, on the overland route to Euboea, a stronghold previously occupied by Thebes. In return for these favours, however, she was required to abandon all other territorial claims, to dissolve the Athenian maritime league, and to become Macedonia's ally – a step which, as things turned out, involved her in rather more than her leaders had anticipated. Their immediate relief, however, was so great that they accepted Philip's terms *en bloc*, without argument. They even went so far, out of sheer gratitude, as to confer Athenian citizenship on Philip and Alexander, and to vote the king a statue in the Agora.

Three envoys – Aeschines, Phocion, and Demades himself – were dispatched north to implement the treaty, and found themselves doing so at dawn, bleary-eyed after one of Philip's all-night drinking-parties.[18] They were in no position to object. Any privileges which Athens might henceforth be granted were an arbitrary favour from the Macedonian king, reversible at will. All the same, the Athenians could at least take comfort from the fact that they had received incomparably better treatment than Thebes. Once again, Philip had good reason for behaving as he did: if he was to hold central Greece, Thebes' very considerable power must be systematically broken up. Her leaders had ignored their treaty obligations once, and might well do so again. They must be taught a sharp lesson – and one calculated to discourage similar ambitions elsewhere. Since they had no fleet worth the name, they, unlike the Athenians, could be coerced with impunity.

Philip therefore began by abolishing the Boeotian League, which was, in effect, an embryo Theban empire. Its member-cities, including Plataea, were given back their independence – a very shrewd stroke of diplomacy. The Thebans themselves were forced to recall all political exiles (a move hardly calculated to stabilize their domestic affairs), and a puppet government was set up, with a Macedonian garrison to watch over it from the Cadmea. Former democratic leaders were liquidated or sent into banishment. Theban prisoners, unlike their Athenian counterparts, had to be ransomed, and at a good price: otherwise they were sold as slaves. At the same time Philip could be magnanimous enough when it suited him. He had no objection to the Thebans raising a great monument at Chaeronea in memory of the Sacred Band: a fine soldier himself, he appreciated truly valorous opponents. He refrained from imposing garrisons on most – though not all – of the leading Greek cities, saying that he 'preferred to be called a good man for a long time rather than a master for a short time'. But despite such fits of jovial generosity, there could be little doubt where the real power now lay. The Greek states retained no more than a pale shadow of their former freedom.[19]

To commemorate his great victory, Philip built and

dedicated at Olympia a circular edifice known as the Philippeum, somewhat similar to the famous *tholos* at Delphi (itself possibly also commissioned by Philip, and for an identical purpose).[20] This building was made of fired brick, with an outer and inner ring of enclosing columns. The roof-beams were tied together by a central bronze clamp, shaped like a gigantic poppy. The Philippeum contained various gold and ivory portrait statues, specially executed by the sculptor Leochares: of Philip himself, of Olympias, of Alexander, of Philip's parents Eurydice and Amyntas. In general appearance it must have resembled nothing so much as a Shinto shrine. What, we well may ask, was Philip's real object in creating so *outré* a monument?

The conclusion seems inescapable: he hoped to establish a quasi-divine cult of himself and his family. (This is by no means the only occasion on which we find one of Alexander's more idiosyncratic actions anticipated by his father.) Other evidence confirms such a hypothesis (see below, pp. 98, 104). That so pragmatic a hedonist ever seriously believed in his own godhead seems unlikely, to say the least of it; at all events, he was very quick to ridicule divine pretensions in others. But he may well have been working towards the essentially political device of a divine ruler-cult. For the Greeks, the gap between men and gods was not so wide as it is for us, and very largely bridged by the 'heroes', semi-mythical champions assimilated to divine status. Here, of course, Philip had good precedent in his own ancestor Heracles. There was also the more recent and intriguing case of Lysander, the Spartan general, in whose honour the Samians appear to have instituted a regular cult, complete with chapel, feast-day, and official sacrifices. On the island of Paros, perhaps somewhat later, we find a parallel cult of the poet Archilochus: his shrine was, similarly, known as the Archilocheum. As we shall see, the citizens of Ephesus encouraged Philip's pretensions to divine status, and it is unlikely, to say the least, that they did so on a mere casual impulse. If, as seems possible, the king was planning his own assimilation to the Olympic pantheon, this fact would have been widely known.[21]

Such a device undoubtedly had great advantages: its subsequent use in Hellenistic and Roman times offers clear proof of this. Philip's fast-expanding power was creating as many problems as it solved, not least as regards his personal status. Like Augustus after him, he was much preoccupied with the problem of converting *imperium* into *auctoritas*, and the policy implicit in the Philippeum constituted an initial step towards this goal. It may also have received some indirect encouragement from Isocrates' last letter to him, written after Chaeronea. The aged pamphleteer – he was now ninety-eight, and died a few weeks later – declared that if Philip subjugated Persia to the Greeks, nothing would be left for him but to become a god.[22]

One thing, however, the statue-group of the Philippeum makes abundantly clear. At the time of its dedication – that is, in or about September 338 – Philip's dynastic plans, now of nearly twenty years' standing, remained firm and unaltered. Olympias was still his wife, and Alexander his legitimate successor, by royal favour no less than by right of primogeniture. Regent at sixteen, and a fully-blooded cavalry general two years later, Alexander could not be taken for anything but the heir-apparent. Indeed, his entire upbringing hitherto had been directed towards that end. No one doubted that he would, in due course, succeed to the throne. If there were any objections lodged against him during those two decades, our sources do not record them. Yet, only a month or two after Chaeronea, the king was to repudiate Olympias as an adulteress, cast open doubts on Alexander's legitimacy (which suggests that the two charges were linked), and marry, as his fifth wife, a blue-blooded Macedonian aristocrat, with the clear object of siring a new male heir. What happened that autumn to produce so sudden and violent a change in Philip's long-matured intentions?

About the same time as Philip's great victory, Artaxerxes Ochus was assassinated by his grand vizier, Bagoas – 'a eunuch in fact but a militant rogue in disposition', as Diodorus pleasantly puts it. Persia remained in a state of near-anarchy until November, while Susa boiled with cut-throat palace intrigue. After all rival claimants had been successfully eliminated, Bagoas placed Ochus' youngest son Arses on the throne, and settled back into his favourite role of puppet-master.[23] These developments are unlikely to have escaped Philip's vigilant eye. Ochus had been a formidable ruler in his own right, whereas Arses was no more than the grand vizier's creature. Between August and November, then, with Greece effectively brought to heel, and Persian leadership seriously weakened, the prospects for an invasion of Asia had improved out of all recognition. Nor was there any need to search around for a formula that would swing the Greek states into line behind Macedonia: Isocrates had provided one ready-made.

Panhellenism now became Philip's watch-word, and the war was projected as a religious crusade, to avenge Greece for Xerxes' invasion a century and a half before. All that remained was to work out the administrative details and logistics, and see how far each individual state was willing to collaborate. Philip's first concern, as always, was with Athens. Immediately after the armistice he sent an official embassy to escort the ashes of Athens' dead home to their last resting-place. In the atmosphere of goodwill which such a gesture would generate, profitable diplomatic exchanges could be expected.[24] As ambassadors extraordinary Philip appointed Antipater, Alcimachus,* and Alexander. This, we may note, was the last occasion on which the crown prince was entrusted with any responsible task befitting his

* Little is known of this man except that he was a trusted general and ambassador who served both Philip and Alexander well: see Berve, *APG*, II, p. 23, no. 47, and Tod, II, no. 180. For his subsequent career see below, pp. 187 ff.

rank – a state of affairs which continued until Philip's death. Alexander's visit to the city of Athens – the only time, so far as we know, that he ever set foot within its gates – seems to have coincided in some way with his fall from official grace.

The embassy itself went off very well, with much exchange of ceremonial courtesies. Philip's statue was officially unveiled; honorary citizenship was conferred both on him – by proxy – and on Alexander. Antipater had useful talks with various influential citizens, including the nonagenarian Isocrates, an old personal friend. (By now Isocrates was tactfully crediting Philip with the whole idea of a Persian invasion: he himself, he said, had merely fallen in with the king's desires.) On the face of it, Athens' leaders must have struck the envoys as cooperative, grateful, and eager to please. At the same time this public conformism clearly had its limits: civility was not allowed to degenerate into mere subservience. When the urns containing the ashes of the fallen were handed over, it was not some safe pro-Macedonian lickspittle who was chosen to deliver the official funeral oration over them, but the diehard Demosthenes, Philip's most intransigent opponent. What he said on that occasion has not survived; but we still possess the moving epitaph composed for their common tomb:[25]

> Time, whose o'erseeing eye records all human actions,
>   Bear word to mankind what fate we suffered, how
> Striving to safeguard the holy soil of Hellas
>   Upon Boeotia's famous plain we died.

The ambassadors had been well briefed before they left for Athens. One of their most important duties was to discuss Philip's future plans, informally, with leading statesmen such as Phocion and Lycurgus, and assess their reactions. The main points they stressed were the establishment of a 'general peace' (*koiné eirené*) between all Greek states; the formation of a new Hellenic League; and the vigorous promotion, under Macedonian leadership, of a

Panhellenic campaign against Persia. Thus Alexander had special and privileged knowledge of all his father's top-secret projects from the moment of their inception. More important, he was familiar with the time-schedule to which they were geared. We know little of his activities in Athens, but that little is interesting. His hosts, having heard of his prowess as a runner, flatteringly matched him against a first-class Olympic athlete. When the latter 'appeared to slacken his pace deliberately, Alexander was very indignant'. It may have been on this occasion that he made his famous remark about only running in the games if he had kings for competitors. He also asked Xenocrates – now head of the Academy, and renowned for his moral pragmatism – to draw him up 'rules of royal government'. How soon, one wonders, did he think he was going to need them?[26]

Meanwhile Philip, who never believed in wasting time, had moved his forces down from central Greece into the Peloponnese. He wrote to the Spartans asking whether he should come as friend or foe, and got the characteristically Laconic response: 'Neither'. On the other hand Sparta's traditional enemies, such as Argos, welcomed him with open arms. Despite his much-publicized disclaimers (see above, p. 80), he left a garrison on Acrocorinth, and probably at several other key-points as well. He parcelled out much of Laconia to anti-Spartan cities, and liberated the serf-state of Messenia. One Spartan official inquired, sourly, whether he had left the Messenians a strong enough fighting force to hold what they had been given.[27]

With each state he made a separate treaty: the maxim of 'divide and rule' had by now become second nature to him. Only Sparta, with defiant stubbornness, refused to negotiate, and here Philip did not force the issue. He may well have felt that an independent Sparta would act as a useful check on those new Peloponnesian allies of his who had acquired slices of Spartan territory. The dedication of the Philippeum was a salutary reminder that from now on, whatever democratic forms might be employed as a salve to the Greeks' self-respect, it was Philip who led and they who followed. When the king announced a general peace conference, to be held at Corinth, Sparta alone abstained.[28]

The delegates assembled about the first week of October; Philip was at great pains to charm them and to soothe their wounded susceptibilities. He needed the Greeks' support for his Persian venture, and was determined to get it. First, he read out a draft manifesto (*diagramma*) of his proposals, which had already been circulated privately through various diplomatic channels. This manifesto formed the basis for all subsequent discussion, and was adopted more or less without change.[29] In essence, it boiled down to the following points. The Greek states were to make a common peace and alliance with one another, and constitute themselves into a federal Hellenic League. This league would take joint decisions by means of a federal council (*Synhedrion*), on which each state would be represented according to its size and military importance. A permanent steering committee of five presidents (*prohedroi*) would sit at Corinth, while the council itself would hold general meetings during the four Panhellenic festivals – at Olympia, Delphi, Nemea, and the Isthmus – in rotation.

Simultaneously, the league was to form a separate alliance with Macedonia, though Macedonia itself would not be a league member. This treaty was to be made with 'Philip and his descendants' in perpetuity. The king would act as 'leader' (*hegemon*) of the league's joint forces, a combined civil and military post designed to provide for the general security of Greece. It was, technically at least, the council that would pass resolutions, which the hegemon then executed. If the Greeks were involved in a war, they could call on Macedonia to support them. Equally, if Philip needed military aid, he was entitled to requisition contingents from the league. In such a case he acquired a second, more purely military role. As well as hegemon he became *strategos autokrator* – that is, general plenipotentiary or supreme commander-in-chief of all Macedonian or league forces in the field, for as long as a state of hostilities might last.

Despite Philip's careful dressing up of his authority in this elaborate quasi-federal disguise, there could be little doubt as to who took the real decisions. One function of the hegemon, for example, was to assess each state's military liabilities in lieu of cash taxation. (The latter would have tarnished the image of freedom and autonomy which Philip was anxious to maintain: besides, at present he needed men rather more than money.) Everyone knew – though for obvious security reasons the topic was not yet discussed openly – that this clause had been inserted for the benefit of Philip's projected Persian crusade. It was an eloquent hint at the king's virtually unlimited *de facto* executive powers that he could thus, at will, dictate the whole future course of Greek foreign policy. Philip's Panhellenism was no more than a convenient placebo to keep his allies quiet, a cloak for further Macedonian aggrandizement.

Most Greek statesmen recognized this only too well. To them, their self-styled hegemon was still a semi-barbarian autocrat, whose wishes had been imposed on them by right of conquest; and when Alexander succeeded Philip, he inherited the same bitter legacy of hatred and resentment – which his own policies did little to dispel. The brutal truth of the matter was that the Greeks, for the most part, knuckled under because, after Chaeronea, they had no alternative. Nor was Philip deceived by their specious professions of loyalty. The military contingents they supplied were, in reality, so many hostages for their good behaviour. As we shall see, whenever they saw the slightest chance of throwing off the Macedonian yoke, they took it. This stubborn, unswerving resentment was something which neither Philip nor Alexander ever managed to overcome. It was always there in the background, a constant threat to their more daring ambitions.[30]

Having thus set the stage for the peace conference, Philip returned to Pella.[31] At this critical point in his career, it might reasonably be assumed, the one thing he had to avoid at all costs was any kind of internal or domestic upheaval. There was far too much at stake abroad to risk a barons' war at home. Yet it was now – and with every appearance of deliberation – that the king embarked on a course of action which split the Macedonian royal house into two bitterly hostile camps, stirred up a whole wasps'-nest of aristocratic intrigue, and drove the hitherto highly favoured crown prince into exile, at a time when his special, indeed unique, talents could ill be spared. To any un-prejudiced outside observer it must have seemed as though Philip had suddenly taken leave of his senses.

The public facts are well known, and not in dispute. Philip announced his intention of marrying Cleopatra, daughter of an aristocratic lowland family; such a move must have caused considerable alarm among the out-kingdom barons, who were bound to assume that this match was aimed, among other things, at undermining their influence in Pella. Cleopatra's uncle, Attalus, a brave and popular general,[32] had himself recently married one of Parmenio's daughters: between them the two families looked like establishing a formidable junta at court. Never-theless, Alexander was, indisputably, Philip's first-born son, and the acknowledged heir-apparent. His claim to the succession remained beyond challenge – until, that is, Philip threw a new light on his marriage-plans by repudiat-ing Olympias on the grounds of suspected adultery, and encouraging rumours that Alexander himself might well be illegitimate.[33]

At this point no one could fail to see what the king's true intentions were. His long-matured plans for the succession had been scrapped, literally overnight. The cooperative integration of lowlands and highlands represented by his marriage to Olympias was similarly being abandoned: with Cleopatra as his regnant queen, the royal house of Mace-donia would be 'no longer a blend between east and west but a dynasty of the plain'.[34] That Philip *really* believed

Alexander to be illegitimate is out of the question. Such charges, as we have seen, were a regular weapon in the dynastic power-game, and recognized as such: both Philip himself and his immediate ancestors had, at one time or another, been smeared in this way.[35] The true problem at issue is why he suddenly chose to adopt such tactics, not least when – on the face of it – he had no apparent justification for what he did, and indeed everything to lose as a result.

The wedding-feast, as might be expected, was a tense occasion. When Alexander walked in, and took the place of honour which was his by right – opposite his father – he said to Philip: 'When my mother remarries I'll invite *you* to *her* wedding' – not a remark calculated to improve anyone's temper. During the evening, in true Macedonian fashion, a great deal of wine was drunk. At last Attalus rose, swaying, and proposed a toast, in which he 'called upon the Macedonians to ask of the gods that from Philip and Cleopatra there might be born *a legitimate successor to the kingdom*'. The truth was finally out, and made public in a way which no one – least of all Alexander – could ignore.

Infuriated, the crown prince sprang to his feet. 'Are you calling me a bastard?' he shouted, and flung his goblet in Attalus' face. Attalus retaliated in kind. Philip, more drunk than either of them, drew his sword and lurched forward, bent on cutting down not Attalus (who had, after all, insulted his son and heir) but Alexander himself – a revealing detail. However, the drink he had taken, combined with his lame leg (see above, p. 69), made Philip trip over a stool and crash headlong to the floor. 'That, gentlemen,' said Alexander, with icy contempt, 'is the man who's been preparing to cross from Europe into Asia – and he can't even make it from one couch to the next!' Each of them, in that moment of crisis, had revealed what lay uppermost in his mind. Alexander thereupon flung out into the night, and by next morning both he and Olympias were over the frontier. After escorting his mother home to her relations in

Epirus, the crown prince himself moved on into Illyria, probably staying with his friend King Langarus of the Agrianians, who afterwards supplied some of his toughest and most reliable light-armed troops (see below, p. 130). These movements are revealing. It seems clear enough that from now on both Alexander and Olympias were actively plotting against Philip, and doing their best to stir up trouble for Macedonia from all the tribes along the western marches.[36]

Philip's behaviour is, at first sight, very hard to explain in rational terms. Our ancient sources, realizing this, assume that he fell so wildly in love with Cleopatra as to more or less take leave of his senses. But Philip, as we have seen, was never the man to confuse marriage with mere casual concupiscence. Even if Cleopatra, like Anne Boleyn, held out for marriage or nothing, there was still no conceivable reason why Philip should repudiate Olympias (he had not done so when he married his fourth wife),[37] much less Alexander, whom he had spent nearly twenty years in training as his chosen successor. Such a step was bound to have the most serious repercussions, and nothing but the direst necessity – some yet greater threat, which it was specifically designed to avert – could ever have driven him to it.

But what could this threat be? Most modern historians fail to suggest any remotely adequate motive. It has been alleged that Philip's turbulent barons were determined to have a pure-blooded Macedonian heir to the throne, and therefore forced the king's hand. This simply will not do. No one had objected to Alexander as the heir-apparent before; why should they suddenly do so now? In any case, succession to the Macedonian throne went exclusively through the male line (see above, p. 28); and, most important, Philip II was not the kind of man to let his hand be forced by anyone, least of all on so personal and politically explosive a matter. Another suggestion put forward has even less to recommend it. If (the argument runs) both

Philip and Alexander were to be killed during the Asiatic campaign, no competent successor would exist, Amyntas being a nonentity and Philip Arrhidaeus half-witted. Thus a second heir had to be produced before the expedition sailed. In that case, we may ask, why begin by wantonly discarding the best available candidate before a replacement was even conceived?[38]

In fact there is one motive, and one only, which could have driven Philip to act as he did: the belief, justified or not, that Alexander and Olympias were engaged in a treasonable plot to bring about his overthrow. Nothing else even begins to make sense. If this *is* what was in the king's mind, his conduct at once becomes intelligible. He could not possibly set out against the Great King leaving Macedonia in the hands of a potential usurper. Equally, he could not entrust his elite cavalry corps to the command of a man whose loyalty had been called in question. Even without proof positive – and proof positive, of a sort, may even have existed – the risk was too great. Alexander would have to be sacrificed, and Olympias with him.

So much seems clear. But the crucial point for a modern reader is whether or not Philip's suspicions were in fact justified, and here the only possible verdict is 'non-proven'. At the same time, it is not hard to see how such suspicions could have been aroused. From the very beginning, Olympias had encouraged Alexander to think of himself as king in his own right, rather than as Philip's eventual successor. This, we need not doubt, was the main source of those 'great quarrels'[39] between father and son, which the queen's jealous temper actively encouraged, and in which she invariably took Alexander's side.

The natural rivalry between Alexander and his father was still further exacerbated by Chaeronea. It could well be argued that it was Alexander who had won Philip's victory for him – a claim which we find Philip going out of his way to deny. Perhaps the king had some grounds for annoyance: Alexander later boasted that 'the famous victory of Chaeronea had been his work, but that the glory of so great a battle had been taken from him by the grudgingness and jealousy of his father'.[40] On the other hand, Philip himself had advanced Alexander to high civil and military office as a matter of deliberate policy. He could hardly complain if the boy discharged his duties with something more than credit. But between jealousy and sedition there is a sharp dividing line. Have we any reason to suppose that Philip's heir crossed it? And if he did, why now rather than at any other time?

We have seen how Alexander thought of himself as the young Achilles, destined from birth to win glory and renown in battle against the barbarians of Asia. His attitude to war was fundamentally Homeric: for him it remained, first and last, the royal road to personal *areté*. He slept with two things beneath his pillow: a dagger, and a well-thumbed copy of the *Iliad*. Olympias had taught him from childhood to regard kingship as his destiny. Aristotle had implanted in his mind the conviction that only through pre-eminent *areté* could that kingship be justified – and by his emphasis on a legitimate war against Persia had shown him how such *areté* might be achieved. But between Alexander and the throne which he held to be his by divine right there still stood one seemingly insurmountable obstacle: his father.

Philip bore a charmed life. For over twenty years he had exposed himself recklessly in every battle he fought. Yet he still survived, lame, scarred, minus one eye, with a fractured collar-bone and a mutilated hand,[41] full of rude and jovial energy, no whit less ambitious than his son, and far more experienced, a veteran still only in his mid forties. When Alexander complained that his father would leave him no great or brilliant *gestes* to achieve, he was very far from joking. After Chaeronea, there was an all too real likelihood that his worst fears might be justified – that he would find himself saying, like Achilles: 'You are all witnesses to this thing, that my prize goes elsewhere.'[42]

It was Philip, not Alexander, who was now preparing to

launch the great Panhellenic crusade against Persia. It was Philip, not Alexander, who would reap the immortal renown that such an enterprise, if successful, must surely confer upon its victor. Unless some chance blow struck the king down, Alexander could expect no more than the lesser glory which falls to a second-in-command – perhaps not even that, since on so crucial an expedition Philip might well turn to his old and trusted lieutenant, Parmenio. Worse still, Alexander might once again be left behind as Regent of Macedonia, and thus play no part at all in the undertaking which he regarded as his birthright. No one could deny that he had powerful and urgent motives for wishing Philip out of the way.

After Chaeronea, it is said, the Macedonians began to speak of Philip as their general, but of Alexander as their king.[43] It is not hard to guess who started *that* rumour – or who put it about that Philip was 'delighted' by such a compliment to his heir. We also have certain cameos – copies, it is thought, of fourth-century originals – which probably show Alexander and Olympias together (the ascription is not proven beyond doubt), rather in the manner of certain Roman emperors and their consorts.[44] Could these have formed part of a propaganda campaign, designed to promote the joint rule of mother and son? After his actual accession Alexander was at some pains to keep Olympias in the background; but at this early stage (and bearing her Epirot connections in mind) he might well have found it politic to encourage her ambitions.

The truth of the matter can never be known for certain. If we apply the *cui bono* principle, then Alexander undoubtedly had everything to gain by staging a *coup* before the expedition was launched. On the other hand, there was a powerful faction at court – including Attalus and Parmenio – which detested this haughty prince and his domineering foreign mother, was actively working to cut the Argead dynasty loose from out-kingdom influence, and would probably stick at nothing to keep Alexander off the throne. Philip's marriage to Cleopatra, and, even more important, his repudiation of Olympias provide eloquent testimony to the degree of success this faction had already achieved. A whispering campaign, hinting at sedition in high places, would have been the most obvious and effective way of undermining Philip's trust in them both.

At all events, by the late autumn of 338 Alexander's hitherto ascendant star seemed in total eclipse. While he and Olympia fumed and plotted in exile, their enemies at home established themselves ever more securely. Preparations for the invasion went ahead, and soon it became known that Philip's new wife was with child. The future now looked clear: few could have seen, at the time, the unexpected turn events were shortly to take.

Throughout the winter of 338/7 the peace conference continued its deliberations at Corinth. In the spring the delegates finally ratified their 'common peace', and formed a Hellenic League along the lines that Philip had suggested in his manifesto. No sooner had the league's representatives been sworn in than they held their first official plenary session. An alliance with 'Philip and his descendants' was thereupon voted, and Philip himself was unanimously elected hegemon – which made him, among other things, *ex officio* chairman of the federal council. In this capacity he proposed a formal motion that the league declare war on Persia, to exact vengeance for those sacrilegious crimes which Xerxes had committed against the temples of the Greek gods.[45]

This proposal too was carried; but then the league had little choice in the matter. Nor could it very well object to appointing Philip supreme field-commander, 'with unlimited powers', of the expedition itself. Another revealing (and very necessary) decree provided that any Greek who henceforth chose to serve the Great King would be treated as a traitor. Some 15,000 Greek mercenaries, not to mention numerous doctors, engineers, technicians and professional diplomats, were already on the Persian pay-roll; more than twice as many men, in fact, as the league ultimately contributed for the supposedly Panhellenic crusade against Darius. The Greek cities of Asia Minor had become more than a little disillusioned with so-called 'wars of liberation', especially when these were conducted by mainland powers like Athens and Sparta. Their main object, it seemed, was to acquire wealthy subject-allies at Persia's expense – though they were ready enough to trade them back to the Great King when they needed Persian support. The Achaemenid regime at least offered mild rule and long-term stability; many Ionian cities actively preferred it, and one can see why.[46]

Philip returned home from Corinth to Pella feeling very pleased with himself, all the more so since there were rumours of a new revolt brewing in Egypt.[47] Anything calculated to keep the Great King's hands full at this point was doubly welcome. His satisfaction, however, was short-lived. About midsummer Cleopatra's child was born, and proved to be not the male heir on which Philip had been counting, but a girl.[48] The king was fundamentally a realistic statesman; he knew, better than anyone, just what this meant. He could not afford to leave Macedonia, during his absence, without a recognized heir to the throne. Nor could he sail for Asia while a dangerous and discontented claimant was stirring up trouble among the Illyrians, and his own discarded wife was similarly employed at her brother's court in Epirus.[49] There was nothing for it: Alexander would have to be brought home and reinstated.

The question was, would he come? While Philip was pondering this problem he received a visit from old Demaratus of Corinth, who was also a close friend of Alexander's (see above, p. 44). After the initial courtesies had been exchanged Philip got down to business. How, he inquired, were the Greek states agreeing with each other now? 'Much right have you to talk of the harmony of the Greeks,'

Demaratus replied, 'when the dearest of your household feel so towards you!' Philip, far from being put out, instantly saw that in Demaratus he had an ideal go-between. Even so, the Corinthian would need all his tact and diplomacy to resolve so prickly a situation.[50]

Somehow Demaratus accomplished his mission successfully (just how, none of our sources reveal), and Alexander came back to Pella with him. The least Philip can have offered was the reassurance that – appearances to the contrary – Alexander remained his chosen successor. On the other hand, the king was determined not to let the boy fall under his mother's pernicious influence again. He therefore left Olympias in Epirus, calculating that any embarrassment she could cause from this distance was negligible in comparison with the havoc she was capable of wreaking at court. Nor, in fact, did he restore Alexander to anything like his old position of trust; and as though to emphasize the fact, he lost no time after Cleopatra's *accouchement* in getting her pregnant for the second time.

During the winter of 337/6 an uneasy peace reigned in the palace. Philip was busy training his forces for an advance expedition into Asia Minor, designed to secure bridgeheads for the main army. He was also running through his reserve funds at an alarming speed. The troops' pay – always an early casualty on such occasions – had fallen badly into arrears. One day when Philip was boxing in the gymnasium, a group of soldiers cornered him, complaining loudly. Philip, dusty and sweating, grinned at them with cheerful effrontery. 'Quite right, boys,' he said. 'But don't bother me just now – I'm in training against the barbarian, so as to pay you off ten times over on the proceeds.' With that he clapped his hands, charged through them, and plunged into the pool, where he splashed around with his sparring-partner until the soldiers got bored with waiting and took themselves off.[51]

This story well illustrates the easy, informal relationship which existed between Philip and his subjects. But it also suggests how badly pressed he was for time and money. At this stage he could not afford to be sidetracked into any minor campaign. Therefore when news came that Olympias had talked her brother into declaring war on Macedonia, he used diplomacy rather than force: not that he under-estimated the man with whom he had to deal. Alexander of Epirus was an independent and ambitious youth. The fact that he owed his throne to Philip weighed not at all with him; he probably regarded this as no more than a fair return for having to put up with his brother-in-law's homo-sexual attentions at an impressionable age. But Philip, pragmatic as always, refused to be discouraged. Though this recalcitrant young man was, it seemed, impervious to the claims of nepotism and paederasty, he might still find some attraction in an incestuous marriage – especially if it carried political advantages.

Philip therefore wrote offering the Epirot king the hand of Cleopatra,* his daughter by Olympias – which meant, of course, that she was also her prospective bridegroom's niece. The offer – for whatever reason – was accepted with alacrity, and the wedding set for June, in the old Mace-donian capital of Aegae. What Cleopatra herself thought about this odd match our sources do not relate. As might be expected of Alexander's sister, she was a tough-minded and passionate girl. She also – unlike her brother – seems to have enjoyed sex. Alexander took a tolerant view of her peccadilloes. Once, when it was reported to him that she had taken some attractive young man as a lover, his only comment was: 'I see no reason why *she* shouldn't get some advantage from her royal status, too.'[52]

---

*To be distinguished from Cleopatra-Eurydice, Philip's new wife. One of the more irritating problems for anyone studying Macedonian history is the endless duplication of too few proper names. All too often it is impossible to be certain just which Amyntas or Pausanias (or, indeed, Philip or Alexander) is under discussion at any given time.

In the early spring of 336 an advance force of 10,000 men, including a thousand cavalry, crossed over to Asia Minor. Its task was to secure the Hellespont, to stockpile supplies, and, in Philip's pleasantly cynical phrase, to 'liberate the Greek cities'. This force was led by Parmenio, his son-in-law Attalus, and Amyntas, son of Arrhabaeus. Here we glimpse one of Philip's more intractable dilemmas, the clash between military and home-front priorities. He had to send out commanders whom he could trust; at the same time, the absence of Parmenio and Attalus meant that two of his strongest supporters were away from Pella when he most needed them. This was a weak point which any would-be usurper – especially a Macedonian – could hardly fail to exploit.

At first Parmenio's campaign went from one success to another. After crossing the Hellespont his army struck south along the Ionian seaboard. Chios came over to him, and so did Erythrae; there were probably other conquests, above all in the Troad and around the Gulf of Adramyttium, which our fragmentary sources do not record. When Parmenio approached Ephesus the inhabitants rose spontaneously, threw out their pro-Persian tyrant, and gave the Macedonians an enthusiastic welcome. They also set up Philip's statue in the temple of Artemis, side by side with the goddess's own image. Whether so curious a tribute was their own idea, or carried out in accordance with Philip's known wishes, remains problematical. One can only say that it fits in uncommonly well with his known ruler-cult propaganda (see above, p. 81). The man who dedicated the Philippeum, and later made a disastrous attempt to have himself enthroned among the twelve Olympians, would scarcely shrink from sharing a pedestal with Ephesian Artemis if he felt political advantage might accrue as a result.

There can be no doubt that he was genuinely anxious to get divine endorsement for his projected invasion. He sent a representative to Delphi (where he was honoured as a benefactor) and with uncompromising directness asked the

Pythia whether or not he would conquer the Great King. The priestess took this blunt approach in her stride. Centuries of experience had made it clear that those who consulted the oracle were quite content with an outrageously ambiguous response – always provided they could read into it what they hoped to find there. The answer Philip got was no exception. 'The bull is garlanded,' he read. 'All is done. The sacrificer is ready.' Philip intrepreted this to mean that the Persian monarch would be slaughtered like a victim at the altar. The actual course of events showed that Delphi (as so often in retrospect) had meant something rather different. Meanwhile Philip 'was very happy to think that Asia would be made captive under the hands of the Macedonians'.[53]

Others, it is clear, shared his conviction, amongst them the various local dynasts of Asia Minor, all anxious to be on the winning side when it came to a show-down. One of these, Pixodarus, a Carian prince, now sent his ambassador to Pella, offering his eldest daughter in marriage to Alexander's half-brother Philip Arrhidaeus. What Pixodarus in fact wanted, of course, was a military alliance with Macedonia. He had usurped the throne by banishing his sister Ada from Halicarnassus, and his relationship with Persia was, to say the least of it, uneasy. Nor did he overrate his eligibility as a potential ally. Though he could claim descent from the great Mausolus,* to Philip he was a mere backwoods baron: none so snobbish as those who have been labelled barbarians themselves. At the same time, with his Persian invasion imminent, the king would find an ally in Caria extremely useful. Besides, Pixodarus must have known very well that Philip Arrhidaeus was a mental defective, and that the king would therefore jump at any chance of marrying the boy off to his own political advantage.

---

* Whose wife (and sister, and successor) Artemisia built the Mausoleum – one of the Seven Wonders of the World – as a sepulchral monument in his memory, and mixed his ashes in her wine daily until her own death two years later.

Alexander, however, whose sense of insecurity was by now showing a somewhat paranoid streak, had managed to convince himself that Philip's real aim, 'by means of a brilliant marriage and a great connection', was to establish young Arrhidaeus as his heir. If Alexander genuinely believed that this local Carian dynast offered a 'great connection', let alone that Philip would ever bequeath the Macedonian throne to an imbecile, he was clearly in no state to think rationally at all. What he *did* assume, beyond a doubt, was that Pixodarus, having sized up Macedonia's dynastic factions, regarded even Arrhidaeus as a more promising son-in-law, politically speaking, than Alexander himself.

This inference could not but confirm all his worst suspicions. It may also explain why he now sent his friend Thessalus the actor[54] on a secret mission to Halicarnassus, with an alternative proposition. Pixodarus, he suggested, should disregard the feeble-minded Arrhidaeus, and take him, Alexander, as a son-in-law instead. On the very kindest interpretation, this was a flagrant case of *lèse-majesté*, and could well have been interpreted as treason. Besides, in the event of Pixodarus accepting Alexander's offer, their secret negotiations were bound, sooner rather than later, to become public knowledge. What did Alexander plan on doing then? And how did he expect his father to react to the news? With a fond parental blessing?

Pixodarus, clearly convinced that he had misjudged the situation at Pella, accepted this new offer with some enthusiasm, on the obvious assumption that it was made with Philip's knowledge and approval. By any reckoning Alexander was a far better catch than his half-brother. But one of Alexander's friends who was privy to these negotiations, Philotas, also happened to be Parmenio's son, and told his father of Alexander's plans. Parmenio, whose personal loyalty to Philip has never been called in question, at once informed Philip what was afoot. The king, seething with fury, took Philotas along as his witness,[55] and had a stormy interview with Alexander. He 'upbraided his son severely,' says Plutarch, 'and bitterly reviled him as ignoble and unworthy of his high estate, in that he desired to become the son-in-law of a barbarian king'. Alexander prudently said nothing; and Philip seems to have taken no direct personal action against him at the time.

Alexander's friends and associates, however, he dealt with very summarily indeed, in a way which suggests that he smelt conspiracy in the air and needed to safeguard his own position. Thessalus the actor had fled to Corinth. Philip, as captain-general of the league, demanded his immediate extradition, and the unfortunate actor was sent back to Macedonia in chains. (Alexander subsequently released him and made good use of his services.) At the same time, a group of men who all afterwards rose to fame and fortune under Alexander – they included Harpalus, his imperial treasurer, Ptolemy, son of Lagus (rumoured to be Philip's bastard), Nearchus the Cretan, Erigyius of Mytilene and his Persian-speaking brother Laomedon – found themselves banished.[56] Behind the illogicalities and tantalizing half-truths of the Pixodarus affair one senses an abortive *coup d'état*. If this is the truth of the matter, Philip's only possible motive for leniency to his son at such a juncture was personal affection – which arguably cost him his throne and his life.

What Philip did, it would seem, was to compromise. He did not execute Alexander's friends; he did not lay a finger on Alexander himself. Perhaps he felt that with the Persian crusade imminent, and a precarious balance of power established at Pella, he dared not yet risk a major purge. Purges, in any case, had never much appealed to him. He would, on occasion, execute known rebels who constituted a direct personal threat to him, like his half-brothers; but the reign of terror, used as a specific instrument of power-politics, was not Philip's style. On the other hand, the most momentous consequence of this episode was, inevitably, to make the king show his hand openly over the succession.

There could no longer be any question of endorsing Alexander's claims. Rumours about the crown prince's illegitimacy began to circulate once more, with Philip's encouragement and approval. More ominous still, the king now arranged a marriage between his brother's son – the amiable but unambitious Amyntas – and Cynane, his own daughter by Audata (see above, p. 27). The ranks were once more closing against Alexander; with Cleopatra due to give birth to her second child in a month or so, his future looked decidedly unhopeful.[57]

The month of June 336 B.C. could hardly, on the face of it, have opened more auspiciously for Philip. First there came encouraging news from Persia, where a fresh outbreak of palace intrigue had culminated in the assassination of the Great King. Once again Bagoas the grand vizier had been responsible: the puppet monarch Arses, it appeared, had threatened to develop a mind of his own. This latest murder finally extinguished the direct Achaemenid line; it looked as though Persia was in for yet another period of anarchy and civil war, with no strong central government, and little will or coordination to resist a determined attack. Such a view, as events turned out, was a trifle optimistic. Bagoas, looking around for some suitably pliable successor, settled on Codoman, a collateral member of the royal house, who now ascended the throne as Darius III. But for once the wily old eunuch had fatally misjudged his man. The new monarch had a good military record (at Issus, as we shall see, he gave Alexander something worse than a *mauvais quart d'heure*), and was clearly made of sterner stuff than the wretched Arses. At all events, his first act on accession was to make Bagoas himself drink the poison he had administered to so many others – a disconcerting gambit which (for the time being at least) put paid to any further court intrigue. Darius III, despite the harsh verdict of posterity, was not an opponent to underestimate.[58]

Meanwhile in Aegae, the old Macedonian capital, preparations were going ahead for the wedding of Alexander's sister Cleopatra to her maternal uncle and Philip's former minion, King Alexander of Epirus. Philip planned to make this state occasion the excuse for much lavish – not to say ostentatious – display and propaganda. Above all, he wanted to impress the Greeks. He felt he owed them appropriate entertainment as some return for 'the honours conferred when he was appointed to the supreme command'. But even more than this, he was anxious to convince them of his goodwill, to win their genuine support. He had to make it clear that he was no mere military despot, but a civilized and generous statesman.

The most important thing, of course, was to pack Aegae with distinguished visitors. Philip summoned all his own guest-friends from Greece, and ordered the Macedonian barons to do likewise. Once the guests were assembled, Philip felt, his munificent entertainment would do the rest.[59] He had organized a non-stop round of rich banquets, public games, musical festivals, and 'gorgeous sacrifices to the gods'. No expense was spared to make this a really impressive and memorable occasion. It was, in fact, to prove more memorable than anyone could have foreseen.[60]

In the midst of these preparations an event took place which, from Philip's point of view, could not have been more opportune: with impeccable timing, the king's young wife gave birth to a son. As though to emphasize the child's future status as his successor, Philip named him Caranus, after the mythical founder of the Argead dynasty.[61] Alexander's reaction to this gesture can all too easily be imagined. His isolation at court was now almost complete. Among the old guard barons only Antipater, 'disgruntled at his own influence diminishing before that of Parmenio and Attalus, and filled with dislike for Philip's pretensions to divinity',[62] could still be regarded as a potential ally. If Alexander did not act soon, it would be too late. However, with the arrival of the bridegroom's party from Epirus, Alexander gained one supporter who, in his eyes, was worth all the rest put together. During these critical months Philip had contrived to keep Alexander beyond the range of his mother's direct influence. But he could hardly prevent Olympias returning to Macedonia as a guest at her own brother's wedding.[63] Alexander, Antipater and the ex-queen must have found a good deal to discuss when they finally met again.

The first day's celebrations went off without a hitch. There was as great a concourse of guests as even Philip could have desired. Not only private individuals but also ambassadors from many important Greek city-states – including Athens – presented the king with ceremonial gold crowns. The Athenian herald announced that 'if anyone plotted against King Philip and fled to Athens for refuge, he would be delivered up'. It was a time-honoured formula; but in retrospect it acquired ominous and pro-phetic overtones. So did the performance of the tragic actor Neoptolemus, during the great post-prandial state banquet. Philip had instructed him to recite various pieces appropri-ate to the occasion, especially with reference to the Persian crusade, and the hoped-for downfall of the Great King. Neoptolemus chose one extract (perhaps from a lost play by Aeschylus) which illustrated the fate in store for excessive wealth and overvaulting ambition. 'Your thoughts reach higher than the air,' he sang. 'You dream of wide fields' cultivation . . . But one there is who . . . robs us of our distant hopes – Death, mortals' source of many woes.' Like the Pythian oracle, these lines were capable of more than one application.[64]

The second day had been set aside for the games. Before dawn every seat in the theatre was taken, and as the sun rose a magnificent ceremonial procession formed up and came slowly marching in. It was headed by 'statues of the twelve gods wrought with great artistry and adorned with a dazzling show of wealth to strike awe in the beholder'. These were accompanied by Philip's own image, 'suitable for a god', an intrusive and unlucky thirteenth. The king's

Greek guests began to see that his propaganda had other purposes besides flattery. Whose, it might well be asked, was the *hubris* now? No one there, it is safe to say, had forgotten the Philippeum at Olympia; many would also recall the setting up of Philip's image in the temple of Ephesian Artemis. The implications of this latest gesture were disconcerting.

Finally, Philip himself appeared, clad in a white ceremonial cloak, and walking alone between the two Alexanders – his son and his new son-in-law. He had ordered the Gentlemen of the Bodyguard to follow at a distance, 'since he wanted to show publicly that he was protected by the goodwill of all the Greeks, and had no need of a guard of spearmen'. As he paused by the entrance to the arena a young man – a member of the Bodyguard itself – drew a short broad-bladed Celtic sword from beneath his cloak, darted forward, and thrust it through Philip's ribs up to the hilt, killing him instantly. He then made off in the direction of the city-gate, where he had horses waiting. There was a second's stunned silence. Then a group of young Macedonian noblemen hurried after the assassin. He caught his foot in a vine-root, tripped, and fell. As he was scrambling up his pursuers overtook him, and ran him through with their javelins.[65]

Those who drew the sword from Philip's side saw that its ivory hilt bore the carved image of a chariot, and some remembered a warning to 'beware the chariot' that he had received from the oracle of Trophonius. Perhaps this was why he had entered the theatre on foot; Philip had his superstitious moments. If so, the oracle – as so often – had brought him little good. Now he sprawled there in the dust, white cloak spattered with blood, his splendid dream broken and forgotten; while beyond him, abandoned now, his statue still stood with those of the other gods, a mute ironic witness to the vanity of human wishes.[66]

Philip's murderer was a King's Bodyguard called

Pausanias, from the out-kingdom of Orestis: an aristocrat, if not of royal blood. A year or two before,[67] Philip, attracted by his remarkable youthful beauty, had taken him as a lover. Later, however, the king transferred his homosexual attentions elsewhere, upon which Pausanias made a great jealous scene with the new favourite, calling him, among other things, a hermaphrodite and a promiscuous little tart. However, the other boy (also, to confuse matters, named Pausanias) proved his manhood by saving Philip's life at the expense of his own, in battle against the Illyrians (? 337). This Pausanias was also a friend of Attalus, whose niece Philip had married.

The incident caused a great scandal in court circles, and Attalus decided to revenge himself on its instigator. The method he chose, though both brutal and revolting, had a certain poetic aptness about it. He invited Pausanias to dinner, and got him dead drunk. Then he himself, and all his guests, took turns to rape the wretched youth, while the rest of the company looked on, laughing and jeering. Finally, Pausanias was turned over to Attalus' grooms and muleteers, who subjected him to the same treatment, and then beat him up for good measure. When Pausanias recovered, he went straight to Philip and laid charges against Attalus. This placed the king in a very awkward position. We are told that he 'shared [Pausanias'] anger at the barbarity of the act', which may well be true. At the same time he could not possibly afford to alienate Attalus, who was not only his father-in-law, but had also just been appointed joint-commander of the advance expedition into Asia Minor (spring 336; see above, p. 98). Cleopatra also pleaded forcefully with Philip on her uncle's behalf. So Philip kept putting Pausanias off, making one excuse after another, or (if we can trust Justin) treating the incident as a joke, until finally he dismissed the charges altogether. The whole affair, he hoped, would soon be forgotten. It was not.[68]

This sordid tale of homosexual intrigue and revenge does

not, at first sight, provide sufficient motive in itself for Pausanias' murderous assault on Philip – nor, indeed, do our ancient sources think so. The grudge he bore the king was legitimate, but secondary. His real enemy was Attalus; but Attalus, luckily for himself, was out of the country. Philip, after all, had merely failed to see justice done for his ex-lover; and though Pausanias did, in the event, kill him for personal motives, he is unlikely to have done so without active help and encouragement from others. His burning and notorious sense of grievance would at once suggest him as the perfect instrument for a political assassination – nor is there any doubt as to who had the strongest motive, now if ever, for wishing Philip out of the way.[69] 'Most of the blame,' Plutarch says, 'devolved upon Olympias, on the ground that she had added her exhortations to the young man's anger and incited him to the deed.' It was she ('beyond any question,' Justin asserts) who arranged for horses to be ready for the assassin, so that he could make a quick get-away. Her subsequent behaviour, indeed, suggests that she not only planned her husband's death but openly gloried in it* – perhaps as a means of diverting suspicion from Alexander himself, who, after all, stood to gain more by Pausanias' action than anyone.

The murderer's corpse was nailed to a public gibbet, and that very same night Olympias placed a gold crown on its head. A few days later she had the body taken down, burnt it over Philip's ashes, and buried it in a nearby grave. Every year she poured libations there on the anniversary of the murder. She obtained the sword which Pausanias had used, and dedicated it to Apollo – under her maiden name of Myrtale. No one, at the time, dared voice a breath of criticism.

*Some of the details which follow here are rejected by most modern historians as wildly implausible fiction. But a woman who subsequently committed at least five political murders (including roasting a baby over a brazier), and ordered over a hundred executions, could hardly be called squeamish; and Olympias was never one to hide or restrain her emotions.

> Treason doth never prosper: what's the reason?
> For if it prosper, none dare call it treason.

Like mother, like son: Olympias, too, never forgave an insult – least of all one directed at Alexander – and when she exacted vengeance it was with a ferocity seldom equalled except in the gorier pages of the Old Testament.[70] Alexander himself also, inevitably, incurred wide suspicion at the time. Cleopatra's new-born son, as everyone knew, represented a dire threat to his succession. Pausanias, moreover, after failing to obtain satisfaction from Philip, had taken his tale of outrage to the crown prince. Alexander heard him out, and then quoted an enigmatic line from Euripides – 'The giver of the bride, the bridegroom, and the bride' – which could be construed as incitement to the murder of Attalus, Philip and Cleopatra.[71]

Modern research can add one or two further details. If Alexander *was* planning a *coup* (aided and abetted by his formidable mother) he chose the best possible time for it. Parmenio and Attalus, with many of their feudal adherents, were away in Asia. Furthermore, ambassadors from all the leading Greek states had conveniently assembled in Aegae for the wedding celebrations. If Philip died, it was vital that his successor should win immediate recognition, not only in Macedonia but also abroad, since the supreme command against Asia would devolve upon him as hegemon of the league. Here was the ideal opportunity to gain such an endorsement.[72] The part played by Antipater in stage-managing the succession suggests that he too was deeply involved.

The assassination itself presents some interesting features. The three young noblemen who pursued and killed Pausanias – Perdiccas, Leonnatus, and Attalus, son of Andromenes – were all close and trusted friends of Alexander. Leonnatus and Perdiccas belonged (as did Pausanias himself) to the aristocracy of Orestis, while Attalus was Perdiccas' brother-in-law. It has lately been argued[73] that Philip's murder was in fact (as Alexander subsequently claimed) the work of disgruntled out-kingdom conspirators, alarmed lest the king's new marriage meant a complete elimination of their own influence at court. The evidence as a whole (not least Alexander's close personal connection with this group of Orestis noblemen) suggests rather that whoever *did* plan the murder cleverly exploited out-kingdom resentment for ulterior motives of their own. Safer to use agents with a known grievance against the Argead dynasty, who could afterwards be identified with some real or imaginary highland attempt to usurp the throne. The best propaganda is that which sticks closest to the truth. Nor would suitable individuals be hard to find: Alexander, as the discarded – and half-Epirot – heir to Philip's kingdom offered a natural figurehead for any such would-be rebels.

From these facts we may perhaps form a hypothesis as to how Philip's murder was planned and carried out.[74] Pausanias – still hot with resentment at the abominable way he had been treated – was approached, probably by Olympias, and promised high rewards and honours if he would join with his three kinsmen from Orestis in assassinating the king. Olympias undertook to have horses[75] ready for all four of them afterwards. But what Pausanias clearly did *not* know was the real role assigned to his fellow-conspirators, those trusted intimates of Alexander. Their business was not the removal of Philip; it was to silence *him*. He knew too much; once he had served his purpose he was expendable. After his death, the propaganda machine could go smoothly into action. The elimination of Pausanias was an essential stage in the plot.[76]

Circumstantial evidence does not amount to proof positive; but men have been hanged on weaker cumulative testimony than that assembled here. The motive was overwhelming, the opportunity ideal. There can be little doubt, in fact, that Alexander 'became king by becoming a parricide'.[77] Once he was established on the throne, of course, all speculation as to his guilt quickly faded away. It is not

[4]

The Keys of the Kingdom

As soon as Philip's body had been removed from the arena, and some degree of order restored, Antipater, with admirable speed, presented Alexander before the Macedonian army, which at once acclaimed him king.[1] Among the first barons to render the new monarch homage was his namesake, Alexander of Lyncestis, one of the three sons of Aëropus. It is sometimes assumed by scholars that Aëropus' sons themselves had a plausible claim to the throne. Such a view has lately been challenged,[2] with very compelling arguments. It is far from certain whether these Lyncestian brothers were in fact of royal stock; they may have simply belonged to the aristocracy. Even if they were, the remote mountain canton of Lyncestis was unlikely to provide any claimant who outranked the surviving male Argeads; and except for one brief usurpation (that by Ptolemy of Alorus: see above, p. 14) the Argead dynasty had ruled at Pella since the beginning of the fifth century.

The Lyncestian Alexander and his two brothers, then, were not *prima facie* serious rivals for the throne. On the other hand, one crucial passage in Plutarch (*Moral.* 327c) links them unequivocally with a man who most certainly was: after Philip's death 'all Macedonia was festering beneath the surface, looking to Amyntas and to the sons of Aëropus'. This was Philip's cousin Amyntas, the son of his elder brother Perdiccas, whom shortly before his death he had married to Cynane, his daughter by Audata of Illyria. Amyntas was not only an Argead with good credentials for the role of pretender, but in all likelihood actively intriguing, with Boeotian assistance, for an eventual take-over.[3] Such a plot would naturally attract out-kingdom support; and here, it would seem, is where the sons of Aëropus came in, rather than as claimants in their own right.[4]

That Amyntas was responsible for Philip's murder is, though not altogether impossible, fundamentally unlikely. Until Philip's death he seems to have lived quietly and happily enough at court. What probably made him seem a danger in Alexander's eyes was his marriage to Cynane. If Philip could, however late in the day, look on Amyntas as a second-string heir to the throne, then so could others. The sons of Aëropus were known to be his friends and associates. Any purges Alexander carried out before leaving Europe, whether of Cleopatra's relatives or of his own, were specifically aimed at eliminating the danger of sedition, and in particular of rival claimants to the throne.[5] As soon as Philip was assassinated, Alexander of Lyncestis (who seems to have been a good judge of men, and knew his Alexander) at once saw how vulnerable his own position was. Without a moment's delay, he 'put on his cuirass and accompanied Alexander into the palace'.

This proved a wise precaution, since the king lost no time in arraigning the Lyncestian's two brothers on a charge of conspiracy. (They were afterwards executed at Philip's graveside.) By so doing, Alexander not only threw the blame for his father's death elsewhere, but got rid of two known supporters of Amyntas. The third brother's swiftness to swear allegiance suggests that he may have been tipped off in advance. He happened to be Antipater's son-in-law, and Antipater at this juncture was crucial to Alexander's plans. This may explain why he did not dispose of the Lyncestian until some years later. Nor, in fact, did he immediately move against the two main candidates for the crown: Amyntas himself and Cleopatra's baby son Caranus. It would have made the worst possible impression, both at home and abroad, if Alexander had carried out a dynastic purge almost before his father's body was cold. For the moment therefore, he left both Amyntas and Caranus untouched: a calculated risk, since though Amyntas may not have plotted a *coup* hitherto, he had every conceivable incentive for doing so now – if only to save his own neck.[6]

Alexander's next move was to address 'the Macedonian people' – or as many of them as he could assemble in Aegae. He assured them that 'the king was changed only in name and that the state would be run on principles no less effective than those of his father's administration' – a somewhat ambiguous promise. He also announced the abolition of all public duties for the individual except that of military service. In other words, Macedonian citizens were to be exempt from direct taxation – a clear bid for popular backing. Having dealt with his own people, Alexander held an audience for the foreign embassies. It was essential to secure their recognition and support: his status as hegemon of the league depended on it. However, he need not have worried. After hearing his carefully affable speech, those delegates present acclaimed him without demur. By way of strengthening his position still further, he now recalled all his close friends from exile (see above, p. 101), and appointed them to key posts in the new administration.[7]

He had every reason to act quickly. The news of Philip's death triggered off a general wave of insurrection, not only among the Greek states, but also in tribal frontier areas such as Thrace. Some cities (including Argos and Sparta) saw this as an ideal opportunity to recover their lost freedom. In Ambracia and Thebes Philip's garrisons were driven out. The Thebans and Arcadians (who had not, we may assume, sent representatives to Aegae) openly refused to recognize Alexander's overlordship. His kingdom was 'exposed to great jealousies, dire hatreds, and dangers on every side'.[8] Perhaps now, but more probably in spring 335, when Alexander went north on his campaign to the Danube, Amyntas son of Perdiccas (together with another Amyntas, Antiochus' son) slipped away from Pella to establish contact with various rebel factions in Boeotia. Epigraphical evidence testifies to their presence in Oropus and Lebadea; they must also have visited Thebes.[9]

But the most active hostility – despite those earlier flowery protestations of allegiance – came from Athens. Demosthenes, who received private intelligence reports on affairs in Macedonia,[10] learnt of Philip's death before the official messenger arrived. He thereupon declared publicly that he had had a dream in which the gods promised some great blessing to his city. When the nature of this 'blessing' became known, the Athenians reacted with almost hysterical enthusiasm. Having just voted Philip a statue, and sworn to surrender any man who plotted against him, they now decreed a day of public thanksgiving, and emulated Olympias by awarding a gold crown to the king's assassin.

On this occasion Demosthenes, whose daughter had died less than a week before, put aside his mourning garb and appeared in white robes, wearing a garland – a gesture which did not endear him to respectable conservatives in Athens. Nevertheless, his uncompromising anti-Macedonian policy won him considerable support. He had been watching every move in the factional struggle at Pella, and knew precisely where Alexander's weakest point lay. If Athens wanted to topple the new Macedonian king, her best hope lay in an alliance with the aristocratic junta that had backed Cleopatra. The assembly, persuaded by his arguments, gave him permission to communicate privately with Parmenio and Attalus in Asia Minor. Demosthenes at once wrote urging them to declare war on Alexander ('a stripling,' he declared airily, 'a mere booby') and promising full Athenian support if they did so.

Attalus, as one might expect, jumped at this proposal; and it is highly improbable that he did so without the approval and backing of his father-in-law Parmenio. Alexander's well-timed *coup* – if such it was – had laid all their dynastic plans in ruins; they would have been less than human (and very much out of character as Macedonians) had they failed to grasp at any opportunity of launching a counter-revolution. The third commander, Amyntas, had even stronger motives for joining an anti-

Alexander faction.[11] His father Arrhabaeus, son of Aëropus, had been one of Alexander's first victims, executed on the very same day as Philip's death (see above, p. 112); this relationship further suggests that the High Command in Asia Minor, through Arrhabaeus' son, was in touch with the Boeotian rebels, and regarded Amyntas son of Perdiccas as a potential ally, perhaps even as a serious alternative to Alexander. No one, at this juncture, could have seriously held out much hope for Cleopatra and her baby while they – and Olympias – remained in Pella. Besides, to establish Caranus as king would have meant a long regency, something every faction was desperate to avoid. Whether Alexander of Lyncestis was also involved in this conspiratorial network is hard to determine; but in the light of subsequent events, and bearing in mind the fact that Parmenio's fellow-general Amyntas was his brother, it seems very likely.

Alexander, however, as Demosthenes and others found to their cost, was a sharper operator than any of them when it came to political in-fighting. He had seen at once that his greatest potential opposition must inevitably come from the High Command in Asia Minor, above all from his implacable enemy Attalus. Amyntas, too, had small reason to love him; Parmenio, on the other hand, was a wily old opportunist who, if offered a tempting enough bait, might well change his allegiance. Alexander therefore chose a trusted friend named Hecataeus, and sent him, with a small picked force, to Parmenio's headquarters: ostensibly as a liaison officer, in fact as an *agent provocateur*. Hecataeus' secret orders were 'to bring back Attalus alive if he could, but if not, to assassinate him as quickly as possible'. What his special instructions were as regards Parmenio we shall see shortly. 'So he crossed over into Asia,' says Diodorus, 'joined Parmenio and Attalus, and awaited an opportunity to carry out his mission.'[12]

Demosthenes, meanwhile, had also persuaded the Athenian government to make overtures to Darius; but

here – for the moment at least – he met with little success.
The Great King had no intention of wasting good Persian
darics on Athens when the power-struggle in Macedonia
would achieve all he wanted at no cost to himself. He
therefore sent back what Aeschines afterwards described as
'a most barbarous and insolent letter', at the close of which
he wrote: 'I will not give you gold; stop asking me for it;
you will not get it.' Events soon made him change his
mind.[13]

Alexander's Macedonian counsellors, led by Antipater,
were all urging him to tread warily. The international
situation, they said, was critical, and might well explode at
any moment. Their advice was that he should leave the
Greek states severely alone, and make an effort to conciliate the barbarian tribes by concessions and diplomacy.
To this Alexander replied, with some force, that if he
showed the least sign of weakness or compromise, his
enemies would all fall on him at once. He intended, he told
them, to deal with the situation by a display of 'courage and
audacity'. It was not a suggestion; it was a flat statement,
and a highly characteristic one.[14] *De l'audace, toujours de
l'audace, encore de l'audace*: all through his life this was to be
Alexander's guiding star, and his first major demonstration
of it has a breathtaking quality which he may have subsequently equalled, but never surpassed.

At the head of a picked corps, the young king rode south
from Pella, taking the coast road through Methone and
Pydna into Thessaly. When he reached the Vale of Tempe,
between Olympus and Ossa, he found the pass strongly
defended. The Thessalians told him to halt his army while
they made up their minds whether or not they should
admit him. Alexander, with dangerous politeness, agreed –
and at once set his field-engineers cutting steps up the steep
seaward side of Mt Ossa. (Traces of these steps, known as
'Alexander's ladder', still survive.) Before the Thessalians
realized what was happening, he had crossed the mountains and was down in the plain behind them. With their

flank thus neatly turned, they chose to negotiate rather than fight. Alexander – having made his point – was all charm and friendliness. He reminded them of the benefits they had enjoyed from Philip's overlordship. He emphasized the fact that he himself was related, through Heracles and the Aeacids, to one of their leading families. 'By kindly words and by rich promises as well' – his father's reliable formula – he persuaded the Thessalian League to appoint him Archon, or head, of their federation for life, as Philip had been before him. They also placed a strong contingent of cavalry at his disposal,[15] and agreed to pay taxes to the Macedonian treasury, which Philip had left so dangerously depleted.

Any ordinary commander would have called a short halt at this point, to be fêted by the nobility of Larissa and to establish his position more securely. But Alexander never wasted time on inessentials. Before Greece learnt of his outflanking stratagem at Tempe, he had already reached the Hot Gates (Thermopylae). Here, relying on his father's ancient privileges, he convened a meeting of the Amphictyonic Council, which at once endorsed his status as hegemon of the league. The council, like the Vatican, had no big battalions behind it; but it enjoyed considerable religious and moral prestige. Few ancient statesmen or generals were more acutely aware than Alexander of the advantages to be got from good publicity.

While he was still at the Hot Gates, some rather flustered envoys arrived from Ambracia in southern Epirus – the first of many such panic-stricken missions. Alexander received them courteously, and 'convinced them that they had been only a little premature in grasping the independence that he was on the point of giving them voluntarily'.[16] Alexander may well have had doubts about his uncle and namesake (now also his brother-in-law): a few independent cities in Epirus would help to limit the Molossian king's ambitions. Philip had used the same technique in Boeotia, as a curb on the power of Thebes. But the main message was clear enough: cooperation would pay off. Quite a few cities took the hint.

Thebes itself, not surprisingly, was Alexander's next concern. As the most powerful and important city in central Greece, its reliability was of paramount importance; and the Thebans' stubborn opposition to Macedonia could hardly be called encouraging. They had expelled Philip's garrison, and refused to acknowledge Alexander. They were also, in all likelihood, already in secret communication with Alexander's cousin Amyntas, son of Perdiccas (see above, p. 111), though whether Alexander himself yet realized this cannot be determined: *prima facie* it would seem most improbable. At all events, he decided to see how far a show of force would overawe them. Startled Theban citizens woke up one morning to find a Macedonian army, in full battle array, encamped before the Cadmea. Alexander's ultimatum was simple: all he asked was recognition as hegemon of the league. If he got it, no more would be said about the expulsion of his father's troops, though they would, of course, be reinstated. Otherwise . . . The Thebans looked down at those grim Macedonian veterans, and capitulated without further argument. Recognition cost them little; a more propitious time for direct action would come in due course, and premature defiance, at this point, was stark lunacy.

Their action caused something of a panic in Athens, which lay a bare forty miles beyond Thebes. Demosthenes' sneering picture of Alexander as a young poltroon, 'content to saunter around in Pella and keep watch over the omens',* was now seen to be perilously wide of the mark. The Athenians, anticipating a siege, brought in their property from the surrounding countryside, and began to repair

* Cited by Aeschines, *In Ctes.* §160. Demosthenes called Alexander 'Margites', a particularly insulting allusion: this was the main character in a pseudo-Homeric pastiche caricaturing Achilles – the implication being that Alexander was no more than a comic imitation of his chosen hero. The 'sauntering around' (*peripatounta*) is a hit at his Peripatetic studies under Aristotle.

the city-walls. However, when Alexander offered them the same ultimatum as he had presented to Thebes, they accepted his terms with alacrity. An Athenian embassy was at once sent north, bearing profuse apologies for so regrettable a delay in acknowledging the king's official status. Among the envoys was Demosthenes himself, very ill at ease about his mission, and small wonder. Quite apart from his public comments on Alexander (which no self-respecting young man could be expected to take kindly) there were those damning letters he had written to Attalus and Parmenio. By now they might well have fallen into Alexander's hands. On top of all this, Demosthenes had already opened private – and, it was said, highly profitable – negotiations with the Great King. With all this in mind he lost his nerve, and turned back home when he had got no farther than Cithaeron.[17]

His natural fears about Attalus were all too well justified. Despite the fact that the Macedonian general 'actually had set his hand to revolt and had agreed with the Athenians to undertake joint action against Alexander', the news of the king's whirlwind advance through Greece, followed by Athens' craven surrender, made him change his mind with some speed. A neat *volte-face*, he calculated, might yet save him. He had kept all Demosthenes' correspondence, and this he now dispatched to Alexander, with many protestations of loyalty. He could have spared himself the trouble. Quite a few people did, in fact, change sides during those early months and get away with it; but Attalus – the man who had publicly insulted Alexander's birth, the uncle of his mother's rival and successor – could expect no mercy, now or ever. That he did not realize this himself was a fatal error of judgement. Besides, by now Hecataeus, in accordance with Alexander's instructions, had come to a private understanding with Parmenio, and (it would seem) with Amyntas as well. It was this double switch of allegiance that finally sealed Attalus' fate.

The old Macedonian marshal – he was now in his mid

sixties – needed little persuasion to change sides. Alexander's masterly display of generalship, followed by the ignominious collapse of all Athenian resistance, made it quite clear that toppling this new king would be no easy matter. Parmenio had not survived so long under Philip without learning a thing or two about life in the political jungle. He therefore decided to cut his losses and back the winning side. His support at this stage was worth a good deal, and he made up his mind to exact a high price for it. What he had to offer, in effect, was the support of most, if not all, of the lowland barons: a move which would leave Amyntas, son of Perdiccas – or any other potential rival – dependent on a coalition of the out-kingdoms and rebellious Greek cities such as Thebes. If Parmenio swung his followers over *en bloc* behind the new king, who could hope to challenge Alexander's position?

Alexander was hard-pressed for time, and could not afford to haggle over Parmenio's terms. This cost him dear later. When the Macedonian army at last crossed into Asia, almost every key command was held by one of Parmenio's sons, brothers, or other kinsmen: it took Alexander six long years to break the stranglehold exerted by this formidable clique. In return for such major concessions, however, Parmenio had to make one sacrifice: Attalus. Here Alexander proved adamant. Perhaps the sacrifice was not really so great: a son-in-law could, after all, be replaced. A few days later Attalus was quietly liquidated – certainly with Parmenio's connivance, and in all likelihood at his express command. The third general, Amyntas, sized up this realignment of forces with a coolly realistic eye, and decided to forget about the execution of his father. He, too, made his peace with Alexander, who afterwards appointed him to various relatively minor commands, including that of the Scouts (*skopoi*) before the Granicus.[18]

In two brief months Alexander had achieved more than anyone would have dreamed possible at the time of Philip's death. Without a blow being struck, he had won recognition from, Thessaly, the Amphictyonic Council, Thebes, and Athens. The murder of Attalus and the transference of Parmenio's allegiance had largely insured him against any attempt at a counter-revolution by the Macedonian nobility. Now the time had come to have his position endorsed in more general terms. He therefore summoned a meeting of the Hellenic League at Corinth. To this were invited (if 'invited' is the right word) not only the existing delegates, but also representatives from such states as had so far refused to acknowledge his overlordship.[19]

The response was all that he could have wished. His actions had thoroughly frightened the Greeks, and their envoys came flocking into Corinth with more haste than dignity. The Megarians went so far as to offer him honorary citizenship; and when (perhaps with Athens' example in mind) he 'made fun of their eagerness, they told him that up to that time they had conferred citizenship upon Heracles only and now upon himself'. Someone at Megara had gauged Alexander's temperament to a nicety. He accepted the honour. A young man who would only run against kings could hardly refuse to share citizenship with a demigod – and his own ancestor into the bargain. Only the Spartans held aloof. The traditions of their country, they informed the king, did not allow them to serve under a foreign leader. (So much for Macedonia's pretensions to Hellenism.) Alexander did not press the point. He could have coerced Sparta easily enough; but in the circumstances this would have been naked despotism. The one thing he needed at the moment was to secure Greek cooperation by strict adherence to constitutional procedure. If he left them the outward semblance of autonomy, the cowed member-states would probably be satisfied.

On the other hand, Alexander had no intention of letting anti-Macedonian powers such as Sparta or Arcadia make any serious trouble for him if he could help it. He therefore appointed tough collaborationist rulers in neighbouring states – Achaea, and above all Messenia – to preserve the status quo. By a flagrantly legalistic quibble, these appointments were made *before* the renewal of the league treaty in Alexander's name, since they violated the clause banning any forcible interference with existing governments. Even so, they caused deep resentment.[20]

So the league duly met at Corinth, and elected Alexander hegemon in his father's place. The treaty with Macedonia was also renewed: once again in perpetuity, so that it applied to the king's descendants as well as to himself. There were no substantial alterations. The Greek states were still to be 'free and independent'; it is not hard to imagine the delegates' feelings as they ratified *that* clause.[21] But they had little choice in the matter. Nor could they very well avoid electing Alexander captain-general of the league's forces for the invasion of Persia. To encourage them, the king introduced a delegate from Ephesus who claimed to be speaking on behalf of 'the Greeks of Asia', and urged Alexander to undertake a war of liberation on their behalf. This appeal, he declared, carried more weight with him than did any other consideration. It sounds like a beautifully stage-managed incident.

But if the Greeks imagined that this last honour was a mere empty formality, they very soon learnt better. The new captain-general at once presented for their ratification a complex schedule 'defining the obligations of the contracting parties in the event of a joint campaign', and covering everything from military pay-scales – one drachma a day for the ordinary infantryman – to the regulation of grain-allowances. The Athenians, somewhat dismayed, found themselves under contract to supply Alexander with ships and naval stores. This clause was opposed by Demosthenes: he saw no guarantee, he said, that Alexander would not employ such a force against those who had furnished it. He was overruled, and Alexander got his way.[22] Since the Macedonian army had escorted him to Corinth, the final issue was never really in doubt.

When the congress was over, 'many statesmen and

philosophers came to [Alexander] with their congratulations'; we can imagine the scene all too clearly. But one famous character was conspicuous by his absence: Diogenes the Cynic. Piqued and curious, Alexander eventually went out to the suburb where Diogenes lived, in his large clay tub, and approached him personally. He found the philosopher sunning himself, naked except for a loin-cloth. Diogenes, his meditations disturbed by the noise and laughter of the numerous courtiers who came flocking at the captain-general's heels, looked up at Alexander with a direct, uncomfortable gaze, but said nothing.

For once in his life, Alexander was somewhat embarrassed. He greeted Diogenes with elaborate formality, and waited. Diogenes remained silent. At last, in desperation, Alexander asked if there was anything the philosopher wanted, anything he, Alexander, could do for him? 'Yes,' came the famous answer, 'stand aside; you're keeping the sun off me.' That was the end of the interview. As they trooped back into Corinth, Alexander's followers tried to turn the episode into a joke, jeering at Diogenes and belittling his pretensions. But the captain-general silenced them with one enigmatic remark. 'If I were not Alexander,' he said, 'I would be Diogenes.'[23] This shows shrewd percipience. Both men shared (and surely recognized in each other) the same quality of stubborn and alienated intransigence. But whereas Diogenes had withdrawn from the world, Alexander was bent on subjugating it: they represented the active and passive forms of an identical phenomenon. It is not surprising, in the circumstances, that their encounter should have been so abrasive.

Having obtained a full mandate from the league, Alexander wound up the congress and set out, at the head of his army, for Macedonia. On the way, however, he made a special detour to Delphi, being anxious to consult the Oracle about the outcome of his Persian crusade. The proceedings at Corinth had taken longer than he anticipated, and by the time he reached Delphi it was late November. Now from mid November to mid February the Oracle did not function. This was a religious matter, and not even for the captain-general of the Hellenes would the priests make an exception. They should have known better. Alexander, ignoring them, sent a peremptory summons to the Pythia. She would not come: it was not lawful, she said. At this Alexander stormed in, seized her physically, and attempted to drag her into the shrine by main force. 'Young man,' gasped the priestess, 'you are invincible!' Alexander promptly released her; this, he said, was a good enough prophecy for him. (Later, the epithet 'invincible' – *aniketos* – became one of his regular titles.) As a mark of his pleasure he donated 150 gold 'philips' to the temple funds; not a princely sum, but by now the captain-general was embarrassingly short of ready cash.[24]

Despite this handicap, however, Alexander refused to hurry or to skimp his preparations. He spent the winter of 336/5 giving his army an intensive training-course in mountain warfare, to prepare them for the campaign which he intended to undertake as soon as the snow was off the passes. He knew that he could not leave Europe until the Balkans had been thoroughly pacified. Though the Greek states no longer presented an immediate threat, the wild tribes to the north and west of Macedonia still had to be reckoned with. Merely to defeat them in battle would do little good. There was only one way in which the northern frontier could be permanently secured, and that was by pushing it forward a hundred miles to the Danube, through some of the roughest fighting terrain in Europe.[25]

The campaign was, therefore, intended to serve a three-fold purpose. It would stabilize the frontiers, and thus leave Antipater – whom Alexander had earmarked for the onerous post of regent – free to concentrate on Macedonia's rebarbative Greek allies during the king's absence abroad. It would force the Thracians and Illyrians to admit that Alexander was no less formidable an opponent than his father. Finally, it would serve as a full-scale tactical exercise in preparation for the assault on Persia. With superb but calculated optimism, Alexander ordered a squadron of warships to sail from Byzantium into the Black Sea, and thence up the Danube, where they were to wait for the army at a pre-arranged rendezvous – probably near modern Ruschuk, south of Bucharest. Then he himself set out from Amphipolis by the overland route: eastward first by Neapolis (Kavalla), across the River Nestus (Mesta) and the Rhodope Mountains, then north to his father's outpost of Philippopolis (Plovdiv, in Bulgaria).

Up to this point he had been marching through friendly territory; but now came the first opposition. To reach the Danube he had to cross the main Haemus (Balkan) range, probably by the Shipka pass. The 'autonomous' Thracians – that is, those who remained independent of Macedonian rule – decided to hold this pass against him: a clever strategical move, since there was no easy alternative route, and Alexander would face a steep, exposed ascent to the main col. The Thracians lined up their waggons at the head of the pass, rather in the manner of a Boer laager, and waited.

One of the qualities which most clearly distinguishes Alexander from the common run of competent field-commanders is his almost uncanny ability to divine enemy tactics in advance. Some of this may have been due to his first-class intelligence service; but at times it looks more like sheer brilliant psychological intuition. Anyone else would have assumed, very reasonably on the face of it, that the Thracians intended to use their waggons as a stockade, and fight behind them. Alexander, however, knew that their favourite battle-manoeuvre was a wild broadsword charge, and instantly deduced what they planned to do. As soon as he and his men were into the narrow section of the gorge, these waggons would be sent rolling down the slope, shattering the Macedonian phalanx; and before its demoralized ranks could close again, the Thracians would charge through the broken spear-line, slashing and stabbing at close quarters, where the unwieldy *sarissa* was worse than useless.

Half the danger from such a manoeuvre lay in the element of surprise; and because of Alexander's inspired foreknowledge, this advantage was now lost. He carefully briefed his men on what to expect, and what avoiding action to take. If they had room, they were to open ranks and let the waggons pass through (a defence measure subsequently employed, with great success, against Darius' scythed chariots at Gaugamela: see below, p. 293). If they found themselves in the narrowest part of the ascent, they were to kneel or lie down close together, shields overlapping above their heads, and with luck the momentum of the waggons (which were, after all, only light mountain carts) would carry them clear. On the face of it, this sounds a wildly impractical scheme. It might work for the front rank (though even here there would surely be a record number of broken legs) but what about those unfortunates immediately behind them? Sooner or later a bouncing waggon must succumb to the force of gravity, and when it does there are better places to be than underneath it. But according to Arrian (1.1.9–10), who is sober about such details, when the waggons came hurtling down as predicted, not a man was lost. Even allowing for partisan exaggeration, this is a remarkable tribute to Macedonian drill and discipline.

After the failure of the Thracians' initial stratagem, the battle itself proved an anticlimax. While Alexander's archers gave covering fire from the rocks above the right wing of the phalanx, and he himself led his *corps d'élite* up the western ridge, the main infantry divisions – doubtless delighted to find themselves still alive – stormed cheering to the head of the pass. The Thracians broke and ran, leaving 1,500 dead behind them, together with many women and children. The road to the Danube lay open.

A great deal of plunder was taken: this Alexander sent back to the coast under escort. Then he and his men descended the far side of the Shipka pass and pressed on across the Danube plain. There was no opposition. When the Macedonians pitched camp on the wooded banks of the Lyginus River (probably the Yantra), the Danube itself was only three days' march away. However, their movements had been watched throughout by the Triballian tribesmen who occupied this area. A large number of their warriors, together with the women and children, the Triballians now evacuated to an island in the middle of the Danube. Then, when Alexander marched on from the Lyginus, a second strong native force slipped in behind him and cut off his retreat.

The moment he got wind of this movement, the king turned back. He found the Triballians established in a wooded glen near the river, where it would be extremely hard to launch a mass attack on them. He therefore sent his archers and slingers to the entrance of the glen, apparently unsupported, while the phalanx and cavalry remained under cover. Exasperated by the arrows and bolts that now began to rain down on their ranks, the Triballians came tumbling out to teach these light-armed gadflies a lesson – and were promptly cut to pieces by the full force of the Macedonian army. Three thousand natives perished in that one murderous charge, while Alexander himself (or so it was claimed) lost only eleven cavalrymen and about forty foot-soldiers. Having given a seemingly effortless demonstration of moral and military superiority, he resumed his march. Three days later his advance scouts drew rein on the southern bank of the Danube, to find the naval squadron waiting at their rendezvous – another remarkable testament to efficient military planning.

Alexander had not chosen this meeting-place at random. It lay opposite the island where the Triballians had taken refuge; and it was this island – Peucé, or the Pine Tree – which, so Alexander claimed,[26] Darius I had used to help him span the Danube with a pontoon bridge, for his Scythian campaign in 514/13. Alexander had, it is clear, been studying Herodotus (as anyone planning to invade

Persia undoubtedly would), and meant to emulate, indeed to surpass, Darius' achievement. Strategic requirements were always adaptable to the needs of heroic *areté*. As though in response to Alexander's *hubris*, things now, for the first time, began to go wrong. Common sense dictated that the island, with its swarms of enemy troops and refugees, should be captured before the Macedonians attempted anything else. But Peucé was rocky and precipitous, with a fast current flowing past it. Alexander's ships were too few and too small to achieve a landing in strength. After several attempts to establish a bridgehead had failed, the king wisely gave up.

Meanwhile a vast horde of Getae nomads – some four thousand horsemen, and between two and three times that number on foot – had appeared at the far side of the Danube. Yet it was now, despite their presence, that Alexander found himself seized by an 'irresistible urge' to cross the river. If baulked by the difficult, try the impossible. The Greek word for this urge is *pothos*; it recurs throughout Alexander's life as a 'longing for things not yet within reach, for the unknown, far distant, unattained',[27] and it is so used of no other person in the ancient world. *Pothos*, in this sense, is an individual characteristic peculiar to Alexander.

> For joy of knowing what may not be known
> We take the golden road to Samarkand.

Flecker's pilgrims were not only following in the great Iskander's footsteps, but doing so for identical reasons.

More prosaically, it could be argued that in this case Alexander had no alternative course open to him – except retreat, which was unthinkable. If he made a successful raid into Getae territory, moreover, there was always the chance that the island's defenders would be sufficiently impressed to come to terms with him. He therefore instructed his patrols to commandeer every dug-out canoe they could lay hands on (these were in plentiful supply along the river for fishing and transport), while the rest of the army was put to work stuffing leather tent-covers with hay, and sewing them into makeshift floats. In this way Alexander contrived to ferry 1,500 cavalry and 4,000 foot-soldiers across the Danube under cover of darkness – a far greater number than would have been possible with the fleet alone.

They landed just before dawn, at a point where the grain was standing high, and acted as camouflage for their disembarkation. The infantry led the way, 'carrying their spears parallel with the ground and obliquely to their line of march, to flatten the grain as they advanced'. When they broke cover, Alexander took command of the cavalry, and the whole phalanx advanced in close order, on an extended front. The mere sight of this grim and disciplined spear-line, appearing as if from nowhere, struck panic into the Getae; and when the cavalry broke into a charge, the whole horde turned and fled. At first they sought refuge in their nearest settlement, some four miles away. But the advance continued, with Alexander's cavalry fanned out on the flanks to watch for ambushes: it was clear that he meant business. As the settlement was unfortified, the Getae hastily loaded women, children and provisions on to the cruppers of their horses and vanished into the steppe – an age-old nomads' trick.

Alexander did not pursue them: he knew better than to press his luck. Instead he plundered the settlement, and then destroyed it. The loot, such as it was, went back to base, while the king made sacrifice on the banks of the Danube to Zeus the Saviour, Heracles, and the river itself, for allowing the army safe passage. Then – *pothos* and prestige duly satisfied – he led his forces back to the southern shore, pitched camp, and waited for the barbarians to make the next move. He did not have to wait long. The Triballians, thoroughly shaken by this display of military expertise, emerged from their island retreat and sent emissaries to seek friendship and alliance with so mighty a warrior. Other independent tribes along the Danube soon heard the story and followed suit. Its echoes even reached the Celts of the Adriatic, and they too made polite overtures – out of curiosity rather than fear, one feels, since they dwelt far away from Alexander's field of operations.

Their envoys, however, have one very special claim to fame: they are the only people on record who found Alexander's pretensions neither awe-inspiring nor horrific, but mildly ridiculous. They were, says Arrian, 'men of haughty demeanour and tall in proportion'. We can imagine them stroking their long moustaches and looking down with patient indulgence at this stocky, blond, dynamic little prince as he asked them, hopefully, what they were most afraid of in the world. The answer he expected, of course, was 'You, my lord'; but the Celts had no intention of falling for so obvious a gambit. After a moment's grave reflection, they said their worst fear was that the sky might fall on their heads – although, they added, with demure insolence, 'they put above everything else the friendship of such a man as he.' Alexander kept a straight face (there was not much else he could do), made a treaty of friendship with the Celts, and sent them on their way. But he was heard to mutter under his breath that for barbarians they had a ludicrously high opinion of themselves.[28]

From the Danube the Macedonians marched back over the Shipka pass, and then turned west instead of south, following the line of the Balkan range by the route which today links Lenskigrad with Sofia. This brought them out of Triballian country, and into the domains of Alexander's old friend Langarus, King of the Agrianians. Langarus himself, together with his finest household troops, had accompanied Alexander to the Danube. They did not operate as an independent auxiliary unit, but were brigaded with the Guards Division (*hypaspistae*) – the earliest known instance[29] of that military integration policy which Alexander afterwards developed more fully in Asia and India.

At this point the most alarming reports began to come in from Illyria – always a dangerous and unstable frontier area. Alexander's original plan, we may assume, was to give his troops a rest in friendly territory – they had already marched and fought for some five hundred miles, over appalling roads, in two months or less – and then to show the flag along the western marches at his leisure. Instead, he found himself thrown headlong into one of the toughest campaigns of his entire career. Cleitus, King of Illyria – son of that Bardylis whom Philip had long ago defeated so crushingly at Lake Okhrida (see above, p. 24) – was up in arms: Alexander's Danubian expedition had given him just the chance he was waiting for. To make matters worse, he had formed an alliance with another chieftain named Glaucias, the leader of the Taulantians – an uncouth and mead-swilling tribe from the Durazzo area, ancestors of the modern Albanians. Yet a third Illyrian tribe, the Autaratians, had agreed to attack Alexander on his line of march.

It was Philip's early days all over again: the entire western frontier of Macedonia stood in the gravest danger. Alexander asked Langarus about these Autaratians, and was told, with cheerful optimism, that they were the feeblest, least war-like fighters in the area. This is not what we learn from one reliable ancient source,[30] where they are described as 'the largest and best of the Illyrian tribes', who had, indeed, at one time emulated Alexander himself by subduing the Triballians. However, Langarus backed his opinion by promising to deal with them himself while Alexander marched against Cleitus. The offer was gratefully accepted. How much confidence Alexander had in the Agrianian's ability to stand this attack off is another matter; but speed, now, was of the essence. Glaucias and his highlanders had not yet joined up with Cleitus, and Alexander strained every nerve to reach the latter's fortress of Pelium before they did. The exhausted Macedonian army took to the road again – if that horrendous mountain track which still links Gor Džumaja and Titov Veles can be so described – and force-marched south-west across the Paeonian ranges. Pelium itself commanded the valley of the Apsus (Devol) and the main trunk road into Macedonia. It was an all but impregnable stronghold, surrounded on three sides by thickly wooded mountains, and approached by a narrow pass, leading to a ford. The small plain before it could, all too easily, become a death-trap for any but the most skilful attacker.

Alexander achieved his initial aim: he got there before Glaucias. The Illyrian advance detachments, after some brief skirmishing, retreated within the walls of Pelium. The Macedonians found eloquent but grisly testimony to the unexpectedness of their arrival: an abandoned altar on which lay the slaughtered bodies of three boys, three girls, and three black rams. This sacrifice must actually have been in mid course when the alarm was given, and Alexander's outriders came galloping through the pass.

The king decided to blockade Pelium, and brought up his siege equipment. This was an odd tactical blunder. He had no time to waste starving Cleitus out, and with so small a task-force his chances of taking this strongly guarded and inaccessible fortress by storm were minimal. Worst of all, at any moment Glaucias would appear at the head of a relief column. In the event he did so less than twenty-four hours later, and promptly occupied the mountains in Alexander's rear. The Macedonians were now cut off, and dangerously short of supplies: a foraging party under Philotas only just escaped annihilation thanks to quick action by Alexander and the cavalry.

But if the young king was to blame for letting himself be cut off in this fashion, the ruse by which he extricated himself must stand as one of the most eccentrically brilliant stratagems in the whole history of warfare. Early next morning he formed up his entire army in the plain – apparently oblivious to the presence of the enemy – and proceeded to give an exhibition of close-order drill. The phalanx was paraded in files 120 men deep, with a squadron of 200 cavalry on either flank. By Alexander's express command, these drill-manoeuvres were carried out in total silence. It must have been an eerie and highly disconcerting spectacle. At given signals the great forest of *sarissas* would rise to the vertical 'salute' position, and then dip horizontally as for battle-order. The bristling spear-line swung now right, now left, in perfect unison. The phalanx advanced, wheeled into column and line, moved through various intricate formations as though on the parade-ground – all without a word being uttered.

The barbarians had never seen anything like it. From their positions in the surrounding hills they stared down at this weird ritual, scarcely able to believe their eyes. Then, little by little, one straggling group after another began to edge closer, half-terrified, half-enthralled. Alexander watched them, waiting for the psychological moment. Then, at last, he gave his final pre-arranged signal. The left wing of the cavalry swung into wedge formation, and charged. At the same moment, every man of the phalanx beat his spear on his shield, and from thousands of throats there went up the terrible ululating Macedonian war-cry – '*Alalalalai!*' – echoing and reverberating from the mountains. This sudden, shattering explosion of sound, especially after the dead stillness which had preceded it, completely unnerved Glaucias' tribesmen, who fled back in wild confusion from the foothills to the safety of their fortress.[31] Alexander and his Companion Cavalry flushed the last of them from a knoll overlooking the ford; then he ordered up the Agrianians and the archers as a covering force, while the rest of the army, led by the Guards Division, began to move across the river at the double.

The tribesmen, their first panic wearing off, suddenly realized that the Macedonians were on the point of breaking out of the trap so carefully laid for them. They rallied, and counter-attacked. Alexander, with the cavalry and his light-armed troops, held them off from the knoll long enough for his siege-catapults to be carried through the ford and set up on the further bank. The archers, meanwhile, again on the king's instructions, had taken up a defensive position in mid stream. While the final units struggled across, a covering fire of arrows and heavy stones (the catapults had a range of several hundred yards) kept Cleitus' men from engaging. Fuller (p. 226, n. 1) observes that 'this is the first recorded use of catapults as field artillery': yet another example of Alexander's extraordinary inventiveness and gift for inspired improvisation. Once again he had concluded a complex and hazardous operation without losing a single man.[32]

At this point any other field-commander, thankful to have extricated himself from so appalling a position, would have blessed his luck and got away as fast as possible. There was still no news from Langarus; for all Alexander knew, his lines of communication with Macedonia might already have been cut. In the circumstances he showed quite incredible *sang-froid*. Calculating, quite rightly, that the barbarians would assume that the Macedonian army had gone for good, he withdrew a few miles, and gave them three days in which to regain their confidence. Then he sent out a reconnaissance party. The news they brought back was just what he had expected to hear. The barbarian camp lay wide open. They had not dug a trench or built a palisade; they were not even bothering to post sentries. Their lines, moreover, were dangerously extended. Over-confidence and lack of discipline in the enemy make powerful allies for any competent general. Besides, as these early campaigns amply demonstrate, the psychological exploitation of tribal indiscipline was one of Alexander's most effective weapons.

He at once marched back, with a specially picked mobile force – including Guards, Agrianians, and archers, his regular commando brigade – and ordered the rest of the army to follow. Then, under cover of darkness, he sent in the archers and the Agrianians (aptly described as the Gurkhas of antiquity) to finish the job for him. It was a massacre pure and simple. Most of the tribesmen were still asleep, and Alexander's troops slaughtered them where they lay. Others were cut down as they tried to escape. The panic and chaos were indescribable. Cleitus, in desperation, set fire to Pelium, and fled with Glaucias to the latter's mountain stronghold near Durazzo. For the time being, at least, the Illyrian threat had been destroyed. It was not until a decade after Alexander's death (314/12) that another Macedonian king, Cassander, became entangled with Glaucias, in an attempt to take over the Durazzo littoral; and his venture proved a failure.

After this annihilating victory, Alexander's first concern was to re-establish contact with Langarus, and, if need be, to deal with the Autaratians. In the event, however, Langarus – true to his promise – had proved more than capable of dealing with them himself. A quick raid on their settlements, a little crop-burning, and they were ready enough to cry quits: it looks as though his judgement on their fighting qualities may not have been so wide of the mark after all. This danger eliminated, Langarus at once set out for Pelium at the head of a relief column, and the two forces met somewhere up-country. (The most likely point is somewhere on the road between Prilep and Bitola in modern Yugoslavia: perhaps at the crossing of the Tscherna River.) It should have been a triumphant reunion; but Alexander's euphoric mood was rudely shattered by the dispatches from Greece which Langarus brought him – the first, apparently, which he had seen since the Danube campaign began. The story they told was far from reassuring.

It would, of course, have been most remarkable had the Greeks (and any Macedonian rivals who fancied their chances) *not* tried to capitalize on Alexander's absence during these crucial months. How far the action of various cities – Thebes and Athens in particular – were consciously coordinated, let alone part of a plan to replace Alexander on the throne of Macedonia by Amyntas, son of Perdiccas,

cannot now be determined with any finality. It does, however, make very good sense of the facts available if we posit
a concerted uprising, with Amyntas as its titular head in the
event of victory, and the removal of Alexander (not to
mention Alexander's aggressive policies) as the conspirators'
prime aim. Alexander's own subsequent actions suggest
very strongly that this was how he, at least, interpreted the
course of events.[33]

The rebels' first task, clearly, was to bring over as many
waverers as possible by means of propaganda minimizing
the threat which Alexander still represented. Demosthenes,
in Athens, went about this task enthusiastically, and
proceeded to stage-manage it with some skill. He announced
in the assembly that Alexander, *together with his whole
expeditionary force*, had been massacred by the Triballians.
To make this fabrication more plausible, he produced the
'messenger', bandaged and bloody, who swore he had
received his 'wounds' in the same battle, and had actually
witnessed Alexander's death.[34] The effect of this dramatic
announcement can well be imagined. If anyone had doubts
about the report, he quickly suppressed them: this, after all,
was just what every patriotic Greek had hoped and prayed
might happen. Throughout the peninsula cities flared up in
revolt. Macedonian garrisons were expelled or besieged.
Even when Alexander's march from the Danube to Pelium
became public knowledge, it was asserted, with equal
confidence, that Demosthenes had simply got his facts a
little muddled, and that the king had in fact been slain by
the Illyrians.[35]

But by far the most potentially dangerous uprising was
that of Thebes. It needed careful planning: Alexander had
left an extra strong garrison on the Cadmea, and had
packed the Theban assembly with pro-Macedonian collaborators. The rebel leaders, however, were in touch with
various political exiles – mostly at Athens – and a group of
these they now smuggled into the city by night. The in-
surgents had their plans worked out in advance, and carried

them through without a hitch. First, they seized and murdered the two senior officers of the garrison. (This not only prevented any effective counter-measures being taken by the garrison itself, but also presented the Thebans with a *fait accompli*: having gone so far, they could not afford to turn back.) They then summoned the assembly and called on all true Thebans to throw off the Macedonian yoke – 'making great play,' says Arrian dourly, 'with the grand old words "liberty" and "free speech"'.[36] They did not appeal in vain.

Had Thebes revolted spontaneously, without external aid, the situation – from Alexander's point of view – would have been bad enough. But by now rumours, at least, of Amyntas' projected *coup* must have reached him; and to make matters worse, the success of the uprising was due in no small measure to arms and gold supplied by Demosthenes, with the open connivance of the Athenian government. It was Demosthenes, too, who had been mainly responsible for persuading the Theban exiles to carry out their part of the plot. When news of its success reached Athens, the assembly, in a burst of enthusiasm, voted to send Thebes military support – again, largely at Demosthenes' instigation. The insurgent cities now formed themselves into an anti-Macedonian league, and it looked as though a full-scale war of rebellion was imminent.

However, cooler heads than Demosthenes now decided that things had gone too far and too fast. Athens at this point was just beginning, under Lycurgus' shrewd administration, to build up her naval and military reserves once more.[37] A premature direct clash with Macedonia might well prove disastrous. The Athenian government therefore decided to wait awhile and 'see how the war would go' before committing troops to the defence of Thebes. Nevertheless, it was all too plain where Athens' sympathies lay, despite this diplomatic fence-sitting; and no one could doubt that the same was true, *a fortiori*, of Sparta and the Peloponnesian states. At any moment the whole of Greece might well go up in flames.[38] With the situation in Macedonia equally explosive – even if Amyntas had not yet shown his hand openly, his plans were widely known – and Pella humming with intrigue, it was plain that the sooner the king returned home, the better.[39]

Yet nothing, it is safe to say, caused Alexander more alarm than the part which Persia was playing in this affair. The Great King had, at long last, taken cognizance of the fact that Alexander not only meant to invade Asia Minor (Parmenio's activities had already made this quite clear) but was, on present showing, singularly well equipped for such a task. Once the situation became clear, Darius reversed his earlier policy of non-intervention, and began to channel gold into Greece wherever he thought it would do most good. He did not, as yet, commit himself to anything more definite: clearly he hoped that the Greek revolt would solve his problem for him. But the mere thought of a Graeco-Persian coalition must have turned Alexander's blood cold.

Darius, through his agents, had offered the Athenian government no less than 300 gold talents as an inducement to support Thebes' bid for freedom. This offer was officially refused: its acceptance would have been no less public an affront to Macedonia than the dispatch of troops. But everyone in Athens knew quite well whose money it was that Demosthenes now began handing out to the Theban exiles. Darius had simply decided (with Athenian connivance) to operate through unofficial channels.[40] He also felt it was high time to crack down on Parmenio's advance expedition: if this force could be wiped out, Alexander's task – especially the crucial business of getting his army across the Hellespont – would become a great deal more hazardous.

Until now Parmenio had had things very much his own way. Many of the Greek coastal cities had come over to him, and those that did not were made to regret their decision. In July 335, for instance, Parmenio stormed the little town of Grynium, on the Ionian coast between Lesbos and Chios, selling its inhabitants into slavery. Alexander's

liberation policy, it seemed, made no allowance for a perverse disinclination to be liberated.[41] Parmenio's force, in
fact, played a far more important part in Alexander's
invasion plans than we might guess from our meagre
sources. Its two main objectives were to keep the invasion-
route open by establishing a bridgehead around it, and to
soften up (by whatever means) the Greek cities of Asia
Minor. It consisted of three operational brigades, covering
respectively Ionia, Aeolis, and the Troad. Parmenio,
besides acting as commander-in-chief, led one of these
brigades himself.

To deal with this nuisance (it is doubtful whether, as yet,
he rated it much higher) Darius now chose his most seasoned and professional strategist, Memnon of Rhodes.
Memnon was given a picked body of 5,000 mercenaries, and
a virtually free hand. He made, first, for the coast south of
the Troad, where Parmenio was now besieging another
small town, Pitane. But on the way an urgent message
reached him from the Great King. Cyzicus, a key port in
the Propontis (Sea of Marmara) was in danger of falling,
had perhaps already fallen: would he go to the rescue?

Memnon's dash north has acquired some fame because,
to save time, he led his troops by the shortest route – straight
across the ranges of Mt Ida. He came within a hair's-
breadth of saving Cyzicus, but was just too late. 'Failing in
this,' says Diodorus, 'he wasted its territory and collected
much booty.' But he did not leave the area without scoring
one major success. His corps made a quick thrust westward
to the Hellespont, and recaptured Lampsacus. Memnon's
main strategy is clear enough: he meant to win control of
the two likeliest crossing-points for a Macedonian army
of invasion. While he himself returned south in search of
Parmenio, a Persian division was called up against the
brigade in the Troad (now commanded by Calas, son of
Harpalus, who had taken over from Attalus after the latter's
execution). Calas fought a defensive action, found himself
heavily outnumbered, and was driven back as far south as

Rhoeteum, near Troy. From here he sent an urgent appeal
to Parmenio. Abydos, the one first-class crossing-point still
in Macedonian hands, must be held at all costs. Its garrison
could not survive unaided. Parmenio instantly raised the
siege of Pitane, eluded Memnon, and went racing north to
the Narrows. He saved Abydos; but many of his earlier
conquests were now lost.[42]

To Darius, this intelligence from Greece and Asia Minor,
though important, formed no more than one strand in the
vast kaleidoscopic pattern of imperial administration. The
armies and fleets he had begun to assemble[43] served other
purposes besides that of halting a possible Macedonian
invasion. Some of them were in Egypt, dealing – very
efficiently – with the last native Pharaoh, and re-establishing
that long-suffering country as a Persian province; while
Darius himself, with what seems, in retrospect, like ironic
prescience, was busy designing and building his royal tomb
at Persepolis.[44] But for Alexander, far away in Illyria, the
news he now learnt constituted a crisis of the first order.

He had no time, at present, to ponder on the lesson it
embodied – that with a regime such as his, personal
ascendancy was all, that professions of gratitude or allegiance could never be taken at their face-value, that he was
committed for life to a policy of charismatic *Machtpolitik*.
All this would come later. What he *did* see, instantly, was
that his first and most urgent task must be to scotch the
rumour of his death. Macedonian rivals and king-makers
he could, and would, deal with in the traditional manner;
but these Greek rebels must be halted at once, before they
had compromised themselves too deeply to turn back.
Alexander did not intend to waste time and effort reducing
desperate last-ditch nationalists: he had more important
tasks on hand. At the same time, Greece must be given an
object-lesson, and one so terrifying that all hope of achieving independence by force would be crushed for ever (a
psychologically erroneous assumption, as modern resistance

movements have made quite clear). There was little doubt in the king's mind as to where, and how, this lesson would be applied. His first move was to dispatch a fast courier to Pella, to spread the news of his imminent return. Besides more routine instructions for Antipater, this courier also carried a private (and probably coded) letter to Olympias – the one person in the world whom Alexander could still trust absolutely. What he asked her to arrange was the immediate liquidation of his two dynastic rivals: Amyntas, son of Perdiccas, and Cleopatra's baby son Caranus. How far this purge was to include Amyntas' known friends and supporters is doubtful. Amyntas, son of Antiochus, seems to have had no difficulty in fleeing the country; he made straight for Asia Minor, where he became one of Darius' mercenary commanders. He also (or so Arrian asserts) took with him a letter to the Great King from Alexander of Lyncestis. Its specific contents are unknown, but may be assumed to have been treasonable, since Darius responded by offering the Lyncestian 1,000 talents, plus full support in a bid for the throne of Macedonia, provided he would assassinate its present occupant.[45] If there is any truth in this assertion, Alexander can hardly have known about it at the time, since he soon afterwards appointed the Lyncestian to a responsible military command. His position as Antipater's son-in-law could protect him so far, but not, one would have thought, against arraignment for high treason.[46]

Olympias carried out Alexander's instructions faithfully, as he knew she would. (Among other honours which he heaped on Langarus, before they parted, was the hand in marriage of his half-sister Cynane, at that time still Amyntas' wife: a nice touch of macabre humour.)[47] Indeed, the queen mother went rather beyond her brief. She dispatched not only Caranus, but also his little sister Europa, probably – accounts differ – by pushing them both face-down into a red-hot charcoal brazier. Finally, she forced their wretched mother to hang herself: not that by now poor Cleopatra can have needed much encouragement. When Alexander heard about this he was furious, and small wonder.[48] Dynastic murder as such had some justification and precedent: but neither Cleopatra nor Europa represented any possible threat to the throne, and Olympias' treatment of them had been dictated by pure spiteful vindictiveness. Alexander's enemies would lose no time in turning it into extremely unpleasant propaganda. When he used the iron hand, the king preferred to be strictly within his constitutional rights – as the events of the next few weeks were to demonstrate in no uncertain fashion.

Having thus settled one urgent piece of business, Alexander struck camp and marched at a cracking pace which shook even Philip's veterans. He struck south-east from Lake Okhrida, 'by way of Eordaea and Elimiotis and the mountain ranges of Tymphaea and Paravaea'. There is, on this description, only one possible route he can have taken: the rough and precipitous mountain trail which still runs from Bilisht in southern Albania over the northern Greek ranges, by way of Kastoria and Greven á, finally debouching in the Thessalian plain near Trikkala. Most travellers, then as now, preferred to enter Greece by the Métsovo pass, from the west – and even this is pretty rough going: modern Greeks still refer to it as the 'Accursed Pass'. But Alexander was in a hurry.

Within seven days he had brought his army safely down to Pelinna, a few miles east of Trikkala. From here he swept on to Lamia, was through the Hot Gates before the rumour of his coming had reached the south, and – less than a fortnight after setting out – bivouacked at Onchestus in Boeotia. He had marched nearly 250 miles, at an average speed of eighteen miles a day. More remarkable still, his time was no better on the flat than it had been in the mountains; anyone who has ever walked from Kastoria to Trikkala will know what a remarkable feat this represents.

Twenty miles beyond Onchestus lay his ultimate destination: Thebes.[49]

The leaders of the revolt – who only learnt that a Macedonian army had passed Thermopylae by the time it lay one day's march from Thebes – could not accept the fact that it was Alexander with whom they had to deal. Alexander, they insisted, with touching faith in Demosthenes' propaganda, was dead. This must be a force under Antipater. When further reports came in, all telling the same story, they still refused to credit them. If the army was led by any Alexander, it was undoubtedly Alexander of Lyncestis – an interesting assumption, which tends to confirm other evidence pointing towards his complicity in the revolt (see above, p. 111). But twenty-four hours later, when Macedonian troops lay entrenched outside the city-walls, no further wishful thinking was possible. Alexander lived and reigned indeed; the only decision, a vital one, left for the rebels was whether to hold out or sue for terms.

Alexander himself is unlikely to have anticipated much serious trouble. It was not so long since a show of force had cowed Thebes into instant submission (see above, p. 118). He had with him a force of over 30,000 men, the cream of Philip's veterans, a superb fighting force scarcely ever defeated in the field: the Thebans would not, surely, be rash enough to challenge them unaided. Besides, as usual he was quite ready to be accommodating provided he got what he wanted without trouble. All his interests were now concentrated on the Persian expedition, and he had not the least desire to waste time and energy coercing recalcitrant Greek city-states. If an example had to be made, he would make it; but it seems probable that his temper had cooled somewhat since leaving Illyria, and his sense of expediency was well to the fore again. As he doubtless reminded them, the Thebans could offer a perfectly acceptable diplomatic excuse for their actions. If Alexander had, in fact, been dead as they believed, the league treaty would at once have become null and void (since he left no issue), and their bid for independence would thus have been quite legitimate. They had acted in good faith; if they now returned to their allegiance, the whole episode could be forgotten, without loss of face on either side.[50]

The Thebans, however, proved unexpectedly stubborn. Their reaction to this overture was not a flag of truce, but a lightning raid on Alexander's outposts, during which quite a few Macedonians lost their lives. Next day the king moved his forces round to the south side of the city, and took up a position outside the Electra Gate, on the road to Athens. This brought him within hailing-distance of his beleaguered garrison, since here the Cadmea rock abutted directly on the city-walls. But still he held off, hoping he might yet force a settlement.

When Alexander's approach was first confirmed, the Theban government had prepared a draft resolution – unanimously approved by the assembly – that they should 'fight it out for their political freedom'. Now the assembly met once more, and this time opinion was by no means unanimous. There was a strong movement – 'from all who had their city's interests most at heart,' says Arrian, that Greek ex-governor of a Roman province – to abandon further resistance, and seek terms. But those most directly responsible for the rising, in particular the returned exiles, held out against any compromise. They put no trust in Alexander's fine guarantees. Their ringleaders had killed two Macedonian officers; many of them were also actively involved with the revived Boeotian confederacy. Such men could scarcely hope to get away with their lives once Alexander laid hands on them.

Besides, they had breathed the heady air of freedom, and did not intend to give it up without a struggle. Indeed, there was always the chance that they might not have to give it up at all. Thebes was well-provisioned, her walls in good repair, her heavy infantry among the best in Greece.

The Cadmea had been isolated by a strong double stockade, so that the Macedonian garrison would find it almost impossible to link up with their countrymen outside the walls. The assembly voted to stand by its earlier resolution.

Alexander saw now what his course must be. It was at this point, Diodorus tells us, that he 'decided to destroy the city utterly and by this act of terror take the heart out of anyone else who might venture to rise against him'. But first, to clarify his own position, and in hope of sowing dissension among the Thebans, he issued a final proclamation. Any individual who so wished might still come over to him, and participate in the Greek 'common peace' (*koiné eirené*). If the two main ringleaders of the revolt were surrendered, he would offer a general amnesty to the rest. This was a clever move. It served to remind the world that Thebes, technically speaking, had rebelled, not against Alexander of Macedon, but against the Hellenic League. By the same token, Alexander himself was acting not as an arbitrary despot, but with impeccable constitutional propriety. He was the league's duly elected captain-general, executing the league's commands. Not a few member-states had old scores to settle with Thebes, and Alexander would not lack for a quorum to back him.

The Thebans, of course, knew this as well as anyone, and their next move deliberately blew Alexander's polite fiction sky-high, in the most public possible manner. By so doing they sealed their own fate. From the highest tower of Thebes, their herald made a counter-demand and a counter-offer. They would, he announced, be willing to negotiate with Alexander – if the Macedonians first surrendered Antipater and Philotas. After this little pleasantry, he went on to proclaim 'that anyone who wished to join the Great King and Thebes in freeing the Greeks and destroying the tyrant of Greece should come over to them'.[51]

The venomous conciseness of this indictment was calculated to flick Alexander on the raw; and the reference to a

Persian entente, which might just conceivably be true, could hardly help striking home. If the Thebans' main object was to provoke the king into discarding his holier-than-thou mask, they succeeded all too well. The word 'tyrant' stung Alexander – no one likes hearing unwelcome home truths about himself, least of all a general whose men are within earshot – and he flew into one of his famous rages. From now on, he swore, he would 'pursue the Thebans with the extremity of punishment'. He was as good as his word. The siege-engines were brought up, and the palisades breached. The Theban army fought a magnificent action outside the walls, and came within an ace of putting Alexander's troops to flight, even when the king threw in his reserves. But at the crucial moment, Alexander saw that one postern-gate had been deserted by its guards. He at once sent a brigade under Perdiccas to get inside the city and make contact with the beleaguered garrison. This task Perdiccas successfully accomplished, though he himself sustained a severe wound during the action.

The moment the Thebans learnt that their city-walls had been penetrated, they lost heart. Alexander counter-attacked; they wavered, broke, and fled in a wild stampede. The Electra Gate was jammed with retreating troops, all desperate to get through. The cavalry followed. Dozens of men were trampled underfoot; the great archway rang with screams and curses and the thudding of hooves. Before the ground could be cleared, or the gates shut and barred, Alexander's veterans were pouring into Thebes. There followed a period of savage street-fighting, which finally degenerated into wholesale butchery. Some of the Theban cavalry broke back and escaped across the plain; but for the most part Thebes' defenders fought and died where they stood, using broken spear-hafts or their bare hands, asking no quarter and certainly getting none. Women and old men were dragged from sanctuary and 'subjected to outrage without limit'. Every house was ransacked, every temple plundered. The dead lay thick along the winding alleys.

Each corner had its piles of loot, its piteously wailing children. This bloodbath was by no means the unaided work of Alexander's Macedonians. Many others whom Thebes in the past had subjected to her own imperious rule – Thespians, Plataeans, the men of Orchomenus: Boeotians all themselves – now took their fearful revenge on the conquered city. By nightfall over 6,000 Thebans had been slaughtered, and something like 30,000 taken prisoner, for the loss of 500 Macedonian and allied troops. Much of the surrounding countryside was also looted and burnt.[52] It was not until the following morning that Alexander finally restored order, but when he did he lost no time about it. A decree was issued banning any further indiscriminate butchery of Theban citizens: they were worth more as slaves, and the Macedonian treasury badly needed an infusion of hard cash. Both sides recovered and buried their dead, the Theban hoplites being placed together in a great common tomb by the Electra Gate.[53] Then Alexander summoned a special meeting of the league council – or such amenable delegates as he could lay hands on at short notice – to determine the city's ultimate fate.

Again, the official responsibility for this decision did not lie with him: he could, and did, claim that he was merely executing the league's verdict. However, most of the available delegates had their own reasons for disliking the Thebans, and could be relied upon to pronounce a suitably harsh sentence. We may take it for granted that the penalties they thought fit to impose were an accurate reflection of Alexander's known wishes. Had he felt it politic to allow Thebes a reprieve, that reprieve would have been forthcoming. In the event, the majority wanted Thebes totally destroyed. Thebes, it was emphasized, had fought on the wrong side in the Persian Wars. The Plataeans recalled their own sufferings at Theban hands; but Medism was the crime to which these delegates returned again and again. No one, of course, had forgotten the Theban herald's ominous words: these sedulous trimmers knew very well what lay uppermost in the king's mind. A dignified and cogent appeal by the one Theban prisoner permitted, for form's sake, to address the council was dismissed out of hand. Then the final voting took place. The delegates' decision was 'to raze the city, to sell the captives, to outlaw the Theban exiles from all Greece, and to allow no Greek to offer shelter to a Theban'. The Cadmea was to retain its garrison, while Thebes' domains were parcelled out among those same Boeotian cities that had encompassed her downfall. The seven-gated city of history and legend, where Oedipus had ruled and Teiresias prophesied, was now, on the authority of a puppet commission, to be blotted from the face of the earth. The sentence was carried out immediately (September 335).[54]

His main objective attained, Alexander was more than willing to make individual concessions – especially if they cost him little, and enhanced his reputation for chivalry, piety, or love of culture. From the general order for mass-enslavement he exempted all priests, any citizens who could prove that they had voted against the revolt, or were guest-friends of Macedonians (including the family which had acted as host to Philip when he was a hostage), and, lastly, the descendants of Pindar the lyric poet. He likewise spared these persons' houses from destruction, together with all shrines and temples. Some statues of artistic celebrities seem to have survived as well: a refugee hid his ready cash in the hollow cloak of one such image, and recovered it intact thirty years later, when the city was being rebuilt.

There was also the celebrated case of the Theban general's widow who appeared before Alexander charged with murder. The officer who had taken over her house first got drunk, then raped her, then demanded her gold and silver. With some presence of mind she said she had hidden all her valuables at the bottom of a dry well in the garden. Down scrambled the Macedonian, still drunk, in his shirt; whereupon the lady, assisted by her maids, dropped rocks on him till he was dead. Alexander, far from punishing her, gave her her freedom, and 'issued orders to his officers that they should take good care no such insult was again offered *to a noted house*'. The italicized words are worth pondering. Alexander, as we shall see, always handled the aristocracy of any occupied area with extreme tact. If they were prepared to collaborate, they could run the administration for him; if not, they could be more nuisance than the rest of the country put together. The moral was clear enough.[55]

No previous disaster of this sort had ever struck the Greek world with quite such horror and amazement as the annihilation of Thebes.[56] The Sicilian catastrophe of 413 took place overseas, and Athens herself survived it. Plataea was a small town, Melos an insignificant island. The Spartan defeat at Leuctra in 371 was a matter of prestige, not of extermination. But Thebes, one of the most ancient and distinguished city-states in all Greece, had been totally destroyed, and her population subjected to the dreadful fate known as *andrapodismós* – wholesale deportation and enslavement. It was, we may note, a by no means unprofitable operation. From the sale of prisoners the Macedonian treasury realized 440 talents, or, on average, 88 drachmas per head.[57]*

The immediate effect of his action was all Alexander could have desired. There was a general rush by the Greek city-states to exculpate themselves and beg forgiveness for their 'errors'. The Athenians, fearing the same fate as Thebes, broke off their celebration of the Mysteries at Eleusis; once more the city was crowded with refugees pouring in from Attica. Demades, the collaborationist

---

*Alexander, who knew his Herodotus, may well have recalled, with grim relish, the story which Cyrus told the Ionians, about the fluteplayer who tried to lure a shoal of fish ashore by playing to them. When they took no notice he put out a net, and hauled them in by the hundred. Seeing the fish jumping about, he said to them: 'It is too late to dance now; you might have danced to my music – but you would not' (Hdt 1.141).

politician (see above, pp. 77 ff.), persuaded the assembly to
pick ten men of known Macedonian sympathies, and send
them as ambassadors 'to assure [Alexander], somewhat un-
seasonably, that the Athenian people rejoiced to see him
safely returned from Illyria and the Triballians, and
thoroughly approved his punishment of the Thebans for
their revolt'. This declaration may have amused the king,
but it certainly did not impress him. He was polite enough
to the envoys; but what they brought back to Athens was a
curt letter requesting the surrender of ten Athenian generals
and politicians 'who had opposed his interest'. Most
prominent among these were Lycurgus, the freebooting
condottiere Charidemus, and Demosthenes. No one doubted
what their fate would be if they went.

A stormy debate took place in the assembly. Phocion –
rather optimistically, one feels – urged the few to lay down
their lives for the many. Demosthenes retorted with a
parable about sheep abandoning their watch-dogs to the
'Macedonian arch-wolf'. 'In surrendering us,' he cried,
'you unwittingly surrender yourselves, all of you.' In the
end Demades (primed, it is said, with five talents from
Demosthenes and his fellow-victims) volunteered to lead a
second embassy to Pella, with the object of begging them
off.

By now Alexander's temper had cooled somewhat, and
his long-term strategic sense reasserted itself. He made it
quite clear to Demades that he held Athens no less responsible than Thebes for the latter's rebellion. He also reminded
him that harbouring Theban refugees was in itself a flagrant
violation of the league's decree. Having rubbed these
points home (in order to leave no possible suspicion in
Demades' mind that he might be climbing down – which of
course he was) Alexander declared himself, with great
magnanimity, willing to forgive and forget. He removed all
the names from his black-list save that of Charidemus, a
licensed privateer whom Demosthenes, for one, was not
sorry to see go; and even in this one case he merely asked

that the Athenians banish him. He also rescinded the order concerning Theban refugees.

Demades returned home in triumph, to be rewarded by a grateful assembly with a bronze statue, and free meals in the Prytaneum (City Hall) for life. Indeed, he deserved them. He had sized up the situation with an uncommonly shrewd eye, and had called Alexander's bluff. Like his father, the king had no intention of embarking on a long and dangerous siege when there were more important things to be done.[58] The concessions he made, moreover, were substantial ones. Charidemus went straight to the Great King, as Alexander must have known he would; so did several other Athenians of note. They did not obtain a military alliance from Darius – the one thing Alexander feared above all else – but they did get massive funds with which to back the growing resistance movement inside Greece itself.[59]

If Alexander expected any gratitude in return for his clemency, he was badly mistaken. In the long run his treatment of Thebes proved one of the worst psychological errors he ever made. Had he spared the city he might, eventually, have reached some genuine accommodation with the Greek states. Now that was out of the question. After their first shocked terror had worn off, the attitude of the Greeks towards Alexander hardened into a bitter and implacable hatred. Outwardly they collaborated, with cynical obsequiousness. But they never forgave him. In public, for the time being, all was quiet. Macedonian notables received honorary citizenships, and garrison commanders were greeted with smiles on the street. A great deal of fulsome and flattering rubbish was turned out by the hack writers. But in private, grim-faced young men fingered their swords and looked forward to the day of liberty and revenge. If Athens and Sparta had ever managed to bridge their differences and achieve a genuine entente, this story might well have had a very different ending.

[5]

The Captain-General

HAVING thus summarily dealt with the Greek revolt, Alexander left the smoking ruins of Thebes behind him, and hurried back north to Pella. There was much to be done, and little enough time in which to do it. His arrival seems to have been marked by fresh purges, this time of Cleopatra's more highly placed relatives: clearly he was taking no chances while abroad.[1] Parmenio was recalled from Asia Minor: as Philip's best and most experienced general, he was to become Alexander's second-in-command. If the king could have found anyone else for the job he almost certainly would have done so, but he had little choice in the matter. The old marshal was indispensable, and knew it.

Alexander next summoned a council to discuss that most burning of issues, the crusade against Persia. When was the campaign to be launched, and what strategy should be followed? Antipater and Parmenio both (as usual) advised him to proceed cautiously. In particular, with the grim struggle for the succession still fresh in their minds, they urged – very reasonably – that before leaving Macedonia he should marry and beget an heir (since both of them had eligible daughters at the time their motives may not have been wholly disinterested). However, the king rejected this notion out of hand, a decision which was to cause untold bloodshed and political chaos after his death. It would be shameful, he told them, for the captain-general of the Hellenes, with Philip's invincible army at his command, to idle his time away on matrimonial dalliance.

It is possible that more calculation entered into his decision than is generally supposed. Whether he chose a wife from the out-kingdoms or the lowland baronies, *someone* was bound to be offended, and thus become ripe for sedition: better to leave such a decision in abeyance until his return. But perhaps this is to flatter the young Alexander unduly. His interest in women was (to put it mildly) tepid, and could not begin to compare with his burning sense of destiny. Once again we hear the young Achilles speaking; once again we glimpse the profoundly apolitical world of Homer's *areté*, in which war remains, first and foremost, an instrument to enhance the hero's personal glory. As time went on, Alexander learnt to temper his vision with political expediency; but there was always a streak of *après moi le déluge* about him. His refusal to marry may not have been 'the most crushing evidence of Alexander's irresponsibility'; on the other hand, it was less than statesmanlike.[2]

At the same time Alexander undoubtedly had one pressing and all too practical reason for his impatience. Philip's attitude to money (which his son inherited) had been more or less that of the Prussian general Von Moltke, who in 1914, when presented with a memorandum on the need for an Economic General Staff, replied: 'Don't bother me with economics – I am busy conducting a war.'[3] But to maintain a professional standing army created economic problems that could not possibly be ignored. When Philip died, he was 500 talents in debt,[4] and the pay of his troops had fallen badly into arrears. Even the 1,000 talents which he drew annually from the Pangaeus mines would only cover one third of the cost of maintaining the Macedonian field army on a standing basis.[5] To make matters worse, Alexander on his accession had abolished direct taxation (see above, p. 113): this may have won him considerable support, but it was also rapidly leading the country into bankruptcy. Every month Macedonia's national debt soared still further. The situation had to be resolved, and quickly.

Alexander in fact found himself facing a very modern dilemma. Retrenchment could only be achieved by dissolving the splendid army on which all his hopes hung. This, for him, was unthinkable. But if he refused to reduce his commitments, he had to increase his resources; and his

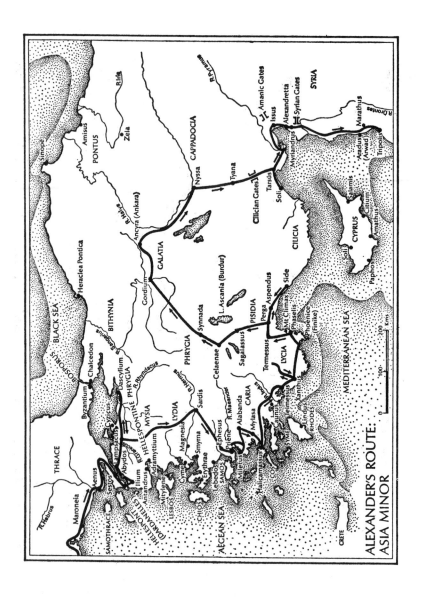

ALEXANDER'S ROUTE: ASIA MINOR

notions of how this could be done were strictly limited (see above, p. 31). To his way of thinking, an empty treasury was best filled at someone else's expense – and the Great King's coffers, as everyone knew, were fabulously well stocked. In other words, to solve his economic crisis, Alexander must either sink back into obscurity, or wage a successful war of aggression. There was never much doubt which course he would choose.

Nevertheless, he had cut things very fine. The Balkan and Illyrian campaigns were almost certainly run at a loss. The sale of Theban captives would just about wipe out Philip's debt; but that still left the problem of finding cash wages for a large field army – at least until they laid hands on some Persian gold. To support them during a minimum six-month training period, even if the allies paid for themselves, would cost 1,000 talents at the very least. It followed that the invasion could not possibly be postponed beyond the following spring (334), and to this date the council reluctantly agreed. Alexander had one obvious recourse, to borrow capital; but in an age when credit-banking was still regarded as a dangerous novelty (a feeling not wholly eradicated from the Greek mind even today) this was something much easier said than done. Besides, most of the bankers and moneylenders were Athenians, if only by adoption; and no Athenian had any intention of lending Alexander money if he could humanly avoid it.

The king therefore turned to his own barons, whose position would make it very hard for them to refuse his demands. Propaganda subsequently romanticized this transaction in a way calculated to enhance Alexander's reputation for generosity and sublime self-confidence. Before the expedition sailed – so the story runs – the king inquired into the financial circumstances of all his friends and Companions, and made over to them the bulk of Macedonia's crown lands, together with their revenue. Indeed, he refused to leave Europe until each man was provided for. When Perdiccas asked him, 'But what have you left for yourself, Alexander?'

he got the famous answer: 'My hopes.' 'In that case,' said Perdiccas, 'we should do the same.' It was not right, he went on, for the barons to accept Alexander's possessions; they should all hold on in expectation of sharing Darius' wealth.

This is a charming story, but it leaves out one central fact. What Alexander was doing, clearly, was *borrowing money* from his Companions, on the only security he had left to offer them. Perdiccas, with true Homeric tact, put down his contribution to the war-chest gratis; others were not so generous. An inscription still survives, for instance, recording Alexander's gift of land to Ptolemy the Bodyguard.[6] By these methods the king managed to raise another 800 talents, but he was still perilously short of ready cash. When the expedition set sail, he took with him no more than seventy talents (which represented about a fortnight's pay, or less, for his troops), and provisions for thirty days. On the other hand, his personal debt, according to one account, had by then been reduced to 200 talents – which suggests that, with a few exceptions only, his barons had followed Perdiccas' lead, and made him outright gifts rather than loans. The bulk of this sum would, of course, have gone to make up arrears of pay.[7]

The final muster-roll of the expeditionary force is a revealing document in more ways than one.[8] Apart from the advance corps already operating round the Dardanelles, which numbered 10,000 foot-soldiers and perhaps 1,000 horse, Alexander's Macedonian army consisted of over 30,000 front-line infantry, and some 3,300 cavalry.[9] Even this by no means exhausted Macedonia's reserves of manpower. From time to time fresh reinforcements were sent out, while numerous agricultural workers remained at home to till the soil and keep the farms productive.[10]* Of these 30,000 troops, perhaps 5–6,000 were on garrison duty

* If we compare these figures with the full-strength army of 10,000 infantry and 2,000 horse which Philip raised in 359, it is clear that twenty-five years of increased prosperity had brought about a remarkable increase in overall population – exactly as happened in Athens after the Persian Wars.

in occupied cities, leaving 24,000 at Alexander's disposal. Yet no less than half this total – a really staggering figure – was earmarked for home defence under Antipater, together with 1,500 of the 3,300 cavalry available. Nothing could show more clearly what Alexander thought of the situation in Greece and the Balkans – or, indeed, what Greece thought of Alexander.

This provides an ironic gloss on the supposed nature of the expedition itself. In theory, Alexander had been commissioned by the league to carry out a Greek war of vengeance against Persia, in retribution for the wrongs which Xerxes had done Greece a century and a half before. This was the Panhellenic crusade preached by Isocrates, and as such the king's propaganda section continued – for the time being – to present it. No one, so far as we know, was tactless enough to ask the obvious question: if this was a Panhellenic crusade, where were the Greek troops? But many must have realized that the resistance movement had already begun to pay off, indirectly, by making the king leave half his army behind as a *de facto* occupation force.

Alexander had a total of 43,000 infantry with him in Asia: the league's contribution to this figure was 7,000. Of cavalry he had over 6,000; the Greek states provided a beggarly 600. The league was responsible for Alexander's fleet, such as it was: 160 ships, of which Athens – with well over 300 triremes in commission – reluctantly supplied twenty. (These, together with 200 cavalrymen, a third of the whole Greek contingent, were all Alexander ever got out of her.) Indeed, despite the league's official veto, far more Greeks fought for the Great King – and remained loyal to the bitter end – than were ever conscripted by Alexander.* What is more, the league troops serving Alexander were never used in crucial battles (another

---

*After Issus Darius arguably had no less than 50,000 Greek mercenaries on his payroll: see QC 5.11.5, Paus. 8.52.5. Scholars generally (not always for convincing reasons) reduce these figures in a drastic manner. See now C. L. Murison, *Historia* 21 (1972), 401 n. 7.

significant pointer) but kept on garrison and line-of-communication duties. The sole reason for their presence, apart from propaganda purposes, was to serve as hostages for the good behaviour of their friends and relatives in Greece. Alexander found them more of an embarrassment than an asset, and the moment he was in a position to do so, he got rid of them (see below, p. 322).

This practice of using troops as hostages Alexander had inherited, like so much else, from his father. It was a simple but highly effective device; perhaps its most successful embodiment was the Royal Corps of Pages – Macedonian youths of good family, kept in personal attendance on the king while training as officer-cadets. But their presence also gave Alexander (as it had given Philip, who initiated the practice) a powerful hold over their turbulent baronial families. Similarly with the allied tribal chieftains: any tough-minded or ambitious warriors among them Alexander took with him – to avoid sedition, as Justin says – leaving home affairs in charge of mild and obsequious conformists.[11]

The overall composition of the expeditionary force can perhaps be most easily understood if set out in tabulated form:

Infantry		*Cavalry*	
12,000	Macedonians (phalanx and Guards Brigade)	1,800	Macedonians
7,000	league troops	1,800	Thessalians
7,000	Odrysian, Triballian, and other tribal levies	900	Thracian and Paeonian scouts
1,000	light-armed troops (archers and Agrianians)	600	league troops
5,000	mercenaries	1,000(?)	advance expedition
11,000(?)	advance expedition	6,100	total
43,000	total		

Overall total: 49,100

The small number of Agrianians and archers is misleading: Alexander used this force continually, in every kind of engagement, and it must have been reinforced by regular drafts from the Balkans. A shortage of mercenaries, on the other hand, is just what we might expect: at this stage Alexander simply could not afford them.[12] We should also note the special status of the Thessalian cavalry, which stood in a category of its own among the allied contingents. Philip had been elected Archon of Thessaly for life, an office which Alexander inherited (see above, p. 117). Ethnically speaking, Thessaly was far more akin to Macedonia than it was to the Greek city-states, being governed by a very similar type of feudal aristocracy. The Thessalian cavalry was, therefore, more or less indistinguishable from its Macedonian counterpart, being identically armed, and organized in the same way – that is, by territorial squadrons.[13] Another vital distinction between this unit and other league forces was the degree of trust which Alexander placed in it – though here his hand may have been forced to some extent. The Thessalians' permanent battle-station was on the left wing, which meant that they came under the direct command of Parmenio. It has been argued, with some force, that 'they virtually formed Parmenio's personal Companion Cavalry, with the Pharsalus squadron in a similar capacity to the Royal Squadron of the Companions'.[14]

This interesting alignment has considerable significance in the light of later events: it fits in very well with what we know of the quiet but deadly struggle that went on between Parmenio and Alexander, right from the beginning, to secure effective control of the army. Every key command must have been fought over tooth and nail. At this stage, however, Parmenio – who even now, perhaps, still thought of the young king as a more than usually active figurehead, dashing but politically immature – was negotiating from strength. He was indispensable in the field, and he had been instrumental in securing Alexander's succession. His bill for these invaluable services proved a costly one. Of his sons, Nicanor obtained command of the Guards Brigade (*hypaspistae*), while Philotas – that same Philotas who had betrayed Alexander's dealings with Pixodarus to Philip –

became colonel of the Companion Cavalry. Parmenio's son-in-law Coenus was allotted one of the six battalions of the phalanx, while the light cavalry probably went to his brother Asander. Since he himself was second-in-command of the entire expeditionary force, Parmenio's position must have seemed virtually unassailable.

Furthermore, when it came to the crucial business of deciding which troops stayed with Antipater, and which were for service in Asia, Parmenio saw to it that a large proportion of the latter was drawn from Philip's old veterans. This particularly applied to the officer corps, at regimental and company level. Though Alexander secured battalion commands in the phalanx for several of his young friends, such as Craterus and Perdiccas, the majority of the officers in 334 were men who had served under Philip, and were not much younger than Parmenio himself. When Justin says that staff headquarters looked 'more like the senate of some old-time republic'[15] he is hardly exaggerating. Alexander may have had his own reasons for agreeing to this arrangement: experienced veterans would be of more use on a major campaign than untried amateurs, while from the political viewpoint it was better, surely, to have Parmenio's old guard – not to mention Parmenio himself – where he could keep a weather eye on their activities. But the fact remains that when Alexander landed in Asia, it was at the head of Philip's army, staffed mainly by Philip's officers and with Philip's old general as his chief of staff. Parmenio had every reason to feel confident.

In addition to front-line troops, the invasion force included large numbers of technicians and specialists. There was a corps of sappers and siege-engineers under Diades the Thessalian: these men were responsible not only for Alexander's artillery and assault-gear, but also for tunnelling, mining, and the construction of roads and bridges. There was a surveying section, the *bematistae*, who 'collected information about routes and camping-grounds and recorded the distances marched'.[16] Staff administration and the secretariat were run by Eumenes of Cardia, Philip's former head of chancery. A more unusual feature – and here Aristotle's influence shows out most clearly – was the surprising number of scholars and scientists who accompanied it in an official capacity. Alexander had always known the value of good intelligence-reports: this military principle he now applied on a far wider scale. His team included architects and geographers, botanists, astronomers, mathematicians and zoologists. All scientific knowledge of the East, for centuries to come, depended, ultimately, on the accumulated information they brought back with them.

Alexander was also, so far as we know, the first field-commander in antiquity to organize an official publicity and propaganda section. Achilles had had Homer to immortalize him, and Achilles' descendant was determined that his own achievements should not go unsung. Besides the day-to-day record of the expedition,* something a little more literary and grandiloquent was called for. To supply it, Alexander appointed Aristotle's nephew Callisthenes as the expedition's official historian.[17] It is generally assumed that this was an unhappy choice, where for once the claims of nepotism prevailed over any considerations of suitability. Callisthenes was a man of principle who believed in speaking his mind – two characteristics not normally conducive to the production of effective propaganda. Aristotle, having heard him in conversation with the king, quoted a line of Homer: 'The way you're talking, my child, you won't last

---

*Normally hitherto attributed (cf. Arrian 7.25–6, Plut. *Alex.* 76; for the fragments see Jacoby *FGrH* 117) to Eumenes of Cardia, and known as the Royal Ephemerides. But scholars have long been embarrassed by the fact that neither Arrian nor Plutarch employs the 'Ephemerides' except for the period immediately preceding Alexander's death. A most convincing explanation of this omission has now been given by A. B. Bosworth in 'The Death of Alexander the Great: Rumour and Propaganda', *CQ* ns21 (1971), 93–105, esp. 117 ff.; if Bosworth's thesis be true, the Ephemerides can be virtually discounted as a source of evidence. At the same time it seems clear that *some* sort of log must have been kept: the scale, scope and complexity of the expedition demanded no less.

long.' Callisthenes had known Alexander as a schoolboy at Mieza, and saw no reason to flatter him. At this stage his young patron was still merely Philip's son, about to embark on a reckless adventure, with an empty treasury, against vastly superior odds.[18]

In fact, however, the king seems to have sized his nominee up with cool, not to say cynical, percipience. Alexander was not by temperament an intellectual himself, but he understood the intellectual mentality, and exploited it – as he did so much else – for his own benefit. Callisthenes was just what he needed at this point: a convinced Panhellenist, a believer (through his uncle's teaching) in the philosophical justification of monarchy through *areté*, above all a political innocent. He had already made some reputation for himself as a historian, while his background (he came from Olynthus) would render him acceptable to his prospective Greek public. He was useful, but inessential. When he had served his purpose he could be, and was, discarded. His prospective task was to chronicle the king's achievements, in a way that would favourably impress Greek opinion. This record was to be sent home by instalments, as the expedition proceeded. Though Alexander reserved the right to check Callisthenes' final draft, and sometimes (as we shall see) suggested a particular slanting of events, it should not be assumed that he virtually dictated all his chronicler wrote. There would be no need to stop Callisthenes setting down the truth as he saw it: it was for his all too predictable intellectual opinions that the historian had been hired in the first place.

Callisthenes himself never realized this; nor, in all likelihood, had he any clear notion of how his work was going to be used. The fact that he was expendable never seems to have occurred to him, either; like so many of his kind, he was not only boorishly outspoken, but a person of quite monumental self-conceit. A little common sense might have told him that he could only rely on staying in favour so long as Alexander needed to conciliate the Greek world. But common sense, as his uncle knew, was not one of

Callisthenes' more outstanding qualities; and the lack of it ultimately cost him his life.[19]

He was, however, a by no means isolated phenomenon. Once it became known that Alexander not only wanted his exploits written up, but would hand out good money for the privilege, a whole rabble of third-rate poets, historians and rhetoricians attached themselves to his train. Their numbers swelled as time went on, since Alexander's unbroken run of successes not only gave them more material, but increased the rewards they could command. In these circumstances it is not surprising that their flattery was gross, and their work for the most part beneath contempt. Alexander himself told one of them, Choerilus, that he would rather be Homer's Thersites than Choerilus' Achilles. But pure artistic merit was no criterion of reward in the propaganda section: another sedulous ape, Pyrrho (who presumably had his employer's foibles better sized up), later received no less than 10,000 gold pieces for one honorific ode. What Philip's veterans made of these chattering civilian *literati* can all too easily be imagined.[20] Alexander himself often derived malicious amusement from playing them off against each other.

His military preparations thus completed, Alexander – in accordance with a tradition established by King Archelaus – celebrated the so-called 'Olympian' Games, a nine-day festival, in honour of Zeus and the Muses, held either at Aegae or Dium. There were lavish sacrifices to the gods, followed by dramatic and musical contests. The king was determined to put his army in a good humour, and a few talents more or less could make little difference now. Indeed, a really lavish display might help to discredit rumours of Macedonian insolvency: one late source claims that Alexander was only stopped from putting an entire bronze proscenium arch in the theatre by his architect, who objected that it would interfere with the acoustics. He certainly ordered a gigantic marquee, large enough to hold a

hundred dining-couches, and gave a splendid banquet in it
for his Companions, his senior officers, and ambassadors
from the Greek city-states. This tent afterwards accompanied him on all his campaigns: the belief that he was only
corrupted by Persian luxury is a myth. There was a free
distribution of sacrificial animals to the troops, 'and all else
suitable for the festive occasion'.[21]

One curious incident – all the more tantalizing in the light
of what was to come – took place during this period. Just
before the great expedition left Macedonia, Olympias is
said to have told Alexander, 'and him alone, the secret of
his begetting, and bade him have purposes worthy of his
birth'. Whatever that secret may in fact have been, there is
no doubt what men afterwards (Callisthenes amongst them)
thought it was. Alexander, so his mother claimed, had been
begotten by a god, in all likelihood Zeus Ammon. Some
confirmation of this belief is provided by an almost identical
story told of Alexander's comrade-in-arms Seleucus, who
afterwards became a king in his own right, giving his name
to the Seleucid dynasty. His mother, Laodice (who in fact
was married to one of Philip's generals), dreamed that she
lay with Apollo, and became pregnant. As a token of the
god's paternity she received a ring with an anchor-device
carved on the stone. This ring he bade her give to the son
she would bear, when he came of age.

Next morning Laodice awoke to find just such a ring in
her bed; and it subsequently transpired that she was, in fact,
pregnant. The son she bore was Seleucus, and, sure enough,
he had the mark of an anchor on his thigh. When he grew
up, and was about to set forth on the great expedition with
Alexander, Laodice 'told him the truth of his begetting,
and gave him the ring'. This whole story is, of course, a
palpable fabrication, probably based on some fortuitous
birthmark, and put into circulation at a time when Seleucus
needed good antecedents for his claim to divine kingship.
For this reason it has had less attention than it deserves.
What is significant is the particular *form* the fabrication

took. There can be little doubt that Seleucus was consciously attempting to emulate Alexander, and transferred to his
own mother a legend first told of Olympias. That he chose
to do so at all suggests not only that the story had wide
currency, but that it was also thought to embody the actual
secret which Alexander heard from his mother before
leaving Europe.[22]

In early spring 334 King Alexander of Macedon set out at
last from Pella at the head of his expeditionary force, and
marched for the Hellespont. Ever since childhood he had
dreamed of this moment: now the dream had been fulfilled,
and he was entering on his destiny of conquest. Few men
can ever have given such solid embodiment to their private
myths. He was the young Achilles, sailing once more for the
windy plains of Troy; but he was also captain-general of the
Hellenes, whose task it was to exact just vengeance for
Xerxes' invasion of Greece. The two roles merged in his
mind, as the two events had merged in history. 'Xerxes
had made it clear that his expedition was the Trojan War
in reverse; Alexander therefore in turn reversed the details
of this most famous of all oriental attacks.'[23]

To begin with, he crossed the Narrows at the same point.
He brought his host the 300 miles to Sestos, by way of
Amphipolis and Thrace, in twenty days, which was good
going. The advance corps had held the bridgehead, and
his crossing took place without Persian opposition. This,
however we look at it, was the most extraordinary piece
of good luck for Alexander. His one great weakness lay
in his fleet. He had only 160 vessels, supplied by the league,
and their crews were far from the best that were available.
Darius' Phoenician navy was almost three times as large,
and far more efficient. A determined attack by sea during
the actual crossing might well have scotched the invasion
before it was well launched. But no such attack took place;
not one enemy ship was sighted. Coordinated strategy could
not be called the Persian High Command's strongest point.

Alexander himself was, it would seem, blithely indifferent to the possibility of such a counter-move: perhaps he had had encouraging reports from his intelligence section. At all events, he left Parmenio to supervise the main crossing to Abydos – a complex but boring operation – while he took off on what has variously been described as a propaganda trip, a romantic religious pilgrimage, and a mere high-spirited youthful lark.[24] It probably in fact contained elements of all three. Accompanied by at least 6,000 men,[25] he made his way overland to Elaeum, at the southern tip of the Thracian Chersonese (Gallipoli Peninsula). Here he sacrificed before the tomb of Protesilaus, traditionally the first Greek in Agamemnon's army who stepped ashore at Troy. Alexander prayed that his own landing on Asiatic soil might be luckier; an understandable request, since he intended to be first ashore himself, and Protesilaus had been killed almost immediately.

He then set up an altar at the point where he was about to leave Europe, made sacrifice, and invoked the gods for victory in his war of vengeance. This done, he and his party crossed the Dardanelles in the sixty vessels which Parmenio had sent down from Sestos to meet him. Alexander steered the admiral's flagship in person. When the squadron was half-way across, he sacrificed a bull to Poseidon, and made libation with a golden vessel, just as Xerxes had done before him: the emphasis could hardly have been clearer. On entering 'the Achaean harbour' – this, I suspect, was in fact Rhoeteum, safely held by Calas' troops – Alexander stood at the prow of his vessel, in full armour, and flung a spear into the sand, 'signifying that he received Asia from the gods as a spear-won prize'. Then he leapt ashore. His ritual spear-throwing gesture has been much disputed. Since it only occurs in one late source, many scholars have denied that it ever took place at all. If it did, was it simply a formal declaration of war? Or was Alexander, with deliberate archaism, employing a long-obsolete symbol of 'conquest by the spear'? Did he, in fact, intend to overthrow the

Achaemenid empire, root and branch, from the very outset?
This last supposition seems the most probable, and what
happened next tends to confirm it.[26]

The king's first act on landing was to set up another altar,
to Athena, Heracles, and Zeus of Safe Landings – throughout his life he showed himself genuinely scrupulous in
religious matters, great and small alike – and to pray that
'these territories might accept him as king of their own free
will, without constraint'.[27] Then he set off on his pilgrimage
to Ilium. This, ironically, was not the true site of Homer's
Troy, but a later foundation, itself by Alexander's day a
mere village, with a 'small and cheap' temple of Athena,
and a collection of relics – bogus in all likelihood – from the
Trojan War.[28] He was welcomed by a committee of local
Greeks, from Sigeium and other towns in the area. Following the lead of his navigator, Menoetius, they presented
him with ceremonial gold wreaths. Alexander then offered
sacrifice at the tombs of Ajax and Achilles, or what local
tradition presented as such. (This was predictable: Xerxes,
too, had visited Troy during his invasion march, and had
poured libations to the spirits of the *Trojan* heroes.) To be
on the safe side, the king also made a placatory offering at
the sacred hearth of Zeus of Enclosures, where, according to
legend, his own ancestor Neoptolemus had slain Priam.

But the oddest ceremony – to our eyes – was when
Alexander and his inseparable companion Hephaestion
laid wreaths on the tombs of Achilles and Patroclus respectively (which Aelian took to mean that they enjoyed a
similar relationship) and then ran a race around them,
naked and anointed with oil, in the traditional fashion. How
fortunate Achilles was, the young king exclaimed, to have
so faithful a friend all his life, and no less a poet than Homer
to herald his fame when he was dead! Later, during a sight-
seeing tour round the town, he was asked if he would care
to inspect a lyre which had belonged to Paris. He refused
curtly, saying that all Paris had ever played on this instrument were 'adulterous ditties such as captivate and bewitch

the hearts of women'. But, he added, 'I would gladly see that of Achilles, to which he used to sing the glorious deeds of brave men.'[29]

Before leaving Ilium, Alexander sacrificed in the sanctuary of Athena. His personal seer, Aristander of Telmessus, observing the overthrown statue of a former rebel satrap which lay outside the temple, predicted a great cavalry victory for the king, in which he would slay an enemy general with his own hands. Aristander's ingenuity at interpreting omens knew no bounds. When a statue of Orpheus was reported to be sweating continually, he explained that this meant 'the writers of odes and the epic and melic poets had hard work coming to celebrate Alexander and his exploits in verse and song'. The king, however, was a glutton for good omens, which may explain why Aristander lasted so long in his service. At all events, he now made lavish sacrifice to Athena, and dedicated his own armour at the goddess's altar. In exchange he received a shield and panoply of guaranteed Trojan vintage, with which he armed himself for his first major engagement on Asiatic soil, at the Granicus River (see below, pp. 176 ff.). However, they got rather badly knocked about during the fighting, and thereafter Alexander merely had them carried into battle before him by a squire.[30]

From Ilium Alexander moved north again, and rejoined the main army at Arisbe, a little way outside Abydos. He made it known that there was to be no looting or ravaging during the advance. This land, he told the troops, was now *theirs*: one should not depreciate one's own property. In particular, they were to respect the estates of Memnon, Darius' Greek general – an act which, it was hoped, might lead the Great King to wonder whether his employee was not perhaps trafficking with the enemy.[31] After reviewing and numbering his host – again, just as Xerxes had done – Alexander led them forth on the road to Dascylium, where the Phrygian satrap had his seat of government. The first town they came to was Percote, still safely in Macedonian hands. But the next major city on their route, Lampsacus, was now controlled by Memnon (see above, p. 139), and to judge from our scanty evidence, quite a number of other Greek towns in Asia Minor were in the same position. The philosopher Anaximenes, acting as his city's official envoy, persuaded Alexander to by-pass Lampsacus, probably with a massive bribe: the king's shortage of money was already public knowledge in Asia. For this service (the nature of which he afterwards embroidered somewhat to increase his dignity)[32] Anaximenes received the honour of a statue at Olympia, dedicated by his grateful fellow-citizens. They could, in fact, have saved themselves the expense. With only a month's supplies – apart from what he could commandeer locally – and enough pay to last a fortnight, Alexander's one hope was to tempt the Persians into a set battle, and win it. He had neither the time nor the reserves to invest a city: if it did not surrender on his approach, he left it severely alone. Colonae, for example, received the same treatment as Lampsacus, without paying anything for the privilege.

When he reached Priapus, however, he was in better luck. His advance scouts reported that the citizens were willing to receive him, and he sent a small force to take the town over. The captain-general had performed his first act of 'liberation', and we may be sure that Callisthenes made the most of the occasion in his dispatches.[33] By now the Persians, who had been too late[34] to stop him at the Dardanelles, saw clearly enough what his intentions were. Arsites, the satrap of Hellespontine Phrygia, sent out an appeal for help to his fellow-governors in Asia Minor: Arsamenes, on the Cilician seaboard, and Spithridates, who ruled over Lydia and Ionia. The three of them established a base-camp at Zeleia (Sari-Keia), east of the Granicus River, and summoned their military commanders to a council of war. They still felt, clearly, that the crisis could be dealt with at provincial level, which shows how badly they underestimated Alexander as an opponent.*

The most sensible plan of campaign was that proposed by Memnon the Rhodian, a seasoned professional mercenary who knew all about Alexander's shortage of money and supplies, and seems, in addition, to have had excellent intelligence concerning the situation in Greece. (His source in both cases was probably the renegade Macedonian general, Amyntas, son of Antiochus.) What he now put forward was a scorched-earth policy: destroy all crops, strip the countryside, if need be burn down towns and villages. Such a policy, as he made clear, would very soon force the Macedonian army to withdraw for lack of provisions. Meanwhile, the Persians should themselves assemble a large fleet and army, and carry the war across into Macedonia while Alexander's forces were still divided.

This was first-class advice; unfortunately it came from a Greek mercenary, whose brilliance and plain speaking did not endear him to his Persian colleagues. A little tact might well have got Memnon all he wanted; but he now went on to say, without mincing his words, that they should at all costs avoid fighting a pitched battle, since the Macedonian infantry was far superior to their own. The plain truth of this assertion hardly made it more palatable. The Persians were hurt in their dignity; Arsites declared, with more patriotism than common sense – he may also have had one eye on Darius, who did not take kindly to reports of satrapal cowardice – that he would not suffer one single subject's house in his satrapy to be burnt.† Memnon's plan was therefore rejected, and the Persians decided to fight it out.[35]

* It is possible that Darius' main forces were still partially tied down in Egypt (see Olmstead, pp. 492–3, 496, and above, p. 140), and that Alexander timed his invasion with this in mind. cf. Davis (Bibl.), p. 36.

† Religious ethics also partly dictated Arsites' response: under the reformed creed influenced by Zoroaster 'a duty of the soldier and nobleman was to protect agriculture' (A. R. Burn, *Persia and the Greeks*, pp. 62–3).

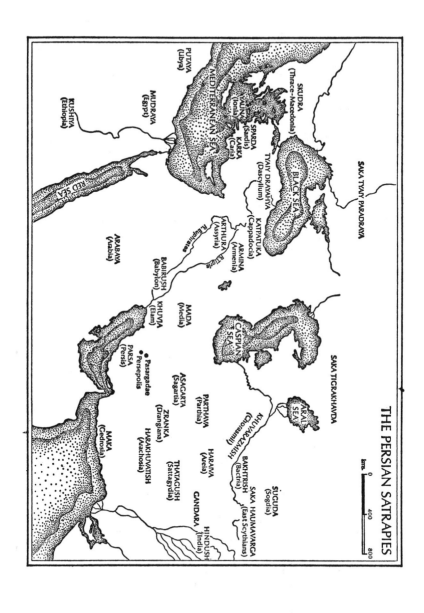

THE PERSIAN SATRAPIES

kms.
0
400
800

PUTAYA (Libya)
MEDITERRANEAN SEA
SKUDRA (Thrace-Macedonia)
MUDRAYA (Egypt)
YAUNA (Ionia)
SPARDA (Sardis)
KARKA (Caria)
KUSHIYA (Ethiopia)
RED SEA
TYAIY DRAYAHYA (Dascylium)
BLACK SEA
SAKA TYAIY PARADRAYA
R. Euphrates
ARABAYA (Arabia)
ARTHURA (Assyria)
KATPATUKA (Cappadocia)
ARMINA (Armenia)
BABIRUSH (Babylon)
R. Tigris
KHUVJA (Elam)
MADA (Media)
CASPIAN SEA
SAKA TIGRAKHAVDA
PARSA (Persia)
● Pasargadae
● Persepolis
ASAGARTA (Sagartia)
PARTHAVA (Parthia)
ARAL SEA
ZRANKA (Drangiana)
HARAKHUVATISH (Arachosia)
KHUVARAZMISH (Chorasmia)
BAKHTRISH (Bactria)
SÚGUDA (Sogdia)
MAKA (Gedrosia)
THATAGUSH (Sattagydia)
HARAIVA (Areia)
GANDARA (India)
SAKA HAUMAVARGA (East Scythians)
HINDUSH (India)

Nothing could have pleased Alexander more. Nevertheless, his opponents still enjoyed one very considerable advantage: choice of terrain. Alexander had marched north-east from Abydos rather than in any other direction (e.g. along the Royal Road to Sardis, which might have seemed more logical) simply and solely because that was where the Persian satraps were mustering their forces. Once his opponents realized how badly he needed a fight – and Memnon must surely have rubbed this point in – they could, without much difficulty, bring him to battle where and when they pleased. In the event, they chose a defensive strategy: once Memnon's scheme had been discarded, this was probably the most sensible alternative. Alexander's dashing reputation had, clearly, preceded him. If he could be lured into attacking a strongly held position, over exposed and dangerous ground, where his cavalry would find difficulty in charging, and the Macedonian phalanx could not hold formation, then that might well be the end of the invasion.

Having collected all available reinforcements, the satraps advanced from Zeleia to the River Granicus (now the Koçabaş), which Alexander would have to cross if he wanted to reach Dascylium – or, indeed, to force an engagement. They chose a position where the stream ran fast and deep, and the bank on the eastern side was high, with thick deposits of alluvial silt beneath it.[36] This offered the best possible conditions for the strategy they had in mind.*[37] At the crossing-point itself Arsites posted Memnon and his mercenaries, about 5–6,000 strong: a solid spear-wall,

---

* The following account of Alexander's victory at the Granicus differs in several important respects from the traditional version, based on official propaganda, and preserved by Arrian (1.13–15.5) and Plutarch (*Alex.* 16.1–3), who utilized the accounts of Ptolemy and Aristobulus. Both make the battle take place that same afternoon, after a direct – and barely credible – frontal assault across the river. The sequence o] events leading up to the engagement, as given here, follows Diodorus' 17.19.1–3. For a full analysis of the problems involved, see my Appendix' 'Propaganda at the Granicus' (below, pp. 489 ff.).

reinforced with light-armed javelin-men, was the best possible defence against a frontal assault by cavalry.[38] Flanking them were the Persian cavalry regiments. Arsites, touchy though he was on this subject, knew better than to hold the front line with his own conscript infantry levies. The cavalry would be immobilized, and in fact acting as mounted infantry for the occasion; but he had to make the best use of what troops were available.

He could, in fact, have been a great deal worse off. His overall force was not much over 30,000 men, whereas Alexander had 43,000 infantry alone. In cavalry, however, he enjoyed a vast superiority of numbers: 15–16,000 to Alexander's 6,000+.[39] This factor dictated much of his subsequent tactics. Whatever he did, he must avoid exposing his inferior infantry to the Macedonian phalanx on open ground. If he was to defeat Alexander, it would be through the skilful use of his cavalry and mercenaries in combination.

Alexander, meanwhile, was advancing on the Granicus, baggage-train in the rear, 'his infantry massed in two groups, both wings protected by cavalry', with a strong detachment of light troops thrown out in front to reconnoitre the ground. When his scouts rode back and informed him that the enemy had been sighted, he drew up his forces in battle-order and moved on at full speed to the river, ready for an immediate engagement. But when they got there, and saw the conditions under which they would be required to attack, Alexander's officers were something less than enthusiastic. Mostly veterans with years of hard campaigning behind them, these men knew a death-trap when they saw one.

Parmenio did his best to reason with the king. The Persians could not be tempted out of their entrenched position: they had every advantage, and knew it. The depth and speed of the river meant that the Macedonians would be unable to advance in extended line. They would have to cross in column, and while they were struggling up that slippery bank on the far side, in general disorder, they would be totally vulnerable. Besides, it was already late in the afternoon. The most sensible course, surely, was to camp where they were for the night. Arsites was so heavily outnumbered in infantry that he might well withdraw; and then the Macedonians could ford the river at dawn without any fear of opposition. Alternatively, they could march downstream under cover of darkness and find an easier crossing-point. 'A failure at the outset,' Parmenio concluded – perhaps his most telling argument – 'would be a serious thing now, and highly detrimental to our success in the long run.'

But Alexander would not listen to reason; he was hell-bent on attacking there and then. The enemy lay before him; his supplies and cash reserves were fast running out;

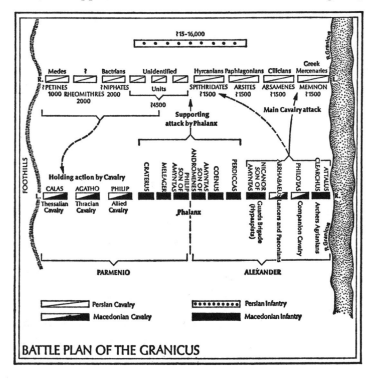

BATTLE PLAN OF THE GRANICUS

it was, he felt, now or never. Parmenio's suggestion that Arsites might decamp during the night must have strengthened the king's resolve more than anything else: this was the one thing he had to prevent at all costs. Besides, his destiny was summoning him, like his exemplar Achilles, to achieve heroic fame through great deeds – and where better, on this occasion, than across the Granicus, against such fearful odds?[40] As a last resort Alexander's staff, knowing their young king's touchy Homeric pride, tried to raise religious objections. It was now May, the Macedonian month Daisios, during which, it seems, military campaigning was taboo – a prohibition originally connected with the need to get the harvest in.[41] Alexander retorted by making an *ad hoc* intercalation to the calendar, so that the month became – by royal decree, as it were – a second Artemisios. He had made up his mind, and nothing, it seemed, would budge him.

If a direct assault in fact took place at this point,[42] it was almost certainly an expensive failure (see below, pp. 508 ff.). Whether it did or not, Alexander was finally forced, however reluctantly, to accept Parmenio's advice. It was the most sensible plan by far, and in his heart of hearts the king knew this as well as anyone. But the loss of face and humiliation which such a decision implied were not things lightly forgotten by a man of Alexander's temper, and may well have played a larger part than most historians allow in his subsequent treatment of Parmenio. From now on, it has been observed, Callisthenes never misses an opportunity, in his official record, of reporting occasions when Parmenio supposedly gave the king bad advice. This advice, needless to say, was always ignored – to the benefit of everyone concerned.

There can be little doubt as to who put such an idea into the historian's head, or why. The fiasco at the Granicus rankled deeply, and this systematic denigration of Parmenio was one of its more unpleasant consequences. Callisthenes, as a progressive Greek intellectual, seems at this stage to have

disliked Philip's old guard barons on principle: it took the
proskynesis affair (see below, pp. 372 ff.) to drive him into
their camp, presumably on the principle that 'my enemy's
enemy is my friend'. At all events he carried out his brief
with partisan thoroughness, in a smear-campaign which
reached its peak at Gaugamela (see below, p. 294). Callisthenes' dispatch on the battle accused the old marshal, quite
unjustifiably, of cowardice and military incompetence.[43]
But by then Alexander was ready to close in on Parmenio,
and in a position to do so. At the time of the Granicus,
Parmenio still held most of the trump cards.

Under cover of darkness – probably leaving all camp-fires
ablaze to deceive the Persians[44] – the army marched downstream till a suitable ford was found. Here they bivouacked
for a few hours. The crossing began at dawn. While it was
still in progress, Arsites' scouts gave the alarm. Several
regiments of cavalry hastily galloped down to the ford,
hoping to catch Alexander's troops at a disadvantage – as
they had done the previous afternoon. But this time they
were too late. The bulk of the army was already on the
eastern bank, and Macedonian discipline had no difficulty
in coping with a surprise attack of this sort. While the
phalanx formed up to cover their comrades in the river,
Alexander led his own cavalry in a swift outflanking charge.
The Persians wisely retreated. Alexander got the rest of his
column across at leisure, and then deployed in battle-
formation (see plan, p. 174). It was rich, rolling plainland,
ideal for a cavalry engagement; on the hills – then as today –
spring wheat rippled in the morning breeze.[45]

Arsites and his colleagues had to think fast. Their initial
advantage was lost. They would now have to fight in open
country – what Justin calls the Adrasteian plain – with the
river on their left flank and their right wing stretching away
towards the foothills. They were strong in cavalry, lamentably weak in infantry. There was only one thing for them
to do. They put all their cavalry regiments into the front

line, deploying them on as wide a front as possible, while the infantry was held in reserve. Then they advanced towards Alexander's position. Their aim, in all likelihood, was to roll up his wings by means of a massive outflanking movement. If they were also, as Tarn believed, determined to kill Alexander, they certainly can have had no trouble in identifying him. He wore the magnificent armour he had taken from Athena's temple at Ilium; his shield was emblazoned as splendidly as that of Achilles, and on his head he had an extraordinary helmet with two great white wings or plumes adorning it (which sounds decidedly un-Homeric in style).[46] All round him thronged an obsequious crowd of pages and staff-officers. The Persians, having observed that he was taking up his battle-station on the right wing, transferred some of their best cavalry regiments from the centre to meet his assault. This was precisely what Alexander had hoped they would do; his conspicuous display (as with so many of his actions) was made with a very practical ulterior motive.

A moment later, with trumpets blaring, while hills and river re-echoed to the terrible battle-cry of the phalanx, the king charged, leading his cavalry in wedge formation. He feinted at the enemy left, where Memnon and Arsamenes were waiting for him; then he abruptly swung his wedge inwards, driving at the now weakened Persian centre. Meanwhile Parmenio, away on the left flank, was fighting a holding action against the Medes and Bactrians. Alexander was making a classic pivotal or echeloned attack (cf. above, p. 24), with his left wing, as usual, forming the axis. When the Persian right moved forward against Parmenio, with the intention of outflanking him, a gap opened in their centre, and it was here that Alexander and the Companion Cavalry punched their way through.[47] The king himself was in the thick of the fighting: blows showered on his shield and body-armour from all sides.

A desperate and truly Homeric struggle now ensued. Mithridates, Darius' son-in-law, counter-charged at the head of his own Iranian cavalry division, accompanied by forty high-ranking Persian nobles, and began to drive a similar wedge into the Macedonian centre. Alexander's spear had been broken in the first onslaught, and old Demaratus of Corinth gave him his own. The king wheeled round and rode straight for Mithridates. The Persian hurled a javelin at him with such force that it not only transfixed his shield, but pierced the cuirass behind it. Alexander plucked out the javelin, set spurs to his horse, and drove his own spear fair and square into Mithridates' breastplate. At this, says Diodorus, 'adjacent ranks in both armies cried out at the superlative display of prowess.' It is all remarkably like a battle-scene from the *Iliad* – which does not necessarily make it suspect testimony.

However, the breastplate held, the king's spear-point snapped off short, and Mithridates – shaken, but still game – drew his sword in readiness for a close-quarters mounted duel. Alexander, with considerable presence of mind, jabbed the broken spear into his opponent's face, hurling him to the ground. He was, however, so preoccupied with Mithridates that he had eyes for no one else. Another Persian nobleman, Rhosaces, now rode at him from the flank, with drawn sabre, and dealt him such a blow on the head that it sheared clean through his winged helmet and laid the scalp open to the bone. Alexander, swaying and dizzy, nevertheless managed to dispatch this fresh assailant; but while he was doing so, Rhosaces' brother, Spithridates, the satrap of Ionia, moved in behind him, sword upraised, ready to deliver the *coup de grâce*. In the very nick of time 'Black' Cleitus, the brother of Alexander's nurse, severed Spithridates' arm at the shoulder with one tremendous blow. It was none too soon; the king collapsed half-fainting to the ground, and a battle-royal raged over his prostrate body.

Meanwhile the phalanx was pouring through the gap in the Persian centre, and had begun to make short work of Arsites' native infantry. Alexander's light-armed troops darted in among the Persian riders, hamstringing their horses and causing general confusion. Somehow the king struggled on to his own horse again, and the Companions rallied round him. The enemy centre began to cave in, leaving their flanks exposed. Many distinguished Persian commanders had already been killed. This was the beginning of the end. Parmenio's Thessalian cavalry, on the left wing, now made a well-timed charge, and in a moment the entire Persian line broke and fled.

Their infantry divisions, except for the mercenaries, put up little resistance. But Memnon and his men retreated in good order to a high knoll above the battlefield, and there made a last stand. They sent a herald to Alexander asking for quarter, but the king (for whatever reason) was in no mood to grant it. He now concentrated his entire attention on destroying them. While the phalanx delivered a frontal assault, his cavalry hemmed them in from all sides to prevent a mass break-out. Seeing they could expect no mercy, Memnon's troops fought with savage and desperate courage: more Macedonians were killed during this stage of the battle than at any other point. Alexander himself, leading the cavalry, had his horse killed under him by a spear-thrust. But there could be only one end to such a struggle. Perhaps 3–4,000 mercenaries died where they stood; the remaining 2,000 laid down their arms and surrendered. Memnon himself somehow contrived to get away: Alexander had not yet seen the last of him. The rest of Arsites' forces were fleeing in wild disorder across the plain, and Alexander let them go. The battle of the Granicus was over, and the captain-general had won a famous victory. His personal conduct during the battle was heroic to a degree; seldom can the palm for valour, awarded him 'by common consent', have found a more deserving recipient.[48]

Casualties among the Persian cavalry units numbered some 2,500, of whom 1,000 were native Iranians. The death-roll included many great noblemen: Darius' son-in-law Mithridates, his son Arbupales, his wife's uncle Pharnaces, together with Spithridates, the Cappadocian commander Mithrobuzanes, and many others. Arsites himself survived and fled into Phrygia, where he committed suicide, believing – justifiably or not – that he was primarily responsible for the disaster. The losses suffered by the Persian infantry have been grossly exaggerated (by Diodorus in particular) and there is no sure way of determining them.[49] However, since they broke and ran without putting up much of a fight, their casualties are unlikely to have been heavy. The losses attributed to the Macedonians are equally suspect. The highest number of casualties said to have been suffered by Alexander's infantry is thirty, and two sources reduce this figure to nine. Similarly with the cavalry: the maximum loss recorded is 120. But the same two authorities (Ptolemy and Aristobulus) admit no more than sixty, of whom twenty-five were Companions who fell 'in the first charge'.[50] Alexander subsequently had statues of these twenty-five erected at Dium in Macedonia: a unique gesture, never to be repeated. He also, characteristically, included his own likeness in the group.[51]

Memnon's 2,000 surviving mercenaries were chained like felons and sent back to forced labour in Macedonia, probably down the mines. Common sense would have suggested acquiring their valuable services for the Macedonian army, at cheap rates: Alexander's action smacks of pure vindictiveness. His ostensible reason – still widely believed – was that 'they had violated Greek opinion by fighting with orientals against Greeks'. In other words, he was making a placatory gesture as captain-general of the league. But Greek public opinion was something of which Alexander took notice only when it suited him; and the league he used as a blanket excuse for a good many underhand actions (the destruction of Thebes is only one example). In fact from now on he enrolled Greek mercenaries – including those who had previously taken service under Darius – whenever he could get hold of them. Aristobulus says he was 'influenced more by anger than by reason', and this, surely, is the plain truth.[52]

From the spoils of victory he selected 300 panoplies, and sent them to Athens for dedication in the Parthenon. The accompanying inscription ran as follows: 'Alexander son of Philip and the Greeks – Lacedaemonians excepted – these spoils from the barbarians who dwell in Asia'. Once more, under cover of executing the league's decrees, Alexander had made it very clear what would happen to any Greeks – Athenians included – who were rash enough to oppose him; the snub to Sparta was merely incidental. Whether the omission of any reference to his own Macedonians was designed to emphasize their Greekness (and his own role as the league's servant), or had some darker and more splenetic motivation, is a question which cannot easily be decided.[53]

On the day following the battle the king celebrated splendid obsequies for his own fallen, who were buried, like true warriors, with their arms and armour. He also granted their immediate relatives exemption from military service, and from all local or property taxes – privileges which, he calculated, would 'create in his men greater enthusiasm to face the hazards of battle': the ulterior pragmatic motive is seldom far to seek in his actions. Perhaps for the same reason he made a point of visiting the wounded, and encouraging them to boast of their personal feats of bravery during the engagement. The bulk of the luxury articles which fell into his hands – purple robes, drinking-cups and suchlike – he sent home to his mother.[54]

After this defeat Darius could no longer fail to take the Macedonian threat seriously. From the very jaws of defeat Alexander had snatched an overwhelming victory. The whole of western Asia Minor now lay open before him: the Persian crusade had begun in grim earnest. As he surveyed the stricken field of the Granicus on that May morning, the captain-general of the Hellenes had good reason to feel pleased with himself. Yet this – as he knew too well – was only the beginning. A long and dangerous journey still lay before him: just how long, and how dangerous, perhaps not even he realized.

⌈6⌉

The Road to Issus

A⊤ the outset of his campaign, how far ahead had Alexander planned, and how clear-cut were the policies which he envisaged? This is a perennially debated point, to which there can be no final answer. At one time it was fashionable to credit him with 'firm long-range intentions and sweeping general policies'; now it is more commonly accepted that 'he almost certainly had no idea how far he would go or what the end would be'.[1] But the Persian Empire, as he well knew, was a vast conglomeration, stretching from the Red Sea to the Caspian, from the Hellespont to beyond the Hindu Kush. Whatever else Alexander had in mind he must have intended to defeat (if not to replace) Darius; and this alone, granted the resources at the Great King's disposal, was liable to prove a gigantic undertaking. Perhaps the simple truth of the matter (to quote his most percipient critic once more) is that 'like other men with full faith in their individual star, he was ready to follow it wherever it should lead'.[2]

This would also account for his flexible attitude towards administration, racial problems, political systems, and military strategy. A man whose one overriding belief is in his own destiny will not be doctrinaire in other matters. All else must be subservient to that one glittering goal. The true obsessional conqueror tends, paradoxically, towards indiscriminate opportunism tempered with propaganda, a phenomenon which Alexander's career amply illustrates. Nothing, in fact, offers a clearer demonstration of his attitude, as we shall see, than the way in which he proceeded to deal with the Greek cities in Asia Minor.

The Hellenic League had been created, in the last resort, as a bulwark against subversive behaviour by the city-states of the mainland. There democracy was the danger, and Antipater in Europe had a free hand to deal with it by imposing tyrants, oligarchies and garrisons. In Asia Minor, on the other hand – conveniently for Alexander – Darius' Greek appointees tended, more often than not, to be oligarchs. This suited Callisthenes' Panhellenic propaganda-line very well indeed. Ostensibly at least, Alexander was pursuing a liberation policy; besides, it was vital that he should not have trouble along his ever-lengthening lines of communication. So in this context (though assuredly for no idealistic motives) his European policy had to be reversed: he overthrew oligarchies or tyrannies and set up democracies in their place. He seems to have had no ideological convictions whatsoever (apart from a determination to shape the world in his own image), and in fact always underestimated those who did. Any instrument that would serve his one compelling ambition he used without scruple.

After the battle Alexander appointed Calas – who already had experience of the area – as governor of Hellespontine Phrygia in Arsites' place. He also offered a general amnesty to those who had fled and taken refuge in the hills. What this meant, in effect, was that the old system continued as before, except that Phrygia had a Macedonian satrap rather than a Persian one: Alexander even instructed Calas 'to maintain the taxes at the same level as before'. Zeleia was occupied, and Alexander took no sanctions against its inhabitants, affecting to believe that it was only through coercion that they had fought on the Persian side. Collaboration, in fact, was to be made more attractive than resistance. Parmenio marched on Dascylium (Eskili) and took it without difficulty, since the Persian garrison had fled before he got there.[3] Alexander lost no time in getting rid of the league forces which accompanied him – another ironic gloss on his role as leader of a Panhellenic crusade. Philip, son of Menelaus, who commanded the allied cavalry, had been killed at the Granicus. The king now appointed Alexander of Lyncestis in his place, and left not only the cavalry but all the league troops, except the Argives, to police Phrygia under Calas' command. News now came in that the shattered remnants of the Persian army, Memnon among them, had retreated down the coast to Miletus, and Alexander promptly marched south in pursuit of them.[4] He did not, however, take the coast road himself, but went south through Mysia. His initial destination was Sardis, capital of the Lydian satrapy, 'bulwark of the barbarian dominion on the sea-coast', and a city of great strategic importance, standing as it did at the head of the Royal Road to Susa.

While he was still some nine miles off, the Persian governor of Sardis, Mithrines, accompanied by a group of leading citizens, came out to meet him. Mithrines offered to surrender not only Sardis itself, but also its acropolis and the treasure stored there. Alexander's victory at the Granicus was beginning to pay off in a gratifyingly literal way.[5] The Macedonian army pitched camp on the River Hermus, a little less than three miles outside the city-walls. Alexander, perhaps suspecting a trap, kept Mithrines with him, and sent an advance party to receive the surrender of the garrison. Everything went off smoothly, and Alexander proceeded to make his arrangements for the administration of Lydia: they repay study.[6]

To govern the satrapy in Spithridates' stead he chose Parmenio's brother Asander: an honour, on the face of it, but the fewer of the old marshal's relatives Alexander had around him, we may surmise, the happier he would feel. As commandant of the fortress he appointed Pausanias, one of his Companions, and gave him as garrison troops the sole remaining allied Greek detachment, that of the Argives. Another slate was thus wiped clean. He also created a separate department to collect taxes and tribute: its first chief finance officer was a Macedonian named Nicias. Lydia's riches were proverbial, and Alexander had no intention of concentrating too much power in too few hands. The other occasions on which he made such an appointment were in Egypt and Babylon: both, it may be noted, provinces of great wealth, and both garrisoned with a military commander in addition to a civilian satrap. In all cases, it is clear, the finance officer was directly responsible to the king, by-passing his fellow-administrators.

Alexander's motives can scarcely be in doubt. He may have wanted to improve financial administration, both for his own benefit and that of his new subjects; but his prime aim, as Griffith points out, was 'to check and limit the powers of the satrap by removing from him the control of the revenues of his province'. Again, Alexander left existing institutions alone as far as possible; he did not, for instance, use the local mint to strike his own currency, a practice which only began – for propaganda motives in the first instance – when he reached Tarsus. He also permitted the citizens of Sardis, and of Lydia in general, 'to observe the old customs of their country, and gave them their freedom'. This was not in fact as munificent as it sounds. The Persians themselves had always, as a matter of policy, left their subjects free to run their own internal administration. There was no need for the Lydians to bring their old constitution out of mothballs, because they had never stopped using it; and by 'freedom' Alexander meant no more than a guarantee against enslavement – a by no means unlikely fate otherwise, as Parmenio's occupation of Grynium (see above, p. 138) had shown. Once again, the king had done no more than ratify the status quo – though this did not stop him taking credit for it.

From Sardis Alexander now advanced to Ephesus – another key communication-centre between Persia and the West – covering the seventy miles' journey in just under four days. At the news of his approach, the city's mercenary garrison fled, taking with them the Macedonian renegade, Amyntas, son of Antiochus. Clearly Alexander's treatment of Memnon's troops at the Granicus had received wide

publicity. Two years before (336) Ephesus had been taken
by Parmenio, and on that occasion its citizens went so far
as to institute a quasi-cult of Philip in the temple of Artemis
(see above, p. 98). But about the time that Alexander had
launched his invasion, Persian sympathizers in the city
had, with Memnon's support, driven out the pro-Macedonian 'democracy', and pulled down Philip's statue. It
was Memnon's garrison which now so hurriedly evacuated
the citadel. Not for the first or last time in their chequered
history, the Ephesians had unwisely chosen the wrong side.

Alexander, naturally, lost no time in restoring the democrats; and until the king put an end to it (not too soon, one
suspects) they carried out a joyous pogrom of their political
opponents. But enough was enough, and after a while
Alexander called a halt to such reprisals, which, we are
told, earned him great popularity in the city. Even so, his
offer (provided he got the credit for it) to restore the temple
of Artemis – burnt down, symbolically enough, on the night
of his birth, and never properly restored – was met with a
polite refusal.[7]

The famous painter Apelles was in Ephesus at the time,
and Alexander commissioned a portrait from him. His first
attempt showed the king astride Bucephalas, and sounds
depressingly like something by David or Ingres at their
worst. Alexander was not at all pleased with it, and said so.
Apelles thereupon had Bucephalas fetched to the studio and
placed by the picture. When the live horse neighed at its
painted likeness, Apelles remarked: 'You see, O King, the
horse is really a far better judge of art than you are.' This
(whatever it may tell us about fourth-century aesthetic,
values) was a very shrewd cut. Alexander prided himself,
erroneously, on his artistic expertise. On one occasion,
while he was holding forth during a sitting, Apelles quietly
suggested that he try some other topic of conversation,
because the young apprentices grinding the colours were
all laughing at him. But over this portrait the king was
adamant, and Apelles had no option but to try again. The

final version showed Alexander as Zeus, wielding a thunder-bolt – a fancy which led the sculptor Lysippus to make some sharp comments on Apelles' lack of taste. But in art designed primarily as propaganda, aesthetic considerations tend to go by the board. The king preened himself, and Apelles collected a fat fee.[8] Already, it is clear, the idea of self-deification (if only as a political instrument) was very much in Alexander's mind.

While he was still in Ephesus, ambassadors came from Magnesia and Tralles, offering their submission. Word had gone round that here at least – whatever he might do at home – the Macedonian invader looked kindly on demo-cracies. Popular factions in the Greek cities, ever on the look-out for a promising *point d'appui*, were not slow to take the hint. Hitherto Alexander may have been feeling his way as regards the administration of conquered territories: now the solution stared him in the face. Two large divisions, under Parmenio and Alcimachus, were sent off to accept the surrender of cities in Ionia, Lydia, and the Aeolid. Before they left Sardis, both commanders were carefully briefed. Oligarchic juntas were to be removed from office, and 'democratic' governments set up in their place. Local laws and customs were to be left untouched. Lastly, the tribute which each city had paid the Persians was to be remitted.

These terms sound, on the face of it, generous enough; but all they really meant was that one lot of puppet rulers was replaced by another. Moreover, despite the acquisition of Sardis' treasure (most of which, in all likelihood, had at once been dissipated on making up arrears of pay) Alex-ander was still very short of ready cash. To forego tribute at this stage was a quixotic gesture he could ill afford. But to call it something else cost nothing. What it seems he did, in fact, was to insist on all 'liberated' Greek cities joining the Hellenic League. Once they had done this they became, under the terms of the league charter, liable for cash 'con-tributions' (*syntaxeis*) to the Panhellenic war-effort in lieu of providing men and ships.[9] The sums involved, we may be sure, differed very little from what they had previously paid the Persians by way of tribute. But the euphemism of a 'contribution' did not carry the same unpleasant associations; and the whole scheme, with its implication of a united Greek front, must have made splendid propaganda for home consumption.

Parmenio and Alcimachus carried out their mission with great success. In city after city – as with Ephesus, as throughout Greek history – the popular party was ready and eager to gain political control with outside assistance, and to carry out a ruthless purge of its opponents in the process. (Alexander, meanwhile, spent most of his time in Ephesus, presumably dealing with problems of administration; though he did make a trip to Smyrna which had far-reaching results after his death. The old city had been destroyed by Alyattes in *c.* 624, and abandoned ever since except for a few squatters. While out hunting on Mt Pagus, Alexander, with his superb natural eye for terrain, found a first-class site for a new city, some two and a half miles south of the old one: built in due course by Antigonus, this city became the New Smyrna of the Hellenistic era.) Another item on Parmenio's brief was, seemingly, to strengthen Ionian coastal defences against possible attacks by the Persian fleet. Clazomenae was linked with the mainland by means of a permanent causeway, and an abortive attempt made to dig a canal through the nearby Mimas peninsula.[10]

Such precautions, as events now showed, were by no means idle. The Great King's squadrons had been sighted off Caria, sailing north, clearly to join the forces – mercenaries and others – now holding Miletus. Earlier, the commandant of the Milesian garrison, thinking his position hopeless, had sent Alexander a letter offering to surrender the city. Now he abruptly changed his mind.[11] The king had to act fast. The league fleet was at once dispatched from Ephesus;[12] if it reached Miletus before the Persians, the harbour could be held and the town saved. Parmenio and Alcimachus were recalled; even so Alexander seems to have marched with what troops he had – over 15,000 were already on garrison duties or detached, not counting casualties[13] – before his second-in-command got back.

Yet he found time, en route, to deal with the problems of Priene: a garrison was imposed, and *syntaxeis* assessed. This, again, reveals Alexander's real attitude to the Greek cities. Priene, we may presume, had resisted liberation. Here, too, the king managed to get what had been denied him at Ephesus: the right of dedicating a great temple. The shrine of Athens was still under construction: Alexander made a generous donation to its building costs, and his reward was the inscription which may still be seen in the British Museum: 'King Alexander set up this temple to Athena Polias.' He generally got his own way in the end. It is revealing that, at a time when he had so many more pressing matters on his mind, he nevertheless found leisure to erase the memory of this minor personal rebuff.[14]

Nicanor, the commander of the Greek fleet, brought his squadrons to anchor by the off-shore island of Lade three days before the Persians arrived. He had only 160 ships to their reputed 400, but his defensive position was superb. Alexander himself also reached Miletus in good time, and fortified Lade with a strong garrison. The Persians were thus forced to anchor off-shore under Mt Mycale. This left them in an exposed position, and cut off from supplies of fresh water, since Alexander posted Philotas at the Maeander estuary to prevent their forage parties landing. He had already captured the outer city, and was now preparing to assault the acropolis.

At this point Parmenio and Alcimachus joined him, and a council of war was held. Parmenio advised risking a naval engagement, even though they were heavily outnumbered. A victory, he argued, would bring them great prestige, while a defeat (since the Persians held so commanding a position at sea) would make very little difference: they had everything to gain and nothing to lose. Alexander opposed this view strongly. Their own crews, he pointed out, were still half-trained (the cities of the league must have been scraping the bottom of the barrel when they chose them); and – a revealing admission – a defeat at this point might well trigger off a general revolt of the Greek states. So much for the Panhellenic crusade. Alexander's main fear, we need scarcely doubt, was that the league fleet might actually desert him if the chance presented itself.

Meanwhile the governor of Miletus sent a representative to his headquarters, offering to 'grant free use of their harbours, and free entry within their walls, to Alexander and the Persians alike', if he would raise the siege. In other words, Miletus was to be made an open city. Alexander turned this proposal down flat, and began his assault. While the league fleet blockaded the harbour-mouth, to prevent any assistance reaching the defenders from their Persian allies, the king's siege-engines battered away at the city-walls. The defences were breached, and the Macedonians surged through. Some of the garrison, including 300 mercenaries, escaped to a small island; the rest surrendered. Alexander, in accordance with his new policy, treated all Milesian citizens mercifully, though any foreigners who fell into his hands were sold as slaves. The Greek mercenaries he offered to spare ('moved to pity by their courage and loyalty,' we are told) on condition that they entered his service. They were, it is clear, part of Memnon's original force; but this time Alexander's supposed deference to the league seems to have been overborne by immediate military requirements.

Nor was there any repetition of the looting and wholesale massacre that had accompanied the destruction of Thebes. Some soldiers who profaned a temple of Demeter were said to have been miraculously blinded. If Alexander did not invent this rumour, he doubtless gave it wide publicity as a deterrent to future offenders. He also went out of his way to emphasize the fact (which local opinion could be forgiven for finding a trifle far-fetched) that this was an ethnic war, a crusade of revenge for the wrongs done to the Greeks by Darius the Great and his son Xerxes. On being shown the statues of those numerous athletes who had won glory for their city at the Pythian and Olympian Games, his only comment was: 'And where were the men with bodies like these when the barbarians were besieging your city?' Miletus had been captured by the Persians in 494, at the close of the Ionian Revolt; this was not, we may guess, a fact of which its inhabitants cared to be reminded in such terms.[15]

For a while the Great King's fleet continued to ride off Mycale, in the hope of provoking an engagement. But apart from some minor skirmishes, their attempts came to nothing; and since they were still cut off from all shore supplies, they found themselves in a virtual state of siege. Finally they gave up, weighed anchor, and sailed away southward to Halicarnassus (Bodrum), where the Persians were establishing a fresh line of defence. But the threat which they represented had not been destroyed. It is in this context that we must view the momentous decision which Alexander now took: to disband his own fleet and stake everything on a land-based campaign. The Athenian detachment, plus one or two other vessels, was retained to serve as a transport-flotilla – and to provide hostages. Alexander also kept his squadrons in the Hellespont. (Six months later they were back on operational service in the Aegean.) But the bulk of the league's naval contingents were now paid off and sent back home.[16]

Various explanations have been advanced for this move. The Greek fleet was inferior, both in numbers and skill (this seems to have been undoubtedly true). Alexander could not afford to keep it on, since it cost him at least 100 talents a month. The Macedonians would fight better if they knew their retreat was cut off. Lastly, Alexander had a new strategy which would render a fleet otiose: he planned to capture all Persian and Phoenician ports from the landward side, thus making it impossible for enemy squadrons to operate in his rear. Nevertheless, he was taking an enormous calculated risk. To put this Persian fleet out of action effectively would mean winning every major harbour from the Hellespont to Egypt, from Cilicia to Tyre. Meanwhile, Darius' squadrons were still at liberty to raid the Greek mainland, cut Alexander's lines of communication, and stir up trouble generally from one end of the Aegean to the other. (Most of these things in due course they did.) With 400 Phoenician warships at large, a Persian-backed Greek revolt was by no means impossible; and if it succeeded, Alexander's chances against Darius would not look at all rosy.

The truth of the matter seems to have been that Alexander distrusted his Greek allies so profoundly – and with good reason – that he 'preferred to risk the collapse of his campaign in a spate of rebellion rather than entrust its safety to a Greek fleet'.[17] He was also banking, again with good reason, on the chronic inability of the mainland city-states to take concerted action of any sort, even to secure their own freedom. But for a time, as we shall see, it was touch and go.

After the fall of Miletus, the surviving Persian forces had withdrawn south to Halicarnassus in Caria – a large, well-fortified stronghold, with a first-class harbour, and every facility for withstanding a prolonged siege.[18] Memnon – who now had a score of his own to settle with Alexander – had already written to Darius, begging for the supreme military command. To forestall the slanders of his enemies at court, he sent his wife and children to Susa as hostages. The Great King granted his request, appointing him 'controller of lower Asia and commander of the fleet'.

Until two years previously, Halicarnassus had been ruled by a local Carian dynasty, which owed allegiance to Persia. It was the last representative of this family, Pixodarus, with whom the young Alexander had made an abortive attempt to ally himself by marriage (see above, p. 99). When the scheme fell through, Pixodarus wisely made his peace with the Great King, and married off his daughter to a Persian nobleman, Orontobates. Now Pixodarus was dead, and Orontobates held Halicarnassus as the Great King's direct representative. Pixodarus himself had originally seized power by an act of usurpation. The legitimate ruler was in fact his elder sister, Queen Ada; and Ada still held Alinda, the strongest fortress in all Caria. These facts were well-known to Alexander, and at once suggested his next move. The Carians had had a Persian administration thrust upon them; nothing would please them more than to see their own dynasty restored. Here was a case where Alexander could offer genuine liberation, and achieve his own ends at the same time.

When he left Miletus, therefore, instead of marching south by the coast road he made a detour over the mountains to Alinda: perhaps he was already in contact with the exiled queen. At all events, she came out to meet him, and voluntarily surrendered her stronghold. In return for her support, Alexander promised to re-establish her on the throne once Halicarnassus had been taken. He also, in due course, since she had a personal grudge against Orontobates, assigned her and her troops the task of besieging the acropolis. The two of them seem to have got on famously. Alexander addressed the middle-aged queen as 'Mother', while she was for ever sending him little presents of cakes and sweetmeats from her own kitchens. Finally she adopted him as her son and official successor.

It is all very touching; but at the same time it once more reveals Alexander's political shrewdness and foresight. Alliance with the opposition – whether Greek or barbarian, popular or reactionary – was a standby that seldom failed him. What this adoption meant was that he had the right, after Ada's death, to impose a viceroy of his own on Caria; and in due course he did so. The local regime had simply been required to transfer its allegiance from the Great King to himself. All Alexander's administrative arrangements in

Asia Minor follow the same basic pattern. He might talk of
a Panhellenic crusade against Persian rule, but he took
over Persian institutions – including satraps and client-
kingdoms – virtually intact.[19] The only differences were
that Persian satraps had been replaced by Macedonians,
the tribute was called a 'contribution', and ultimate authority now resided, not with the Great King, but with Alexander himself.

The Carians, however, merely saw that this Macedonian
adventurer had come to deliver them from the Persians, and
to restore their rightful queen. When the news of Alexander's adoption became known, 'straightway all the cities
sent missions and presented the king with gold crowns and
promised to cooperate with him in everything'.[20] Alexander
had already sent on his siege-equipment by sea, perhaps to
Iasus: time was pressing. He now bade farewell to Ada,
and marched south-west, over the Latmus range, by way of
Labranda and Euromus.[21] The towns through which he
passed welcomed him with open arms, though his role as an
adoptive Carian must have been a trifle embarrassing when
he came to any predominantly Greek settlement. On such
occasions he took care to emphasize that 'the freedom of the
Greeks was the object for which he had taken it upon
himself to war against the Persians'.[22]

He reached the coast at Iasus, where again he was well
received: this port had seemingly already given a friendly
reception to his transport squadron. At all events, when the
citizens petitioned him for the restoration of certain territorial fishing-grounds they had lost under the Persian regime,
their request was at once granted.[23] At Iasus, too, Alexander met a local celebrity, a schoolboy who had won the
devoted affection of a dolphin. According to one account,
the king afterwards 'made the boy head of the priesthood
of Poseidon at Babylon, interpreting the dolphin's affection
as a sign of the deity's favour'.[24] There was a strong streak
of superstition about Alexander, and he certainly now,
if ever, needed luck at sea.

From Iasus he took the coast road through Bargylia, and thus approached Halicarnassus from the north-east, pitching camp about half a mile outside the Mylasa Gate.[25] A scouting party, sent forward to reconnoitre, was met by a volley of missiles from the walls. Memnon's troops then made a sudden sortie, timing their attack so well that they were back through the city-gates before anyone realized what was going on. It was not a happy omen; and the more Alexander studied Halicarnassus' defences, the less he liked what he saw. It is possible that he had made contact with a pro-Macedonian group inside the city.[26] If so, the intelligence thus obtained must have been discouraging. Memnon had several thousand Greek mercenaries with him (including two Athenian commanders, Ephialtes and Thrasybulus, whose surrender Alexander had demanded after the destruction of Thebes). The stores and magazines were full, and Memnon's defence equipment included siege artillery.

On the landward side of the fortress rose huge crenellated walls, with guard-towers at regular intervals, protected by a moat forty-five feet wide and over twenty in depth. There were no fewer than three fortified citadels, which could – and did – hold out long after the city itself had fallen. One stood on the ancient acropolis, at the north-west bastion. The other two – the fortress of Salmacis, at the southernmost tip of the promontory, and the so-called 'King's Castle', on the tiny offshore island of Arconnesus – commanded the harbour entrance. This harbour was further protected by the Great King's fleet, which now rode at anchor there.

Since Alexander had disbanded his own squadrons, he could not enforce a blockade from the seaward side. Thus Halicarnassus was not liable to run short of supplies, let alone be starved into surrender. Alexander himself, on the other hand, for the first time since landing in Asia Minor, found himself up against a serious provisioning problem. Hellespontine Phrygia had been harvesting when his troops came through; a fertile region, it was also watered by three major rivers, including the Granicus and the Scamander (which alone, according to General Sir Frederick Maurice, had sufficed to water Xerxes' host in 480). Similar conditions prevailed on the march south as far as Miletus: rich arable land, and ample watering from the Greater Maeander. Even so, Curtius tells us, the Macedonians made such locust depredations that a return journey along the same route would have been impossible. Now they were encamped on the rocky Bodrum peninsula (a notoriously barren region) at the tail-end of the dry season. The nearest source of water – probably inadequate for their needs – was twenty miles away. Food, water and forage all probably had to be brought in from Miletus – a two or three days' journey.[27]

The king's one hope, clearly, was to take Halicarnassus by direct assault. But here he faced another difficulty: his siege-equipment had not arrived. Persian squadrons were patrolling the coast, and Alexander's transport-vessels had so far failed to elude them. His original plan had been to land this heavy gear at Myndus, a small port ten miles west of Halicarnassus. He had made contact with the usual opposition party, whose leaders assured him that if he brought his forces there on a certain night the gates would be opened, and the city placed in his hands. But – as so often with such arrangements – something went wrong. Alexander arrived at midnight, only to find the gates shut and the walls bristling with defenders. Nevertheless, he set his infantry to undermine one of the guard-towers. During this operation heavy naval reinforcements arrived from Halicarnassus, and the Macedonians were forced to retreat. Treachery or careless talk had led Alexander straight into a prepared trap.

For some days, deprived of a harbour at which to land his siege-train, Alexander made fruitless attempts to breach the city's defences without it. But at last the transport squadron got through, presumably beaching in some deserted cove along the coast of the Ceramic Gulf. From that moment the siege was on in earnest. Under cover of sheds or mantlets, Alexander's men filled in one section of the moat. He then brought up his mobile towers to bombard the defenders with stones and other missiles, while battering-rams were swung at the walls, and sappers undermined the guard-towers. By these methods he contrived to breach Halicarnassus' fortifications, and the phalanx went storming in over the rubble. But this time they had met their match. Memnon's mercenaries were equally well trained, and had the further advantage of heavy covering fire from catapults set up on the walls. Several such assaults were made, and all, after a tremendous struggle, driven back. During the night, while builders worked in relays to mask the gaps with demi-lune curtain-walls, Memnon sent out a commando force to burn Alexander's towers and engines. Another desperate battle ensued. Finally the Persians were forced to retreat – but not before some three hundred Macedonians had been severely wounded.

Alexander now moved his siege-train against the northern side of the city. Relentless pounding by rams and artillery at length brought down two towers and the intervening curtain-wall, and Alexander decided to attempt a night-attack.[28] This operation proved an expensive failure, largely because the Macedonians found their way blocked by an inner curtain-wall. They managed to extricate themselves, but next morning Alexander was forced to ask Memnon for a truce so that he could recover his dead.

The commanders of the garrison – Memnon, Oronto-bates, and the two Athenians, Ephialtes and Thrasybulus – now held a council of war. Ephialtes, a man of great personal strength and courage, insisted that if Halicarnassus was to be saved they must take the offensive themselves. Memnon, reasonably enough, agreed. Between them they worked out a highly ingenious operation, which came very close indeed to success. From the mercenaries in the garrison they selected 2,000 men, the pick of their troops. These they divided into two commando forces. The first group, armed

with torches and pitch-buckets, sallied out from behind the
curtain-wall at dawn, and set fire to Alexander's siege-
equipment, 'causing a great conflagration to flare up at
once'. The king, as Memnon had anticipated, brought up
his infantry battalions to deal with this threat, and detailed
other troops for fire-fighting operations. Once the phalanx
was engaged, Memnon's second mercenary force charged
out from the main city-gate nearby – 'the last place,' says
Arrian, 'that the Macedonians looked for a sally' – and took
them in flank and rear. At the same time Memnon brought
a new piece of siege-equipment into play: a wooden tower
150 feet high, every platform bristling with artillery and
javelin-men. While Ephialtes led the attack below, laying
about him with murderous energy, a shower of missiles
rained down on the phalanx from above.

Memnon, who had been watching the progress of this
engagement with close attention, now threw in his Persian
infantry reserves. Alexander, on the face of it, had as good
as lost the battle: hemmed in on all sides, he could do nothing but fight a desperate last-ditch action. He was saved,
finally, by his reserve battalion of veterans, men who had
campaigned with Philip but were now exempt from combat
duty. Roused by the chaotic struggle they had been forced
to witness, they decided to show these unlicked youngsters
how a battle should really be fought. Shields locked, spear-
line bristling, they now moved into the fray, a solid, un-
breakable line. The psychological effect on Ephialtes and
his men was considerable. Just as they thought victory within their grasp, they found themselves faced with the prospect
of fighting a second action. They wavered; the Macedonians
pressed home their advantage; and by a great stroke of luck
Ephialtes himself was killed.

In a matter of minutes the whole Persian assault-group
crumbled, and began a stampede back to the city. There was
savage hand-to-hand fighting by the curtain-wall, while so
many men crowded on to the bridge crossing the moat that
it collapsed. The defenders inside the city-gate panicked,

and – in their eagerness to stop the Macedonians forcing an entry – shut out considerable numbers of their own men.[29] Some were trampled to death in the rush; the rest died by the spears of their Macedonian pursuers. By now night was falling, and Alexander had the retreat sounded: in the circumstances he was lucky to have scraped a victory at all. The Macedonians withdrew to their camp: Alexander knew when not to press his luck.

But the defenders, too, had had enough. Their casualties, especially during that final sortie, had been immense. The city-walls were seriously breached in a number of places. That night Memnon and Orontobates decided to pull out. Their best surviving troops they left behind to garrison the harbour-fortresses. The remainder of the defence force, together with all easily removable stores and equipment, they evacuated by sea to Cos. (Presumably – though no ancient source records this – a large proportion of the civilian population went with them.) Before leaving, they set fire to the armouries, to the great wooden tower that contained their siege artillery, and to houses abutting on the walls. A strong wind was blowing – the autumn *meltemi* that still scours Bodrum – and the blaze rapidly spread.

Alexander saw it, but was helpless. Nor – a telling comment on his total lack of naval power – could he do a thing to stop the evacuation. He had no fleet of his own worth mentioning, and in any case the strong-points at the harbour mouth were still in Persian hands. He and his troops were forced to stand and watch, by the lurid glare of the conflagration, while Memnon shipped out all the personnel, stores and equipment he could cram aboard. At dawn the Macedonians entered the still-burning city. They had strict orders to treat all civilians with respect, and to rescue any cut off by the fire. Halicarnassus was, after all, the capital of Alexander's ally and adoptive mother Queen Ada. The tradition that he razed the city to the ground, as he had done in the case of Thebes, is, for this very reason, highly improbable. At most, his sappers may have done some emergency demolition-work to prevent the fire spreading further. He surveyed the fortresses still in enemy hands, saw how impregnable they were, and wisely decided to leave them alone: Salmacis he surrounded with a high wall and a ditch, but there was nothing he could do about the island stronghold of Arconnesus.[30] He had gained his main objective, and it had cost him dear. Now he must move on.

Queen Ada duly became satrap of Caria, though little can have remained of her once-proud capital save walls and smoking rubble. Alexander left her a force of 3,000 mercenaries and 200 cavalry under Ptolemy, their task being to mop up any remaining pockets of Persian resistance in the area. (These operations, including the reduction of the garrison fortresses in Halicarnassus itself, took them a full year.) All newly-married men were now sent home on winter leave, an act which won the king much popularity. Cleander and Coenus, who went with them as escorting officers, were instructed to collect fresh reinforcements from Macedonia and the Peloponnese.[31] These two men were brothers; Cleander, moreover, was Parmenio's son-in-law. Alexander had already got rid of the old marshal's brother Asander by appointing him satrap of Lydia: no Macedonian baron could resist promotion.

The expeditionary force was now divided into two separate commands – one reason probably being to ease the supply-problem during a winter campaign. Parmenio, with the Thessalian cavalry, the allied contingents, and the baggage-train – including Alexander's heavy siege equipment – was to march back north as far as Sardis, and from here conduct a campaign against the tribes of the central Anatolian plateau. The king himself, meanwhile, would advance eastward into Lycia and Pamphylia, 'to establish control of the coast and so immobilize the enemy's fleet'. Having done this, he would take his column up through the Pisidian hinterland, and rejoin Parmenio early the following spring, at Gordium. This was also to be the rendezvous for the troops coming back off leave.[32]

So the two commanders parted, each, perhaps, glad to be
rid of the other's uneasy company for a while. Alexander
marched south-east from Halicarnassus,[33] skirting the
eastern shore of Lake Köyejiz, and by-passing the coastal
strongholds of Caunus and Cnidos, which were still in
Persian hands (they later fell to Ptolemy). He crossed the
Dalaman River, captured a town – still unidentified – called
Hyparna, and reached the coast at Telmessus. This town
fell to him without any trouble; both Nearchus the Cretan
and Aristander, his personal seer, had friends there. One
of these met Nearchus, and asked how he could best help
him. Nearchus sent a group of dancing-girls and their
slave-attendants up into the acropolis, as a present for the
Persian garrison-commander. They had daggers hidden
in their flutes, and small shields in their baskets. After
dinner, when the wine had circulated freely, they proceeded
to massacre their hosts, and the acropolis fell without further
trouble.[34] For his part in this ruse Nearchus was afterwards
rewarded with the satrapy of Lycia and Pamphylia.

From Telmessus Alexander advanced to the Xanthus
River, where he received the submission of some thirty
towns and villages. Meanwhile, however, he had completely
lost touch with Parmenio's division: a great rampart of
mountains, now rapidly becoming snowbound, lay between them. He therefore struck north, up one of the passes
which circumvent the Xanthus gorges, with the object of
breaking through to the trunk road linking Phrygia with the
coast. Here, between mountain snows and hostile tribesmen,
he bogged down, still short of his objective. Envoys from
Phaselis and other towns in eastern Lycia now arrived,
'bringing him a gold crown and offers of friendship':[35]
they also must have told him of the easier route to the
north which he eventually followed, by way of Sagalassus
and Celaenae.

Alexander weighed up the odds, and decided to let his
communications go hang for the time being. He marched
back to the coast (no one but a lunatic would have

attempted the direct route across the mountains in mid winter), and here, at Xanthus, an incident took place which convinced him that the risk he was taking was justified. As the result of some subterranean upheaval, a spring near the city boiled up like a geyser, spewing forth a bronze tablet inscribed with ancient symbols – perhaps some long-lost *ex-voto* offering. For any diviner with his wits about him, this must have come as a godsend. Aristander duly interpreted the mysterious inscription: it said (and who was to contradict him?) that 'the empire of the Persians would one day be destroyed by the Greeks and come to an end'. Much encouraged, Alexander set off again, in an easterly direction this time, by the coast road as far as Phoenice (Finike), and thence across the Chelidonian peninsula to Phaselis.[36]

The only land-route between Phaselis and Side began with a stretch which presented no difficulty to peasants on mule-back, but would make hard going for an army on the march. This was the pass over Mt Climax, a narrow, precipitous track rising from the Kemer Chay through high-walled limestone defiles, and emerging on the Pamphylian plain south of Beldibi. Alexander, remembering the device he had employed to negotiate Mt Ossa (see above, p. 116), now set his Thracian pioneers to work, cutting steps and widening the gorge.[37]

It was during his short stay in Phaselis that Alexander first got news from Parmenio (the old general seems to have had better intelligence than his master concerning the routes of the central Anatolian plateau). A small detachment arrived, bringing with them a Persian prisoner named Sisines. This man had a circumstantial and disquieting story about Alexander of Lyncestis, at present serving under Parmenio as commander of the Thracian cavalry (see above, p. 184). According to Sisines, the Lyncestian had sent a letter to Darius, offering his services to Persia. The Great King had written back promising him 1,000 gold talents and full support in a bid for the Macedonian throne if he would assassinate Alexander. Sisines himself had been chosen to act as confidential intermediary. But (he now told the king) he had been picked up by Parmenio's guards before he could accomplish his mission, and to save his own life had confessed the truth under interrogation.[38] This was a matter for the king himself to decide.

Sisines' report left Alexander (as it may indeed leave the modern historian) in something of a quandary. Was he to believe it or not? Olympias, it would seem, had been warning him about the Lyncestian in recent letters – or so he later alleged. While the latter's alleged claim on the throne was, as we have seen, flimsy in the extreme, that would not necessarily stop Darius from encouraging his ambitions. With Amyntas son of Perdiccas dead, the lure of power might look very enticing. Another possibility was that the whole story had been fabricated by Persian agents, to foster suspicion and dissension in the Macedonian High Command. On the other hand, Alexander can hardly have helped wondering why Parmenio, of all people, was being so suddenly solicitous on his behalf; and one possible explanation instantly suggests itself.

At the outset of the expedition Alexander had made the Lyncestian commander of the Thracian horse. Now the Thracians served under Parmenio, so that this was one appointment in his own corps which Pausanias did *not* dictate, and to which he almost certainly took strong exception. He treated the Thracians and Thessalians more or less as his own Companion Cavalry (see above, p. 159) – a potentially dangerous set-up which Alexander was determined to neutralize. The appointment of the Lyncestian can be seen as a first step towards this goal. Nor was it the only one. Until the Granicus, the Thessalians were under Calas, Parmenio's own nominee, who had served with him on the advance expedition. After the battle, however, Alexander, with admirable speed, removed him from this command and made him satrap of Hellespontine Phrygia – a promotion to which he could scarcely object. The vacant

Thessalian command was filled by one of Alexander's own lieutenants, Philip, son of Menelaus – a move which undercut Parmenio's authority still further.

The old general, then, had an excellent reason for wanting to get rid of the Lyncestian; and the latter's out-kingdom background (coupled with the execution of his two brothers, ostensibly for treason), suggested one obvious way in which this end could be attained. If Parmenio fabricated a convincing story designed to prove that Alexander of Lyncestis was a traitor, some of the mud was bound to stick – enough, in the long run, as things turned out, to secure his execution (see below, pp. 345 ff.). It might even be true that Sisines *had* been sent to approach him, as a potential renegade, but without his knowledge. The Persian would not be over-fussy about the story he told Alexander if the alternative was a knife in his back. Besides, what chance had Alexander, away in Phaselis, of investigating such a case thoroughly? With any luck he might order the Lyncestian's immediate execution – and indeed, if he had followed the advice his staff now gave him, that is precisely what would have happened.

The king was clearly made suspicious and nervous by such a circumstantial story. At the same time he had no intention of sacrificing a good officer without making very careful inquiries into the case. He therefore adopted a compromise solution. One of his staff officers, Amphoterus, accompanied Sisines back to Parmenio, with instructions that the Lyncestian was to be held under close arrest pending further investigations. Any designs Parmenio might have on that vacant cavalry command the king forestalled by giving it to one of his own oldest and most trusted friends, Erigyius of Mytilene.*

Meanwhile the Thracians had cleared a fair trail over Mt

---

*Just how precarious Alexander's communications were is shown by the fact that Amphoterus and his party had to make their way through the interior with local guides, and disguised in native costume to avoid being recognized (Arrian 1.25.9).

Climax. Alexander now sent the main body of the army toiling in column up the gorge, while he himself, accompanied by a small escort, made his way along the shore. This passage was only negotiable with a strong north wind blowing; at other times the sea came rolling in under the headland, where a narrow path wound its way among rocks and shingle to the beach on the farther side. For some while now there had been heavy southerly gales, which made this short cut impossible. However, Alexander decided to trust his luck. According to Callisthenes and others, the wind veered round to the north at the appropriate moment, so that the king and his party negotiated the passage without trouble.

Callisthenes, naturally enough, made the most of this in his official dispatches. The change of wind was attributed to divine intervention: the very sea had recognized Alexander's royal presence, and had withdrawn as an act of obeisance (*proskynesis*).[39] It is, in fact, possible that this miraculous wind-change did not occur at all, but was mere fictional propaganda. Alexander said nothing about it in his dispatches; but then it was not the sort of embellishment that would appeal to Antipater. Besides, if Strabo's version of the incident be the true one (which seems likely) it was a case for censorship rather than propaganda. According to him, Alexander 'set out before the waves had receded; and the result was that all day long his soldiers marched in water submerged to their navels'.[40]

Once past Mt Climax, the army emerged into the rich and beautiful Pamphylian plain – the modern Turkish Riviera – a well-watered crescent some sixty miles long by eighteen deep, in splendid isolation between the sea and a high enclosing rampart of mountains. This marked the eastward limit of Alexander's foray along the coast. From Side as far as Cilicia stretched a wild, rugged, uninhabited region, without harbours or adequate land-communications. No military intervention was needed here.[41] However, as Alexander advanced through this plain towards

Perga, his rearguard was attacked by a horde of Pisidian brigands. These marauders had established themselves on a strong rock-fortress in the foothills, whence they made regular incursions into the lowlands, terrorizing the farmers and robbing travellers. Their sudden descent caused havoc in Alexander's baggage-train. The Macedonians suffered heavy casualties; their assailants got away with numerous captives and pack-animals.

This time, however, the Pisidians had picked the wrong man to meddle with. Coldly furious, Alexander held up his advance while he laid siege to their rocky stronghold. For two days they held out against his assaults. Then, when it became clear that he would never give up until the rock was in his hands, the young men among them resorted to desperate measures. Ignoring their elders' advice to surrender, about six hundred of them burnt their families alive in their houses to prevent them being taken prisoner, and themselves slipped through Alexander's lines to the mountains under cover of darkness.[42]

The king had more than one reason for smoking out this robbers' nest. Now that he had secured the coast as far east as Pamphylia, his main concern was to strike inland and link up with Parmenio once more. He seems not yet to have learnt of the comparatively easy route north to Gordium, through Sagalassus and Celaenae; as a result he was still attempting to force his way north-west over the passes, to link up with the Cibyra highway. This rock-fortress – convincingly identified by Dame Freya Stark as Chandir – lay on his direct route thither. Nor, we may surmise, were the inhabitants of Phaselis or the Pamphylian littoral in any hurry to tell him about the shorter route. They saw this Macedonian army as a providential instrument for clearing out hostile mountain strongholds on their behalf; so far it had done so in the most obliging manner. If Alexander was set on thrusting up the Cibyra road, they would do even better. When this road left the coast it ran through a gorge overlooked by the powerful city of Termessus. To force this

defile, Alexander would have to deal with the Termessians –
something the coastal townships had notably failed to do
on their own account.

Before the king struck into the interior, however, he had
to complete his settlement of the coastal littoral. Perga
surrendered without fuss, and the Macedonians pushed on
towards Aspendus. Outside the city they were met by a
deputation, offering submission, but asking at the same time
to be spared the indignity of a garrison. Alexander – who
had been well briefed on Aspendus' resources, and was by
now running short of cavalry mounts as well as cash – agreed
not to garrison the city; but he exacted a steep price for the
privilege. The Aspendians were to turn over to him all the
horses they bred for Darius in their famous stud-farms, and,
on top of this, to 'contribute fifty talents towards the men's
pay'. Wealthy the Aspendians may have been, but this was
sheer extortion. The envoys, however, had no choice in the
matter. They accepted Alexander's terms, and returned
home. The king marched on to the important port of Side,
where he left a garrison. He then turned back north-west
through the mountains to Syllium, an isolated fortress
held by mercenaries. This looked a tough proposition, and
was off his direct line of march. Alexander therefore decided
to by-pass it.

This decision was partly caused by news from Aspendus.
The citizens, hearing his outrageous terms, had repudiated
the treaty made in their name. When Alexander's commissariat party arrived to collect horses and 'contributions',
they found the gates barred against them. Aspendus stood
on a hill overlooking the Eurymedon, with a walled suburb
down by the river itself. The citizens now evacuated this
lower quarter, shut themselves in the citadel, and hoped
against hope that the king would be too busy elsewhere to
come back and deal with them himself. Unfortunately for
them, he was not. He needed money and horses, and had
every intention of getting both. All too soon, the Aspendians
saw Alexander and his troops bivouacked in the empty

lower town. At this their nerve failed them, and they sent down a herald, asking permission to surrender on the terms previously agreed.

But Alexander had no intention of letting them off so lightly. The horses, he said, they were to supply as before. Their already exorbitant 'contribution', on the other hand, was now doubled, and in addition they had to pay an annual sum as tribute – not, be it noted, to the league, but to Macedonia. Aspendus was placed under direct satrapal control, a step which almost certainly included the imposition of a garrison. All leading citizens were to be surrendered as hostages. Lastly, the king ordered a public inquiry concerning land Aspendus was accused of filching from her neighbours: small doubt what the commission's findings would be.[43] The case of Aspendus exposes, with harsh clarity, Alexander's fundamental objectives in Asia Minor. So long as he received willing cooperation, the pretence of a Panhellenic crusade could be kept up. But any resistance, the least opposition to his will, met with instant and savage reprisals. *Sois mon frère ou je te tue*: Alexander's conduct has since become a grim cliché, an anti-revolutionary joke. But it was no joke for those who, like the Aspendians, happened to become its victims.

His business on the coast thus satisfactorily concluded, with fresh mounts for his cavalry and a few weeks' pay in hand, Alexander returned to Perga. From here he struck inland towards Termessus. His route lay through a narrow gorge, and the Termessians held the cliffs on either side of it – a well-nigh impregnable position. But Alexander, now as always, showed himself a shrewd judge of 'barbarian' psychology. He made no attempt to force the pass; instead, he ordered his men to pitch camp for the night. As he had anticipated, the Termessians, observing this, withdrew their main force to the town nearby, leaving only a small detachment guarding the defile. A quick commando raid soon dealt with these sentries. Alexander thereupon advanced through the gorge – only to find his way barred once more by the commanding citadel of Termessus itself, 3,000 feet above sea-level. Nothing would help here but a prolonged siege, the one thing he was at all costs anxious to avoid. At this moment, providentially, envoys reached him from Selga, a mountain town lying to the north of Aspendus. The Selgians were fine fighting men, and hostile to Termessus: they offered Alexander their friendship and support. They also told him – a piece of vital information which he had hitherto lacked – about the easier alternative route through central Anatolia. He promptly abandoned Termessus, and marched back, under Selgian guidance, striking north through Kirkgöz and Dösheme towards Lake Burdur.[44] The last real opposition he encountered in this region was at Sagalassus. Here he had to fight that most tricky of all engagements, an uphill attack against an entrenched position – and without cavalry support, since the ground was too steep and rough. But Macedonian training and discipline proved their worth here, and after a fierce struggle Sagalassus fell.

Alexander, having taken time to mop up a few minor hill forts, now pressed on over the plateau, through regions 'where waters flow naked through sandy landscapes, and villages are screened in poplars, and few tracks wind among stones'.[45] Skirting Lake Burdur, with its desolate salt-flats, he came in five days to Celaenae. This city lay at the headwaters of two rivers, the Maeander and the Marsyas. The latter had its source in a great limestone cavern, and streams came tumbling down through the rocks to the plain beyond. Cyrus had had a palace here, and a great park full of wild animals. To the Macedonians, weary after their long march, it must have been a welcome sight: lush and green, an oasis in the barren Anatolian wilderness.

But its position also made it of great strategical importance. Celaenae lay at the junction of the main roads crossing the plateau – south to Pamphylia, by the route Alexander had followed; west to the Hermus and Maeander valleys;

north to Gordium. The two latter itineraries formed a section of the Persian Royal Road: Xerxes had passed through Celaenae on his march to Sardis. Before Alexander moved on, Celaenae had to be made secure. Through this narrow 'corridor', with unsubdued tribes to the north and south, would run his only true lines of communication between the Middle East and Ionia.

The city possessed a high, strongly fortified acropolis, which Alexander knew better than to assault. On his approach, the inhabitants abandoned the lower town, and prepared to defend this citadel. The king sent a herald, threatening all manner of savage reprisals if they did not surrender. They thereupon took the herald on a conducted tour of the defences, and informed him that Alexander did not, apparently, appreciate what he was up against. The herald came back with the news that the fortress was impregnable, and its occupants ready to fight to the death. Alexander did nothing dramatic; he merely sealed the acropolis off from the outside world, and waited. Ten days sufficed to shake the defenders' confidence, mostly on account of inadequate provisions.

At this stage they made a proposition to Alexander. If no relief force arrived from Darius within the next two months, they would surrender. Alexander accepted this offer: time was precious, and he had little alternative. Nevertheless it was a dangerous gamble. He therefore left behind in Celaenae one of his very best generals, Antigonus of Elimiotis, known as 'One-Eyed', who afterwards became a monarch in his own right. He gave Antigonus 1,500 troops, all he could spare, to guard his lines of communication, and appointed him satrap of Central Phrygia (this despite the fact that Darius' nominee was still holding out on the acropolis). A messenger was dispatched west to Parmenio, confirming the rendezvous in Gordium. Then Alexander set out thither himself, marching north by the Royal Road.[46]

He and his men covered the 130-mile journey without further incident, reaching Gordium early in March 333.

The last stages of his journey followed the Sangarius River, looping northward past the tombs of long-dead Phrygian kings; and the great Assyrian gateway through which he and his Macedonians passed into Gordium itself had been old when Midas reigned. There was no opposition: the city surrendered of its own accord. Here in due course* he was joined by Parmenio's corps, together with the troops who had been sent home on leave for the winter. They brought him welcome reinforcements – 3,000 Macedonian infantrymen, 500 cavalry, 150 volunteers from Elis. But the general situation in Greece and the Aegean, as his returning officers now reported it, was clearly disastrous, far worse than anything he could have feared; and once again the man responsible was Alexander's most dangerous opponent, that resourceful and elusive mercenary commander, Memnon of Rhodes.

After his masterly but unavailing defence of Halicarnassus, Memnon had been confirmed by Darius as commander-in-chief over all Persian forces in Asia Minor. The Great King now authorized him – better late than never – to implement the strategy he had proposed before the Granicus: that of carrying the war over into Macedonia and Greece. The Persian (or, more accurately, Phoenician) fleet was already at his disposal; Darius furnished him, in addition, with funds substantial enough to raise a professional mercenary army. This Memnon duly did – which may partially account for the shortage of volunteers that Cleander encountered in the Peloponnese.

With a strong amphibious force at his disposal, Memnon systematically set about reducing the islands of the eastern Aegean: an essential first step in any campaign directed against the Greek mainland. Cos and Samos had already come over to him, and Chios soon followed suit. It is possible that he also won back Miletus and Priene; he badly needed

---

* In late April, according to Murison, *Historia* 21 (1972), 404, who bases his calculations on seasonal weather conditions.

a base on the Ionian coast. Certainly he did not face a violent or entrenched opposition. Alexander had scarcely endeared himself to the Greek cities on his march south: many of them must have regarded Memnon as a more genuine liberator, if only because he was himself a Greek. The rest probably saw nothing to choose between one occupying force and another. While the Rhodian general moved on north from Chios to Lesbos, his agents were busy in Greece itself, handing out the Great King's gold to prospective supporters, and promising them that Memnon would soon descend on Euboea, with a large army and a fleet of 300 vessels.

This was indeed an enticing prospect. In Athens, military preparations went ahead day and night: no less than 400 triremes were now in commission. Many other Greek states, Sparta included, were ready to rise in revolt the moment Memnon gave the word. Their enthusiasm knew no bounds when, after a fierce struggle, the vital port of Mytilene fell to him. On receipt of this news, nearly all the islands in the Cyclades sent missions offering their allegiance.[47] It looked very much as though the promised invasion of Euboea and the mainland would soon become reality.

Alexander was thus faced with a crucial decision. If he went on, he might well lose the Hellespont, perhaps even Macedonia itself: Greece stood on the very brink of general revolt. But if he turned back, the odds against his carrying the Persian crusade through to a successful conclusion would lengthen immeasurably. Quite apart from the psychological loss of face involved, it was unlikely that either Darius or Memnon would fail to exploit such a reprieve. While Memnon undid all Alexander's work in Asia Minor, the Great King would have leisure to build and train a really formidable defence force. Worse still, Macedonia remained perilously near bankruptcy, and so far very little of Darius' fabled wealth had found its way into Alexander's hands. It was now, while the young king was still debating this problem, that the famous episode of the Gordian Knot took place. Like many men faced with a seemingly impossible choice, Alexander was ready to stake everything on a divine portent: now, if ever, was the moment for the voice from heaven.

In Gordium, by the temple of Zeus Basileus, he found what he sought. This was an ancient waggon – supposedly dedicated by Gordius' son Midas when he became King of Phrygia – which still stood, a much-revered relic, on the acropolis. It had one very odd feature: its yoke was fastened to the pole with numerous thongs of cornel-bark, in a complex multiple knot of the kind known by sailors as a Turk's-head. An ancient oracle had foretold that anyone who contrived to loose this knot would become lord of all Asia.* This was a challenge which Alexander found irresistible. Indeed, to leave Gordium *without* attempting the Gordian Knot was out of the question. Hostile propaganda would not be slow to suggest that he had doubts about the eventual outcome of his crusade.

So when he and his attendants made their way up to the acropolis, a large crowd of Phrygians and Macedonians followed him, impelled by something more than mere

---

*The two legends concerning the original dedication of the waggon are of interest in this connection. Both were handed down by the Phrygians themselves. The first ran as follows. Long ago, during a period of civil strife, it had been foretold that a man in a waggon would come to end the Phrygians' quarrels, and reign over them. Midas, a poor husbandman, drove up in his ox-cart while the assembly was discussing the oracle, and thus became king. According to the second account, the Phrygians had originally dwelt on the marches of Macedonia – indeed, in the Gardens of Midas (see above, p. 55), which were named after their king. Afterwards they migrated to Asia Minor, and settled in the area round Gordium. This hints at a successful conquest of the original inhabitants, a story Alexander would undoubtedly have heard from Aristotle during his schooldays at Mieza. When Midas dedicated his waggon to Zeus, it was in gratitude for having been granted rule over Phrygia (and presumably symbolized an end of wandering nomadism for him and his people).

casual curiosity. The atmosphere was taut and expectant; many of the king's courtiers were alarmed by his rash self-assurance, and, on the face of it, with good reason. One characteristic of a Turk's-head knot is that it leaves no loose ends visible. For a long while Alexander struggled with this labyrinthine tangle, but to little effect. At last he gave up, 'at a loss how to proceed'. A failure would have been the worst possible propaganda: something drastic had to be done. Aristobulus says that Alexander drew out the dowel-peg which ran through pole and yoke, thus releasing the thongs. This sounds like *ex post facto* rationalization. According to our other sources (far more in character psychologically) Alexander, exclaiming 'What difference does it make *how* I loose it?'* drew his sword and slashed through the tangle at a single stroke, thus revealing the ends carefully tucked away inside.

That night there came thunder and lightning, which Alexander and the seers took to mean that Zeus approved the king's action (it could, of course, equally well have signified divine wrath).[48] In any case, Alexander's mind was now made up. He would continue his campaign, whatever the cost. Amphoterus was appointed admiral of the squadrons guarding the Hellespont, while Hegelochus took command of the land-forces based on Abydos. Alexander gave them 500 talents to raise a fresh fleet from the Greek allies (a singularly thankless task) and sent 600 more to Antipater for garrison pay and home defence. Such makeshift arrangements hint all too clearly at his expanding ambitions. He was now prepared, if need be, to sacrifice Macedonia altogether in pursuit of the greater goal. He had never taken the office of captain-general very seriously, except as a temporary convenience, and it paled into in-

---

*It could be argued – no doubt this was the line Alexander took – that the wording of the oracle was ambiguous, since *luein* in Greek can mean not only 'untie', 'unfasten', but also 'sunder', 'break up', 'resolve'. In any case his use of a sword was symbolically appropriate, since if he was to become lord of Asia, it would be by force of arms.

significance beside the prospect of becoming lord of Asia. At the moment his homeland must have seemed very small and far away.

The latest intelligence reports confirmed that Darius was still in Susa, but had begun to assemble a large army. Alexander could not afford to waste time. Almost immediately after the cutting of the Gordian Knot, he and his troops took to the road again (May 333). Before they left, a singularly ill-timed embassy arrived from Athens, begging the king to release those Athenian prisoners captured at the Granicus, and now held in Macedonia. The request was refused. When circumstances proved more favourable, Alexander told the envoys, with grim ambiguity, they might approach him again (see below, p. 279).[49]

From Gordium he marched north-east to Ancyra (Ankara), on the borders of Cappadocia and Paphlagonia. The Paphlagonians sent him an embassy, offering submission and asking him, in return, not to invade their country. Since the last thing Alexander wanted at this point was a mountain campaign in the north, he readily agreed. He also exempted them from tribute (which they had not paid the Persians anyway); as a face-saving gesture, he informed them that they were now responsible to Calas, the new satrap of Phrygia, a formality which neither side can have taken very seriously. He also received the 'surrender' of all Cappadocia west of the River Halys, and 'a good deal of the far side'. Here he did not even impose a Macedonian administration, but appointed a local baron, Sabictas, to govern the area on his behalf – the first attested instance of a practice on which he was afterwards to rely more and more. In this case (as so often) it did not work out well. The natives were getting wise to Alexander's methods: they met him with bland promises of cooperation, and then raised hell the moment he had moved on. A year later (see below, p. 264) Antigonus the One-Eyed was obliged to fight at least three major battles in the area to keep Alexander's lines of communication open.

While he was still in Ancyra, the king received one more than welcome piece of news: shortly after the siege of Miletus, Memnon had fallen sick and died. He was the only first-class general Darius possessed in Asia Minor, and his disappearance from the scene was an extraordinary piece of luck for Alexander. The threatened invasion of Greece had depended entirely on the Rhodian's skill and initiative. With his death the whole project might well collapse overnight. At the same time (mid July) reports came in that Darius had at last moved from Susa to Babylon, and was busy preparing the Imperial Army for active service. By now, however, Alexander had a fairly shrewd idea of the leisurely way in which the Great King went about such matters, and saw no reason to alter his original strategy.[50] From Ancyra he would march south through the Cilician Gates to Tarsus, and thence down the coast by way of Tyre and Sidon to Egypt. Only when all the main ports of the Eastern Mediterranean were in his hands, and the Phoenician fleet thus eliminated as an active threat, did he intend to tackle Darius.

After Memnon's death the command of his expeditionary force passed to two Persian noblemen: his nephew by marriage, Pharnabazus, and Autophradates. They began by garrisoning Mytilene with 2,000 mercenaries, and imposing a heavy fine on the citizens to pay for their maintenance. Then the two new commanders separated. While Autophradates went on with the campaign among the Aegean islands, Pharnabazus took a strong mercenary force by sea to Lycia, with the clear aim of winning back Alexander's conquests along the coast. But this very promising strategy was soon cut short by Darius, who knew as well as Alexander that Memnon's invasion plans had appreciably less chance of success without Memnon himself to direct operations. He therefore summoned a meeting of his privy council and put the problem before them. Should he still attempt to carry the war into Europe? Or would it be better to force a direct trial of strength with the Macedonian army?

The general reaction among his Persian councillors was that Darius should bring Alexander to battle. They also emphasized that it would boost the troops' morale if he led them in person. This view was opposed, with more force than tact, by the Athenian captain Charidemus (see above, p. 150). He pointed out, quite rightly, that it would be lunacy for Darius to stake his throne on such a gamble. The Great King should remain at Susa, in charge of the war effort as a whole, while a professional general dealt with Alexander. When asked how many men would be necessary for this operation, Charidemus put the figure at 100,000 – provided one-third of them were Greek mercenaries. He also hinted, in pretty broad terms, that he was more than ready to assume supreme command himself. It is all very like Memnon before the Granicus; no Greek seems to have been capable of stifling his contempt for the Persian soldier's fighting abilities, even to carry a point in conference.

Darius' councillors, as might have been predicted, reacted sharply to this slur. Charidemus, they hinted, only wanted the command so that he could the more easily betray them to the Macedonians. At this point Charidemus, fatally for himself, lost his temper: as a mercenary he was more vulnerable than most to such allegations. The meeting degenerated into a shouting match. Some of his remarks about Iranian cowardice and incompetence so incensed Darius (who could speak Greek fluently) that he 'seized him by the girdle according to the custom of the Persians' and ordered his instant execution. As he was dragged away, Charidemus cried out that Darius would pay for this unjust punishment with the loss of his throne and kingdom.

Once Darius' temper had cooled, he bitterly regretted having killed his best surviving general, and ordered Charidemus to be given special funeral rites. But this hardly solved the problem of Memnon's replacement. In the end he was forced to admit that no suitable candidate could be found. As a result, the European invasion was now officially abandoned in favour of a direct confrontation with Alexander: this decision arguably changed the entire outcome of the war. Pharnabazus found himself officially confirmed as Memnon's successor; but the empty nature of this honour was made plain by the simultaneous recall of all his mercenaries, whom Darius badly needed to stiffen the Persian infantry line. Pharnabazus, making the best of a bad job, rejoined Autophradates with his reduced forces, and together they continued their naval operations. While ten triremes under Datames were detached to raid the Cyclades, the remainder sailed north and captured Tenedos. The Macedonians had still failed to raise an adequate fleet, and there was little opposition. One of Antipater's naval patrols did manage to destroy Datames' squadron off Siphnos; but this minor success could not conceal the fact that the Persians now virtually controlled the entire Aegean.[51]

While Darius awaited his reinforcements in Babylon, Alexander was thrusting south across the rocky, volcanic uplands of Cappadocia, under a burning August sun. For some seventy-five miles, water and provisions were virtually unobtainable: as on other similar occasions, over comparable distances, Alexander seems to have force-marched his men on iron rations and the bare minimum of water. Between them and the coastal plain stretched the great rampart of the Taurus mountains. The only pass was a deep, twisting canyon, overshadowed by high crags. At one point some long-dead king had set his engineers to hack a narrow cut through from gorge to gorge, thus saving a vast detour. This grim defile was known as the Cilician Gates. Until a modern highway was blasted through it, there was barely room for two laden camels to pass abreast. A single regiment, with archers to provide enfilading fire, could hold off an army by the simple expedient of rolling rocks down on them. The defile was also crossed at several points by gulleys and mountain water-courses.

Alexander, understandably, anticipated trouble at the Gates; but there was no other feasible route. He was saved a good deal of trouble – unintentionally – by Arsames, the Persian governor of Cilicia. Arsames had been one of the commanders at the Granicus, and was also present when Memnon proposed his scorched-earth policy. The disaster which followed its rejection had made a deep impression on him. Arsames is a striking instance of that too-common phenomenon, the second-rate commander who gets one idea into his head, and keeps it there. Unfortunately, what would have been admirable strategy at the Granicus was sheer disaster in Cilicia.

The Gates provided him with a defence-line of unparalleled strength. If he had brought up all his troops, and staked everything on holding the pass, Alexander would have had no option but to retreat. Instead, bent on imitating Memnon's strategy and avoiding a head-on collision, Arsames left only a small force at the Gates, and devoted much time and energy to laying waste the Cilician Plain in their rear. This can hardly have inspired his advance guard to make a heroic last stand, in the manner of Leonidas at Thermopylae. Indeed, they very soon began to suspect that Arsames had deliberately abandoned them; so when Alexander launched a night-attack on their positions, they took to their heels and ran for it. At dawn, the Thracians went ahead to flush any possible ambushes, while archers climbed the ridge to give them covering fire. Then the entire Macedonian army advanced through the Gates, four abreast, and down into the plain. Alexander himself said afterwards that he never had a more amazing piece of luck in his entire career.

He now heard reports that Arsames was evacuating Tarsus. In accordance with his chosen policy, the Persian intended to loot the city of its treasure, and then burn it down. Alexander at once sent Parmenio on ahead with the cavalry and the light-armed troops. Arsames, learning of his approach, took off in some haste, leaving both city and treasure intact. Darius was on the march from Babylon, and the satrap now made his way eastward to join him.[52]

Alexander entered Tarsus on 3 September 333, sweating, hot and exhausted after a rapid forced march from the foothills of the Taurus. In late summer the Cilician Plain, ringed on three sides by mountains, becomes a torrid oven. Through the city itself ran the River Cydnus (Tersus-Tchai), clear, fast-flowing, and ice-cold with melted mountain snows. When he reached its banks, the young king dismounted, stripped off his clothes, and plunged in. Almost immediately he suffered an attack of cramp so severe that those watching took it for some sort of convulsion. His aides rushed into the water and pulled him out half-conscious, ashen-white and chilled to the bone. Before he took his bathe he seems to have been suffering from some kind of bronchial infection, which now quickly turned into acute pneumonia.

For days he lay helpless, with a raging fever. His physicians were so pessimistic about his chances of recovery that they refused to treat him, in case they should be accused of negligence – or, worse, of murder. (They had some reason for their alarm: the Great King was now proclaiming publicly that he would give a 1,000-talent reward to any man who slew Alexander.) One doctor only, Philip of Acarnania, offered to treat him. This was Alexander's confidential physician, whom he had known since childhood. There were certain quick-acting drugs, Philip told him, but they involved an element of risk. The king, his mind running feverishly on Darius' advance, raised no objection. He knew enough about pharmacology himself to realize that Philip's medicine might just achieve the desired result. Then, after the dose had been made up, a note was brought to Alexander from Parmenio – again, as in the case of Alexander of Lyncestis, that odd and ambivalent solicitude – warning him that Philip had been bribed by the Great King: the purge he administered would be strong poison.

Alexander handed this letter to Philip, picked up his

medicine, and drank it while Philip was still reading. The physician, with considerable *sang-froid*, merely remarked that if Alexander followed his advice he would make a good recovery. But it was touch and go. The purge had an immediate and violent effect: the king's voice failed, he began to have great difficulty breathing, and presently lapsed into a semi-coma. Philip massaged him, and applied a series of hot fomentations. Alexander's tough constitution pulled him through the crisis, and the drug did the rest. Presently his fever dropped, and after three days he had sufficiently recovered to show himself to his anxious troops. One cannot help wondering how matters would have turned out – both for him and for Parmenio – had he heeded the old marshal's warning.[53]

In the event, Parmenio was kept fully occupied during the king's convalescence. Alexander sent him, with the allied infantry, the Greek mercenaries, and the Thracian and Thessalian horse, to report on Darius' movements and to block the passes. Parmenio swept round the Gulf of Alexandretta, and captured the little harbour-town of Issus, which he made his advance base. There were two passes, and two only, by which Darius could bring his army into Cilicia. Parmenio proceeded to reconnoitre them both. First he struck south along the coast, with the mountains on his left flank. He crossed two rivers, the Deli and the Payas, and occupied a narrow defile known today as the Pillar of Jonah. About fifteen miles farther on lay the Syrian Gates (Beilan pass), through which a road ran by way of the Orontes Valley to Thapsacus on the Euphrates. When he reached the Gates, Parmenio learnt that Darius had crossed the Euphrates by means of a pontoon bridge, and was now advancing towards the coast. On receipt of this news, he left a scouting party to watch the Syrian Gates, stationed his main holding force at the Pillar of Jonah, and then hurried back north to secure the Great King's other possible entry-point. This was the Bahçe pass – known in antiquity as the Amanic Gates – which traverses the mountain ranges

due east of Tarsus, and now carries the railway line between
Konia and Aleppo.* Here, as at the Syrian Gates, he
mopped up a few enemy outposts and established his own:
probably in Castabala, close by the entrance to the pass.

Alexander, realizing from Parmenio's reports that the
situation was not as urgent as he had feared, spent another
week or two convalescing in Tarsus. Even so, he was far
from idle. For the first time, he took over a major mint,
and used it to strike his own coins – a highly significant
innovation. Until he crossed the Taurus, he could still
claim to be 'liberating the Greeks'. But from Cilicia onwards he came as a conqueror. If he wanted Syrians or
Phoenicians to acknowledge his overlordship, he had to
build up an authority similar to that wielded by the Great
King himself. The imposition of a new coinage was an
obvious step in this process.[54] Old issues were called in,
melted down, and restruck with Alexander's name and
type: what began at Tarsus was very soon copied by mints
on Cyprus and all down the Phoenician coast. Some old-
type coins continued to exist alongside the new ones; but
Alexander undoubtedly achieved his main object – to get
himself 'recognized as the master in all parts of his new
territory'. He also had a convenient centre from which to
pay the army.

It was now, too, that Harpalus, his treasurer and quarter-
master general, supposedly defected – though the evidence[55]
is ambiguous, and Harpalus may, in fact, have been on a
secret mission to watch the political situation in Greece,
with defection as his cover-story. All we are told is that he
was 'persuaded' to leave Alexander by a 'bad man',
Tauriscus. The two men travelled to Greece together, but
then parted company, Harpalus remaining in the Megarid,
while Tauriscus went on to southern Italy, where he joined

---

*An alternative candidate is the slightly more southerly Hasanbeyli
Pass, which now carries the main highway: Murison, op. cit., p.
408. From here the smaller pass of Kaleköy led into the plain of Issus.

an expedition led by Alexander of Epirus,* and was subsequently killed. The whole affair remains shrouded in mystery and propaganda. Whatever Harpalus was up to in Greece did not prevent his subsequent reinstatement (see below, p. 281): he is by far the most enigmatic of Alexander's entourage, and we have by no means heard the last of him.

The news from Parmenio meant that there was time to make at least a perfunctory show of 'subjugating' Cilicia. Alexander first visited Anchialus, a day's march west of Tarsus. Here he was shown what purported to be the tomb of Sardanapalus (Assurbanipal), with a relief of the king in the act of snapping his fingers. Underneath was an inscription which (or so the guides told him) read 'Sardanapalus . . . built Tarsus and Anchialus in one day. Eat, drink, copulate! The rest is not worth *that*.' This story the king sent back to Aristotle, who said of it that the epitaph might just as well have been written on the tomb of a bull.[56] From Anchialus Alexander advanced to nearby Soli, where the inhabitants proved a good deal less cooperative. As a result they were forced to accept a garrison, and found themselves fined 200 talents for their 'pro-Persian attitude'. The king had to spend a week dealing with Cilician guerrilla forces in the nearby hills, which is unlikely to have improved his temper.[57] But when he got back to Soli he found excellent news awaiting him. Ptolemy, Asander, and Queen Ada (see above, pp. 193 ff.) had at last defeated Orontobates at Halicarnassus, Cos had been recaptured, and the entire Carian coast was now in Macedonian hands.

* Alexander had been invited to Italy by Tarentum; he crossed over with fifteen ships and numerous horse-transports, leaving his wife Cleopatra (Alexander the Great's sister) as regent. After campaigning successfully in Italy until 331 (there is evidence that his venture had his brother-in-law's approval, if not his active backing), he was finally killed in battle. At one point he is said to have remarked that while he encountered men in Italy, Alexander in Asia had fought against women. See n. 55 to this chapter, below, p. 538.

Alexander was more concerned over events in the West than he liked to admit, and his relief found expression, as so often, in an outburst of official festivities. (His enthusiasm might have been a little dampened had he known that within a month or two Miletus, Halicarnassus and most of the islands would be Persian-occupied once more.) There were lavish sacrifices to Asclepius, the god of healing, in gratitude for the king's recovery. There were public games, and a relay race, and a torchlight tattoo, and literary competitions. These celebrations concluded, Alexander made his way back from Soli to Tarsus. Philotas and the cavalry were sent ahead as far as the Pyramus River, on the west side of the Gulf of Alexandretta. The king himself followed with the Royal Squadron and the infantry. He seems to have been much concerned to win support from the Cilician towns en route, but this did not noticeably delay his advance.

At Castabala Parmenio met him with the latest news. Darius had pitched camp at Sochi, somewhere east of the Syrian Gates (Beilan pass) in the open plain. It looked as though he meant to stay there: the terrain was admirable for large-scale cavalry manoeuvres. His presence had much impressed the local cities, which were all turning pro-Persian once more. Parmenio urged Alexander to marshal his forces at Issus, and wait for Darius there. In so narrow a space, between the mountains and the sea, there was less danger of the Macedonians being outflanked. Curtius, who tells this story, does not mention one other obvious argument, which must surely have been uppermost in Parmenio's mind: from Issus Alexander could anticipate Darius *whichever pass he chose to come through*. Nevertheless, Alexander seems to have convinced himself that if Darius moved at all, it would be by way of the Syrian Gates. Perhaps the Persians had deliberately 'leaked' false information, which Alexander's intelligence section picked up and treated as genuine.

At all events, the king did not wait at Issus. He left his sick and wounded there – which shows that he believed the place safe from attack – and force-marched the rest of the army south through the Pillar of Jonah to Myriandrus. Here he pitched camp, opposite the pass, and waited for an enemy who never came.[58] This, clearly, was just the move that Darius had been hoping he would make. The Great King had already rendered his own task-force lighter and more mobile by sending the baggage-train, all non-combatants,

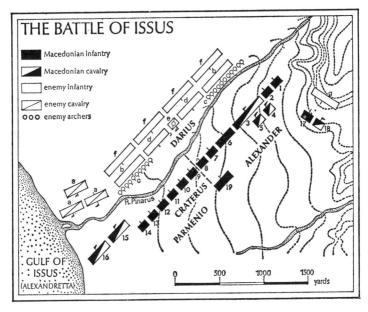

THE BATTLE OF ISSUS

- Macedonian infantry
- Macedonian cavalry
- enemy infantry
- enemy cavalry
- ooo enemy archers

GULF OF ISSUS (ALEXANDRETTA)

R. Pinarus

DARIUS
ALEXANDER
CRATERUS
PARMENIO

0 500 1000 1500
yards

Macedonians
1 Agrianians
2 Macedonian Archers
3 Companion Cavalry
4 Paeonian Light Horse
5 Lancers
6 Hypaspists
7 Phalanx Coenus
8 Phalanx Perdiccas
9 Phalanx Craterus
10 Phalanx Meleager
11 Phalanx Ptolemy
12 Phalanx Amyntas
13 Cretan Archers
14 Thracian Javelin-men
15 Thessalian Cavalry
16 Allied Greek Cavalry
17 Group of Agrianians
18 Squadron of Light Horse
19 Greek Mercenaries

Persians
a Cavalry under Nabarzanes
b Cardaces
c Archers
d Greek Mercenaries
e Darius and Bodyguard
f Asiatic Levies
g Detachment

and the bulk of his treasure under guard to Damascus. While Alexander was held up at Myriandrus by a violent thunderstorm (a very lame excuse, this: the Macedonian army afterwards marched mile after mile through Indian monsoon rains) Darius set out north on a lightning dash for the Amanic Gates.*

Having got through the pass unobserved and unopposed, Darius swooped down from Castabala on Issus, where he captured most of Alexander's hospital-cases. Their hands were cut off and seared with pitch; they were then taken on a tour of the Persian units, turned loose, and told to report what they had seen to Alexander (Xerxes had done much the same with a group of Greek spies caught in his camp during the Persian Wars). From Issus the Great King advanced as far as the Pinarus River – probably the Payas rather than the Deli[59] – and took up a defensive position on its northern bank. He now lay in Alexander's rear, squarely across his lines of communication, and could thus force him to fight a reversed-front engagement.

Alexander had been caught in an almost perfect trap. South of him lay the potentially hostile cities of Phoenicia. If he retreated through the Syrian Gates, and struck north along the route Darius had taken, the Great King would have ample warning of his approach, and could close the Bahçe Pass against him. There was nothing for it but to fight, and in highly unfavourable circumstances. For the

* His Greek mercenaries, led by the renegade Macedonian, Amyntas, are said to have urged him to stay and fight it out in the plain, where he would have the advantage of numbers. This is a most improbable story. Darius' vast horde (600,000 according to some sources) was pure fiction, invented by Macedonian propagandists. The army he commanded at Issus was no bigger than Alexander's, and may, indeed, have not been as large, since he had been in too much of a hurry to wait for contingents from the more remote provinces. In any case, no professional soldier would have had anything but praise for the Great King's strategy. cf. Arrian 2.7.1; QC 3.8.11–13; Plut. *Alex.* 20.1–3. Murison (op. cit., pp. 400–403) appreciates Darius' underrated talents as a strategist, though his version of events differs in several essential respects from that given here.

Persians, a drawn battle would be as good as a victory. As Tarn says, they 'only had to hold the line, and Alexander's career was ended'. Nor did he have much choice of tactics: it was a frontal assault or nothing. Darius' army had to be squarely defeated, and the sooner the better. His own Macedonians had marched over seventy miles in two days, and at the end of this marathon effort torrential rains had washed them out of their tents. They were sodden, exhausted, and resentful. Yet somehow Alexander's outrageous optimism – well conveyed in the rousing address he now gave them – proved infectious. When he finished his speech with a reference to Xenophon and the Ten Thousand, they cheered wildly.

It was now after midday, and Alexander (who knew, long before Napoleon, that an army marches on its stomach) saw to it that his troops had a good hot meal. He then sent on a small force of cavalry and mounted archers to reconnoitre. When darkness fell, he marched his whole army as far as the Jonah pass, and by midnight had established himself in a commanding position on the heights overlooking it, from where he could see Darius' camp-fires twinkling far and wide across the plain. While his troops snatched a few hours' rest, Alexander himself went up the mountain and made sacrifice by torchlight to the tutelary deities of the region. Next morning, if ever, he was going to need their aid. Before leaving Myriandrus he had also driven a four-horse chariot into the sea as an offering to Poseidon – perhaps in hope of averting any untimely intervention by Darius' Phoenician fleet.[60]

At dawn the Macedonian army began its descent towards Issus. It took Alexander three miles to get clear of the Jonah pass, after which he had to march another nine before reaching the Pinarus River. The line of the mountains was irregular, with numerous outlying spurs and ridges. The plain, nevertheless, slowly widened as he went on, like a very narrow isosceles triangle. By the time the Macedonians had reached a point about 1,000 yards from the river, there was a front of over three miles in which to manoeuvre. Even if the phalanx was driven back into the apex of the wedge, at least it would not be outflanked. Alexander began this march in column of route; then, as the ground opened out before him, he deployed battalion after battalion of the infantry into line, keeping his left flank close by the shore (Parmenio had strict instructions never to lose contact with the sea) and pushing his right up into the foothills.

When all the line-regiments had been brought up, Alexander began to feed in the cavalry squadrons. Most of these, Thessalians included – Parmenio, for the moment, had to make do with the Greek allies – he massed on the right wing, this being where he originally assumed that Darius would deliver his main attack. Scouts had reported enemy troop concentrations up in the hills; these Alexander took to be part of a general encircling movement directed at his right flank and rear. But it was very hard to be certain just what Darius had in mind, since he had cleverly thrown a large screen of cavalry and light-armed troops forward across the river to mask his dispositions.

As usual, the Persians' great weakness lay in their infantry. Darius' Asiatic levies were worse than useless against the Macedonian phalanx; he sensibly lumped them together in the rear as reserves and camp-guards. To make up his front line (see plan, p. 225) was something of a problem. In the very centre he placed his Royal Bodyguard, a crack Iranian corps 2,000 strong, whose spear-butts were decorated with golden quinces. He himself, as tradition required, was stationed immediately behind them, in his great ornamental chariot. Flanking the Bodyguard on either side were Darius' indispensable Greek mercenaries: 30,000 of them, according to our sources, though this figure is generally regarded as an exaggeration. Finally, on the wings, came two divisions of light-armed Persian infantry, the so-called 'Cardaces': Iranian youths who were undergoing, or had just completed, their military training.* As a further defence, he had built palisades of sharpened stakes at any point where the river-bank was dangerously low (they must have been very hard to anchor in that damp, shifting gravel).

By the time Darius had moved all his infantry units into battle formation it was mid afternoon, and the Macedonians were getting uncomfortably close. Not that Alexander showed any impatience. He led his troops forward at a very leisurely pace, with frequent halts to check their dressing and observe enemy movements. Darius' intentions were still far from clear. Then, abruptly, the Persian cavalry squadrons that had been acting as a screen were signalled back across the river, and dispatched to their final battle-stations. At this point Darius' intentions became very clear indeed, and Alexander had to carry out a quick last-minute reorganization of his own line, since instead of massing the Iranian cavalry opposite Alexander's right, where it had been expected, the Great King was moving all his best squadrons down to the seashore, against Parmenio.

Alexander at once sent the Thessalians back across to his left, as reinforcements, ordering them to ride behind the phalanx so that their movements would remain unobserved. Reports now came in that the Persian forces up on the ridge had occupied a projecting spur of the mountain, and were actually *behind* the Macedonian right wing. Alexander sent a mixed force of light-armed troops to deal with them,

---

* To employ the Cardaces as front-line troops was a new experiment – and one which the Great King never repeated. How far he trusted their military prowess, even before the battle, we can infer from the strong force of archers he posted in front of them on either flank. See Tarn, vol. II, pp. 180–82. The reported numbers of Darius' mercenaries (30,000), and, *a fortiori*, of the Cardaces (60,000), drew critical comment from Polybius (12.18), who argued that such masses of men could not be contained in the coastal strip. This objection has appealed to many modern scholars, but it ignores the factor of phalanx–depth. How many ranks were these units disposed in? The question remains open.

though he himself (for whatever reason) was still far more concerned by the possibility of a frontal outflanking movement. He pushed forward his cavalry patrols, and brought across two squadrons from the centre to strengthen his right wing. The Persians in the hills, however, made no attempt to fight, and a quick commando assault soon routed them. Alexander left 300 cavalry to watch their movements, but recalled the archers and Agrianians as extra protection for his flank.

So the Macedonian army, now deployed on a three-mile front, continued its steady advance. Alexander rode up and down the line, checking his more impetuous troops with a quick, characteristic gesture of the hand, anxious that they should not be out of breath when they joined battle. Almost within bowshot, he halted once again, in the hope that the Persians might charge. They did not. There was some grumbling among Alexander's staff officers about the Great King's lack of spirit. In fact, of course, Darius had a first-class defensive position, and – very reasonably – was not in the least inclined to abandon it. At this point Alexander saw that any further delay would be useless. It was already late afternoon. After a final inspection he led on once more, slowly at first, in close formation, until they came within range of the Persian archers. These now loosed off a tremendous volley, 'such a shower of missiles that they collided with one another in the air'. Then a trumpet rang out, and Alexander, at the head of the Companions, charged across the river, scattering Darius' archers and driving them back among the light-armed Persian infantry. It was a magnificently successful assault: the battle on the right wing was won in the first few moments.

In the centre, things did not go nearly so well. Here the phalanx had great difficulty in getting across the river at all. They found themselves confronted by a steep bank, some five feet high in places, and all overgrown with brambles – not to mention the Persian stake-palisades. Macedonian infantrymen were soon locked in a bloody hand-to-hand struggle with equally tough, equally professional Greek mercenaries, who on this occasion were fighting for something more than their pay. For a while neither side could advance more than a few feet. Then came the inevitable aftermath of Alexander's headlong charge: a dangerous gap opened up on the right flank of the phalanx. This was too good a chance to miss. A spearhead of mercenaries drove a deep wedge into the Macedonian line: during the desperate fighting that followed, Ptolemy, son of Seleucus, and some 120 Macedonian officers lost their lives.

Meanwhile Alexander, having rolled up the Persian left wing, now swung his wedge of cavalry inward against the rear files of the mercenaries and the Royal Bodyguard. If the Persians at the Granicus had aimed at killing Alexander, Alexander now, with even more certainty, strained every nerve to kill or capture Darius. The Great King offered the best – perhaps the only – focal point for any future resistance involving all the provinces of the empire. His loss would cripple the Persian cause. Besides, the vast majority of his subjects cared little who ruled them so long as their own local interests were left intact.[61] The man who toppled Darius should have little trouble in winning general recognition as his successor.

The moment he located the Great King's chariot, Alexander charged straight for it, and every Macedonian warrior that day shared his ambition. The defence was equally heroic: Darius certainly knew how to command loyalty among the Iranian barons. Oxathres, his brother, leading the Royal Household Cavalry, fought desperately to protect him. Dying men and horses lay piled in wild confusion. Alexander received a wound in the thigh – from Darius himself, or so it was claimed. If this is true, it shows how close he came to attaining his objective.* The horses

---

* However, in his dispatch to Antipater written after the battle (Plut. *Alex.* 20.5, *Moral.* 341C) Alexander merely noted: 'I myself happened to be wounded in the thigh by a dagger. But nothing untoward resulted from the blow ...'

of Darius' chariot, covered with wounds and terrified by the corpses lying all about them, plunged and reared, half berserk. For a moment there was a real danger that they might carry the Great King headlong through Alexander's lines. Darius, abandoning royal protocol in this emergency, grabbed the reins with his own hands. A second, lighter chariot was somehow found and brought up. Darius, seeing himself in imminent danger of capture, scrambled into it and fled the field.

At the very moment of his departure, Alexander received an urgent appeal from the phalanx, still bogged down beneath the river-bank, and now in desperate straits. Nor were things much better on the left wing, where Parmenio's Thessalians had been having a hard time of it against the Persian heavy cavalry under Nabarzanes, and were still barely holding their own. With both centre and left thus seriously threatened, Alexander had no option but to postpone his pursuit of the Great King. He must have been in a fury of frustration; nevertheless he acted promptly and with crushing effectiveness. He swung his whole right wing round in a wedge against the mercenaries' flank, and drove them out of the river with heavy casualties. When Nabarzanes' cavalrymen saw their own centre being cut to pieces, and heard of the Great King's flight, they wheeled their horses about and followed him. The retreat soon became a rout.

Unutterable chaos ensued. Nabarzanes' men were encumbered by their heavy scale-armour, and the Thessalians harried them relentlessly. The Persian foot-levies, who had played no serious part in the battle, were already flying for their lives towards the safety of the mountains. Many were ridden down by their own cavalry, and the horsemen themselves, hard-pressed from the rear, and jostling together as they approached the defiles, offered an easy target to Alexander's archers. Ptolemy reported afterwards that he and his squadron rode across one deep water-course over the piled-up bodies of the dead.

As soon as Alexander saw that the phalanx and the Thessalians were out of danger, he and his Companions set off on a headlong chase after Darius. But everything was against them. It was now between five and six o'clock of a November evening, and already dusk had begun to fall. The Great King had over half a mile's start on them. Worse, the route he had taken – probably the mountain track to Dörtyol and Hassa – was now jammed with the disorganized remnants of the Persian Imperial Army.[62] Despite these hazards, the pursuers kept going for some twenty-five miles. Only when darkness had fallen did Alexander give up and turn back. Despite everything, he did not reach camp empty-handed. Darius had very soon abandoned his chariot, and fled over the mountains on horseback, stripping off his royal mantle and all other insignia by which he might be recognized. These, together with his shield and bow, Alexander found and kept as battle-trophies.

Meanwhile the Macedonians had overrun Darius' base-camp, and found it a looters' paradise. Every tent was chock-a-block with vessels of gold and silver, with jewelled swords and inlaid furniture and priceless tapestries. Even though the main baggage-train and treasure had been sent to Damascus, the victors still collected no less than 3,000 talents in gold, a fantastic haul. The ladies of the Persian court – who, according to custom, had accompanied Darius on his campaign – were stripped of their valuables and severely manhandled by Alexander's troops. Only the Great King's pavilion, together with his immediate family, were kept untouched, under strict guard. These, by right of conquest, belonged to Alexander himself.

Alexander got back to camp about midnight, dusty and exhausted after his breakneck ride. When he had bathed (in the Great King's tub) and changed (into one of the Great King's robes, which must have been a great deal too large for him) he entered Darius' huge pavilion, and found it ablaze with torches. On the tables the royal gold plate had been set out, and a celebratory banquet was in preparation. As he stretched himself out on a luxurious couch, Alexander turned to his dining-companions and said, with that ambiguous irony which marks so many of his recorded utterances: 'So this, it would seem, is to be a king.'

Just as he was settling down to dinner there came the sound of wailing and lamentation from a nearby tent. Alexander dispatched an attendant to find out what all the uproar was about. It appeared that one of the Persian court eunuchs, having seen the Great King's chariot and royal insignia, had jumped to the conclusion that he was dead; and now Darius' mother, wife and children were mourning for him. Alexander hastened to clear up this unfortunate misunderstanding. His first thought was to employ Mithrines on this errand, he being a Persian. It was, however, pointed out to him that the sight of a traitor (Mithrines had surrendered Sardis [see above, p. 184] and was now collaborating with the Macedonians) might upset the ladies still further. He therefore sent Leonnatus, a Gentleman of the Bodyguard who was also his close personal friend.

As Leonnatus and his guards appeared at the entrance of the queen mother's tent, her attendants ran inside screaming. All the captive women, they at once assumed, were to be butchered, and this was the execution squad. When Leonnatus, somewhat embarrassed, went inside, Darius' wife and mother both flung themselves at his feet, and begged permission to bury their lord's body before dying themselves. Leonnatus told them, through an interpreter, that they had nothing to fear. Darius was not dead; Alexander, moreover, had not fought against him out of personal enmity, but 'had made legitimate war for the sovereignty of Asia'. They were to retain all the titles, ceremonial, and insignia befitting their royal status, and would receive whatever allowances they had been granted by Darius himself. As Tarn well observes, 'later writers never tired of embroidering the theme of Alexander's treatment of these ladies; their praise of what he did throws a dry light on what he was expected to do.'[63]

On the other hand it is unlikely that this generous treatment was dictated by wholly altruistic motives. Alexander had learnt a good deal from Aristotle about Persian customs and religion. He would have known that in the Achaemenid royal house succession to the throne depended very largely on establishing a claim through the distaff side[64] – one reason why the queen mother was so powerful a figure in Persian dynastic politics. No wonder he treated Darius' family well: they offered him a unique chance, when the time came, to legitimize his position as a usurper. The compassion he showed them was not only laudable, but politic. When he returned to camp after his long ride, he said to one of his companions: 'Let us go and wash off the sweat of battle in the bath of Darius' – only to be reminded that the bath now belonged not to Darius, but to him. The same applied, *a fortiori*, to these extremely valuable hostages.

Issus was a great victory, but by no means a decisive one. It had enabled Alexander to extricate himself from a highly dangerous position. It brought in welcome spoils, and had excellent propaganda value. But more than 10,000 mercenaries had got away, in good order, to form the Greek nucleus of another Persian army; the Eastern provinces, such as Bactria, were still intact; and – most important of all – so long as Darius himself remained at large, there was no question of the war being over.

[7]

Intimations of Immortality

HOUR after hour Darius kept up his headlong flight, over bad mountain roads, in pitch darkness, accompanied only by a few staff officers and attendants, determined to put as many miles between himself and Alexander as he could before daybreak. Next morning he was joined by other disorganized groups of fugitives, including some 4,000 Greek mercenaries. With this scratch force he rode on eastward, never slackening rein until he had crossed the Euphrates and reached Babylon (Arrian 2.13.1; QC 4.1.1–3; Diod. 17.39.1). The Great King was, for the moment, a very frightened man. He clearly expected Alexander to be hammering at the gates of Babylon within a matter of days, and his own shattered forces were in no condition to fight another battle. The administration of the empire had been totally disrupted; most of the Great King's Council of Friends were also serving as corps commanders, and where they were now only time would tell.

Darius therefore had no option but to act on his own initiative. Since he could not fight within the immediate future, he decided, he must try diplomacy. So – doubtless with many misgivings – the fugitive lord of Asia now drafted a memorandum to Alexander proposing terms for a settlement. The offer he made was, as we shall see (below, p. 240), extremely generous: it can never have occurred to him that his adversary might reject it out of hand. He had yet to learn the scope and intensity of Alexander's ambitions.

On the morning after the battle Alexander, accompanied by his *alter ego* Hephaestion, went to visit Darius' womenfolk himself. Both men wore plain Macedonian tunics; Hephaestion was the taller and more handsome of the two. The queen mother, Sisygambis, naturally enough mistook him for Alexander, and threw herself at his feet in supplication. When her error was pointed out to her by an attendant, she was covered with confusion, but nevertheless gamely 'made a new start and did obeisance to Alexander'. The king brushed aside her apologies, saying: 'Never mind, Mother; you didn't make a mistake. He is Alexander too.' Then he personally confirmed all the promises he had conveyed through Leonnatus: he even undertook to provide dowries for Darius' daughters, and to bring up the Great King's six-year-old son with all the honours befitting his royal status. The child was not in the least frightened; when Alexander called him over he came at once, and put his arms round the king's neck for a kiss. Alexander, touched by this gesture, remarked to Hephaestion what a pity it was that the father lacked his son's courage and self-possession.[1]

After this, in his customary fashion, he visited the wounded, and also held a splendid military funeral for the fallen, with the whole army on ceremonial parade. Decorations were awarded to those who had distinguished themselves during the battle. Balacrus, son of Nicanor, was appointed satrap of Cilicia, while Harpalus' vacant post as treasurer and quartermaster-general Alexander divided between Philoxenus and Coeranus. Among their other duties they became responsible for supervising the various mints (in Cilicia and at Myriandrus, later to be augmented by those of Aradus, Byblos and Sidon) from which Alexander now began, as a general policy, to issue his own coinage.

The Macedonians were revelling in their first real taste of oriental luxury: Darius' camp (even with the heavy baggage already removed to Damascus) had yielded plunder beyond their wildest dreams. Alexander himself might despise such fripperies, but his officers and men did not. From now on their passion for good living steadily increased. After the near-Spartan hardships of life in Macedonia they fell, all too easily, into an orgy of ostentatious affluence. One officer had his boots studded with silver nails. Another gave audience to his troops on a carpet of royal purple. They also laid hands on large numbers of Persian concubines and camp-followers, who swelled the ranks of Alexander's army as it progressed farther into Asia. Sometimes this proved a mixed blessing. Antigone, the girl whom Parmenio's son Philotas now took as his mistress, was later suborned to spy on him and report his private conversations (see below, pp. 339–40). But it is small wonder that the Macedonians were now, as Plutarch says, 'like dogs in their eagerness to pursue and track down the wealth of the Persians'.

The battle once over, Alexander had told them, 'nothing would remain but to crown their many labours with the sovereignty of Asia'. This in the event, proved an infinitely expandable programme. If they were expecting a quick chase after Darius, another share-out of Persian loot, and a triumphant homecoming, they were doomed to disappointment. At this critical stage in the campaign Alexander had to consider his future strategy very carefully indeed. The Persian army he had defeated was by no means totally destroyed, nor did it represent Darius' last reserves of manpower. Its survivors had scattered to the four quarters of the compass. Some, including the cavalry, had made their way north of the Taurus, and were liable to cut Alexander's always tenuous lines of communication across Anatolia. The eastern provinces remained intact; their contingents had not been present at Issus at all, and it was from them that Darius would recruit the backbone of his new defence force.

No one could say, for the moment, exactly where the Great King had gone, and Alexander did not intend to plunge into a hazardous guerrilla campaign through the wilds of Asia, against an all-too-elusive enemy. Besides, the Phoenician fleet was still at large, and Persia continued to control most of the Aegean. While Issus was bound to make a considerable psychological impact on the Greek states, its effect could easily be over-estimated. The situation in Asia Minor remained highly fluid, and Alexander's immediate strategy bore this fact fully in mind. The one way in which he could finally crush Darius was by provoking him into another set battle – a battle, moreover, in which the full strength of the Persian empire was deployed. He therefore decided, very shrewdly, to attend to other matters for the time being. The Great King's pride was such that there would be no difficulty in forcing a show-down when the time came. Meanwhile he had to be given ample leisure to reassemble and strengthen his shattered forces.

This suited Alexander's own plans very well. While Darius was thus occupied, he himself – undisturbed by any major opposition – would complete his interrupted project of reducing the Phoenician seaboard. As usual, he wasted no time. Only a few days after Issus, the Macedonian army struck camp and set out down the coast road into Syria. Before Alexander left, as a gesture he remitted the fifty talents still outstanding from the fine he had imposed on Soli. He was liable to have quite enough trouble in his rear as it was without stirring up more bad blood gratuitously. Besides, from now on he could afford, when he so chose, to be generous.[2]

From Myriandrus the Macedonian army marched south, by the old Phoenician road: inland at first, through the Orontes Valley – where he left Menon as governor of Lowland Syria – and then along the coast by way of Gabala (Jebleh) and Paltos (Arab el Melik) towards Marathus, with its fortified offshore island, Aradus (Arwad). Marathus could have caused Alexander considerable trouble. But once again his luck held. The local princes of Phoenicia and Cyprus had mustered their squadrons and sailed west to support Pharnabazus in the Aegean. Among them was the ruler of Marathus, who had left his son Straton to hold the city during his absence. With a depleted garrison and virtually no naval forces, there was very little

Straton could do in the event of an attack. When he heard that the Macedonians were approaching, he decided that resistance would be futile. He therefore rode out to meet Alexander, who graciously accepted his offer of a gold crown, together with the formal surrender of Marathus, Arwad, and all dependent territories as far inland as Mariamne. The last-named city was a most valuable acquisition. Not only did it control first-class farming territory, but also lay on the vital caravan route to Palmyra and Babylon.

When Alexander reached Marathus, he was met by two Persian envoys bearing Darius' armistice proposals. The Great King protested that Philip and Artaxerxes had been in peace and alliance; that Philip had committed acts of aggression against Artaxerxes' successor Arses; that Alexander himself had wantonly invaded Asia in defiance of 'this ancient friendship'. He, Darius, had done no more than defend his country and his sovereignty. The battle had gone 'as some god willed it'. If Alexander would restore his wife, mother, and children, he was ready to pay an appropriate ransom. Furthermore, if Alexander agreed to sign a treaty of friendship and alliance with Persia, the Great King would cede him 'the territories and cities of Asia west of the Halys River'. What Darius now offered him, in fact, was all that Philip had aimed to conquer – 'Asia from Cilicia to Sinope', as Isocrates phrased it.

Alexander thus found himself in a somewhat delicate predicament. If he revealed the Great King's terms to his war council, Parmenio and the old guard would argue, irrefutably, that the Persian crusade had gained all its objectives, and that this offer should be accepted without delay. But Alexander's own ambitions looked far beyond so modest a goal. Nothing would satisfy him, ultimately, but the utter overthrow of Darius, and his own establishment as lord of Asia, heir by right of conquest to the Achaemenid throne and empire. With this end in view, it was essential that the Persian offer should be turned down. Alexander therefore suppressed the original document, and forged a substitute, which was not only offensively arrogant in tone, but – more important – omitted any reference to territorial concessions. This, not surprisingly, the council rejected on sight.

Alexander then drafted a reply which began, very much *de haut en bas*, 'King Alexander to Darius'. He treated the Great King as a mere vulgar usurper, who had conspired with Bagoas to win the throne 'unjustly and illegally'. He raked over all the old accusations against Xerxes and his successors. He accused Darius of having procured Philip's murder, which was not true, and of running an anti-Macedonian fifth column in Greece, which was. He professed himself willing to restore the queen mother, the queen, and her children, without ransom – provided Darius came to him humbly, as a suppliant. But it is his concluding words which are most remarkable:

> In future [he wrote] let any communication you wish to make with me be addressed to the King of all Asia. Do not write to me as an equal. Everything you possess is now mine; so, if you should want anything, let me know in the proper terms, or I shall take steps to deal with you as a criminal. If, on the other hand, you wish to dispute the throne, stand and fight for it and do not run away. Wherever you may hide yourself, be sure I shall seek you out.

The envoy chosen to deliver this scathing broadside had strict instructions 'to discuss no question whatever which might arise from it' – a very necessary precaution.

If Alexander's letter reveals how far-reaching his aims had become, it also displays very shrewd psychological insight.[3] That final threat was, at the time of writing, no more than a monumental, if calculated, piece of bluff; yet it might well sting Darius – whose prestige had taken a bad battering – into doing the one thing that would enable Alexander to bring about his final downfall – that is, amass another imperial army, and challenge the Macedonians to a second trial of strength. Cool heads at Susa must have realized that success depended on avoiding such a direct confrontation; but honour and prestige were now involved. Meanwhile, the mere fact that Darius had offered to surrender Asia Minor showed how badly Issus had shaken him. It was an encouraging sign for any future negotiations which Alexander might undertake.

When Darius received Alexander's reply, he at once began planning a fresh campaign. The eastern provinces contained vast untapped reserves of manpower. All he needed was time in which to organize them. Meanwhile, Memnon's scheme for carrying the war into Europe – temporarily shelved at the instance of the Persian High Command – was now given a fresh airing. If Darius could cut Alexander's land-communications in Asia Minor, win complete control of the Hellespont, and persuade the Greek states to launch a general revolt against Antipater, the Macedonian army's position would (it was thought) become virtually untenable. In this way, the Great King calculated, he might force Alexander to withdraw without fighting another major engagement. At the very least he would win valuable time to rebuild his own shattered forces.

He therefore sent out an order of the day alerting his commanders on the Ionian seaboard. The Aegean campaign had, not surprisingly, been holding fire since Issus; as a result of Darius' directive it once more acquired top priority. Pharnabazus (who had recaptured Miletus and Halicarnassus, and was now using the latter as his operational headquarters) had already been privately in touch with King Agis of Sparta, now actively planning a nationalist rebellion. On receipt of Darius' order he summoned the Spartan to Halicarnassus, and sent him home equipped with Persian ships, Persian gold ('to change the political situation in Greece in favour of Darius') and no less than 8,000 mercenaries, who had found their way from Issus to Caria since the battle.* It was now, too, that the port of

---

* At least 4,000 mercenaries had joined Darius in Babylon, and were thus available for immediate service. After Issus some 12,000 more had

Taenarum, in the deep Mani, became established as a landing-point and recruiting-centre for rebel volunteers. At the same time – again on Darius' orders – another mercenary force was sent to recover the Hellespont area.

A number of important cities in Asia Minor (our sources do not name them) were recaptured for Persia. Most important of all, those units – including Nabarzanes' crack cavalry divisions – which had escaped north of the Taurus now raised a full-scale revolt in Cappadocia and Paphlagonia. Alexander's lines of communication, as we have seen (cf. above, pp. 209–10), ran through a narrow bottleneck by way of Celaenae. With the aid of the mountain tribes, Darius calculated, it should not take long to close this bottleneck altogether. Antigonus the One-Eyed, who had been left as governor of central Anatolia, was dangerously short of troops. If Alexander found himself cut off from Europe, he might prove somewhat more amenable to argument. But this (though Darius could not have known it) was a false assumption. Alexander had already made his own crucial decision, at Gordium: Greece and Macedonia were, in the last resort, expendable. The victory of Issus can only have reinforced such an attitude.[4]

Meanwhile Parmenio had – as so often – been given the most tiresome and dangerous job going, with wholly

----

withdrawn in good order and force-marched down the Phoenician coast to the port of Tripolis, where the fleet that had transported them from the Aegean still lay at anchor (Arrian 2.13.2–3; Diod. 17.48.2; QC 4.1.27). They loaded up all the ships they needed, burnt the rest to prevent them falling into Alexander's hands, and then put to sea. The Macedonian renegade Amyntas took 4,000 of them to Cyprus, where he won over some local garrisons (Diod. 17.48.3; QC 4.1.27), and thence to Egypt, where the entire force, Amyntas included, was wiped out by Persian garrison troops from Memphis (Arrian 2.13.3; Diod. 17.48.2–3; QC 4.1.29–33). This is the only case of wholesale defection by Greeks in Darius' service. (Amyntas, as a Macedonian, stood in a special category of his own.) Most of them remained loyal to the bitter end, even when it was obvious that the Great King's struggle could not possibly succeed.

inadequate forces for its safe execution. His orders, received the day after Issus, were to march through lowland Syria on Damascus, receive the city's surrender, and secure the Great King's baggage-train. He had no first-class troops with him apart from the Thessalian cavalry, and felt understandably nervous. Winter was setting in: if the citizens of Damascus decided to close their gates and stand siege, that would be that. His column advanced through a flurry of snowstorms. Even when the snow stopped, the ground remained frozen solid with hoar-frost. It was bitterly cold. But when they were about four days' march from the city, a letter reached them from the governor, saying that 'Alexander should speedily send one of his generals with a small force, to whom he might hand over what Darius had left in his charge'.

On the excuse that Damascus' walls and fortifications were too dilapidated to resist attack, the governor now ordered a general evacuation – timing it so that treasure, baggage, and distinguished prisoners should be there for the picking when Parmenio arrived. All went off as planned. The Macedonians were met by a long column of refugees plodding through the snow (it was so cold that the porters bearing the treasure had wrapped themselves in Darius' gold and purple robes). The Thessalian cavalry charged. Baggage-carriers and armed escort fled, leaving the Persian royal treasure scattered in the snow: coined money, gold ornaments, jewelled bridles, chariots. Each item was carefully listed by Parmenio in an inventory he prepared fo. Alexander. It included 2,600 talents of coined money, and 500lb. of wrought silver. The total weight of gold cups was about 4,500lb., or something over *two tons*, if we can trust our sources; of cups inlaid with precious stones, 3,400lb. In addition, all Darius' household staff was captured: the inventory showed, amongst others, 329 concubines (musically trained), 277 caterers, and seventeen bar-tenders. Other prisoners, if less exotic, had greater political significance: various high-ranking Persians, the wives and children of Darius' commanders and blood-relatives, and Memnon's widow Barsine, the daughter of Artabazus. Most interesting of all, there were ambassadors from Thebes, Sparta, and Athens.

Parmenio sent Alexander a detailed dispatch on all these matters, together with a richly wrought and jewelled gold casket, by general agreement the finest *objet d'art* in Darius' collection. (Alexander, characteristically, used it as a travelling-box for his *Iliad*.) What, he asked, were the king's instructions now? Alexander's reply was very crisp and practical. He commissioned Parmenio to organize the military defences of lowland Syria, in collaboration with Memnon, the new governor. Darius' treasures were to be kept under guard in Damascus, and the captive envoys sent on to Marathus for interrogation. Parmenio was further authorized to issue Macedonian coins from the Damascus mint. He had asked, in his dispatch, what action should be taken against two Macedonians accused of raping mercenaries' wives. If found guilty, Alexander wrote, they were to be 'put to death as wild beasts born for the destruction of mankind'.

In the same letter he informed Parmenio – perhaps a little too insistently – that he had neither seen nor wanted to see Darius' wife, and would not even allow people to discuss her beauty in his presence (presumably she had been veiled on the morning after Issus). He went on to describe the Great King's harem, in general, as 'an irritation to the eyes'. Parmenio, who seems to have had a sophisticated sense of humour, sent Alexander the three ambassadors, as requested; but he also sent him Barsine, now in her late thirties or early forties, whose aristocratic Persian breeding had been reinforced with an impeccable Greek education. This experiment (if we can believe Aristobulus) proved a striking success – even though the hypothetical son born of the union is more often than not dismissed as pure fiction.[5]

Early in January 332 Alexander continued his march from Marathus. Byblos surrendered without any trouble,

The Macedonians tramped on south by the sea, through
Nahr-el-Kalb, where their predecessors from Babylon and
Assyria and Egypt had carved inscriptions in the rock-face
as they passed, to the great commercial port of Sidon. Here
the inhabitants welcomed Alexander – out of hatred for
Darius and the Persians, says Arrian (2.16.6); but Sidon's
long-standing rivalry with Tyre, a few miles farther down
the coast, must surely have been the deciding factor. The
Sidonians repudiated their reigning prince (he appears to
have been executed) and left the appointment of a successor
to Alexander. Alexander, we are told, asked his friend
Hephaestion to select a suitable candidate. Hephaestion's
choice fell on a collateral member of the royal house, now
living in reduced circumstances and working as a market
gardener.

This man, Abdalonymus – his Phoenician name means
'servant of the gods' – duly ascended the throne, and
ancient moralists never tired of citing his history as a classic
instance of 'the incredible changes which Fortune can
effect'. (Alexander doubtless calculated that so dramatic an
elevation would give him a permanent sense of compliant
obligation to his god-like benefactor.) Abdalonymus has a
further claim to fame: it was he who subsequently commissioned the great 'Alexander-sarcophagus' now in
Istanbul, with its hunting and battle scenes. These depict
not only Alexander himself, but also, in all likelihood
(though the identifications have been contested), Hephaestion and Parmenio. One especially interesting feature of the
sarcophagus reliefs, as of the coins which Alexander now
began to issue from Sidon's ancient mint (active since 475
B.C.) is the king's portrayal as the young Heracles – a
vigorous, handsome figure wearing Heracles' traditional
lion-skin helmet.

There was ample precedent for this in Macedonian tradition: Argead monarchs often found it useful to underline
their Heraclid descent. But Alexander's new gold staters
and silver decadrachms reveal significant modifications.

The conqueror is shown being crowned by Nike (Victory), who bears a wreath in her outstretched hand; and the serpent of earlier issues is replaced by the Persian lion-headed griffin. Heracles, moreover, was generally identified with the Phoenician god Melkart.[6] Alexander could hardly have made his assumption of eastern sovereignty less ambiguous; and indeed this calculated Heraclid propaganda campaign sheds an interesting light on the events of the next few days.

From Sidon Alexander continued south towards Tyre, the most powerful naval and commercial port between Cilicia and Egypt. It stood on a rocky island half a mile offshore, protected by great walls which on the landward side rose to a height of about 150 feet. As his army approached, a group of ambassadors, including the king's son, came out to greet him, with the usual gold crown and many protestations of allegiance.[7] But their hospitable manner was deceptive. They had not the slightest intention of handing over Tyre to the Macedonians: on the contrary, they meant to hold this island fortress for Darius and the Phoenician fleet. If they could avoid trouble by a little diplomatic bribery, well and good (the lavish gift of provisions they brought with them might at least stop these uncouth and unwelcome visitors from ravaging the countryside). But they were not prepared to compromise. If Alexander proved obdurate, he could go ahead and besiege them. They had worn out besiegers before, and the Macedonians did not even have the advantage of a fleet. Besides, the longer they delayed Alexander, the more time Darius would have to mobilize a new army and carry out his military operations in Asia Minor.[8]

Before very long Alexander saw that the Tyrians were 'more inclined to accept an alliance with him than to submit to his rule'. He thanked the envoys for their gifts. Then, very blandly, he said what great pleasure it would give him, as a royal descendant of Heracles, to visit the island and sacrifice to their god Melkart, in his great temple there. The Tyrians were well aware of the Heracles–Melkart equation, and probably also knew just how Alexander hoped to exploit it for his own benefit. This was the time of Melkart's great annual festival,[9] which attracted many visitors, especially from Carthage. To let Alexander have his way would be tantamount to acknowledging him as their rightful king. (If other Near Eastern parallels apply here, to sacrifice to Melkart during this festival was strictly a royal prerogative.) So the envoys, with charming aplomb, told him that this was, unfortunately, out of the question. However, another temple, just as good, existed on the mainland, at Old Tyre. Perhaps he would like to sacrifice there?[10] They meant no offence, they said; they were merely preserving strict neutrality. Till the war was over they would admit neither Persians nor Macedonians to their city.

At this patent evasion Alexander's always uncertain temper got the better of him. He flew into a murderous rage and dismissed the envoys out of hand, with all manner of dire threats. On returning home they advised their government to think twice before taking on so formidable an opponent. But the Tyrians had complete confidence in their natural and man-made defences. The channel between Tyre and the mainland was over twenty feet deep, and frequently lashed by violent south-west winds. Their fortifications, they believed, would resist the strongest battering-ram yet devised. The city-walls stood sheer above the sea: how could any army without ships scale them? Shore-based artillery was useless at such a range. The Tyrians decided to stand firm, encouraged by their visitors from Carthage,[11] who promised them massive reinforcements.

Even Alexander himself appears to have had second thoughts about embarking on so hazardous a project – perhaps because his officers showed something less than enthusiasm for it. He therefore sent heralds to Tyre, urging the acceptance of a peaceful settlement. The Tyrians,

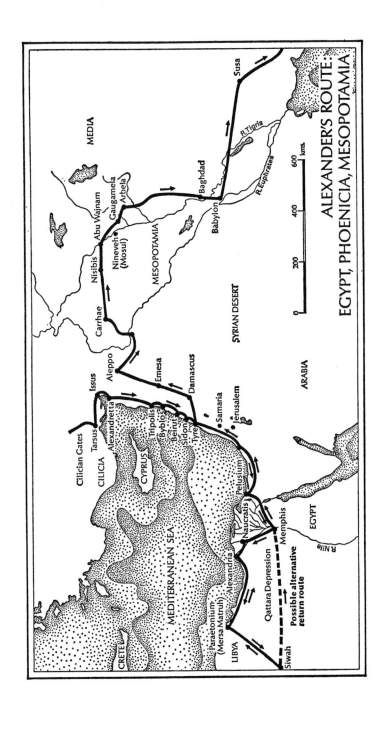

ALEXANDER'S ROUTE:
EGYPT, PHOENICIA, MESOPOTAMIA

however, mistaking this move for a sign of weakness, killed the heralds and tossed their bodies over the battlements.[12] If this senseless atrocity did nothing else, it at least got Alexander a solid vote of confidence from his staff. The speech he now made to them (reported *in extenso* by Ptolemy, who was present)[13] shows a solid grasp of strategic realities. There had been some talk of leaving a garrison at Old Tyre to 'contain' the island, and marching straight on to Egypt. Others were anxious to abandon Phoenicia altogether and continue the hunt for Darius. Either course, Alexander emphasized, was out of the question so long as Tyre remained a potential base for the Great King's fleet. But once naval supremacy had been achieved in the eastern Mediterranean, Egypt would offer no resistance; and then, with both Egypt and Phoenicia safe, they could take the road to Babylon.*

Such arguments might convince Alexander's corps commanders; the Macedonian rank and file, on the other hand, cared not a jot for strategy. What *they* saw was the work they would have to undertake, and they did not fancy it. Alexander had made it known that he intended to reach Tyre by building a mole across the strait. They took a good look at the deep, windswept channel, and the fortress of Tyre beyond it, and the artillery that their opponents were already mounting on the walls. Never can Alexander's lack of a fleet have seemed so obvious and insurmountable a handicap. A mole half a mile long, through *that*? This time

---

* Both Egypt and Cyprus (as Alexander reminded his audience) were still Persian-occupied. Sparta stood on the very brink of rebellion, and Athens had only held aloof till now through fear, not out of any sense of loyalty. If the Macedonian army left Tyre unconquered, and struck inland, Darius would have little trouble in recovering the whole Phoenician coast – after which a full-scale naval assault on Greece was a virtual certainty (though one which probably alarmed Alexander rather less than it did his officers: see above, p. 214). If Tyre fell, on the other hand, the Phoenician squadrons, deprived of their bases, would very soon desert to the winning side – a shrewd prediction which events were soon to vindicate: see below, p. 254.

the king was asking too much.[14] But Alexander – who, as Curtius observes, 'was by no means inexperienced in working upon the minds of soldiers' – now announced that he had had a dream, in which he saw Heracles standing on the walls of Tyre and beckoning to him. Aristander interpreted this as meaning that the city would be taken, but only after labours worthy of Heracles himself: an obvious enough deduction.[15]

All opposition was finally overcome, and Alexander began what was to prove the longest and most gruelling military operation of his entire career.[16] He began by demolishing Old Tyre to provide foundation-stones and rubble.[17] A pioneering party was sent inland through the lower Beqaa Valley to fetch timber, cedars in particular, from the slopes of Antilebanon. It is possible that both this expedition and Alexander's own subsequent raid into the same area (see below, p. 255) were in search not only of timber – essential for mole-building operations – but also of grain-supplies. Though adequate water was provided by the River Litani, about five and a half miles from the city, local resources would clearly be inadequate to victual Alexander's forces over a long period. Before the siege was over, Josephus tells us, Alexander wrote to the high priest in Jerusalem, 'requesting him to send him assistance and supply his army with provisions'.[18] Meanwhile not only Alexander's own troops, but all able-bodied men from the surrounding towns and villages found themselves drafted into a vast emergency labour force, estimated at 'many tens of thousands'.

The early stages of the project,[19] across mud-flats and through shallow water, presented no particular problems. Alexander's siege-engineers sank piles in the mud, packed down rocks between them, and on this foundation laid huge baulks of timber. The mole, in its final form, is said to have reached a breadth of no less than 200 feet: Alexander wanted to assault the fortifications on as wide a front as possible. He himself was always on the spot, ready to solve any technical problem, encouraging the men and handing out rewards for conspicuously good work.

At first the Tyrians treated his project as a joke. They would row across to watch, and sit there, just out of range, making rude comments. They jeered at the soldiers for carrying loads on their back like beasts of burden. They inquired, facetiously, whether Alexander had become so swollen-headed that he was now setting up in competition with Poseidon.[20] But the rapid, efficient progress of the work soon made them change their tune. They evacuated some of their women and children,[21] and began to construct extra artillery for the landward defences.[22] Far from laughing at Alexander's mole, they now made a vigorous attempt to destroy it before it could become a real menace. Eight vessels crammed with archers, slingers, and light catapults sailed down either side of the construction, and poured a concentrated cross-fire into the thousands of labourers swarming over it.[23] At such short range they could hardly miss, and Alexander's men, who wore no armour while working, suffered heavy casualties.*

As a counter-measure the king rigged up protective screens of hide and canvas, and placed two tall wooden towers near the end of the mole. From these his archers and artillerymen could shoot straight down into the enemy's boats. Such precautions were now doubly necessary. The work was so far advanced that very soon it would come within range of the catapults on the walls; but at the same time, since it had now reached the deepest part of the channel, its rate of progress had slowed almost to a standstill.[24] Endless tons of rock went into the sea without appreciably raising the foundation-level. Supplies of timber were not coming

---

*Both Curtius (4.4.3–4) and Diodorus (17.41.5) report that a large sea-monster appeared from the deep and crashed into the mole during these operations, though without doing it any damage. Tyrians and Macedonians alike took this as a favourable omen, the former going so far as to hold all-night revels in celebration, and to man their ships the following morning while still tipsy and garlanded.

through as fast as they should, since the forestry section had constantly to fight off attacks by Arab marauders.[25] On top of everything else the Tyrians, whose resourcefulness was only matched by their sense of timing, chose this moment to carry out a highly successful commando raid.

They took a broadbeamed old horse-transport and crammed it to the gunwales with dry firewood, over which they poured large quantities of liquid pitch. Two new masts were rigged well forward in the bows, and from the projecting yard-arm of each they hung a cauldron full of some highly inflammable substance, probably naphtha. Finally, they ballasted this curious vessel so heavily aft that its bows rose clear of the water, despite the extra load they had to carry. When a good on-shore wind began blowing, they put a skeleton crew aboard, and towed this improvised fireship towards the mole with a pair of fast triremes, the crews rowing flat out so as to work up maximum speed. At the last moment the triremes sheered off, to port and starboard respectively, while those aboard the transport let go the tow-ropes. Then they hurled flaming torches into the midst of the combustible material, and quickly dived overboard.

The barge, now a mass of flames, bore straight down on the mole, its bows crunching and grinding over the outermost foundations, close to Alexander's wooden towers. These caught fire at once. Meanwhile the two triremes had put about, and now lay alongside the mole, sniping at any Macedonian who put his head outside the towers or attempted to extinguish the fire. Then the ropes holding the cauldrons burnt through, and a torrent of naphtha came pouring down. The result must have been like a small-scale explosion in an oil-refinery: both towers were at once engulfed in a raging inferno. At the same time a flotilla of small craft which had been following the fireship ran in on the mole from all sides. One commando party slaughtered the men carrying rocks from the shore. Others tore down Alexander's protective palisades and set fire to any siege equipment that had escaped the original conflagration. The whole attack was carried out in a matter of minutes. Then the raiders withdrew, leaving behind them a smoke-blackened trail of carnage and destruction. For its entire length the mole was littered with charred corpses and blazing, shapeless piles of timber.[26]

Alexander, nothing daunted, gave orders for new towers and artillery to be built, and directed that the mole itself should be widened still further. He then left Perdiccas and Craterus in charge of operations, and himself returned to Sidon, with the Guards Brigade and the pick of the light-armed troops. This expensive setback had made one thing abundantly clear: without a strong fleet he might as well give up altogether. Only an amphibious assault stood any real chance of success. To obtain ships, moreover, was not so hopeless a task as might be supposed. In his speech to his corps commanders, Alexander had predicted that when news of Issus – and subsequent successes – reached the Aegean, many of the Phoenician squadrons serving with Pharnabazus would defect. This optimistic hunch now vindicated itself in the most remarkable fashion.

The kings of Byblos and Aradus (Arwad), learning that their cities were in Macedonian hands, both withdrew their contingents and sailed back to Sidon. Ten triremes arrived from Rhodes (hitherto a Persian stronghold), ten more from Lycia, and three from Soli. Together with Sidon's own squadrons, this at once gave Alexander 103 vessels. But better still was to come. A day or two later the kings of Cyprus sailed in, leading a combined flotilla of no less than 120 warships. Desertions on this scale meant that the Persian fleet would very soon cease to be an effective force. At the same time a fifty-oared Macedonian galley, having successfully dodged Pharnabazus' blockade, arrived with the welcome news that a strong naval counter-offensive, under Amphoterus and Hegelochus (see above, p. 214), was now developing in the Hellespont area.[27]

Alexander had every reason to be pleased. In a week or two he had mustered a far more powerful fleet than that of the Tyrians; and the situation in Greece and Ionia seemed to be, at long last, taking a turn for the better. He at once collected fresh engineers from Cyprus and Phoenicia, who were set to work mounting siege artillery (including rams) on barges or old transport vessels. While the fleet was being fitted out, Alexander himself took a flying column up into the rough, snow-clad wastes of the Lebanon ranges, and spent ten days harrying the tribesmen who had threatened his supply-lines.

One evening he and his immediate entourage fell behind the main troop, chiefly because of Alexander's old tutor Lysimachus, who had insisted on accompanying them, but proved unable to stand the pace they set. When night fell they were lost, and shivering with cold. Beyond them twinkled the camp-fires of their elusive opponents. Alexander went out alone, Indian scout fashion, crept up on the nearest encampment, knifed two natives, and got away with a large flaming branch. They built their own fire, bivouacked for the night, and rejoined the others in the morning. This episode (if true: it bristles with improbabilities) offers a fairly typical instance of the gratuitous personal risks which Alexander continued to take throughout his career. It excites our admiration: yet what would have happened if one of those Arab mountain guerrillas had been a little quicker off the mark? As so often, it is hard to decide at what point courage merges into sheer exuberant irresponsibility. One stroke of a dagger amid the Lebanese snows could have changed the entire course of Greek history.[28]

His minor punitive expedition successfully concluded, Alexander hurried back to Sidon. Here he found further welcome reinforcements awaiting him.[29] Cleander was back at last from his recruiting drive in the Peloponnese (see above, p. 200), accompanied by no less than 4,000 Greek mercenaries. Word had got about that Alexander's expedition was now not merely solvent, but also paying handsome dividends. The king never again had any real trouble in recruiting as many mercenaries as he wanted. The fleet was ready for active service. Alexander at once put to sea in battle formation, using the fifty-oared Macedonian galley as his flagship, with half the large Cypriot contingent stationed on each wing to strengthen his overall striking power. The Tyrian admiral's first thought, on hearing of Alexander's approach, was to force an engagement. But the appearance of this gigantic armada, far larger than anything he had anticipated, soon made him change his mind: Alexander, spoiling for an immediate trial of strength, saw the enemy squadrons put about and make for home. At this he crammed on all speed in a bid to reach the north harbour before them, and a desperate race ensued. Most of Tyre's best troops had been packed aboard the galleys to fight as marines, and if Alexander could force his way into the harbour, he had an excellent chance of capturing the city there and then.

The Tyrians, in line-ahead formation, just managed to squeeze through the harbour entrance in front of Alexander's leading vessels. Three Tyrian triremes put about to hold off the attack, and were sunk one after the other. Meanwhile, behind them, a solid array of ships was jammed bows on across the harbour mouth. Similar defensive tactics were adopted at the Egyptian harbour, on the south-east side of the island.[30] Alexander, seeing there was nothing he could do to force an entry, brought his fleet to anchor on the lee side of the mole. However, if it was impossible for him to get in, he had, equally, no intention of letting the Tyrian fleet get out. Early next morning he sent the Cyprian and Phoenician squadrons to blockade both harbour mouths. This effectively bottled up Tyre's entire naval force, and at one stroke gave Alexander mastery of the sea.[31]

He was now free to press on at full speed with the mole, his workers protected from attack by a thick defensive screen of ships.[32] But Poseidon, it seemed, was fighting on the Tyrian side. A strong north-west gale blew up, which not only made further progress impossible, but caused serious damage to the existing structure. Alexander, however, refused to admit defeat. A number of giant untrimmed Lebanon cedars were floated into position on the windward side, and absorbed the most violent impact of the waves. After the storm subsided, these huge trees were built into the mole as bulwarks. The damage was soon made good, and Alexander, surmounting every obstacle, at last found himself within missile-range of the walls.[33]

He now proceeded to launch the ancient equivalent of a saturation barrage.[34] Stone-throwers and light catapults were brought up in force to the end of the mole. While the stone-throwers pounded away at Tyre's fortifications, the catapults, reinforced by archers and slingers, concentrated on those defenders who were manning the battlements. At the same time, no less vigorous an assault was being pressed home from the seaward side. Alexander's engineers had constructed a number of naval battering-rams, each mounted on a large platform lashed across two barges. Other similar floating platforms carried heavy catapults and manganels. All were well protected against attack from above.[35] These craft, escorted by more orthodox vessels, now formed a tight circle right round the island fortress, and subjected it to the most violent, unremitting assault. The great rams smashed their way through loose blocks of masonry, while a deadly hail of bolts and arrows picked off the defenders on the walls.

The Tyrians fought back as best they could. They hung up hides and other yielding materials to break the force of the stone balls. They built wooden towers on their battlements, and filled them with archers who shot fire-arrows into the assault-craft below. They worked at feverish speed to repair the breaches made by Alexander's rams, or, where this proved impracticable, to build new curtain-walls behind them.[36] At the end of a long day's fighting their position did not look at all encouraging. They had one consolation, however: the defences opposite the mole still stood firm. Here the walls were tallest, and built of great ashlar blocks set in mortar; even the heaviest Macedonian artillery had so far made no impression on them. Alexander, well aware of this, but determined to press home his advantage, now attempted a night-assault from the seaward side. Under cover of darkness his whole task-force moved into position. Then, for the second time, Tyre was saved by bad weather. Clouds drifted across the moon, accompanied by a thick sea-mist. A gale got up, and violent waves began to pound Alexander's floating platforms. Some of these actually broke up: they were unwieldy at the best of times, and quite unmanageable in a storm. Alexander had no choice but to cancel the operation.[37] Most of his fleet got back safely, though many vessels had suffered serious damage.

This setback gave the Tyrians a brief but valuable breathing-space. With considerable ingenuity, they now dumped heavy blocks of stone and masonry in the shallow water below the walls – probably demolishing large numbers of houses to supply them with the necessary material. Such a protection should, with luck, suffice to keep Alexander's floating rams out of range. Their engineers and smiths, who seem to have been of an inventive turn of mind, kept the forges working late to devise ever more *outré* and horrific weapons. They had to face the fact that very soon (unless something quite unforeseen happened) Alexander's mole would reach the island. This is why many of their devices were designed for hand-to-hand combat. They included drop-beams (which swung down on the ships from a derrick), grappling-irons or barbed tridents attached to cords, with which assailants could be hooked off their towers, fire-throwers that discharged large quantities of molten metal, scythes on poles to cut the ropes which worked the rams, and – simple but effective – lead-shot fishing-nets to entangle any who might rush the fortifications by means of bridge-ladders.[38]

One reason for all this urgent work was an embassy which had just arrived from Carthage, bearing highly unwelcome news. Those Carthaginians still in the city had doubtless sent home increasingly gloomy reports on Tyre's chances of survival. Their government, sensing an imminent débâcle, did not want to involve Carthage in what might prove a long and expensive war. They remembered, suddenly and conveniently, that Carthage had troubles of her own at home, and would not, therefore, much though they regretted it, be able to send Tyre any reinforcements.[39] This news caused considerable alarm throughout the beleaguered city. One man was rash enough to announce that he had had a dream in which he saw a god (probably Baal: our classical sources say Apollo) departing Tyre, and it was at once assumed that he had made up this tale in order to curry favour with Alexander. Some of the young men actually tried to stone him, and he was forced to seek sanctuary in the temple of Melkart. Others, more superstitious, reserved their anger for the god, and tied his image down securely with golden cords to prevent him deserting to the enemy.[40]

Alexander, meanwhile, was making vast efforts to winch up the heaps of stone and masonry which had been dropped in the sea beneath the walls. This work could only be done from securely anchored transport vessels with strong derricks. Tyrian divers held up the salvage work by cutting these ships' anchor-cables. Only when Alexander replaced the cables with chains could the crews go ahead. They finally cleared all the stones, catapulting them into deep water where no one could retrieve them.[41] Now, once again, the assault-craft could come in close under the walls. About the same time, after a sustained effort of which Heracles himself might well have been proud, the mole finally reached Tyre: Alexander's promise that he would join Tyre's fortress to the mainland had been fulfilled.[42] At this point he would have been less than human had he not attempted a direct assault. The great siege-towers, over 150 feet high, were wheeled into position, the boarding-gangways were made ready, and a tremendous attack launched against the walls.[43]

The Tyrians, who had been long awaiting this moment, fought back with ferocious courage. The most ingenious and horrific device at their disposal was also the simplest. They filled a number of huge metal bowls with sand and fine gravel, and then heated this mixture until it was almost incandescent. The bowls were mounted on the parapet, each with a tipping mechanism, so that its contents could be emptied over any assailant who came within range. The red-hot sand sifted down inside breastplates and shirts, burning deep into the flesh: an appallingly effective forerunner of napalm. Finally Alexander was forced to retreat: the assault had proved an elaborate and expensive failure. At this point, from utter weariness it is said,[44] he felt seriously tempted to abandon the siege and march on to Egypt. It was now high summer: for nearly six months he had laboured before the walls of Tyre, and all in vain. The wastage of manpower and materials had been prodigious; and day by day Darius was steadily building and training a new Grand Army. If Alexander held on, it was because he had long ago passed the point of no return. To give up this siege now would be more costly than to go through with it.

It was the Tyrians who finally gave him what he needed. Their fleet made an all-but-successful sortie during siesta-time, but after a sharp engagement was driven back and bottled up in the north harbour – where it remained for the duration of the siege. Alexander was now able to move round the island without any trouble, looking for a weak point on which to concentrate. He brought up his seaborne artillery and rams against the fortifications by the north harbour, but once again a solid barrage failed to breach them.[45] The king then moved his entire task-force round to the south-east side of Tyre, just below the Egyptian harbour. Here he had better luck. Concentrated bombardment broke down one section of the wall, and badly shook what remained. Alexander, desperate to follow up this opening, at once threw assault-bridges across from his ships, and ordered a spearhead of crack troops into the breach. They were driven back by a violent and well-aimed hail of missiles.[46] Yet despite this he knew, beyond any doubt, that he had at last found the vulnerable point in Tyre's defences.

It was now 28 July. Alexander decided to rest his men for a couple of days before the final assault. Something of his suddenly increased confidence must have communicated itself to Aristander the seer, who after taking the omens announced that without a doubt Tyre would fall within the current month. The sea had become choppy again; but on the third night the wind dropped, and at dawn Alexander began a tremendous bombardment of the wall, choosing the same point that he had breached earlier.[47] When a wide section had been battered into rubble, he withdrew his unwieldy artillery barges, and brought up two special assault craft crammed with shock-troops. While this was going on the Cypriot and Phoenician squadrons launched a powerful attack against both harbours, and numerous other vessels, loaded with archers and ammunition, kept circling the island, lending a hand wherever it might be needed.[48]

As soon as the assault craft were in position, and the gangways run out, a wave of Macedonians charged across on to the battlements. First came the Guards Brigade, closely followed by Craterus' battalion of the phalanx. The commander of the spearhead, Admetus, had his skull split by an axe. When he fell, Alexander took over in person. Stubbornly the Macedonians fought their way along the battlements. Then there came a sound of cheering from the harbours below them: the Cypriot and Phoenician squadrons had successfully smashed their way through.[49] The Tyrians on the walls, afraid of being caught front and rear, now retreated to the centre of the city, barricading the narrow streets as they went. Tiles came pelting down on their pursuers from the roof-tops. By the Shrine of Agenor Tyre's defenders turned at bay, and fought it out to the death.[50]

When the last organized resistance was broken, Alexander's veterans ranged through the city on a ferocious manhunt, all restraint abandoned, hysterical and half-crazy after the long rigours of that dreadful siege, mere butchers now, striking and trampling and tearing limb from limb until Tyre became a bloody, reeking abattoir.[51] Some citizens locked themselves in their houses and committed suicide. Alexander had ordered that all save those who sought sanctuary were to be slain, and his commands were executed with savage relish. The air grew thick with smoke from burning buildings. Seven thousand Tyrians died in this frightful orgy of destruction, and the number would have been far higher had it not been for the men of Sidon, who entered the city alongside Alexander's troops. Even though Tyre had been Sidon's rival for centuries, these neighbours of the victims, horrified by what they now witnessed, managed to smuggle some 15,000 of them to safety.[52]

The great city over which Hiram had once held sway was now utterly destroyed. Her king, Azimilik, and various other notables, including envoys from Carthage, had taken refuge in the temple of Melkart, and Alexander spared their lives. The remaining survivors, some 30,000 in number, he sold into slavery. Two thousand men of military age were crucified. Then Alexander went up into the temple, ripped the golden cords from the image of the god (now to be renamed, by decree, Apollo Philalexander), and made his long-delayed sacrifice: the most costly blood-offering even Melkart had ever received.[53] Afterwards came the feasting and the processions, a lavish funeral for the Macedonian dead, torch-races, public games, and a splendid naval review. The ram which finally battered down Tyre's bastions Alexander dedicated to Heracles, with an inscription which not even Ptolemy could bring himself to repeat.[54]

But it was Zachariah, a Jewish prophet crying in the wilderness, who had already composed the city's epitaph:

Burden of the Lord's doom, where falls it now? . . . This Tyre, how strong a fortress she has built, what gold and silver she has amassed, till they were as common as clay, as mire in the streets! Ay, but the Lord means to dispossess her; cast into the sea, all that wealth of hers, and herself burnt to the ground! [Zachariah ix, 1–8]

Against Alexander's mole, quiet now under the summer sky, sand began to drift from the coastal dunes, softening the sharp outline of blocks and joists, linking Tyre ever more closely to the mainland. The flail of the Lord had done his work all too well. With each passing century the peninsula grew wider. Today, deep under asphalt streets and apartment blocks, the stone core of that fantastic causeway still stands: one of Alexander's most tangible and permanent legacies to posterity.

Zachariah was not alone in foreseeing the destruction of Tyre. Darius, too, must have realized that the city could not hold out much longer. Unfortunately he was in no position to relieve its garrison. Rumours to the contrary, he had done very little about raising a new imperial army, preferring to stake everything on the success of his campaign in Asia Minor and the Aegean. All the front-line troops he had available were committed to one of these two theatres. By the summer of 332, however, shortly before Alexander stormed Tyre, Darius was forced to recognize that this campaign had proved an expensive failure. Alexander's commanders on the Hellespont, Amphoterus and Hegelochus, had at last succeeded in raising a powerful fleet (the news of Issus probably helped here, too). They defeated Aristomenes' squadrons off Tenedos, and then swept south through the Aegean, recapturing Lesbos, Chios and other islands. Wholesale desertions from Pharnabazus' fleet by the Phoenician contingents made their task progressively easier as they advanced.

On land the situation (from Darius' point of view) was no better. Balacrus had defeated the Persian satrap

Hydarnes, and won back Miletus. Calas was campaigning successfully against the Paphlagonians. Most important of all, the Persian drive to cut Alexander's lines of communication across central Anatolia had proved a complete fiasco. Antigonus the One-Eyed had fought three pitched battles against Nabarzanes' crack cavalry divisions, and won them all.[55]

After a careful assessment of this deteriorating situation, Darius decided to approach Alexander again.[56] The terms of his second offer were somewhat more generous. Territorial concessions remained unaltered: he would cede all the provinces west of the Halys. But the ransom proposed for his family was now doubled, from ten to twenty thousand talents; and on top of this he offered Alexander the hand in marriage of his eldest daughter, with all the fringe-benefits proper to the Great King's son-in-law. His letter ended on an admonitory note. The Persian Empire was vast: sooner or later Alexander's small army would have to emerge into the steppes, where it would be far more vulnerable. Alexander, however, securely in control at Tyre, had no qualms about rejecting these new proposals. Darius, he told the Persian envoys, was offering him a wife he could marry whenever he so chose, and a dowry which he had already won for himself. He had not crossed the sea to pick up such minor fringe benefits as Lydia or Cilicia. His goal now was Persepolis, and the eastern provinces. If Darius wanted to keep his empire, Alexander repeated, he must fight for it, because the Macedonians would hunt him down wherever he might take refuge.

On receipt of this message, the Great King abandoned his attempt to secure a settlement by diplomatic means, and 'set to work on vast preparations for war'.[57] He summoned all the provincial satraps to join him in Babylon, with their full war-levies. The strongest force was that of the Bactrians: he could not afford to dispense with their help, though he profoundly distrusted the Bactrian satrap, Bessus, who had ambitions – and some genealogical claim – to be Great

King himself. Conscious that his earlier failures had been due in part to inadequate equipment, Darius this time took far greater care over the arming of his troops. Whole herds of horses were broken in to provide mounts for regiments that had previously fought on foot. Men who had had to make do with javelins were now issued swords and shields. More of the cavalry got protective chain-mail. As a special shock-force, the Great King ordered two hundred scythed chariots, to 'cut to pieces whatever came in the way of the horses as they were swiftly driven on'.

While Alexander was still at Tyre, fifteen delegates arrived from the Hellenic League. Its member-cities, they announced, had voted Alexander a gold wreath, as a prize for valour and in recognition of all he had done 'for the safety and freedom of Greece' [*sic*]. The king was far too realistic to accept this flattery at its face value; but it did offer a valuable pointer as to how much the Greek political climate had been changed by the news of Issus. At the same time Parmenio returned to base from Lowland Syria, having handed over his duties as military commander to Andromachus. Alexander was thus ready to continue his march again.

When the fall of Tyre became known, every coastal city along the direct route south to Egypt had made its submission – with one important exception. This was Gaza, a powerful walled stronghold at the edge of the desert, built on a tell a couple of miles inland, with deep sand-dunes all round it. Besides controlling the approaches to Egypt, Gaza stood at the head of an age-old caravan route, and thus formed a natural clearing-centre for the eastern spice-trade. Its inhabitants, a mixed group of Philistines and Arabs, had thus acquired enormous wealth – another reason for not by-passing it. The city's governor, Batis, believed it to be impregnable. While Alexander was besieging Tyre, Batus had hired a strong force of Arab mercenaries and laid in vast stocks of provisions. Like the

Tyrians, he now awaited Alexander's approach with cheerful confidence, secure in the knowledge that the last commander to take Gaza by direct assault had been Cambyses, two centuries previously.

Untroubled by such considerations, Alexander sent Hephaestion ahead by sea with the fleet and the siege-equipment, while he himself led the army thither by land. It seems likely that one of Hephaestion's tasks was to keep the army supplied with food and water: during August and September most of the wadis on the 160-mile stretch between Tyre and Gaza would be dry, while Batis had already efficiently stripped Palestine of its immediate grain-reserves. Alexander could not rely solely on the wells and granaries of the few cities along his route, and the only major river available was the Jordan: the obvious solution was to ferry in regular supplies by sea from Tyre and beyond. The line of march lay down the coast, which made the use of tenders easy: Alexander's troubles in the Gedrosian desert (see below, pp. 433 ff.) began when he was forced inland by the mountains of the Makran Coast Range. The Macedonians marched south through Ake (once used by the Persians as a stronghold for attacking Egypt)· where Alexander set up another mint; past Mt Carmel, sacred to Baal, and Joppa, where Andromeda had patiently awaited the arrival of her sea-monster, and Ascalon, on the borders of Lowland Syria. Samaria surrendered – for a while; but the tradition that Alexander made a pilgrimage to Jerusalem is mere pious legend.

At Gaza this easy progress was brought to an abrupt halt. Alexander's sappers went to work undermining the walls, but their task proved harder than they had anticipated. When the siege-towers were brought up, they sank axle-deep in fine, shifting sand. During a sally by Batis's mercenaries, Alexander was shot in one shoulder, the arrow piercing clean through his corslet. He lost a great deal of blood – it sounds as though the wound severed an artery – and had to be carried off the field half-conscious. The defenders made constant raids on his lines, trying to burn the siege equipment. In the end he was forced to build a mound all round Gaza, to the same height as the tell itself – a monumental undertaking. Then, at last, he could bring his most powerful catapults into play, hauling them up a ramp to the summit of the mound. After a prolonged pounding with heavy stone balls, a breach was opened in the fortifications. While one assault-group scrambled across on gangways, another broke in through an underground tunnel. After some savage hand-to-hand fighting, the city finally fell.

Alexander, whose first wound was still only half-healed, had his leg cracked by an artillery stone during the action. This, combined with the fact that Batis had held up his advance for a further two months, did not leave him in the best of tempers. The defenders, some 10,000 in number, he slaughtered wholesale, while their women and children were sold into slavery. He also captured vast quantities of spices from Gaza's warehouses – which provided him, *inter alia*, with his memorable present to old Leonidas (see above, p. 42). Batis himself was captured alive, by Leonnatus and Philotas, who brought him before Alexander for judgement. He stood there, grimly defiant, covered with dust and sweat and blood, a huge corpulent dark-skinned eunuch. Interrogated by Alexander, he refused to utter a word; he would not even beg for mercy. The king, who actively disliked ugly people (and was himself in a very ugly mood) seems to have lost control of himself at this point; the ordeal before Tyre had left him more than a little frayed. Curtius asserts that he had Batis lashed by the ankles behind a chariot and dragged round the walls of Gaza till he was dead: a grim variant on Achilles' treatment of Hector's dead body in the *Iliad*.[58]*

---

* Alexander must have suffered heavy casualties during his Phoenician campaign: much heavier, certainly, than those put out by the propaganda section, which (for example) admitted a mere 400 Macedonian casualties at Tyre. Before moving on, therefore, he sent Amyntas, son of

From Gaza Alexander marched for the Nile delta, covering the 130 miles to Pelusium in a week – a remarkable
forced march which, once again, was probably due to the
difficulty of obtaining water and supplies en route, from a
region that was nothing but barren desert. As before, the
fleet must have been responsible for provisioning his land
forces. At some point it was sent on ahead, and when the
Macedonians reached Pelusium it was already there to
welcome them – together with a rapturous throng of
Egyptians, for whom Alexander truly came as a liberator.
The Persians had maintained an uneasy and intermittent
regime in Egypt ever since 525, when Cambyses had first
acquired it for his empire. He made a disastrous start by
attempting to break the power of the Egyptian priesthood –
destroying their temples, mocking their beliefs, and with
his own sword dispatching the sacred bull, Apis.

The Egyptian fellaheen would endure more abuses than
most people; but any affront to their religion meant trouble.
For two centuries they had regarded the Persians as godless
oppressors against whom they revolted whenever the
opportunity presented itself. The most successful of these
insurrections lasted for some sixty years, during which time
Egypt was, to all intents and purposes, an independent
country. Three successive attempts to reconquer the province met with little success. It took that brutal autocrat Artaxerxes Ochus to break down the last elements of resistance
(see above, pp. 51–2). Small wonder, then, that the Egyptians,
having endured Persian rule again since 343, now hailed
Alexander as their deliverer. The Persians had treated this
province all the more harshly because they – like the
Romans after them – regarded it as little more than a
gigantic free granary, to be exploited by every means at

Andromenes, home to Pella, with ten triremes, on a fresh recruiting
drive (Diod. 17.49.1; QC 4.6.30–31). Local volunteers and mercenaries
were well enough in their way; but the backbone of Alexander's army
remained the phalanx, and only Macedonians – as yet – could adequately fill the many gaps in its ranks.

their disposal. Even during the fifth century Egypt's tribute-quota had been set at 700 talents, the second highest of any province in the empire. This did not include the free grain it was required to provide for Persia's 20,000 resident garrison troops.

Alexander, therefore, had everything in his favour when he arrived. If he took care not to offend local religious susceptibilities – better still, if he participated in some kind of public ritual to symbolize the transfer of power – he could count on enthusiastic support from the entire population. In the event, he got rather more than he bargained for. What had been conceived as a piece of political diplomacy turned into a profoundly felt emotional and spiritual experience. It is no exaggeration to say that the months Alexander spent in Egypt, from late October 332 till April 331, marked a psychological turning-point in his life.

From Pelusium the Macedonian fleet and army advanced up the Nile in stately procession towards Memphis. The Persian garrison offered no resistance. Mazaces, Darius' governor, came out to meet Alexander, presenting him with '800 talents and all the royal furniture'. This obliging service won Mazaces an administrative post in the new regime. But when Alexander reached Memphis, he found a still greater tribute awaiting him. The Persian kings had been, *ex officio*, Pharaohs of Egypt, by right of conquest over the native dynasty. Alexander had put down Darius: in the priests' eyes he now became their legitimate ruler. So, on 14 November 332, the young Macedonian was solemnly instated as Pharaoh. They placed the double crown on his head, and the crook and flail in his hands. He became simultaneously god and king, incarnation and son of Ra and Osiris; he was Horus the Golden One, the mighty prince, beloved of Amen, King of Upper and Lower Egypt.

The impact of this revelation on Alexander can well be imagined. Here, at last, Olympias' belief in his divine birth found a wholly acceptable context. Pharaonic dogma closed the gap between mortal and immortal, fused godhead and royal supremacy in one person. Soon Alexander's new subjects – primed, no doubt, by the propaganda section – absorbed the old rumours of his begetting into their own theocratic system. The god who had visited Olympias in the guise of a snake (the royal uraeus?) was Nectanebo, the last native Pharaoh; and the child of this union was Alexander.

Too much success can be dangerous: power breeds its own special isolation. There are signs that after Issus Alexander began to lose touch with his Macedonians, and such an infusion of superhuman charisma must surely have accelerated the process. Already his achievement had out-rivalled those of Heracles. Now, amid the ancient splendours of Egypt – a civilization which invariably bred semi-mystical awe in the Greek mind – he learnt that he was in truth a god, and the son of a god. Greek tradition dis-tinguished sharply between the two; Egypt did not. For Alexander this was to have interesting consequences.

After the coronation ceremony, Egypt's new Pharaoh made public sacrifice to Apis and the other Egyptian gods. Then, to show that despite everything he remained a Hel-lene at heart, he held splendid athletic contests and literary festivals, inviting many distinguished artists from Greece to take part in them. His growing number of local and not-so-local roles raised serious problems for the future. Already he was King of Macedonia, hegemon of the Greek League, Queen Ada's adopted son in Caria, and now Pharaoh of Egypt. In the last-named capacity he hastened to emphasize the contrast between his own regime and that of his Persian predecessors. Before leaving Memphis, in January 331, he ordered the restoration of at least two temples, at Karnak and Luxor (both of them, in all likelihood, destroyed by Cambyses). Then he sailed back down the Nile, this time along the western, or Canopic, tributary.

Here he was following a long-established Greek pre-cedent. For centuries all sea-borne commerce had entered the Nile by its so-called 'Canopic mouth', sailing some fifty miles through the delta to Naucratis, the international

Greek trading-port. Alexander's object, clearly, was to visit Naucratis and assess its value as a commercial centre. Having eliminated Tyre, he now meant to divert the Eastern Mediterranean's highly profitable flow of maritime traffic from Phoenicia to Egypt. Naucratis, perhaps because of its isolated inland position, did not impress him. When he reached the coast, and sailed round Lake Mareotis, he found a far better site, on a narrow limestone ridge between lake and sea, opposite the island of Pharos. The harbour here was deep, and provided excellent shelter. Both land approaches could be easily blocked against invasion. Cool prevailing winds would ensure a pleasant, healthy climate, even at the height of summer. There were no steamy marshes, no dust-storms, no malaria. Once more Alexander had a prophetic dream, in which some hoary sage declaimed Homer's lines alluding to Pharos. As his first royal act, Egypt's Macedonian Pharaoh decided to build a city there – Alexandria, the most famous of all those many foundations which afterwards bore his name.[59]

About this time Hegelochus arrived in Egypt, with a more than welcome report on Macedonian naval successes in the Aegean. He also brought with him a number of 'hard-core' oligarchs from Chios, who had ruled the island during Pharnabazus' ascendency. These he judged too dangerous to be left to the unpredictable mercies of the League Council, and Alexander agreed with him: they were promptly banished to Elephantine, far up the Nile. This, of course, constituted a flagrant breach of the League Treaty; but by now Alexander cared very little for Greek opinion, and one technical illegality more or less made little difference to him. The most important news that Hegelochus brought, however, concerned Athens. Demades, who was now in charge of Athenian state revenues (while remaining a good friend to Antipater) had persuaded the Athenian assembly not to make their powerful fleet available to King Agis of Sparta for the revolt he was now planning.

If they did so, he pointed out, they would lose 50 drachmas apiece: these funds, at present earmarked for public distribution during the Anthesteria (a religious spring festival) would go towards the expedition instead. Even Demosthenes kept quiet at this point; it seems possible that there was some private connection between him and (of all people) Hephaestion.[60]

It was now that Alexander expressed a particular desire, a *pothos* (see above, p. 128) to consult the oracle of Zeus-Ammon in the Siwah Oasis.[61] Since Siwah lay some three hundred miles distant across the burning wastes of the Libyan desert, his motives must have been very compelling. He did not make a habit of wasting six weeks or more on some mere casual whim. On the other hand, he did tend to consult an oracle before each major advance in his career of conquest. He had made a special detour to Delphi; the incident at Gordium had left a profound impression on him. Now once again he hoped to lift the veil that covered his future. In this connection it is significant that, though 'Ammon' was a Hellenized form of the Egyptian deity Amen-Ra, nevertheless Siwah's reputation stood highest in the Greek-speaking world.[62]

The oracle had been consulted by Croesus, and before him – or so legend related – by Alexander's ancestors Perseus and Heracles. Pindar had composed a hymn to Ammon, and dedicated his temple in Thebes. The Athenians had consulted his oracle during the Peloponnesian War; Aristophanes bracketed Siwah, for reliability, with Delphi and Dodona. Since then its reputation had risen still further. Many distinguished Greeks, including Lysander the Spartan, had sought its guidance. The Greeks in general regarded Ammon as parallel to, if not precisely identical with, their own Zeus: the very existence of an 'Ammonium' in Athens shows how far he had been acclimatized. If Alexander, as Pharaoh, had wished to consult an *Egyptian* oracle, he could have done so without setting foot outside the Nile Valley – at hundred-gated Thebes, for example. But despite his long flirtation with orientalism, he remained in many ways surprisingly parochial, not least in religious matters. What he wanted was the most trustworthy *Greek* oracle within marching-range. He may have felt himself specially favoured by the gods; but for him they were Greek gods, and would only speak through a suitably Hellenized mouthpiece.

Alexander had several obvious motives for making such a pilgrimage. Despite the scepticism expressed by some modern scholars, there can be little doubt that he was anxious to clear up the very serious question of his divine parentage. If he was in truth son of Ammon – or of Zeus – as the priests had declared him at his coronation, then let the oracle endorse their claim. Quite apart from this, he was about to embark on a crucial stage of his campaign, and would have been less than human had he not shown concern as to its ultimate success or failure. Would Siwah confirm the judgement of Gordium, and declare him the future lord of Asia? There was also the question of this new city he hoped to found at the mouth of the Nile: no Greek would dream of attempting such a task without endorsement from an oracle. Lastly – one question on which almost all our sources are agreed – he wanted to know *whether all his father's murderers had been punished.* If he was indeed a party to the assassination himself, this carefully oblique query affords us a horrifying glimpse into his mind. The fear of divine retribution hung over him; Philip's angry ghost, like Orestes' ineluctable Furies, haunted him still. And if he were declared the son of a god, parricide would *ipso facto* become mere murder, a venial offence which (to judge by the number of occasions on which he committed it) caused him few if any qualms.

So, probably in late January, he set out westward with a small party, following the coastal road immortalized by another great general, in a more modern war. He passed through the village known today as El Alamein, and after travelling about 170 miles reached the Libyan border settlement of Paraetonium (Mersa Matruh). Here he was met by a group of envoys from Cyrene, bringing expensive gifts, and an offer of friendship and alliance. Alexander duly made a treaty with them, which may have included an agreement for the purchase of North African wheat. He was always meticulous about securing his frontiers.[63] From Paraetonium he struck south-west into the desert, along an ancient caravan-trail. Siwah was still nearly 200 miles away.

This part of Alexander's journey proved both hazardous and uncomfortable.[64] After four days the party's water-supplies gave out, and only a providential rainstorm saved them. Later the *khamsin* – that terrible south wind of the desert – blew up, obliterating all landmarks in a blinding sandstorm. Alexander's guides completely lost their bearings, until a migrant flight of birds making for the oasis enabled them to pick up the trail again. They finally reached Siwah in late February, some three weeks after setting out. It must have been a welcome sight: an abundance of olives and date-palms, and everywhere the sound of water from innumerable springs.[65] But Alexander had no time for relaxation. He went straight to the temple, where the chief priest, warned of his approach, was waiting for him.[66] The new Pharaoh received a traditional greeting as 'Son of Ammon, Good God, Lord of the Two Lands'. His first query, then, was solved before he ever set foot inside the holy of holies.

Since none of his followers was admitted with him, and Alexander never revealed what took place during that famous oracular consultation (though it is just possible that the priests may have done so for a consideration) the responses he received must remain problematical.[67] When he came out, all he would say in answer to a chorus of eager questions was that 'he had been told what his heart desired'. In a subsequent letter to his mother, he wrote that he had learnt certain secret matters which he would impart to her, and to her alone, on his return. Since he died without ever again setting foot on Macedonian soil, these secrets went to the grave with him. Nevertheless, it seems very likely that the traditional answers are not too wide of the mark. Alexander's status as son of a god now became more generally known and accepted: other oracles hastened to endorse the claim. If Ammon did not actually promise him the Achaemenid empire, at least he was told to which gods he should sacrifice if, or when, he became lord of Asia (see below, p. 429). The future site of Alexandria must have been approved. Tradition asserts that he had to rephrase his question about Philip's murderers, since he had spoken of 'his father', and it was impious to describe the god as suffering a violent death. But whatever Alexander heard at Siwah, one thing is certain: it struck him with the force of a revelation, and left a permanent mark on his whole future career.

His purpose thus accomplished – and Ammon's priests suitably rewarded – Alexander left Siwah and returned by the way he had come: across the desert, and then eastward along the coast road to Lake Mareotis. He could have taken a more direct route, straight through the Qattara Depression to Memphis; but this would entail a 400-mile journey across unrelieved desert, which no more appealed to Alexander than it did to Rommel in 1941.[68] Besides, he was impatient to supervise the planning of his new city: time enough to revisit Memphis later. By the time he got back the king clearly had the whole plan of Alexandria worked out. It was to be built along the isthmus, in the symbolically appropriate shape of a Macedonian military cloak. Deinochares, the city-planner who had re-designed Ephesus, persuaded Alexander to adopt the axial-grid system, with a great central boulevard running from east to west, intersected by numerous streets at right-angles. But the king had his own ideas about such matters as the exact line of the outer fortifications, the position of the central market, and the sites to be reserved for various temples – including a shrine to the Egyptian goddess Isis.

He strode about the ridge at a breathless pace, marking-chalk in hand, equerries and surveyors panting along behind him. The dock area and harbours would be opposite Pharos, and the island itself was to be linked with the mainland by a great mole (later known as the Heptastadion because it was seven stades or furlongs in length). The grid was to be placed at such an angle that the streets got the full benefit of the Etesian winds. Presently Alexander ran out of chalk, and helpful attendants provided him with baskets of barley-meal that had been intended for the workers' rations. Full of town-planning zeal – what the workers had to say about it is not recorded – the king scattered flour by the handful, wherever the fancy took him. His main object appears to have been a quasi-ritual outlining of the city-wall. Presently flocks of hungry gulls and other birds descended *en masse* and made short work of this unexpected feast, till every last grain was devoured.

Alexander, being superstitious to a degree, was seriously alarmed, and at first regarded the incident as an unfavourable omen for his project. But that ingenious seer Aristander quickly reassured him. The city, he foretold, would have 'most abundant and helpful resources and be a nursing mother to men of every nation'. For once he hit the mark better than he knew, and those familiar with Alexandria's cosmopolitan splendours can fully endorse his verdict. The city's official foundation-date was 7 April: after the first bricks had been laid, Alexander left the builders to get on with it and sailed back up-river to Memphis,[69] where the atmosphere of divine royalty enfolded him once more. On temple walls at Luxor and Karnak and Khonsu Egyptian artists were busy depicting their new Pharaoh, 'king of the south and north, Setep-en-Amon-meri-re, son of the sun, lord of risings, Arksandres', a god among gods, in the act of sacrifice.

Nor, indeed, was this new line in flattery confined to Egypt. Once the Greeks learnt what had taken place at Memphis and Siwah, they very quickly saw how Alexander's position could be exploited for their own benefit. Among many embassies awaiting him on his return was one from Miletus, with remarkable news concerning Apollo's oracle at nearby Didyma. No prophecies had issued from this shrine since its destruction during the Persian Wars. Even the sacred spring dried up. But with the coming of Alexander – or so the envoys said – miracle of miracles, the spring began to flow again, and the god to prophesy. Since the Milesians were anxious to excuse themselves for having supported Pharnabazus during his Aegean campaign, the king probably took all this with a fairly large grain of salt. Nevertheless, it made undeniably useful political propaganda. Apollo ratified Alexander's descent from Zeus, predicted great future victories for him (not to mention the death of Darius), and saw no future in King Agis' threatened Spartan revolt.[70]*

From now on Alexander began to take a noticeably softer line with embassies from mainland Greece. All those who waited upon him in Memphis, for instance, had their petitions granted out of hand. Success – combined with what he had learnt at Siwah – may have put the king in a more generous mood; but it is hard not to believe that he was also influenced by the potentially explosive situation in the Peloponnese. Anything that might prevent a general revolt of the Greek states was worth trying.

The administration of Egypt presented special problems. The country's size, wealth, and enormous strategic importance had made a deep impression on Alexander. He also knew that its history as a province revealed two recurrent hazards: nationalist insurrections, and take-over bids by ambitious satraps. The arrangements he now put into force aimed to avoid both, their cardinal principle being com-

---

* King Agis' activities in the Peloponnese were, nevertheless, causing Alexander some anxiety. The small number of reinforcements which now arrived from Antipater – a mere 400 mercenaries and 500 Thracian horse (Arrian 3.5.1) – shows that the regent took an equally serious view of the situation.

plete separation of the civil and military arms. As far as possible Alexander left the actual running of the administration in Egyptian hands – a move which won him considerable popularity. Municipal government went on exactly as before, operating through a network of district commissioners. Thus, though taxes were now paid into the Macedonian war-chest, they continued to be collected by native officials: if the fellaheen grumbled, it would not be against Alexander. The existing structure was retained even in the higher echelons, so that an Egyptian 'nomarch', in true Pharaonic style, ruled over Upper and Lower Egypt. But since he controlled neither troops nor taxes, he had little chance of acquiring real power.

A similar system of divide and rule was employed on the military side. The eastern and western frontier districts were commanded by two Greeks, one of whom, Cleomenes of Naucratis, was further responsible for receiving taxes after collection. Alexander installed Macedonian garrisons at Memphis and Pelusium; the mercenaries remained under their own officers and were stationed elsewhere. Supreme command over these various units – some 4,000 men in all – was divided between two (possibly three) generals. Even they, however, had no authority over the naval squadron left to guard the Nile delta. Yet, despite all these precautions, a clever man – in this case Cleomenes – could, and did, very soon make himself *de facto* satrap of Egypt. He saw that the key to success here was hard cash, and (with the help of his military-cum-fiscal office) proceeded to amass it in vast quantities. The story of his rapid rise to power, through robbery, blackmail, grain-profiteering and wholesale extortion, is too complex, and marginal, to relate here. What does call for comment, however, is Alexander's reaction to it.

It was not long, a year or two at most, before this typical Middle East success story reached the king's ears. Far from removing his subordinate, or charging him with gross corruption, Alexander tacitly accepted Cleomenes' enhanced status. Later, this official recognition was still further extended, and all the Greek's past misdemeanours written off. Cleomenes, crook though he might be, was highly efficient and (more important) completely lacking in political ambition. He had nothing to gain from disloyalty to his master. He might make huge profits for himself, but he was sensible enough to give Alexander the lion's share. As a result he was the only Macedonian-appointed governor (apart from Antigonus the One-Eyed, who had different methods of making himself indispensable) to hold office uninterruptedly until the king's death. There is a moral of a sort here.[71]

The holiday in Egypt was now over. Callisthenes, who had been travelling round Ethiopia and speculating (with remarkable prescience) on the sources of the Nile, prepared to resume his more serious official labours. Alexander – having first had the river and its tributary canals bridged just below Memphis – set out on the road back to Tyre. It was now mid April. Just before the army marched north one of Parmenio's sons, Hector, was drowned during a boating expedition. Though Alexander is said to have been much attached to the young man personally, he doubtless consoled himself with the reflection that Hector's death meant one less place which Parmenio could fill. As he advanced up the coast, he learnt that Andromachus, his military commander in Lowland Syria, had been burnt alive by the Samarians. One swift, savage raid sufficed to smoke these guerrillas out of the caves in the Wadi Daliyeh where they had taken refuge. The murderers were surrendered and executed.

At Tyre Alexander found the fleet awaiting him, together with envoys from Athens, Rhodes and Chios. The Athenians had come to make a second application for the release of their fellow-countrymen captured at the Granicus (see above, p. 215). This time the request was granted at once, without argument. The Chians and Rhodians had complaints about their Macedonian garrisons: these complaints, after investigation, the king upheld. He also reimbursed the citizens of Mytilene for their expenses during the Aegean campaign, and granted them a large stretch of territory on the mainland opposite. All the king's actions at this point suggest that he was especially anxious to conciliate the Greeks as far as possible before heading east after Darius. Hence the high honours he paid to the independent princes of Cyprus, whose fleet had proved so invaluable during the siege of Tyre.

This policy of Alexander's shows diplomatic foresight, but must also have been to a great extent dictated by the alarming news from mainland Greece. During the winter Agis and his brother Agesilaus had managed to win over most of Crete. Before leaving Egypt, Alexander dispatched a naval task-force under Amphoterus (who had reported back from the Hellespont) with orders to 'liberate' the island and clear the sea of 'pirates' – the latter term doubtless including, if not specifically designating, any pro-Spartan squadrons they might encounter. But at Tyre Alexander learnt that Agis was now in open revolt. He had gathered a large mercenary force, and was appealing for all the Greek states to join him. A number of them, however – as might have been predicted – were either undecided, or anxious to stay clear of trouble. This gave Alexander his opening. A hundred Cypriot and Phoenician triremes now sailed to Crete to rendezvous with Amphoterus. The combined flotilla would then move into Peloponnesian waters, and do everything possible to unite the still uncommitted city-states against Sparta. Further rumours were coming in about a revolt in Thrace. But Alexander could waste no further time or reserves on Greece; from now on it was up to Antipater.

Before he finally left Tyre, Alexander made several important administrative changes. Menon, the satrap of Syria, had died shortly after taking office, and his stop-gap successor did not come up to Alexander's high standards of efficiency over organizing supplies for the army's forth-coming march inland. The king replaced him with a more carefully chosen nominee. However, the incident also suggested to him that he might do well to appoint two senior finance officers, with jurisdiction respectively over Phoenicia and coastal Asia Minor. Their main task would be to collect taxes (or rather *syntaxeis*) from the countless 'independent' city-states under Macedonian rule.

These new appointments were due in part to the mysteri-ous reappearance of Harpalus, Alexander's former quarter-master-general and treasurer, who had supposedly defected just before Issus (see above, p. 222), but was more probably on a secret mission to Greece. (He may well have brought Alexander intelligence concerning Agis' activities in the Peloponnese; and it is tempting, in view of later develop-ments [see below, pp. 308–9], to associate him with Athens' abstention from the revolt.) During his absence the Trea-sury had been run by two men, Coeranus and Philoxenus. Alexander, we are told, invited Harpalus back himself, promising him not merely a free pardon, but also – far more extraordinary, on the face of it – reinstatement in his old office, which carried enormous power and responsibility.[72]

Unless Harpalus' 'defection' was in fact some kind of cover-story, it is hard to credit Alexander, of all people, with so touching a faith in human repentance, especially regarding a post which involved access to vast stores of plunder and bullion. Whatever the truth of the matter, Harpalus, not surprisingly, accepted the king's offer without hesitation. His return, however, meant that new positions would have to be found for his stand-ins. It seemed a pity to waste their newly-acquired expertise: by appointing them regional finance officers Alexander solved the prob-lem very neatly. This, of course, left them as Harpalus' direct subordinates.

In early summer 331 Alexander led his whole army north-east through Syria, reaching Thapsacus on the Euphrates not earlier than 10 July.[73] By now the Mesopotamian summer was at its height. Temperatures in the plain reached a steady 110°F – not exactly ideal conditions for men carrying battle equipment, and in all likelihood heavy waterskins (not to mention iron rations) as well.* An advance party led by Hephaestion had constructed two pontoon bridges, leaving the final span incomplete as a safeguard against attack. Their operations were observed by a cavalry force some 3,000 strong under Mazaeus, the satrap of Babylon. Darius knew very well that Babylon itself must be Alexander's next objective. This great city on the Lower Euphrates was the economic centre of the empire, the strategic bastion protecting Susa, Persepolis, and the eastern provinces. Nor was there much doubt in the Great King's mind as to the route his adversary would take. Alexander, he knew, struck hard, fast, and with maximum economy. It was therefore odds-on that he would come straight down the east bank of the Euphrates – just as Cyrus had done in 401, to meet disastrous defeat at Cunaxa.

There are signs that Darius had studied the battle of Cunaxa with some care, and hoped to repeat it in detail. Mazaeus' advance force was similarly ordered to retreat before the invader, burning all crops for fodder as it went. Even the famous scythe-chariots (a long outmoded method of warfare) had been re-introduced because Artaxerxes used them against Cyrus. Darius clearly thought he had found the magical formula for victory. The plain at Cunaxa, some sixty miles north-west of Babylon, was ideal for cavalry manoeuvres – and the Great King now had some 34,000 armed horsemen at his disposal. Alexander's troops, he calculated, would reach Cunaxa hot, exhausted, and

---

*That Alexander anticipated commissariat difficulties on this march is clear: Arimmas, the satrap of Syria, had been ordered to set up supply depots for the army in advance, and was removed from office when he failed to organize sufficient provisions (Arrian 3.6.8, describing the journey between Tyre and Thapsacus). There is a sixty-mile waterless stretch on the Hamah-Aleppo section.

underfed. Between Mazaeus' scorched-earth policy and the blazing Mesopotamian sun, they would fall easy victims to his own fresh, well-armed, and numerically superior divisions. This whole elaborate fantasy, however, depended on Alexander's doing just what he was expected to do: always a dangerous assumption, and especially foolish in the present instance. It might surely have occurred to the Persian High Command that their opponent was at least as familiar with the Cunaxa débâcle as they were. Alexander, who undoubtedly knew his *Anabasis*, was the last man to walk into such a trap when he had Cyrus' example to warn him off. Besides, the narrow green strip of the Euphrates valley would barely support his army even if Mazaeus failed to lay it waste. So when the bridges were built, the Macedonian army, instead of marching downstream as predicted, struck out in a north-easterly direction across the Mesopotamian plain.

Mazaeus watched them go, horror-struck. Then he rode the 440 miles back to Babylon with the news. Darius could forget his dream of a second Cunaxa; a quick change of strategy was imperative. The Great King thereupon made up his mind to hold Alexander at the Tigris: a bold but hazardous plan, since no one could be certain where the Macedonian intended to cross. Four main fords could be regarded as possibilities. The nearest of these to Babylon was at Mosul, 356 miles away. From Thapsacus the march to Mosul was slightly longer, 371 miles. But as one went farther north, the ratio of distances changed in Alexander's favour. The most remote crossing-point from Babylon was also the nearest to Thapsacus, 308 miles as opposed to 422.

Darius' plan looks competent enough on paper. Fast mounted scouts were at once sent out to reconnoitre all the main crossing-points; these would report back to an advance force under Mazaeus, who would in turn notify Darius himself. The main body of the imperial army – now perhaps 100,000 strong – would march north by the Royal

Road to Arbela, due east of Mosul. This was where the Great King hoped and expected that Alexander's crossing would take place. However, if he chose a different ford, Mazaeus and his cavalry were to fight a holding action until the main force, under Darius himself, came up and finished the Macedonians off. In point of fact the Great King had no option but to concentrate on the Mosul ford. With his unwieldy army this was the only crossing-point where he could hope to get into position before Alexander arrived. Even so, he was going to have remarkable luck if he made it with any margin to spare. The overall plan depended on perfect coordination between Mazaeus, the scouts, and command headquarters. The imperial army had, at all costs, to reach Arbela on schedule. Most important of all, Alexander must get no inkling of this revised strategy: a security leak would be fatal.

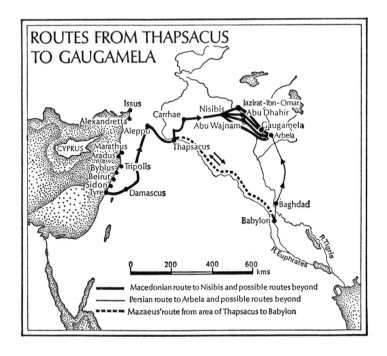

ROUTES FROM THAPSACUS
TO GAUGAMELA

Issus
Carrhae
Nisibis
Jazirat-Ibn-Omar
Abu Dhahir
Alexandretta
Aleppo
Abu Wajnam
Gaugamela
Arbela
CYPRUS
Marathus
Aradus
Thapsacus
Byblus
Tripolis
Beirut
Sidon
Tyre
Damascus
Baghdad
Babylon
R. Tigris
R. Euphrates

0   200   400   600
kms

———— Macedonian route to Nisibis and possible routes beyond
——— Persian route to Arbela and possible routes beyond
▪▪▪▪ Mazaeus' route from area of Thapsacus to Babylon

The Great King got his forces to Arbela, and prepared to march on Mosul. Meanwhile Alexander, following the northern route across Mesopotamia, had been lucky enough to capture some of Darius' scouts. Under interrogation they not only revealed the entire Persian plan of campaign, but also provided valuable details concerning the size and composition of the Great King's army. (How far Alexander believed what he was told is, as we shall see, quite another matter.) If the Macedonians had, in fact, been making for the Mosul ford, which seems quite probable, there was now a quick change of route: they turned off in the direction of Abu Wajnam, some forty miles to the north.[74]

Alexander reached the Tigris on 18 September, having suffered none of the hardships predicted by Darius. Northern Mesopotamia was not only cooler than the Euphrates valley, but far better supplied with grain and fodder. His men were neither starved nor wilting from heat-exhaustion. Even the perils of the crossing itself have been much exaggerated. Tradition paints a graphic picture of the Macedonian phalanx struggling breast-deep through a raging torrent, arms linked to stop themselves being swept away. There might have been a sudden flash-storm; but modern travellers report the average depth of the Tigris in September, between Jazirat and Mosul, as about a foot. In any case, the Macedonians encountered no opposition at Abu Wajnam. A few frightened scouts fled south with the news, and the Great King – already across the Greater Zab and approaching Mosul – had to change his plans yet again. He no longer had the Tigris between Alexander's army and his own. The Macedonians were little more than fifty miles away. His best chance now was to locate another open plain, suitable for cavalry and chariots, and bring Alexander to battle there.

Persian scouts found what he needed at Gaugamela (Tell Gomel), a village between the Khazir River and the ruins of Nineveh. Darius brought up his troops, inspected the plain, and at once set sappers to work clearing it of any trees, rocks, or awkward hummocks. What he did *not* do – an omission which afterwards cost him dear – was to occupy the low hills some three miles to the north-west. From this convenient vantage-point Alexander's reconnaissance troops subsequently observed, and reported on, all his military dispositions.

Shortly after crossing the Tigris, Alexander made contact with a regiment of Mazaeus' cavalry. The Paeonian mounted scouts, under their leader Ariston, were sent up to deal with this nuisance. The Persians fled; Ariston speared their commander, cut off his head, and 'amid great applause laid it at the king's feet'. The Macedonians were then given two days' rest. On the night before they resumed their march (20–21 September, at 9.20 p.m.) a near-total lunar eclipse took place. Aristander, optimistic as always, interpreted this as meaning victory for Alexander 'during that self-same moon'. Duly reassured, the army set off once more. Four days later (24 September) Mazaeus' cavalry was sighted again. Could this indicate the presence of the whole Persian army? A quick cavalry raid, led by the king in person, secured one or two prisoners. These soon told him what he wanted to know. Darius now lay at Gaugamela, no more than eight miles away beyond the hills. His ground-levelling operations showed that he did not intend to budge far from his present camp. Alexander therefore, very sensibly, gave his own troops another four days' rest (25–8 September). The heat down in the plain was gruelling, and he wanted them as fit and fresh as possible for the final battle.

During this period Darius' agents tried to smuggle in messages offering the Macedonians rich rewards if they would kill or betray Alexander. These were intercepted and (on Parmenio's advice) suppressed. The camp was also strengthened with a ditch and a palisade.[75] It was now, too, that the Great King's unfortunate wife fell ill and died –

either in childbirth or as the result of a miscarriage. Since she had been separated from her husband since November 333, almost two years before, Alexander may conceivably not have found her quite such an 'irritation to the eyes' (let alone to his long-term dynastic ambitions) as he liked to proclaim. This sad news was brought to Darius by a eunuch of the queen's bedchamber, who escaped from the Macedonian camp, stole a horse, and so reached the Persian lines.

The Great King's reaction was interesting. After an understandable outburst of sorrow and passion, he pulled himself together, and made his third and final attempt to reach a settlement with Alexander by peaceful negotiation. This time he offered more, far more, than previously – all territories west of the Euphrates; 30,000 talents as ransom for his mother and daughters; the hand of one daughter in marriage, and the retention of his son Ochus as a permanent hostage. Alexander placed these proposals before his war council – though this time the decision was never seriously in doubt. Parmenio, as spokesman for the old guard, observed sourly that dragging so many prisoners around ever since the capture of Damascus had been a great nuisance: why not ransom the lot and have done with it? As for one old woman and two girls, they were a bargain at the price offered. No man hitherto had ever ruled from the Euphrates to the Danube – and here was Darius proposing to ratify all these conquests without a fight! 'If I were Alexander,' Parmenio concluded, 'I should accept this offer.' 'So should I,' said Alexander, 'if I were Parmenio.' Then he turned to Darius' envoys. Asia could no more support two monarchs, he told them, than the earth could exist with two suns. If Darius wanted to keep his throne, he would have to fight for it. The Persian terms were rejected out of hand, and Darius 'gave up any hope of a diplomatic settlement'.[76]

Alexander had not yet actually set eyes on Darius' new army for himself, and was clearly sceptical of what he had heard concerning it. He seems to have assumed that it would be neither very much larger nor noticeably more efficient than the force which he had broken at Issus. Prisoners' reports and similar sources always tended to exaggerate. His own army had been built up since then to a total of about 47,000 men. Before dawn on 29 September he breasted the low ridge of hills above Gaugamela, and got the first glimpse of what he was up against. It shocked him considerably. Darius' army consisted, to all intents and purposes, entirely of cavalry, and armoured cavalry at that. Looking down through the morning haze, Alexander could see countless thousands of mailed horsemen, this time including the crack eastern divisions from Parthia and Bactria. A snap count suggested that in this vital arm the Macedonians were outnumbered by at least five to one. The Great King, unable to raise a competent infantry force, had decided to give up the idea of front-line foot-soldiers altogether.

Not only was this highly unconventional force stronger and better-armed than Alexander had anticipated; its order of battle also slightly took him aback. Darius, this time, was clearly determined that the Macedonians should not repeat those tactics which had brought them victory at Issus and the Granicus. On his left wing he had stationed a considerable force of Bactrian and Scythian cavalry, together with half his scythed chariots. The more he studied these Persian dispositions, the less Alexander liked them. He therefore assembled his staff-commanders, and solicited their advice. Should they attack now, or wait till tomorrow? Without any overt suggestion that the Persian army was more formidable than had been supposed, he argued that perhaps the terrain needed closer reconnaissance. There had been rumours of hidden pits with sharpened stakes fixed in them, of caltrops and other similar devices. Most of his officers were keyed up for immediate action, but Alexander – with Parmenio's backing – managed to talk them out of it.

He spent much of 29 September riding round the prospective battlefield with a strong cavalry escort, examining

the ground – and Darius' lines – with a very sharp eye. The
Persians made no attempt to stop him. Then (like his hero
Achilles, but for very different reasons) he retired to his
tent. While his men ate and slept, Alexander sat up hour
after hour, 'casting over in his mind the number of the
Persian forces', considering and discarding one tactical
scheme after another. During the night Parmenio visited
him, with the suggestion of a surprise night-attack. The
king retorted, snubbingly, that to steal victory was a cheap
trick (and, he might have added, bad propaganda):
'Alexander must defeat his enemies openly and without
subterfuge.' Besides, as Arrian reminds us, a night-attack is
of all operations the most dangerous and unpredictable.
This did not stop Alexander from carefully 'leaking' the
possibility of such an attack, so that the rumour very soon
reached Darius' lines. As a result the Persians stood to arms
all night and were exceedingly sleepy in the morning.

After much thought, Alexander worked out the last
details of his master strategy – and having done so, at once
fell into a deep untroubled sleep. The sun rose, but the king
did not. Company officers, on their own initiative, sounded
reveille and issued orders for the men to take breakfast. Still
Alexander slumbered on. Finally Parmenio shook him
awake. It was high time to form up in battle order – and
only Alexander himself knew what that order was. The
king yawned and stretched. When Parmenio expressed
surprise at his having slept so soundly, Alexander retorted:
'It is not remarkable at all. When Darius was scorching the
earth, razing villages, destroying foodstuffs, I was beside
myself; but now what am I to fear, when he is preparing to
fight a pitched battle? By Heracles, he has done exactly
what I wanted.'

This in one sense was true, as it had been at the Granicus,
and for much the same reasons (see above, pp. 170–71); but it
was also the most superb bravado. Darius had 34,000 front-
line cavalry to Alexander's 7,250: no amount of strategy –
or so it might have been thought – could get round that one

basic fact.[77] Alexander was going to be outflanked, and
knew it. There were no mountains to protect him as at
Issus, and no sea either. The Persian line overlapped his
by nearly a mile. So while his basic order of battle remained
unchanged, he took special pains to protect his flanks and
rear – and also to make his line appear weaker there than it
in fact was. He stationed a powerful force of mercenaries
on his right wing, carefully masking them with cavalry
squadrons. He echeloned both wings back at an angle of
45° from his main battle-line. Finally, he placed the league
infantry and the rest of the Greek mercenaries to cover his
rear.

He was, in fact, making a virtue of necessity. Alone in his
lamplit tent, by sheer intuitive genius, he had invented a
tactical plan that was to be imitated, centuries afterwards,
by Marlborough at Blenheim and Napoleon at Austerlitz,
but which no other general (so far as is known) had hitherto
conceived. To reduce the vast numerical odds against him,
and to create an opening for his decisive charge, he planned
to draw as many Persian cavalry units as possible away from
the centre, into engagement with his flank-guards. When the
flanks were fully committed he would strike, hard, at Darius'
weakened centre. Such a plan, of course, was going to need
the most delicate timing. Alexander had no spare cavalry
with which to provoke Darius. The Great King himself must
make the first move, must be edged into taking the bait
which those massively outflanked and deceptively weak-
looking wings offered him. Furthermore, the decisive attack
itself had to be delivered at just the right moment. 'If he
charged too soon, his offensive weapon would be blunted; if
he left it too late, the wings might cave in and the heavy
cavalry become involved in a fight for its very existence.'[78]

Both commanders made a speech before the battle,[79] and
in each case an interesting theological angle was involved.
Darius, invoking Mithra, emphasized to his troops that this
was a Holy War rather than a mere struggle for power:
his description of Alexander and the Macedonians sounds

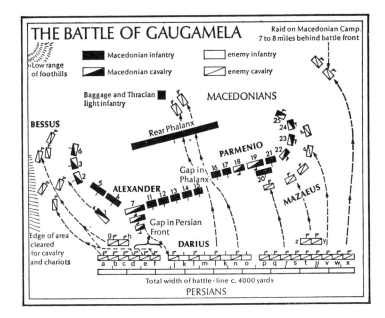

THE BATTLE OF GAUGAMELA

Raid on Macedonian Camp.
7 to 8 miles behind battle front

Low range
of foothills

Macedonian infantry enemy infantry
Macedonian cavalry enemy cavalry

Baggage and Thracian
light infantry

MACEDONIANS

BESSUS

Rear Phalanx

PARMENIO

Gap in
Phalanx

ALEXANDER

MAZAEUS

Gap in Persian
Front

Edge of area
cleared
for cavalry
and chariots

DARIUS

Total width of battle-line c. 4000 yards

PERSIANS

Macedonians

Right flank guard
 1 Greek Mercenary Cavalry—
    Menidas
 2 Lancers—Aretes
 3 Paeonian Cavalry—Ariston
 4 ½ Agrianians—Attalus
 5 ½ Macedonian Archers—
    Briso
 6 Veteran Mercenaries—
    Cleander

Right wing
 7 Companion Cavalry—Philotas
 8 Javelin-men—Balacrus
 9 ½ Macedonian Archers—
    Briso
10 ½ Agrianians—Attalus
11 Hypaspists—Nicanor
12 Phalanx—Coenus
13 Phalanx—Perdiccas
14 Phalanx—Meleager
15 Phalanx—Polyperchon

Left wing
16 Phalanx—Simmias
17 Phalanx—Craterus
18 Allied Greek Cavalry—
    Erigyius
19 Thessalian Cavalry—Philip
20 Cretan Archers—Clearchus
21 Achaian Mercenary Infantry

Left flank guard
22 Greek Mercenary Cavalry—
    Andromachus
23 Thracian Horse—Sitalces
24 Allied Greek Horse—
    Coeranus
25 Odrysian Horse—Agathon

Persians

Left wing
 a Bactrian Cavalry
 b Dahae Cavalry
 c Arachosian Cavalry
 d Persian Cavalry
 e Susian Cavalry
 f Cadusian Cavalry
 g Bactrian Cavalry
 h Scythian Cavalry
 i Chariots

Centre
 j Carian Cavalry
 k Greek Mercenaries
 l Persian Horse Guards
 m Persian Foot Guards
 n Indian Cavalry
 o Mardian Archers

Right wing
 p Coelo—Syrian Cavalry
 q Mesopotamian Cavalry
 r Median Cavalry
 s Parthian Cavalry
 t Sacian Cavalry
 u Tapurian Cavalry
 v Hyrcanian Cavalry
 w Albanian Cavalry
 x Sacesinian Cavalry
 y Cappadocian Cavalry
 z Armenian Cavalry

uncommonly like later Persian diatribes against the Demons
of the Race of Wrath (which may, indeed, have influenced
Curtius' account). Alexander, attended by a white-robed,
gold-crowned Aristander, delivered a long exhortation to
the Thessalians and league troops – not, be it noted, to his
own Macedonians – praying the gods 'if he was really
sprung from Zeus, to defend and strengthen the Greeks'.
It was the morning of 30 September 331 B.C. These pre-
liminaries once over, the Macedonian and Persian armies
moved forward, crabwise and with apparent reluctance,
into an engagement which, as it turned out, 'gave Alexander the chance to secure the whole Persian Empire from
the Euphrates to the Hindu Kush': his military master-
piece, alike in design and execution.

The Macedonians advanced, as usual, with their left
wing progressively echeloned back, trying to lure the Persian right, under Mazaeus, into a premature flank engagement. At the same time the Persian left – commanded by
Bessus, satrap of Bactria and would-be Great King – outflanked Alexander so far that he and the Companion
Cavalry were almost opposite Darius' central command-
post. Neither side wanted to initiate the engagement: both
Alexander and Darius – who by now had learnt the secret
of his opponent's 'oblique' advance – kept edging forward
and sideways, till they were very near the edge of the terrain
which the Persians had cleared for their chariots and
cavalry. Someone had to act; and in the end it was Darius.
Anxious to halt this dangerous drift towards rough ground,
he ordered Bessus to launch a flank attack against Alexander's advancing right wing.

This was the move for which Alexander had been waiting.
Once Bessus' cavalry was committed, the king, with superb
timing, kept feeding in further units from his deep flank-
guard. To counter this increasing pressure, Bessus brought
up squadron after squadron, determined now to penetrate
or roll up Alexander's flank, and probably still unaware of
the 6,700 mercenaries waiting in reserve behind the Mace-

donian cavalry. A point came when this force – Alexander's cavalry numbered no more than 1,100 – was holding, for just long enough, ten times its own strength of front-line, heavily armoured Persian horsemen. Meanwhile Darius, as a diversionary measure, launched his scythed chariots, which proved, on the whole, remarkably ineffective. The screen of light-armed troops which Alexander had posted in front of his main line caused havoc amongst them by pelting the horses with javelins, and stabbing the drivers as they whirled past. A few limbs and heads were lopped off, to provide, in due course, a field-day for Graeco-Roman rhetoricians; but the well-drilled ranks of the phalanx opened wide, and the survivors were rounded up by Alexander's grooms, with the help of a few agile volunteers from the Guards Brigade.

By now almost all the Persian cavalry on both flanks was engaged. Parmenio was fighting a desperate defensive action against Mazaeus, while Alexander had just flung in his last mounted reserves, the Rangers, to hold Bessus. At this crucial moment the king's keen eye detected a thinning of the ranks, perhaps even a gap, momentarily opening in Darius' left centre. It was now or never. Gathering all his remaining forces into one gigantic wedge, Alexander charged. The spearhead of this wedge was formed by the Companion Cavalry, Alexander himself leading with the Royal Squadron. Behind him came seven more squadrons, together with the Guards Brigade and any disengaged phalanx battalions, followed by a fierce rush of light-armed troops.

The Companions smashed through the weakened Persian centre towards Darius, shattering his household cavalry division and the Greek mercenaries. In the course of two or three minutes the battle was completely transformed. Bessus, still fully engaged against Alexander's right, found his own flank dangerously exposed by the force of the Companions' charge; he had lost touch with Darius, and feared that at any moment Alexander's wedge might swing round to take him in the rear. He therefore, with good justification, sounded a retreat, and began to withdraw his forces. At the same time Darius, hard-pressed by Alexander's cavalry and infantry, and seeing himself in danger of being cut off, fled the field as he had done at Issus. This time he only just managed to get away before the ring closed on him. It was now, at this crucial moment, that an urgent message reached Alexander from Parmenio, informing him that the left was heavily engaged; it had probably been dispatched just before the king's charge with the Companions.*

A gap had opened between Parmenio's Thessalians and the charging battalions of the phalanx. Into this gap a body of Indian and Persian cavalry charged headlong, probably with the original intention of taking Parmenio in the rear. In the event, however, perhaps carried on by their own momentum, they swerved neither to left nor right, but rode straight on through the reserve infantry, and made for Alexander's baggage-camp. After looting for a while, and releasing some Persian prisoners (the queen mother, wisely, decided to sit tight until the situation clarified itself) they were driven out again. On their way back they ran into Alexander and the cavalry, and put up the toughest fight of the entire battle. During this scrimmage no less than sixty Companions lost their lives, and Alexander himself was in serious danger.

By now, however, the whole Persian line was rapidly breaking up. Once again the Great King's personal withdrawal had proved decisive. Darius vanished across the plain towards Arbela, dust-clouds swirling behind his chariot. Mazaeus, seeing him go, at once broke off the long and desperate struggle against Parmenio. Bessus was already withdrawing, in comparatively good order, on the farther

* This incident was afterwards turned, by Callisthenes and others, into something much less creditable to Parmenio. His conduct in the battle was represented as 'sluggish and inefficient'; he was 'envious and resentful' of Alexander, and his message – probably a pre-arranged signal with the king to determine the timing of the main charge – became an abject appeal for help, which delayed Alexander just long enough to prevent his capturing Darius; cf. Marsden, p. 62.

flank. Parmenio's Thessalians, who had fought superbly all day against heavy odds, now found themselves surging forward in pursuit of a beaten foe.[80] For the second time, Alexander's efforts to kill or capture Darius were frustrated. While Parmenio rounded up the Persian baggage-train, with its elephants and camels, the king rode on into the gathering dusk, still hoping to overtake Darius' party. When darkness fell, he rested his weary men and horses for an hour or two, resuming the chase about midnight. The Macedonian troop rode into Arbela as dawn broke, having covered some seventy-five miles during the night, only to find Darius gone. However, as at Issus, he had left his chariot and bow behind him, together with no less than 4,000 talents in coined money. This was a substantial consolation-prize; and in any case the Great King's prestige had suffered such a catastrophic blow that his personal escape was of comparatively little moment. The Achaemenid empire had been split in two, and its ruler's authority ripped to shreds. If Alexander now proclaimed himself Great King in Darius' stead, who except Bessus would deny his right to the title?

Macedonian intelligence officers soon pieced together the story of the Great King's escape. He and his retinue had retreated headlong to Arbela, not even bothering to break down the river-bridges as they fled. Here they were joined by Bessus and the Bactrian cavalry, 2,000 loyal Greek mercenaries, and a few survivors from the Royal Guard. The defeated monarch gathered them around him, and made a short speech before continuing his flight. He predicted, correctly, that Alexander would press straight on to the rich cities of southern Iran, 'since all that part was inhabited and the road itself was easy for the baggage trains, and besides, Babylon and Susa naturally seemed to be the prize of the war'. He himself, he said, intended to take the road over the mountains into Media and the eastern provinces, where he would recruit yet another army. Let the Macedonians glut themselves with gold, idle their time away amid concubines and luxury: nothing was better calculated to weaken them as a fighting force.

It may be doubted whether Darius' audience took this apologia very seriously, though it was about the best he could do in the circumstances. They had suffered a massive and humiliating defeat,* which no mere words could palliate. The prospect of abandoning Babylon, for whatever reason, came as an added indignity. However, the Greeks remained doggedly loyal; even Bessus was not confident enough – yet – to discard Darius altogether. As a symbolic figurehead he still counted for something. So, soon after midnight, these battered remnants of the Persian Grand Army set out together from Arbela, taking the road east through the Armenian mountains, and eventually descending on Ecbatana from the north. Here Darius halted for a while, to let stragglers rejoin him. He made sporadic efforts to re-organize and re-arm them; he also sent palpably nervous notes to his governors and generals in Bactria and the upper satrapies, urging them to remain loyal. But Gaugamela had broken his nerve, and he was never to recover it.[81]

---

* Alexander had not only defeated a far stronger army on its own chosen terrain, but had done so without over-heavy losses. His highest recorded casualties (P. Oxyrh. 1798) are 1,000 foot and 200 horses (other estimates range from 300 [QC 4.16.26] to a mere hundred [Arrian 3.15.6, probably drawing on Ptolemy]) – as against Persian losses, according to the same source, of some 53,000.

[8]

The Lord of Asia

THE oracle at Gordium had foretold that Alexander would
become 'lord of Asia' – that is, king of the Persian Empire
and Darius' legitimate successor. It was thus, somewhat
prematurely, that he had bidden Darius address him when
they exchanged letters. After Gaugamela the claim looked
a good deal more plausible. As Plutarch says, 'the empire of
the Persians was thought to be thoroughly dissolved'.
Alexander made his wishes known to the army, which
thereupon acclaimed him 'lord of Asia' as part of the victory
celebrations. Thus Gaugamela marked a turning-point for
Alexander in more ways than one. The Greeks, who had
never taken his democratic professions very seriously, found
this new development absolutely in character. For them he
had always been a type-cast example of the ambitious
tyrant, and now he was proceeding to vindicate their
judgement.

The effect on his Macedonian troops, however, was profound. From this time on, relations between Alexander and
the army steadily deteriorated, culminating – as we shall see
– in ugly episodes of mutiny and murder. The Macedonian
old-guard barons, in particular, were shocked by their
king's visible drift towards oriental despotism. For them
Alexander's task in Asia was done, and the sooner he took
them all home again the better. Parmenio told him, bluntly,
that he ought rather to look back upon Macedonia than
fix his gaze on the East. But Alexander's horizon of conquest
was continually expanding; Macedonia, for him, had begun
to seem very small and far away.

The king himself understood his dilemma all too well.
He would not, could not, abandon the vision of glory and
empire that drove him on; but he went out of his way to

conciliate those who opposed him most vehemently. Before leaving Arbela he made lavish distributions of 'wealth, estates, and provinces' to his senior officers. At the same time, anxious to win favour among the Greeks – not surprisingly, with the Peloponnese in revolt – he wrote telling them that all their tyrannies were abolished, and they could henceforth live under their own laws. This sounded a fine and generous gesture; but the king's private instructions to Antipater seem to have been rather different. At all events, the tyrants of Sicyon, Pellene and Messenia continued in office; it would be simple enough, later, when all danger was past, to make Antipater himself the scapegoat for their retention (see below, pp. 458–9). Alexander's promise to rebuild Plataea, however, was eventually

honoured, perhaps as a safeguard against any resurgence of ambition by Thebes.[1]

One of the trickiest problems the king had to face would only begin with his invasion of Persian soil. Hitherto he had been able to present himself as a liberator. In Asia Minor and Egypt the claim could be made to look convincing enough, despite those outbursts of pure terrorism down the Phoenician coast. Even for Babylonia, once proudly independent, the formula might just work. But once he set out on the road to Susa and Persepolis, he would have to think of a different formula. He could hardly claim to be liberating the Persians from themselves. Thus Alexander soon became, as the Marxists say, involved in a contradiction; which may well explain why his dispatches home now placed more emphasis on revenge than liberation as a motive for the crusade. Doubtless he took the same line with his Macedonian troops.

However, if he was to prevent trouble in his rear – let alone pose as Darius' successor – he would have to conciliate the Persian nobility in no uncertain fashion; and this, again, would not endear him to his own men. A good many Iranian grandees did not hesitate to collaborate with the invader. There nevertheless remained a hard core of opposition, led by Persia's priestly caste, the Magi, whose hostility to Alexander was primarily religious in origin, and who regarded him as a mere heathen aggressor. He did not worship Ahura Mazda; he was not a Persian aristocrat of Achaemenid stock, nor even from one of the 'Seven Noble Families'. In the eyes of this powerful group, his claim to the throne rested on force, and force alone. Their propaganda presented him, naturally enough, as a common usurper, a ravening lion sent for Persia's destruction.

Alexander, who had studied the teachings of the Magi under Aristotle, seems to have been well aware of these objections. If he hoped to get himself accepted as Great King, he would need to make very large concessions to national religious and dynastic sentiment. His only chance of legitimizing himself as an Achaemenid was by removing Darius and marrying into the royal family: hence his careful cultivation of the queen mother.[2] Though any immediate plans he may have had for a dynastic alliance were disrupted by Stateira's untimely death, and Darius' second escape, the king's Achaemenid ambitions were bound to cause an eventual breach between him and his fellow-countrymen. He could hardly lay claim to the throne of Persia, for instance, without observing Persian court etiquette. The Great King was hedged about with endless taboos and religious ritual – in sharp contrast to the easy-going relationship which prevailed between a Macedonian monarch and his peers. To combine these roles was, ultimately, impossible; sooner or later he would have to choose between them.

Alexander stayed no more than a day or two in Arbela. He buried his own dead, but left the Persians where they lay: one excellent reason for a rapid departure. A force under Philoxenus was sent ahead to Susa, by the direct route, with orders to accept the city's surrender and safeguard its treasure. Meanwhile Alexander himself crossed the Tigris and marched for Babylon, some 300 miles away to the south. His route led through the most fertile region of Mesopotamia: the country was criss-crossed with irrigation canals, so that water and shade were both plentiful. At Mennis, near modern Kirkuk, Alexander was shown a great bitumen lake, and also a well of crude petroleum or naphtha. The local inhabitants, anxious to demonstrate the marvellous properties of this liquid, one evening sprinkled it all along the street leading to Alexander's quarters, and then set a torch to the ground, so that 'with the speed of thought the flame darted to the other end, and the street was one continuous fire.'[3]

Meanwhile some hard private bargaining was going on between Alexander and Mazaeus, who after Gaugamela had returned to his duties as satrap of Babylon. Alexander wanted a bloodless surrender of the city; Mazaeus hoped to continue in office under the new regime. Some sort of provisional deal was worked out during the march south. Nevertheless, Alexander did not trust his late opponent, and therefore approached Babylon in battle-formation, ready for any kind of treachery or surprise attack. To those dusty soldiers trudging along beside the Euphrates, the city must have appeared like some shimmering mirage

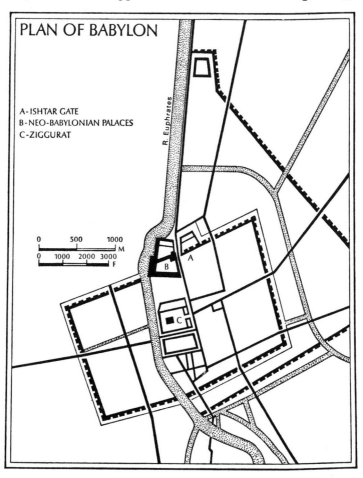

PLAN OF BABYLON

A-ISHTAR GATE
B-NEO-BABYLONIAN PALACES
C-ZIGGURAT

R. Euphrates

0   500   1000
|___|___|___| M
0 1000 2000 3000
|__|__|__|__| F

across the plain: a vista of high white terraces, luxuriant greenery, great crenellated walls and towers. Babylon formed a rough square (each side being about fifteen miles long) bisected by the river and the processional way. Its outer fortifications were of mud-brick bound with bitumen, and so broad on top that two four-horse chariots could pass abreast on them.

Hardly less impressive was the colourful procession which now came trailing out along the royal road – with much trumpet-blowing and clashing of cymbals – to greet Alexander and his men. At its head rode the renegade satrap Mazaeus, who formally made over city, citadel and treasure into the king's hands. Behind him crowded Babylon's chief citizens, with a motley collection of livestock as gift-offerings: not only horses and cattle, but also caged lions and leopards. There followed a solemnly chanting group of Babylonian priests, and lastly, as escort, several magnificently accoutred squadrons of the Great King's household cavalry. Alexander now mounted a chariot, formed his men into hollow columns (he still seems to have suspected some sort of trap) and made a superb triumphal entry. The whole route was strewn with flowers and garlands. Silver altars, heaped high with rich spices, burnt sweetly in honour of the conqueror. As Alexander rode under the high gold and lapis splendours of the Ishtar Gate, with its heraldic bulls and dragons, crowds on the parapet cheered and showered roses down on him.

Ironically enough, when Cyrus the Great had entered Babylon two centuries earlier (29 October 539) he too had been welcomed as a liberator by Marduk's priests. But in 482, after a nationalist rebellion Babylon had received terrible punishment. The fortifications built by Nebuchadnezzar were demolished; worst of all, the seven-storey ziggurat, 300 feet high, on which stood Esagila, Marduk's temple, the 'House of the Foundation of Earth and Heaven', was pulled down, never to be rebuilt. The god's solid gold statue, eighteen feet high and weighing nearly 800 lb., was carried off by Xerxes' troops and melted down for bullion. Babylon's walls had been rebuilt, but Esagila remained a lost memory. Alexander's enthusiastic welcome was due in part to his promise – which no doubt Mazaeus had passed on – that he would restore the ziggurat and shrine of the god. Once more, and for the last time, he could present himself as the deliverer from Persian injustice and oppression.

In any case the cheerful, luxury-loving citizens of Babylon, reflecting (with good reason) that it was better to collaborate than to suffer the fate of Tyre, went out of their way to give these Macedonian troops a month's leave they would never forget. Officers and men alike were billeted in luxurious private houses, where they never lacked for food, wine, or women. Babylon's professional courtesans were reinforced by countless enthusiastic amateurs, including the daughters and wives of many leading citizens. (After-dinner striptease seems to have been very popular.) Their guests were shown the usual tourist sights, including the fabulous Hanging Gardens – a stone-terraced forest of trees and shrubs, built by an Assyrian king whose wife pined for the forests and uplands of her native Iran.[4]*

While his troops enjoyed themselves, and Callisthenes supervised the transcription of the Babylonian priests' astronomical records (if they really went back for 31,000 years he must have had his time cut out) the king plunged into problems of administration. His first and undoubtedly most important step was to confirm Mazaeus as satrap of Babylon, with the traditional right of coining silver. What Parmenio and the Macedonian diehards thought about this re-instatement of an ex-enemy can all too easily be

---

*Alexander was scornfully amused by the statutory regulations – inscribed on a brazen pillar in the palace – for Darius' breakfast and dinner. These included such items as 100 geese or goslings, 400 bushels of wheaten flour, and a talent's weight (57½lb.) of garlic (Polyaenus 4.3.32). The interpreter perhaps neglected to inform him that this (admittedly extravagant) outlay was for the Great King's entire palace household and all his retainers.

imagined; but it was a very practical step. If Alexander intended, from now on, to put himself forward as the legitimate Archaemenid successor, he had to get the support of the Persian aristocracy; and this implied more than suppressing potential opposition. Iran's noble families provided the empire's traditional administrators, and Alexander had no trained (much less bilingual) civil servants with which to replace them.

From this point of view Mazaeus' appointment can be seen as a particularly astute move: the satrap had a Babylonian wife, and strong local connections. Thus Alexander contrived to improve his image with the Persians, while at the same time posing as a liberator for the benefit of nationalists in Babylon. Not that he was foolish enough to give Mazaeus a completely free hand. The garrison commander in Babylon was a Macedonian; so was the officer left in charge of the satrapal levies, with responsibility for further recruiting. Mazaeus might have the right to issue coins, but not to collect taxes. This job went to a Macedonian finance officer, working under Harpalus. It was now, too, that Alexander first developed his keen interest in Babylonian religion and astrology (perhaps erroneously equating Egyptian Sarapis with Bel-Marduk, because the latter was sometimes referred to as Sarri-rabu, 'the great king'). He may have ordered the restoration of Marduk's temple and ziggurat, in the first instance, for purely political reasons; but after a while he seems to have acquired a genuine respect for these Chaldaean priests. Whatever rituals they prescribed he carried out, and when the army moved on a number of them joined his retinue.[5]

Susa, the second of the Great King's palatial capitals, lay some 375 miles south-east from Babylon, close to the Persian Gulf. The plain in which it stood was immensely fertile, but ringed with mountains, so that for nine months of the year it formed a natural oven. Strabo wrote that 'when the sun is hottest, at noon, the lizards and the snakes could not cross the streets in the city quickly enough to prevent their being burnt to death'. One reason why Alexander waited a month in Babylon was to let Susa cool down. By mid November, when he finally set out, the winds had veered round to south or south-east, and the first rains had fallen.* The army was overtaken en route by massive reinforcements from Greece, under Amyntas (see above, pp. 267-8, n.): 1,500 cavalry and no less than 13,500 infantry, of whom nearly a third had been recruited in Macedonia itself. There were also fifty new royal pages: the king had certainly gone out of his way to insure himself against trouble at home, though the pages were later (see below, p. 378) to prove something of a trouble in their own right.

The arrival of this force prompted Alexander to halt his march for a day or two and carry out certain innovations in the command structure. Infantry reinforcements were still distributed territorially among the battalions of the phalanx, and a new additional seventh battalion was now formed. But with the cavalry Alexander went out of his way to break down all territorial groupings. The squadrons were now subdivided into two troops (*lochoi*), each under its own troop commander, and brought up to strength with replacements chosen on a random, non-regional basis. Promotion in future was to be by merit rather than seniority – which again gave the king far closer control over all military appointments. This kind of shake-up, taken in conjunction with the donations at Babylon, suggests that Alexander was already faced by considerable lack of enthusiasm – to put it no more strongly – among his officers and men. The

---

*To judge from the massive donations which we find Alexander paying out at this point (Diod. 17.64.5-6; Plut. *Alex.* 34, 39; QC 5.1.45) he must have had some difficulty in persuading his troops to abandon the fleshpots of Babylon and take to the road once more – especially since they were marching east rather than west, deeper into Asia and not back home. Each Macedonian cavalryman received 600 drachmas – not far short of a year's pay – and other ranks proportionate amounts. The total expenditure came to well over 2,000 talents, but the Babylon treasury would appear to have footed the bill.

reorganization had two objects: increased efficiency and increased loyalty. 'He brought the whole force,' Diodorus says, 'up to an outstanding devotion to its commander and obedience to his commands, and to a high degree of effectiveness.' The order of priorities is revealing.

While Alexander was still on the road to Susa, a messenger reached him from Philoxenus with the news that the city had capitulated, and all its treasure was safely under guard. Once again the Macedonian army received a royal welcome. The satrap, Abuleites, sent out his son to escort Alexander's troops as far as the Choaspes River, where he was awaiting them in person. His gifts included camels, dromedaries, and a dozen elephants: by this time the Macedonian baggage-train must have begun to resemble a travelling menagerie. When Alexander entered Susa he was at once conducted into the royal palace, passing through the great hypostyle hall with its vivid glazed-brick reliefs – horned lions, winged griffins, long rows of gorgeously apparelled Persian archers – to the treasury. Here Abuleites formally made over to him 40–50,000 talents of gold and silver bullion, together with another 9,000 talents of minted gold darics. So fabulous a hoard was something beyond even Alexander's wildest dreams.

But this was only the beginning. The treasury also held more than a hundred tons of purple-dyed cloth from Hermione, nearly two centuries old, its colour still bright and unfaded. There was all the loot which Xerxes had amassed from Greece, including the famous 'tyrannicide' statue-group of Harmodius and Aristogeiton. There were jars of Nile and Danube water, sent in by vassal monarchs as tokens of fealty. There were the furnishings, gold plate and jewellery in the palace itself: when Alexander sat down to dine with his Companions, the scene must have resembled that recorded, for an earlier period, in the Book of Esther:

On every side, fastened by ivory rings to marble columns, hung canopies, some white, some flaxen, some violet, with cords of fine linen and purple thread; couches of gold and silver were set here and there on a floor of malachite and marble, wondrously patterned. From golden cups they drank, and the very trenchers on which the meat was served were ever of new design.

If Darius was, in fact, hoping to distract Alexander with dazzling riches while he himself once more prepared for battle, he could hardly have baited the trap more effectively.[6]

Alexander's personal ambitions, however, reached farther than mere loot, which never held any great attraction for him. After he had inspected the treasury, his first act – no doubt a calculated gesture – was to seat himself on Darius' throne, under its famous golden canopy. This, as he well knew, meant death for any other than the legitimate occupant. Old Demaratus of Corinth shed tears of joy at the sight, and died shortly thereafter: *nunc dimittis*. But despite its symbolic impact, this incident also had a streak of unintentional comedy about it. Darius was a tall man, and Alexander somewhat under average height; when Alexander sat down, his feet dangled in space above the royal footstool.

One of the pages, with considerable presence of mind, snatched away the footstool and substituted a table. At this a Persian eunuch standing by began to weep noisily. When Alexander asked him what the trouble was, he explained that this was the royal table from which his master Darius had formerly eaten. Alexander, anxious not to offend against any Achaemenid religious taboos, was on the point of having the table removed again; but Philotas, with shrewd perspicacity, pointed out that his act, being committed unknowingly, counted as an omen. Alexander had, in true biblical style, made his enemy's board his footstool. The table stayed where it was.

An even more ludicrous *faux pas* which Alexander committed about this time came as a timely reminder of the vast gap which still existed between upper-class Persian and Macedonian customs. Olympias had sent her son, as a present, a large quantity of purple cloth, together with the women who wove it. Alexander offered both to the Persian queen mother, Sisygambis. If she liked the material, he informed her, these women would teach her granddaughters how to make it for themselves. This kindly, if somewhat naive, offer was construed by Sisygambis as a calculated insult of the most deadly sort. The mere idea of any royal lady performing so menial a task almost gave the old Achaemenid matriarch apoplexy. The king, she thought, must be sneering at her servile status: it took a great deal of explanation and many elaborate apologies before good relations were restored between them. Alexander assured her that his own sisters had helped to weave the bale, but Sisygambis is unlikely to have regarded this claim as anything more than gallant fiction.[7]

Amyntas' report on the situation in Greece was anything but encouraging. King Agis of Sparta, he told Alexander, continued to gain ground. Tegea, Elis, Arcadia and other states had gone over to him. His total force was now estimated at nearly 30,000 men, of whom about one third were professional mercenaries. Meanwhile Alexander's governor in Thrace, Memnon, had also decided to revolt – the timing was not, in all likelihood, accidental, but correlated with Agis' movements – while Zopyrion (who held the same office for Pontus) had been defeated and killed while on a wholly unauthorized expedition into Scythia. Antipater was thus facing imminent trouble on two fronts simultaneously (and must have cursed the king for depriving him of so many badly-needed front-line troops). The situation on the home front was, clearly, critical.

Alexander, well aware of this, did what he could to help his hard-pressed regent. Menes, who was now appointed inspector-general for Syria, Phoenicia and Cilicia, took 3,000 talents back to the coast, with orders to pay Antipater as much as should prove necessary for the expenses of the Lacedaemonian war (Alexander clearly anticipated a long campaign). At the same time, the king was much concerned to keep Athens neutral: the fear of a Spartan–Athenian *détente* was never far from his mind. He had the sculpture-group of the tyrannicides carefully shipped back to Athens as Persian war-reparations (a gesture which cost him nothing and emphasized his role as captain-general of the league); at the same time large grants (or bribes) ranging from 50 to 100 talents were offered to various distinguished Athenian citizens, including Phocion and Xenocrates, both of whom refused them.

Ironically enough, Alexander could have spared himself all this worry and expense. Had he but known it, the crises in Thrace and the Peloponnese were already resolved. Antipater had marched out in full strength against Memnon, thus calling the rebel's bluff: to fight a full-scale battle was the last thing Memnon had in mind, and he cheerfully came to terms with the regent in return for confirmation as governor. (He must have been an astute diplomat, since he held this post until 327/6, when he was summoned out to India – still in good odour – with a draft of reinforcements.) King Agis of Sparta went down before Antipater's infantry outside Megalopolis – fighting heroically to the end, still without any help from Athens – at about the same time that Alexander himself defeated Darius at Gaugamela.

Before this final campaign got under way, however, Amyntas had left Greece. Alexander may not have learnt of Agis' defeat and death until he reached Persepolis – and his touchy military ego would not let him give Antipater the credit for any great achievement when he did: 'It seems, men,' he announced, 'that while we have been conquering Darius here, over there in Arcadia there has been a battle of mice.' It was the summer of 330 before Antipater's full dispatches on the campaigns in Greece (and Alexander of Epirus' death in Italy) finally caught up with him.[8] Nothing more sharply distinguishes ancient from modern warfare than the degree of time-lag in passing on vital information.

By now it was January, and bitterly cold up in the passes. Any reasonable person (a category which included Darius) could have predicted what Alexander would do now. Between Susa and the two major provinces of Iran, Persis and Media, lay the great snowbound rampart of the Zagros Mountains, towering in places to 15,000 feet. The Macedonians, it was safe to assume, would go into winter quarters at Susa. With the coming of spring they would set out again: either north-east to Ecbatana, where Darius now lay, or south-east to Persepolis and Pasargadae. But Alexander, as so often, shattered all reasonable expectations. He made a speciality of winter campaigns, and he meant to exploit his victory at Gaugamela to the full: this did not include offering Darius a gentlemanly three months in which to get his wind back.

Alexander left Susa for Persepolis in mid January.* The only Persian who seems to have divined his intentions in advance was the satrap Ariobarzanes. Since Gaugamela this determined and energetic officer had raised an infantry force of 25,000 men, together with 700 cavalry. The moment he learnt that the Macedonian army was on the move, Ariobarzanes occupied a deep mountain gorge known as the Susian Gates, and built a defensive wall across it. There were two possible routes to Persepolis, of which this was the more direct. If Alexander made a frontal assault up the gorge, he was bound to be repelled with heavy losses. On the other hand, if he chose the easier southern route (more or less identical with the modern highway through Kazerun and Shiraz) there would be ample time for the Persians to fall back on Persepolis. The city itself could be evacuated, and its gold-reserves removed to safety, long before Alexander

---

*The Great King's mother, daughters and son were left behind: they would be a serious encumbrance during the guerrilla campaign which Alexander had in mind, and something worse than an embarrassment when he finally reached his destination. To keep them occupied, he appointed tutors to instruct them in the Greek language (Diod. 17.67.1; QC 5.2.17–22).

got there. This admirable plan contained only two fallacies. Ariobarzanes believed his position at the Susian Gates to be impregnable; and he did not allow for the possibility that Alexander might divide his forces.

The king's initial route lay through a district inhabited by mountain tribesmen, the Uxians. Like several clans in the area, they habitually levied tolls from all travellers passing through, the Great King included, and saw no reason to make an exception for this foreign invader. They therefore informed Alexander that if he wanted to take his troops through to Persepolis, he must pay for the privilege. Alexander blandly told them to wait for him at the pass, 'there to receive payment at his hands'. Craterus, with a strong detachment, was sent up into the heights above this defile. Before dawn Alexander, descending by a little-known hill-track, made a brisk *razzia* through several still-sleeping Uxian villages. He then assaulted the pass. Its defenders lost their nerve and fled into the mountains, where Craterus' men annihilated them. Henceforth the Uxians paid tribute rather than exacting it – 100 horses, 500 pack-animals, and 30,000 sheep annually.

Alexander now sent off Parmenio, with the baggage-train, the Thessalians, and all the heavy-armed troops, by the main southern road, while he himself took a light mobile column of shock-troops over the mountains to deal with Ariobarzanes. After five days' hard marching this force reached the Susian Gates. An attempt to carry the wall by direct assault failed disastrously. Ariobarzanes had artillery mounted above the wall; his men rolled great boulders down on the Macedonians and poured a hail of arrows and javelins into their ranks from the steep spurs of the gorge. Alexander suffered heavy casualties, and was forced to retreat. He had, however, taken some prisoners during this foray, and one of them, a local herdsman, volunteered to guide him by an extremely difficult pass over the mountains, which would bring him out behind Ariobarzanes' position. The king left Craterus at the entrance to the gorge, with

500 cavalry and two battalions of the phalanx. In order to deceive the enemy, he was to burn the normal number of camp-fires. When he heard Alexander's trumpets, he was to assault the wall. Ariobarzanes would thus be caught between two attacking forces.

The mountain detour was only twelve miles round, but it took Alexander's commando force a gruelling day and two nights to negotiate it. They got there just before dawn on the third day. Two guard-pickets were silently massacred. Then the trumpets blared out, and Craterus' waiting troops at once launched a fierce frontal attack against the wall. At the same moment Alexander and his men came swarming down the crags from behind Ariobarzanes' camp. The Persians, finding themselves pressed hard from both front and rear, tried to escape by scrambling up the sides of the gorge. Alexander, anticipating this, had stationed a force 3,000 strong at the top. Most of these fugitives were cut down during the close-quarters fighting that followed: there seems to have been a fearful massacre. Only Ariobarzanes himself, with a mere handful of his 700 horsemen, managed to get away.

Even after Alexander's column had passed through the Gates, it made slow going for a while. Its route was seamed with lateral ravines and watercourses, and often obliterated by heavy snowdrifts. It was now that a messenger got through to the king from Tiridates, the garrison-commander of Persepolis. Tiridates promised to surrender the city, but warned Alexander that he and his Macedonians must get there without delay: otherwise the inhabitants might well plunder the royal treasury before they left. Alexander acted at once. Ordering the infantry to follow as best they could, he set off on an all-night, breakneck cavalry dash which reached the Araxes River at dawn. There was no bridge (or else it had been broken down). The king and his men built one in record time by the simple expedient of knocking down a nearby village, and using the timbers and dressed stone blocks from the houses they demolished. Then they rode on.

A little way beyond the river their first deputation met them. But these shabby creatures were very different from the elegant, time-serving collaborators with whom Alexander had hitherto dealt. Their cries of welcome, and the suppliant branches they bore, revealed them as Greeks: middle-aged or elderly for the most part, perhaps mercenaries who had fought on the wrong side against that ferocious monarch Artaxerxes Ochus (see above, pp. 51–2). What made them so ghastly and pitiable a sight was the fact that each one of them had been appallingly mutilated. Ears and noses had been lopped off wholesale, a typical Persian practice. Some lacked hands, others feet. All were disfigured by brand-marks on the forehead. 'They were,' says Diodorus, 'persons who had acquired skills or crafts and had made good progress in their instruction; then their other extremities had been amputated and they were left only those which were vital to their profession.'

Alexander at first offered to repatriate them. After discussion, however, they told him they would rather stay where they were and form a separate community. Back in Greece they would be isolated objects of pity, social pariahs. Here they at least were among their own kind, companions if only in misfortune. The king applauded their choice, provided them with all they needed to set up as small farmers – oxen, seed-corn, sheep, cash subsidies – and made them tax-exempt in perpetuity. The local administration became directly responsible for their safety and well-being.[9] We need not doubt the truth of this curious episode, which is recounted in circumstantial detail by all our main narrative sources except Arrian. At the same time Alexander must surely have seen, and duly emphasized, its value as propaganda when justifying his own subsequent conduct at Persepolis. The systematic looting and burning of Parsa's shrines would look better if presented, in part at least, as a *quid pro quo* for Persian atrocities committed against Greeks.

Alexander entered Persepolis on 31 January 330 B.C. This city was the traditional burial-place of the Achaemenid kings, the repository of their accumulated treasure, the religious capital of the empire (and thus outside normal satrapal jurisdiction). It was here, in April, that the solemn Akitu New Year festival took place, during which the Great King underwent a ritual ordeal – symbolized by reliefs representing his fight with a monstrous Death Demon – and emerged victorious, his office renewed, to be fêted as Ahura Mazda's vice-regent on earth. Persepolis, in fact, was a Holy City, akin to Mecca or Jerusalem, and equally rich in solemn religious associations. If Alexander still cherished hopes of inheriting the Achaemenid crown according to legitimate precedent, backed by the Great King's nobles and the priestly caste of the Magi, he would treat this, of all cities, with extreme propriety and respect. Anything less would permanently antagonize those whom he most needed to conciliate.

There are signs, however, that by the time Alexander reached Persepolis he had become considerably less optimistic about persuading the Iranian elite to endorse his claims. What he had not reckoned on was the stubborn resistance generated by a purely religious or ideological opposition – something to which his own pragmatic nature tended to blind him. Many Iranian aristocrats were ready enough to collaborate: no country has ever lacked its political opportunists. But to recognize Alexander as the Chosen One of Ahura Mazda was quite another matter. We know something of the propaganda which the Magi organized against him,[10] and which was echoed by Darius in his speech before Gaugamela. To them, Alexander and his unkempt Macedonians were 'the Demons with Dishevelled Hair of the Day of Wrath'. There is an echo of this attitude in the Book of Daniel, where the Macedonian empire is symbolized as a beast, 'terrible and dreadful and exceeding strong; and it had great iron teeth; it devoured and broke in pieces, and stamped the residue with its feet' (vii, 7).

There is one Sibylline Oracle which presents an even clearer picture of Alexander as the godless, violent, foreign usurper:

> One day shall come to Asia's wealthy land an unbelieving man,
> Wearing on his shoulders a purple cloak,
> Wild, despotic, fiery. He shall raise before himself
> Flashes like lightning, and all Asia shall have an evil
> Yoke, and the drenched earth shall drink in great slaughter.

Ever since Issus Alexander had tried to change this image, but without success: episodes such as the sack of Tyre confirmed it all too well. Disaffection among his troops, Agis' revolt, and, worst of all, this stubborn, intangible atmosphere of moral hostility – all had combined to fray his all-too-edgy temper. Even his diplomatic overtures to Darius' womenfolk seem to have broken down in the end. This may explain why, despite Tiridates' formal surrender, he now gave his troops *carte blanche* to sack Persepolis – all but the palaces and the citadel, where Darius' treasures were stored. What he could not bend, he would break. If the Achaemenid crown was denied him, he would take it by main force, and show himself such a terrible Lion of Wrath as even the Magi had not dared to predict.

He now made an inflammatory speech to his officers, ranting on about Persian crimes against Greece – the incident of the mutilated mercenaries must have helped here – and describing Persepolis as 'the most hateful of the cities of Asia'. The Macedonians needed no further encouragement. Their last real taste of wholesale rape and plunder had been at Gaza. Ever since then, at Babylon and Susa in particular, Alexander's policy of conciliation had placed them under heavy disciplinary restraint. Now, unleashed at last, they went completely berserk. The king authorized them to kill all adult males they encountered, 'thinking that this would be to his advantage'. Presumably he now meant to secure Persian compliance through sheer terrorism. But he was also giving his hard-worked troops a holiday before leading them on the long, hard road through the eastern provinces. For a whole day the Macedonian army gave itself up to an orgy of plunder and destruction. Every private house was full of gold and silver ornaments, rich tapestries, beautiful inlaid furniture. Priceless works of art were smashed up wholesale to give rival looters a share of the precious metal and jewellery that adorned them. Frequent fights broke out, and those who amassed especially rich loads of booty were often killed by jealous rivals. No one bothered to take prisoners: they were not worth ransoming, and many committed suicide to save themselves from worse indignities.

Alexander, meanwhile, was busy inspecting the royal treasure-vaults, which contained an accumulated surplus of no less than 120,000 talents, dating back to the time of Cyrus the Great. From the Great King's bedchamber came 8,000 talents in gold, besides the jewelled golden vine – which, as Alexander surely knew, was also a symbolic Tree of Life, representing 'the rightful, proper continuity of Achaemenid government under Ahura Mazda'. This fantastic fortune was now destined to finance Alexander's further adventures in the East. Some of it he kept with him, but the bulk was transferred to Susa and thence, ultimately, to Ecbatana. Its removal called for every pack-animal that could be commandeered from Susa and Babylon, together with no less than 3,000 Asiatic camels. Taking the pound sterling at its 1913 value, this bullion was worth something like £44,000,000 – which represents the national income of the Athenian empire, in its fifth-century heyday, for very nearly three hundred years.[11]

Alexander's supremacy was now assured. With brilliant

panache he had struck, through freezing winter snows, at the very heart and nerve-centre of Darius' crumbling empire. The Zagros mountains had been neatly by-passed; the fall of Persepolis opened the road to Ecbatana. Once again, any reasonable person, working on precedent, could have deduced what Alexander would do next – head straight north, capture Darius whatever the cost, and wind up this already overlong Persian campaign. But – once again – Alexander's behaviour proved totally unpredictable. He did not leave Persepolis until the late May or early June of 330. The climate was pleasant, and he spent much time out hunting. He visited the old capital of Pasargadae, fifty miles to the north (it had surrendered soon after his arrival, netting him a further 6,000 talents) and was shown the tomb of Cyrus the Great. He continued to hand out over-lavish gifts to his friends, a practice which brought him warnings not only from Olympias, but also from the Persians collaborating with him.[12]

The unmistakable impression one gets is that he was killing time. But why? Though Ecbatana was five hundred miles distant, his route thither would follow the course of the river-valleys, through a predominantly fertile region: he was unlikely to sit waiting patiently until the crops ripened. What possible reason could he have for so prolonged a delay? (Plutarch's four-month estimate seems, after all, to be about right.) It has recently been suggested[13] that throughout the winter of 331/30 his communications with Europe were totally disrupted; that he dared not move before he learnt the outcome of the Greek revolt; that his reinforcements were not even certain whether he was in Ecbatana or Persepolis. This is hardly a compliment to any competent general, let alone to Alexander, who made a fetish of good communications and intelligence. Agis had died the previous September, and Persepolis did not fall until late January. Some delay is very likely; but even if his land-communications with Greece had been cut (which is by no means certain) Alexander now controlled the whole eastern Mediterranean. It is inconceivable that the news of Antipater's victory reached him later than February, and it may have done so much sooner – probably by mid December. There was only one motive that could possibly have kept him in Persepolis until April and beyond: the Persian New Year festival. He had shown his Iranian subjects that he was not a man to be trifled with: the sacking of Persepolis proved that. But the vandalism of the Macedonian army had been most carefully controlled. The palaces and temples, the great *apadana* or audience-hall, the whole complex of buildings which formed the city's spiritual centre, on that vast, stage-like terrace backed by the Kuh-i-Rahmet mountains – none of these had been touched. In other words, the New Year Festival could still be held. Perhaps after such a lesson, Alexander argued, these proud nobles and priests might change their minds. Perhaps even now common sense would prevail, and he, Alexander, be acclaimed, with all due ceremonial, as Ahura Mazda's representative on earth. The psychological effect produced by such an act of recognition would be incalculable. Its impact would reach the remotest corners of the empire.

But more was at stake here than mere political propaganda. Alexander found himself up against a people who took their religion (including the divinity that hedged the Great King) very seriously indeed. If negotiations were ever opened on this tricky subject, they soon broke down. March passed into April, and soon it became clear that Persepolis would see no procession that year, no ritual renewal of kingship. About 20 April Alexander finally gave up hope. While deciding what his next step should be, he took an expeditionary force up into the mountains, and spent a month pacifying the province (one of his favourite relaxations when under strain: he reacted similarly after Hephaestion's death [see below, pp. 467–8]). His victims included a group of shockheaded troglodytes whose womenfolk were expert slingers. The spring rains had begun, and the

Macedonians suffered badly from slush and sleet, especially at high altitudes.[14]

Alexander returned to Persepolis in late May, his mind finally made up. The city must be destroyed. It symbolized centuries of Achaemenid rule: once Alexander moved on eastward it would form an obvious rallying-point, both religious and political, for any nationalist resistance movement. Its great friezes and palaces and fire-altars embodied something to which the Macedonian conqueror had no effective answer: a purely spiritual and ideological opposition. He was to come up against the same problem again amongst the Brahmins of the Punjab (see below, p. 425).

Parmenio, on being told what he planned to do, replied bluntly that the king would be a fool if he destroyed his own property (a recommendation which, as the old marshal doubtless recalled, Alexander himself had made to his troops on first landing in Asia Minor). Nor was he likely to impress the Iranians by mere conquest and destruction. Since Alexander had already failed to impress them in any other way, he could only reiterate that burning Persepolis would avenge Xerxes' similar destruction of the Greek temples. 'My own view,' says Arrian, stung into voicing a personal opinion for once, 'is that this was bad policy.' Scholars down the ages have echoed Arrian's verdict (generally throwing in a charge of gross vandalism as well), though they sometimes differ as to the king's motivation. What remains indisputable is that such an act finally destroyed any chance Alexander might have had of legitimizing himself as an Achaemenid by peaceful means. It also provoked a desperate last-ditch stand in the eastern provinces. Because of this, many have been tempted to see the burning of the palaces as an accident, suggested during a drunken orgy, and regretted immediately afterwards.

Such is the version of events which has passed into history (or legend), and no arguments now are likely to dislodge it. The *mise-en-scène* is justly famous. Alexander held a great feast, at which he got very drunk. Thaïs, Ptolemy's mistress, speaking as an Athenian, said what a wonderful gesture it would be to burn down Xerxes' palace – thus, of course, shifting the initial onus of responsibility away from Alexander himself. Torches were called for, and a wavering, garlanded procession set off, to the skirling of flutes and pipes. As the revellers approached the palace doors there was a moment's hesitation. This, cried some sedulous ape, was a deed worthy of Alexander alone. The king, with drunken enthusiasm – and perhaps glad to feel himself once more the champion of Hellas, a role he had been progressively abandoning – cast the first torch. Flames licked out, consuming rich tapestry-work, eating into the dry cedar cross-beams. Guards who came hurrying up with water-buckets stayed instead to watch the fun. Very soon the entire terrace was one roaring inferno.

Premeditated arson or drunken accident? The odds are heavily in favour of the former. As at Thebes, as at Tyre and Gaza, Alexander's royal will had been thwarted – something which tended both to cloud his judgement and produce the most drastic sort of retaliation. That he lived to regret his decision seems likely enough: it meant that his future hold over the Persian empire depended on *Machtpolitik* alone. But that he willed – and with his own hand initiated – the destruction of Persepolis seems a virtual certainty. It agrees too well with too many other aspects of his character and career.[15]

The palaces had already been systematically looted before their destruction – another tell-tale hint. Macedonian soldiers found and removed almost all the coins, gold-work and jewellery. They raided the armoury for swords and daggers, but left thousands of bronze and iron arrow-heads behind. Innumerable exquisite stone vases, which had no immediate market value, they carried out into the court-yard and deliberately smashed up. They decapitated statues and defaced reliefs. The Hellenic crusade against Asiatic barbarism was now approaching its final triumph. What remains today, solid and indisputable, is the evidence of the fire itself – and all that it preserved. 'Burned beams of the roof still lay their print across stairways and against sculptures. Heaps of ashes are all that remain of the cedar panelling.'[16] But that vast conflagration also hard-baked hundreds of clay tablets (which would otherwise long since have crumbled to dust), besides firing the marvellous glaze on Xerxes' processional reliefs. When Alexander left these smoking ruins behind him, he could hardly know that his act of incendiarism had immortalized Persepolis for all time.

At this point the king's immediate strategy was clear enough. He could no longer hope to legitimize himself as an Achaemenid by cultivating the queen mother (of whom from now on virtually nothing is heard). His best hope was to capture Darius alive: this would at least give him a good bargaining-counter. If the Great King abdicated in his favour, the hard-core nobility and the eastern satraps might yet be persuaded to endorse his claims rather than fight it out. So at the beginning of June Alexander struck north from Persepolis, leaving 3,000 Macedonians behind to garrison the city and province – an unusually strong force. On his way to Ecbatana (Hamadan) he was met by further reinforcements, who must have taken a short cut over the Kurdish mountains: 5,000 foot and 1,000 horse, under an Athenian commander. With them came Antipater's dispatches on the situation in Greece, Thrace, and South Italy.

Rumours began to come in that Darius, who had assembled 3,000 horse and 30,000 infantry, including his faithful 4,000 Greek mercenaries, was determined to offer battle once more. But three days' march from Ecbatana, after Alexander had already covered more than 400 miles, a renegade Persian nobleman appeared with the news that Darius was in retreat. His expected reinforcements had failed to arrive; he had therefore taken off eastward, five days before, with the Bactrian cavalry, 6,000 picked infantrymen, and 7,000 talents from the Ecbatana palace treasury. His immediate destination seemed to be the Caspian Gates,* where his harem and baggage-train had been dispatched some time before. Alexander had to move fast. Darius' intention (his informant said) was to retreat by the shores of the Caspian as far as Bactria, ravaging the land as he went. This would leave the Macedonians with a serious supply-problem, since their route lay round the northern edge of the great salt desert. If they could be lured into the desolate wilderness of mountain and steppe beyond Hyrcania, a fresh satrapal army, familiar with local conditions, might very easily wear them down.[17]

When he reached Ecbatana, Alexander took rapid stock of the situation. He was now embarking on a new phase of his campaign. The burning of Persepolis had written *finis* to the Hellenic crusade as such, and he used this excuse to pay off all his league troops, Parmenio's Thessalians included. The crisis in Greece was over: he no longer needed these potential troublemakers as hostages. What he now envisaged was a streamlined professional army, loyal to him alone, and prepared to follow him wherever he might lead. The immense wealth he had gleaned from Persepolis also showed him how such an imperial force could be recruited and kept in order. When he dismissed the league troops, he paid each cavalryman, over and above his expedition pay, a bonus of one talent (6,000 drachmas). The bonus paid to the infantry, though smaller (1,000 drachmas) was still munificent. The first represented about eight years' accumulated pay, the second three.

A still more tempting bait was dangled before these demobilized troops. Any man who wished might re-enlist with Alexander as a soldier of fortune, and those who did so received a bounty of no less than *three talents* (18,000 drach-

---

* Probably the pass between the Dasht-i-Kavir and the Kuh-i-Surkh mountains, which runs east past the northern spur road to Firuzkuh and the Guduk pass, turning north-east to Damghan after Aradan: see now J. F. Standish, *G&R*, 17 (1970), 17–24.

mas) on enrolment. It would take a very high-minded veteran to resist such princely terms. The whole deal cost Alexander some 12–13,000 talents, but he probably regarded it as a valuable long-term investment. Almost as much again was embezzled by his light-fingered financial officers – an ominous symptom of things to come. Had he known about this at the time, Alexander might still have thought himself in credit. Money as such meant very little to him (and less than ever now); but by applying it so skilfully – the Macedonians likewise appear to have received fat donations – he had bought himself a mercenary army overnight. He had also fatally loosened Parmenio's hold on the military command structure. In future, he calculated, his troops' first allegiance would be to their royal paymaster.[18]

The demobilized league forces were given a cavalry escort back to the coast, and from there took ship home, remaining under safe-conduct as far as Euboea. Alexander probably reckoned that they would form a useful pro-Macedonian leaven in the various Greek states, not to mention their value as free recruiting propaganda. Once they were out of the way, he lost no time in cutting Parmenio down to size. The old general remained behind at Ecbatana as area military commander: his career as chief of staff was over. Alexander dealt with him very tactfully. Parmenio was, after all, seventy years old, and – as the king doubtless assured him – had earned a rest from front-line campaigning.

This did not mean that he was off the active list: in fact his first task *qua* area commander would be to convoy the Great King's treasure to Ecbatana, after which he was to take an expeditionary force – Alexander had left him something like 6,000 mercenaries – and pacify the tribes round the south and south-west Caspian. During his absence the treasure would be guarded by four battalions of the phalanx, left behind on light duties. When he got back, these battalions would rejoin Alexander: their commander

was to be Cleitus the Black, at present on sick-leave in Susa.
It all sounded very sensible: on the face of it Parmenio's
position had lost nothing in dignity or prestige. But the old
man's effective power – as he himself well knew – had been
drastically curtailed. Of his close relatives, only Philotas and
Nicanor still held key operational commands. He had lost
his Thessalian cavalry as a unit, and it was to Harpalus,
as imperial quartermaster-general, that the mercenaries
who had replaced them now looked for their pay. When the
treasure-convoy reached Ecbatana it was Harpalus who
would have charge of it and issue Alexander's coinage from
the royal mint. Parmenio's own new second-in-command,
Cleander, was the king's nominee.

Slowly, ruthlessly, Alexander was closing in on Parmenio;
and from this point onwards he held all the trump cards. It
has been said that Ecbatana marked the point at which
Alexander's tragedy began, 'the tragedy of an increasing
loneliness, of a growing impatience with those who could
not understand'.[19] In point of fact his Macedonian officers,
Parmenio included, understood all too well. Military
success had increased Alexander's self-confidence, and
sharpened his appetite for power. His coronation as Pharaoh,
followed by that mysterious visit to Siwah, had made him
acutely conscious of his supposedly divine antecedents. But
in the last resort it was the capture of Darius' millions which
removed all effective limitations from his authority, and
left him free to indulge his fantasies as he chose.

All absolute autocrats end in spiritual isolation, creating
their own world, their private version of the truth: to this
depressing rule Alexander was no exception. From now on,
those few friends who dared criticize him to his face most
often paid a heavy price for their honesty. Such a state of
affairs encouraged gross adulation among the king's more
sycophantic courtiers; and this, in turn, reinforced Alexander's own latent delusions of grandeur. Thoughts of
conspiracy were thereby engendered amongst the resentful,
and the discovery of plots, or rumours of plots, brought out

all Alexander's lurking paranoia. In 330 the process was barely begun. But during the years that followed – aided by the king's increasing addiction to drink – it developed with alarming speed and intensity.

Alexander wasted not a moment more than was necessary in Ecbatana. His arrangements made, he at once went on after Darius. With luck he might yet overtake the Persians before they were through the Caspian Gates. But it was now mid July, and his main problem was the appalling heat. He covered the 200 miles between Ecbatana and Rhagae (near Tehran) in eleven days. This was good going, but far from exceptional: Napoleon, marching through worse terrain, averaged twenty-eight miles a day. Even so, men fell out by the wayside, and their horses died under them. Arrian contrives to suggest that this was the result of the cracking pace Alexander set. In point of fact they must have been suffering from dehydration and heat-stroke.*

At Rhagae, about fifty miles short of the Gates, Alexander learnt that Darius had already passed through them, and was now making for Hecatompylus (Damghan) – later to become the summer residence of the Parthian kings. To continue his forced march under that burning sun, without rest or adequate preparation, would be suicidal as well as pointless. Alexander bivouacked at Rhagae for five days, and then pressed on as far as the Gates. Beyond them, south of the Elburz Mountains, lay that desolate tract of salt-desert known today as the Dasht-i-Kavir. Before the column could proceed further, Alexander needed fresh provisions.

* For Alexander's march-rates see C. Neumann, *Historia* 20 (1971), 196–8, defending Tarn and Hammond against R. D. Milns, *Historia* 15 (1966), 266, who had argued that a daily march-rate of 36 miles was a 'physical impossibility' and the 52-mile dash from Rhagae to the Caspian Gates 'absurd'. Neumann cites some highly interesting march-rates from modern as well as ancient history (Antigonus, 44 miles per 24 hours; Scipio Africanus, between 46 and 54 miles per 24 hours; Gen. Craufurd, perhaps 52 miles in 24 hours). Cf. now C. L. Murison, *Historia* 21 (1972), 409 n. 32.

Coenus was therefore given some cavalry and sent out on a foraging expedition.

During his absence two Babylonian noblemen – one of them Mazaeus' son – rode in with the dramatic news that Darius had been deposed, and was now a prisoner. The *coup* had been planned jointly by Bessus, satrap of Bactria, and the grand vizier, Nabarzanes. Alexander, it seemed, was not the only person to think of using this wretched royal fugitive as a political bargaining counter. What he heard spurred the king into immediate action. Without even waiting for Coenus to get back, he set off after the Persian column, taking his best cavalry and the Guards Brigade. They force-marched all night, when it was cooler, and all the next morning too. After a brief siesta they resumed the chase, and did not call a halt until dawn, when they reached the camp where Darius had been put under arrest.

Here they found his aged Greek interpreter, who gave Alexander further details. Nabarzanes had suggested, to begin with, that the Great King might – temporarily, of course – resign his title in favour of Bessus. This proposal made good practical sense. Bessus was well-known and respected in the eastern provinces; he had Achaemenid blood; and if there was to be a national resistance movement, he would make a far more effective leader for it than the twice-defeated and wholly demoralized Darius. But the Great King, weakly resentful, flew into a rage, drew his scimitar, and tried to kill Nabarzanes. The council-meeting broke up in some disorder. This left the retreating army split into two hostile camps. The Bactrians and other eastern contingents looked to Bessus as their natural leader, while the Persians, under Artabazus, and the Greek mercenaries stuck loyally to Darius.

An open trial of strength at this juncture was out of the question. The conspirators therefore swore formal oaths of fealty to Darius, and were officially reconciled. With old Artabazus haranguing them on the importance of a united front, no one dared question their sincerity. A night or two later, however, they abducted Darius to the Bactrian camp and placed him under close arrest. His Greek mercenary commander had warned him what was afoot, but he refused any offer of protection. The loyalists were left with only two alternatives, to pull out or to capitulate. At first they chose the former. Artabazus, the Persian contingents and the Greeks made off east towards Parthiene, 'thinking anything safer than a retinue of traitors'. But two days later most of the Persians drifted back to Bessus, seduced by his lavish promises, and 'because there was no one else to follow'.[20]

Bessus now declared himself Great King, taking the title of Artaxerxes IV, and was enthusiastically acclaimed by his troops.[21] His predecessor found himself chained up in an old covered waggon: as good a way as any of camouflaging his whereabouts on the march. Darius was also, of course, the rebels' insurance ticket: as Arrian says, they 'had determined to hand him over if they heard that Alexander was after them, and thus get favourable terms for themselves'. On the receipt of this information, Alexander saw that there was not a moment to lose. Again, he marched all through the night and the morning which followed it. About noon the Macedonian party reached a village where Darius and his captors had rested the previous day. At this rate the pursuers were going to collapse from fatigue and heat-exhaustion before they overtook their quarry. At all costs Alexander had to head the Persians off. Was there, he inquired, any kind of short cut?

Yes, the villagers told him, a trail did exist, but it ran through uninhabited desert, and there were no water-holes. Alexander swept these objections aside, commandeered local guides, dismounted 500 of his cavalrymen, and gave their horses to his toughest, fittest foot-soldiers. Then he set off on a fantastic all-night dash across the desert, covering over fifty miles by dawn, and overtaking the Persians just as first light broke. They were trailing along unarmed, and put up no more than a token resistance.

Clearly they had believed themselves to be at least two days' march ahead of him still, and his sudden appearance completely shattered them. Yet, according to Plutarch, only sixty horsemen had in fact kept up with the king. If Bessus' men had not panicked – numerically they were far superior – they might well have made history by bagging Alexander in addition to Darius.*

Instead, their one thought was to get away, and as fast as possible. Darius' heavy waggon slowed them down considerably. Bessus and Nabarzanes urged their prisoner to mount a horse and escape with them. The Great King refused. If he could not hold his empire, at least he would die with dignity. He would not, he said, accompany traitors. Divine vengeance lay at hand: he cast himself on Alexander's mercy. There was no time for prolonged argument. At any moment the retreating column might be surrounded. Bessus and Nabarzanes could do nothing now but ensure that Darius did not fall into Alexander's hands alive. So they and their fellow-conspirators ran him through with their javelins, and then fled, each by a different route – Nabarzanes to Hyrcania, Bessus to his own province of Bactria, while others made off southward, to Areia and Drangiana (Seistan).

This set Alexander a nice problem. If the Great King was still a prisoner, which of the various retreating columns had charge of him? It was impossible to tell. Weary Macedonian officers rode up and down the abandoned baggage-train, hoping against hope. Meanwhile the oxen pulling Darius' now driverless waggon had wandered about half a mile off the road, down into a valley where there was water. Here they came to a standstill, bleeding from numerous wounds, and weakened by the heat. A thirsty Macedonian soldier called Polystratus, directed by peasants to the spring in the valley, saw this waggon standing there, and thought it odd that the oxen should have been stabbed rather than rounded up as booty. Then he heard the groans of a dying

---

* For another incident of the same sort, see below, p. 369.

man. Naturally curious, he went over and drew back the hide curtains. There on the floor lay King Darius, still in chains, his royal mantle sodden with blood, the murderers' javelins protruding from his breast, alone except for one faithful dog crouching beside him. He asked, weakly, for water. Polystratus fetched some in his helmet. Clasping the Macedonian's hand, Darius gave thanks to heaven that he had not died utterly alone and abandoned. Soon after this his laboured breathing dwindled into silence, and all was over. Polystratus at once took his news to the king. When Alexander stood, at last, before the broken corpse of his adversary, and saw the sordid, agonizing circumstances in which he had died, his distress was obvious and genuine. Taking off his own royal cloak, he placed it over the body. At his express command, Darius was borne back in state to Persepolis, and given a kingly burial, beside his Achaemenid forebears.[22]

However, this chivalrous gesture of Alexander's, though prompted in part by personal remorse, had other, more practical, motives as well. With Darius dead, and therefore unable to abdicate in his favour, Alexander's claim on the Achaemenid throne remained that of a foreign invader. Worse still, he was now up against a genuine and far more formidable Achaemenid competitor in the person of Bessus (or King Artaxerxes, as he now styled himself). This was a most dangerous development. If Bessus managed to rally the West behind him, Alexander could still be in serious trouble. As it was, he would have to fight for the eastern provinces instead of receiving their surrender under the terms of a general settlement. The war, in other words, was very far from over.

Alexander's only possible line was to behave, from the moment of Darius' death, as though he were in fact the Great King's chosen and legitimate successor. He must hunt down Bessus, not as a rival for the throne, but as a rebel and a regicide. Having pursued the Great King to his death, he must now rapidly switch roles and pose as his avenger. When he took possession of the Eastern empire it must be as Darius' heir.[23] But what he had originally anticipated was a public endorsement by Darius himself. Hence, perhaps, the dubious tradition, recorded by several sources,[24] that the Great King, *in extremis*, acknowledged Alexander as his successor, solemnly adjuring him to avenge his death on the traitors who had slain and abandoned him. It is even suggested that Alexander found Darius still breathing, and received this last vital message in person. The whole episode sounds far more like an improvised story put out by the propaganda department, suddenly faced with the fact of Darius' death, and forced to make the best of a bad job at short notice.

Alexander's own reaction to the loss of his bargaining-counter was prompt and characteristic: he took the cavalry straight on after Bessus. If this powerful rival for the throne could be caught and destroyed before he got away to his Bactrian province, all might yet be well. Bessus, unfortunately, had too long a start on them, and the chase was soon abandoned. Alexander thereupon took his troops back to the nearby city of Hecatompylus, and gave them a few days' rest. A rumour – very understandable in the circumstances – got around the camp that this was the end of the crusade, that they would all soon be back in Macedonia. The Great King was dead, the allied troops had already been dismissed. Wishful thinking crystallized into firm belief. Alexander woke one morning to hear the sound of waggons being loaded up for the homeward march.

Since he was already planning ahead in terms of a long Eastern campaign, this attitude caused him considerable alarm. He summoned his staff-commanders, 'and, with tears in his eyes, complained that he was being recalled from the mid course of his glory'. They agreed to do what they could, but advised the king to be tactful and conciliatory when he made his general address to the troops. If he tried to get tough at this point, they said, he might well have a mutiny on his hands. In the event Alexander did something even more effective: he scared them silly. His whole speech emphasized the insecurity of the conquests they made, the unwillingness of the Persians to accept their overlordship. 'It is by your arms that they are restrained, not by their dispositions, and those who fear us when we are present, in our absence will be enemies.' Nor should they underestimate Bessus. Fine fools they would look if they went home now, and a few months later found this rebel satrap crossing the Hellespont to invade Greece! Until he was crushed, their task remained undone.

Now came the clinching peroration. 'We stand on the very threshold of victory,' Alexander told his men. Once Bessus was destroyed, Persian submission would be a foregone conclusion. Besides, the satrap's capital lay no more than four days' march away (a plain lie: the distance was 462 miles). What was that after all they had been through together? His troops cheered him to the echo: another crisis had been surmounted by a judicious application of charisma and rhetoric.

Despite the gloomy picture he drew of Persian national resistance, despite the burning of Persepolis, Alexander was still on the look-out for collaborators among the Iranian nobility. Before leaving Hecatompylus he carefully went through his prisoners, singled out those of high birth and rank (about a thousand in all) and henceforth treated them with special consideration, as potential administrators or governors under his new regime. Apart from anything else, he no longer had a surplus of trained Macedonians to spare for such posts; and the farther east he went, the more acute this problem would become.[25]

Two days later the army struck camp and marched north into Hyrcania, a wild, mountainous, but fertile district bordering on the Caspian. They were suffering from a shortage of horses: many had died of heat during the chase after Darius, and more were now lost as a result of eating poisonous roots. During his march on Zadracarta (Sārī), the capital, Alexander received a letter from Nabarzanes. The grand vizier, after much specious self-exculpation for the part he had played in Darius' murder, offered to give himself up if he was granted a safe-conduct and reasonable terms. Alexander at once sent him the assurances he required. Every additional defection at this level would leave Bessus weaker and more isolated.

On his arrival in Zadracarta the king found a number of high-ranking Persians, Artabazus among them, waiting to offer him their submission. This was a most encouraging sign. There were also envoys from the Greek mercenaries. The Persians – especially old Artabazus, as a former guest-friend at Philip's court – were received with every honour. But Alexander flatly refused to do a deal with the mercenaries' representatives, saying that Greek soldiers who fought for Persia against their own flesh and blood 'were little better than criminals and all proper Greek feeling was against them'. From these 1,500 he would accept nothing but unconditional surrender. His unexpected reversion to the post-Granicus line sounds like propaganda designed for public consumption, and he may well have shown himself more accommodating in private. At all events, the mercenaries accepted his terms without demur – and the whole 1,500 were afterwards incorporated in the Macedonian army *en bloc*, at standard rates of pay.

The king now conducted a rapid punitive expedition against the Mardians, 'a people of rude habits of life and accustomed to brigandage', who later supplied him with some first-class archers. His main object was probably to round up new cavalry mounts without paying for them: the Mardians were great horsemen. They retaliated, in kind, by stealing Bucephalas – a joke Alexander failed to appreciate. He let it be known that if the horse was not returned 'they should see the country laid waste to its furthest limit and its inhabitants slaughtered to a man'. The Mardians, realizing that he was in deadly earnest, sent Bucephalas back at once. They also dispatched no less than fifty tribal elders, bearing

rich gifts, to convey their profound apologies. Alexander
accepted the presents – and coolly retained the leaders of
this delegation as hostages for the tribe's future good conduct.[26] Soon after the king's return to Zadracarta, Nabarzanes
arrived on the scene. The grand vizier had brought numerous costly offerings with him to sweeten his reception,
including 'a eunuch of remarkable beauty and in the very
flower of boyhood, who had been loved by Darius and was
afterwards to be loved by Alexander'.[27] The name of this
sinister youth was Bagoas: as time went on he acquired
great influence over the king. Alexander had in fact already
promised Nabarzanes his life; but Bagoas' attentions are said
to have tipped the scales still further in the grand vizier's
favour. Again, it was a dangerous omen of things to come.

A far more immediate problem, in Macedonian eyes, was
Alexander's ever-increasing orientalization: his adoption of
Persian dress and protocol, the way he was beginning to
confer on Iranian noblemen honours previously reserved
for Macedonians, the progressive infiltration of ex-enemy
troops into his own field army. As we have seen, his motives
for such innovations were severely practical; this will not
have increased their popularity. By now he was employing
Asiatic court ushers, and had even admitted some Persians
(including Darius' brother Oxathres) to the ranks of his
Companions. He had taken to wearing the Persian blue and
white royal diadem, though not the upright tiara which
went with it – a typically uneasy compromise. He had, in
like fashion, adopted a quasi-Persian style of dress, which
drew the line at anything so barbaric as trousers, but
retained the characteristic white robe and sash.

At first he only wore these exotic clothes in private, or
with Persian friends; but very soon they became his regular
attire, even on such occasions as a public audience, or when
he was out riding. His court, in general, began to bear an
ever-closer resemblance to that of the Great King. Macedonian horses were decked out in Persian harness; Alex-

ander even took over the traditional retinue of 365 concubines (one for each night of the year) who had served Darius, and were hand-picked from the most beautiful women in all Asia. Alexander is unlikely to have made any of these innovations from active choice or preference. Concubines bored him; so (at least to begin with) did Persian court ceremonial. But he needed new administrators and officers; and if the Persians were ever to accept his dynastic pretensions, he must play the part of Great King in an acceptable manner. By so doing, of course, he risked alienating his own Macedonians.

Fatally, he tried to compromise: this did him no good with anybody. If he adopted the diadem, he should have had the courage of his convictions and worn the high tiara as well. If he chose to surround himself with concubines, no one thought the better of him for not sleeping with them. The fact that he 'employed these customs rather sparingly' would cut no ice with the Macedonians, who objected to his employing them at all; while the Persians were unlikely to admire a monarch who followed their traditions in so gingerly a fashion (quite apart from having burnt and sacked their Holy City). Alexander's dilemma is well symbolized by the two seal-rings he used from now on. For European correspondence he employed his old Macedonian ring, while letters for delivery inside the Persian Empire he stamped with the royal signet of Darius. He made his Companions – much against their will in some cases – wear purple-bordered white Persian cloaks, and (when all else failed) tried to silent his more vociferous critics with increasingly lavish hand-outs and bonanzas.[28]

However, any ruler who made so blatant an effort to run with the hare and hunt with the hounds could hardly avoid trouble in the long run. A few of Alexander's close friends, such as Hephaestion, together with the usual clique of court toadies, actively supported his new integrationist line. The professional career officers – Craterus is a good example – were indifferent so long as their own status and prospects did not suffer. But Philip's hard-lining veterans bitterly resented the whole experiment.[29] The sight of their young king parading in outlandish robes, and on intimate terms with the quacking, effeminate, barbarian nobles he had so lately defeated, filled them with genuine disgust. The idea of accepting their ex-enemies as comrades-in-arms was equally repugnant to them. So far as they were concerned, the war had ended with Darius' death, and Alexander's grandiose dreams of further eastern conquest left them cold. The sooner they got home, the better.

This widening rift between them and the king is underlined by the fact that Alexander now began to employ two separate aides on liaison duties: Hephaestion for all dealings with the Persians, and Craterus when Macedonians and Greeks were involved. If Parmenio still hankered after his old proconsular powers – to put it no more strongly – this situation gave him a most promising basis of support. There were many, many Macedonians (including almost all the most experienced officers) who violently disapproved of the turn events had taken. Any leader offering a reversal of Alexander's policy, coupled with speedy repatriation, could almost certainly count on their backing. The king had only just soft-talked his troops into going on as it was; there would be no shortage of barrack-room lawyers to emphasize the inconsistency between his alarmist speeches and his fraternizing tactics. The air was electric, ready to spark an explosion at any moment.

Alexander took several steps to lessen the tension. Like most personally austere leaders, he had an ill-disguised contempt for humanity in the mass, and seems to have felt he could manipulate his troops as he pleased simply by indulging their grosser appetites. It was now that vast luxurious feasts and drinking-parties first became a regular feature of camp life: the idea of bread-and-circuses was by no means a Roman invention. At the same time, the king actively encouraged his Macedonian rank and file to marry the concubines they had picked up on their travels, offering them what sounds like a primitive family welfare scheme by way of bait.[30]

This was a shrewd and very farsighted move. Soldiers with their own domestic establishment in camp were less likely to clamour for immediate repatriation. They would put up with greater hardships, over a longer period. Eventually, indeed, they would come to regard their military existence as a permanent way of life: Alexander, it seems, looked to these liaisons for future recruits. Such a notion, if true, is highly revealing. It means that the king regarded conquest and exploration as an end in themselves, the natural condition of man; that he anticipated a state of affairs which would still be fundamentally unchanged in twenty years' time.

Immediate action, however, was the best antidote to any threat of mutiny.[31] The army marched on eastward, from Zadracarta to Susia in Areia. Here the satrap, Satibarzanes, who had been one of Darius' murderers, came forward and made his submission (presumably after putting out diplomatic feelers to see whether he would be well received). The news he brought was that Bessus – who, unlike Alexander, did not hesitate to assume the upright tiara, and indeed had a far better claim to it – was now being widely acclaimed as lord of Asia. Recruits were joining him, not only in Bactria itself, but also from the wild nomadic tribes beyond the Oxus.

This was a threat that had to be dealt with as soon as possible, before it got completely out of hand. Alexander therefore confirmed Satibarzanes as satrap – a decision he soon had cause to regret – and pressed on at top speed towards Bactria. During this march Parmenio's son Nicanor, the commander of the Guards Brigade (*hypaspistae*), fell ill and died. Alexander was in too much of a hurry to bury him with full military honours; he continued the march eastward, leaving Philotas to arrange his brother's funeral, and overtake the main body afterwards as best he could – an absence which, as we shall see, conceivably cost him his life.

At the Margus (Murghab) River,* Alexander heard that
Satibarzanes had massacred his Macedonian garrison, and
was raising Areia in revolt. The king at once halted his
advance into Bactria. Leaving Craterus in command of the
main army, he took a flying column southward towards
Artacoana, the satrapal seat, where Satibarzanes was
gathering his forces. In two days Alexander covered nearly
a hundred miles. Satibarzanes, caught off-guard, fled to
Bactria with 2,000 cavalry. His remaining troops dug themselves in on a nearby wooded mountain (Kālat-i-Nādiri).
It was now August: Alexander simply set the forest alight
and roasted the lot of them.

Another Persian, Arsaces, was appointed satrap of Areia
in Satibarzanes' place. To help prevent further trouble,
Alexander founded a settlement near Artacoana, which he
called Alexandria-of-the-Areians (Herat) – the first of many
such military garrisons planted at strategic points throughout the eastern provinces. The Macedonians were now
advancing into regions where towns, as a Westerner
would conceive them, were largely non-existent, and of
which their geographical knowledge was hazy in the
extreme. They thought, for example that the Jaxartes
River (Syr-Darya) formed the upper reaches of the Don,
and that the Hindu Kush range was somehow an extension
of the Caucasus. From the moment they plunged into

* Mr Don Engels, in an unpublished communication, argues that the
river Alexander reached at this point was not the Murghab but the
Kushk, some 180 miles from Susia (Tus); Arrian (3.25.6) states that
Artacoana was 600 stades (70 miles) from the point where Alexander
changed direction to deal with the treacherous Satibarzanes, 'which
gives a location on the Kushk and not the more northerly Murghab'.
Mr Engels argues, with some force, that Alexander 'would probably
skirt the south edge of the Dasht-i-Chol, descend the Kashaf Rud to the
Tedjen River (Ochus), and thence to the Kushk ... If Alexander
struck due east from Tus there would be only one river, the Tedjen,
before he reached the Murghab, the rivers being 100 miles apart,
50 miles of which are over the Dasht-i-Choe. It is more likely that he
chose the southern route.' Likely, but in the face of the evidence not
certain.

eastern Iran they were off the known map. It was now that the legends and tall stories began to proliferate – starting with the well-attested report that Alexander received a visit, during his stay at Zadracarta, from the queen of the Amazons, anxious to conceive a child by him. There was, on the other hand, nothing romantic or mythical about the three years of mountain guerrilla fighting (330–27) which followed, from Afghanistan to Bokhara, from Lake Seistan to the Hindu Kush, against the fiercest, most indomitable opposition Alexander had yet been called upon to face. Bessus, and his successor Spitamenes, were fighting a nationalist war, with strong religious overtones: between them they gave Alexander more continuous trouble than all the embattled hosts of Darius.[32]

The foundation of Herat had been made easier by a timely arrival of reinforcements – 3,000 Illyrians from Antipater, and almost the same number of Lydian mercenaries. Craterus now rejoined Alexander with the main army (including the four phalanx battalions that Cleitus the Black had brought back from Ecbatana), and together they marched on south. For the moment Alexander's original plan of a direct assault on Zariaspa, otherwise known as Bactra (Balkh) was abandoned; yet another rebellious regicide had to be dealt with first. This was Barsaëntes, satrap of Drangiana and Arachosia, a vast area extending eastward from Seistan as far as the Indus.

After this thousand-mile diversion Alexander planned to march north-east through Arachosia, and reach Bessus' stronghold by way of the Hindu Kush. Barsaëntes, hearing that Alexander was at hand, fled towards the Indus, but the local inhabitants seized him and sent him back. The king ordered his immediate execution, on charges of treason and murder. Nationalist opposition in this remote area was thus crushed without much effort (for the time being, that is: Alexander was to have more trouble from Satibarzanes a few months later). The Macedonian army now rested for a while at the capital of Drangiana, on the eastern shore of

Lake Seistan – a city afterwards occupied by the Parthians, who called it Phrada. It was here, during the autumn of 330 (in circumstances hardly less mysterious than those surrounding the Dreyfus Affair), that Alexander finally destroyed both Parmenio and his one surviving son, the arrogant, ambitious Philotas.[33]

For a long while now, as we have seen, the king had been steadily undermining Parmenio's power and authority. Quite apart from the personal vendetta between them, Parmenio symbolized Macedonian conservatism in its most uncompromising form. Alexander's new pretensions deeply antagonized the whole old guard, his second-in-command perhaps more than anyone. This was not a crucial matter so long as the rank and file remained loyal; but there were disturbing signs, now, that their allegiance too had begun to wear dangerously thin. Victories, loot, and glory were not, in the end, enough for them. The war had gone on too long already, and peace continually receded over the eastern horizon. Worse still, the leader they had hero-worshipped was rapidly turning into an unapproachable oriental despot. 'We have lost Alexander,' one old soldier lamented. 'We have lost our king.'

With the death of Darius, and its obvious implications regarding the succession, some kind of showdown became inevitable. Alexander, characteristically, made up his mind to strike first. Parmenio enjoyed great popularity with the troops, and any direct move against him might well provoke a riot, or worse. Alexander's obvious line was to get at the old marshal through his son, Philotas, a far less likeable character. Tactless, overbearing and ostentatious, Philotas caused deep resentment among officers and men alike by his caustic tongue and high-handed manners. Parmenio had warned him about his behaviour: Philotas took no notice. For some while now Alexander had been steadily advancing Craterus and Perdiccas at his expense.

He had also – on Craterus' suggestion – suborned

Philotas' mistress Antigone to report any treasonable remarks her lover might make.[34] Presumably Alexander meant to build up a dossier of careless talk and then stage a show-trial. This approach, however, produced surprisingly little hard evidence. Philotas once vehemently asserted, while drunk, that he and his father between them were responsible for all Alexander's finest achievements – a remark which might perhaps smack of *lèse-majesté* but which could hardly be construed as conspiratorial or subversive. Philotas' worst fault, indeed, seems to have been his outspoken bluntness – something very different. If we can believe Curtius,[35] he wrote to Alexander after the Siwah episode, congratulating the king on his divine parentage, and commiserating (perhaps only half in jest) with all those who would in future be under such more than human authority.

This kind of shrewd deflation was hardly calculated to increase Alexander's liking for him. On the other hand, one quality Philotas possessed guaranteed him immunity – at least until after Gaugamela. He was a brilliant cavalry commander, who led the Companions with superb panache and assurance. Now, however, as Alexander's destiny called him away from the plains into the mountains, and guerrilla fighting became the order of the day, Philotas had lost his usefulness – could, indeed, be regarded as expendable. What was more, the death of his last remaining brother, Nicanor, left him dangerously isolated; and Parmenio was far away in Ecbatana. All Alexander needed was a good excuse to act, and fate – or some discreet manipulation behind the scenes – obligingly produced it.

Philotas rejoined the army at Lake Seistan, after attending to Nicanor's funeral. A day or two later he was buttonholed outside Alexander's headquarters by a young man called Cebalinus, who poured out some confused and unconvincing story about a plot against the king's life. Cebalinus' brother, it seemed, was in love with a man named Dymnus, who had invited him to join the plot, but of course (Cebalinus said) he had refused . . . We can imagine Philotas tapping his foot impatiently during this long-winded recital, and thinking: Another homosexual quarrel, with the usual bitchy accusations: obviously nothing in it. Cebalinus now proceeded to name several important persons, including Demetrius, a Gentleman of the Bodyguard. Worse and worse, Philotas must have thought. No witnesses, no proof: the boy had not even come in person, but had sent his brother. Now he was accusing friends of the king. Best not to get involved: this kind of gossip made for endless trouble.

Cebalinus was tiresomely importunate, and to get rid of him Philotas promised that he would pass on his information to Alexander without delay – probably calculating that the whole affair would die a natural death soon enough. Perhaps, too, at the back of his mind there stirred the unacknowledged thought that if by any remote chance the rumour *was* true, events should be allowed to follow their natural course:

> Thou shalt not kill, yet need'st not strive,
> Officiously, to keep alive.

At any rate, though he had several interviews with Alexander during the next two days, the subject of this alleged conspiracy was never brought up.[36] Each time Cebalinus saw Philotas, he asked him whether he had told Alexander yet; each time Philotas (who had no intention of feeding the king's all-too-inflammable paranoia with mere malicious tittle-tattle) made the usual polite excuses that one tends to reserve for ultra-persistent bores. In the end Cebalinus, understandably suspicious, carried his tale to one of the royal pages instead.[37]

This time he got immediate action. The page hid Cebalinus in the armoury, and told Alexander his story while the king was bathing.[38] Alexander at once ordered Dymnus' arrest, and then proceeded to grill Cebalinus himself. Why, he asked, very reasonably, had there been forty-eight hours' delay before he was informed – especially since the *coup* had been planned for the third day after Cebalinus first learnt of it?[39] At this point Philotas' name was brought into the discussion for the first time. Cebalinus made no attempt to implicate him in the plot, and he had not figured in Dymnus' list of conspirators.[40] All that Cebalinus complained of – more to excuse himself than for any more sinister reason – was Philotas' dilatoriness in passing on his message.

But Alexander saw, instantly, that here was the opening he had been waiting for, the perfect instrument with which to encompass Philotas' downfall. By the time Dymnus was dragged in, barely alive (he had fallen on his sword when arrested) the king had a breathtaking punch-line ready: 'What great wrong have I planned against you, Dymnus,' he exclaimed, '*that you should think Philotas more worthy to rule the Macedonians than I am myself*?' Dymnus, however, was by now past speech, and died leaving this extraordinary question unanswered.[41] Next, Alexander summoned Philotas, who at first made light of the whole affair, 'fearing besides,' as Curtius says, 'lest he should be laughed at by the rest if he reported a quarrel between a lover and his favourite'. The news of Dymnus' suicide took him aback. He admitted that perhaps he ought to have reported the matter, and apologized for not having done so. Alexander accepted his apology, the two men shook hands, and that, on the face of it, was that. Philotas walked out a free man.[42]

In fact, of course, the king simply needed a little more time in which to perfect his plans. He called a private council meeting from which Philotas was conspicuously absent.[43] Amongst those present were Hephaestion, Craterus, Coenus – Parmenio's son-in-law, but ready enough to swim with the tide – Erigyius of Mytilene, and two Gentlemen of the Bodyguard, Perdiccas and Leonnatus. All were subsequently raised to high command; four became marshals of the empire. These, if anyone, constituted Alexander's inner circle of faithful friends. Cebalinus' brother Nicomachus was brought before them and made to repeat his story in detail.[44] Craterus then rose and made a virulent attack against both Philotas – his personal rival – and Parmenio, asserting that Alexander would never be safe so long as they were left alive. The other members of the council agreed. Philotas must surely be implicated in this plot: why else had he been so reluctant to report it? He should be tortured; perhaps he would then confess the names of other accomplices.

Having thus secured the support of his staff, Alexander struck at once. The actual arrest of Philotas would be the most dangerous step in the whole operation, since there was always an outside chance that the troops might stand by him. The king took all possible precautions. A route-march was announced for the following morning. Cavalry patrols were stationed at every gate of the camp, and on the road outside, to make sure no messenger got away to Parmenio during the night. Philotas himself, to disarm suspicion, received a dinner-invitation from Alexander. About midnight a picked detachment of troops set out from the king's tent to arrest both Philotas and the other conspirators whom Cebalinus' brother had named. Philotas' house was quietly surrounded while he lay asleep, and all the arrests were carried out with smooth efficiency.[45]

Next morning Alexander summoned a general parade of his Macedonian troops. In cases of high treason, the king acted as prosecutor, but it was the army which passed final judgment. After a long silence, during which the atmosphere became progressively more strained, Alexander began his speech. Dymnus' body lay there before him; Philotas, for the moment, he kept out of sight. By now he was ready to declare, as proven fact, that Parmenio had been the master-mind behind the conspiracy, with Philotas and the rest as his agents. The best evidence he could produce for this assertion was an intercepted letter from the old man, containing the ambiguous injunction: 'First, look out for yourselves, then for yours: for thus we shall accomplish what we have planned.'[46]

Cebalinus, his brother, and the royal page who had broken the news to Alexander were all produced as witnesses: none of them incriminated Philotas. Alexander was reduced to raking up old gossip and tittle-tattle; not even the dossier supplied by Philotas' mistress gave him any really solid ammunition. The accused man was now, at last, brought in, hands tied behind him, wearing an old threadbare cloak. His appearance excited murmurs of pity from the troops. One officer, Amyntas, jumped up and attempted to counter this wave of sympathy by claiming that the prisoner had betrayed them all to the barbarians, that because of him none of them would see their wives or homes or children again.* Amyntas was followed by Coenus, Philotas' own brother-in-law, who damned him as a traitor to king, country, and army, and was only with difficulty restrained from stoning him.

Philotas was, according to custom, allowed the privilege of speaking in his own defence, though Alexander – after a cheap gibe about his refusal to speak in Macedonian dialect – did not stay to listen. This was perhaps just as well, since Philotas, with contemptuous ease, tore the whole prosecution case to shreds. The hostile feeling of the assembly was only restored, with difficulty, by an ex-ranker general, who reminded them what an arrogant snob Philotas was, how he evicted troops from their billets to make room for his own stores. This produced an angry uproar, during which one of the guards was heard shouting that he would tear the traitor to pieces with his own hands.

Alexander, with his usual faultless sense of timing, now reappeared, and dismissed the assembly till the following day. At a second council meeting that evening it was agreed

---

*This may have stirred up the troops, but it infuriated Alexander, who had been working very hard to undermine the whole idea of early repatriation.

that Philotas and his fellow-prisoners should all suffer the traditional penalty – death by stoning. But there were two things Alexander wanted to get first: a written confession from Philotas himself, and some sort of statement implicating Parmenio. Craterus, Hephaestion and Coenus were therefore authorized to torture Philotas until he provided both. The king had a private briefing-session beforehand with Craterus ('the subject of which has not been made public,' says Curtius, and small wonder). Then he withdrew to his quarters and let them get on with it – or, according to Plutarch, observed the proceedings from behind a curtain.[47]

Before morning the torturers had their written confession, and probably enough extra details, imagined or remembered, to implicate Parmenio as well (at one point Philotas asked Craterus, with weary cynicism, to explain just what it was he wanted said). When their victim was brought before the assembly to hear sentence pronounced, he had to be carried, since he could no longer walk. Our main source, Curtius, alleges that he suffered further torture even after his confession had been wrung out of him. As soon as he and the rest of those accused had been executed, Alexander (never averse – in the most literal sense on this occasion – from killing two birds with one stone) ordered his own namesake, the Lyncestian, to be brought in for final judgment.[48] But three years of close confinement seem to have addled this once-proud aristocrat's wits. When ordered to defend himself, he hesitated, stumbled, and finally dried up after a few meaningless words. The guards standing nearby grew impatient (or perhaps had their orders) and ran their spears through him without more ado.

Three of Andromenes' four sons were also arraigned now; mainly because they had been on close terms with Philotas, and Alexander had received warning letters about them from his mother. The fourth brother, Polemo, had fled on hearing of Philotas' arrest – enough, one might have thought, to damn them all out of hand. But Amyntas, the eldest (and the main target for Olympias' venom), put up a vigorous defence, pointing out, *inter alia*, that the queen mother's main grudge against him was due to his having conscripted several of her young palace favourites – at the king's express command – while recruiting in Macedonia.[49] Alexander, surprisingly, allowed them all to go free. (One brother, Attalus, was Perdiccas' brother-in-law, which perhaps had some bearing on the matter.) The king may well have felt that a scrupulous acquittal in one instance would suggest that all the trials had been fairly conducted.* When Demetrius the Bodyguard protested his innocence, Alexander let him go – and then quietly re-arrested him a little later, after all the fuss had died down.[50]

However, the king had no intention of carrying out a wholesale pogrom of dissident Macedonian officers. He had attained his immediate objective, and knew when to stop. Only one thing – perhaps the most important – still remained to be done. Polydamas, one of the Companions, was dispatched across the deserts of central Iran, in Arab costume and with two Arabs as guides, bearing Parmenio's death-warrant. To ensure that they reached Ecbatana before the old marshal could hear any rumour of his son's death, the party travelled on racing camels, covering the distance in eleven days rather than the usual thirty.

It was evening when Polydamas reached his destination. He changed back into Macedonian dress, and went straight to Cleander, Parmenio's second-in-command. One glance at Alexander's warrant was enough. Cleander alerted his staff-officers, and made arrangements for Polydamas to meet Parmenio early the following morning, in a grove of the Royal Park. Polydamas had brought two letters for Parmenio himself, so that this sudden visit should not arouse any untimely suspicions. One was from Alexander, while the other bore Philotas' seal, and may, indeed, even have been written by him at the same time as his 'con-

---

*At least one modern scholar has fallen for this old propaganda trick: see Tarn, vol. I, pp. 63–4, and Badian's comments, *TAPhA* 91 (1960), 334–5.

fession'. As the old general opened it, in evident delight, Cleander stabbed him twice, first through the ribs and then in the throat. His fellow-officers followed suit. Blows continued to rain down on him even after he was dead. The guards outside the grove hurriedly roused their comrades in camp, and came back threatening lynch action. An ugly situation was only just averted by Cleander, who showed their leaders 'the letters which contained an account of the plots of Parmenio against the king and Alexander's prayers that they should avenge him'. The soldiers, only partially mollified, demanded their old commander's body for burial. At first Cleander, afraid that such a concession might offend the king, refused point-blank. But when a near-riot ensued, he agreed to compromise. The head was hacked off and sent back to Alexander, while the decapitated trunk received a military funeral in Ecbatana.[51]

Parmenio's troops, with whom he had been extremely popular, never forgot or forgave his death. Years later, when those responsible were purged in their turn (see below, pp. 438–9), the occasion called forth general rejoicing. For Alexander it had been touch and go. He had got the army to act against Philotas, and had destroyed both Parmenio and Alexander of Lyncestis in the backwash of that carefully staged condemnation. The incubus that had lain on him for so long was now at long last removed. But the whole episode left an unpleasant aftermath of suspicion and hatred behind it. From now on Alexander never completely trusted his troops: the feeling was mutual.

To keep abreast of what the rank and file were thinking, he instituted the first known system of military postal censorship. Men and officers alike were encouraged to write letters home: they would, the king intimated, get the chance less and less often as they marched farther east. These mails were dispatched with his own couriers. After three postal stages they were recalled, and Alexander went through every letter at his leisure. All those who expressed criticism of him and his policies, or were (in his opinion) unduly distressed by Parmenio's death, or groused about their prolonged military service, he 'assembled into one unit which he called the Disciplinary Company, so that the rest of the Macedonians might not be corrupted by their improper remarks and criticism'. The ultimate purpose of this group, Justin alleges, was to supply men for particularly dangerous missions, or to garrison remote military settlements on the eastern frontiers.[52]

At the same time Alexander decided (though he later revoked the decision) never again to leave his all-important Companion Cavalry under one man's control. He therefore split Philotas' command between Black Cleitus – an appointment clearly designed to placate old guard conservatives – and his own closest personal friend, Hephaestion.[53] This was Hephaestion's first major post. From now on his rise to power was steady, progressive, and by no means based entirely on nepotism: he seems to have been a competent, if uninspired, cavalry commander.

When Antipater learnt of Parmenio's death, he said: 'If Parmenio plotted against Alexander, who is to be trusted? And if he did not, what is to be done?'[54] It was an understandable reaction, and one with echoes for the future. The whole episode remains tantalizingly ambiguous. Plutarch assumed that the only plot was that *against* Philotas; most recent historical studies tend to agree.[55] Both Philotas and Parmenio, according to this view. were innocent victims of Alexander's personal vindictiveness and political absolutism. There may be an element of truth in this, but to present it as the *whole* truth is, surely, a dangerous oversimplification.

Unless we decide to jettison our sources altogether, it is evident that some sort of conspiracy against Alexander *was* in the air. Moreover, the way in which the king subsequently divided Philotas' vacant command between two officers suggests that – rightly or wrongly – he had convinced himself, if no one else, of the dead man's guilt. Whether he also regarded Parmenio as a traitor is more problematical. Disaffection was in the air, and Parmenio would be a natural focus for it. Furthermore, he controlled a key sector of Alexander's communications, and was admirably placed, in the event of a *coup*, to seize the accumulated treasures from Susa and Persepolis. Whatever his personal feelings, the king could not possibly afford to leave him in so powerful a position after the execution of his last suriving son.

If a plot existed at this juncture, it could have only one object: to overthrow Alexander, reverse his unpopular policies, and wind up the expedition as soon as possible. The natural instigators of such a programme were the Macedonian old guard: its natural leaders would be men like Parmenio and Philotas. So much Alexander could have deduced for himself; he might well have decided to get his own blow in first – especially since he had old scores to settle with both father and son. Yet certain details make one wonder. Philotas' obstinate refusal to report what he had been told remains – despite all his plausible explanations – undeniably odd. The extract from Parmenio's letter to his sons (if not a mere forgery) is, on the kindest interpretation, ambiguous. The sudden, apparently unmotivated decision to execute Alexander of Lyncestis would make more sense if there was any risk of his being used as a potential figurehead.

The truth, now, can in all likelihood never be recovered. Perhaps even at the time no one man – least of all Alexander himself – held all the clues. Our verdict over the 'Philotas affair', then, should be a cautious 'Not Proven' rather than a confident 'Not Guilty'. At the same time we should not waste too much liberal sympathy on Parmenio, whose own record of judicial murder (see above, p. 120) will not bear over-close examination. Those who live by the sword shall perish by the sword; this tough and wily old Macedonian opportunist merely lasted longer than most.

[9]

The Quest for Ocean

IT was winter by the time Alexander resumed his march. If he had simply wanted to pursue Bessus, with no other considerations in mind, he could have back-tracked north to the point where he left the Murghab (or the Kushk) River, and then have continued his advance on Zariaspa. Instead, he swung north-east through Arachosia, which meant that he would now be forced to cross the Hindu Kush. His main reason for picking this long, difficult route seems to have been the still-unpacified state of the southern satrapies, including Arachosia itself. Dissension, indeed, was widespread. No sooner had he set out than reports reached him of a fresh rising in his rear, once again under Satibarzanes' leadership. An expeditionary force was at once sent back to Areia to deal with the rebels, and its commander, Erigyius of Mytilene, won great distinction by killing Satibarzanes in single combat.

The revolt collapsed, but Areia continued to give trouble. Its Persian governor had subsequently to be replaced by a reliable Macedonian. Alexander appointed another Macedonian, Menon, as satrap of Arachosia: Menon's authority was further reinforced by a new military settlement, probably near the site of modern Kandahar. The whole region, it is clear, was very far from subdued, much less reliable.

Alexander reached Kandahar in February 329, and began his crossing of the Hindu Kush about the beginning of April. During their winter march through the highlands of eastern Afghanistan his troops had suffered severely from frostbite, snow blindness, and chronic fatigue – the latter probably due to oxygen shortage at high altitudes.[1] Somewhere near Kabul the king gave them a short and well-earned rest. Then, after establishing a third garrison town (which received the name Alexandria-in-the-Caucasus) he took his army over the Khawak pass (11,600 ft), and struck north along the line of the Surkhab River towards Drapsaca (Kunduz). The crossing is said to have been accomplished in seventeen days – a remarkable feat, and one which must have required the most careful planning and accumulation of supplies at Alexander's base-camp. North of the Hindu Kush Bessus had adopted a scorched-earth policy; all supplies had been either destroyed or else concealed in pits by the local inhabitants. This caused the Macedonians considerable hardship, but failed to hold up their advance.*

Bessus himself, together with 7,000 Bactrians and some strong Soghdian levies – the latter under two great feudal barons, Spitamenes and Oxyartes – was confidently awaiting Alexander at Aornus (Tashkurgan). There are no less than seven passes from Kabul to the Oxus valley: Bessus assumed, very reasonably, that the Macedonians would choose the lowest one. But Alexander, unpredictable as always, did nothing of the sort. The Khawak pass is not only the easternmost of the seven (which was why he chose it) but also the highest and the most heavily snowbound. His army negotiated it with fantastic speed, and Bessus, eighty miles away to the west, found himself outflanked. He therefore decided to abandon Bactria altogether, retreat across the Oxus, and base his defence on Soghdiana.[2]

When this plan was announced, most of his Bactrian cavalrymen promptly deserted, peeling off home to their own villages. Yet Bessus' strategy – as subsequent events

---

*Throughout the period 330–326 Alexander may very well have been commandeering or bulk-purchasing grain from some at least of Greece's normal sources of supply (which in his day, according to the Elder Pliny, *HN* 18.12.63–5, were – in that order – Sicily, North Africa, Egypt and Pontus) to keep his large army fed during its eastern campaigns. For the general grain shortage in Greece at this point, and the relief consignments (up to 805,000 Aeginetan, or over *one million* Attic, *medimni*, the *medimnus* being about one and a half bushels) obtained from Cyrene, in N. Africa, see the remarkable inscription recorded in Tod, II (no. 196), with the editor's commentary, pp. 273–6.

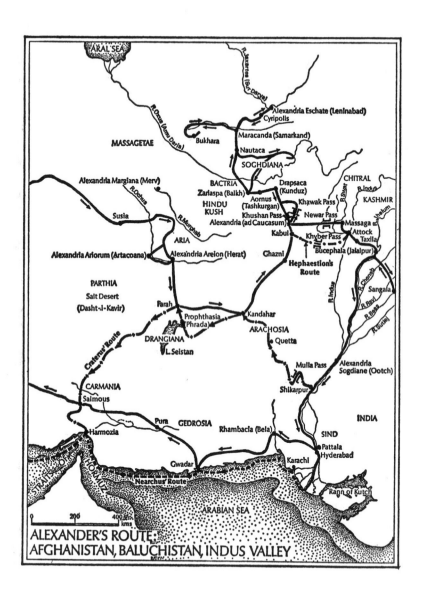

ALEXANDER'S ROUTE:
AFGHANISTAN, BALUCHISTAN, INDUS VALLEY

proved – was neither cowardly nor unintelligent. Bactria, being for the most part a seamed and rugged mass of pathless mountains, offered almost impossible fighting terrain. Beyond the Oxus, however, conditions were very different. Soghdiana (Bokhara and Turkestan) consisted largely of plain and desert. Its inhabitants were fierce, independent tribesmen who could ride almost before they could walk. This offered the perfect combination for a hit-and-run campaign of attrition (cf. Fuller, p. 117), carried out by mounted guerrillas who could swoop down on a marching column, and vanish into the steppe when pursued.

After a short rest at Drapsaca, Alexander went on to occupy both Tashkurgan and Zariaspa, the capital of Bactria – and Zoroaster's birthplace – without encountering any real opposition. Then, leaving old Artabazus as satrap of the newly conquered province, he passed on towards the Oxus. It was now June, the dry season, and his route lay across a burning waterless desert, where the frostbitten suddenly found themselves suffering from heatstroke. Marching by night made conditions less unbearable, since the temperature then dropped considerably (from 100°+ to 70° or even 60°F). Even so, the bulk of the army trailed behind badly during this gruelling marathon – so much so that when Alexander finally reached the Oxus, about sunset, he had to light beacon-fires for them: otherwise they might have missed his camp in the darkness.

After this experience the Thessalian volunteers (already restive enough as a result of Parmenio's murder) mutinied *en masse*, and many of Philip's older veterans followed their example. They were four thousand miles from home: they had had enough. The king had no alternative but to release them all, with severance pay and bonuses. This unexpected demobilization left him dangerously short of first-class troops. To make matters worse, a great number – more than he had lost in any battle – now died as a result of dehydration followed by frenetic over-drinking. He therefore took a gamble and, for the first time, recruited local

'barbarian' auxiliaries on a large scale. The gamble paid
off handsomely – though how Alexander's remaining Macedonians reacted to it is quite another matter.

The Oxus (Amu Darya) presented a formidable obstacle.
Rising in the high Pamirs, it carries down a vast quantity
of snow-water from the mountains of central Asia. At Kelif,
where Alexander made his crossing, it was three-quarters
of a mile wide, and deep in proportion, with a sandy
bottom and a swift-flowing current. The king's engineers
tried to sink piles for a bridge, but these were quickly
carried away. In any case the countryside was barren and
treeless: to collect enough timber would have taken far too
long. Finally Alexander fell back on the expedient he had
adopted at the Danube (see above, pp. 128–9) – except that
this time he had no fleet to help him. All the leather tent-
covers were stuffed with dry chaff and then stitched up
carefully to make floats.

By this makeshift method the king got his forces across the
river. But it took him five days: if Bessus had chosen to
attack during this period he would have had Alexander at a
very serious disadvantage. He might also, as things turned
out, have saved his own life.[3] Instead, he assumed that
Alexander would be held up at the Oxus until he could
collect a transport fleet – just as he had earlier deduced,
with erroneous confidence, which pass the Macedonians
would follow from Kabul. His military reputation, already
shaky after the evacuation of Bactria, sank to zero when
Alexander's latest exploit became known. Spitamenes and
the Soghdian barons decided, at this point, that a change of
leadership was advisable. They therefore placed Bessus
under arrest, and sent messengers to tell Alexander that if a
Macedonian officer and escort came to a certain rendezvous, the regicide would be handed over to them. This was
an extremely clever move. It not only rid the new junta
of Bessus himself, but convinced Alexander of their willingness to collaborate.

Nevertheless he reacted cautiously: the message might

prove to be some sort of trap. Ptolemy, son of Lagus (who had been made a Bodyguard after the liquidation of Demetrius), was entrusted with this delicate mission. As an insurance against possible trouble, he had a very strong force with him – about 1,600 cavalry and 4,000 infantry.[4] Spitamenes and his colleagues, who no more trusted Alexander than he did them, carefully avoided any personal contact with his party. Ptolemy was directed to a remote village, where he found Bessus under armed guard. He thereupon sent a dispatch back to Alexander, asking how Bessus should be brought into his presence.

The king's instructions were very specific. Bessus was to be placed by the roadside where Alexander and his troops would pass, naked, bound to a post, and with a slave's wooden collar round his neck. This was duly done. When Alexander (whose treatment of Bessus seems to have been mainly dictated by a desire to impress the recalcitrant Iranian nobility) came abreast of his prisoner, he stepped down from his royal chariot, and asked why Bessus had first enchained and then slain Darius 'his king, kinsman and benefactor'. Bessus replied that it had been a joint decision, 'to win Alexander's favour and so save their lives'. But such favours (as everyone knew) would only be welcomed as such by a foreign usurper – the one title Alexander was anxious to avoid. As proof of the abhorrence with which he regarded Bessus' act of betrayal, Alexander first had him scourged, and then sent back to Zariaspa, where in 328 he stood trial as a regicide. His nose and ears were cut off – a Persian practice, which Darius I had previously used against a pretender to the throne, but here done on Alexander's express orders – and he finally suffered public execution in Ecbatana,[5] before a full assembly of the Medes and Persians. How far Alexander's display of Achaemenid justice impressed them is a debatable point.

Both the crossing of the Hindu Kush and the desert march which followed it had taken heavy toll of the Macedonians' cavalry mounts. Alexander now re-equipped his squadrons with local Turkestan horses, bigger and stronger than any breed they had encountered hitherto. Then, under the happy but mistaken impression that Spitamenes was now his subject-ally, and all south-west Soghdiana peacefully subdued, he struck north for Maracanda (Samarkand) and the Jaxartes (Syr-Darya). This river marked the furthermost north-eastern boundary of the Persian Empire. Beyond it lay limitless 'Scythian' steppe and mountain, inhabited by wild nomadic tribesmen – Dahae, Sacae, Massagetae. Here Alexander found an outpost and a chain of forts, seven in number, supposedly built by Cyrus. These he garrisoned with mercenaries. He also planned to construct a new military settlement of his own, 'both as an excellent base for a possible future invasion of Scythia and as a defensive position against raiding tribes from across the river'. Its name was Alexandria-the-Furthest (Leninabad or Khodjend).

Various 'Scythian' tribes had sent delegations to him, seeking alliance. Alexander received them graciously. A number of Macedonian officers accompanied these envoys home, with instructions to ratify treaties of friendship – while at the same time picking up all the information they could get about local topography, military equipment, and troop-numbers. The practice of using diplomats as intelligence agents is by no means an exclusively modern phenomenon.

It was now that the real trouble began. Alexander summoned Spitamenes and his colleagues to a meeting in Zariaspa. Spitamenes, probably afraid that the king meant to take hostages for their future good behaviour, refused. The whole province now rose in revolt under him. Local commandos recaptured Cyrus' outpost and its string of forts, massacring Alexander's garrisons. Spitamenes himself laid siege to Maracanda. On receipt of this news the king acted promptly enough, but he does not seem, as yet, to have fully appreciated what he was up against. The relief force he sent to Maracanda was hopelessly inadequate for its task. Indeed, its titular commander, Pharnuches, a

Lydian interpreter, had probably been chosen with an eye to diplomatic negotiations rather than fighting. He knew the local language, 'and had often shown a skilful hand in dealing with the natives'. All he had with him were sixty Companion Cavalry, and 2,000 mercenaries, 800 of them mounted, under three Macedonian officers. Alexander dealt with the river-forts himself. He had been shot through the leg-bone by a stray arrow on the march to Maracanda: this is unlikely to have improved his temper. Five of the seven forts he retook in three days, butchering their defenders by way of reprisal. The main outpost, Cyropolis, fell after a raiding-party squeezed in along a dry river-course that ran under the wall. Eight thousand men died in a last desperate stand. Seven thousand survivors, together with the garrisons of the two remaining forts, were (says Aristobulus) afterwards executed *en masse*. During the hand-to-hand fighting Alexander was struck on the face and neck by a large stone. For a while both his vision and his vocal chords were impaired, and there was a fear that he might actually go blind.

What he needed more than anything was the chance to rest and recuperate. Bone-splinters kept working out of his wounded leg, and he must have suffered the most excruciating migraines. Yet though he could barely stand, he spent the next three weeks supervising the construction of Alexandria-the-Furthest's new city-walls. Towards the end of this period, irritated by the taunts and threats of the tribesmen across the river, he carried out a tactically brilliant raid into their territory. The encircling nomad horsemen were outmanoeuvred and encircled in their turn, and a thousand of them cut down by Alexander's heavy cavalry. During the retreat which followed, the king drank some infected water. When he recrossed the Jaxartes he had gastro-enteritis to contend with on top of his other troubles.

But the worst news was yet to come. When Pharnuches and his relief column approached, Spitamenes had withdrawn from Maracanda, skilfully luring his pursuers on towards Bokhara, across the Zarafshen River, into the wild territory of the Massagetae. Here they were ambushed, surrounded, and shot down almost to a man (accounts differ as to the exact circumstances). Only 300 infantry and about forty mounted troopers escaped. Spitamenes at once took his troops back to Maracanda, and resumed the siege. When Alexander heard this grim story from the survivors, he threatened them with the death penalty if they breathed a word about what had happened. Knowing his Herodotus, he probably also had in mind Cyrus' equally ill-fated expedition among the Massagetae, which ended with a similar massacre – in which the king lost his life. One thing stood out clearly: Spitamenes was the most dangerous opponent Alexander had been called upon to face since Memnon of Rhodes.

Once again the king moved with quite extraordinary speed. Taking a column of cavalry and light-armed troops, he force-marched along the Jaxartes, across the Golod'naya Steppe, and into the valley of the Zarafshen, reaching Maracanda at dawn on the fourth day – a distance of about 160 miles. Spitamenes and his horsemen promptly raised their siege and faded away into the desert. Alexander pursued them for a while, but in the end gave up the chase as hopeless. On his way back he systematically ravaged the land bordering on the river: without fodder and provisions hostile raiders would find it difficult to attack Maracanda during the winter. He also made a detour to the spot where Pharnuches had been ambushed, and buried the dead soldiers still lying there.[6]

This done, he recrossed the Oxus and went into winter quarters at Zariaspa (329/8). Here final sentence was pronounced on Bessus (see above, p. 355); and here Alexander also dealt with the rebel satrap of Areia, who was brought back in chains by his collaborating fellow-nobles. Welcome reinforcements, mostly mercenaries, arrived from the coast. With them came such men as Parmenio's brother Asander (who, perhaps fortuitously, is never heard of again), and

Nearchus, Alexander's boyhood friend, till recently satrap of Lycia (see above, p. 201), and now appointed a battalion commander in the Guards Brigade. The winter months were also enlivened by various embassies, including a personal visit from Pharasmenes, King of the Chorasmians, a large tribe dwelling along the Oxus towards the Aral Sea.

Though it was probably from Pharasmenes that Alexander first learnt of the Aral's existence, faulty notions of geography and over-imaginative interpreting seem to have got the two men quite splendidly at cross-purposes. Pharasmenes was eager to enlist so great a conqueror's support against his western neighbours on the Caspian; but somehow Colchis and the Amazons were brought into the picture, and Alexander became convinced that what Pharasmenes had in mind was an expedition to the Black Sea. What is most interesting about this *malentendu* is the king's reaction to it. He told Pharasmenes that his first concern was to round off the conquest of Asia by subduing India. When he returned to Greece, however, he planned, he said, to make a full-scale naval and military expedition into the Black Sea; and for this Pharasmenes' offer would be most useful.[7] Here is the first hint in our sources of Alexander's plans for ultimate world-conquest, of the further expeditions that would follow when the East had been fully subdued.

Meanwhile, before he could think of moving on to India, there was the elusive Spitamenes to be dealt with. Early in the spring of 328 Alexander, leaving Craterus and four battalions of the phalanx to police Bactria, recrossed the Oxus and set about this singularly frustrating task.[8]* He split up his forces into five mobile columns, under Hephaestion, Ptolemy, Perdiccas, Coenus and himself. These columns ranged through the countryside, mopping up

* At the crossing of the Oxus two springs, one of water and the other of oil, were revealed when a trench was being dug for the king's tent. Aristander the seer, with his usual glib and platitudinous self-assurance, interpreted this as 'a sign of difficulties to come and of eventual victory'.

pockets of local resistance and establishing a linked network of military outposts. Either now or shortly afterwards a similar system was set up in Margiane (western Bactria). Existing hill-forts were taken over and fresh ones built, all within easy reach of each other. Justin lists no less than thirteen such posts in Soghdiana alone.[9]

Spitamenes, meanwhile, had kept well beyond Alexander's reach, among the Massagetae nomads, where he was reputed to be raising a large cavalry force. When the five Macedonian columns made their pre-arranged rendezvous in Maracanda, about midsummer, the king sent off Coenus and old Artabazus to keep an eye on his activities. Spitamenes dodged their scouts with insolent ease, swept south into Bactria, captured a border fortress, ravaged the land round Zariaspa, and carved up a scratch force of Macedonian veterans who ventured out against him. When this news reached Craterus (who had been up-country with his four phalanx-battalions) he hurried after Spitamenes, overtaking him just on the edge of the desert. There was a fierce engagement, during which about 150 Massagetae horsemen lost their lives. But the remainder, Spitamenes included, did their usual vanishing-trick into the steppe, where Craterus found it impracticable to pursue them.[10]

The atmosphere in headquarters that summer was strained and irritable. What should have been a quick minor campaign continued to drag on inconclusively. Two unprecedented defeats did not improve matters. The hatred and jealousy between Philip's old guard and the king's Graeco-Oriental courtiers reached a fresh peak of intensity. Maracanda sweltered dustily under a burning sun. Everyone, Alexander included, had begun to drink rather more than was good for them. Under such conditions it needed very little to bring overstrained tempers to flash-point. The heavy carousing which followed a Macedonian banquet soon set resentful tongues wagging freely. *In vino veritas* – and the truth came out with more violence for being so long suppressed, as it had done during Philip's last and fatal marriage-feast. Sooner or later there was bound to be an explosion; and when it came, it assumed a particularly ugly form.[11]

The evening began, like so many others, with a lavish banquet – perhaps in honour of Black Cleitus, who was setting out next day to take up his new appointment as governor of Bactria, a hazardous and responsible post.[12] Presently the banquet degenerated into the usual uproarious drinking-party. Alexander, more than half-tipsy, and egged on by the sycophants who crowded round him, began to boast immoderately of his own achievements. Flatterers compared the king's exploits – favourably – with those of Heracles. This vainglorious attitude might have been calculated to provoke the old guard. If so, it achieved its object.[13] Cleitus (who found Alexander's orientalism and the gross adulation of his courtiers equally repellent) now remarked, sourly, that such talk was blasphemous. In any case, he went on, they were exaggerating. Most of Alexander's successes were due to the Macedonian army as a whole (a theme to which Cleitus returned later, with fatal consequences).[14] When he heard this the king was 'deeply hurt'. One can imagine the scene all too clearly.

Alexander's clique, by no means averse to fanning the flames, now launched into a wholesale denunciation of Philip, suggesting that what *he* had done 'was, after all, quite ordinary and commonplace'. The king himself needed little encouragement to develop this theme. Philip had grudged him credit for the victory at Chaeronea, even though he, Alexander, personally saved his father's life during the battle. Other long-cherished grudges came tumbling out.[15] Cleitus, by now angry-drunk himself, vigorously upheld Philip's achievements (and with good reason), 'rating them all higher than the present victories'. He even spoke out in defence of Parmenio, accusing Alexander of winning easy victories for which he depended on Philip's veterans.

'From this,' says Curtius, 'there arose a dispute between the younger and the older soldiers.'[16] But the division was not merely one of youth and age; it was fundamental, irreconcilable – nationalism against the orientalizing policy, simplicity against sophistication, blunt free speech against sedulous conformism. It is by no means impossible that Alexander (who had become ultra-sensitive of late, perhaps with reason, about plots against him) deliberately provoked this kind of outburst to learn what old guard officers such as Cleitus were really thinking and feeling. At all events, he poured fuel on the flames by giving the floor to a Greek singer,[17] who proceeded to entertain the company with a malicious skit aimed at certain (unnamed) Macedonian commanders who had recently been defeated in battle against Spitamenes (see above, pp. 357–60 and n. 10). This provoked an outcry among the older Macedonians present, but Alexander and his courtiers, hugely delighted, told the singer to go on.

Cleitus, stung beyond endurance, cried out that it was a shameful thing, in the hearing of enemies and barbarians (by which he meant the king's Persian guests) 'to insult Macedonians who were far better men than those who laughed at them, even though they had met with misfortune'. We see now why Alexander timed this after-dinner *jeu d'esprit* when he did. Cleitus, clearly, had been one of the commanders involved – and was now rising to the bait. Silkily, the king murmured that to call cowardice 'misfortune' sounded like special pleading. 'It was my cowardice, as you call it, that saved your life at the Granicus,' Cleitus shouted. 'It is by the blood of the Macedonians, and these wounds of ours, that you have risen so high – disowning Philip, claiming Ammon as your father ...' He also, significantly, reproached Alexander with the murder, not of Parmenio, but of *Attalus*, which suggests where his own sympathies may have lain during the struggle for power.[18]

Alexander's reply, too, is highly revealing. '*That's how you talk about me the whole time, isn't it?* That's what causes all this bad blood between the Macedonians. You needn't think you're going to get away with it . . .' 'Look, Alexander,' Cleitus said, carefully addressing the king by his bare name, according to Philip's practice, 'we *don't* get away with it, even now. What rewards have we for our labours? Those who died are the luckiest – they never lived to see Macedonians thrashed with Median rods, or kow-towing to Persians before they could have an audience of their own king.' This speech caused a tremendous uproar, during which Alexander, perhaps not quite so drunk as he made out, turned to two Greek courtiers, sitting beside him and observed, scathingly: 'Don't you feel that Greeks go about among Macedonians like demi-gods among wild beasts?' – a remark which might have been calculated to make any old-guard Macedonian lose his last vestige of self-control.

There was so much noise that Cleitus missed the king's exact words – which may in fact have been a deliberate aside, designed to provoke him further. The old warrior bellowed at Alexander that he should either say what he meant openly, or else not invite to supper 'men who were free and spoke their minds', but rather consort with slaves and barbarians, creatures who would prostrate themselves before his white robe and Persian sash. Alexander, half out of his mind with rage, picked up the first thing that came to hand, an apple,[19] hurled it at Cleitus, and began looking round for his sword. One of the Gentlemen of the Bodyguard had prudently removed it. The king's closest friends – Perdiccas, Lysimachus, Leonnatus – scenting trouble, crowded round and forcibly held him down. A violent struggle developed, with Alexander screaming that this was a plot, that he had been betrayed like Darius.

Meanwhile other guests, led by Ptolemy son of Lagus, managed to drag Cleitus out of the banqueting-hall by main force. The king finally broke loose, and began shouting in broad Macedonian, 'Turn out the Guard! Turn out the Guard!' He ordered his trumpeter to sound a general alarm: with great courage and presence of mind the man refused – an act which afterwards won him great praise, since he arguably avoided a riot – and was knocked flat for his pains.[20] At this point Cleitus, who had broken loose once more, lurched back in by another door, shouting a line from Euripides' *Andromache*: 'Alas what evil government in Hellas!' Euripides was a popular playwright in Macedonia, and schoolboys learnt long stretches of his work by heart. Alexander would have had no trouble in continuing Cleitus' all-too-apt quotation:

> When the public sets a war memorial up
> Do those who really sweated get the credit?
> Oh, no! Some general wangles the prestige! –
> Who, brandishing his one spear among thousands,
> Did one man's work, but gets a world of praise.
> These self-important fathers of their country
> Think they're above the people. Why, they're nothing!

Alexander, flicked on the raw by this indictment, and in no mood now (if ever) for Stoic theories about the Brotherhood of Man if they in any way diminished his ego, sprang up, seized a spear from one of his guards, and ran Cleitus through, killing him instantly.[21]

Struck by sudden overwhelming remorse, the king plucked the spear from his old comrade's dead body and tried (not very energetically, it would seem) to impale himself on it. His friends, however, once more closed in and forcibly restrained him.[22] He now shut himself up in his private quarters, where he continued to lament all night, recalling, *inter alia*, the omission of a sacrifice to Dionysus, which sounds like an attempt to divest himself of responsibility for his murder by laying it at the door of an angry god.[23] At dawn he had Cleitus' body brought to him, and mourned over it for a while, though it was later removed again.[24] For a considerable period – estimates range between Plutarch's thirty-six hours (the most likely) and Justin's four days (a characteristic exaggeration), with Curtius and

Arrian settling for a quasi-canonical three-day retirement[25] – he remained in seclusion, without food or drink. The point at which genuine grief began to merge into calculated play-acting is very hard to determine: perhaps the two elements co-existed up to a point throughout. We can only judge by results, and the results were of great interest and significance. Once it sank into the minds of Alexander's followers that he might *really* starve himself to death, leaving them leaderless in this remote and barbarous country, they did everything they could to make him change his mind. What the king sought, in effect, was a combined absolution and vote of confidence: he got both. Callisthenes tried tactful philosophical comfort. This was not a success.[26] Anaxarchus, however, a political realist, saw at once that Alexander needed not intellectual placebos but philosophical justification. He therefore marched into the king's bedroom and told him, with cheerful brutality, to get up and quit snivelling: the king stood above mere human laws.

This, of course, was precisely what Alexander hoped to be told: from now on Anaxarchus enjoyed increasing favour at Callisthenes' expense. The Macedonians, taking their cue from the king's reaction, now 'decreed that Cleitus had been justly put to death', presumably for treason. Soothsayers complicated the issue by ascribing his end to the anger of Dionysus: various premonitory omens were 'remembered' (i.e. manufactured) confirming such a view, and implicitly transferring the burden of responsibility from Alexander to 'Fate's decrees' (Aristander played a useful role here). His crime thus retrospectively legitimized – and conscious that henceforth he could, at a pinch, get the army's endorsement for almost anything – Alexander consented to sit up and take nourishment.[27] Nevertheless, every man present at that fatal banquet knew the truth. Cleitus had been killed for daring to express open criticism of the king, and for no other reason. What was worse, Alexander's act of murder had not been forgiven so much as publicly justified. From now on there would be no holding him. The death of Cleitus, coming so soon after that of Parmenio, did indeed, as Curtius says, mark the end of freedom.[28]

Alexander had now spent two campaigning seasons in Bactria and Soghdiana, with very little to show for them. Spitamenes remained as elusive as ever. The king was grimly determined to finish him off before spring came: he had no intention of holding up his projected invasion of India a moment longer. There had been far too much delay as it was. Alexander himself took over Cleitus' vacant command in the Companion Cavalry. While the bulk of the army moved into winter quarters at Nautaca, Coenus, with two battalions of the phalanx and a strong mixed cavalry force, was sent to cover the north-west frontier.

The network of Macedonian hill-forts now began to prove its worth. Spitamenes was finding ever greater difficulties in obtaining provisions and horses, let alone a secure base. Finally, in desperation, he enlisted the support of three thousand Massagetae horsemen and attempted a mass breakthrough – just as Alexander had foreseen when making his dispositions. Coenus cut this large but ill-disciplined horde to pieces with professional zest, killing 800 enemy horsemen at almost no loss to himself. Those few Soghdians who had followed Spitamenes now came over to the Macedonians – in whose ranks many of their fellow-countrymen were already serving. Spitamenes himself fled into the desert with the nomads, his prestige much lowered by this ignominious defeat. Indeed, when the Massagetae learnt that Alexander himself was coming after them, they lost no time in executing Spitamenes, whose head they then dispatched to the king by way of a peace-offering.* Their desert neighbours, the Dahae,

* According to Curtius (8.3.1 ff.) the execution was carried out by Spitamenes' wife, playing Jael to his Sisera because she was tired of their fugitive guerrilla existence but could not persuade him to sur-render.

hearing what had happened, promptly turned in Spitamenes' second-in-command, thus winning themselves a free pardon.[29]

With Spitamenes' death all organized resistance on the northern frontier collapsed. Though the Soghdian leader's military qualities have been overrated, he was undoubtedly an excellent guerrilla general who saw, just as Memnon had done, that the best way to deal with Alexander was by commando raids and *maquis* tactics. He tied down a large and hitherto invincible army in Turkestan for over two years; and if he had had more reliable supporters than desert nomads in search of easy loot, he might have done even better.

It was now midwinter, and Alexander had still to deal with the wild mountainous district of the south-east (Paraetecene, between modern Tadzhik and Badakhshan) where at least four great barons continued to defy him from their remote rock-fortresses. After only two months at Nautaca the Macedonian army set off once more. It was early January, and weather conditions proved appalling; torrential rain, electric storms, and violent hail, turning to hard ice overnight as the temperature dropped below zero. During this march some 2,000 men froze to death or died of pneumonia. Alexander, as always, showed his best qualities in a crisis. Somehow he rallied the demoralized Macedonians: trees were cut down, fires lit, icy limbs thawed out. One soldier, lost in the forest, at last reached camp, barely able to stand, let alone hold his weapons. The king sat him down on his own chair by a blazing fire. When the man had recovered, and saw whose seat he was occupying, he sprang up at once, with the reflex instinct of a well-trained guardsman.

Alexander's reaction was characteristic – and revealing. He looked kindly at the soldier and said: 'Now do you see how much better a time you have of it under a king than the Persians do? With them, to have sat in the king's seat would have been a capital offence – but in your case it proved a life-saver.' Even on a freezing mountainside the king was still preoccupied (even allowing for Curtius' Roman rhetoric) with the insoluble problem of how, politically speaking, to be all things to all men. His mother's hints, his Pharaonic enthronement in Egypt, even the flattering predictions of Isocrates – who after Chaeronea told Philip that, once he had subdued the Great King, nothing would remain for him but to become a god – pointed towards one increasingly attractive answer.[30] After all, had he not already eclipsed the achievements of Heracles?

The first mountain stronghold to face Alexander's assault was that known as the 'Soghdian Rock'. Oxyartes, the local baron, had garrisoned it strongly (with 30,000 troops, we are told, but this sounds a suspiciously high figure), and had sent his own wife and children there to ensure their safety. Provisions were stored up against a two-years' siege. Deep snow not only hampered the Macedonians' advance, but also ensured abundant drinking-water for the defenders. The rock itself was sheer-faced and, or so its occupants believed, absolutely impregnable. Their optimism became apparent when Alexander, at a preliminary parley, offered them safe conduct to their homes if they would surrender the fortresses. They laughed rudely and asked whether his men could fly, adding that they would only surrender to winged soldiers, 'as no other sort of person could cause them the least anxiety'. The king's reputation should have made them think twice before issuing such a challenge: far from discouraging him, it simply put him on his mettle.

He at once combed through the entire army for experienced cragsmen and mountaineers, of whom he found some 300. Reconnaissance had shown that the defenders only guarded the direct approach to the fortress. Alexander now called for volunteers to scale the sheer rockface on the far side, offering vast rewards to the first twelve men up. They were to take swords, spears and provisions for two days. When they reached the summit, above the fortress itself, they were to wave white flags as a signal.

Every man of them volunteered for this perilous operation. The details recorded by Arrian and Curtius suggest that Alpine climbing techniques have changed comparatively little in over two millennia. The raiders roped themselves together and scaled the most difficult overhangs with the aid of iron wedges and *pitons* driven into cracks in the rock-face. They made the ascent by night, an extra hazard. About thirty of them plummeted down into the snowdrifts below, and their bodies were never recovered. But at dawn a flutter of white flags broke out from the very summit of the rock, and Alexander sent a herald to tell the defenders that if they looked up, they would see he had found his winged men. Oxyartes' troops were so taken aback by this *coup de théâtre* that they capitulated on the spot, even though they outnumbered the mountaineers by something like a hundred to one, and Alexander's main forces still had no clear road to the summit. Once again psychological insight had paid off handsomely.[31]

But better still was to come. After the surrender of the Soghdian Rock Alexander let it be known that he took a personal interest in Oxyartes' daughter Roxane, whom all the Macedonians regarded as 'the loveliest woman they had seen in Asia, with the one exception of Darius' wife'. Whether Alexander was genuinely in love with her is a debatable point, though several sources allege it; she only became pregnant in the last year of his life, after Hephaestion's death.* In any case, the political advantages of such an alliance were very considerable indeed, for all parties concerned. So Alexander and Roxane were duly married: bride and bridegroom shared a ritual loaf, which Alexander sliced in two with his sword. This custom may have been Macedonian; it was certainly symbolic.

---

* Unless, that is, we accept the dubious testimony of the Metz Epitome (c. 70), according to which Roxane bore Alexander a son who died soon afterwards, at the R. Jhelum (Hydaspes), in the summer of 326.

Romance has cast a distorting haze over the details of what was undoubtedly, as one French scholar says, *'un habile acte de propagande'*.[32] Immediately afterwards, Alexander renewed his winter offensive – accompanied, now, by an influential father-in-law who, as the most powerful of his late enemies, could be relied upon to talk over-stubborn resistance leaders into submission. Oxyartes' presence proved a godsend at another even more inaccessible fortress, perched on a rock some 4,000 feet high, and no less than seven miles in circumference. After making vast efforts to bridge the ravine which led to this stronghold, the king sent Oxyartes to convince its commander that further resistance was useless, and that if he surrendered he would receive honourable treatment. The trick worked, and the bargain was duly kept. Alexander allowed this baron, Chorienes, to remain in command of the fortress; Chorienes, as a *quid pro quo*, provided Alexander with two months' rations for his entire army. (He could not resist pointing out that this was no more than one-tenth of the rock's reserves, the implication being that he had surrendered from choice rather than necessity.) Soghdiana's reduction was now almost complete.[33] The king detached a force under Craterus to deal with any remaining opposition, and took the main army back to Zariaspa, in preparation for his long-delayed invasion of India.

Alexander was under no illusions as to the nature of his hard-won victory. He had, at last, subdued the two great north-eastern satrapies; but unless he took very special precautions there would be serious trouble the moment he recrossed the Hindu Kush. By marrying Roxane – a gambit that would surely have won his father's approval – he had purchased himself a certain measure of local support, albeit (once again) at the risk of alienating the Macedonian old guard. What else could he do to strengthen his position? One answer was provided by the network of military garrisons he had built up. Some of these could be turned into permanent cities. At least six major foundations, all named Alexandria, are known from this area, including those of Margiane (Merv), Tarmita (Termez) on the Oxus, and Alexandria-the-Furthest, or Alexandria Eschate (Leninabad, or Khodjend). Their primary function was that of frontier defence; but several became important trading-centres, and they also served as a convenient dumping-ground for numerous* Greek mercenaries, time-expired or of suspect loyalty.[34]

In addition, ample drafts of reinforcements (16,000 infantry alone during 328) made it possible to allow for an extra-strong garrison. Amyntas, who had replaced Black Cleitus as the new satrap of Bactriana, was eventually given 10,000 foot and 3,500 horse, a vast figure by previous standards. But the most significant step which Alexander took at this time (and the one which most clearly reveals Philip's influence) was the recruitment of 30,000 native youths, to be taught the Greek language and given a thorough Macedonian-style military training. All the boys were carefully selected for their strength, fitness and intelligence, and chosen from the best families in every province.

This scheme had two primary aims, one immediate, the other long-term. Eventually, these trainees would furnish replacements for Alexander's officer corps, now much depleted by casualties, sickness, and garrison or administrative appointments along the line of march. The king later referred to them as his 'Successors', by which, *bien entendu*, he meant successors to the Macedonian old guard. For the moment, however, while he marched on to India and the shores of Ocean. they would serve as admirable hostages.[35]

It was, clearly, impossible to keep this innovation a secret, even had Alexander wished to do so. Doubtless he emphasized the role of the 'Successors' as hostages when discuss-

---

*At least 26,000 subsequently revolted (see below, pp. 421, 450), but we do not know how many remained in the settlements.

ing the matter with his staff officers; but the whole idea, from their viewpoint, was too uncomfortably reminiscent of the Royal Corps of Pages – and on a far larger scale. Yet another section of the king's original Macedonian command-structure, the 'training-school for generals and governors',[36] saw itself threatened by direct competition from barbarian upstarts. Indeed, it must have looked as though Alexander planned (for obvious reasons) to purge his royal *apparat* of all Macedonian influence whatsoever. The leaders of the old guard, the only group which continued, with xenophobic stubbornness, to oppose and ridicule the king's imperial pretensions, had one by one been eliminated. Persian nobles were now coming to occupy more and more important posts in Alexander's administration, and Persian court protocol had rendered him increasingly inaccessible to his titular peers.

Nevertheless, one major snag still remained. It was all very well to brigade Iranian and Bactrian troops with Macedonians or with Greek mercenaries; but where, except among the ranks of the Companions, the Guards Brigade, and the phalanx, were first-class battalion or divisional commanders to be found? Like it or not, Alexander had to put up with his officer corps; and it was these same officers whose blunt Macedonian irreverence kept pricking the bubble of his oriental self-aggrandizement.

Nothing better exemplified this fundamental division in court circles than the matter of *proskynesis* or obeisance. To Persians this was normal prescriptive etiquette, though the manner of greeting varied considerably according to the relative social rank of the parties involved. Equals received a kiss on the mouth, near-equal superiors on the cheek, whereas, in Herodotus' words, 'a man of greatly inferior rank prostrates himself in profound reverence'. As we might expect, the one person entitled to *proskynesis* in its most extreme form, from all his subjects, whatever their rank, was the Great King. To the Greeks, however, *proskynesis*, if practised at all, was a gesture reserved exclusively for the adoration of a god. In any merely social context it struck them as comic, humiliating, and blasphemous – 'the typical indication of oriental servility'.[37] Callias, after the battle of Marathon, was astonished to see a Persian prisoner greeting him in this way. Ambassadors to Persia found the act a source of constant embarrassment. One ingenious diplomat dropped his seal-ring at the crucial moment, and told himself he had merely gone down on hands and knees to pick it up. At Persepolis, the relief of a Mede doing obeisance to the Great King was deliberately defaced by Alexander's troops, a clear pointer to what *they* thought of the practice.

To make matters worse, since the Greeks viewed *proskynesis* as an act of *religious* adoration, they came to the erroneous conclusion that Persians, by thus prostrating themselves before the Great King, must be *acknowledging his divinity*. It is easy to picture the confusion and resentment which these conflicting beliefs must have aroused in Alexander's court. His Persian grandees prostrated themselves before him as a matter of course – just as they in turn expected *proskynesis* from their own inferiors. Alexander could not abolish the custom without having his own *bona fides* as Great King called in question. On the other hand, there were far too many incidents of Macedonian officers roaring with laughter or otherwise showing unmannerly contempt when the act of obeisance was performed. Polyperchon, in what sounds like a parody of some well-known Macedonian drill-sergeant, called out to one prostrate Persian: 'Come on, don't just *touch* the floor with your chin! Bang it, man! *Bang* it!'[38]

Obviously this kind of situation could not be allowed to continue. To have half the court performing *proskynesis* while the other half treated the whole thing as a huge joke was intolerable. But what was to be done? Alexander could hardly imprison or execute all his best officers. (He did gaol Polyperchon for a while, but soon released him again; Leonnatus, another offender, seems to have got off scot-free.) The only hope was, by slow degrees and careful stage-managing, to make the Macedonians accept this gesture as a mere polite formality. A great deal of quiet discussion went on behind the scenes, mostly between Alexander himself, his Greek propaganda section (including both Callisthenes and Anaxarchus), and various high-ranking Macedonians.

Echoes of these discussions have been preserved for us in the stylized debates set out by Arrian and Curtius.[39] Anaxarchus, backed by a group of sedulous propagandists,[40] and well aware that the main Macedonian objection to *proskynesis* was its implication of divinity, put forward a bold but eminently logical proposal (which doubtless had the king's own less-than-modest blessing). Why not, he asked, recognize the obvious *fait accompli* and treat Alexander as a god? He was bound to receive divine honours posthumously. 'Would it not, therefore, be in every way better to offer him this tribute now, while he was alive, and not wait till he was dead and could get no good of it?' His exploits had already outstripped those of Heracles and Dionysus, with whom his links were loose enough anyway. Would it not be preferable – a sop to nationalist vanity, this – to think of him as a purely *Macedonian* god?

But Anaxarchus' attempt to woo the Macedonians proved a failure: they obstinately refused the bait he offered them. What was more, they got support from a most unexpected source. Callisthenes, the court historian, came out with a flat rejection of Anaxarchus' proposals, on traditional religious grounds. Why? He had shown no qualms whatsoever about glorifying his employer as the *son* of Zeus or Ammon. He had spent the past six or seven years publicizing Alexander's exploits, not always in the most scrupulous or veracious fashion. He disliked the old guard, and had been quite ready to help run a smear-campaign against Parmenio (see above, pp. 175, 294). His whole previous career, despite modern apologias,[41] reveals him as a pliant and conceited intellectual time-server.

What brought about his abrupt change of heart? He *may*, as he himself implied, have found the idea of deifying Alexander genuinely repugnant to his religious sensibilities, though for him (as for most Greek sophists) physical reality and hyperbolic literary rhetoric had, at best, a tenuous connection. It seems far more likely that he was reacting to a change in the balance of power at court. Hitherto, it seems clear, he had anticipated a Greek take-over once the old guard had been finally cleared out; he only embraced the cause of Macedonian conservatism, we may surmise, when it became clear that any future take-over would be not Greek, but Persian.

Whatever his personal motives, Callisthenes had judged the immediate situation with some percipience. In the last resort Alexander depended on his Macedonian commanders; and they were strongly against *proskynesis* if it involved treating the king as a god. Callisthenes had backed the winning side, and Alexander's project was, for the moment, abandoned. What the Greek historian failed to understand, however, was that by this untimely opposition he had dug his own grave. For Alexander, Hellenism was now virtually a dead letter; and Callisthenes' ideological *faux pas* after Cleitus' death (see above, p. 365) had hardly endeared him to the king, who expected his yes-men to say 'yes' not only loud and clear, but also in the appropriate form of words. Anaxarchus managed this side of things far better, and his stock now rose accordingly. The model for success in this field was, of course, Aristander, and we need not doubt that Anaxarchus had watched and carefully imitated his methods.

Since the deification scheme, thanks to Callisthenes' intransigence, had fallen through, Alexander – together with Hephaestion and one or two other close friends – now devised an alternative plan for introducing *proskynesis* on a more or less secular basis. It was arranged that at one particular banquet, when the loving-cup passed round, those who were privy to the scheme should drink, rise, prostrate themselves before the king, and receive in return – to take the sting out of any humiliation this act might imply – the royal kiss of equality. Then, it was hoped, other guests would feel constrained, if only out of politeness, to follow suit.

History has known worse diplomatic compromises; and in fact everything went off without a hitch until – once again – it came to Callisthenes' turn. After spending his whole life playing with words, Aristotle's nephew failed to realize that he was now playing with fire. He seems to have convinced himself that the pen was, literally, mightier than the sword; that Alexander, exploits and all, could be made or broken by his, Callisthenes', version of events – a common, but in this case fatal, delusion. He therefore drank, but did not prostrate himself. Alexander, deep in conversation with Hephaestion, failed to notice; but a nearby courtier quickly pointed out the omission. Alexander refused Callisthenes his salutation, whereupon the Greek said, loudly, as he turned away: 'Well then, I'll leave the poorer by a kiss.'[42] Once again he had killed Alexander's *proskynesis* scheme stone dead. Hephaestion, to protect himself, was forced to claim that Callisthenes had accepted the idea, but afterwards went back on his word.

This little exhibition sealed Callisthenes' fate, though the philosopher himself seems to have been blissfully unaware of the fact. He realized, in a vague way, that he had alienated Alexander; but his overnight popularity with the Macedonians seems to have gone straight to his head. He began to see himself, head still in the philosophical clouds, as the defender of freedom against tyranny, upholding traditional Hellenism against decadent barbarian innovations.

Alexander did not relish having his carefully laid plans blown sky-high by this posturing literary ass. Already the propaganda section had begun a whispering campaign against Callisthenes, attacking his prim abstemiousness, and reporting a number of so-called 'subversive' remarks he had made (mostly anti-tyrannical clichés straight out of the rhetorical stockpot). He had also been heard to mutter, on leaving the king's presence: *'Patroclus also is dead, who was better by far than you are.'* The king's main task, however, was to undermine Callisthenes' newly-won popularity with the old guard. In the event this proved absurdly easy. By playing on the innate conceit of the one and the ingrained prejudice of the other he achieved his end in a single evening. After dinner Callisthenes was invited to display his oratorical skill by making an impromptu speech in praise of the Macedonians. This he did so successfully that he got a standing ovation, and was showered with garlands. Alexander now had Callisthenes where he wanted him, in a position from which sheer conceit would not let him back down. Quoting a provocative tag from the *Bacchae* ('Give a wise man an honest brief to plead/and his eloquence is no remarkable achievement'),* the king challenged Callisthenes to show his skill in eristics (see above, p. 61), by taking the other side of the argument and making an equally persuasive *denunciation* of the Macedonians, 'that they may become even better by learning their faults'. The philosopher, a born preacher and teacher, rose to this lure without further encouragement, and launched into a swingeing indictment of Macedonian *mores* and Greek factionalism, culminating with the proverbial line 'But in a time of sedition the base man too is honoured' – a clear gibe (or so his hearers assumed) at Philip. The old-guard barons, who could not distinguish between an exercise in eristics and a speech from the heart, were mortally offended,

---

* The quotation itself (*Bacchae*, 266 ff.) was a well-chosen insult. The passage continues:

> But you are glib; your phrases come rolling out
> smoothly on the tongue, as though your words were wise
> instead of foolish. The man whose glibness flows
> from his conceit of speech declares the thing he is:
> a worthless and a stupid citizen.

while Alexander (who could) made matters worse by saying that what Callisthenes had demonstrated was not eloquence so much as personal malice.[43]

After that, it was simply a matter of finding some convenient plot in which the historian could be implicated: what had been good enough for Philotas was certainly good enough for a mere Greek civilian. An opportunity arose soon enough. One of the royal pages, with a personal grudge against Alexander, laid a plot to assassinate him. Four other pages joined this conspiracy. The attempt misfired, one of the pages talked, and all five were put under arrest. None of them, when interrogated, made any attempt to deny their guilt. In fact, with the courage of despair, their ringleader Hermolaus took this opportunity to deliver a scathing broadside against Alexander's arrogance, alcoholism, and dictatorially criminal behaviour. But none of them, equally, even under pressure, would implicate Callisthenes, whom the king had arraigned as an accessory the moment he heard of the plot.

Callisthenes, like any Greek philosopher, had inveighed against tyranny in general terms, but that was all. His indictment rested on the flimsiest circumstantial evidence. It was alleged against him that when Hermolaus complained about a flogging he had received from Alexander, Callisthenes told him to remember he was a man now. The prosecution interpreted this as incitement to murder; it sounds far more like a piece of Spartan stiff-upper-lip morality. Callisthenes was nevertheless found guilty. As Alexander himself remarked at the time, 'often even what has been falsely believed has gained the place of truth'.[44] The five pages suffered immediate execution by stoning. Callisthenes – accounts vary – was either hanged, somewhat later, or else dragged around with the army in a prison-cage until he died of disease.

In a letter to Antipater, the king related the execution of the pages, but said that he himself would take personal responsibility for punishing 'the sophist' – as he contemptuously described Callisthenes – 'together with those who sent him to me and those who now harbour in their cities men who conspire against my life': words[45] which must have given both Aristotle and Antipater himself considerable pause for thought (see below pp. 459–60).

Alexander's ideas concerning India were, at this point, still sketchy in the extreme. To the Greeks of his day the land across the Indus was a shallow peninsula, bounded on the north by the Hindu Kush, and on the east by the great world-stream of Ocean, which ran (or so they believed) at no great distance beyond the Sind Desert. Of the main Indian sub-continent, let alone the vast Far Eastern land-mass from China to Malaysia, they knew nothing whatsoever. Aristotle, indeed, believed that Ocean was actually visible from the summit of the Hindu Kush. That fallacy, at least, Alexander had now disproved by personal observation; but in general his ignorance of Indian geography remained profound, and his whole eastern strategy rested on a false assumption. When enlightenment came, it was too late. The great Ganges plain, by its mere existence, shattered his dream more effectively than any army could have done.

Two centuries earlier, Cyrus the Great had created an 'Indian province' between Peshawar and the northern Punjab, which was subsequently alleged to pay the fantastic annual tribute of 360 talents – in gold-dust. About 517 Darius I commissioned a Greek, Scylax of Caryanda, to explore the Indian trade-routes. Scylax sailed down the Indus and reached home by way of the Persian Gulf, afterwards writing a book on his voyage. Herodotus and Ctesias (a Greek doctor at the Persian court during the latter part of the fifth century) both wrote in some detail about India. All three works would be easily available to Alexander and his staff; it is unlikely in the extreme that they did not familiarize themselves with such obviously relevant material. Not that they would have been much the wiser for doing so:

by the fourth century Persia had abandoned her Indian satrapies, and even while 'Hindush' was part of the empire, it remained largely *terra incognita*, a region of myth and fable, like medieval Cathay. Herodotus believed that the Indians' gold was dug up by gigantic ants, larger than foxes; and with Ctesias we are in a fairy-tale world akin to that portrayed by Hieronymus Bosch.[46]*

Alexander had several cogent motives for invading this mysterious wonderland. As self-proclaimed Great King, he meant to recover Cyrus' lost satrapies. The existence of the Khyber pass meant that he had to protect Turkestan from possible eastern attack. His main impulse, however, seems to have been sheer curiosity, a *pothos* for the unknown, coupled with his determination to achieve world-dominion in the fullest sense. When he stood by the furthest shore of Ocean, that ambition would be fulfilled. As he had told Pharasmenes (see above, p. 359), India once conquered, 'he would have Asia entirely in his hands'. *Ever to strive to be best*: no previous mortal ruler, not the great Cyrus, not even that semi-legendary figure Queen Semiramis, had ever invaded India with complete success. Hitherto such a triumph had fallen to gods alone. Dionysus had passed through the country with his Bacchic rout, carrying out a programme of conquest and civilization (he was supposed, *inter alia*, to have brought India the vine). Fifteen generations later, according to tradition, came Alexander's ancestor Heracles, who through his daughter sired a long line of Indian kings. Alexander was determined to outshine them both; perhaps even to win acceptance – here if anywhere – as a god himself.[47]

*In his *Indica* Ctesias describes men with tails and dogs' heads, and that fearful anthropophagous beast the martichora, and pygmies whose penises hang down to their ankles, and eight-fingered archers with ears large enough to shade them from the sun, and a tribe where the babies are born sans anus, only acquiring this essential feature later, at puberty – all those weird tales, in fact, which later turn up *rechauffé* in the *Travels of Sir John Mandeville.*

Before setting forth, the king greatly enlarged and modified the structure of his original cavalry arm. Each of the eight Companion squadrons was now brigaded, separately, with Iranian cavalry units from the central satrapies to form a whole new independent division, known as a 'hipparchy'. This policy of integration made for greater military efficiency; but it also struck one more blow at the old guard. If every Macedonian cavalry commander was operating with an international unit, his chances of forming any sort of junta were considerably reduced.

The final size of the army which recrossed the Hindu Kush in spring 327 is almost impossible to estimate with any degree of accuracy. Alexander had with him not more than 15,000 Macedonians, of whom 2,000 were cavalrymen. Total cavalry estimates, however, range between 6,500 and 15,000. The infantry figures are equally uncertain, varying from 20,000 to 120,000. Tarn's guess of 27–30,000 operational troops is almost certainly too conservative. On the other hand it has been suggested, with some plausibility, that 120,000 represents an overall total, including campfollowers, traders, servants, grooms, wives, mistresses, children, scientists, schoolmasters, clerks, cooks, muleteers, and all the other members of what had by now become 'a mobile state and the administrative centre of the empire'.[48]

This vast horde, we are asked to believe, streamed over the (?)Salang pass (12,000 ft) to Alexandria-of-the-Caucasus in a mere ten days: more probably the advance guard took this time to establish a forward base camp, leaving the rest to follow as and when they could. While he was still in Bactriana, Alexander had been joined by an Indian rajah, Sasigupta (Sisicottus), a deserter from Bessus who presumably had briefed him on the political situation beyond the Khyber. At all events, the king now sent envoys ahead to Ambhi (Omphis), the rajah of Taxila (Takshaçila) and 'the Indians west of the Indus', asking them to meet him, at their convenience, in the Kabul valley. Ambhi and several other minor princes duly arrived, with gifts, flattering speeches of welcome, and twenty-five elephants. It was the elephants which caught Alexander's eye, and eventually – under a certain amount of pressure, one suspects – the Indians agreed to make him a present of them. However, Ambhi had good reasons for keeping in with Alexander: he wanted the Macedonian army's support against his great rival Porus, a powerful monarch whose domains lay beyond the Jhelum (Hydaspes) River.

Alexander now divided his army. Hephaestion and Perdiccas, with rather more than half the cavalry, three battalions of the phalanx, and the baggage-train, were to proceed down the Khyber pass to the Indus. 'Their instructions', Arrian reports, 'were to take over either by force or agreement all places on their march, and on reaching the Indus to make suitable preparation for crossing' – probably a pontoon bridge of portable boats, such as (till very recent years) could still be seen in this area. Ambhi and his fellow-Indians would accompany them as guides. Meanwhile Alexander himself, with Craterus as his second-in-command, planned to take a mobile column up the Choaspes (Kunar) River and to march through the hill-country of Bajaur and Swat, reducing enemy strongholds en route, and giving cover to the main army's left flank. The two forces would finally rendezvous at the Indus.[49]

Hephaestion's part in this operation, except for one month-long siege, proved straightforward and uneventful. Alexander, on the other hand, had a very rough passage indeed. The mountain terrain he passed through was difficult to negotiate, and most of the tribesmen he came up against showed themselves first-class fighters. During one engagement he got an arrow through his shoulder; and by the end of the campaign (which lasted from November 327 till about February 326) his condition can perhaps best be described as jittery. Most of the walled towns he attacked, far from obligingly opening their gates at the first onset, put up a violent resistance.* By way of retaliation, when they finally fell he took to butchering the inhabitants wholesale: crossing his will, as always, brought violent retribution. At Massaga he treacherously massacred 7,000 Indian mercenaries together with their wives and children – and after guaranteeing them safe conduct – because they refused to join him against their fellow-countrymen. Plutarch said that this act 'adhered like a stain to his military career'; modern Indian historians, understandably, echo Plutarch's verdict.[50]

It is now, too, that we first find signs of the propaganda section promoting Alexander's divinity rather than his divine sonship. During the siege of Massaga the king received a slight wound in the ankle, and an Athenian bystander, Dioxippus, quoted Homer's line: 'Ichor, such as floweth from the blessed gods'. Alexander at once snubbed his flatterer with the testy remark: 'That's not ichor, that's *blood*.' Enough, clearly, was enough.[51] For a Greek to make such a comment had been a *faux pas*; the interesting thing from our point of view is that he thought of making it at all, or supposed it would prove welcome. The idea of Alexander's godhead must at least have been under serious discussion, if only as a device to impress the Indians. It is also significant that the two best-known episodes from this campaign (which probably means those given most official publicity) both had divine associations, one with Heracles, the other with Dionysus.

After dealing with the Aspasians (Açvakas) along the Kunar and Bajaur valleys, Alexander moved on north, into the rich forest-clad mountain region below Chitral. One

* One remark of Cleitus' which had particularly annoyed Alexander was a reminder of what Alexander of Epirus reputedly said in Italy: that he had fought men, whereas Alexander of Macedon had won victories over Asiatic women (QC 8.1.37). Hitherto the gibe had come uncomfortably close to the truth. From now on it was to be a very different matter. The warrior-tribes of Hindush gave Alexander the toughest opposition he had ever experienced, and in Porus he found an opponent who out-classed both Memnon and Spitamenes.

night the column pitched camp in a wood. It was so bitterly cold that they gathered fuel and built a number of camp-fires. The flames spread, and engulfed what turned out to be cedar-wood coffins hanging among the trees. These went up like tinder. There was a great barking of dogs from beyond the wood, which revealed that the Macedonians were near a town – had, indeed, accidentally stumbled on its somewhat exotic cemetery.

This town surrendered after a short siege. It was called Nysa, a name intimately associated with Dionysus, and the god who founded it had (to judge from what the local inhabitants told Alexander) decidedly Dionysiac charac-teristics. Dionysus' presence was further confirmed for the Macedonians by a great mountain outside the town, where there grew not only vines but also ivy – a plant they had found nowhere else in the Far East. Alexander and his men climbed this mountain, crowned themselves with ivy-wreaths, and went (or so our sources allege) on a ten-day Bacchic spree, feasting and drinking and revelling in splendid style. 'Hence,' says Curtius, 'the mountain heights and valleys rang with the shouts of so many thousands, as they invoked the god who resided over that grove.'

It used to be thought that this whole episode was pure fantasy, put out as propaganda either by Alexander himself, or else (in the view of more puritanical scholars) by his enemies. Yet the mountains south of Chitral – abounding in wild game, lush with vines and ivy, walnut and plane, mulberry and apricot – exactly match the description given by our ancient sources. Furthermore, they are still inhabited by a unique and isolated people known as the Kalash Kafirs, who make wine (a skill known to no other tribe in the area), sacrifice goats for religious purposes – and expose their dead in wooden coffins hung among the trees.[52] As so often, it is the most improbable anecdote which turns out to rest on a bedrock of sober fact.

The second episode was Alexander's remarkable capture of the fortress which Arrian calls Aornus: perhaps a Greek attempt at Sanskrit *avarana*, 'a place of refuge'.[53] This fortress stood on the great massif known as Pir-Sar, in a bend of the Indus about seventy-five miles north of Attock, and over 5,000 feet above the river. Arrian gives its circumference as roughly twenty-five miles. It was well provided with water, and had only one ascent, which was steep and difficult. Local legend told how a god (whom the Macedonians identified with Heracles) had tried, unsuccessfully, to capture this inaccessible stronghold. Arrian's comment – perceptive if cynical – is that 'people like to make difficulties look much more difficult than they really are, and to this end start a legend about Heracles' failure to overcome them'. Alexander, of course, at once conceived a violent desire (*pothos*) to capture Aornus himself; as we might predict, 'the story about Heracles was not the least of his incentives'.

After making contact with Hephaestion (their rendezvous-point was to be at Ohind, some sixteen miles upstream from Attock) he at once set off to tackle this officially ultra-Herculean labour. He brought to his task what Sir Aurel Stein adjudged 'such combined energy, skill and boldness as would be sought rather in a divine hero of legend than in a mortal leader of men'.[54] If people were willing to deify Alexander, this stemmed in large part from his desire, and ability, to perform more than godlike feats – which he meant, moreover, as a deliberate challenge to divine precedent. At Aornus, in order to bring his catapults and artillery within range (hauling them up the 8,721 feet of the Una-Sar massif was a remarkable enough achievement in itself) he found himself obliged to run a great wooden cribwork causeway across the ravine between Una-Sar and a small hill dominating Pir-Sar. This extraordinary structure must have somewhat resembled an early American railroad trestle bridge. When the causeway was built, and Alexander's artillery in place, the defenders fled. With some difficulty a group of Macedonians reached the summit, and thus 'Alexander was left in possession of the rock which had baffled Heracles himself'.[55] If the king's propagandists gave him good publicity, at least they had something out of the ordinary to publicize.

Leaving Sasigupta as garrison commander of Aornus, Alexander carried out a quick reconnaissance of the surrounding countryside. His patrols were ordered to interrogate the natives and, 'in particular, to get what information they could about elephants, as this interested him more than anything'. Most of the Indians had fled across the river. Alexander, whose retinue already included a group of hunters and mahouts, rounded up thirteen abandoned elephants (two others fell over a cliff) and attached them to his own column. He then built rafts and shipped the entire force, elephants included, downstream to Ohind. His engineers had completed the bridge[56] some while before – a notable feat, since even in the dry season the Indus was seldom less than a mile across, and generally much wider – while Hephaestion had also collected a number of boats, including two thirty-oar galleys.

Various rich presents, ranging from bar silver to sacrificial sheep, had arrived from Ambhi, escorted by a crack native cavalry regiment seven hundred strong. The rajah also promised to surrender his capital, Taxila, the greatest city between the Indus and the Jhelum, and a former Persian satrapal seat. This was a rare prize indeed. Taxila's reputation in antiquity as a wealthy centre of trade and the arts has been confirmed by modern excavation: its ruins extend over some twelve square miles, and the countryside round it, between Attock and Rawalpindi, has just that spaciousness and fertility which Strabo claimed for it.

It was now March (326). Alexander gave his troops a month's rest, ending with athletic contests and a cavalry tattoo. Then, after lavish sacrifices – and correspondingly favourable omens – the entire army crossed the Indus, and set out towards Taxila. Ambhi came out to welcome them, at the head of his own forces, in full battle-array and parading an impressive number of gaily caparisoned war-elephants. As they advanced across the plain they must have presented a most striking spectacle. Alexander, however, still tense and nervous after his gruelling Swat campaign, at once assumed that this was a dangerous trap. All Ambhi's gifts and diplomacy, he thought, had been aimed at lulling the Macedonians into a sense of false security. Now this perfidious Indian meant to massacre them while they were off their guard. Trumpets blared out, orders were barked down the line, and the Macedonians hurriedly moved into battle-order.

That the king could have entertained this nonsensical idea for one moment tells us a lot about his state of mind at the time. The rajah's army was five miles distant, and coming on in full view; it is hard to see how he could have hoped to surprise anyone. In fact, the moment Ambhi saw 'the excited activity of the Macedonians' and guessed its cause he galloped ahead, alone except for a small cavalry escort, and formally submitted his person and army to Alexander.[57] The king, much relieved, thereupon reinstated him, with full sovereign rights, as rajah of Taxila. For the next three days Ambhi entertained the Macedonians royally, adding further lavish gifts to those he had already sent.

But Alexander, as usual, had the last word. No one must outshine him, whether in warfare or munificence. He returned all Ambhi's presents, adding on his own account thirty horses, a collection of rich Persian robes, some gold and silver vessels, and no less than 1,000 talents in cash from the military chest.[58] Over dinner the following night Meleager, one of his battalion commanders,[59] congratulated the king, with sour irony, on having at last found a man worth that amount, even if it had meant coming all the way to India. Meleager was a trusted Companion, and drunk; Alexander – very much on his guard after the Cleitus affair – merely remarked, with unwonted restraint, that jealous men were their own worst enemies. The comment, nevertheless, carried a sting in its tail: Meleager never got another promotion while Alexander lived.

The king's generosity to Ambhi had one obvious and highly practical motive. By now his intelligence service must have provided a preliminary report on the size and strength of enemy forces beyond the Jhelum. It was all too clear that Porus, the warrior-king whose territories extended from Gujrat to the Punjab, and Abisares, the dissident rajah of Kashmir, could between them provide a formidable opposition to Alexander's further advance. Ambhi of Taxila might be their traditional enemy; but in the circumstances they were more than likely to hold out a tempting olive-branch in his direction. Alexander had to ensure that if this happened, Ambhi would stand firm. A combination of all three local kings against the Macedonians could well prove, if not fatal, at the very least a most serious hazard.

Hence, of course, the king's dazzling generosity (a point which should have been obvious to any quickwitted staff officer: if Meleager never reached field rank this was, in a sense, just retribution for plain stupidity). Nor did Alexander's munificence imply uncritical trust. Despite all the superficial honours and rewards heaped on Ambhi – including the right to assume the royal diadem – Alexander nevertheless appointed a Macedonian as military governor of Taxila, with a strong garrison at his disposal. There was no point in taking needless chances. On the other hand Alexander himself delayed at Taxila for between two and three months, which in one respect at least was a near-fatal mistake: it meant that by the time he embarked on the next stage of his expedition, in early June, the monsoon rains would already have begun. Even so, if he could reach some diplomatic accommodation with Abisares and Porus, thus avoiding another major campaign, it would have been time well spent.

Early in April came ambassadors from Abisares, with gifts and promises of submission. These Alexander accepted: their sincerity was highly questionable, but at least they made good propaganda. The rajah's real object, in all likelihood, was to insure himself against an immediate attack while he mobilized his army. Nevertheless, the arrival of Abisares' mission prompted Alexander to send his own envoys to Porus, on whom the timing of such a gesture would not be lost. The Paurava monarch was requested to meet Alexander at the Jhelum (which formed his frontier) and to pay tribute in token of vassalage. The reply to this proposal was exactly what Alexander had feared and expected. Porus would indeed, he said, meet Alexander at the Jhelum – but in full military strength, and ready to do battle for his kingdom. Intelligence reports put his muster at 3–4,000 cavalry and up to 50,000 infantry. together with some 200 elephants and 300 war-chariots.[60] Reinforcements were expected from Abisares, and Indian troops had already begun to move up along the eastern bank of the river. Alexander, it was clear, could not afford to waste time. His first urgent need was for a transport flotilla. Taxila lay miles from the nearest navigable river, and in any case building ships from scratch would take too long. Coenus was therefore sent back to the Indus, with orders to dismantle Alexander's pontoon-bridge, cut up the boats into sections, and load them on to ox-carts. They would then be carried overland for reassembly by the Jhelum.[61]

While Coenus was thus occupied, Alexander made his final military and administrative arrangements. Five thousand Indian troops were now drafted into the infantry, and the king received thirty more elephants, captured with the rebel satrap of Arachosia. About the beginning of June the monsoon broke; and a few days later Alexander led his army southward to meet Porus, through steaming, torrential rains that continued almost without a break for over two months. His route lay across the Salt Range, by way of Chakwal and Ara; when he was through the Nandana pass, he turned south-west, and reached the Jhelum near Haranpur, having marched about 110 miles since leaving Taxila, in an estimated two days.[62] Even if this time applied only to his advance guard, its achievement under monsoon conditions was a quite extraordinary feat.

Alexander knew, from intelligence reports on the terrain ahead, that Haranpur was one of the few points at which he could hope to ford the Jhelum under monsoon conditions. (This is confirmed by its choice as the site of a modern railway-bridge.) Porus, clearly, had been thinking along very similar lines. When Alexander reached the Haranpur ford, he found the opposite bank held in strength by a large force that included archers and chariots. Most alarming of all – especially to the horses – were Porus' elephants. A squadron of these great beasts, eighty-five strong, kept guard over the approaches, stamping and trumpeting as they moved ponderously to and fro. The river itself, swollen by monsoon rains, came roaring past in muddy spate, a good half-mile wide. There was no sign of the promised crossing-point.[63]

Even if it were physically possible, to negotiate the river against such mass opposition would be suicidal: Alexander's cavalry horses would go mad with fright if brought anywhere near the elephants.[64] Further reconnaissance revealed that Porus had put strong guard-detachments at every other nearby point where a crossing could be made.

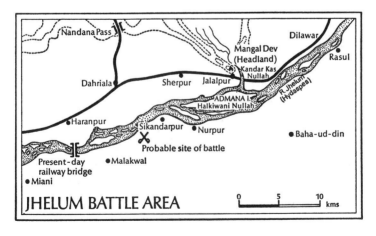

JHELUM BATTLE AREA

It looked very much like stalemate, and Alexander deliberately encouraged this impression by having endless wagonloads of grain and other supplies brought to his camp, in full sight of the enemy. This would, with luck, convince Porus that his opponent meant – as he publicly declared – to sweat it out on the Jhelum until the rains were over and the river became fordable once more.

At the same time Macedonian troop activities continued to suggest the possibility of an immediate attack. Cavalry detachments rode from one outpost to another. Battalions of the phalanx marched and counter-marched along the river-bank, squelching dismally through thick red mud. Boats and assault-craft sailed up and down, occasionally landing raiders on one of the many small islands near Haranpur which might serve Alexander as a bridgehead.[65] But after a while, when no attack materialized, Porus began to pay less attention to all these distracting manoeuvres – which was, of course, just what Alexander had intended. Meanwhile Macedonian cavalry patrols were discreetly exploring the higher reaches of the Jhelum, as far east as Jalalpur. It was here, over seventeen miles upstream from their base-camp, that they found what Alexander wanted: a large, wooded island (Admana), with only a narrow channel flowing past either side of it, and a deep nullah on the near bank where troops and assault craft could be conveniently hidden.[66]

Since the king had decided to force the Jhelum under cover of darkness, he spent much time and ingenuity confusing Porus as to his real intentions. Every night fires would be lit over a wide area, with plenty of noise and bustle. Every night Ptolemy would take a large cavalry force 'up and down the bank of the river, making as much noise as possible – shots, war-cries, and every sort of clatter and shindy which might be supposed to precede an attempted crossing'.[67] At first Porus took these demonstrations very seriously. He followed every sound and movement on the opposite bank, bringing up his elephants at the first alarm, while his cavalry patrolled the river wherever a landing seemed imminent. After a while, however, when he found that nothing came of all the noise and clatter, he relaxed his vigilance. This was not merely a case of familiarity breeding contempt. Endless false alarms in the middle of the night, followed by chaotic sorties carried out under lashing monsoon rain, must have wrought havoc with the Indian troops' morale. Porus probably decided that this was Alexander's real aim. At all events, he stopped all nocturnal troop-movements, relying solely on his chain of look-out posts up and down the river.

Alexander now learnt that Abisares, the rajah of Kashmir, was on his way south at last – was, indeed, no more than fifty miles off – with 'an army little smaller than that of Porus'.[68] To let them join forces was out of the question. Porus, then, must be dealt with in the next forty-eight hours. Alexander's flotilla had already been transported piecemeal to Jalalpur and reassembled in the Kandar Kas nullah. The king now held an emergency staff conference and outlined his plan for the assault. The element of secrecy would only work up to a point. Alexander might deceive Porus as to where and when he intended crossing the river; but once the actual crossing had begun, Porus' scouts would very soon observe and report it.[69]* Any assault-plan, then, must discount the chance of a surprise attack. The only way to keep Porus guessing was by a division of forces which left him uncertain, until the very last moment, where the main blow would fall.

Alexander made his dispositions accordingly. The larger part of the army, together with the baggage-train and the non-combatants, was to remain at base-camp by the Haranpur ford, under Craterus' command. Preparations for crossing the river were to be carried out quite openly. The king's pavilion was to be pitched in a conspicuous position

---

*Alexander had guards posted *within earshot of each other* all the way from his base-camp to Jalalpur – a new device seemingly based on the Indian look-out system.

near the bank, and a certain Macedonian officer, a near-double of Alexander's, was to appear wearing his royal cloak, 'in order to give the impression the king himself was encamped on that part of the bank'.[70] In actual fact the king, together with the main assault group (or 'turning force', as Fuller calls it), would already be on his way to Jalalpur. This force, numbering 5,000 horse and at least 10,000 foot, would cross the river before dawn, and advance down the southern bank on Porus' position. A second group – three battalions of the phalanx plus the mercenary cavalry and infantry – was to take up a position between Haranpur and Admana Island, opposite the main fords, and only cross when battle had been joined.[71] Craterus' holding force, meanwhile, was not to attempt a crossing 'until Porus had moved from his position to attack Alexander' – and only then provided no elephants were left behind to defend the ford, 'or until he was sure that Porus was in retreat and the Greeks victorious'.[72]

This was a brilliant plan, and the dilemma in which it placed Porus has become something of a classic for military historians.[73] Whichever way he moved, he left himself open to attack from the rear, either by Alexander or by Craterus. His one possible defence move was to detach a strong but limited force that could destroy Alexander's assault-group before it established a bridgehead, thus still leaving Porus himself in full control at Haranpur. To counter such a gambit Alexander built up his 'turning force' from the crack divisions of the Macedonian army: the Royal Squadron of the Companions, three hipparchies, or cavalry brigades, under Hephaestion, Perdiccas and Demetrius; the Guards Brigade, two phalanx battalions (commanded by Coenus and Cleitus the White), the archers and Agrianians, cavalry units from Bactriana and Turkestan, and a special force of Scythian horse-archers.

This whole body, some 15–16,000 strong, he brought to the crossing-point, and embarked on boats and rafts, by about 3 a.m. on the morning of the assault. Scholars sometimes take such operations for granted – a great mistake. One of the crucial factors behind Alexander's continuous and unbroken success was the unparalleled efficiency of his supply and transport commands. When we reflect that in 1415 it took Henry V *three days* to disembark 8–10,000 men at Harfleur, and that to ferry 2,000 horse and 3,000 foot across the English Channel William of Normandy needed some 350 boats, we can the better appreciate Alexander's achievement at the Jhelum.[74] He had to get this large force out of camp in broad daylight, without their departure being noticed by Porus' scouts; march them over seventeen miles (which in monsoon conditions can hardly have taken less than six hours); reassemble and launch enough vessels to convey them across the river; and embark the entire assault-group, horses included, well before dawn.

To complicate matters further, the crucial part of the operation was carried out not only in darkness, but during a particularly violent electric storm. In one way this storm came as a godsend. The steady roar of torrential rain, interspersed with deafening thunder-claps (Alexander lost several men struck by lightning) completely masked the noise of the embarkation.[75] When dawn broke, and the wind and rain had become less violent, the flotilla was already sailing down the northern channel, still hidden from Porus' scouts by the wooded mass of Admana Island. But the moment they passed beyond its western tip, the alarm was given, and messengers rode off at full speed to warn Porus.[76]

It was now that Alexander made a miscalculation which could have cost him the battle. When he was clear of Admana Island he put in to shore and disembarked all his forces, cavalry leading. But, as he presently found, what he had taken for the river-bank was in fact another long, narrow island. Either his intelligence was badly at fault, or else the storm during the night had created a fresh channel. There was no time to re-embark; their only hope lay in finding a ford. At first the task seemed hopeless. It was not a wide channel, but the Jhelum was roaring down in spate, over a muddy, shifting bed that gave no sure foothold. Finally they managed to struggle ashore, the infantry – weighed down by their armour – fighting against a breast-high torrent, the horses with little more than their heads visible. Sodden and exhausted, the assault group was at last ready for its advance – cavalry massed on the right, infantry on the left, with a fringe of light-armed troops to cover their flank, and a screen of horse-archers thrown out in front.[77]

To get such a force ashore must have taken several hours, at the very least, by which time Porus would have known all about it. Was Alexander's move a feint, or the prelude to a major attack? At this point no one could tell. Craterus' camp was a mass of activity: whichever way Porus moved, he would inevitably find himself in trouble. The Indian rajah, however, was no mean strategist himself. Without hesitation he detached a force of 2,000 cavalry and 120 chariots, under his own son, to ride east with all speed and, if possible, destroy Alexander's assault-group before it was clear of the river. In the circumstances this was his only feasible move; unfortunately he had made it too late.[78] His son, moreover, was heavily outnumbered, and in the event proved no match for the best cavalry units in the whole Macedonian army.[79] After a brief skirmish – during which Bucephalas received the wound from which he subsequently died – the Indians fled, leaving four hundred dead behind, including young Porus himself.[80] The chariots bogged down in thick mud and had to be abandoned. It was at this point, in all likelihood, that the reserve battalions, under Meleager, Attalus and Gorgias, crossed by the main fords and joined Alexander's advance. The king was pressing on ahead with the cavalry, leaving the infantry to follow at their own speed. By now there was a gap of over two miles between them.

When the news of his son's defeat reached Porus,[81] the rajah had a brief moment of indecision. Either as a feint, or because they took the minor engagement across the river for a full-scale victory, Craterus' men were making vigorous preparations to force the Haranpur crossing. Finally, however, Porus decided correctly that his showdown must be with Alexander. He left a holding force, with elephants, to keep Craterus in play,[82] and marched the rest of his army upstream, ready for battle. At this point – allowing for detachments and losses – he probably had at his disposal 20,000 infantry, 2,000 horse, 130 elephants and 180 war-chariots. He picked his ground carefully: a level sandy plain, free from mud, where elephants and cavalry would have ample room to manoeuvre.*

Porus drew up his infantry battalions on a wide central front, stationing an elephant every hundred feet or so to strengthen them. (Our ancient sources say that this produced the appearance of a castle, with the elephants as towers and the infantry as curtain-walls.) On either wing he placed, first, a flanking body of infantry, and then his cavalry, with a squadron of chariots masking them.[83] The overall Indian battle-line must have been nearer four miles than three in length, of which the infantry accounted for at least two-thirds. This formation, as Burn correctly points out,[84] lacked flexibility, a weakness Alexander was never slow to exploit. While he was waiting for the infantry to catch up with him, he carried out a detailed reconnaissance of Porus' dispositions, carefully keeping his own forces out of sight behind trees and broken ground. A frontal attack was impossible: Alexander could not risk having the horses panic when brought up against elephants. But if the phalanx was to deal with Porus' centre, his Indian cavalry had to be knocked out first; otherwise the Macedonians

---

*The exact site has not been identified, but it must have been somewhere between Nurpur and Malakwal. In this area there is still a village known as Sikandarpur ('Alexanderville'), and though the name recurs frequently throughout the Punjab, it seems more than possible that the battle of the Jhelum was in fact fought here, or not more than a mile or two away to the south.

could be outflanked and ridden down while pressing home their attack.[85]

To defeat Porus' cavalry, Alexander adopted a highly ingenious stratagem. If he launched a cavalry attack of his own against the Indian left wing, *with numbers just sufficiently less than Porus' own total mounted force to convince the rajah that an all-out retaliation would annihilate them,* then Porus might well, as they say, take a swinger – which in this case would mean shifting his right-wing cavalry across to the left in the hope of achieving total victory. The success of such a scheme depended on Alexander keeping two full cavalry divisions hidden from the enemy until Porus had committed his own forces irrevocably to a left-flank engagement. The commander of these divisions, Coenus, received very specific instructions.[86] He was to circle Porus' right wing, still out of sight, and wait until battle was joined on the opposing flank. If Porus transferred his right-wing cavalry to feed this engagement, Coenus was to charge across behind the enemy lines,[87] and take them in the rear. Otherwise he would engage them normally. The phalanx battalions and the Guards Brigade, in similar fashion, had orders 'not to engage until it was evident that the Indians, both horse and foot, had been thrown into confusion by the Macedonian cavalry'.[88]

His dispositions thus made, Alexander attacked at once. The mounted archers, a thousand strong, were launched against the Indian left, and knocked out almost all Porus' chariots – a very useful softening-up process.[89] Then the king charged, at the head of his massed cavalry divisions.[90] Porus did just what Alexander had hoped he would. From the howdah on top of his great war-elephant (an excellent command-post) the rajah made a lightning assessment of Macedonian cavalry strength, and brought across his own right-wing squadrons to deliver the *coup de grâce*. Coenus, with his two fresh divisions, at once broke cover and rode in pursuit. The Indians engaged against Alexander suddenly found themselves forced to fight a rearguard action against

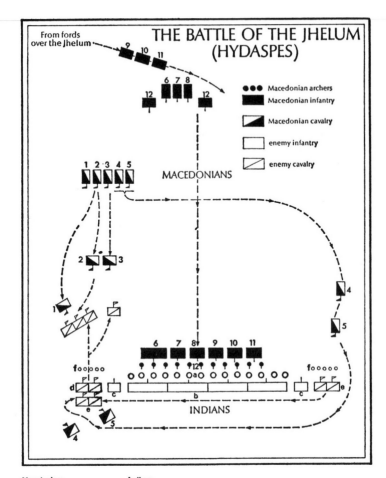

THE BATTLE OF THE JHELUM (HYDASPES)

From fords over the Jhelum

Macedonian archers
Macedonian infantry
Macedonian cavalry
enemy infantry
enemy cavalry

MACEDONIANS

INDIANS

Macedonians
1 Horse-Archers
  Companion Cavalry
2 Hephaestion
3 Perdiccas
4 Coenus
5 Demetrius
6 Hypaspists-Seleucus
  Phalanx
7 Antigenes
8 Cleitus
9 Meleager
10 Attalus
11 Gorgias
12 Agrianians, Archers, and Javelin-men

Indians
a Elephants
b Infantry
c Flanking Infantry
d Left-wing Cavalry
e Right-wing Cavalry
f Chariots

Coenus as well.[91] 'This, of course,' says Arrian, 'was disastrous not only to the effectiveness of the Indians' dispositions, but to their whole plan of battle.'

Alexander pressed home his charge just as they were facing about, and the Indians fell back on the protection of the elephants. By now, all danger removed from their flanks, the Macedonian heavy infantry, strongly reinforced with archers and javelin-men, were advancing on Porus' centre. They had one stroke of luck. The Indian archers used a long heavy bow: the leaf-headed clothyard shaft it discharged was capable – as Alexander later found to his cost – of great penetration at medium range. But they usually rested the foot of this bow on the ground when drawing it, and the earth had become so slippery that their effective fire-power was seriously reduced.[92] The real nightmare facing the phalanx, though – one which haunted them for the rest of their days – was that line of maddened, trumpeting, ferocious elephants. Alexander had worked out a technique for dealing with these beasts: encircle them, let the archers pick off their mahouts, and then discharge volleys of spears and javelins into the most vulnerable parts of their anatomy, while infantrymen slashed through their trunks with Persian scimitars, or chopped at their feet with axes.

The elephants had several very effective tricks of their own. Some Macedonian soldiers they stamped underfoot, crushing them to a bloody pulp, armour and all. Others they caught up with their trunks and dashed to the ground. Others, again, found themselves impaled on the great beasts' tusks. Quite apart from the elephants, they were also engaged in a desperate struggle with the Indian infantry (though here the long Macedonian *sarissa* once more proved its worth). To preserve any sort of military discipline in that hell of mud and blood and driving rain, with such terrible carnage going on all around, was in itself a most remarkable achievement – and one which made victory possible. An Indian cavalry counter-attack failed.

As Porus' squadrons were pressed back, the elephants, hemmed in a narrowing space, began to trample their own side: the cavalry suffered particularly heavy losses because of them.[93]

Porus led one last elephant-charge in person. It was not a success. By now the Macedonians were learning how to deal with these lumbering creatures at least risk to themselves, dodging them like so many huge bulls, relentlessly slashing and shooting at them and their riders. Presently the elephants decided they had had enough. They 'began to back away, slowly, like ships going astern, and with nothing worse than trumpetings'.[94] At this Alexander drew his cavalry ring tighter round Porus' battered divisions, and signalled the Guards Brigade and the phalanx 'to lock shields and move up in a solid mass'.[95] This final stage of the battle was pure butchery, but the Macedonians, after so traumatic an experience, were in no mood to give quarter. Indian casualties are variously estimated at 12,000 or more and 23,000 (of which 3,000 were mounted troops). Some managed to break through Alexander's cavalry – only to be mopped up by Craterus, who had crossed the river and now continued the pursuit with his fresh units.[96] Losses among Porus' commanders and officer corps were particularly heavy: both his sons were killed.

Porus himself fought to the bitter end. Then, when he saw further resistance was hopeless, he slowly rode off the field on his great elephant, weak from loss of blood (a javelin had pierced him through the right shoulder). Alexander, 'anxious to save the life of this great and gallant soldier', sent Ambhi after him with an immediate offer of terms. This was an appalling diplomatic blunder. Porus regarded Ambhi as a traitor and turncoat; when he approached, the wounded rajah made a valiant attempt to pig-stick him with his lance. Eventually, however, a more suitable messenger reached Porus, who now dismounted from his elephant, weak and thirsty, and was brought to Alexander.

No one could better Arrian's description[97] of that momentous meeting (certainly not our other sources,[98] which bury it under the usual dreary rhetorical floss): 'When they met, Alexander reined in his horse, and looked at his adversary with admiration. He was a magnificent figure of a man, over seven feet high and of great personal beauty; his bearing had lost none of its pride; his air was of one brave man meeting another, of a king in the presence of a king, with whom he had fought honourably for his kingdom.' When Alexander asked him how he wished to be treated, the dignified Paurava warrior said: 'Like a king.' Alexander pressed him further. Was there nothing else he wanted for himself? He had only to ask. 'Everything,' Porus told his captor, 'is contained in that one request.'

The anecdote – surely true in substance – forms a fitting epilogue to Alexander's last major battle, and one which many students regard as his greatest. Gaugamela was fought against heavier odds, and far more hung on its outcome. But at the Jhelum Alexander displayed a flexible resourcefulness of strategy which he never equalled on any other occasion, from his brilliant initial dispositions to the final ruse by which he outmanoeuvred Porus' cavalry. In addition, he had to cope with appalling weather, and – worst of all – with the Indian war-elephants. In the circumstances we need not wonder that he played down his undoubtedly heavy losses. The highest casualty-figures recorded are 280 cavalry and something over 700 infantry; but close scrutiny of the evidence suggests that an overall figure of 4,000 might well come nearer the truth,[99] with especially heavy losses among the battalions of the phalanx.

This frightful struggle left its mark on Alexander's men. Their nerve, if not broken, had been severely shaken, and nothing Alexander said or did would ever reconcile them to facing elephants in battle again.[100] They had come very near the end of their endurance, and perhaps it was the monsoon almost as much as the elephants which finally undid them. Only those with personal experience of the rainy season in India or Burma can fully appreciate its effects on equipment, terrain, and morale. When every piece of metal (be it sword or gun) rusts in five or six hours after polishing; when canvas, leather and fabric become patched with damp green mould, and rot in a matter of weeks; when every soldier in uniform suffers agonies from foot-rot and prickly heat (not to mention the likelihood of contracting malaria or amoebic dysentery); when the ground is a steaming morass, and the air whines like a band-saw with mosquitoes – then, in Alexander's day or Wingate's, there is mutinous talk in camp, and a damp collective *cafard* descends on old sweats yearning for the long voyage home.[101]

After the battle, says Diodorus, 'the Macedonian army rested for thirty days in the midst of a vast plenty of provisions'. Even so, some of them got less rest than others. During this month the king found time to make a quick *razzia* through the territories of any neighbouring Indian tribes who had not yet submitted. These new conquests were turned over to Porus, who had been reinstated in his own kingdom with every mark of honour.[102] Indeed, Alexander's chivalrous treatment of Porus led the Indians to regard him as a *Dharmavijayi*, or 'conqueror through righteousness'[103] – a concept which still casts its spell over some modern historians. While the king undoubtedly felt strong and genuine admiration for his defeated opponent, he also saw him as a most useful ally, a source of first-class recruits, and the ideal counterweight to Ambhi of Taxila. Though Alexander staged a public reconciliation between the two rajahs, he meant each of them to keep a watchful eye on the other.

Bucephalas had died at last, of old age and wounds: Alexander gave his faithful charger a state funeral, leading the procession himself. One of the two new cities he founded, on the actual site of the battle, was named Bucephala, as a memorial tribute (Alexander called another settlement Perita, after his favourite dog). The second,

Nicaea ('Victoria') – probably modern Jalalpur – went up at the point where he had made his night-crossing. (Both were mud-brick settlements, quickly completed: coolie labour, Alexander found, was dirt-cheap and inexhaustible.) Thus while Porus was spared the indignity of a resident Macedonian satrap, it would nevertheless be possible, through these military garrison-towns, to keep some kind of check on the rajah's activities.

Such fears proved groundless. Porus, an honourable man, repaid Alexander's confidence with unswerving loyalty during the king's lifetime – which was more than could be said for most of the conquered Indian tribes, especially in Bajaur and Swat, where Alexander now had to put down a serious rising.[104] His great victory at the Jhelum, however, had considerable effect on such potentates as Abisares – who, wisely, arrived too late for the battle. The rajah of Kashmir now sent his brother on an embassy to Alexander, with treasure and elephants (the king's favourite gifts), offering anything short of personal submission – 'for he would not live without royal power, nor reign as a captive.' The king replied, briefly, that if Abisares did not come to him, then he would come to Abisares, and with an army behind him.[105]

A four-horse chariot statue-group of Alexander was erected to mark the battlefield, and the king made lavish donations, in gold, to his officers and men in recognition of their valour at the Jhelum. But this, for him, was no more than the prelude to yet another chapter of conquest and exploration. 'He intended,' says Diodorus, 'to reach the borders of India and to subdue all of its inhabitants, and then to sail downstream to the Ocean.' Arrian presents a substantially similar view.[106] Here, I submit, we have an accurate summing-up of his aims *immediately after the victory over Porus*. What is more, this urge to mop up the remaining regions of India makes strategical sense only if Alexander was, at the time, still convinced that there was no great distance between his advancing forces and the shores of

Ocean. In other words, the existence of the Ganges was still unknown to him while he was planning his overall eastern campaign,[107] and the fleet being made ready by Craterus had been ordered with a view to finding Ocean shortly after crossing the River Hyphasis (Beas).

Alexander and his staff, as we have seen, took their fundamental notions on the geography of India from Aristotle. First-hand observation (above, p. 379 with n. 46) had already disproved some of Aristotle's basic facts. However, from a study of the *Meteorologica* Alexander might well still infer that the Eastern Ocean lay only a short way beyond the Punjab.[108] When, exactly, was this erroneous notion dispelled? By now Alexander must have been well aware, through long discussions with Ambhi, Porus, and other Indian dignitaries, that Greek beliefs concerning the eastern stream of Ocean (see above, p. 379) were at complete variance with local information on the subject. This does not necessarily mean that he rejected Aristotle's guidance at once: axioms are often cherished long after reason would counsel their abandonment. Yet though Alexander's notions of world geography might be vague, he never failed to amass accurate intelligence about the regions through which he planned to pass, and undoubtedly did so on this occasion. It has been argued that he 'continued eastward from the Hydaspes [Jhelum] waiting for his accumulating geographical intelligence to clarify the matter',[109] and up to a point this may be true; but the suggestion of our ancient sources, that his first intuition of the truth only came when his troops were on the verge of mutiny before reaching the Beas (see below, p. 407), is flatly incredible.

Such lack of immediate intelligence would have implied inefficiency of a sort that Alexander never tolerated for one moment. What seems far more likely is that by now he knew the truth very well – had, indeed, suspected it for some time – but kept it a close secret for fear of the effect it might have on his troops' already low morale. Alexander was not a man to be deterred by mere geographical considerations. If he could lure the army forward one river at a time, with Ocean a glittering goal always just over the next hill, he might yet attain his end. Such a confidence-trick depended entirely on his knowing more than the army about local conditions, and this he usually did.* But at the Beas there were no more hills to deceive his men, only a vast expanse of plain stretching away eastward, and beyond that – visible on a fine day from Gurdaspur, where Alexander probably reached the river – the great rampart of the Western Himalayas.[110] No more potent incitement to mutiny could well be imagined. A diplomatic lie had been nailed, once and for all, by the brute facts of geography.

This, however, remained an unforeseeable hazard during Alexander's immediate advance from the Jhelum. He meant to rely, for as long as he could, on the substantial gap between his own intelligence and the hearsay information which filtered through to the troops. With this in mind, he had the propaganda section minimize the scope and extent of his coming campaign. He also put out a rumour (which he himself could not have believed for one moment) that the Jhelum and the Chenab in some mysterious way formed the headquarters of the Nile, because crocodiles had been seen in them, and 'Egyptian' beans grew along their banks.[111]

Why did he do this? The answer seems clear enough. Alexander knew his Herodotus; he may even have possessed a copy of Scylax's *Periplus*. His next project after reducing India was to explore the coasts of Arabia and the Persian Gulf. Ample supplies of fir, pine, cedar and other shipbuilding timber were available in the nearby

---

*Strabo (2.1.6, c. 69) remarks that 'those who made the expedition with Alexander acquired only cursory information about everything, but Alexander himself made accurate investigations, since the men best acquainted with the country had described the whole of it for him'. In modern parlance, that is, he made a habit of personally debriefing local leaders, from Mazaeus to Porus: one important reason for his strategical successes.

mountains: Craterus had already been set to work on the construction of a vast fleet.[112] So much was public knowledge. But to spell out for his troops just how long and hazardous a voyage they would be undertaking obviously struck Alexander (and with good reason) as most inadvisable. The propaganda line that was used on this occasion is recorded by Strabo: Alexander 'thought of preparing a fleet for an expedition to Egypt, *thinking that he could sail as far as there by this river*'. But unfortunately the truth soon leaked out. Numerous Greek, or Greek-speaking, traders and settlers were in touch with Alexander's commissariat; the king, after a while, grudgingly admitted that a voyage down the Jhelum would, indeed, lead in the first instance to the Indian Ocean.[113] It was just such a leakage of unwelcome topographical information which finally precipitated Alexander's showdown with his troops.

The king resumed his march eastward in early July, before the end of the monsoon – a great psychological blunder, but by now he would seem to have been more than a little frayed himself. He crossed the Chenab and Ravi rivers, defeating some tribes and terrifying others into submission. One city, Sangala, was razed to the ground. Rain fell heavily from a grey sky; the air was steaming and humid.[114] The Macedonians trudged on, sodden, desperate, marching and fighting like automata, plagued by snakes, and sleeping in tree-slung hammocks to avoid being bitten. As they advanced, they too began to pick up more precise information about what lay ahead – not the shores of Ocean, but an interminable plain, peopled by fierce warrior-tribes.

While the king himself and his intimates were entertained by pliable local princelings, who pressed everything on them from women to Indian hunting dogs, morale in camp dropped daily – and with good reason. Alexander's veterans were no longer the same eager youths who had set out from Pella eight years before. They had marched over 17,000 miles and fought in every kind of battle and siege.

Few can have come through this ordeal unscathed. Their arms and armour were worn out, fit only for the scrapheap. Their Macedonian clothes had long since been thrown away. By now they were perilously near breakingpoint. Obedience, discipline, loyalty had brought them so far. But there is a limit to what men will stand without a clear end in view, and Alexander's Macedonians had reached it.[115] The siege of Sangala had been a hard and bloody affair: even Ptolemy (who minimizes Macedonian losses with monotonous regularity) admitted that 1,200 men were seriously wounded during the fighting.

Now, as Alexander and his troops approached the rainswollen Hyphasis (Beas), wild rumours began to circulate about the territory and people which lay ahead. Twelve days' march after the Beas they would come to a far greater river (presumably the Sutlej), and beyond this dwelt a fierce, warlike nation, with vast armies, chariots, and – worst of all – not less than *four thousand* fighting elephants.[116] Furthermore, the Beas appears to have formed the eastern frontier of Darius I's empire, a fact which (despite some modern claims to the contrary) would not be lost on any Macedonian.[117] Up to this point Alexander could at least claim to be acting as Darius' successor, and recovering lost provinces that were his by right of conquest and inheritance. The end, however remote, had always been in view. But once he crossed the Beas, there was no predictable limit to his ambitions, only a constantly receding horizon *ad infinitum*. What he intended now was (in the most literal sense) a march to the world's end: small wonder that his veterans baulked at such a prospect.

Hitherto Alexander's innate contempt for the common run of mankind had not led him into serious trouble: his extraordinary personal charisma saw to that. Soldiers, in particular, he seems to have dealt with on the assumption that they were motivated exclusively by fear, greed, and ambition; on most occasions this hypothesis worked well enough. Between the stick of tough discipline and the carrot of rich plunder he had kept his army efficient and loyal for a decade. Why should the formula not work once again? The men were tired, he understood that: they had had a gruelling two months. Mutinous talk was nothing new. All they needed was some sort of special bonus: that would soon shift them.

But the geographical horizons revealed when Alexander finally halted his advance at the Beas made any such solution quite hopeless. To reach even the westernmost tributary of the Ganges, the Jumna, meant crossing some two hundred miles of the northern Indian desert. The subsequent march from the Jumna to the Ganges, and from the Ganges to Ocean, would add well over a thousand miles more. Yet Alexander still seems to have believed, with a kind of insane optimism, that a little indulgence would induce his veterans to march on through this limitless *terra incognita*. He therefore gave the army a holiday, with *carte blanche* to ravish and plunder the surrounding countryside. He could not offer them another Persepolis, but this was the next best thing. The local rajah had entertained Alexander for two days, and was now officially his ally – a consideration which bothered the king not at all. When his veterans' loyalty hung in the balance, to lose local goodwill was a cheap sacrifice.[118]

While the Macedonians were off on this legalized looting spree, Alexander, like any political demagogue, wooed their wives with a promise of free monthly rations and child-allowances.[119] Nothing could better demonstrate his failure to appreciate what he was up against. This time it was different: this time the usual bribes, threats and blandishments would no longer work. After the troops got back from their expedition, laden with plunder, he thought they would have changed their minds about going on. They had not. A speech exhorting them to further glorious exploits fell very flat indeed. They did nothing loudly or aggressively mutinous, merely stood in sullen silence and refused to budge.[120]

Having failed with the men, Alexander called a private meeting of his senior officers. He was now on very dangerous ground, since at this stage he needed his Macedonians more than they needed him – a fact which they doubtless realized. Without their unrivalled training and experience, his entire command-structure would be in danger of collapsing overnight. There was – as yet – no comparable Iranian officer-corps to replace them. If they struck, he could not possibly go on. His address to this key group shows, and all too clearly, what the main points of grievance were.[121] The unknown, he assured his sceptical audience, always sounded worse than in fact it was. They should beware of exaggeration. The rivers were not so wide as rumour made out, the Indian warriors neither so numerous nor so valiant. As for elephants, they had beaten them once and could beat them again. In any case, their journey was almost over. Soon, very soon, they would reach Ganges and the Eastern Ocean. Why turn back now, when their goal lay so near? And if they *did* turn back, they risked losing all they had won.

After Alexander had finished speaking, there was a long embarrassed silence; and small wonder. To challenge this farrago of nonsense and special pleading without provoking the king's formidable wrath seemed out of the question. In any case he had made his own attitude all too clear: 'For a man who *is* a man,' he declared, 'work, in my belief, if it is directed to noble ends, *has no object beyond itself.*' There was no arguing with Alexander; in the last resort one could only agree to differ, and even that had its dangers. Nevertheless, after he had several times invited comment, Coenus – old now, and perhaps already in the grip of his last illness – made a valiant effort to get the truth through to him.[122] The veterans, Coenus reiterated, were worn out, done for, pushed beyond the last limits of human endurance. Many had died of sickness or in battle. What survived was 'a small remnant broken in health, their old vigour and determination gone'. They wanted one thing only: to get home before it was too late. Alexander could mount other expeditions from Greece, with younger men. 'Sir,' Coenus said, 'if there is one thing above all others a successful man should know, it is *when to stop*.'

This speech was greeted with thunderous applause. Furious, Alexander dismissed the conference. Next day he summoned his officers once more, and tried another gambit. *He* was going on, he told them, whether they did or not – and so would many others. They were not necessary to his plans. If they wanted to return home, they could do so. 'And you may tell your people there,' he added, 'that you deserted your king in the midst of his enemies.' With that he retired to his tent, as he had done after the Cleitus affair, refusing to see anyone for the next two days.[123] It was pure bluff; and this time the bluff was called. Alexander's Macedonian officers, far from undergoing a change of heart, as the king confidently expected, kept up their angry, obstinate silence. If Alexander meant to starve himself to death, they at least had no intention of stopping him. They could, they now realized, quite well get the army back home without his assistance. Professional soldiers to a man, they were indispensable and knew it.

By the third day Alexander saw that there was going to be no tearful reconciliation, no offer to follow him wherever he might lead. For once his infallible charisma had failed him. Indeed, unless he walked very warily, he might well find himself in danger of being deposed by a military junta. Coenus was, after all, the last surviving member of Parmenio's old guard. He had changed sides once, and could do so again. The king therefore emerged from his self-imposed retreat, announced that he still meant to go on, and proceeded to offer sacrifice 'in the hope of favourable omens for the crossing'. The omens, of course, were all against him: a convenient face-saving device behind which, yet again, one senses Aristander's tireless prophetic diplomacy. To climb down under pressure was unthinkable, but to bow before the will of heaven indicated both prudence and piety.[124]*

Twelve great commemorative altars, in honour of the twelve Olympian gods, were erected by the river. Their hyperbolic dimensions, together with those of various special outsize fortifications, pieces of military equipment, and even dining-couches, which Alexander now had made and left behind, were designed to provide the natives with evidence that their enemies had been 'men of huge stature, displaying the strength of giants'.[125] One late and erratic source, Philostratus,[126] further asserts that the altars bore the inscription 'To Father Ammon and Brother Heracles and Athena Pronoia and Olympian Zeus and the Cabeiroi of Samothrace and Indus and Helios and Apollo of Delphi' – so odd a collection of dedicatees that I am sorely tempted to believe Philostratus, for once, an honest reporter, and the inscription genuine. He also records the existence of a brass obelisk, put up, he suggests, by the Indians, and bearing the legend 'Alexander stopped here.'

When the king's decision to retreat was first made known, a laughing, tearful mob, hysterical with relief, thronged round his tent, calling down blessings on him for so generous a surrender. If he ever felt like murdering the entire Macedonian officer corps with his own bare hands it was, surely, at this moment. He never got over his humiliation by the Beas, nor did he forgive those responsible for it. 'In Alexander's reaction to the thwarting of his desires by his unhappy soldiers one may see most clearly the despot's spite, egotism and ingratitude . . . they had crossed him, and that was all that counted.'[127] He was determined, by whatever means, to make the long homeward trek a hell on earth for them all; and in this aim he unquestionably succeeded.[128]

---

*Craterus (who was not there) wrote a letter home claiming that Alexander had actually reached the Ganges – a hint of what the king's expectations may well have been at the time when the two men parted company. See Strabo 15.1.35, c. 702.

[10]

How Many Miles to Babylon?

ALEXANDER's return march to the Jhelum began in autumn 326. While the army lay at the Chenab, a fresh embassy arrived from Abisares, with thirty elephants and other rare gifts. Once again the rajah of Kashmir failed to present himself in person: this time he pleaded illness as an excuse. (The illness may have been more than diplomatic, since a year later Abisares was dead.) Alexander, however, proved surprisingly lenient. He not only accepted the rajah's apologies, but confirmed him as governor of his own 'province'. In point of fact there was little else he could do. To whip Abisares into line would call for another campaign, and the Macedonians were unlikely to relish the prospect of chasing elusive tribesmen up the Himalayas. Alexander's sudden loss of interest in northern India was largely due to circumstances beyond his control. To save time and trouble, all conquered territory as far as the Beas was simply made part of Porus' kingdom.[1] Thus the Paurava monarch now found himself – paradoxically enough – more powerful than he had been before his defeat at the Jhelum.

During the eastward advance Hephaestion, like Craterus, had been on detachment – not, fortunately, to the same place, since the two men detested each other, as only personal rivals for power can do. Hephaestion had 'pacified' a large area, rejoining Alexander just before the mutiny. One of his tasks had been to build a fortified garrison-town at the Chenab crossing. This 'town' (probably little more than a mudbrick compound and a market) was now ready. Alexander settled it with the usual mixed population: unfit or time-expired mercenaries reinforced by local native volunteers – an abrasive formula, which seldom made for either peace or permanence. Craterus, with remarkable efficiency, had Alexander's naval flotilla ready and waiting by the time the Macedonians returned to the Jhelum.[2] There were eighty triakonters (thirty-oar vessels), 200 undecked galleys, 800 service ships – horse-transports, grain-barges, lighters – and a multitude of rafts and smaller river-craft. Crews had been drafted from Phoenician, Cypriot, Carian and Egyptian volunteer units accompanying the expedition. The larger vessels were built on the spot, from timber cut in the Himalayas; the rest had been commandeered. Massive reinforcements – 30,000 infantry and about 6,000 cavalry – had also arrived from Thrace, Greece, and Babylon. The Babylonian contingent dispatched by Harpalus brought, in addition, badly needed medical supplies, and 25,000 suits of new armour, all beautifully inlaid with silver and gold. These Alexander issued to his men, ordering the old equipment to be burnt – an eloquent comment on its condition. Presumably the king had sent Harpalus an urgent request for replacements.[3] Whether he also requisitioned a transfer of bullion or coined money we do not know. Certainly none would seem to have been sent. This (like so many things connected with Harpalus) is both puzzling and suspicious.

Despite the legendary wealth of the Indians (mostly in jewels and gold-dust, it was believed), Alexander did not acquire much loot during his eastern campaigns. His expenses, on the other hand (not least in bribes, bonuses and donations), were very heavy, and sometimes – as in the case of his thousand-talent gift to Ambhi – caused active ill-feeling. His daily mess-bill alone came to 10,000 drachmas, and he never had less than sixty or seventy officers at dinner with him. Obviously he could well afford this scale of living: Darius' treasures had made him the wealthiest potentate in the known world. Yet by the end of his Indian campaign there are definite signs that he was hard-pressed for ready cash. The cost of his river-flotilla he partly defrayed by appointing thirty 'trierarchs' on the Athenian model (that is, wealthy men who were made responsible for outfitting vessels and paying their crews). By the time his flotilla entered the Indian Ocean, Alexander was once more, as in Macedonia at the outset of his career (see above, p. 155), reduced to raising loans among his friends.[4] Wherever the Persian treasure might be, it was not coming through to India. Yet if Harpalus' 7,000 men brought 25,000 suits of armour with them, they could just as easily have convoyed gold bullion. The inference, especially in the light of subsequent events, seems clear enough: Harpalus had other, more personal, plans for its use. This ties in very well with the alarming rumours which now began to reach Alexander about his imperial treasurer's general conduct.

At first, it seems, Harpalus had done nothing more adventurous than make experiments in exotic gardening. (He imported a number of Greek plants and shrubs for the royal park, all of which flourished except ivy.) But after a while this lame quinquagenarian discovered that money, in unlimited quantities, could buy a good deal more than hardy annuals. He brought over a glamorous Athenian courtesan, on whom he proceeded to throw away Alexander's gold with lavish generosity. When she died he built her two monuments, one in Babylon, the other in Athens: between them these cost him over 200 talents. Harpalus seems to have been an affectionate, not to say uxorious, patron: he never had more than one mistress at a time, and invariably became devoted to her. His next acquisition, Glycera, was likewise an Athenian. What she felt about her predecessor being worshipped as a local variant of Aphrodite one can only surmise; but as she herself was set up *en princesse* in the palace at Tarsus she had little cause for complaint. The besotted Harpalus gave her a gold crown, and made visitors prostrate themselves when they greeted her. Jokes began to circulate about the 'Queen of Babylon'.

All this might, just conceivably, have been the product of infatuation and nothing more. But the introduction of *proskynesis* (whether in jest or earnest) carried ominous political overtones. Furthermore, in 327/6 the Tarsus mint began striking a series of Persian-type silver coins without reference to Alexander. Independent issues also appeared about the same time in Phoenicia and Cyprus. True or not, it was widely thought that Harpalus, given half a chance, meant to revolt against the king. In this connection his links with Athens – which went rather beyond the acquisition of courtesans – are highly significant. During the great grain-famine which hit Greece between 330 and 326, perhaps in part as the result of Alexander's military requisitions (see above, p. 351 n.), Harpalus, on his own initiative, had sent Athens a large consignment of wheat, for which he was rewarded with honorary Athenian citizenship.

Though we know little of the details, it seems pretty clear that Harpalus, like many other men in authority, was hedging his bets on the king's political future. If Alexander never came back from the Far East – which to observers in Europe or Asia Minor must have seemed more likely than not – then Harpalus, with his immense financial reserves, could easily emerge as the most powerful man in the empire. Given Greek support, he could go on to dispose of Antipater. But if Alexander *did* come back, crowned with victory, then his embezzling (and possibly seditious) imperial treasurer would undoubtedly need all the friends he could raise. On either count, Athenian citizenship would not come amiss.[5]

When these rumours first reached Alexander he threw the messengers in jail. But a detailed report from the Chian historian Theopompus seems to have convinced him that some, at least, of the charges were true. During the flotilla's voyage down-river, at the time of the Rural Dionysia (December 326), a satirical sketch was performed, lampooning Harpalus, Glycera, the Athenians, and the Persian Magi – a revealing series of targets. This sketch, the *Agen*, fragments of which survive, must have had the king's endorsement; indeed, according to one tradition he wrote it himself.[6] But there was little more he could do about Harpalus' activities till he got back to Babylon. In any case he does not appear to have taken them over-seriously. His exploration of the Persian Gulf went through as planned. He probably saw Harpalus as comic rather than dangerous: a hobbling, elderly, Hephaestus-like pasha, a spendthrift victim of the male menopause. Before the departure downriver, Coenus sickened and died. Those who crossed Alexander's will seldom – whether by design or accident – outlived his displeasure for long. 'So far as circumstances permitted,' Arrian observes drily, 'Alexander gave him a splendid funeral.' Curtius adds that though the king was grieved by his death, he 'could not forbear to remark that Coenus for the sake of a few days had begun a long harangue, as if he alone were destined to see Macedonia again'. Porus, on the other hand, Alexander's late opponent, was now proclaimed king of all subjugated Indian territories except for Taxila: the contrast must have suggested, forcibly, to Coenus' surviving friends that defeat at Alexander's hands brought greater and more immediate rewards than long years of hardship in his service. Moreover, whereas the pliable Ambhi had to put up with a Macedonian 'resident' to keep a watchful eye on his activities, Porus (like the dynasts of Caria) ranked as an independent vassal-prince, responsible directly to Alexander.[7] This distinction indicates, with some clarity, the relative degree of trust which the king placed in each of them.

The flotilla set out from Jalalpur early in November 326. Nearchus of Crete had been appointed admiral-in-chief, with a grand total of 1,800 vessels under his command. At dawn on the day of departure some 8,000 troops – no more than a small fraction of the total expeditionary force, but including the Guards Brigade and the Companion Cavalry – began to file aboard. The remainder were divided into three separate columns, under Craterus, Hephaestion and Philip, the newly-appointed 'resident' (or satrap) of Taxila. When all was ready Alexander made sacrifice, and standing in the bow of his flagship poured libations from a golden chalice to various appropriate deities: Ocean,

Poseidon, the Nereids; the rivers which the fleet would traverse – Jhelum, Chenab, Indus; his ancestor Heracles, his divine father Zeus Ammon. Then a trumpet sounded, hawsers were cast off, and in perfect formation Alexander's armada began to glide downstream, bright with gaily coloured flags and bunting, each vessel's oars rising and dipping as its coxswain called the stroke.

The Jhelum, here and as far as its confluence with the Chenab, was at least two and a half miles wide – space enough for over forty oared galleys to travel abreast. It must have been a highly impressive spectacle. The natives had never seen anything like it, and followed the flotilla's progress for miles (they were particularly astonished by the horse-transports). At various points, says Arrian, 'other friendly tribesmen who were near enough to hear the cries of the rowers and the dash and the clatter of the oars came running to the river-banks and joined in the procession, singing their barbaric songs'. The fleet advanced at a very leisurely pace, no more than five miles a day, with frequent disembarkations.

Craterus and Hephaestion went on ahead, Craterus marching along the right bank, and Hephaestion (with the main body and 200 elephants) along the left: a sensible arrangement, considering the feud between them. Philip at first followed on with the baggage-train, but was afterwards sent east to march along the line of the Chenab, thus covering Hephaestion's left flank.[8] While the flotilla cruised down-river, Aristobulus entertained the king by reading out his freshly composed account of the battle at the Jhelum – a sensational piece of fiction, which made Alexander fight out an epic duel against Porus, and kill the rajah's elephant with one javelin-thrust. Alexander (still proof, it would seem, against the grosser sorts of flattery, especially those with a built-in credibility-gap) pitched this effusion overboard, remarking that Aristobulus himself deserved to follow it for writing such rubbish.[9]

Rapids and whirlpools at the confluence of the Jhelum

and the Chenab gave the king a very rough passage. His light galleys in particular were tossed about like corks, quite out of control, oars snapping off as they swung broadside-on to the turbulent current. At one point the royal flagship nearly foundered, and Alexander (who could not swim) only just managed to struggle to safety with the help of his friends. However, the fleet got through in the end. Alexander now could – and did – boast that, like his hero Achilles, he had done battle with a river. Once safely through to the broad waters of the Chenab, the fleet put ashore at a pre-arranged rendezvous, and the whole expeditionary force was once more united.

So far Alexander had met very little serious resistance; but now reports came in that two powerful tribes, the Malli (Mālavas) and the Oxydracae (perhaps the Kshatriyas or Kshudrakas, a Hindu warrior caste) were mobilizing in force to block his advance. They were said to have about 100,000 men under arms – not to mention 900 chariots. Alexander, on receipt of this intelligence, sent Nearchus and the fleet on ahead to the meeting-point of the Chenab and Ravi, divided his forces into three major assault-groups, and got ready to make a clean sweep of the Malli before they could link up with their allies.

At this point Alexander's veterans, realizing that they were about to be pitched into yet another tough campaign (when all they had bargained for was an uneventful voyage), once again threatened to mutiny. They complained, with some justification, that they 'were exposed to unconquered nations in order that at the cost of their blood they might open up a way for him to the Ocean'. Not – as their spokesman hastened to point out – that Ocean itself ('a deep teeming with schools of savage sea-monsters') was all that attractive a goal in any case, even if they did eventually fight their way through to it. They were sick of glory and honour. They had endured more in eight years than most men are called upon to face in a lifetime. Now all they wanted was a quick, safe journey home. By a charismatic

mixture of blarney, romantic rhetoric, and the most outrageous lies (Ocean lay so close they could almost smell the
sea-breeze; the tribes facing them were 'unwarlike')
Alexander somehow talked them into going on. But though
they cheered him, their morale was still perilously low – a
fact which became all too clear during the tough campaign
which followed.

The king himself had lost none of his tactical flair and
panache (once again he scored a notable victory by marching fifty miles through waterless desert before dawn), but
his men were at the end of their tether. Like frightened and
desperate troops the world over, they began to fight with
savage, almost hysterical cruelty. Rapine and wholesale
massacre became commonplaces: even Tarn, for whom
Alexander can do little wrong, claims (with some exaggeration) that 'among Alexander's campaigns this is unique in
its dreadful record of mere slaughter'.[11] Resistance, stimu-
lated by the Brahmin priestly caste, became correspondingly
more stubborn, and this in turn revealed the demoralization
of Alexander's hitherto invincible phalanx.

Twice they refused to mount the scaling-ladders during a
siege, until the king himself led the way, and shamed them
into following him. On the second occasion a soothsayer
(doubtless sensing the troops' reluctance) warned Alexander against pressing this attack: the omens indicated
danger to his life. Alexander looked at him sharply. 'If
anyone interrupted *you* while you were about your professional business,' he snapped, 'I have no doubt you would
find it both tactless and annoying, correct?' The seer
agreed. 'Well,' said the king, '*my* business – vital business –
is the capture of this citadel; and I don't intend to let any
superstitious crackpot stand in my way.' With that he
shouted for the scaling-ladders to be brought up. The men
hung back, hesitating. Furious, Alexander snatched a ladder
himself – there would seem to have been no more than two
or three available – leaned it against the parapet, and went
straight up, holding a light shield over his head as protection.

When he reached the top, he quickly cut down the defenders barring his way, and stood alone for a moment on the battlements – a perfect target for any archer. His friends shouted to him to come back. Instead, with splendid but foolhardy bravado, he jumped down *inside* the citadel. His back against the wall, and protected on one side by a large tree (which suggests that the struggle took place at ground-level) he proceeded to take on all comers singlehanded. After a moment he was joined by three other Macedonians: Leonnatus, Peucestas his shieldbearer, and a highly decorated Guards officer named Abreas. These should have been the first of many – his gesture had had its desired effect – but such a crowd of soldiers now came swarming up the ladders that they collapsed into matchwood, leaving Alexander temporarily cut off.

While frantic Macedonian sappers battered their way through a postern-gate, with mattocks and axes, the king and his three faithful aides held off a multitude. Stones, bolts, every kind of missile clattered on their shields and helmets as they laid about them. Abreas fell, shot in the face. Then a long Indian arrow drove clean through Alexander's corslet and breast, just above the lung. He dropped on one knee, half-fainting, but still had the strength to run his sword through another assailant before he collapsed altogether. Peucestas stood over the king as he lay there, covering him with the sacred shield of Ilium, hemmed in by eager attackers. But by now rescue was on the way. One assault-group scaled the wall on a series of improvised *pitons*. The postern-gate yielded, and a crowd of furious Macedonians charged through into the citadel, killing every man woman and child they found there. Meanwhile Alexander was borne away on his shield to the royal pavilion; word went round that he was either dead or dying.[11]

To extract the arrowhead proved a perilous operation. It was leaf-shaped and barbed, about three inches long by two wide, and lodged deep in the breastbone beside the heart.

When it had been finally cut out – one account says that Perdiccas did the job with his sword, because no surgeon could be found, or was willing to take the risk – a major haemorrhage followed, and Alexander lost consciousness. His attendants barely succeeded in staunching the flow of blood; for a week the king hung between life and death.[12] No one believed he could survive, and a premature but circumstantial report of his death spread rapidly through the area. The Indians at once recovered confidence, while in Alexander's base camp (now established at the junction of the Chenab and the Ravi) the news caused sheer consternation.

His men could not imagine themselves under any other leader. No one else seemed qualified to replace him. Now he was dead they would never get home again. At the Beas they had had a comparatively safe line of retreat. Here they were surrounded on all sides by hostile and war-like tribes, who would fight all the more fiercely without Alexander's name to sap their courage. Even the rivers suddenly looked wider. 'Every difficulty seemed hopelessly insoluble without Alexander to get them through' (Arrian 6.12.2). Nothing could more clearly demonstrate the personal and charismatic quality of the king's leadership – or its fundamental limitations.

All he had built up depended on the awe and inspiration caused by his physical presence; the moment he was gone, his empire split into anarchic warring fragments, without any central principle or authority to hold it together, or halt the centrifugal explosion which followed so soon upon his death. When this false rumour reached Bactria, some three thousand Greek mercenary-settlers at once revolted, and set out westward for home – an ominous foretaste of things to come. At the same time his prestige and personal authority were so overwhelming that men who afterwards founded royal dynasties and became great generals in their own right – a Seleucus, a Ptolemy, a Perdiccas – were wholly eclipsed by him. He had perhaps the most extraordinary and talented team of subordinates in all history; yet till the day of his death subordinates they remained, competent staff-officers and nothing more. Only Alexander could control them – yet so masterfully did he do the job that his troops saw none of them as his natural or pre-destined successor.

Almost the moment he recovered consciousness, the king wrote a public letter to the troops at headquarters, squash-ing the rumour of his death, and promising he would be with them as soon as he was fit to travel. But by now the men were in such a state that they flatly refused to credit what they heard. The letter, they said, was a forgery, something concocted by Alexander's officers as a device for boosting morale. When this news reached the king's ears, he knew that only his personal appearance could forestall a serious breakdown of discipline. His wound was still uncicatrized; but, fit or not, he must move to base camp at once. He was carried on a litter to the Ravi; two vessels were lashed together, and his daybed set on a high platform between them, where he could easily be seen from the river-bank. Let the Indians learn that Alexander still lived, and lose their false hopes.

But he was still dreadfully weak: so weak, indeed, that his boat travelled some distance ahead of the others, 'in order that the quiet which he still needed . . . might not be inter-fered with by the beat of the oars' (QC 9.6.2). As they approached base camp, he ordered the stern awning to be removed, so that he was plainly visible in the sunlight. Even now the troops remained dubious. This motionless figure was Alexander's corpse, they muttered, not a living man, not their commander. Then the king raised his hand, weakly, in greeting, and a great cheer went up. But something more was needed, some proof that Alexander not only lived, but was indeed *aniketos*, invincible.

When the boat put in to shore, a litter was waiting for him. He told his attendants to take it away and to bring him his horse. With what iron exercise of will one can scarcely imagine, he got up, mounted, and slowly rode into camp in full sight of his troops. A sudden spontaneous storm of applause broke out, 'so loud that the river-banks and neighbouring glens re-echoed with the noise' (Arrian 6.13.3). As he drew near his pavilion he dismounted, and walked the rest of the way. His veterans crowded around him, touching his arms and clothes with superstitious awe, as though to make sure he was not a ghost. Wreaths and flowers were showered on him. Then he passed out of sight into his tent – where, after this supreme effort, he probably at once lost consciousness. Even Alexander's extraordinary physique had its limitations, and there are signs that he never fully recovered from the effects of this appalling wound.

The king's friends took him seriously to task afterwards. He had no business, they said, to risk his life – and hazard the outcome of the entire expedition – by so gratuitous a display of heroics. It was company officers, not the commander-in-chief, who should be first up a scaling-ladder. To this Alexander doubtless replied that if his company commanders had not all shown themselves arrant cowards, he would have been under no compulsion to set them an example. The old Boeotian who told him 'Action is a man's job, my lord' was not altogether wrong. Alexander might well have pointed out, in addition, that his personal feat of valour had (apart from anything else) considerably shortened the campaign. The Malli were so shattered by the loss of their chief stronghold, and – equally important – the circumstances in which it had fallen, that they felt further resistance against this godlike figure was useless, and surrendered. At the same time numerous ambassadors arrived from the Oxydracae, who were so impressed by Alexander's campaign against the Malli that they made their own submission without striking a blow.[13]

If the king had deliberately set out to demonstrate just how indispensable he was, he could not have succeeded in a more striking fashion. From now on he was able to get away with almost anything, and showed an increasing inclination to do so. Perhaps his survival, against all reasonable odds, convinced him that he really *did* possess superhuman powers. When Craterus and Ptolemy, back off detachment, came to pay him their respects during his convalescence, the subject uppermost in his mind was the posthumous deification of Olympias.[14] Once again Alexander had become preoccupied with divine aspirations; and this time the idea was not put aside, but grew into a major obsession.

A great banquet was held to celebrate the king's full recovery. This occasion gave rise to an unpleasant but all too characteristic incident. One of Alexander's most distinguished Macedonian veterans, Corragus, challenged the famous Athenian boxer Dioxippus to single combat. Dioxippus fought naked, armed only with a club, while Corragus was in full armour, and carried both sword and spear. Dioxippus, defter than any Roman net-fighter, finished off his opponent in a matter of seconds. Alexander (who had backed Corragus) was so furious he left the feast: this had been a matter of national prestige. From now on his sycophants made endless trouble for Dioxippus, even going so far as to plant a gold cup on him at a dinner-party, and then accuse him of stealing it. In the end the wretched athlete committed suicide rather than endure further persecution.[15] When Alexander learnt the truth of the matter he was, as so often, filled with remorse. But by then it was too late.

The southward advance now continued, interspersed with a number of minor campaigns. About February 325 Alexander's much-enlarged flotilla emerged from the Chenab into the Indus. The confluence of these two great rivers marked the southern limit of Philip's satrapy. A frontier garrison-city, with dockyards, was built here, and new thirty-oared galleys laid down for the fleet. At the same time, to strengthen his communications with eastern Iran,

Alexander replaced the unreliable Persian satrap of Paropamisus (Hindu Kush) by his own father-in-law, Oxyartes.
It took the king another five months to reach the head of
the Indus delta. During that period he fought a whole
series of bloody battles against various independent rajahs
who blocked his advance, or rose in revolt once he had
passed on. Again, the record of sheer slaughter is appalling.
Diodorus (17.102.5) does not exaggerate when he says that
Alexander 'spread the terror of his name throughout the
entire region', with fire, destruction, and wholesale enslavement. The ultra-fierce resistance he encountered was
due in large part to holy-war propaganda spread by the
Brahmin priests. As before, Alexander's only answer to
ideological opposition was sheer terrorism. Many Brahmins who fell into his hands were hanged as a deterrent.
One, on being asked why he had instigated a certain leader
to revolt, replied: 'Because I wished him to live with
honour or die with honour.' Here the king badly misjudged
his opponents. Resistance, far from being crushed by his
strong-arm methods, took on a new lease of life: before
300 B.C. every Macedonian garrison in the Land of the
Five Rivers had been wiped out.[16]

Perhaps near modern Shikarpore (details are uncertain:
the Indus has changed its course a number of times over the
centuries) Alexander divided his forces. Craterus, with
Polyperchon as his second-in-command, was to take three
battalions of the phalanx, the elephants, and all time-
expired Macedonian veterans, and march overland into
the province of Carmania. Here the fleet and the rest of the
army would rendezvous with him, either at the mouth of
the Euphrates, or at some nearer point along the Persian
Gulf. The route Craterus was to follow ran through the
Mulla pass to Quetta and Kandahar, thus traversing the
ancient satrapy of Arachosia. From here he was to march
south-west, by Lake Seistan, the Kerman Desert, and the
Jebal-Barez. Once again Alexander had been at some pains

to keep him well away from Hephaestion – who, we may note, took over his post as deputy supreme commander the moment he was gone. The most interesting aspect of this move, however, is the detailed geographical knowledge it reveals on Alexander's part. Desert conditions and shortage of available supplies in the regions which lay ahead made a division of forces essential: so much is obvious. What comes as a surprise is the degree and extent of the king's advance information: clearly he had the whole voyage of exploration already planned, complete with rendezvous-points. It is easy to forget the immensely valuable work which his intelligence section and surveyors and scientists were always doing in the background throughout his campaigns: mapping, measuring, collecting specimens, studying natural resources, sifting information of every type.* Without their constant assistance, their reports on everything from salt-mines to desert routes, the expedition would have gone a great deal less smoothly: might, indeed, have met with irreparable disaster.[17]

Alexander reached Pattala, at the head of the Indus delta, in July 325. The governor of the city had previously come to him with an offer of surrender, but was so alarmed by the king's punitive methods that he now evacuated both Pattala itself and the surrounding countryside. Since Alexander planned extensive harbour and dockyard works here (for which he would need coolie labour), he sent word to the refugees that they were welcome to come back and till their fields as before. Most of them did so. With the appointment of Peithon as governor of lower India to the

---

*Alexander himself, as we might expect, took great interest in Indian medical lore: when Ptolemy was hit by a poisoned arrow the king cured him with a plant now identified as *rauwolfa serpentina*, 'the first of the modern tranquillizers but used in India for thousands of years to cure snakebite, among other things' (Snyder, pp. 163–4, with note). The detailed attention which our sources lavish on this comparatively trivial incident testify to the widespread influence of Ptolemy's own memoirs, from which it was certainly drawn.

sea, Alexander's campaign of subjugation was complete. Greek writers, bedazzled by the glamour of this exotic and unknown region, vastly exaggerated the importance of what was, in fact, little more than a large-scale raid. Alexander penetrated no farther than West Pakistan, nor does his name once figure in the later Indian literary tradition. For a very brief period his representatives ruled – in theory if not always in fact – over a region extending from Kashmir to Karachi. But their hold on the country remained precarious, and to the Indians themselves they were never anything but mere barbarian aggressors. Indeed, no sooner had Alexander moved on than the destruction of his work began. Philip the satrap was killed by a group of mercenaries. Resistance gathered in the Punjab, under the leadership of a young Kshatriya commoner, Chandragupta. After Alexander's death Chandragupta was joined (ironically enough) by a Punjabi king named Parvataka, who is almost certainly Porus. Between them these two conquered the empire which Alexander had dreamed of, but never won.[18] The Mauryan dynasty founded by Chandragupta held sway eastward to Bengal and the Ganges, southward as far as Mysore.

Nor did Alexander ever appreciate how fundamentally alien the Indian temperament was to anything he had hitherto encountered. When he first reached Taxila he was struck – like every visitor from the West – by the naked Jain ascetics and teachers, who became known in Greek as *gymnosophistae*, or 'naked philosophers'. Numerous stories, most (but not all) apocryphal, are told about this confrontation of cultures. Alexander and his advisers, having the characteristic Greek taste for syncretic interpretations, seem to have convinced themselves that the *gymnosophistae* preached a local variant of Diogenes' Cynicism. There was just enough truth in this notion to prevent any serious examination of what they *did* think; and zealous Cynics had no scruples about filling in the gaps. (Only Pyrrho, who afterwards founded the Sceptic school, seems to have grasped something of their philosophy: his doctrines of inaction and contempt for external phenomena bore a considerable resemblance to Jain teaching.) Like so many aspects of Alexander's career, his encounters with the *gymnosophistae* soon became a topic for romance or myth. Yet certain anecdotes still have an unmistakable ring of truth about them. Alexander persuaded one holy man to abandon his life of ascetic contemplation and accompany the expedition – presumably as a tame travelling sage, an exotic addition to Alexander's Greek seers and Chaldaean astrologers. This person was written off by more high-principled ascetics as 'a slave to fleshly lusts' for choosing to serve any lesser master than God; he later burnt himself alive, a remorseful act of self-immolation. On another occasion, Alexander with his retinue passed a meadow where the *gymnosophistae* gathered for philosophical discussion. At the approach of the troops 'these venerable men stamped with their feet and gave no other sign of interest'. When Alexander, through an interpreter, inquired the reason for their curious behaviour, this was the reply he got: 'King Alexander, every man can possess only so much of the earth's surface as this we are standing on. You are but human like the rest of us, save that you are always busy and up to no good, travelling so many miles from your home, a nuisance to yourself and to others. Ah well! You will soon be dead, and then you will own just as much of the earth as will suffice to bury you.'[19] Alexander is said to have applauded such sentiments; he had reacted in much the same way after his encounter with Diogenes (see above, p. 123). However, as Arrian reminds us, 'his conduct was always the exact opposite of what he then professed to admire'.

At Pattala the Indus split into two main channels before reaching the sea. Alexander now left Hephaestion to fortify the citadel and supervise the construction of docks and harbours, while he himself set out on a reconnaissance voyage down the right-hand or western arm. The south-west monsoon was blowing, and the fleet suffered considerable damage from storms. At one point, very near the sea, they had to run for shelter up a side-channel, only to find themselves left high and dry by the tide – a phenomenon which, as Mediterranean sailors, they regarded at first with considerable alarm. They wandered helplessly about the mudflats, avoiding giant crabs and other unpleasant creatures, imagining they were stranded there for ever. Though this illusion lasted only a few hours, the fast tidal bore that lifted them off was just as frightening and caused further damage to the boats. Alexander carried out what running repairs he could, and sailed on. The fleet found good anchorage off an island in the mouth of the estuary. They had reached Ocean at last.

During his visit to Siwah, one question Alexander must have put to the Oracle was whether he would conquer all of Asia. Ammon, it seems, not only gave the hoped-for response, but also laid down what sacrifices Alexander must make to which gods when the prophecy should be fulfilled. That moment had now come, and the king duly honoured – with open acknowledgement – such deities as Ammon had prescribed. His campaign of eastern conquest could clearly go no farther. Nevertheless, he had to display his authority over Ocean, however, perfunctory or symbolic the gesture. He therefore sailed out to a second island, some twenty-five miles offshore, where – again on instructions – he set up altars to Ocean and Tethys. After a brief exploratory cruise along the coast, he returned to his anchorage in the estuary. Here he sacrificed bulls to Poseidon for a safe voyage home, and set off back up-river. Though the eastern arm of the Indus would give his fleet an extra 200 miles to sail, it might, he hoped, prove somewhat less hazardous.

In the event it gave him just what he was looking for. It was sheltered from monsoon winds. Its waters discharged into the Rann of Kutch, which at this period extended far further inland, as a vast landlocked salt-water lake. Having reconnoitred the passage through to the sea, Alexander took his cavalry a three days' journey westward along the coast. Parties were left at various points to dig fresh-water wells. A harbour and dock were built by the salt lake, and provided with a garrison.[20] This done, the king returned to base and began organizing his projected expedition in detail.

If the fleet was to make a voyage from the Indian Ocean into the Persian Gulf, it would need wells and supply-depots prepared for it at regular intervals. All reports agreed that the coast, for several hundred miles, was barren desert, a wind-scoured, dusty, red-rock wilderness known today as the Makran. Alexander planned to march by this route, hugging the coast as far as possible, with the main body of the army and all non-combatants. As they went they would dig wells and lay down supply-dumps. Provisions for four months were secured (Arrian 6.20.5: presumably grain and salted fish). From a close study of our evidence (see n. 22 below) it becomes clear what Alexander's strategy was. Fleet and army would advance according to a coordinated plan. The fleet would carry bulk supplies; the army would be responsible for finding water.* This was the highly successful amphibious strategy adopted by Xerxes in 480 for his invasion of Greece; but Alexander (who had doubtless borrowed it after studying Herodotus) should have noted that any lengthy separation of fleet and army was liable to have unfortunate consequences. In the event it directly occasioned the most catastrophic episode of his entire career.

Alexander's motives for undertaking this hazardous venture were somewhat mixed. He probably regarded the plan he had worked out as the best and safest method of getting both fleet and army through a peculiarly barren

---

*This becomes clear from the fact that when the fleet reached Hormuz, its crews were in perfectly good shape; whereas once the army had lost touch with its floating supply-depot, Alexander's starving troops were very soon reduced to eating their pack animals.

stretch of territory. He was genuinely concerned about the revictualling of the fleet: otherwise he might well have sent the entire expeditionary force by sea. Further, it would be dangerous to leave any unsubdued territory in the Iran–Baluchistan area: this meant reducing Gedrosia, the primitive satrapy bordered by the Makran. He also may well have been curious, as Arrian (8.32.11) suggests, to find out whether a viable trade-route could be opened up between India and the Euphrates.

Such considerations seem reasonable enough. But Nearchus (who was in a better position than most to know the truth) recorded that Alexander, *although aware of the difficulties,* nevertheless conceived a burning desire, a *pothos,* to march by this route (Arrian 8.20.1–2). According to tradition, both Queen Semiramis and Cyrus the Great had attempted the feat: the queen got through with twenty survivors, Cyrus with no more than seven. Once again Alexander was seized by the spirit of emulation: *ever to strive to be best.* Would it not stand as a glorious achievement if he were to succeed where they had failed, and bring his entire army safely through the Makran? So far Nearchus: it may also have occurred to Alexander, after studying the intelligence reports of what lay ahead of them, that his by now unwieldy host could do with a little trimming and pruning, especially among the non-combatants. This march, in fact, would be a survival of the fittest.

The king's most immediate problem was purchasing supplies. For whatever reason (see above, p. 414) the military chest had little left in it, and once again Alexander was reduced to making a whip-round among his friends. He asked Eumenes, his chief secretary, for 300 talents. Eumenes somewhat grudgingly protested that he could only spare a third of the sum required. Alexander, in a flash of fury, set fire to Eumenes' tent, and waited for him to rescue his hidden valuables. In this way he obtained over a thousand talents in gold and silver. At the same time many of the expedition's documents and records were destroyed (Plut.

Eum. 2.2–3). Some, perhaps, Alexander was not sorry to see lost, even though he afterwards wrote round to his various satraps and generals asking for duplicates. Since the treasures of the Persian campaigns were still intact, and the mints of Asia Minor in active production, it seems clear that (whether by accident or design) at least one consignment of bullion, and probably more, had failed to arrive. After some hesitation on Alexander's part, Nearchus was appointed admiral of the fleet. The king at first showed reluctance (says Nearchus) to hazard one of his closest friends on so perilous a mission; but persistence was finally rewarded, and Nearchus got the command. Troop morale was still low; Nearchus' presence would reassure the crews that they had a fair chance of survival. However, the fleet could not leave until the end of the monsoon, when the prevailing winds were due to veer round from the southwest and give them a following breeze – that is, in late September at the earliest. Alexander and the army, however, set out well ahead of Nearchus, towards the end of August. Thus, since no one could exactly foresee when the monsoon would terminate, a random time-element entered the relations between land and sea forces *ab initio*.

To begin with, however, all went as planned. Alexander and his men were marching through comparatively fertile territory. They dug wells along the shore, and a brisk punitive expedition brought the tribes immediately west of modern Karachi to heel. A city, Rhambacia, was founded here, some way from the sea. Apollophanes became satrap of the region, and Leonnatus also stayed behind, as military governor, with a considerable force at his disposal. Their instructions were to keep the natives docile and make preparations for the fleet's arrival.[21] At this point Alexander clearly had no shortage of supplies, since he collected, and left behind for Nearchus and the fleet, no less than ten days' rations of grain (Arrian 8.23.7–8).*

---

*So, at least, Nearchus alleges: as we shall see (below, p. 441) it is by no means impossible that this ambitious Cretan had good personal

Now Alexander moved on into Gedrosia, keeping as close to the shore as possible. His first encounter was with a grisly Stone Age tribe whom the Greeks nicknamed Ichthyophagi, or Fish-Eaters. They were hairy all over, with long matted locks and uncut nails like wild beasts' claws. Diodorus (17.105.3–4) calls them 'unfriendly and utterly brutish'. They wore animal pelts or shark-skins, and built their houses from the skeletons of stranded whales. Even their cattle lived off fish-meal, and had a fishy taste when eaten. To obtain provisions from them was virtually impossible. Nothing grew here except thorn and tamarisk and the occasional palm-tree.

As they pressed on into the Makran, the land became still more inhospitable. For a while Alexander kept advance-parties digging wells; but presently he reached the mountains of the Talar-i-Bund, the Makran coast range, which stretched all the way down to the sea. Because of this he was forced to make a long detour inland, away from any chance of rendezvous with the fleet, even supposing the fleet overtook him. It was now, predictably, that the real suffering began. They ran desperately short of water, and often had to march anything from 25 to 75 miles between one brackish well and the next, for the most part at night. When they got there, the men were so maddened with thirst that they often plunged straight into the pool, armour and all. Many died from the effects of over-drinking after de-hydration. Many more succumbed to heatstroke. In the end Alexander was forced to bivouac at least three or four miles from a water-point.

reasons for falsifying the record when he afterwards came to compose his account of the Gedrosian disaster. *Inter alia*, he had to explain why fleet and army never achieved a rendezvous en route, and justify himself for failing to provide Alexander with supplies. The first omission he could blame on the monsoon's vagaries; for the second he seems to have been reduced to the assertion that Alexander in fact had supplies and to spare: if he left ten days' rations for the fleet, how could the fleet's commander then be held responsible for the army's near-starvation?

Nevertheless, he contrived to preserve his prestige and popularity by sharing the men's worst hardships. Once, when a helmetful of muddy water had been found for him in some nearby gully – but no more was to be had – he laughed, thanked the donor, and then tipped the water out into the sand. 'So extraordinary was the effect of this action that the water wasted by Alexander was as good as a drink for every man in the army' (Arrian 6.26.3). It was ironic that during this terrible march the army should have passed through a region rich in myrrh and spikenard: the Phoenician merchants accompanying the expedition loaded up their pack-mules with these precious herbs, while soldiers hung branches of myrrh from their tents, and the spikenard roots they trampled as they advanced gave off a delectable aroma.

Under a brazen sky the long column struggled forward, up and down the sides of soft, shifting sand-dunes, endlessly repeated like waves of the sea, where wagons sank to the axles, and boots filled with burning grit. Poisonous snakes lurked in the herbage, poisonous plants were all around – prickly cucumbers that squirted a blinding juice, laurel-like shrubs which made pack-animals die foaming at the mouth. Date-palms, with their succulent 'cabbages', provided some relief, but too many unripe dates frequently choked the eater to death. Soon Alexander's troops were surreptitiously killing pack-animals and breaking open sealed stores. Alexander – wisely – affected not to notice: the problem now was sheer survival. Men fell out hourly, dying in the sun from exhaustion, or left behind when they were no longer fit to march.

Too much water could be as dangerous as too little. One night the baggage-train and non-combatants were encamped in a dry wadi – something any Macedonian officer should have known better than to permit – when a sudden flash-storm broke in the hills. Down roared a great torrent of water through the darkness, carrying away tents, baggage (including the royal pavilion), almost all the women and children, and large numbers of the remaining transport animals. Many soldiers had narrow escapes from drowning, and survived with nothing but their weapons and what they stood up in. Alexander at once sent off emergency requests to all the surrounding satrapies for food-stuffs and other essential suppies. These were to be dispatched (as presumably the messages had been sent) by racing camel, and await the army's arrival in Carmania. Whether it would be humanly possible for the satraps to carry out such orders in time seems more than doubtful. Perhaps Alexander's main object, even at this point, was to find some handy scapegoats for the disasters that had overtaken him.

The final catastrophe was a violent sandstorm, which obliterated all landmarks, so that even the guides lost their bearings and took a path which led farther and farther away from the coast. Alexander, realizing what had happened, set off south with a small cavalry detachment, and eventually reached the sea. Here he and his men dug wells in the gravel – and to their incredulous delight struck pure fresh water. For a week the whole army marched along this coastal strip, always finding water when they dug for it. Then Alexander's guides picked up the road that led inland to Pura, the Gedrosian capital. Sixty days after first entering the Makran, that ragged column of gaunt, sun-blackened weary men reached safety.[22] Their losses were appalling. Alexander had begun the march with perhaps 85,000 persons in all, a majority of them non-combatants: of these not more than 25,000 now survived. His Companion Cavalry was reduced from 1,700 to 1,000.[23] Horses, pack-mules, stores, equipment – all were lost. This disastrous march through the desert has been compared, and with good reason, to Napoleon's retreat from Moscow in 1812.

If Alexander had set out with the idea of surpassing Cyrus and Semiramis, his hubristic ambition had received something more than a sharp rebuke. If – as seems only too likely – he had by now come to regard himself as superior to all natural hazards, his pride and self-confidence must have been badly shaken. On both counts he had to find a scapegoat, and perhaps more than a scapegoat. Since he normally took intelligent and practical precautions to ensure that superiority, we may well ask ourselves whether he did not, in fact, have legitimate cause for complaint against certain key subordinates who (for whatever reason) had failed to carry out the orders assigned them. As we have seen (above, p. 426), his advance intelligence concerning Gedrosia and the adjacent regions was thorough, his planning (as always) meticulous. It is inconceivable that he did not know of the Talar-i-Bund's existence, or realize that it would necessitate a long detour inland.

From this there emerges the inescapable conclusion that Alexander (as we might assume in any case) had arranged at least one rendezvous with Nearchus before leaving the coast, to draw iron rations for his march through the desert. When the fleet did not appear on schedule, Alexander had no option but to press on without further delay. Every day he waited ate into his minimal reserves. Neither Nearchus nor the governors of Gedrosia, Susiana, Paraetecene and Carmania had sent him the supplies he so desperately needed. Nearchus could, and did, make convincing excuses for his failure – excuses into which Alexander, through sheer relief at seeing the fleet back at all, probably did not inquire over-closely. The satraps, who presented a correspondingly greater potential threat, were not so lucky.[24]

Alexander's subsequent behaviour makes it clear enough that he, at least, thought something worse than mere negligence was involved. Nor is it hard to see why. Harpalus had failed to send him consignments of bullion when he needed them, was giving himself royal airs and graces (see above, p. 414), and was widely held to be contemplating defection.[25] At least two, and probably several more, of his provincial governors had let him down badly during a crucially dangerous march. The fleet had vanished when he most needed it. A far less naturally paranoiac mind than Alexander's might well have deduced from these circum-

stances that Harpalus, Nearchus and the rest of them were
all in a widespread conspiracy against him, the object of
which was to encompass his death in the burning wastes of
the Gedrosian desert. The question is, were his suspicions
justified? At this distance in time, and with the limited
evidence at our disposal, we cannot return a firm verdict;
but the evidence for satrapal disaffection after Alexander
vanished into India should not be minimized,[26] and
Nearchus certainly had ample leisure to polish his own
version of the fleet's vicissitudes for Alexander and posterity.[27]

The king's first, and most obvious, victim was the wretched
Apollophanes (see above, p. 432), in whose satrapy the
disaster had taken place. Alexander now sent a letter
formally deposing him. This crossed with a dispatch from
Leonnatus, who reported that local tribal levies had attacked
his division, inflicted severe losses, and then withdrawn.
Among those killed was Apollophanes. Alexander, baulked
of his prey, did what he could by converting this defeat into
a propaganda victory, with Leonnatus destroying 6,000
natives for the loss of fifteen horsemen and a few footsoldiers.
Troop morale was not yet up to digesting another defeat.[28]

A more cheerful dispatch arrived from Craterus, who had
defeated two Persian nobles attempting a revolt, and was
bringing them on to Alexander in chains. But the general
news was far from encouraging. Rumours of treachery,
inefficiency, and large-scale embezzlement came in from
every side. Nothing, as yet, had been heard of the fleet.
Many officials, confident that Alexander would never
return from his Indian venture, had set up as independent
oriental despots, and equipped themselves with powerful
private armies. Every kind of luxurious excess and administrative corruption was reported. Here was a dangerous
situation – and one which made Harpalus look far less like
a figure of fun (not that by now Alexander can have had
many illusions left on *that* score). Nor could it have arisen
at a worse time. After the fearful casualties sustained in

Gedrosia, Alexander's own prestige had lost much of its charismatic lustre; the epithet *aniketos* (invincible) now bore a large interrogation mark after it. Unless the king acted with speed and decision, he might find himself up against something far worse than mere dereliction of duty. Frightened, guilty men make natural conspirators.

After a short rest period at Pura, Alexander set out again: clearly there was no time to be lost. His immediate destination was Salmous (Tepe Yaḥyā: cf. *Iran* 7, 1969, p. 185) in Carmania, some way inland from the Strait of Hormuz. Wisely, he relaxed discipline during this march. There is a persistent tradition that for seven days he and his army reeled through the rich countryside in a splendid Dionysiac rout. Alexander, like Philip, was much addicted to such quasi-religious revelry, and the story is by no means incredible.

Such junketings, however, did not distract him from more important business. When the army entered Carmania it was welcomed by Astaspes, the Iranian satrap. Alexander already had a dossier on this man, who (quite apart from failing to get supplies through) had allegedly been plotting treason during the expedition's absence in India. For the moment nothing was said. Alexander greeted Astaspes warmly, took everything he had to offer, and confirmed him in his position. By the time he reached Tepe Yaḥyā, however, the king had collected more evidence. He had also felt the mood of sullen hostility in the province as a whole. Astaspes was abruptly put under arrest and then executed. Alexander's satrapal purge had begun. In fact it might be said to have begun earlier; the satrap of Paropamisus (Hindu Kush), whom he replaced by his father-in-law Oxyartes, was likewise afterwards executed for treason.

Alexander's recent summons to the various satraps to meet him in Carmania with provisions and transport animals plainly had more than one purpose. As soon as the Ecbatana contingent arrived, their leaders (Cleander, Sitalces, and two deputy commanders) were arrested and clapped in irons. As Parmenio's murderers (see above,

p. 346) they were by no means popular with the troops, so that Alexander found no shortage of witnesses, both Persian and Macedonian, to testify against them, 'alleging that they had plundered temples, disturbed ancient tombs, and committed other crimes of a violent and tyrannical nature against the people of the province' (Arrian 6.27.4; cf. QC 10.1.1–5). Cleander and Sitalces were condemned to death; we hear nothing more of their subordinates, who presumably suffered the same fate. Cleander, of course, was Coenus' brother. All of them had been potentially involved with the elusive Harpalus (Cleander, indeed, belonged to the same family as the imperial treasurer, the royal out-kingdom House of Elimiotis).

The independent control exercised by this group over the great central satrapies was dangerous enough in itself, without proof positive of treason. But if a junta did in fact exist, Alexander lost no time in eliminating it. Harpalus himself, however, escaped capture: he knew better than to go anywhere near Alexander from now on. When the summons came, he fled to the coast, with a body of 6,000 mercenaries and some 5,000 talents in silver. (Why did he not take more – scoop the pool, in fact? Is it possible that Alexander had in fact pre-empted such a move by dividing his treasure up among more independent custodians than our sources would suggest?) From here he sailed for Athens, hoping to cash in on his benefactions and honorary citizenship.

Harpalus' sudden panic-stricken flight, coming so soon after the execution of Cleander and Sitalces, removed any real fear of an organized *coup*. Alexander was playing an extremely shaky hand with his usual cool flair and psychological insight. Perhaps, too, he remembered the technique adopted by Artaxerxes Ochus in 358, when faced with a very similar situation. One of the first things which that bloodthirsty monarch did (having killed off his relatives and put down a provincial revolt) was order his satraps in Asia Minor to disband their mercenaries. In Artaxerxes' case this decree provoked a rebellion. Alexander, however, had prepared the ground somewhat better, and when he 'wrote to all his generals and satraps in Asia, ordering them, as soon as they had read his letter, to disband their mercenaries instantly' (Diod. 17.106.3) the order was obeyed without question.

On the other hand, only dire political necessity could have dictated it. There were quite enough unemployed mercenaries loose in Asia as it was, without adding to their number (see above, p. 421). The social consequences of this policy were only too predictable. If they lacked a paymaster, they would turn to freelance marauding for a livelihood. Soon all Asia was full of such wandering bands, and the moment the resistance movement began to develop again in Greece, they naturally made their way across the Aegean and joined it. Again, when heads began to roll, it was not simple corruption that invariably brought Nemesis in its wake: there had to be a political angle as well. Cleomenes, the Greek who had made himself *de facto* satrap of Egypt (see above, pp. 278–9), had about the most scandalous record for graft and general financial huckstering of all Alexander's administrators. But he was loyal, efficient, and – best of all – *not Macedonian*. The king confirmed him in his command. Philoxenus in Cilicia also got away with a great deal – though he nearly ruined his chances by offering Alexander a pretty boy-prostitute as a present. The implications were hardly flattering, and Alexander was not the man to let anyone choose his lovers for him.[29]

It was now December (325). Craterus arrived safely, with his troops and elephants; shortly afterwards came a report that Nearchus had been seen in the vicinity. At first Alexander could not credit this news, and actually arrested the provincial governor for spreading false rumours. Even when Nearchus appeared – in ragged garments, hair long and matted with brine – the king's first thought was that he and his five companions were the only survivors. Bitter distress at the presumed loss of the fleet eclipsed any pleasure he might have felt at his admiral's escape. But as soon as Nearchus revealed that the fleet had come through intact, and now lay at Hormuz undergoing a refit, while the crews were well and fit, Alexander's delight knew no bounds.

Those who made the sea-voyage had their own adventures to tell. Nearchus, with breathtaking effrontery, had (he said) been forced to weigh anchor *earlier* than he originally intended, because of attacks by the natives: on Alexander's departure the natives had lost their terror and begun to behave like free men. Later, of course, the monsoon, and storms, and various accidents had combined to delay him for up to a fortnight beyond Alexander's marching time of sixty days, but there was, clearly, to be no suggestion of deliberate loitering. Nor did Nearchus intend to admit that he and his men had had a comparatively easy time of it. The coast, he claimed, had proved barren and inhospitable. He even went so far as to assert that supplies had begun to run out (not much more than two of those four months' rations were accounted for: what had become of the rest?). In their hunger, so the story ran, they had been compelled to raid a friendly town and strip it of provisions. When on the very verge of starvation they killed and ate seven camels. Nor were the perils of the deep forgotten in this recital. The sudden appearance of a school of whales caused great alarm, but Nearchus – rising nobly to the occasion – had all the trumpets of the fleet blown simultaneously, and charged them, on which they dived out of sight.

Alexander now made sacrifice to the gods, and held a great athletic and musical festival, in thanksgiving for the safe return of his fleet, and (according to Aristobulus) '*for his conquest of India and the escape of his army from Gedrosia*' (Arrian 6.28.3). What the survivors made of this stunning if pious lie one can only surmise. Nearchus was the hero of the hour: he headed the ceremonial procession, while the troops showered him with ribbons and flowers. The prize for singing and dancing went to Alexander's favourite, the eunuch Bagoas (see above, p. 333). Everyone in the audience told the king he should kiss the winner. Alexander duly obliged.

It would be interesting to know how Bagoas got on with Hephaestion: perhaps their spheres of ambition and influence were so different that they could not regard one another as genuine rivals. Hephaestion's bickering with Craterus, on the other hand, broke out the moment they were in contact again. The two men actually drew swords on each other. Alexander, who separated them, rebuked Hephaestion publicly, 'calling him a fool and a madman for not knowing that without Alexander's favour he was nothing'. (Plut. *Alex.* 47.6). Craterus received *his* dressing-down in private.[30] An official reconciliation now took place; but the sooner these two touchy individuals could be separated again, clearly, the better. Before Alexander set out for Persepolis, in January 324, he placed Hephaestion in charge of the baggage-train, the elephants, and the bulk of the army, and dispatched them by the long, easy coast road, where they would find plentiful supplies. He himself, with the Companion Cavalry and the light infantry, travelled overland. We may be tolerably certain that Craterus went with him. Nearchus, at his own request, had stayed with the fleet: their next rendezvous was to be at Susa.[31]

The satrap of Persis had died, and his place was now filled by a wealthy Iranian nobleman named Orsines, who claimed descent from Cyrus. As Alexander approached Pasargadae, Orsines came out and met him with rich gifts of every kind, including many for his friends and commanders. To Bagoas, however, he gave nothing. When told, discreetly, that the eunuch was Alexander's favourite, he replied with aristocratic contempt that 'he was honouring the friends of the king, not his harlots' (QC 10.1.26). This remark soon got back to Bagoas, who at once began a vicious smear-campaign, systematically poisoning Alexander's mind against Orsines. When it was found that the tomb of Cyrus at Pasargadae had been looted by vandals, and all its rich gold and silver treasures stolen, Bagoas saw his chance. It was not hard to convince the all too suspicious king that Orsines had been, as it were, robbing dead Peter to pay live Paul. The satrap was arrested, convicted, and hanged – with a last scornful word for the minion who had brought about his downfall.

After the Gedrosian disaster, a change for the worse seems to have taken place in Alexander. He became increasingly paranoiac and suspicious, ready to believe any calumny against his officials, however unlikely its source. He would now punish even minor offences with sternness, on the grounds that an official guilty of minor irregularities might easily progress to more serious crimes. This line may have been dictated in part by the purge he was carrying out; but it hints at something rather more fundamental. There is a tendency nowadays to pooh-pooh the belief (universally held in antiquity) that Alexander's character had by this time undergone very considerable degeneration. This does not imply a fundamental *change* in his nature: the man who burnt Persepolis was also the boy who had destroyed Thebes. From the very beginning his ambition had been insatiable, and murderous when thwarted. But in any consideration of his later years, the combined effects of unbroken victories, unparalleled wealth, power absolute and unchallenged, continual heavy physical stress, and incipient alcoholism cannot be lightly set aside. Abstemious as a boy, he now regularly drank to excess. Nor was it political pressure alone which now dictated the king's actions, but his own increasingly dominant and uncontrollable megalomania.[32]

From Pasargadae Alexander moved on to Persepolis, where Orsines was executed. To succeed him as satrap the king appointed his shieldbearer, Peucestas, who had recently been made a supernumerary Gentleman of the Bodyguard. Peucestas was utterly loyal and of undistinguished origins: two first-class qualifications in Alexander's eyes. He had, moreover, dutifully adopted the king's orientalizing habits, and spoke fluent Persian. At the same time Harpalus' vacant post as imperial treasurer went to a competent nonentity, a Rhodian accountant named Antimenes. Sensitive administrative appointments, Alexander seems to have decided, were safer (and indeed more efficiently discharged) in the hands of anonymous Greek bureaucrats or sedulously loyal underlings.

Towards the end of February 324 Alexander reached Susa, where he made a lengthy halt, and his satrapal purge finally ran its course. The governor of Susiana and his son were both put to death on the usual charges: maladministration, extortion, and, most important, failure to deliver supplies to the army in Gedrosia. The satrap, Abulites, offered Alexander 3,000 talents in cash as a substitute. The king had the money thrown to his horses. 'What kind of provisions do you call these?' he asked, when they refused to touch it. He is said to have dispatched Abulites' son in person, transfixing the wretched youth with a spear. The ghost of Cleitus, it seems had ceased to trouble him. At the same time he was already full of plans for further campaigns of conquest, this time in the western Mediterranean. Carthage, Spain and Italy were all mentioned as possible targets. There was even a rumour that he meant to circumnavigate Africa. Nearchus arrived safely with the fleet, and the two men discussed this new project. The king sent orders for the construction of no less than 700 large new galleys at Thapsacus on the Euphrates. The kings of Cyprus were commanded to provide this flotilla with copper, hemp and sailcloth.[33]

All organized opposition in Asia was now effectively crushed, and Alexander felt free to proceed with his systematic policy of orientalization. Despite some ingenious special pleading by modern scholars,[34] it is safe to say that this did *not* imply any ideological belief in racial fusion or the brotherhood of man. The arguments used to promote such a view have been adequately disposed of elsewhere,[35] and need no more than a brief mention in this context. Plutarch (*Alex.* 27.6) has a story about Alexander's conversation with the priest of Zeus-Ammon at the Siwah Oasis – where, we recall, he had just been proclaimed the son of god. The priest observed, platitudinously but undeniably, that God was the common father of mankind; to which Alexander replied 'that though God was indeed the common father of all mankind, still he made peculiarly his own the noblest and best of them'. From this statement Tarn somehow contrived to extract an endorsement by Alexander of the brotherhood of man. In fact, of course, it points in another direction altogether, and suggests a far more sinister slogan, given wide currency by George Orwell's *Animal Farm*: 'All animals are equal, but some animals are more equal than others.'

Apart from this curious assertion, Tarn's case rests largely on two passages: the sixth chapter of Plutarch's first rhetorical treatise *De Alexandri Magni Fortuna aut Virtute* (*Moral.* 329A–D), and Arrian's account of the supposed 'international love-feast' which followed Alexander's reconciliation with his men after the mutiny at Opis (Arrian 7.11.8–9). The latter episode will be scrutinized in its proper context (see below, pp. 453 ff.); of the former disquisition one need only say that Plutarch wrote it when very young, as an exercise devoted to proving the highly dubious proposition that Alexander, by his deeds, showed himself a true philosopher of action. By the time he came to compose the *Life*, Plutarch had discreetly abandoned this unprofitable paradox; Tarn, of course, interprets the change of attitude as middle-aged loss of idealism – 'the fire had burnt low and was half swamped by his much reading.'[36] Any reader who has followed Alexander's career with attention this far should be able to assess the nature, and extent, of the king's idealism for himself.

That Alexander (or his propaganda section) used various philosophical notions concerning the unity of mankind to put an acceptable gloss on what otherwise has been construed, with justice, as mere political or militaristic opportunism is by no means impossible. Such ideas had been circulating at least since the fifth century,[37] and could obviously be utilized to justify an expansionist policy of conquest. One promising propaganda line still in use today can be extrapolated from Plutarch (*Moral.* 328E), who argued that those defeated by Alexander were luckier than those who escaped him, since the former received the blessings of Greek culture and philosophy, whereas the latter were left in their backward and uncouth primitivism. A publicist such as Anaxarchus may well have used these arguments on Alexander's behalf, thus starting a tradition which Plutarch in due course picked up; but for a modern historian to take them *au pied de la lettre*, to mistake propaganda for honestly held beliefs, shows political naivety of a very high order.

Any steps which Alexander took towards racial integration were strictly limited, and with immediate, purely practical ends in view. His policy, far from being dictated by the impulses of philanthropic idealism, was restricted to the higher echelons of government service and the army (the officer corps in particular); its two main objectives were to assimilate Persian generals and colonels into the existing command structure, and to create a joint Perso-Macedonian administrative class. Indeed, it could plausibly be argued that Alexander's ultimate aim was to discard his Macedonian cadres altogether. After the heavy losses sustained in India and the Makran, he reduced the number of Companion Cavalry divisions from eight to four, and then added a fifth, based on the Royal Squadron. For the first time, Iranians were not only brigaded with these units at squadron level, but fully integrated. Some privileged Persians were actually admitted to the Royal Squadron, and issued with Macedonian arms.

To make matters worse, the 30,000 Iranian youths whom Alexander had sent to be given a Macedonian military training (see above, pp. 371–2) now reappeared at Susa, having completed their long and arduous course. They were superbly equipped, bursting with energy and enthusiasm, never weary of displaying their expertise at weapons-drill, their marvellous fitness and discipline. Alexander was loud in their praises. He not only called them his 'Successors', which was bad enough, but made it clear that if necessary they could be used as a 'counterbalance [*antitagma*] to the Macedonian phalanx' (Diod. 17.108.3). It is hardly surprising, then, that their presence caused deep alarm and resentment among Alexander's veterans, who with a mixture of scorn and envy nicknamed them 'the young wardancers'. On top of Alexander's autocratic behaviour and Persian dress, the unapproachable pomp and protocol of his court life, all this became 'a cause of deep resentment to the Macedonians, who could not but feel that Alexander's whole outlook was becoming tainted with orientalism, and that he no longer cared a rap for his own people or his own native ways' (Arrian 7.6.5).

To a large extent this fear was well-grounded. Babylon had long since replaced Pella as the centre of Alexander's universe; he cared little more about what happened in Greece, now, than he would about any other province on the periphery of his vast empire. It was reported about this time, for instance, that Olympias and Cleopatra had raised a faction against Antipater, with Cleopatra taking Macedonia for her province, while Olympias kept Epirus. Alexander's only comment on this was that his mother had made the more sensible choice, since Macedonians would never agree to be ruled by a woman.[38]

The king's high-handed, not to say dictatorial, efforts to enforce top-level integration reached a climax with the famous Susa mass-marriages. At a ceremony of extraordinary splendour, between eighty and one hundred high Macedonian officers took Persian or Median brides, from the noblest families in Iran. The weddings were all solemnized in Persian style. The bridegrooms sat on chairs, in order of precedence; then, after a toast, their brides came in, took them by the hand, and kissed them. Every guest who sat down to the banquet which followed had a gold cup before him. The celebrations went on for no less than five days. Alexander himself took *two* wives at this ceremony, the daughters respectively of Darius and of Artaxerxes Ochus. If he was going to strengthen his claim on the Achaemenid throne he might as well make a thorough job of it – even if this meant being saddled with no less than three regnant queens. Hephaestion he also married to a daughter of Darius – ostensibly because he wanted their children as his own nephews and nieces.

Hephaestion's rivals, however, would not be slow to see another, more ominous, explanation for this royal favour. Already the office of Chiliarch, or grand vizier, had been revived for him. He had recently taken over as sole commandant of the Companion Cavalry, despite Alexander's earlier resolution never again to entrust this post to one man (see above, p. 348). Whatever Alexander may have said to him in a moment of anger (see above, p. 442), he was now, beyond any doubt, the second man in the empire and the king's most likely successor. None of this increased his popularity. Nor did the marriages themselves have the effect which Alexander hoped to achieve. They had been made willy-nilly, at the king's express command, and almost all of them were repudiated soon after his death. To the Macedonians they symbolized Alexander's oriental despotism at its very worst. His idea of creating 'a new ruling class of mixed blood, which would be free of all national allegiance or tradition' proved an utter failure.[39]

His troops now thoroughly distrusted him, and he was reduced to pacifying them by means of wholesale bribery. Sometimes this worked; sometimes it proved unexpectedly disastrous. The men had no objection to his compiling a register of those who had married Asiatic wives, since his purpose in doing so was to give them all belated wedding-presents (the total number involved was over 10,000). But his next step, though clearly meant as a *douceur*, was not nearly so well received. Most of the men were heavily in debt to the traders, merchants, horse-copers and brothel-keepers who accompanied the expedition (the situation would doubtless have been worse had not a number of outstanding debts been written off in the burning sands of the Gedrosian desert). Now that Alexander once more had access to ample funds – Harpalus, as we have seen, embezzled a small fraction only of the 180,000 talents realized after Persia fell – he decided it was high time these accounts were settled, and to win favour he announced that he would settle them himself. He therefore called for a detailed schedule, with names, so that payment could be made at once.

The response was minimal: hardly anyone put his name down. All ranks assumed, instantly, that this was a trick of Alexander's, to find out which of them had overspent their army pay. Furious, Alexander informed them that a king always, in duty bound, spoke the truth to his subjects, and that they had no right to presume otherwise. After this somewhat breathtaking assertion, he had banking-tables set up in camp, and instructed the pay-clerks to settle all outstanding claims on the production of a bond or IOU. No names were to be taken. Convinced at last, and with grudging gratitude, the men now came forward. This piece of open-handed munificence cost Alexander 20,000 talents.[40]

A far more urgent problem, and one largely created by Alexander's own policies, was that of the countless unemployed Greek mercenaries still at large. From a merely social menace (which was bad enough) they looked like becoming a serious political and military threat. Many of them were exiles, victims of those puppet oligarchies which Antipater, on the king's orders, maintained in Greece. Their sole means of livelihood had been to take service under Darius. By so doing they virtually outlawed themselves, since their allegiance to Persia was regarded as treason against the Hellenic League. Alexander had very soon learnt that a tough line against mercenaries did not pay off; but this made little difference to the Greek cities of the league, which were in no mood now or ever, to re-absorb their old political enemies. There was thus created a large body of homeless and drifting men who could only be kept out of mischief so long as they had regular military employment. The king had already taken steps to ease this problem. He enrolled all the mercenaries he could find room for in his own army, and, as we have seen, planted numerous garrison-colonies throughout the Far East. This by no means accounted for them all, however; and some, in any case, loathed Alexander and all he stood for so much that they refused to serve under him whatever the inducement. What brought the crisis to a head, of course, was the king's emergency decree ordering the satraps to dissolve their private armies (see above, pp. 439–40). This at once threw a vast body of well-trained, ruthless toughs out of work, and made them available on the international market. Moreover, when Alexander began his purge of imperial administrators, quite a few Persian satraps and commanders seized what funds they could and fled to Taenarum, in southern Laconia, now being organized as an anti-Macedonian recruiting-centre.

This conjunction was too good an opportunity to ignore, and an Athenian general, Leosthenes – probably with the connivance of his government – started running an under-ground ferry-service for mercenaries, from Asia Minor to the Peloponnese. Here was a potentially explosive situation indeed. The mercenaries had found a centre, an organiza-tion, and leaders who could pay them – Harpalus among others, who now reached Taenarum with his 5,000 talents still intact. The 3,000 rebel settlers from Bactria (see above, p. 421) also made their way back to Greece about this time. Unless Alexander took firm action, fast, he looked like having a major crisis on his hands.

But what action could he take? Professor Badian (*MP*, p. 220) puts the problem in a nutshell: 'He could not disband the concentrations of desperadoes; he knew that

he could not, on the whole, re-enlist them; he had found
that he could not resettle them. The only solution was to
send them home.' Most of these men were his implacable
enemies; but even they might well feel better disposed
towards him if he was responsible for terminating their exile.
On the other hand, the puppet governments backed by
Antipater would sing a very different tune when compelled
to take back all their radical opponents: that could not be
helped.

Alexander now drafted a proclamation, addressed directly
to the exiles themselves. It read as follows: 'King Alexander
to the exiles from the Greek cities. We have not been the
cause of your exile, but, save for those of you who are
under a curse [i.e. for sacrilege or murder: Alexander also
made an exception in the case of the Thebans], we shall be
the cause of your return to your own native cities. We have
written to Antipater about this to the end that if any
cities are not willing to restore you, he may constrain them'
(Diod. 18.8.4). In other words, the king was preparing,
with great finesse, to ditch his Greek quislings (who were
expendable); to shift the blame for the exiles' plight, by
implication, on to Antipater (who was not expendable yet,
but soon would be); and to collect some easy popular
credit by reversing the previous Macedonian party line
and supporting democrats for a change. The decree was
bound to produce a whole spate of litigation and administrative tangles; detailed instructions were therefore drawn
up for those who would be required to implement it.[41]

In March the final draft was read out to Alexander's
assembled troops. The king wanted an official announcement made at the Olympic Games that summer, and his
special envoy Nicanor – Aristotle's adopted son – left on
this mission soon afterwards. With him he took a second,
unrelated decree, which has aroused considerable controversy among scholars, but seems to have been regarded by
the Greeks themselves as a joke – and one in somewhat
questionable taste, at that. Alexander now required that the

cities of the league should publicly acknowledge him as a god. That this was a mere political device[42] is unlikely in the extreme: in fact the *practical* advantages that Alexander could derive from his own deification were virtually nil. It would inevitably antagonize the Macedonians (a prospect however, which by now he must have regarded with some equanimity), and Persian opinion was bound to consider it sheer blasphemy. Sophisticated Greeks would ridicule the king's pretensions with mocking epigrams. Perhaps the best (certainly the most ironic) comment came from Damis the Spartan. When the question of divine honours was under debate, he said: 'Since Alexander desires to be a god, let him be a god.'[43]

Whatever his divination meant to anyone else, it is plain that Alexander himself took it very seriously indeed. All his life, in a sense, he had been moving towards this final apotheosis. Divine blood ran in his veins; heroes and demigods were numbered among his ancestors; his mother's dark hints concerning his begetting had been given fresh dimensions by the Pharaonic coronation ceremony in Memphis, and Ammon's revelations during his pilgrimage to the Siwah Oasis. If superhuman achievements conferred godhead (as Anaxarchus had suggested in Bactria) then Alexander had unquestionably earned himself a place in any pantheon: his deeds by now far outshone those of Achilles or Heracles. Aristotle had taught him that the true king was a god among men. The dying Isocrates had argued that nothing would remain for the conqueror of Asia but deification.

Year by year, with that growing isolation from one's fellow-men (and hence from reality) that is the penalty of an unbroken ascent to absolute power, Alexander's control over his own latent megalomania had grown progressively weaker. What finally broke it were the psychological shocks inflicted by the mutiny at the Beas and the nightmare of the Gedrosian desert. 'He took refuge from the insecurity of power in the greater exercise of power: like a god intervening in the affairs of mortals, he would order the fate of princes and of nations.'[44] He became a god when he ceased wholly to trust his powers as a man, taking the divine shield of invincibility to combat his inner fear of failure, the divine gift of eternal youth as a talisman against the spectres of old age, sickness, death: the perils of the flesh that reminded him of his own mortality. Alcoholism bred paranoia: his dreams became grandiose lunacies. He was formidable still; but he had come very near the end of the road.[45]

In spring 324 Alexander left Susa. Hephaestion, with the bulk of the infantry, was dispatched west to the Tigris, by the overland route. The king himself sailed down the River Eulaeus, cruised along the coast until he reached the Tigris estuary, and then made his way upstream to Hephaestion's camp. From here he continued as far as Opis, the highest navigable point on the river, some 200 miles north of Babylon. The Persians had built a series of weirs to prevent enemy squadrons raiding upstream; Alexander's engineers systematically cleared these dams as he advanced, and built others off the main stream to ensure efficient irrigation of the delta.[46] It was probably during this journey, somewhere between the Eulaeus and the Tigris estuary, that the king founded Alexandria-in-Susianis (Charax), a port which subsequently became the main entrepôt for Babylon. The removal of the weirs similarly suggests, among other things, a wish to encourage trade and commerce.

At Opis, Alexander assembled his Macedonian troops, and announced the imminent demobilization 'of all men unfit through age or disablement for further service' (Arrian 7.8.1). He promised them lavish bonuses and severance pay, enough to make them the envy of their fellow-countrymen when they returned home (not to mention a walking advertisement for future recruits). 'Doubtless,' Arrian observes, 'he meant to gratify them by what he said.' Doubtless. But he knew their cumulative

grievances, the rebellious state they were in. If they mutinied again, he was going to make sure they did so when the
odds were all in his favour.[47] In any case, his words produced a near-riot.[48] Those he proposed to release shouted
that it was an insult to wear men out with long service and
then throw them on the scrap-heap. The younger time-
expired veterans demanded their own discharge. They had
served as long, fought as hard; why discriminate between
them? All the pent-up resentment against the king's
orientalizing policy burst out in ugly heckling and barrack-
ing.[49] Underneath it all they were scared: scared that he no
longer needed them, that they would become a tiny isolated minority in a virtually all-Persian army, that he had
the whip-hand at last, and knew it.

Their worst fear (and with good reason) was that 'he
would establish the permanent seat of his kingdom in
Asia', that they would not see home again for years, perhaps never. In the end they threatened to walk out on him
en masse. 'Go on and conquer the world with your young
war-dancers!' one veteran shouted – a bitter allusion to the
Persian 'Successors'. '*With his father Ammon, you mean,*'
retorted another.[50] The cry was taken up generally, amid
jeers and laughter. It certainly had its effect. In a blinding
fury[51] Alexander sprang down from the dais, accompanied
by his officers of the guard, and strode through the ranks
pointing out the chief troublemakers. Thirteen men were
arrested, and dragged off to summary execution.[52]

A horrified silence fell. Then the king, with that psychological flair which never deserted him in a crisis, went
straight back to the platform, where he began a cuttingly
contemptuous speech by listing all the benefits and favours
the Macedonian army had received *from his father Philip*.[53]
Philip, he said, had found them a 'tribe of impoverished
vagabonds' dressed in sheepskins, unable to defend their
own frontiers. When he died, they were masters of the
greatest state in the Aegean. 'Yet,' Alexander went on,
'these services are small compared with my own' – which

he then proceeded to enumerate in full. He reproached his
men bitterly for their disloyalty and cowardice. Then came
the final thrust. 'You all wish to leave me,' he cried. 'Go,
then! Out of my sight!' With that he swept off to his private
quarters, leaving the assembled troops silent and dumb-
founded: for some while they stood there like sheep, at an
utter loss what to do next.[54]

As usual on such occasions, Alexander shut himself up
incommunicado, and waited. Like his hero and exemplar
Achilles, he could think of no worse punishment to inflict
on his fellow-warriors than to deprive them of his incomparable and indispensable presence. Crowds of veterans
stood about hopelessly outside his pavilion. He refused to
see them. His psychological shock-tactics had never been
more skilfully employed.[55] On the third day he let it be
known that he was using the 'Successors' to form new
Persian units on the lines of the old Macedonian *corps
d'élite* – a Persian Royal Squadron and Companion Cavalry,
a Persian Guards Brigade. At the same time he summoned
the cream of the Iranian fighting nobility, and appointed them to all brigade commands previously held by
Macedonians.[56] These high dignitaries were also, in
Achaemenid fashion, termed the king's 'kinsmen', and entitled to exchange the kiss of friendship with him.[57]

When the troops learnt what was happening their resistance broke down altogether: this kind of brutal emotional
blackmail got clean past their guard. They all rushed to
Alexander's pavilion, weeping and shouting and begging to
be let in, condemning themselves as worthless ingrates,
asking for any punishment rather than this barbarian
usurpation. They offered to surrender both the instigators
of the mutiny and 'those who had led the cry against the
king'. They refused to disperse until Alexander dealt with
them: it was a sitdown strike in reverse.[58] Having thus
manoeuvred them into a suitably contrite mood, Alexander
emerged from seclusion prepared to be magnanimous. At
the sight of all those battle-scarred old toughs crying their

eyes out he shed tears himself – probably from sheer relief. One elderly, grizzled cavalry officer, who acted as spokesman, said their main grievance was Alexander's having made Persians his kinsmen, privileged to exchange the kiss of friendship, when no Macedonian had ever received such an honour. Here was one occasion that cost nothing. 'But I regard you *all* as my kinsmen,' the king exclaimed. At this many of those present, led by the old cavalry officer, came forward and kissed him: as a symbol of public reconciliation the gesture left little to be desired.[59] Afterwards they all picked up their arms (thrown down at the doors in token of supplication) and marched back to camp, bawling the victory paean at the tops of their voices; though one might have thought that if anyone had a right to sing that particular song just then it was Alexander himself.

Nevertheless, the Macedonians were still by far his best troops, and he had no hesitation in flattering them with a grandiose public gesture once he had gained his point. Another vast banquet now took place,[60] to celebrate a double reconciliation: between Alexander and his veterans, between Persians and Macedonians. By addressing the mutineers as 'kinsmen' the king had raised them, socially speaking, to the level of any Persian noble: this privileged status was emphasized at.the banquet itself, where they had the seats of honour beside him and drank from the royal mixing-bowl. There is no hint here of that international love-feast, that celebration of the Brotherhood of Man which at least one scholar[61] has professed to find in the banquet at Opis. Persians were placed firmly *below* Macedonians in order of precedence, and other races, again, below them. When Alexander made his famous prayer at the feast for 'harmony [*homonoia*] and fellowship [*koinonia*] of rule between Macedonians and Persians' he meant precisely what he said, and no more – nor is there much doubt which race he meant to be senior partner.*

---

*The evidence of Plutarch (*Alex.* 71.4–5, *Moral.* 329A–D), combined with the use of the terms *homonoia* and *koinonia*, both philosophical

As soon as the celebrations were over, Alexander went ahead with his demobilization scheme – but on a far more massive scale than he had originally planned.[62] No less than 11,000 veterans were discharged, a total which suggests that most of the younger time-expired men went with them. Alexander's intention had been to retain a Macedonian nucleus of 13,000 infantry and 2,000 cavalry in Asia for garrison duties. After such an exodus he may well have had to supplement even this basic figure from Persian sources. The terms of discharge, moreover, were extremely generous. Active-service pay was to be continued throughout the period spent travelling home – an eloquent hint as to the probable conditions to be encountered en route. Over and above this, each man received a severance bonus of one talent. Alexander sent instructions to Antipater that special seats must be reserved for them in the theatre and at all public contests. Orphaned children of men who had died on campaign were to receive their father's pay.

At the same time, the king insisted that all native wives or concubines, together with their offspring, should be left behind – to avoid friction (he said) between them and the men's original families in Macedonia. He promised that the sons of these unions would receive, gratis, a good Macedonian-style education – 'with particular attention to their military training'.[63] When they were grown up, he added, somewhat vaguely, he would bring them back to Macedonia. In fact, from these boys – there were about 10,000 of them – he meant to create 'a royal army of mixed blood and no fixed domicile – children of the camp, who knew no loyalty but to him'.[64] He clearly did not plan any end to his

commonplaces, does indeed suggest that Anaxarchus and his associates had been busy creating a suitable intellectual background for the reconciliation at Opis, which on both military and political grounds was absolutely essential for the implementation of Alexander's future projects. But the king's own beliefs, insofar as they can be determined at all, rest on the Deification Decree. All men might well be brothers; but – as Plutarch (*Alex.* 27.6) eloquently suggests – they were to be brothers under *him*.

campaigns in the foreseeable future. Aristobulus commented on his insatiable thirst for conquest, and his plans for western conquest as far as the Atlantic were well known.[65]

As commander of the discharged veterans on their long homeward march Alexander chose Craterus, with Polyperchon as his second-in-command. But this apparently routine appointment was merely a prelude to the most coveted post in the empire. When Craterus reached Macedonia, he was 'to assume control of Macedonia, Thrace and Thessaly, and *assure the freedom of Greece*' (Arrian 7.12.4). In other words, he would supersede Antipater as regent – or rather, now, as viceroy. Antipater himself received orders to hand over his command, raise fresh drafts of Macedonians as replacements for those lately discharged, and bring them out to Babylon.

Antipater had known for a long time that the next blow might well be aimed at him. He had had a decade now in which to consolidate his position. His defeat of King Agis had left him supreme in Greece, without fear of opposition: it was after this victory that Alexander began to denounce him for 'affecting royal pretensions'. He seems to have won his battle of wills with Olympias about the same time; the queen mother now retired to Epirus, whence she kept up a non-stop smear-campaign against Antipater in correspondence with her son. It is plausibly suggested (though by late and untrustworthy sources) that it was these letters from Olympias which finally drove the king to take action against his deputy in Europe.[66] Were there any more substantial grounds for suspicion?

Antipater had been deeply and genuinely shocked by Alexander's request for deification, and would have nothing to do with it: indeed, he opposed the entire orientalizing policy, root and branch. The king was jealous of his achievements: that remark about the victory at Megalopolis having been 'a battle of mice' must have warned the viceroy what was in store if he showed himself too successful a leader. Furthermore, he enjoyed the close friendship of Aristotle, who took equal exception to Alexander's divine pretensions. The king had lately (see above, p. 379) been dropping uncomfortable hints and threats to both of them in his correspondence. He seems to have convinced himself (or to have been bent on convincing others for his own ends) that Antipater, the one really powerful old guard noble left, was plotting to seize his throne. When someone praised the viceroy's frugal way of life, Alexander snapped: 'Outside Antipater is plain white, but within he is all purple.'[67]

Remarks of this nature would not take long to get back to Macedonia. Nor would the ambiguous text of the Exiles' Decree, or – if it came to that – the news of Craterus' sudden promotion to the office of viceroy, which almost certainly reached Antipater's ears before the official dispatch. It must have very soon become apparent to him that, on top of everything else, he was to be made the scapegoat for Alexander's repressive government in Greece, though he had done no more than carry out the king's own orders. His replacement by Craterus would be publicized as the dawn of a new democratic era, an argument to which the return of perhaps 40,000 democratic exiles would lend a certain superficial plausibility.

On the other hand, if Antipater obeyed the royal summons to Babylon he was a dead man, and knew it. Even at seventy-odd he had no great desire to be lopped off by another of Alexander's rigged treason trials. The executions of Callisthenes, Philotas, Parmenio, and his own son-in-law, Alexander of Lyncestis, had shown only too clearly which way the wind was blowing. The king's increasingly unpredictable temper, the disturbing signs of paranoia and megalomania which now characterized his actions, the ruthless purges he had so lately carried out – such things made it abundantly clear that Antipater must, at all costs, stay out of his clutches. Since the viceroy enjoyed considerable popularity in Macedonia (not least, we may surmise, through handling Olympias with such exemplary firmness), and, more important, had the whole Home Army behind him, he could afford to temporize. He may even have used these advantages to take some private counter-measures of his own.[68]

Calculating that Alexander, for the moment at any rate, had no more desire for an open trial of strength than he did, Antipater ignored the king's summons, and instead sent out his eldest son Cassander to negotiate on his behalf (see below, pp. 472–3). Cassander's brief was a tricky one. Almost certainly he had instructions to make an on-the-spot assessment not only of the king's intentions but also of his mental state. He may, in addition, have had the delicate task of sounding out some likely senior officers, such as Perdiccas, regarding the possibility of a take-over. It is very probable that at some point on his journey he met Craterus and did a private deal with him, since when Alexander died, a year later, the veterans were still no nearer home than Cilicia. Antipater, we may take it, was not the only far-sighted man who hedged his bets during those last few crucial months.

Nor is it hard to see why a persistent, widespread tradition in antiquity should claim that he and Aristotle now began plotting to remove the king by means of a fatal dose of poison.[69] One modern scholar, indeed, has advanced the very plausible theory that Alexander was eliminated by a junta of his senior commanders, including Perdiccas and Antipater (working, for the moment at least, in close co-operation), with Cassander as their liaison officer, and a share-out of the empire carefully agreed on in advance.[70] Even without such powerful support, Antipater's chances in the event of a straight showdown were by no means negligible. He was well-known (and well-liked) in Macedonia, whereas Alexander had been an absentee ruler for ten years. His troops were efficient, loyal, and *fresh*; Alexander's were worn out after endless campaigns, had been largely replaced by orientals (whom they detested), and had underlined their attitude by staging two full-scale mutinies. Antipater had every reason to feel confident. Meanwhile he began, very discreetly, to look round for potential supporters among the Greek states. There were two powers, Athens and Aetolia, which strongly opposed the Exiles' Decree, because its enforcement would involve them in territorial losses (they were determined to prevent exiles being returned to Samos and to Oeniadae respectively). Alexander had plans to crush both of them for their stubbornness, and this made them potentially susceptible to a secret approach by the viceroy. Antipater negotiated a private alliance with the Aetolians, and may well have approached Athens as well: with her vast fleet and impregnable naval arsenals, the violet-crowned city would be indispensable to any general organizing the defence of Greece.[71] But here Antipater had to tread warily. Until he learnt the result of Cassander's negotiations, he could not afford to commit himself too far.

It was now, early in July 324, that Harpalus appeared on the scene again, a political hot potato with a genius for mistiming his intrigues. If he offered his cash and troops to Antipater (as he must surely have done when he heard of the viceroy's dismissal) they were doubtless refused with more haste than politeness. As a revolutionary Harpalus showed himself peculiarly inept. No one else could have gone round peddling open revolt to men who were pinning their hopes on secret diplomacy. With bland cheerfulness, he next descended on Piraeus, followed by his entire private army, apparently in the naïve expectation of receiving a hero's welcome. Instead, he found the harbour closed against him. Many Athenians were only too anxious to do a deal with Alexander's defaulting treasurer – but not at the price of having their activities made quite so glaringly public.

By the middle of the month, however, Harpalus was back again. This time, more tactfully, he presented himself as a suppliant, with only three ships – plus 700 talents in cash.

Since he still enjoyed honorary Athenian citizenship, such a formula more or less guaranteed his admission. Once inside the city he made contact with various leading politicians, and very soon collected massive support for his projected revolt. At this point envoys arrived, in rapid succession, from Antipater, Alexander, and Olympias, each firmly demanding Harpalus' extradition. (When the king's ambassador, Philoxenus, appeared in the assembly, Demosthenes said: 'What will they do on seeing the sun who are dazzled by a lamp?') Harpalus appealed for help to his old friend Phocion, even offering to deposit all his money in trust with him. Phocion prudently declined.

Argument raged as to whether Harpalus should or should not be surrendered – and if so, to whom. In the end Demosthenes devised a formula to stall everybody and leave the situation open. Harpalus himself was taken into what amounted to protective custody, and held under guard. His funds were turned over to a special commission (which included Demosthenes) and stored for safekeeping on the Acropolis. This move drew bitter recriminations from the war-party. Hypereides even complained that by arresting Harpalus they had thrown away the chance of a satrapal revolt. Though that chance had in fact been lost much earlier, and through no action of Athens', at least Harpalus was still alive and safe from Alexander's hands.

Demosthenes now left for Olympia, where the Exiles' and Deification Decrees were proclaimed about the beginning of August. As an official Athenian delegate, he was empowered to negotiate with Nicanor, Alexander's representative, on any matters arising from the decrees which affected Athens. Apart from territorial problems (in particular the status of Samos, where Athens had settlers) the future of Harpalus must surely have come up during these talks. Whatever agreements the two men made were, for obvious reasons, kept secret. But Alexander – somewhat grudgingly, it is true – *did* leave the Athenians in possession of Samos, so there was probably a *quid pro quo* involved, and the most obvious would be the surrender of Harpalus. If Demosthenes in fact struck such a bargain, he clearly did not intend to honour his side of it. No sooner was he back in Athens than Harpalus – with the connivance of persons officially unknown – contrived to escape. This, of course, triggered off a major political scandal, which hardly diminished when it became known that of the original 700 talents only half had found their way to the strongroom on the Acropolis. Demosthenes was widely thought to have pocketed no less than fifty talents himself. Charges and counter-charges, involving most of the best-known public figures in Athens, were hurled to and fro with angry abandon. At first Demosthenes admitted receiving money from Harpalus, but said he had spent it on public business which he was not at liberty to divulge (perhaps as pay for Leosthenes' Peloponnesian mercenaries). Then he changed his mind and denied the whole thing. Finally, at Demosthenes' own suggestion, that venerable body the Areopagus – with which he had close and friendly ties – appointed a commission to investigate the affair: then as now a reliable stalling technique. Six months later its members still had not published their findings. Like everyone else, they were waiting on events.[72]

Except in Athens and Aetolia, where it met with united hostility, the Exiles' Decree seems to have had a mixed reception (depending in each case on the political colour of the ruling party). Everywhere it brought a vast amount of administrative and legal problems in its wake.[73] Alexander's request for deification was quite another matter. Since it had little practical impact on their lives, most Greeks seem to have regarded it with tolerant indifference, a subject for witty aphorisms. Positive reactions varied from angry contempt to amused disdain. Only a few elderly conservatives, like Antipater, were genuinely shocked.

As we might expect, the debate at Athens – on the motion that Alexander should be recognized as a thirteenth god in the Olympian pantheon, like Philip – was a particularly lively affair. The most outspoken comment was that by the Athenian statesman Lycurgus. 'What sort of god can this be,' he asked, 'when the first thing you'd have to do after leaving his temple would be to purify yourself?' One opponent of the motion retorted, on being rebuked for youthful presumption, that at least he was older than the prospective deity. Demades, however, proposing – an act which cost him a ten-talent fine when Alexander was safely dead – uttered one shrewd word of warning to the opposition. While they were concentrating on heavenly matters, he told them, they might well lose the earth – meaning Samos. The hint went home. Even Demosthenes, a convinced opponent of deification on principle, now gave Demades his grudging support, 'All right,' he said, 'make him the son of Zeus – and of Poseidon too, if that's what he wants.'[74] The motion was carried.

To escape the torrid heat of the plains, Alexander moved on east from Opis to Ecbatana, the Great King's traditional summer retreat. During this journey a ridiculous quarrel broke out between the touchy Hephaestion – clearly not at all sweetened by Craterus' removal – and Eumenes, the chief secretary. Eumenes' staff had requisitioned a house for their master. Hephaestion threw them out and gave the billet to a Greek flute-player. Once again Alexander was forced into the role of peacemaker over a shrill and petty private quarrel.

At Ecbatana, as soon as all urgent business had been settled, the king staged a lavish and protracted festival in honour of Dionysus, with athletics, music, and 3,000 Greek performers specially brought over to provide entertainment. Every evening there would be an epic drinking-party. After one of these Hephaestion (whose capacity for alcohol seems to have at least equalled Alexander's) collapsed and was put to bed with a high fever. His physician prescribed a strict plain diet, and for a week Hephaestion followed it obediently. Then he began to feel better. Early one morning, as soon as the doctor's back was turned, he got up, wolfed a whole boiled chicken, drank about half a gallon of chilled wine, and – not surprisingly – became very ill indeed. Alexander, warned that he had taken a turn for the worse, came hurrying back from the stadium, where he was watching the boys' athletics. By the time he reached his friend's bedside, Hephaestion was already dead.

The king's *alter ego* has not gone down to posterity as a very sympathetic figure. Tall, handsome, spoilt, spiteful, overbearing and fundamentally stupid, he was a competent enough regimental officer, but quite incapable of supporting great authority. His most redeeming quality was his constant personal devotion to Alexander. To someone who asserted that Craterus showed him equal loyalty, the king replied: 'Craterus loves the king; Hephaestion loves me for myself.' Olympias, as one might expect, was violently jealous of her son's inseparable companion. When she was through with denigrating Antipater in a letter, she would often throw off a barbed or threatening paragraph directed against Hephaestion. In the end, with overweening self-assurance, Hephaestion sent her a personal rebuke, couched in the royal plural. Its final words were: 'Stop quarrelling with us and do not be angry or menacing. If you persist, we shall not be much disturbed. You know that Alexander means more to us than anything.'

If Alexander meant more than anything to Hephaestion, so did Hephaestion to Alexander. The violence and extravagance of the king's grief went beyond all normal bounds. For a day and a night he lay on the body, weeping: no one could comfort him. General mourning was ordered throughout the East. All flutes and other musical instruments were banned in camp. Alexander cut his hair in token of mourning, as Achilles did for Patroclus, and even had the manes and tails of his horses docked. Hephaestion's wretched physician was crucified, and the temple of Asclepius in Ecbatana razed to the ground – a brisk gesture of retribution by one god against another. In heaven as on earth,

Alexander gave incompetence very short shrift indeed. The body was embalmed, and sent on ahead to Babylon, with a royal escort commanded by Perdiccas. A funeral of the magnificence which Alexander had in mind would take some time to prepare. It was finally celebrated in the early spring of 323, and every province of the empire contributed to its cost. The pyre was five storeys high and a furlong square at the base, a vast Wagnerian monstrosity decorated with gilded eagles and ships' prows, lions, bulls and centaurs. 'On top of all stood sirens, hollowed out and able to conceal within them persons who sang a lament in mourning for the dead' (Diod. 17.115.4).

After Hephaestion's death, no official appointment was ever made to the vacant command of the Companion Cavalry: it was still known as 'Hephaestion's Division'. Many of the Companions – led by Eumenes – tactfully dedicated themselves and their arms to the dead man. Alexander had sent envoys to Siwah asking if it would be lawful to worship Hephaestion as a god. This was a little too much even for Ammon. No, the oracle replied; but it was permissible to establish a hero-cult in his honour. Alexander at once wrote off to the rascally Cleomenes, now his governor of Egypt (see above, p. 440), promising him a blanket pardon for all his many misdeeds provided he built appropriate shrines to Hephaestion in Egypt, and ensured that the name 'Hephaestion' appeared on all merchants' contracts. It now became fashionable to swear oaths 'by Hephaestion', while stories of visitations, cures and prophecies began to multiply. Finally, in disregard of Siwah's instructions, Hephaestion was actually worshipped as 'God Coadjutor and Saviour'.

All this orgy of grief came remarkably expensive. The funeral pyre alone set Alexander back by 10,000 talents, and the elaborate tomb which he subsequently commissioned cost rather more than that: the millionaire's resources went to realize the megalomaniac's dreams. Just what sort of future the king had in mind for his lost favourite we can only surmise; but one fact is worth noting. During the month after Hephaestion's death, Roxane became pregnant, and the son she subsequently bore was Alexander's sole legitimate heir.[75]

After his providential escape from Athens, Harpalus returned to the Peloponnese, collected his squadron, and sailed for Crete – that home of all lost causes – where he was promptly assassinated. The murderer appears to have been a Macedonian agent, acting in collusion with Harpalus' second-in-command, and very probably at Alexander's direct instigation. The king would have been less than human had he let his defaulting and treacherous imperial treasurer go scot-free. Harpalus' steward, however, got away to Rhodes, where the ever-watchful Philoxenus, now governor of Cilicia, soon had him picked up and interrogated. In this way Philoxenus acquired a full dossier on all Harpalus' private contacts. He thereupon – clearly with Alexander's approval, if not on his express orders – sent an official dispatch to Athens, listing every Athenian citizen whom Harpalus had bribed, together with the sums involved.

There is some doubt as to whether Demosthenes' name originally figured on this list, but it was undoubtedly there by the time (February 323) that the Areopagus finally published its findings on the Harpalus affair. With the death of Hephaestion Demosthenes had lost his friend and contact at court; the murder of Harpalus now removed any excuse for hushing matters up on security grounds. In March 323 an Athenian jury found Demosthenes guilty of accepting bribes, and fined him fifty talents. The sum was more than he could raise, and he suffered imprisonment instead. Later, however, he escaped – like Harpalus, with the connivance of his guards – and got away to Aegina, where he remained until Alexander's death.[76]

The best panacea for grief is work; and there was only one kind of work which Alexander knew. In the winter of 324/3, by which time his misery had subsided into moody aggressiveness, he launched a whirlwind campaign – his last, as it turned out – against the Cossaeans. These were mountain tribesmen dwelling south-west of Ecbatana. The Achaemenid kings had paid them an annual sum for undisturbed passage through their territory, a practice which Alexander regarded with contempt (see above, p. 311). It took him about five weeks to exterminate them; this he called 'an offering to the shade of Hephaestion' (Plut. *Alex.* 72.3).[77] His mind was already full of plans for new conquests and adventures. Before leaving Ecbatana he sent a reconnaissance expedition off to the Caspian Sea, complete with carpenters and shipwrights. They were to cut timber in the great Hyrcanian forest, and build a fleet of Greek-style warships – ostensibly for a voyage of exploration, but in fact, no doubt, as a preliminary to that long-deferred campaign against the Scythians (see above, p. 359). Other projects, including one for the subjugation of the whole vast Arabian peninsula, were in active preparation.

By the time Alexander had finished with the Cossaeans, spring was approaching. The whole army now set out for Babylon, marching in easy stages, with frequent rest-periods. Embassies from Libya and South Italy – the first of many such – met them on the road, with honorific gold crowns and flattering speeches. A less cheerful note was struck by the Chaldaean seers, who warned the king that a great disaster would befall him if he entered Babylon. However, they added, he would escape this danger if he undertook to restore Bel-Marduk's ziggurat and temple. In any case he should avoid making his entrance into the city from the eastern side, i.e. facing the setting sun.

Here was a splendid piece of effrontery. Alexander had, in fact, ordered work to begin on this vast undertaking at the time of his first visit, seven years before (see above, pp. 303–4). Expenses were to be met from temple funds – the usual procedure in such cases. However, clearing the mound alone was estimated as two months' work for 10,000 men; and what funds there were had been going straight into the priests' pockets for a century and more. Once the project got started, this profitable source of income would dry up overnight. As a result, of course, almost nothing had been done. Now the priests were belatedly attempting to scare Alexander into footing the bill himself. The remarkable thing – and a significant general pointer to the climate of fourth-century religious belief – is how seriously he still took them. Though he must have known quite well, in his heart of hearts, what they were up to, nevertheless after some hesitation he decided to play safe.

While the bulk of the army marched on into Babylon, Alexander himself, together with his immediate entourage, pitched camp a safe distance outside. Philosophical sceptics like Anaxarchus, astonished by this display of superstitious nerves on the king's part, very soon talked him into a more rational frame of mind, and he made up his mind to ignore the Chaldaeans' warnings. Yet even now he still tried (though finally without success) to find a way into Babylon through the swamps and marshes lying west of the river. His entry was, it seems, followed by several appalling omens, and Alexander's opinion of Greek philosophers dropped to zero.[78]

However, he had other distractions to take his mind off the machinations of Fate. Ambassadors arrived daily, from every corner of the Mediterranean world – and in particular (as we might expect when Alexander's plans for future conquest became known) from Sicily, Italy, Spain, North Africa, and Carthage. Some were in search of profitable alliances, some came to defend their governments against various accusations or claims, all bore hopeful official tributes and the statutory gold crowns or wreaths. In the end Alexander was so swamped by them that he laid down a strict – and revealing – order of priorities for granting audiences. Religious matters were dealt with first, gifts second. Next it was the turn of those with disputes for arbitration, or – less important – internal domestic problems. Right at the bottom of the list (a popular category, one suspects) were 'those who wished to present arguments against receiving back their exiles' (Diod. 17.113.3).

One country which, curiously, sent no delegation to Babylon was Arabia: ample excuse for a punitive expedition, Alexander claimed. Even Arrian finds this a little hard to swallow, and is prompted to comment that the real motive was simply 'Alexander's insatiable thirst for extending his possessions' (Arrian 7.19.6). Ships sent out to reconnoitre the Arabian coastline now came back with glowing reports of the country's size and prosperity, the heady scent of spice-trees blowing out to sea, well-placed islands and anchorages. Phoenician galleys were dismantled, carried across country on pack-animals, and reassembled on the Euphrates. A vast new harbour-basin was dug at Babylon, large enough, allegedly, to accommodate a thousand vessels. The Arabs, Alexander was told, worshipped two gods only, Uranus and Dionysus. On learning this, he pronounced that he himself was entitled to make a third in their somewhat limited pantheon, since 'his achievements surpassed those of Dionysus' (Arrian 7.20.1).[79]*

While his naval preparations went forward, Alexander busied himself with the celebration of Hephaestion's funeral. This pious task once discharged, he lost no time in getting outside the city-limits once more. Boarding a flotilla of small boats, he and his friends sailed down to inspect the marshy lower reaches of the Euphrates, with its canals and dykes and floodgates. Irrigation was a problem that had always interested him: before leaving Greece he had found time to organize the partial drainage of Lake Copaïs. He also wanted to examine the navigational facilities for his Arabian fleet, which included two vast Phoenician quinqueremes.

---

*One motive generally assigned to his urge for further conquests (not in Arabia only but also, as here, in Italy) was a presumed 'wish to rival and to pass beyond the limits of Dionysus' and Heracles' expeditions': see Plut. *Moral.* 326B, and Wilcken, pp. 225–6. He may also have planned to link India with Egypt.

By entering Babylon and then quickly leaving again before any disaster could befall him, the king felt he had finally disproved the Chaldaeans' prophecy. But as the boats pushed their way through those stinking, overgrown, malaria-haunted swamps, an incident took place which caused both him and the soothsayers considerable uneasiness. As he sat at the tiller of his boat, a stray gust of wind blew off the sun-hat he was wearing, with its royal blue-and-white ribbon. The ribbon fluttered away, and caught in the reeds by an ancient royal tomb: all the old kings of Assyria were said to be buried here among the marshes. This was a grim enough portent for anyone. But the sailor who swam across and rescued the sun-hat unwittingly made matters worse by putting it on his own head to avoid getting it wet. Alexander gave him a talent as reward for his kindness, and then a sound flogging for *lèse-majesté*. Some accounts claim that he actually had the wretched man beheaded, 'in obedience to the prophecy which warned him not to leave untouched the head which had worn the diadem'.[80]

When the king returned to Babylon he found Peucestas there, with a force of 20,000 Iranians from Persia. Philoxenus had also arrived, at the head of a Carian contingent; so had Menander, from Lydia. The Arabian invasion force was beginning to take shape. Alexander now carried his integration policy one step farther. He re-brigaded the infantry battalions of the phalanx, using four Macedonians – as section-corporal and file-leaders – to twelve Persians. Macedonians were still to be armed with the *sarissa*, Persians with the bow or javelin. Perhaps it was fortunate that this extraordinary mixed force was never tried in action: it would surely have taken the most rigorous training and discipline (let alone the linguistic problem of communication) to make it even remotely effective. On the other hand, it did undoubtedly provide an effective safeguard against mutiny.

On the day that Alexander was organizing the re-allocation of men to their new units, he left his parade-ground dais for a moment, with his aides, to get a drink. During his absence an escaped Babylonian prisoner mounted the dais, put on the king's royal cloak and diadem, and seated himself on the throne. When interrogated under torture as to his motives, he would only say that the god had put the idea into his head. Alexander suspected some kind of nationalist plot; and the incident is so oddly reminiscent of the Rite of the Mock King in the Babylonian *Akitu* (New Year) Festival, due at this time, that he may even have been right.[81] Our sources, at any rate, are unanimous in reporting a number of such ominous portents shortly before Alexander's death. These are worth more consideration than they normally get. It is most often taken for granted that they were *ex post facto* propaganda, manufactured after the event. But in this case they are at least as likely to have been manufactured *before* the event, by those most interested in getting Alexander out of the way. They would certainly suggest that the king's death was due to divine or natural causes, rather than to human agency. The best prophet (to adapt Euripides) is he who knows what will happen in advance.

More embassies now arrived, this time from Greece, and their delegates behaved in Alexander's presence 'as if their coming were a ritual in honour of a god' (Arrian 7.23.2): from the king's viewpoint, of course, it was, and Greeks – in Alexander's day as in Juvenal's – would not be slow to fall in with the monarch's whims. *In caelum iusseris, ibit.* 'And yet,' Arrian adds, with ironic hindsight, 'his end was not far off.' With these envoys came Cassander, to negotiate with the king on his father's behalf, and very probably (if Alexander proved impervious to reason, or showed alarming signs of mental instability) to arrange, in concert with Perdiccas and other senior officers, for his discreet removal (cf. above, p. 460).[82]

Antipater's son got off to the worst possible start in Babylon by bursting into nervous laughter when he saw a Persian prostrate himself before the royal throne. At this Alexander sprang up in a paroxysm of rage, seized Cassander by the hair with both hands, and beat his head against the wall. Later, when Cassander tried to rebut various charges that were now being brought against his father, the king accused him of philosophical hair-splitting, and threatened both of them with dire retribution if the accusations were well-founded. By so doing he may well have signed his own death-warrant; he certainly scared the young negotiator almost witless. Years afterwards, when he was himself King of Macedonia, Cassander still trembled and shuddered uncontrollably at the mere sight of Alexander's portrait, and the hatred engendered during that visit to Babylon lasted until his dying day.[83]

The fleet's training programme was now in full swing, with competitive races up and down the river between triremes and quinqueremés, and golden wreaths for the winning crews. But Alexander, despite the prospect of a new campaign, was sunk deep in *accidie*, and drinking so heavily as to cause his Greek doctor serious concern. He was, he admitted on one occasion, 'at an utter loss to know what he should do during the rest of his life' (Plut. *Moral.* 207D 8). On this the Roman emperor Augustus (himself no mean empire-builder) made a comment that many historians have since echoed. He felt astonishment, he said, 'that Alexander did not regard it as a greater task to set in order the empire which he had won than to win it'. But for Alexander conquest and *areté* were all. The dull but essential routine of administration held no charms for him. The chaos he had left behind him in the East, even the threat of civil war at home, could not distract him from the lure of Arabia.[84]

But the dream, this time, was to remain unfulfilled. On the evening of 29 May[85] Alexander held a banquet for his admiral Nearchus. The usual deep drinking took place. After dinner the king wanted to go to bed: an uncharacteristic preference, and one which, combined with his *accidie*, suggests that (for whatever reason) he had during the past week or two been feeling some kind of malaise. However, his Thessalian friend Medius[86] was giving a late party, and persuaded him to attend it: those sources which relate the poisoning theory (see below, p. 476) make Medius one of the conspirators.[87] After further carousing – in commemoration of Heracles' death – the king was given a large cup of unmixed wine, which he drained straight down, and instantly 'shrieked aloud as if smitten by a violent blow'.[88] On this he was carried back to his quarters and put to bed.

Next day he had a high fever. Despite this he got up, bathed, had a siesta, and once more wined and dined with Medius. That night his fever was so intense that he slept in the bathing-house for the sake of coolness. The following morning (31 May) he went back to his bedroom, and spent the day playing dice. By the night of 1 June he was in the bathing-house again, and here, on the morning of the 2nd, he discussed the projected Arabian voyage with Nearchus and other senior officers. He was now in constant and increasing fever. By the evening of 3 June it became clear that he was critically ill. Nevertheless he had himself carried out next morning to perform the daily sacrifice, and to hold a briefing for his officers. On 5 June he himself was forced to recognize the gravity of his illness, and ordered all high officials to remain within call of his bedside.

By the evening of 6 June he was almost past speech, and gave his ring to Perdiccas, as senior marshal, so that routine administration would continue to function smoothly. At this, not altogether surprisingly, a rumour spread through the camp that he was in fact dead. His Macedonian troops crowded round the palace, threatening to break down the doors if they were not let in to see him. Finally a second entrance was knocked through his bedroom wall, and an endless file of veterans passed slowly through to take their leave of him. Sometimes he would painfully raise his head a little; more often he could do no more than move his eyes in token of greeting and recognition.

During the night of 9–10 June a group of his officers kept vigil on his behalf in the nearby temple of 'Sarapis' (probably in fact that of Bel-Marduk). But when they asked the god if it would help Alexander to be moved into the shrine, the oracular response came that it would be better for him if he stayed where he was. At this the king's friends, gathered round his bedside, asked him – it was, after all, a vital question – to whom he bequeathed his kingdom. Weakly Alexander whispered: 'To the strongest.' His last, all too prophetic words were: 'I foresee a great funeral contest over me.' Early in the morning of 10 June 323 B.C., his eyes closed for ever.

There is an extremely circumstantial story told about one of the king's companions, Apollodorus of Amphipolis, who served in Babylon and Ecbatana while Alexander was away in the East. On the king's return from India, Apollodorus was scared (as well he might be) by the ruthless purge of high officials which followed. He therefore consulted his brother, Peithagoras, a distinguished soothsayer, as to his own future, saying that those he particularly feared were Alexander and Hephaestion. Peithagoras wrote back telling him not to worry: both men would soon be removed from his path. Common sense suggests that whatever this seer may have said (by way of justifying his prescience) about lobeless sacrificial livers, the truth was that he had inside information of some sort; perhaps he had also been encouraged to create some suitable prophecies before the event (see above, p. 472). Hephaestion in fact died no more than a day or two after Apollodorus got Peithagoras' tip-off, and the manner of his death – heavy drinking followed by an inexplicable high fever – exactly duplicates Alexander's own end.

Now our ancient sources all record a tradition that Alexander was in fact poisoned: that Aristotle prepared the drug, that Antipater's son Cassander brought it to Babylon, and that it was administered to the king, in unmixed wine, by his cupbearer Iolaus – another of Antipater's sons.[89] Till recently this tradition was dismissed out of hand as preposterous propaganda. Obviously, it is not susceptible of proof. Equally obviously, when marshals like Craterus, Antipater and Perdiccas later fell out, they would not hesitate to use smear-techniques against each other: it has lately been argued, with some cogency, that our tradition represents an attempt by Perdiccas to incriminate Antipater.[90] But it is not a justifiable inference from this that no murder was committed: we may well be dealing with a smoothly executed *coup d'état* involving numerous conspirators.

The poisoning charge, as Badian rightly says, 'if true . . . was bound to be denied or ignored, and if false, bound to be asserted'.[91] But we must at least regard it as a strong possibility; and though the attempt to make Antipater and his clique exclusively responsible sounds like *ex post facto* propaganda, it nevertheless remains plausible enough *per se*, on the *cui bono* principle if for no other reason. Antipater had, after all, been superseded and summoned to Babylon. Aristotle's nephew had been executed, and he himself may well have been in danger. Both men were appalled by the king's orientalizing extravagances (as they saw them), and even more by his assumption of godhead. For them he had become an arbitrary, unpredictable tyrant; and as Aristotle himself wrote (*Pol.* 1295a), 'no free man willingly endures such rule.'

A recent biographer, R. D. Milns, has also pointed out[92] that the symptoms of Alexander's last illness, especially his lassitude and high body temperature, are compatible with slow strychnine poisoning. Strychnine is easily extracted, and can be kept effective for a long period – in a mule's hoof or any other less exotic container (the former being

alleged by some of our ancient sources). Aristotle's friend
Theophrastus describes its uses and dosage,[93] remarking
inter alia that the best way to disguise its bitter taste is by
administering it *in unmixed wine*. There is, then, much
circumstantial evidence (and some direct testimony) which
suggests that neither Alexander nor Hephaestion died from
natural causes. If they did not, the odds are that both were
eliminated by a junta of senior commanders (with Craterus,
Perdiccas and Antipater prominent among those involved),
in a 'successful *coup d'état*, cleanly and ruthlessly executed'.[94]

If the king was not poisoned, the chances are that he
succumbed either to raging pleurisy, or else, more probably,
to malaria (the latter picked up during his boat-trip through
the marshes). In either case, advanced alcoholism, combined
with the terrible wound he sustained in India, had finally
lowered even his iron resistance to a point where he could
no longer hope to survive. Whatever the truth concerning
his last days, it is clear enough that at the time (a point not
stressed as much as it should be) there were few men, and
a fortiori fewer women, who lamented Alexander's passing.
In Greece and Asia alike, during his lifetime and for several
centuries after his death, he was regarded as a tyrannous
aggressor, a foreign autocrat who had imposed his will by
violence alone. When the news of his death in Babylon
reached Athens, it was the orator Demades who crystallized
public reaction. 'Alexander dead?' he exclaimed. 'Impossible; the whole earth would stink of his corpse.'[95]

The reaction was an all too predictable one. For 25,000
miles Alexander had carried his trail of rapine, slaughter,
and subjugation. What he achieved of lasting value was
largely unintentional: in political terms his trail-blazing
activities through the Near East had a curiously ephemeral
quality about them. The moment he moved on, rebellion
tended to flare up behind him; and when he died – just as
he himself predicted – the empire he had carved out at once
split apart into anarchic chaos, while the next forty years
saw an indescribably savage and bloody struggle between

his surviving marshals. At a fairly early stage in these 'funeral games' (310) Cassander liquidated Roxane and her thirteen-year-old son, Alexander IV, so that the king's direct line became extinct.

Alexander may have demanded deification in his own lifetime, but by a kind of ironic rough justice he got mythification after he was dead. While his physical remains, smoothly hijacked by Ptolemy to Alexandria, lay on view in a glass coffin, a tribute to the local embalmers' art, his legend took root and flourished. When Aristobulus (see above, p. 417) could concoct pure fiction about recent and known events, to be recited in the presence of their actual protagonist, what would later romancers not achieve, once freed from the fear lest Alexander himself should pitch their effusions into the nearest river, and threaten to deal with them in similar fashion?[96] Immediately after his death, the king's character, reputation, and career were taken in hand by endless propagandists, would-be monarchs, historians, and a whole series of interested parties with some axe or other to grind.

He was not popular in Hellenistic times (though in art his portraiture, especially that by Lysippus, started a widespread iconographic trend, and rulers were fond of using his head on their coinage as a species of political endorsement), which may partially account for the fact that none of our main surviving accounts of him was written less than three hundred years after his death. By the time world-conquest came into fashion again, with Augustus, Alexander was already well on the way to becoming a giant, a demigod, the superhuman figure of romance who figured during the Middle Ages as Iskander the Two-Horned (a description which started from coin-portraits showing him wearing the ram's horns of Zeus Ammon).

Nothing did more to accelerate this process than the so-called 'Alexander-romance'. Perhaps in the second century A.D., perhaps much earlier – some details suggest propaganda of a date not long after the king's death[97] – an anonymous writer who borrowed the name of Callisthenes wrote a sensationalized, semi-mythicizing version of Alexander's career which at once ousted all the more sober versions, and spread like wildfire not only through the Greek and Roman world, but far into the East. In this work, for example, Alexander was alleged to have been sired on Olympias by the Egyptian Pharaoh Nectanebus, himself changed into a magician for the occasion. By the fifth century A.D. Syriac and Armenian versions of this weird farrago were in circulation. Arabic and Persian poets drew on it, with the result that cities like Secunderabad in the Deccan preserve Alexander's name although he never came anywhere near them.

Yet the uncomfortable fact remains that the Alexander-romance provides us, on occasion, with apparently genuine material found nowhere else, while our better-authenticated sources, *per contra*, are all too often riddled with bias, propaganda, rhetorical special pleading, or patent falsification and suppression of the evidence. Arrian drew for the most part on Ptolemy and Aristobulus, who both (as we have seen) had powerful motives for preserving a *parti pris* version of the events in which they had taken part. No one has yet worked out a satisfactory analysis of the eclectic tradition on which Plutarch and Diodorus drew.[98] Curtius, for all his tedious rhetorical hyperbole, contains valuable material not found elsewhere, and not all of it can be written off as hostile material invented by Cleitarchus or the 'Peripatetic tradition', as Tarn would have us believe.[99]

The truth of the matter is that there has never been a 'good' or 'bad' source-tradition concerning Alexander, simply *testimonia* contaminated to a greater or lesser degree, which invariably need evaluating, wherever possible, by external criteria of probability. This applies to all the early fragmentary evidence quoted in extant accounts as well as, *a fortiori*, to the authors of those accounts themselves. A. E. Housman's strictures, in the field of textual criticism, against 'the reigning fashion of the hour, the fashion of leaning on one manuscript like Hope on her anchor and trusting to heaven that no harm will come of it' could equally well be applied, *mutatis mutandis*, in the field of Alexander studies, where until recently Arrian received similar treatment. This was due, as Borza acutely noted,[100] to a process whereby scholars formed a rigid estimate of Alexander's character, and then 'began to reject or accept evidence depending upon whether that evidence was consistent with their characterization'.

Such a circular process of argument will also leave judgement very much at the mercy of contemporary fashions and preoccupations, a fate to which Alexander (who has always tended to involve his interpreters' emotions at least as much as their reasoning faculties) is, to judge by the record, peculiarly prone. Everyone uses him as a projection of their own private truth, their own dreams and aspirations, fears and power-fantasies. Each country, each generation, sees him in a different light. Every individual biographer, myself included, inevitably puts as much of himself, his own background and convictions, into that Protean figure as he does of whatever historical truth he can extract from the evidence. The power and fascination of Alexander's character are undeniable, and operate as strongly on modern scholars as they did on his Macedonian veterans. The king's personality is so strong, so idiosyncratic, that it comes through despite all the propaganda, pro or con: the smears, the eulogies, the star-struck mythologizing.

Something can be done, by careful analysis, to sort out truth from propaganda and legend.* But this is where the real difficulties begin, since each student inevitably selects, constitutes criteria, according to his own unconscious assumptions, social, ethical or political. Moral conditioning, in the widest sense, plays a far greater part in the matter than most people – especially the historians themselves –

---

*The most comprehensive attempt has been that of Lionel Pearson, n *The Lost Histories of Alexander the Great*, I (Providence, 1953).

ever realize. So, indeed, does contemporary fashion. To the Romans of Augustus' day Alexander was the prototype of fashionable world-conquerors; they could call him 'the Great' without any sense of creeping inferiority, since their own Princeps had so signally eclipsed his achievements, both in scope and durability. Juvenal, writing slightly later, at a time when imperial pretensions had become something of a cliché, saw Alexander rather as a supreme instance of the vanity of human wishes.[101]

The medieval world, which enjoyed Juvenal's savage sniping at wealth and ambition, developed much the same theme. 'And where is Alisaundir that conqueryd al?' asked Lydgate; many other poets echoed his rhetorical question. With the Renaissance came a reversion to the Augustan picture. Great Captains – as the popularity of Plutarch's *Lives* demonstrates – were once more in the ascendant: the prevailing mood was summed up for all time by that marvellously evocative line of Marlowe's:

Is it not passing brave to be a king, and ride in triumph through Persepolis?

Such an attitude survived largely unchallenged until the early nineteenth century. One event which then heralded a change in Alexander's reputation was undoubtedly the Greek War of Independence, following close on the French Revolution and the American War of Independence. The climate of educated liberal opinion had swung sharply round against the concept of imperialism; the fashion now was to endorse all subject races struggling for liberty, an ideological programme into which it would be hard to fit Alexander's career without some fairly thorough-going (not to say casuistic) reappraisal of the evidence.

This trend reached its logical climax in the famous – and still eminently readable – *History of Greece* by George Grote, a professional banker and passionate liberal, two things less mutually exclusive then than they have, it would seem, since become. Grote's hero in the fourth century is Demosthenes, whom he sees as embodying the true spirit of independence in the face of brazen and calculated imperialist aggression. He writes off both Philip and Alexander as brutalized adventurers simply out for power, wealth, and territorial expansion, both of them inflamed by the pure lust for conquest. Earlier historians, of course, had said much the same thing, but without Grote's note of moral censure. Committed liberalism, however, was not a universal feature of nineteenth-century scholarship. European history moved in various channels, some more authoritarian than others: as usual, Alexander's reputation varied according to context. One milestone in Alexander studies was the publication of Johann Gustav Droysen's still immensely influential biography, *Alexander der Grosse* (1833). It has often been said, with justice, that this is the first work of modern historical scholarship on Alexander: Droysen was, undoubtedly, the first student to employ serious critical methods in evaluating our sources, and the result was a fundamental study. Once again, however, Droysen's own position largely dictated the view he took of his subject.[102] Far from being a liberal, he was an ardent advocate of the reunification of Germany under strong Prussian leadership and after 1848 served for a while as a member of the Prussian parliament.

Thus we have a biographer of Alexander imbued with a belief in monarchy and a passionate devotion to Prussian nationalism: how the one aspect of his career influenced the other is, unfortunately, all too predictable. For the aspirations of independent small Greek states (as for their German counterparts) he had little but impatient contempt. In his view it is Philip of Macedon who emerges as the true leader of Greece, the man destined to unify the country and set it upon its historical mission; while Alexander carried the process one step farther by spreading the blessings of Greek culture throughout the known (and large tracts of the unknown) world. Plutarch's early essay on Alexander had made much the same point, contrasting the untutored savage who had not benefited from the king's civilizing attentions with those happy lesser breeds who had, the result of their encounter being that blend of Greek and oriental culture which Droysen, perhaps rather misleadingly, christened Hellenism.

As one contemporary scholar says,[103] 'Droysen's conceptions were propounded so forcefully that they have conditioned virtually all subsequent scholarship on the subject.' Whatever their views on the nature of his achievement, most subsequent biographers tended to see Alexander as, in some guise or other, the great world-mover. This view held up surprisingly well until after the Second World War. The late nineteenth century, after all, saw the apogee of the British Empire, and scholars who got misty-eyed over Kipling in their spare time were not liable to argue with Droysen's view of Alexander. But this was also the heyday of the English gentleman, and much of that fascinating if often legendary figure's characteristics also now began to figure in their portraits – Alexander's becoming lack of interest in sex, his chivalrous conduct to women, his supposed ideals and aspirations towards the wider and mistier glories of imperialism.

The climax of this trend was, of course, the famous and enormously influential biography by the late Sir William Tarn, first published in the *Cambridge Ancient History* (1926) and then again in 1948, the narrative more or less unchanged, but this time supported by an immense volume of specialist research on various key topics. Tarn's basic picture resembled that of Droysen, but he added something new: a social philosophy, a belief on Alexander's part in the Brotherhood of Man. Why he took this line is clear enough. Tarn had an ethical dilemma to solve when he set about his task. By the time he came to write, imperial expansionism was no longer a tolerable programme in the minds of progressive intellectuals unless it had some sort of idealist or missionary creed to underwrite it. Tarn could not possibly, therefore, treat Alexander as a conqueror pure and simple and still regard him with unqualified approval. He had to find some ulterior goal for this imperial adventurer to pursue, and duly did so.

His solution, as it happened, lay conveniently ready to hand. The early 1920s were the heyday of the League of Nations, and as a gentlemanly late-Victorian liberal Tarn – along with Sir Alfred Zimmern, Gilbert Murray, and many others – was instantly swept away on a wave of international idealism. As in the case of Droysen (though with rather different results) Tarn's personal political convictions strongly affected his subsequent treatment of his hero. The League of Nations was proclaiming the Brotherhood of Man. Tarn brooded over the feast at Opis, laced it with some hit-and-miss proto-Stoicism, added a pinch of dubious early rhetoric from Plutarch (see above, p. 445), and duly evolved what I have always thought of as the League of Nations Alexander.

We can, if we so wish, criticize Tarn on the grounds of political naïvety, and this is, of course, the most significant and damaging weakness in a *magnum opus* which, by any standards, remains a major scholarly achievement. But in this connection there are two important points we should remember. The first, and perhaps the most important, is that his version proved immensely popular. True or not, it was what a vast majority of people actively *wanted* to believe, and they therefore believed it, despite the critical small-arms fire with which various hardheaded historians, both at the time and later, riddled Tarn's central thesis. The second consideration to bear in mind is this. Tarn passed his formative years at the close of a century of peace and affluence, which enjoyed a stability – financial, social, political – such as the world had seldom seen since the days of the Roman Empire under the Antonines. This epoch, which those who lived through it regarded as the climax of a rational process with its roots in the eighteenth century, we now know for the unique phenomenon it was. This awareness, it goes without saying, has profoundly modified our attitude to the problems of history.

Tarn and those like him held that the devils of emotion and irrationalism had been chained and tamed for ever. They believed in the supremacy of human reason, the essential goodness of human nature. The grim events of the past sixty years have taught us that man's life, alas, remains much the same as Thucydides or Thomas Hobbes saw it: nasty, brutish and short. The optimistic idealism characteristic of so much Victorian thinking bears little relationship to the overall sweep of human history. Towards the end of his life Tarn, in a groping way, began to realize this. The final paragraph of his original study in the *Cambridge Ancient History* was an impassioned plea for the ultimate indestructibility of the Brotherhood of Man as a perennial concept. In his 1948 edition, however, he appended a footnote which read: 'I have left the latter part of this paragraph substantially as written in 1926. Since then we have seen new and monstrous births, and are still moving in a world not realized; and I do not know how to rewrite it.'

There we have the humanist's *cri de coeur*, the last despairing utterance of an idealist mind at the end of its tether. Behind the clumsy abstractions there stalk ghosts not laid but merely sleeping: horrors like the gas-chambers and the hydrogen bomb, the world of double-think and ruthless power-politics and Orwell's *1984*, things which Thucydides and Alexander and Augustus understood very well in their own terms, but which Western Europe or America in the early years of this century simply could not conceive. Tarn further suffered from a sternly *simpliste* attitude to the psychological facets of morality: in his eyes murder was wrong, promiscuity was wrong, homosexuality was especially wrong, pure aggression without justification was wrong. Alexander, as a great man and a great hero, *had* to be cleared of such imputations as far as possible. It was only a short step from this axiom to the corollary that those traditions which presented Alexander in a morally good light were sound, while hostile testimony could be with confidence dismissed as false propaganda.

In short, the rise of psychology as a scientific discipline, combined with the return of totalitarianism as an instrument of politics, left Tarn's approach almost totally bankrupt in principle, if still a most impressive achievement over matters of detail (e.g. Alexander's eastern foundations) where ethical considerations did not apply. It is impossible to have lived through the middle decades of this century and not apply its lessons to the career of Alexander, which in so many ways shows remarkable parallels with those of other would-be world-conquerors who used propaganda as a deliberate tool and believed that truth was a commodity to be manipulated for their own ends.

Our picture of Augustus, as those who have read Sir Ronald Syme's classic work *The Roman Revolution* will be well aware, has been altered out of all recognition by this traumatic modern experience. It was hardly to be expected that the old rose-tinted view of Alexander would remain unaltered either. For post-war historians the king has once more become a world-conqueror *tout court*, the act of conquest being regarded not as a means to an end but an end in itself, carried out by a visionary megalomaniac serving the implacable needs of his own all-consuming ego.* At the same time, perhaps inevitably, a Freudian element has crept into the study of Alexander's personality during recent years. Critics now point out that his distaste for sex, the rumours of his homosexual liaisons – in particular his lifelong friendship with that rather lumpish character Hephaestion and the sinister but beautiful young eunuch Bagoas – coupled with his partiality for middle-aged or elderly ladies and the systematic domination of his early years by that formidable matriarch Olympias, all suggest

---

* Scholars who in one way or another would seem to endorse such a view include Badian, Bosworth, Burn, Hamilton, Milns and Schachermeyr (see Bibliography); perhaps one should also add Andreotti, *Historia* 1 (1950), 583 ff.

the presence in his nature of something approaching an Oedipus complex.

It hardly needs saying that this generation is no more free from the influence of its own overriding assumptions than any previous one; that perhaps once again we are reading into that chameleon personality what we ourselves fear or desire or find of obsessional concern in our own lives and society. As I suggested earlier (see above, p. 56), the Freudian interpretation of Alexander's motives can easily be overdone: an Adlerian power-complex would seem to fit the facts better. The real virtue of the new approach, it seems to me, is its basic pragmatism: it at least begins by looking at the historical facts without trying to fit them to a preconceived moral theory based on some arbitrary assessment of character. The picture which emerges in the course of such an investigation is hardly one to please idealists; but it makes a great deal of political and historical sense. To strip away the accretions of myth, to discover – insofar as the evidence will permit it – the historical Alexander of flesh and blood: this must be the task of any contemporary historian, and to the best of my ability I have attempted it.

For me, in the last resort, Alexander's true genius was as a field-commander: perhaps, taken all in all, the most incomparable general the world has ever seen.[104] His gift for speed, improvisation, variety of strategy; his coolheadedness in a crisis, his ability to extract himself from the most impossible situations; his mastery of terrain, his psychological ability to penetrate the enemy's intentions – all these qualities place him at the very head of the Great Captains of history. The myth of the Great Captains is wearing rather thin these days, and admiration for their achievements has waned: this is where we too become the victims of our own age and our own morality. Viewed in political rather than military terms, Alexander's career strikes a grimly familiar note. We have no right to soften it on that account.

Philip's son was bred as a king and a warrior. His

business, his all-absorbing obsession through a short but crowded life, was war and conquest. It is idle to palliate this central truth, to pretend that he dreamed, in some mysterious fashion, of wading through rivers of blood and violence to achieve the Brotherhood of Man by raping an entire continent. He spent his life, with legendary success, in the pursuit of personal glory, Achillean *kleos*; and until very recent times this was regarded as a wholly laudable aim. The empire he built collapsed the moment he was gone; he came as a conqueror and the work he wrought was destruction. Yet his legend still lives; the proof of his immortality is the belief he inspired in others. That is why he remained greater than the measurable sum of his works; that is why, in the last resort, he will continue an insoluble enigma, to this and all future generations. His greatness defies a final judgement. He personifies an archetypal element, restless and perennial, in human nature: the myth of the eternal quest for the world's end, memorably summed up by Tennyson in the last line of *Ulysses*: 'To strive, to seek, to find, and not to yield.'

Appendix:
Propaganda at the Granicus

THE battle of the River Granicus has at least two special claims on our interest: it was not only the first engagement fought by Alexander on Asiatic soil, but also, apparently, one of the most dramatic. Yet it is, on the whole, poorly documented; and the accounts we possess of it[1] contain inconsistencies and anomalies which have never been satisfactorily explained. Motives remain impenetrable; tactical dispositions range from the wilful to the lunatic. The baffling nature of the evidence was strikingly demonstrated in 1964 by E. W. Davis,[2] who, after analysing the inadequacies of no less than four previous accounts – those by Tarn, Beloch, Fuller and Schachermeyr – concluded that the problem was, ultimately, insoluble, 'for with the information at our disposal we cannot read the minds of the Persian leaders'.[3] Davis handicapped himself needlessly by his curious assumption[4] that the Persian army was under the command not of Arsites, but of a committee – perhaps in an effort to excuse the indubitably irrational Persian strategy as reported by our main sources. At the same time his pessimism is all too understandable, and his three basic questions – 'why the battle was fought, why it was fought where it was fought, and why it was fought as it was fought'[5] – must be squarely faced by any student of this enigmatic engagement.

The first two points need not detain us overlong: on them there exists a fair (if not unanimous) consensus of agreement. It is the third which has always been the real difficulty. From Alexander's viewpoint, an immediate engagement was essential. He had to secure Hellespontine Phrygia before moving on south; more important, he urgently needed the cash and supplies which only a victorious battle could give him. His debts were crippling. When he crossed into Asia he had a bare seventy talents (perhaps representing two weeks' pay for his troops) and provisions for no more than a month at the outside.[6] Memnon, well described by Diodorus as 'famed for his understanding of strategy', διαβεβοημένος ἐπὶ συνέσει στρατηγικῇ, had accurately assessed Alexander's predicament: hence his shrewd proposal that the Persians should avoid battle, implement a scorched-earth policy, and if possible carry the war across into Greece. Alexander would then be forced to withdraw for lack of supplies.[7] As his invasion strategy had already made clear, he possessed neither the time nor the equipment to besiege cities en route. If they did not come over to him at once, of their own will, he simply by-passed them.[8]

The Persians, however, rejected Memnon's advice, and chose instead to establish a defensive line on the Granicus River, with the object of holding up Alexander's eastward advance towards Dascylium, and, if possible, of cutting short this Macedonian invasion 'as it were at the gateway of Asia', ὥσπερ ἐν πύλαις τῆς 'Ασίας. This may have been, as most modern scholars argue, a mistaken decision; but it was a perfectly understandable one. Pride entered into it: Arsites declared he would not let a single house in his satrapy be burnt. So did distrust of Memnon, the Greek mercenary, who made no secret of his contempt for Persian infantrymen, and was thought, rightly or wrongly, to be 'deliberately procrastinating over this campaign for the sake of [i.e. to prolong] his commission from the King',[9] τριβὰς ἐμποιεῖν ἑκόντα τῷ πολέμῳ τῆς ἐκ βασιλέως τιμῆς ἕνεκα.

Modern scholars have found other additional or alternative explanations, not all equally convincing. Tarn's I will deal with in a moment. Schachermeyr argues that the Persians' aristocratic code forbade them to retreat without a fight, so that Memnon's advice was by definition unacceptable.[10] Though the Iranian nobility undoubtedly, like all aristocrats, did observe a strict code of honour,[11] this had not prevented them, half a century previously, from using very similar tactics against Agesilaus; and as Davis says,[12] 'there is no evidence that Persian standards of knightliness had risen noticeably in the interval'. Davis himself suggests, rather more convincingly, that the satraps must answer not merely to their code but also to Darius; that Alexander was, as yet, merely a young Macedonian leader, Philip's son, and not the charismatic world-conqueror of later years; while the threat of revolt by the Greek cities of Ionia would undoubtedly become reality unless a firm stand was taken against the invader.[13]

However, once the decision to fight had been made, the Granicus line, it might well be argued, was the natural one to hold. This river, today the Koçabas, flows in a north-easterly direction from Mount Ida to the Sea of Marmara, through flat rolling country, ringed by low mountains, and ideal for a cavalry engagement such as the Persians were used to fighting. In May, when Alexander made his advance through Asia Minor, the Granicus would be swollen, though still fordable at its main crossing-points.[14] The Persians now advanced from their base-camp at Zeleia (Sari-Keia), and established themselves on the high, steep eastern bank of the river. As Fuller points out,[15] 'the southern flank of its lower reach was safeguarded against a turning movement from its western side by a lake, now called the Edje Göl.' Granted the Persians' decision to stand and fight, Arsites and his colleagues had chosen about the best possible terrain for their purpose.

But one point which has worried every student of this battle is the strategy – if we are to believe our sources – which they then proceeded to adopt. They drew up their forces along the river-bank, on a broad front, with high ground behind them. According to Arrian, their infantry was kept at the rear, virtually out of action, and their cavalry posted in front, where it could not charge.[16] As Davis understandably remarks,[17] 'either error is bad enough, but both together seem almost too much'. The Persians had hitherto acted without comparative good sense, and such a move makes them appear stupid almost past comprehension. It does not need Tarn's assurance[18] to convince us that this was not the proper way to hold a river-bank. Wilcken's comment ('a glaring error of tactics')[19] is typical of most historians' reaction to this strange aberration, which wasted a perfectly good body of professional Greek mercenaries during the battle, and resulted in its near-annihilation afterwards.

Various attempts have been made to explain, if not to justify, such a move. All, as Davis notes without comment, 'try to puzzle out some rational explanation as to what could have been the Persians' purpose behind this apparently mad act of folly'[20] – i.e. they rest on the initial premiss that our evidence is to be taken at its face value. None is in the slightest degree convincing. Tarn, for instance, argued that the Persian leaders 'had in fact a very gallant plan; they meant to strangle the war at birth by killing Alexander'.[21] Elsewhere[22] he developed this thesis more fully, claiming that 'the extraordinary formation they adopted was to induce Alexander himself to charge'. But Alexander, like all commanders of antiquity, led his own troops as a matter of course; nor, granted his position at the Granicus, could he refuse battle even if he so wished. The Persians had no need to adopt a special formation – let along a patently suicidal one – to make him attack, or do their best to kill him when he did.[23]

Furthermore, how the king's death would be more surely encompassed by pulling the Persians' only first-class infantry unit out of the fighting-line is left to our imagination. Fuller, with his usual acumen in tactical matters, pointed out [24] that 'if the sole aim of the Persians was to kill Alexander, then the best way to do so was to meet his cavalry charge with a hedge of spears; let him shatter himself against it, and then, should he break through, over-whelm him with javelins.' Elsewhere[25] he spells out just what they should have done by telling us what they did *not* do: 'They did not deploy the Greek mercenaries along the eastern bank, with the Persian cavalry on their flanks, and also in their rear to counter-attack any force that might break through the infantry.' Fuller, like Tarn, takes this failure as fact, and simply casts around for an explanation.

The answer he comes up with is almost identical to that proposed by Schachermeyr, and we may conveniently deal with both together. This is the Military Etiquette or Medieval Tournament theory. According to Schachermeyr, this was to be a formal contest of *Junker gegen Junker*, where only the cavalry would participate, and both sides would observe rules of knightly warfare: *Im Ritterstil bot sich der Gegner zur Schlacht an, im Ritterstil wollte ihm der König begegnen.*[26] But infantry and light-armed troops did, in fact, take part in the battle, while no knightly code known would require the Persians to adopt the formation they did. Then (we may legitimately ask) why pay several thousand Greek mercenaries for doing nothing? Fuller's answer is that 'throughout history the cavalry soldier has despised the infantryman, and to have placed the Greek mercenaries in the forefront of the battle would have been to surrender to them the place of honour. Military etiquette forbade it.'[27] In support he cites parallels from Taganae (A.D. 552) and Crécy. What he does *not* emphasize, though it is only too apparent from his own subsequent narrative,[28] is the crucial role played by these supposedly despised Greek mercenaries, very much in the forefront of the battle, at Issus and Gaugamela. Nor, obviously, did Cyrus have any such social qualms when deploying his forces at Cunaxa.[29] Greek mercenaries, in fact, very often enjoyed the place of honour in Persian tactical dispositions, unhampered by any hypothetical requirements of knightly precedence. This theory, then, will not do either.

There are in fact three possibilities, and three only.
1. The Persian commanders were sheerly incompetent.

2. Their known dislike and distrust of Memnon, the mercenaries' commander, were so great that they deliberately threw away a battle rather than let him and his troops win it,[30] even while keeping them on what must have been a very expensive payroll. 3. Our surviving accounts of the battle contain, for whatever reason, substantial inaccuracies. 1 and 2, though not by definition impossible, do not readily lend themselves to analytical investigation. Let us see what can be done with 3. The first, and most obvious, fact which emerges from a detailed comparison of our three main versions is that whereas Arrian and Plutarch (with certain exceptions I shall come to in a moment) agree well enough, Diodorus tells a quite different story, and may therefore be assumed to depend, in part at least, on a different source: not necessarily Cleitarchus, as was formerly thought to be the case,[31] certainly not Tarn's hypothetical 'mercenaries' source',[32] though perhaps a case of a sort could be made out for Trogus.[33]

Arrian and Plutarch both make the battle take place in the late afternoon; Diodorus puts it at dawn.[34] Arrian and Plutarch describe an engagement where the Persians are holding the high eastern river-bank against a direct assault through the river itself; in Diodorus Alexander gets his whole army across the river unopposed, and draws it up in battle-formation before the Persians can do anything to stop him.[35] There are other discrepancies, but these remain by far the most important.[36] It is worth noting at this point that though comparatively few scholars have thought the Diodorus version worth serious attention, they include Konrad Lehmann, Julius Beloch, Helmut Berve, and, most recently, R. D. Milns.[37] Beloch complained of the difficulty involved in finding an account that was '*unbeirrt durch den Arrian-Kultus*';[38] it is hard not to remember this remark when reading Davis's assertion[39] that Beloch 'contents himself with rewriting the entire battle' – though in fact Beloch has simply utilized the testimony of Diodorus.

Now Arrian and Plutarch both allude to the *possibility* of a dawn attack. This was, according to them, the strategy recommended to Alexander by Parmenio when the army first reached the Granicus. It was late in the afternoon; the Persians were entrenched in an extremely strong position; while the Granicus itself, with its steep banks and deep, fast-flowing stream, presented a formidable initial hazard (I am leaving on one side, for the moment, the actual disposition of Arsites' forces). There was, it seems, something of a panic among Philip's old officers, thus called upon to launch an assault under highly unfavourable conditions, while exposed to concentrated enemy fire. Nor would it be the first time their youthful leader had made a dangerous error of judgement: his campaign against Cleitus and Glaucias had come within an ace of ending in total disaster.[40] Tactfully, they argued that Daisios was a taboo month for Macedonians to fight a battle; Alexander replied by performing an *ad hoc* intercalation on the calendar, so that the month was now (officially at least) a second Artemisios.[41]

This point being settled – again, according to Arrian and Plutarch – battle was joined, and after a hard initial struggle the Macedonians won their great victory. Yet few modern students would disagree with Plutarch's verdict that the strategy which Alexander employed 'seemed to be crazy and senseless rather than the product of reason', ἔδοξε μανικῶς καὶ πρὸς ἀπόνοιαν μᾶλλον ἢ γνώμῃ στρατηγεῖν.[42] In fact the one thing which, so far as we can judge, prevented it ending in total disaster was the even more lunatic strategy adopted by the Persians on the other side. This gives one food for thought, especially since Diodorus offers us not only a quite different picture but an eminently sane one.

Here, beyond any doubt, we have a situation in which *Parmenio's advice has been followed.* Alexander moves at dawn, and gets his whole army across the Granicus undisturbed – which makes it a virtual certainty (assuming, for the moment, the validity of the report) that during the night he had moved away from the Persian position, and found an easier alternative fording-point. In which direction? Welles (see n. 36) claims that Diodorus, or his source, probably 'located the battle farther upstream, in the foothills'. He cites no evidence for this view, and the topography of the area is, on balance, against it. There is also the (admittedly ambiguous) evidence of Polyaenus[43] to consider in this context. At his crossing of the Granicus, Polyaenus reports, Alexander Πέρσας ἐξ ὑπερδεξίων ἐπιόντας (αὐτούς) αὐτὸς ἐπὶ δόρυ τοὺς Μακεδόνας ἀναγαγὼν ὑπερεκέρασεν. The Persians, that is, were *advancing*, ἐπιόντας, which they could scarcely have been doing in the engagement as described by Ptolemy and Aristobulus; and they were advancing ἐξ ὑπερδεξίων. While this phrase came to mean simply 'from above' or 'from higher ground' in many cases, its root meaning was 'from above on the right', and in various well-attested instances[44] it could signify 'from upstream'. Alexander then proceeded to outflank his attackers on the right wing, another significant departure from the canonical version of the battle: ἐπὶ δόρυ . . . ὑπερεκέρασεν. Whatever meaning we attach to ἐξ ὑπερδεξίων, what Polyaenus would seem to be describing is an engagement fought at right-angles to the river rather than parallel with it, which suggests that he too drew on the Diodoran tradition.

Now in Diodorus' account, the Persian order of battle, far from being a mere unaccountable whim, makes very good sense indeed. Here it is only after Alexander has crossed the river, and deployed his forces,[45] that Arsites and his fellow-commanders decide to counter the Macedonian attack with an all-out cavalry front, and to hold their infantry in reserve. This plan bears some resemblance to Darius' battle order at Gaugamela (see above, pp. 289–90), and was adopted for very similar reasons. In the first place, Persian infantry (or indeed any infantry if sufficiently outnumbered) was 'unsuitable for a pitched battle in the plains either against hoplites or charging horsemen'.[46] Secondly, and more important, in cavalry the Persians were overwhelmingly stronger than their opponents, a fact which went some way to balance out their shortage of first-class foot-soldiers.

To calculate the actual number of troops which the Persians had available at the Granicus is a highly conjectural task, but in ways a most revealing one. Arrian (1.4.4) states that they had 20,000 cavalry and 20,000 infantry, the latter consisting exclusively of mercenaries. Diodorus (17.19.5) gives the figure as over 10,000 cavalry, plus 100,000 infantry. This latter figure, improbably enough in itself, is contradicted by Arrian's statement elsewhere (1.13.3) that the Persian infantry was 'outnumbered', and thus even at an outside estimate lower than the overall Macedonian total of 43,000[47] – some at least of whom were probably on line-of-communication duties. Plutarch gives no figures at all, while Justin (11.6.11) offers an all-in total of 600,000 (*sic*).

Let us now compare these figures with the casualty lists. Diodorus (17.21.6) claims that the Persians lost over 2,000 cavalry and 10,000 infantry. Plutarch (*Alex.* 16.7) places the infantry losses at 20,000, those of the cavalry at 2,500. Arrian (1.16.2) makes no assessment of infantry losses at all, except to say that the Greek mercenary phalanx, all but some 2,000 men, was totally wiped out. Diodorus further records the number of prisoners taken – and in the context it is clear that means *infantry* prisoners – as 20,000. In contrast, Macedonian losses, according to our sources, are unbelievably small. The highest cavalry losses recorded (Justin 11.6.12) are 120; Arrian (1.16.4) puts the figure at 60, including 25 Companions, while Plutarch (16.7), on the authority of Aristobulus, cites the 25 Companions alone. Infantry losses, on the testimony available, were even smaller: thirty, according to Arrian, no more than nine by Plutarch's and Justin's reckoning. The historian, remembering the circumstances in which the battle was putatively fought, may perhaps permit himself a brief smile of incredulity.

There is, however, one even more striking and paradoxical fact which instantly stands out about these figures. In an engagement where the Persians are often said to have relied exclusively on their cavalry, their heaviest losses – or so we are asked to believe – took place among the infantry. Yet according to the same sources, these troops, except for the Greek mercenaries, put up little resistance: they fled in a rout, and there was no pursuit (Plut. *Alex.* 16.6; Arrian 1.16.1–2). This would at once seem to dispose of those 10,000 corpses and 20,000 prisoners: the first law of propaganda is to make your story consistent. Yet in sharp contrast to this, the cavalry losses recorded are, as we shall see in a moment, perfectly plausible. What, one well may ask, lies behind so striking and blatant a discrepancy?

First, let us see if we can find any evidence from which the true size of the Persian forces can be deduced. Diodorus (17.19.4) gives Arsites' order of battle in some detail, certainly as regards the cavalry: whatever source he is here utilizing at least had access to Persian as well as to Macedonian records, if only in the form of captured intelligence-files (always presuming that such things existed in the fourth century, for which there is little evidence).[48] On the left wing was Memnon, with his Greek mercenaries: an exclusively mounted contingent, it is assumed. Next to him came Arsamenes with his Cilicians; then Arsites, commanding the Paphlagonians; then Spithridates, with the eastern cavalry from Hyrcania. At this point Diodorus has a moment of infuriating vagueness: the centre, he says, is also occupied by 'other national cavalry contingents, numerous and picked for their valour', τὸν δὲ μέσον τόπον ἐπεῖχον οἱ τῶν ἄλλων ἐθνῶν ἱππεῖς, πολλοὶ μὲν τὸν ἀριθμὸν ὄντες, ἐπίλεκτοι δὲ ταῖς ἀρεταῖς. Beyond them the right wing was held by 1,000 Medes, 2,000 Bactrians,[49] and 2,000 unidentified horsemen under Rheomithres.

If this catalogue is at all trustworthy, we can make a very fair guess at the size of the Persian cavalry arm. Seven regiments are named and described; the other 'national contingents' provided at least two more, probably three. We read of two that are 2,000 strong, and one of half that number. If we strike a (conservative) average of 1,500, we obtain a round total of about 15,000 – a median figure, as it happens, between the estimates given respectively by Diodorus and Arrian. Losses of 2,000+ or 2,500 (i.e. of 14–16 per cent) would be just about what one might expect.[50] When we turn to the infantry, however, it is a very different matter. To begin with, there can be no doubt that Arrian (or Ptolemy) has vastly exaggerated the numbers of mercenaries involved.[51] When Memnon was first commissioned by Darius, he got no more than 5,000 mercenaries; Polyaenus puts the figure as low as 4,000.[52] It is unlikely that the troops at his disposal were substantially increased until he obtained the supreme command in western Asia Minor; and Darius lost no time in recalling what mercenaries he did have immediately after his death – which shows that, as a commodity, they were still in short supply.[53] Indeed, it was only in 333, when Alexander had already conquered most of Anatolia, that the Great King began recruiting in earnest. By the time of Issus he had arguably raised the number of mercenaries to 30,000, and the force on his payroll later reached an attested total of 50,000.[54]

But in May 334, when Alexander reached the Granicus, it is doubtful whether Darius had more than 15,000 Greek mercenaries all told, in Egypt, Asia Minor, or anywhere else, including the eastern provinces. 5,000, in fact, would be just about what he could spare Memnon to deal with Parmenio's advance force, and it is doubtful whether, at this stage, he thought Philip's untried son dangerous enough to justify any further reinforcements. There are two additional points to bear in mind here. That Alexander massacred 18,000 out of 20,000 mercenaries at the Granicus is not an absolute impossibility *per se*; but it is, to say the least, unlikely.[55] The sack of Thebes, a far more general and unrestrained piece of mass-slaughter, produced a death-roll only one third the size;[56] even the butchery of the Athenians at the Assinarus was on a lesser scale.[57] Secondly, it is quite incredible, on any reckoning, that the Persians, with so wide a variety of units to draw upon, should have had *no infantry whatsoever* apart from the mercenaries; and indeed neither Aristobulus nor Diodorus' source assumed this to be the case.[58]

On the other hand, if we are in search of hard figures, the case is almost hopeless. Arrian's 20,000 is the only remotely plausible estimate: we should not reject it out of hand because of Ptolemy's assertion that it consisted of mercenaries alone. But even this figure may well be too large. Justin's overall estimate of 600,000 is so ludicrously inflated that it suggests textual corruption rather than propaganda. At some point a scribe might well have misread $\widehat{M}$ (30,000) in his Greek source as $\overset{x}{M}$ (600,000); but though this would give us a very plausible round figure, it is not a theory on which one can build with any confidence. If we allow for an infantry force of, say, 15–16,000, of which up to one third were Greek mercenaries, that is about as close as we are likely to get.

Let us now turn back to the battle itself, as reported by Ptolemy and Aristobulus. Against Parmenio's considered advice, and amid general reluctance on the part of his Macedonians, Alexander disdainfully insisted on pressing home the attack (Arrian 1.13; Plut. *Alex.* 16.1–3). He then, according to Aristobulus (16.3), plunged precipitately into the river with no more than thirteen squadrons accompanying him. Ptolemy, on the other hand, makes him order his whole battle-line in a way that agrees with Diodorus' account of the dawn engagement,[59] and emphasizes at the same time the disposition of the Persians: lined up along the bank, cavalry to the fore, infantry in rear – again, duplicating Diodorus. One or the other of them, it is fair to assume, has mistaken his occasion. At this point, according to Ptolemy, there was a short pause, while both sides eyed each other and did nothing. Then Alexander sent the Scouts, the Paeonians, one Companion squadron and one file of infantry ahead, and followed in person at the head of the whole right wing, advancing obliquely with the current towards the Persian centre. This seems a far more deliberate and well-organized manoeuvre; it also sounds far more appropriate for a normal land-battle. Both sources are in general agreement as to what happened next. The Macedonian spearhead found itself up against the Persian cavalry, who were, very gallantly but for no good apparent reason, doing a job that could have been done far better by Memnon's hoplites and light-armed javelin-men (cf. Fuller, above). Curiously, it is javelins (ἀκοντία, βέλη) which now rained down on them from the banks; the Persians are described as ἐσακοντίζοντες, while the Macedonians resist with spears – δόρατα or ξυστά. When Alexander is struck[60] he is ἀκοντισθείς. We may note, however, that when there is a specific reference to the Persian *cavalry*, these are not, apparently, their weapons. They, like their Macedonian counterparts, use spears, δόρατα, and the sword, ξίφος, when their spears are broken. Some of them are also armed with the scimitar or sabre, κοπίς, a traditional cavalry weapon. Diodorus also mentions the σαυνίον.[61] Only Ptolemy refers to παλτά in this context,[62] and though it remains uncertain just what kind of spears or javelins these were, they are specifically associated with cavalry usage.

The initial attack suffered badly, as we might expect (how this setback is reconciled with the minuscule Macedonian casualty-list remains a mystery) and part of the credit for the repulse is specifically attributed to Memnon.[63] There follows another interesting discrepancy between Ptolemy's version and that of Aristobulus. While the cavalry was engaged upon this heroic hand-to-hand struggle, the latter tells us, 'the Macedonian phalanx crossed the river and the infantry forces on both sides engaged' (Plut. *Alex.* 16.6). But according to Ptolemy, the Persian infantry (whether mercenaries or not) remained in rear of the cavalry throughout. Which of them is telling the truth? And who (if Aristobulus is correct) are these ghostly foot-soldiers, with their javelins and darts, that we glimpse here for a moment (under Memnon's orders, it can scarcely be doubted), first resisting Alexander's cavalry charge, and then grappling with the phalanx: καὶ συνῆγον αἱ πεζαὶ δυνάμεις?[64] In the next sentence we read that they 'did not resist vigorously, nor for a long time, but fled in a rout, *all except the Greek mercenaries*' – a clear enough statement that Memnon's troops were not the only infantry fighting on the Persian side.

Ptolemy is at least consistent: according to his version, Alexander only dealt with the enemy infantry after the main cavalry engagement had been won – a view, be it noted, which is also that of Diodorus.[65] But Diodorus, as he makes very clear, is dealing with a battle which supposedly took place at dawn the following morning, and in very different circumstances: not across the river, but in the open plain on the far side – *in campis Adrasteis*, as Justin says (11.6.10); a small pointer, but not without its significance. Nevertheless, once Alexander and his men are up the further bank of the Granicus, and firmly established – it is just at this crucial point, suggestively enough, that the narratives of Ptolemy and Aristobulus become momentarily blurred in detail – the three accounts all go forward in close agreement. We have the famous duel between Alexander, Mithridates, and Rhosaces; Alexander's split-second rescue by Black Cleitus; the final rout and victory. Alexander himself is handled a little more roughly, a little less like the invincible hero, in Diodorus' version: at one point he seems actually to be down on the ground, with Spithridates and his royal kinsmen assailing him from all sides.[66] But that all three sources are from now on dealing with the same battle seems beyond dispute.

It will be convenient, before proceeding further, to recapitulate the facts that have emerged in the course of this investigation. Firstly, we have two separate (and on the face of it irreconcilable) accounts of the battle which Alexander fought at the Granicus. In the one he is advised to wait until dawn rather than launch an impossible frontal assault against heavy odds; he refuses the advice, attacks, and ultimately triumphs. In the other, he *does* wait till dawn. In the one he attacks across the river and up a steep bank on the farther side; in the other he gets his troops across unseen by the Persians (at least till the very last minute) and then fights a classic Macedonian-style engagement. In the one, both sides' tactics are ill-advised, and those of the Persians flatly incredible; in the other they are appropriate and excite no comment. Up to the crossing of the river, Ptolemy and Aristobulus disagree not only with Diodorus, but also, on occasion, with one another, in a way which suggests that they may well be suppressing vital evidence (e.g. the possible role played by Memnon's infantry during the initial assault). After the crossing, their account of the battle merges smoothly into that given by Diodorus, though the latter is, on the face of it, describing a quite different occasion. Lastly, we have the remarkable exaggeration of Persian infantry numbers and losses, together with a suggestion on Ptolemy's part that they were *all* Greek mercenaries; and, balancing this, an estimate of Macedonian losses so small that it can hardly be explained away as propaganda. Propaganda, after all, is meant to be believed.

What are we to make of all this? We may argue, and with some confidence, that Diodorus' version of events has a good deal more to be said for it than is generally allowed. This at once raises the question of why most scholars dismiss it out of hand. The most illuminating answer to this question is contained in Davis's criticisms of Beloch:[67]

The Arrian – Plutarch version of the battle he dismisses as merely a romantic picture designed to exhibit Alexander in the light of a Homeric hero. What he is doing here is not merely preferring the poorer to the better authority; he is also setting the Granicus against the evidence of Alexander's whole career. He is making Parmenio out of Alexander the Great. Why should this be the one occasion when Alexander chose the more cautious over the bolder course? And it is impossible to explain either the rest of

Alexander's career or the history of the years after his death if Alexander is reduced to a mere colorless competence. Alexander *was* a Homeric hero.

Now whatever our feelings about a mechanical reliance on 'better' as against 'worse' sources, we may willingly concede Davis's central point. The Diodorus account does indeed run counter to Alexander's known life-style in every possible way. But does that justify us in rejecting it out of hand, without further consideration? I think not. Circumstances may arise in which even an Alexander is forced to act against his own wishes, or, worse, to admit a serious error of judgement. On such an occasion his immediate instinct will be to falsify the record in his own interests. Our problem, I would submit, is a more complex one than merely deciding between two alternative traditions. What we are faced with here is deliberate, unmistakable, and systematic manipulation of the evidence.

Thus we cannot, like Gulliver, opt for one end or other of the egg, since propaganda (contrary to popular belief) avoids direct lies whenever possible. It normally prefers to save the appearances, aided by those two time-honoured devices *suppressio veri* and *suggestio falsi*. The carefully slanted half-truth is far more effective than any mere fabrication, if only because it becomes much harder to expose for what it is.* If we provisionally accept the hypothesis that our main account of the Granicus has been doctored to conceal some kind of initial failure, then a completely new light is shed not only on Alexander's behaviour, but also on the

---

*There are, of course, exceptions to this rule. Professor Badian reminds me of a splendid instance in Cicero (*De Orat.* 2.241), discussing a speech by L. Crassus which claimed that Memmius chewed up his opponent Largus' arm. 'You see how witty this kind of story is,' Cicero says, 'how elegant, how worthy of an orator – whether you have a true incident you can tell, which yet must be coloured by a few little lies, or whether you just make it up.' Perhaps the counter-principle, exemplified by the totally fictitious 'Protocols of the Elders of Zion', is that if you *are* going to invent, do it on a really staggering scale, and thus disarm incredulity.

supposedly divergent *testimonia*, which it may prove possible to reconcile in an unlooked-for fashion. What we seem to have here is, on the one hand, the 'official' version of the Granicus battle; and on the other an independent account which, while accepting some of the 'official' record's more dubious claims (e.g. those concerning Persian infantry losses), nevertheless disagrees with it at several crucial points.

If we ask ourselves who was ultimately responsible for doctoring the record utilized by Ptolemy and Aristobulus (both of whom, incidentally, must have been well aware of the truth), the only possible answer is Alexander himself, aided in all likelihood by Eumenes, his chief secretary, and the expedition's official historian, Callisthenes. So much seems clear enough. But our most important task is to find out not only *how* the truth was distorted, but also *why*. After all, the battle of the Granicus *was won*: that fact remains solid and undeniable. But it also poses an obvious dilemma. If Alexander won in the way suggested by Diodorus, why should he bother to make up a completely false version of events which does no credit to his strategic sense?[68] And if Ptolemy and Aristobulus are telling the truth, how did the eminently sane and unromantic account utilized by Diodorus ever get into circulation at all? Diodorus, significantly, makes the king out as Homeric a figure as anyone could wish during the actual battle (whenever and wherever that may have taken place); it is only beforehand that caution comes to the fore.

Here we may pertinently recall Davis's question: 'Why should this be the one occasion when Alexander chose the more cautious over the bolder course?' Might it not be that in the first instance he did nothing of the sort, but acted, characteristically, like the Homeric hero on whom he modelled himself, and with disastrous consequences? A hypothesis of *two* battles at the Granicus,[69] one, abortive, in the afternoon, the second, overwhelmingly successful, the following morning, would not only enable us to reconcile our conflicting evidence; it would also provide the strongest possible motive for Alexander to falsify the record afterwards. An initial defeat, at the very outset of his Asiatic campaign – even though recouped immediately afterwards – would make the worst possible impression, not least on the still undecided Greek cities of Asia Minor. Delphi had pronounced Alexander ἀνίκητος,[70] unconquerable, and ἀνίκητος he had to be, on every occasion. Herein lay the ultimate secret of his extraordinary personal charisma: the quasi-magical belief that he could not fail, that his leadership in itself guaranteed victory.

Now throughout his life, as we have seen,[71] Alexander reacted very badly indeed to any direct thwarting of his will and ambition. His instinct was to destroy those who stood in his path; he would, if need be, wait years for an appropriate and satisfying revenge. A setback, even a temporary one, at the Granicus would bode ill for all persons responsible once victory had been secured. The most competent and experienced troops fighting on the Persian side were, of course, Memnon's Greek mercenaries. Can we regard Alexander's special, and singularly vicious, animus against this particular unit as mere coincidence? He slaughtered them wholesale, and sent the survivors, chained like felons, to forced labour in Macedonia, at a time when common sense would have suggested acquiring their valuable services for himself at preferential rates. Moreover, this was an isolated action: from then on he enrolled Greek mercenaries whenever he could get hold of them.[72]

His ostensible reason (published by Ptolemy and accepted by most modern scholars) was that 'they had violated Greek public opinion by fighting with orientals, as Greeks, against Greeks' – ὅτι παρὰ τὰ κοινῇ δόξαντα τοῖς "Ελλησιν "Ελληνες ὄντες ἐναντία τῇ 'Ελλάδι ὑπὲρ τῶν βαρβάρων ἐμάχοντο.[73] In other words, he was making a gesture as captain-general of the league. But Greek public opinion was something of which Alexander took notice only when it suited him; and the league served him as a blanket excuse for various questionable or underhand actions, the destruction of Thebes (see above, pp. 147 ff.)[74] being merely the most notorious. A little good publicity in Greece never came amiss; but it is improbable, to say the least, that this was his primary motive. Aristobulus tells us that Alexander was 'influenced more by anger than by reason', θυμῷ μᾶλλον ἢ λογισμῷ,[75] and this sounds far more like the truth. His behaviour, indeed, bears all the signs of that terrible rage which could, at times, sweep away the last vestiges of his self-control, and was invariably caused by some personal insult, some thwarting of his destiny, some affront to his will, dignity, or honour.

The falsification of the record in this respect is highly suggestive. The infantry were made out to be more numerous than they were; in Ptolemy's account (see above) they are no mere Persian conscripts either, but highly trained mercenaries to the last man. We have already seen how improbable a claim this was. As propaganda, however, its meaning is clear. The threat which the Greek mercenaries represented was to be highly exaggerated, and the glory of overcoming them correspondingly increased. Yet at the same time *any part they may have played in the actual crossing of the Granicus* was to be deleted from the official account, even if it meant crediting the Persians with a wholly unbelievable battle-plan. This double reaction, coupled with Alexander's savage treatment of them afterwards, suggests that they somehow thwarted his plans in a way which showed him up in a very bad light, and which he was determined should be forgotten. In any case the odds against him were to be dramatically increased: if he *had* failed, he was determined to show that no mortal man could have succeeded.

Now if Alexander had in fact simply followed Parmenio's advice, crossed the river at dawn, and won his victory, there would have been no pressing need for him to invent the long dramatic rigmarole recounted by Ptolemy, with its wealth of circumstantial detail: the Macedonian panic, the intercalation of a calendar month, the argument with Parmenio, the details of that first suicidal assault across the river. These things really happened; and they happened in the late afternoon, just as Ptolemy says they did. If, at this point, we are prepared to argue that Diodorus' account is *likewise substantially true*, then the nature of Alexander's propaganda at the Granicus at once reveals itself, and all the apparently unmotivated discrepancies fall into place. Here, then, is a reconstruction of what I believe may have been the true course of events.

When Alexander reached the Granicus, he found that Arsites had made his dispositions not perversely but all too well. He did, indeed, have his cavalry along the river-bank, since this was by far his strongest native arm; but it was not alone. At the crossing-point itself he had placed Memnon's redoubtable mercenaries, just as any competent commander might be expected to do. The Persians knew the strength of their defences; they simply sat tight and waited to see whether Alexander (whose dashing reputation, clearly, had preceded him) would be rash enough to try a frontal assault. They had gauged their man well. Alexander was determined to cross the river at once; any further delaying tactics on the part of his officers would leave the man who used them facing a charge of cowardice, if not of treason.[76] For the second, and last, time in his life, the king's youthful impetuosity, coupled with the dire need to force an engagement at all costs, got the better of that cool strategic head. Parmenio suggested, hopefully, that the enemy might decamp during the night.[77] This, of course, was the one thing Alexander had to prevent, and it was probably a major factor in deciding him to reject his second-in-command's advice.

Besides, his Homeric destiny was summoning him to achieve heroic deeds, like his exemplar Achilles; and where better, here and now, than across the Granicus River, in the face of fearful odds? He charged headlong into the stream, and thirteen squadrons went with him. Perhaps the phalanx followed; just possibly it did not. There had been panic in the ranks; Parmenio's advice had been flouted;

and almost every key command – including those of the Hypaspists and the Companion Cavalry – was held by one of Parmenio's sons, relatives, or personal nominees.[78] If there was a power-struggle between Alexander and Parmenio from the first, Burn asks,[79] why did the army not simply 'make a Uriah' of Alexander at the Granicus? Nothing, he adds, could have been easier. In fact, I would submit, they may well have attempted to do so; but Alexander, as his subsequent exploits make abundantly clear, had an even more remarkable talent for survival than his father Philip.[80]

For a while, with furious resolve, Alexander and his squadrons battered at Memnon's mercenaries, while a deadly blizzard of javelins rained down on them.[81] If other Macedonian units, whether of foot or horse, supported this attack, they still made very little headway. At last, forced to admit defeat, they turned back across the river. This is the central fact which Ptolemy and Aristobulus are at such pains to conceal. Alexander's first brush with the Persians had ended in humiliating failure. Worse still, Parmenio had been proved right; and with all the weight of his sixty-five years behind him, he would not be slow to emphasize the fact. Yet Alexander, though he never forgot or forgave an injury, was also a realist, who never lost sight of his ultimate goal. He swallowed his pride; it must have taken some doing. During that night the army marched downstream and forded the Granicus. Perhaps Alexander simply intimated to his staff that if the troops distinguished themselves in battle next morning the matter would be regarded as closed. After all, he had as much reason for wanting the first assault forgotten as anyone.

So, indeed, it turned out: the Macedonians, perhaps a little ashamed of themselves, won an overwhelming victory. But that, from Alexander's point of view, was by no means the end of the matter. There were scores to settle, and an episode to be hushed up. Not for several years yet would the king feel himself strong enough to try conclusions with that indispensable figure Parmenio;[82] but Memnon's mercenaries, who had been instrumental in achieving his humiliation, were quite another matter. On them he took prompt and savage vengeance, camouflaging his personal motives by the pretence that he was executing justice on behalf of the Hellenic League. His initial *débâcle* may also provide a possible explanation for the minuscule size of the Macedonian casualty-lists in our sources. As an overall estimate they are ludicrous, a fact which every scholar has acknowledged. If the final battle took place in the way Ptolemy claims it did, by direct frontal assault, the one thing we can say with absolute assurance is that Alexander's losses would have been murderously heavy, almost on the scale of those suffered (in not dissimilar circumstances) by the Light Brigade during the Crimean War. But if we take them as the casualties suffered *by the thirteen squadrons which charged across the river with Alexander*, and by them alone, they at once fall into place – even down to the nine foot-soldiers, who will have belonged to that 'one file of the infantry', καὶ τῶν πεζῶν μίαν τάξιν, included in the spearhead.[83] Alexander had statues erected at Dium to the twenty-five Companions who fell at the Granicus – another unique gesture, never to be repeated: it is significant that *all* of them are said to have been killed 'in the first assault', ἐν τῇ πρώτῃ προσβολῇ.[84] To commemorate the faithful few, and them alone, would have been a superbly contemptuous gesture, very much in line with all we know of Alexander's character.

Now it only remained to put the record straight for propaganda purposes. There was no need to tamper with the final battle; only to transfer its setting. What had to be eliminated, at all costs, was that disastrous, ill-conceived, and humiliating initial charge. So the two separate engagements were run into one, and the scene of the final conflict changed from dawn to evening, from the Adrasteian plain to the river-bank of the Granicus. Callisthenes (or whoever was responsible) had to do the job in a hurry; small wonder that some loose ends and tell-tale inconsistencies remained, that the stitching of the join could be seen by those who cared to look for it. Memnon's role in the defence was carefully obliterated, though (as we have seen) not quite carefully enough; the Persian battle-plan was put, unchanged, into a new context which made it appear perverse to the point of insanity (itself an excellent piece of propaganda); and the king's deed of personal ἀρετή was increased beyond measure as a result.

No one would dare to publish the truth during Alexander's lifetime: too many high officials had connived at its falsification. Nor, indeed, was the real story one that reflected overmuch credit on anyone concerned – except, perhaps, on Parmenio. The battle had, after all, been won; and human memory is mercifully short. But discrepancies – mostly caused by unthinking adherence to the truth except at specifically sensitive points – were bound to find their way into the official version. Lastly, one of Diodorus' sources utilized a tradition which put on record the true facts of Alexander's dawn manoeuvres. The genesis of this tradition can be no more than a matter for speculation; but it appears, severely truncated, in Diodorus' own narrative, and is hinted at by Justin and Polyaenus.[85] If this hypothesis should be correct, it shows us the one occasion in his whole career when Alexander suffered a personal defeat – and by so doing renders him one degree more credible as a human being.

I do not for one moment suppose that the theory here put forward solves the enigma of the Granicus beyond any reasonable doubt, and I am well aware of the arguments that can be brought against it. Diodorus is a notoriously uncritical and unreliable source (or transmitter of sources); his contaminated account of the battle of Issus would hardly encourage one to accept him on the Granicus were it not for the (to me) unavoidable considerations advanced above. Nor, let me freely confess, do I find it intrinsically plausible that – as one of my more cogent critics represents the case I propose – 'of our two accounts one (Arrian) is a deliberate falsification, combining (roughly) the first half of the first battle with the second half of the second; while the other (Diodorus), coincidentally but by pure accident, omits the first battle and gives us only the second one'. I simply find this less unlikely than the alternative possibilities. Again while the motives of Ptolemy and Aristobulus in this matter are clear enough, why should any source *hostile* to Alexander not have instantly jumped on the first, abortive, attack on the Granicus, and given it maximum detrimental publicity – as indeed happened with so many other incidents, known to far fewer people, which Alexander's propagandists afterwards suppressed or distorted? To this question I can see no answer – any more than I understand how, supposing Arrian to be telling the truth, the Diodorus version (so much saner and more commonsensical by comparison) ever got launched. The one postulate raises just as many problems as the other. It may be that there was no botched afternoon attack, and that Alexander crossed at dawn without further demur. It may even be true (a point hard to determine without on-the-spot topographical investigation) that he forced the crossing *ab initio*, though I find this improbable, to say the least. But in either case the very real difficulties I have outlined still need to be explained. (It will not do, for instance, to dismiss Diodorus' account of the battle's pre-liminaries as a piece of rhetorical fiction straight from the Issus stock-pot. Alexander repeated his basic dispositions in almost every major battle he fought: the cliché, if cliché there be, is tactical rather than rhetorical.) I would claim no more than that my hypothesis answers more questions than it raises. Perhaps in the last resort Davis was right, and the enigma must be pronounced insoluble.

Notes and References

Chapter 1

1. See C. F. Edson, *AM*, p. 44.
2. For the chronology see Hamilton, *PA*, p. 7.
3. Philip's supposed regency for his brother Perdiccas' son Amyntas rests on dubious evidence, that of Justin 8.5.9–10, and has lately been challenged in a penetrating article by J. R. Ellis, 'The Security of the Macedonian Throne under Philip II', *AM*, pp. 68–75.
4. cf. A. Aymard, 'Le protocole royal grec et son évolution', *REA* 50 (1948), 232–63.
5. See now S. Marinatos, *AM*, pp. 45–52.
6. *Suda* s.v. Κάρανος.
7. The sixth day of the Macedonian month Loïos; cf. Hamilton, *PA*, p.7, and E. J. Bickerman, *Chronology of the Ancient World*, London, 1968, pp. 20–26, 38–40. But surely the news had reached Philip earlier.
8. Plut. *Moral.* 177c 3 (= 105a, 666a).
9. Hdt 3.40–41.
10. Seltman, *GC*² p. 200 with pl. xlvi, nos. 11–14; Head-Hill-Walker, *Guide*, p. 39 with pl. IIIB, no. 20.
11. This account is much indebted to the excellent survey in Hammond, *HG*, pp. 533 ff. I have also drawn on Edson's useful article 'Early Macedonia', *AM*, pp. 17–44.
12. Appian, *Syr.* 63; Diod. 7.15; Thuc. 2.99.3; Edson, *AM*, pp. 20–21.
13. Despite some late *testimonia* (e.g. schol. Clem. Alex. *Protrept.* 2.8, Justin 7.1.10) which claim that the Argeads simply renamed Edessa Aegae, it seems clear that the two sites, though close, were distinct. See Hammond, *AM*, pp. 64–5, and Edson, ibid., p. 21 n. 18, who points out that our ancient sources 'always associate the royal tombs with Aegae, never with Edessa': cf. *AP* 7.238; Diod. 19.52.5, 22.12; Pliny *HN* 4.33; Plut. *Pyrrh.* 26.12; *FGrH* no. 73, fr. 1.
14. See A. B. Bosworth, 'Philip II and Upper Macedonia', *CQ* 21ns [65] (1971), 99–100.
15. Strabo 7.7.8, C. 326.
16. Hammond, *HG*, p. 534.
17. Hdt 5.22; Justin 7.22.
18. Green, *The Year of Salamis, 480–479 B.C.* (1970), pp. 258–60.

19. Demosth. 23.200; [Demosth.] 12.21, cf. Hdt 8.121.2, and Edson, *AM*, p. 26, with nn. 50–53.
20. Edson, *AM*, pp. 26–9.
21. Plato *Gorg.* 471; Athen. 5.217d; Aelian *VH* 12.43, 8.9; Arist. *Pol.* 5.811–12, 1311b.
22. Edson, *AM*, pp. 34–5 and reff. there cited.
23. Aelian *VH* 7.12.
24. Hdt 5.22; Thuc. 2.99.3, 4.124.1; Paus. 7.25.6; Pindar frs. 120–21 (Snell); Bacchylides 20B (Snell).
25. *SEG* 10.138; Andoc. 2.11.
26. *AM*, pp. 30–31. For the reforms in general see Harpocration and the *Suda* s.v. πεζεταῖροι, citing Anaximenes of Lampsacus.
27. Thuc. 2.100.2.
28. Archelaus' attachment to Greek intellectuals: Dio Chrys. 13.30. Zeuxis: Aelian *VH* 14.17, cf. Athen. 8.345d, Plut. *Moral.* 177B. Evidence for the 'Olympian' festival at Dium collected in W. Baege, *De Macedonum Sacris* (Halle, 1913), pp. 10–12. Agathon: Aelian *VH* 13.4, 2.21; cf. Aristoph. *Thesmoph.* 100–130, 191, and *passim*, also Plato *Protag.* 156b. Euripides: *AP* 7.51.4, Aelian *VH* 13.4. Socrates' refusal: Arist. *Rhet.* 2.23.8, 1398a; Seneca *De Benef.* 5.6.6; DL 2.25.
29. Arist. *Pol.* 1324b; Athen. 18a.
30. For a vivid (and probably not much exaggerated) vignette of Macedonian court life see Theopompus ap. Polyb. 8.9.6–13, and the same writer cited by Athenaeus, 4.167a–c; cf. Demosth. *Olynth.* 2.18–19.
31. On this episode see now A. B. Bosworth, *CQ* 21ns [65] (1971), 100–101 with n. 7.
32. Justin 7.4.7–8, 7.5.5. The *testimonia* for this entire period are collected in F. Geyer, *Makedonien bis zur Thronbesteigung Philipps II*, Historische Zeitschrift, Beiheft 19 (Munich/Berlin, 1930), ch. 5, pp. 105–39.
33. Diod. 15.71.1. It is possible that Ptolemy was the son of *an* Amyntas; the name was common enough in Macedonia (see e.g. Berve *APG*, vol. II, nos. 56–65).
34. Aeschin. *De Fals. Leg.* 29; Plut. *Pelop.* 26–7: Marsyas ap. Athen. 14.629d; Justin 7.5.1–3; Diod. 15.60–61, 67, 71, 77, 16.2 (with n. 2 in Loeb edn, pp. 236–7). Our sources are highly confused. One says that Philip was taken as a hostage by the Illyrians after a battle with Amyntas; most agree that he was ransomed by Alexander II and then sent to Thebes. But this makes little sense. The present version depends largely on Aeschines, *De Fals. Leg.* 26 ff., and is that accepted by most modern historians.
35. M. Cary, *CAH*, vol. VI, p. 82.
36. QC 6.8.25; cf. Tarn, vol. II, p. 138, n. 1, and Edson, *AM*, p. 32.

37. Hammond, *HG*, p. 535.
38. Tarn, vol. II, p. 141.
39. Thuc. 2.100; Xen. *Hell.* 5.2.39; cf. Milns, p. 46, Fuller, p. 47, n. 1, Hammond, *HG*, p. 536, n. 1, and Snodgrass, pp. 119–20.
40. Other candidates include Alexander II and Archelaus; but the first had too brief a reign to carry out any lasting military reforms, while the second is only introduced by means of textual emendation. See Edson, *AM*, p. 31, n. 80.
41. Snodgrass, pp. 118–19.
42. Carystius ap. Athen. 11.506e–f, 508d–e.
43. Diod. 16.2–3; Polyaenus 4.2.1, 10; Aelian *VH* 14.48; Tarn. vol. II, pp. 135 ff.
44. Tod II, nos. 143, 147, 148.
45. Even so moderate and generally conservative a historian as Hammond can say of Athens at this period that 'her methods in diplomacy and war were comparable to those of pirates' (p. 503). For Timotheus' activities see Diod. 15.81.6; Isocr. 15.108 ff.; Demosth. *C. Aristocr.* 150 ff.; Tod, II, no. 143. The *Antidosis* of Isocrates, here cited, is especially revealing.
46. Aeschin. *De Fals. Leg.* 29–30.
47. Diod. 16.2.4–6.
48. Diod. 16.3.4.
49. Diod. 16.3.5–6; Demosth. *C. Aristocr.* 121.
50. Polyaenus *Strat.* 4.10.1.
51. Diod. 16.4.3–7; Justin 7.6.7; Front. *Strat.* 2.32; Polyaenus *Strat.* 4.2.17; cf. Beloch, *GG²*, III, i, p. 226 and n. 2, Hammond, *HG*, p. 538 (an excellent tactical account).
52. cf. Burn, *AG*, pp. 34–5.
53. cf. Plut. *Alex.* 3.4–5, Justin 12.16.6.
54. For an excellent account of this aspect of Philip's reign see now Harry J. Dell, 'The Western frontier of the Macedonian monarchy', *AM*, pp. 115–26, esp. 118–19, 121–2, with reff. there cited. Our main sources are Demosth. *Olynth.* 1.13, 23, *Phil.* 1.48; Justin 8.3.7–8; Diod. 16.69.7.
55. For Audata, Phila and Philinna see Satyrus ap. Athen. 13.557c–e. The whole passage repays close study, since it both indicates the chronological order of Philip's marriages, and makes a clear distinction between those women he married, and those he did not (particularly the two Thessalians, Philinna and Nicesipolis, by whom he merely had offspring). This distinction is not always observed by modern scholars: see e.g. G. T. Griffith, *CQ* 2ons [64] (1970), 70 with n. 1. The passage also explains why Justin, for instance, refers to Philinna (13.2.11) as a *scortum* (whore). We have no reason to query his description of her elsewhere (9.8.2) as a *saltatrix*, or dancing-girl.

56. E. Badian, *Phoenix* 17 (1963), 244. He also quotes that delightful Latin hexameter applied to the Habsburg dynasty in its heyday: *Bella gerant alii: tu, felix Austria, nube* ('Leave others to make war, while you, lucky Austria, marry').
57. Diod. 16.4.1–2; Justin 7.6.6–9; Beloch, *GG²*, III, ii, pp. 68 ff.; Tod, II, p. 146.
58. Demosth. *In Leptin.* 33; Strabo 7.4.6 (C. 311); Tod, II, no. 151. The price of grain had doubled since 393. In 357 Athens imported no less than 2,100,000 *medimni* (the *medimnus* was about a bushel and a half) from Leucon, ruler over the Cimmerian Bosporus. For special privileges granted to Leucon and his sons see Tod, II, no. 167. Similar considerations at this time prompted an Athenian expedition to keep the Thebans out of Euboea: Demosth. *Olynth.* 1.8, *Chers.* 74; Tod, II, nos. 153, 154.
59. Isocr. *Phil.* 2; Aeschin. *De Fals. Leg.* 21, 70, 72, *In Ctesiph.* 54; *IG*, ii², 127.
60. Diod. 16.8.3–4; Tod, II, no. 158.
61. Plut. *Alex.* 2.1–6, 9.3–4; Arrian 7.12.6–7. The marriage may also have had political motivations. See Bosworth, op. cit., p. 102, for the special ties between Epirus and Upper Macedonia: 'The two powers to the east and west of the Pindus range were now allied in marriage, and any progeny would be hybrid – so Attalus was to remark later.'
62. Diod. 16.3.7, 16.8.6–7, 16.53.3; Theopompus ap. Athen. 4.167a; Tod, II, p. 170; Bellinger, pp. 35–6; Griffith, *GR*, p. 127.
63. Plut. *Moral.* 177C2.
64. cf. Hammond, *HG*, pp. 497–8, a vigorous and just condemnation of Spartan methods. For Philip's attitude see, e.g., Plut. *Moral.* 177C–D4.

Chapter 2

1. Plut. *Alex.* 3.1–4; Cicero *Nat. Deorum* 2.27, 2.69.
2. e.g. Plutarch, who despite his use of contemporary sources was dominated by the urge to present Alexander as a type-figure, the 'spirited' man ruled by passion and ambition. See in particular Plutarch's two early essays *On the Fortune or the Virtue of Alexander*, *Moral.* 326D–333C, 333C–345B, together with the perceptive comments of A. E. Wardman, *CQ* ns5 (1955), 96 ff., E. Badian, *Historia* 7 (1958), 436 f., and J. R. Hamilton, *GR*, p. 123, *PA*, pp. xxxviii ff. On the subject of unconscious bias in historians of Alexander, see above, pp. 480 ff.
3. cf. S. K. Eddy, *The King is Dead*, pp. 11–12, 23 ff., 65–9; and below, pp. 314–15.
4. Hamilton, *GR*, pp. 123–4.

5. Plut. *Alex.* 5.1–3; *Moral.* 342B–C; Diod. 16.52.3, cf. QC 6.5.2, and Hammond, *HG*, p. 548. cf. Polyt. 12.22.

6. For Philip's siege and capture of Olynthus see Demosthenes' three Olynthian orations, *passim*; Diod. 6.53.2–3, 55 *passim*; Justin 7.4, 8.3. For Alexander of Epirus ('the Molossian'), see Demosth. *Olynth.* 1.13; Paus. 1.11.3; Justin 8.6.5.

7. *Olynth.* 1.13.

8. Theopompus ap. Polyb. 8.9.6–13 and Athen. 4.167a–c; Demosth. *Olynth.* 2.17–19; cf. Parke, *Greek Mercenaries*, p. 160.

9. For their attitude see, e.g., Theophrastus ap. Athen. 10.435a.

10. Tarn, vol. II, p. 326.

11. See, e.g., Isocrates, *Philippus*, 32–4, 111–20.

12. *Iliad* 3.179 and 6.208; the latter line is quoted, very tellingly, by P. A. Brunt in *GR*, p. 208. For Alexander's pedigree see Plut. *Alex.* 2.1; Diod. 17.1.5. The anecdote about achievement: Plut. *Moral.* 179D1.

13. Arrian 4.9.3; Plut. *Alex.* 5.4–5, 7.1.22.5, 25.4–5.

14. Plut. *Alex.* 6.1; Arrian 5.19.5; Pliny *NH* 8.154; cf. A. R. Anderson, *AJPh* 51 (1930), 1 ff. For Philip's celebration of games at Dium in 347 see Demosth. *Fals. Leg.* 192–5. In assessing the Bucephalas story I am much indebted to the expert advice of Major E. N. Barker, M.C., general manager of the Lazarina Stud Farm at Trikkala in Thessaly. For the reputation of Thessalian horses in antiquity see Hamilton, *PA*, p. 15 and reff. there cited. We have no instance on record of a higher price being obtained for any horse in antiquity. The nearest is the 100,000 sesterces (about 4 talents) paid by Dolabella: see Aul. Gell. *NA* 3.9.

15. This anecdote is related at length and in circumstantial detail by Plutarch, *Alex.* 6 *passim*. I have done little more than paraphrase it. For Demaratus' role in the affair see Diod. 17.76.6, and Chares of Mytilene ap. Aul. Gell. *NA* 5.2. Other sources in Berve, no. 253, p. 133.

16. Aeschines *In Timarch.* 166–9; Plut. *Per.* 1.5.

17. Diod. 16.53.2–3, 55 *passim*; Justin 7.4, 8.3; Demosth. *Fals. Leg.* 233, 237, 264 ff.; Tod, II, no. 166; Aeschines *Fals. Leg.* 18–19.

18. The main sources are the rival speeches *On the False Embassy* composed by Demosthenes and Aeschines. For the general reader, the Loeb editions of both works can be recommended; each has an excellent introduction.

19. The preserved speeches of Demosthenes, Aeschines, Hypereides and others illustrate this outburst of vindictive litigation in some detail. For Philocrates' impeachment see Demosth. *Fals. Leg.* 114–16, 145–6. For Aeschines' trial see the speeches cited in n. 18, *passim*.

20. Diod. 16.59.3–4, 60 *passim*; Justin 8.4.12–8.5.6; Tod, II, no. 172; Demosth. *Fals. Leg.* 111–12, *Peace* 22, *Philip* 3.32.

21. Justin 8.2.1; Isocr. 5.2.0; Demosth. 1.21–2; cf. Griffith, *CQ* ns20 [64] (1970) 73 and n. 6, cf. 74 ff. Most historians place this appointment now, in 344.

22. On Nicesipolis and her daughter see Plut. *Moral.* 141B23, 178F22; Satyrus ap. Athen. 13.5573, Paus. 9.7.3, 8.7.7; Diod. 19.52; Strabo 7 fr. 24; Steph. Byz. s.v. Θεσσαλονίκη.

23. On the Peace of Antalcidas see Norlin's analysis in the Loeb edn of Isocrates, vol. I, pp. xxv, 116–17, which the non-specialist will find clearer and more succinct than the accounts given in most standard histories.

24. Diod. 15.9.19; cf. Isocr. *Paneg.* 15.

25. *On the Peace*: see esp. §§29, 34, 103, 120; and *Areopag.* 4.

26. *Paneg.* 182; *Archidamus, passim*; cf. Norlin, Loeb edn, vol. I, p. xl, with note.

27. *Paneg.* 140–43, 187–8, 166–8; *Philip* 99–105, 132–6, 95–8, 120–23.

28. *Philip* 127.

29. e.g. the settling of Greek mercenaries by Alexander in the cities of Asia (§§122–3) and the articles accepted by the League of Corinth in 337 (see p. 94).

30. Isocrates *Philip* 101–2; cf. Olmstead, pp. 424–9.

31. Diod. 16.44–50 *passim*; Demosth. *Phil.* 4.33–5, *Ep. ad Phil.* 6–7; Arrian 2.14.2; cf. Olmstead, pp. 436–7, 486, Cloché, *Philippe II*, p. 274. I do not accept the theory that Artaxerxes offered Philip a free hand in dealing with Thrace as a *quid pro quo* for his nonintervention; there is no evidence that Persia exercised any effective control in the Thraceward regions during this period.

32. cf. Jaeger, *Aristotle*, p. 119.

33. Jaeger, ibid., pp. 105 ff.; A.-H. Chroust, *Historia* 15 (1966), 189, and 21 (1972) 170 ff.; *GR* 14 (1967) 39–44.

34. Strabo 13.1.57; Diog. Laert. 5.1.3–4; Jaeger, ibid., pp. 112 ff., 288–90.

35. Plut. *Alex.* 7.1–2.

36. Plut. *Alex.* 4.1–3; Aelian *VH* 12.14; Plut. *Moral.* 53D, 179D, 331B; Ps-Call. 1.13; Jul. Val. 1.7; Bieber, *Portraits*, pp. 24–5, pl. v. The characteristic poise of Alexander's head has been variously ascribed to congenital tortocollosis, compensation for imperfect vision in one eye, and plain affectation. For the girlish impression given by the statue-portraits cf. J. H. Jongkees, *Bull. Ver. Ant. Beschaving* 29 (1954), 32–3, and R. A. Lunsingh-Scheurleer, ibid., 40 (1965), 80–83.

37. Fredricksmeyer, *CPh* 56 (1961), 162–3.

38. For Marsyas see the *Suda* s.v. Μαρσύας Περιάνδρου Πελλαῖος, and Berve *APG* no. 489, pp. 247–8.

39. Plut. *Moral.* 178E–F 22; cf. *Alex.* 7.4.

40. e.g. Burn, pp. 16–17; Milns, pp. 19–20; cf. Philip Slater, *The Glory of Hera*, pp. 98, n. 9, 132.

41. Plut. *Alex.* 4, *Moral.* 179D, 331B.
42. Plut. *Alex.* 7.4–5; Aul. Gell. *NA* 20.5.
43. Aristotle *Pol.* 1284a–b, cf. 1288a 28 ff.; cf. Balsdon, *MP*, pp. 185–6. For the pre-eminent man as god, cf. *Pol.* 1253a 4–5, 25–9; and see also Jaeger, *Aristotle*, pp. 288–90.
44. Slavery natural: *Pol.* 1252a 32, 1254b 20, 1253b 32, 1278b 33. Persians ('barbarians') as slaves by nature: *Pol.* 1252b 8; Eur. *IA* 1400, cf. Ehrenberg, *Alexander and the Greeks*, pp. 89–90, and for the advice to Alexander, Aristotle fr. 658 Rose.
45. Didymus on Demosth. 5.64, 6.50 [Jacoby *FGrH* 2b, p. 640]; Diod. 16.52.5; Polyaenus 6.48; Ps-Arist. *Oecon.* 2.2.28; Demosth. *Phil.* 4.31–3. It is not necessary to assume, with Chroust, *Historia* 21 (1972) 175, that Philip's prime motive for recalling Aristotle in 343/2 was the protection of an agent whose cover was in danger of being blown, rather than the genuine need to find a highly qualified tutor for his son.
46. Ehrenberg, *Alexander and the Greeks*, p. 98, Hamilton, *GR*, p. 119.
47. Tarn, *CAH*, vol. VI, p. 357, repeated *AG*, vol. I, p. 8.
48. Eur. *IA* 1400; Plato *Rep.* 470c–471a; Isocr. *Paneg.* 3, 184, *Panath.* 163; Arist. *Pol.* 1256b 25.
49. *Eudem. Ethics* 1215b 35 (cf. Jaeger, pp. 253–5); Plut. *Alex.* 8.3.
50. Plut. *Alex.* 22, *Moral.* 65F, 717F.
51. Plut. *Alex.* 8.1.
52. See below, pp. 377 ff. For Alexander's interest in eristics see the excellent article by Philip Merlan, *Historia* 3 (1954/5), 60 ff., and esp. p. 76 for the comment here cited.
53. Merlan, ibid., pp. 60–63.
54. Demosth. *Chers.* 2; Diod. 16.71; Satyrus ap. Athen. 13.557b–e; cf. *CAH*, vol. VI, p. 251.
55. Demosth. *Halonn.* 16, *Chers.* 43–5, repeated in *Phil.* 4, 15–16.
56. Demosth. *Chers.* 6, 24–7; Isocr. *Ep. Phil.* 2 *passim*.
57. Demosth. *Chers.* 3, 11–13, *Phil.* 3, 9, 18, 25–7, and *passim*.
58. Demosth. *Halonn.* 16, *De Cor.* 87.
59. Demosth. *Phil.* 3.70–72, *Phil.* 4.52–3, *De Cor.* 87.
60. Diod. 16.72.1; Justin 8.6.4–8; Demosth. *Halonn.* 32; Tod. II, nos. 173–4.
61. Demosth. *Phil. Ep.* 6; [Plut.] *X Orat.* 847F–848A; cf. Demosth. *De Cor.* 76–7.

Chapter 3

1. Theophrastus ap. Athen. 10.435a. The earliest known portrait of Alexander is by no means inconsistent with this anecdote; see Bieber, pp. 24–5.

2. Diod. 16.74.2–76.4; Plut. *Alex.* 9.1 (cf. Hamilton, *PA*, pp. 22–3).
3. Plut. *Moral.* 178B 16–17 = 806B; Val. Max. 7.2.ext.§10.
4. Demosth. *De Cor.* 73, 76–7; *Ep. Phil.* 6; Diod. 16.76.4–77.2; Justin 9.1; Plut. *Phoc.* 14.
5. Demosth. *De Cor.* 145 ff.; Justin 9.2–3 *passim*; Plut. *Moral.* 174F, 331B, 334A.
6. He had already bribed one man, unsuccessfully, to set fire to the Piraeus dockyards: see Demosth. *De Cor.* 132.
7. Demosth. *De Cor.* 169 ff.; Plut. *Demosth.* 18; Diod. 16.84.2–5; cf. Grote, *HG*, vol. XI, pp. 287 ff.
8. The *Panathenaicus*, published during the crisis, compares Philip to Agamemnon before Troy, and contains several very cool allusions to Thebes, Sparta, and Argos. See esp. §§74–83, 91 ff., 121 ff.
9. A small squadron under Phocion did, in fact, sail to the North Aegean and attack Macedonian shipping there; but it was negligible as a threat, and in any case soon returned to Athens. See Plut. *Phoc.* 14.8, 16.1.
10. Aeschin. *De Fals. Leg.* 148; Plut. *Demosth.* 18.3; Polyaenus 4.2.8.
11. For the following account of Chaeronea I am much indebted to the masterly analysis by N. G. L. Hammond, 'The two battles of Chaeronea', *Klio* 31 (1938), 186–218, together with his more succinct account in *HG*, pp. 567–70. For the relative size of the armies, cf. Diod. 16.85.7 with Justin 9.3.9.
12. Plut. *Demosth.* 18.4, 20.1, *Phoc.* 16.1–3, cf. Hammond, *HG*, p. 567. The date is most often given as 2 August or 1 September (Metageitnion 7); I follow Plut. *Camill.* 19.5, which dates the battle Metageitnion 9. A new moon was visible at Athens on 26/7 July (Bickermann, *Chronology*, p. 119; cf. C. B. Welles, Loeb Diodorus, vol. VIII, pp. 78–9, n. 1), so 4 August must be considered the most likely date.
13. See on this the analysis by Polyaenus, 4.2.7.
14. Diod. 16.86.1–5; Plut. *Alex.* 9.2, *Demosth.* 20–21, *Moral.* 845F; Polyaenus 4.2.2, 4.2.7–8; Hammond *ut supr.* n. 75 *passim*; W. K. Pritchett, 'Notes on Chaeronea', *AJA*, 62 (1958), 307–11, with pls. 80–81.
15. Diod. 16.86.6–87 *passim*; Plut. *Demosth.* 20.3, *Moral.* 715C, 849A.
16. Hypereides fr. B 18 [=*MAO* II, pp. 575–7, cf. pp. 364–5]; Lycurg. *In Leocr.* 16; Demosth. *De Cor.* 195, 248; Aeschin. *De Fals. Leg.* 159; [Plut.] *Vit. X Orat.* 848, 849A, 851–2.
17. Quintil. *Inst. Orat.* 2.17.2; Deinarch. *In Demosth.* 104; Sext. Emp. *Adv. Math.* 2.16; *Suda* s.v. Δημάδης; Plut. *Phoc.* 1; Aelian *VH* 5.12; Demades, *Twelve Years* frr. 29, 51; cf. Pierre Lévêque, *The Greek Adventure*, pp. 326–7, also Pytheas ap. Athen. 2.44a and Aul. Gell. *NA* 11.10.
18. Diod. 16.87; Justin 9.4; Demades, *Twelve Years* frr. 9–10; Aelian

VH 6.1; Plut. *Moral.* 177E–F, *Demosth.* 10, 13, *Phoc.* 96; Hypereides *Eux.* 16–17 (cols. 12–13); Demosth. *De Cor.* 285; Theopompus ap. Athen. 10.435b–c.

19. For Philip's treatment of Thebes see Diod. 16.87–8; Arrian 1.7.11; Justin 9.4.6–10; Paus. 9.1.8, 9.37.8, 4.27.10. His treatment of Greek cities generally: Plut. *Moral.* 177C–D4, cf. Burn, *AG*, p. 42, who cites the parallel modern aphorism that 'you can do almost anything with bayonets except sit on them.'

20. Paus. 5.20.9–10; cf. Bieber, p. 19, and literature there cited.

21. See Badian, *Phoenix* 17 (1963), 246–7 and n. 16, with reff. there cited; Diod. 16.92.5, and C. B. Welles *ad loc.* (Loeb edn, vol. VIII, p. 101, n. 3): 'The implication of this claim on Philip's part was that he was in some fashion the equal of the Twelve and entitled like them to worship.' The episode involving the Twelve Gods is discussed more fully on p. 104. For Lysander see Plut. *Lys.* 18; Paus. 6.3.14–15; Athen. 15.696; Hesychius s.v. Λυσάνδρια. For the Archilocheum see F. Lasserre and A. Bonnard, *Archiloque* (Paris, 1958), pp. lxxviii ff. For Philip's contempt of divine pretensions in others, as exemplified by his dealings with Menecrates, the self-styled 'Zeus-physician', see Hegesander ap. Athen. 7.289c–e; Aelian *VH* 12.51.

22. Isocrates, *Epist.* 3, §5. For the Ephesus incident see p. 98 and n. 53.

23. Diod. 17.5.3–4; cf. Olmstead, pp. 489–90.

24. Justin 9.4.5; Polyb. 5.10; Plut. *Demosth.* 22; Hypereides fr.B 19.2–5 (cols. 77–80).

25. Paus. 1.9.4; Clem. Alex. *Protrept.* 4.54.5; Isocr. *Epist.* 3.3; Tod, II, no. 176; Demosth. *De Cor.* 285 ff. (Demosthenes quotes a different and longer epitaph, which he says was inscribed on the monument at public expense.) For that cited here see *Anth. Pal.* 7.245.

26. Plut. *Moral.* 471E, cf. 331B, 1126D. The sprinter's name is wrongly given as Crison, who flourished in the 440s (unless this is another man of the same name, perhaps called after his great predecessor); such a slip does not necessarily invalidate the anecdote itself.

27. Plut. *Moral.* 217F, 233E 29, 760A–B; Paus. 8.7.4; Diod. 17.3; cf. Roebuck, *CPh* 43 (1948), 73–92, Wilcken, p. 41, Burn *AG*, pp. 43–4. Wilcken argues that any garrisons which Philip imposed had league sanction, but this is no more than to say that the league tactfully endorsed the king's wishes.

28. E. Badian, *Hermes* 95 (1967), 172. For the Spartan abstention see Plut. *Moral.* 240A. Phocion attempted to make Athens follow Sparta's example, but was overruled by Demades: Plut. *Phoc.* 16.4.

29. This account of the league, and of the peace conference at Corinth, necessarily simplifies – perhaps oversimplifies – an immensely complex and controversial topic. The main source is a fragmentary inscription recording the terms of the treaty (Tod, II, no. 177,

pp. 224–31). Literary sources are scanty and misleading: Diod. 16.89.1–3; Justin 9.5. The best modern treatment is still Wilcken's (pp. 42 ff.); see also Borza's notes *ad loc.*, pp. 328–9, with more recent bibliography. Few scholars would probably now endorse J. A. O. Larsen's verdict, *CPh* 39 (1944) 160, that the league as organized by Philip 'must be ranked among the great achievements of statesmanship in the world's history', but it does offer ample evidence for his shrewdness and skill in political manoeuvring.

30. Diod. 17.22.5; cf. F. Mitchel, *GR*, p. 190.
31. Diod. 16.89.3.
32. Diod. 16.93.9; 17.2.4. For Attalus' marriage see QC 6.19.17; cf. Badian, *Phoenix* 17 (1963), 245.
33. For Philip's divorce of Olympias, and his declaration that Alexander was illegitimate, see Justin, 11.11.3–5.
34. See Bosworth, *CQ* ns21 (1971), 102, with n. 2. While realizing the bad effects such a match would inevitably have on the out-kingdoms, he side-steps any discussion of the true motives which led Philip to contract it in the first place.
35. Aelian, *VH* 12.43; cf. above, pp. 12, 22.
36. Satyrus ap. Athen. 13.557d–e; Plut. *Alex.* 9.3–7; Justin 9.5.9, 9.7.3–4; Ps-Callisth. 1.20–22; Jul. Val. 26–8. Cleopatra's maiden name before her marriage seems to have been Eurydice; see Arrian, *Succ.* 22.3; Justin 9.7.3.
37. Meda, daughter of King Cothelas of the Getae; see Satyrus ap. Athen. 13.557d, and above, p. 62.
38. For these various views see, e.g., Milns, p. 27, Badian *ut supra*, p. 244, Bosworth loc. cit., and Hammond, *HG*, p. 573. Burn, p. 44, seems to accept the tradition that Philip was merely suffering from acute infatuation.
39. Plut. *Alex.* 9.3. Note also Alexander's implicit claims to actual royalty in his refusal to run except against kings, and perhaps in his application to Xenocrates for rules of royal conduct (see above, p. 85).
40. QC 8.1.23.
41. Demosth. *De Cor.* 67.
42. Homer, *Iliad* 1.120.
43. Plut. *Alex.* 9.3.
44. Bieber, p. 23, and figs. 3–4, with earlier literature there cited.
45. Wilcken, pp. 47–9; Hammond, *HG*, p. 572, with reff. The idea of a 'sacred war' against Persia was not new: Pericles had suggested it long before, when moving his so-called 'Congress Decree': Plut. *Per.* 17.
46. See the admirable analysis by Milns, pp. 14–15. For the declaration of war by the league see Diod. 16.89.1–3; Justin 9.5.1–7; Plut. *Phoc.* 16.4; Demosth. *De Cor.* 10.

47. See Olmstead, pp. 491–2, with reff.
48. Satyrus ap. Athen. 13.557e; cf. Justin 9.7.12. This reconstruction of events assumes that Cleopatra bore *two* children before Philip's death: a daughter, Europa, and a son, Caranus. Since our various sources never mention both children together, many scholars assume that only one in fact existed (see, e.g., Tarn, vol. II, pp. 260 ff., who uses much special pleading to argue Caranus out of existence) and place Philip's marriage to Cleopatra later, in the spring or summer of 337. This thesis does not affect my main conclusions. On the other hand, it makes the recall of Alexander in 337 considerably harder to explain.
49. Justin 9.7.7.
50. Plut. *Moral.* 179c 30, cf. *Alex.* 9.6. For the difficulty experienced by Demaratus in persuading Alexander to come back see Justin 9.7.6.
51. Polyaenus 4.2.6.
52. Justin 9.7.6–7; Plut. *Moral.* 818b–c.
53. Justin 9.5.8; Diod. 16.91.2, 17.2.4, 17.7.1–2; Polyaenus 4.4.4; Arrian 1.17.11; Tod, II, no. 192, and commentary, p. 265; cf. Badian, *Stud. Ehrent.*, pp. 40–41 and Brunt, *JHS* 83 (1963), 34–5. For Erythrae see *SIG*³ 284 with Dittenberger's notes *ad loc.*
54. For fourth-century actors as diplomats see A. W. Pickard-Cambridge, *The Dramatic Festivals of Athens* (1953), p. 287. They travelled freely, and their status seems to have given them some sort of diplomatic immunity, which made them ideal agents. Thessalus was the head of a troupe which gained prizes at Athens in 347 and 340; he also accompanied Alexander's expedition, performing in Tyre, and probably also in Egypt (Arrian 3.1.4). cf. Berve, *APG*, II, p. 180, no. 371, and Hamilton, *PA*, p. 25.
55. The text of Plutarch is uncertain; but this would seem to be the best interpretation of a vexed passage (10.3). See Hamilton, *PA*, pp. 25–6 *ad loc.*
56. On the Pixodarus affair see Plut. *Alex.* 10.1–3; cf. Strabo 14.2.17, C.656–7; Arrian 3.6.5; Badian, *Phoenix* 17 (1963), 245–6; Hamilton, *PA*, pp. 25–7. On Ptolemy's parentage (perhaps the claim that he was Philip's son is no more than propaganda put out to justify his subsequent position as King of Egypt) see QC 9.8.22; Paus. 1.6.2. His mother was said to have been one of Philip's concubines.
57. Polyaenus 8.60; Justin 11.11.3–5.
58. Diod. 17.5–6; cf. Olmstead, p. 490.
59. One may, perhaps, profitably compare this occasion with the recent (1971) junketings laid on by the Shah of Persia at Persepolis.
60. Diod. 16.91.4–6; Justin 9.6.1–3.
61. Diod. 17.2.3; Justin 11.2.3; Paus. 8.7.7. For Caranus as founder of the Argead dynasty see Diod. 7.15.1–3; Plut. *Alex.* 2.1; Justin 7.1.7–12, 33.2.6, Vell. Pat. 1.6.5. A different version is found in

Herodotus (8.137-9, and Thucydides (2.100), who reckon Perdiccas I as the first king of the line. It has been argued (e.g. by Tarn, vol. II, pp. 260 ff.) that the 'Caranus-genealogy' was mere fourth-century propaganda, but this is pure speculation. Philip would surely have taken an existing tradition, however mythical, to make his point rather than manufacture a brand-new piece of fiction for the occasion.

62. Milns, p. 31.

63. It is generally assumed – e.g. by Badian, *Phoenix* 17 (1963), 249, and Hamilton, *PA*, p. 28 – that Olympias remained in Epirus until after the wedding, and therefore could have played no direct part in the plot against Philip's life. This is hard to credit when we consider who was getting married, and it is directly contradicted by the evidence of Justin 9.6.8–10, and Plut. *Alex.* 10.4.

64. Diod. 16.92.3–4.

65. On the basis of a highly fragmentary papyrus (P. Oxy. 1798 = *FGrH* 148) it has recently been argued by Bosworth, *CQ* ns21 (1971), 93 ff., that Pausanias was handed over for execution to the Macedonian army. He is not in fact named in this text, and the person referred to could equally well be a brother of Alexander the Lyncestian (cf. Arrian 1.25.1–2; QC 7.1.6–7).

66. Badian, *Phoenix* 17 (1963), 244 ff., Milns, pp. 29–31.

67. Justin, 9.6.5, says that he was *primis pubertatis annis* at the time, i.e. a young adolescent; and the last *recorded* campaign which Philip fought against the Illyrians (there must have been many more) had been in 344/3 (Diod. 16.69.7). On this somewhat flimsy evidence the whole episode is normally placed in 344, i.e. *eight years* before Philip's murder. This is to strain credulity well past breaking-point – and unnecessarily so, since both Plutarch (*Alex.* 10.4) and Diodorus (16.93.8–9) make it quite clear that the event was of recent occurrence. It seems more likely that the battle with the Illyrians was a skirmish provoked by Alexander's activities there in exile (and for that reason perhaps afterwards suppressed), which would date it to 337, just the right period. Justin's phrase can then be treated as mere rhetorical hyperbole. Valerius Maximus (8.14.ext. §4) has a dubious anecdote of Pausanias asking a philosopher named Hermocles (otherwise unknown: the sculptor commissioned by Seleucus Nicator will hardly fit the bill) what he must do to reap immediate fame, and being told to kill a famous man.

68. Diod. 16.93 *passim*; Plut. *Alex.* 10.4; Justin 9.6.4–8; Arist. *Pol.* 1311b 2.

69. We may note the parallel case of Harmodius and Aristogeiton, the murderers of Peisistratus' son Hipparchus; here, again, homosexual jealousy was neatly harnessed to political ends: see Hdt 5.55–6, 6.109, 123; Thuc. 1.20, 6.5.54–57.

70. Plut. *Alex.* 10.4; Justin 9.7.8–14.
71. Plut. ibid.; Justin 9.7.3. The Euripides citation is from *Medea*, 288, where it refers to Creon, Jason, and Creusa. This was not to be the only occasion on which a passage from Euripides was to be associated with murder in Alexander's life: see below, p. 364 and notes *ad loc.* I do not (as I am quite sure some scholars must have done, or will do in due course) deduce from this parallelism that both instances are mere rhetorical fiction.
72. cf. Diod. 17.2.2, and below, p. 113.
73. By Bosworth, in *CQ* ns21 (1971), 93–105. Though there is slight evidence (Plut. *Moral.* 327C) for factions in Macedonia, as well as in Greece at large, causing Alexander some trouble *after his accession*, Bosworth fails to make out a convincing case for either Amyntas or the Lyncestian brothers having been behind the assassination itself.
74. See Welles's acute remarks in the Loeb Diodorus, vol. VIII, p. 101, n. 2.
75. The use of the plural (Diod. 16.94.4) is suggestive. Pausanias himself needed only one horse; the implication, surely, is that the original plan envisaged several murderers – nor can there be much doubt as to who was involved.
76. For similar interpretations see Milns, p. 31, and Badian, *Phoenix* 17 (1963), 249.
77. Milns, ibid.

Chapter 4

1. This seems to have been the traditional method of confirming the succession: see Berve, *APG*, II, pp. 46 f.; Badian, *Phoenix* 17 (1963), 248, citing Ps-Call. 1.26. The smooth take-over implied here has lately been challenged by Bosworth, *CQ* ns21 (1971), 103 and n. 1; but it gains confirmation both from Diod. 17.2.2 and Justin 11.1.8.
2. By Bosworth, op. cit., pp. 96–7.
3. See J. R. Ellis, 'The Security of the Macedonian Throne under Philip II', *AM*, pp. 68–75, further developed in *JHS* 91 (1971), 15–24.
4. Darius' supposed offer of 1,000 talents to Alexander, plus help in securing the Macedonian throne for himself (Arrian 1.25.3 ff.: see above, pp. 202–3, even if not a mere fictional libel invented afterwards to justify the Lyncestian's condemnation, hardly proves more than that he was an acceptable usurper – to Darius.
5. See Justin 11.5.1–2, 12.6.14.
6. Arrian 1.25.1–2; QC 6.9.17, 6.10.24, 7.1.6–7; Justin 11.2.1–2, 12.16.4; Diod. 17.2.1; Plut. *Alex.* 10.4, *Moral.* 327C.
7. Diod. 17.2.2–3; Justin 11.1.8–10; Arrian 3.6.6; cf. Wilcken, pp. 63–4.

8. Plut. *Alex.* 11.1, cf. *Moral.* 327C–D; Diod. 17.3.3–5; Justin 11.1.2–3.
9. Ellis, op. cit., esp. pp. 72–3 and testimony there cited.
10. Aeschines, *In Ctesiph.* 77. His source was the mercenary general Charidemus: cf. Plut. *Demosth.* 22.
11. For the relationship see Berve, *APG*, II, nos. 59 and 144; cf. Justin 11.5.8 for his Asia Minor command.
12. Plut. *Demosth.* 22–3 *passim*, *Phoc.* 16.6 [*X Orat.*] 847B; Diod. 17.2.3–6, 17.3.2, 17.5.1; Aeschin. *In Ctesiph.* 77, 160; Justin 11.3.3–4.
13. Aeschin. *In Ctesiph.* 238; cf. Diod. 17.7.12; Plut. *Phoc.* 17.1–2. Refusing Greek applications for gold subventions had become second nature to Persian monarchs and their officials: see, e.g., the amusing passage in Aristophanes' *Acharnians* (98–114), where almost the only intelligible remark the Great King's Eye makes is: 'No getty goldy, nincompoop Iawny [Ionian]'.
14. Plut. *Alex.* 11.2, cf. *Moral.* 327C.
15. Diod. 17.4.1–2; Justin 11.2.4, 11.3.1–2; Polyaenus 4.3.23; cf. Fuller, p. 82.
16. Diod. 17.4.3; Aeschin. *In Ctesiph.* 160–61.
17. Diod. 17.4.2–7; Plut. *Demosth.* 23.2–3, *Moral.* 327D; cf. Wilcken, p. 65, Olmstead, p. 495.
18. Diod. 17.5.1–2; Plut. *Demosth.* 23.2; QC 7.1.3, 8.7.5; Justin 11.5.1; Arrian 1.12.7, 1.17.9; cf. Badian, *Phoenix* 17 (1963), 249–50, *Stud. Ehrenb.*, pp. 41–3, Berve, *APG*, II, no. 59, pp. 29–30. I can see no grounds for Badian's statement that the execution of Attalus took place after the fall of Thebes.
19. On this important distinction see Wilcken, p. 65.
20. Megarian offer of citizenship: Plut. *Moral.* 826C–D. Spartan abstention: Arrian 1.1.2. Tyrannies in Achaea and Messenia: Demades, *Twelve Years*, 4–7, 10–11; Paus. 7.27.7.
21. See Ps-Demosth. *On the Treaty with Alexander, passim*, esp. §§10, 15, 16, 19–20, 26. Ironically enough, we only know most of the terms of the treaty because Macedonia was afterwards accused of breaking them.
22. For the league's meeting at Corinth see, in general, Diod. 17.4.9; Arrian 1.1.1–3; Plut. *Alex.* 14.1–3; Justin 11.2.5; cf. Hamilton, *PA*, pp. 33–4, Wilcken, pp. 65–6. The schedule of military obligations: Tod, II, no. 183, with commentary, pp. 240–41; Plut. *Moral,* [*Vit. X Orat.*] 847C. The mission from Ephesus: Plut. *Moral.* 1126D.
23. Plut. *Alex.* 14.1–3, *Moral.* 331F, 605D, 782A; Diog. Laert. 6.32; cf, Berve, *APG*, II, p. 417, n. 3. The story was extremely popular in antiquity; Berve (loc. cit.) has collected no less than twenty-two references. Modern scholars, for reasons not entirely clear to me, regard it as fiction, seemingly on the grounds that it is designed to illustrate character. Why such anecdotes should automatically be

taken as unhistorical is hard to see; even on the law of averages one would expect *some* of them to have a basis in fact.

24. Plut. *Alex.* 14.4; Diod. 17.93.4; cf. Tarn, vol. II, pp. 338 ff., who argues – rightly, in my opinion – for the authenticity of the anecdote; also Hamilton, *PA*, pp. 34–5. For the donation to the temple see *SIG* 251H.

25. For what follows I am much indebted to the excellent strategic analysis by Fuller, pp. 219–26. The only detailed source is Arrian, 1.1.4–1.6.11, *passim*; cf. the brief notices given by Diod. 17.8.1–2; Plut. *Alex.* 11.3, *Moral.* 327A; and the modern discussions of Tarn, vol. I, pp. 5–6, Burn, pp. 55–9, Wilcken, pp. 66–70, and Milns, pp. 35–8.

26. It is impossible to identify this island with any certainty. All we know is that Strabo's identification (7.3.15, C. 305) is undoubtedly wrong, since he places it 120 stades (= 15 miles) from the mouth of the Danube; it must have been at least 100 miles further upstream. Alexander's opponents on the farther bank were the Getae, and two other countries (those of the Sauromatae and the Scythians) lay between them and the sea: cf. Arrian 1.3.2 – though he is describing the Danube tribes as they were in his own day. There may well have been several islands with the same name. Whether Alexander did in fact cross by Darius' route (see Hdt 4.90, with the note by How and Wells, vol. I, p. 334, and H. L. Jones's note on Strabo, Loeb edn, vol. III, pp. 216–17) seems highly doubtful; he had no time to waste on so vast a detour, and Arrian's text (1.2–3, *passim*) suggests a march of no more than five or six days at the most from the Shipka to the Danube. Note also that the current is said to flow swiftly round Peuce because of the narrows, which would not be the case near the delta. Lastly, Darius' opponents were not the Getae, but the Scythians: in his case Strabo's identification may well be right.

27. Ehrenberg, *Alexander and the Greeks*, p. 60. The whole chapter, 'Pothos' (ibid., pp. 52–61) is full of valuable psychological insights. It is reprinted complete in Griffith, *MP*, pp. 74–83. I am not ignoring the possibility that on occasion Alexander's *pothos* may simply have been an excuse for motives which he preferred to keep private.

28. Arrian 1.4.7–8; Strabo 7.3.8, C. 301–2. Tarn, vol. I, pp. 5–6, points out that the reference to the sky falling is an allusion to the form of oath used by the Celts (and by the Irish Gaels a millennium later): 'We will keep faith unless the sky fall and crush us or the earth open and swallow us or the sea rise and overwhelm us.'

29. Arrian, 1.5.2, is quite specific on this point. The earliest brigading of Macedonians and Orientals seems to have begun immediately after Issus: see Griffith, *JHS* 83 (1963), 69. But we have here an interesting pointer in the same direction; and, be it noted, in the Guards Brigade (*hypaspistae*) rather than the cavalry, though as

Griffith remarks (ibid., p. 74), 'the horsemen of the Companions might be expected to be a little more sympathetic towards [Alexander's] political plans.' With the Agrianians, of course, the object was more purely military.

30. Strabo 7.5.11, C. 317–18.
31. As Fuller (p. 225, n. 3) acutely remarks, 'an unexpected and tremendous shout can at times be as effective as a volley of musketry'. He compares Alexander's ruse with a similar incident at the storming of the Alamo in 1836. Marius employed the same device during his Numidian campaign: Sallust, *Bell. Iug.* 99.
32. Arrian 1.5.5–1.6.9, *passim.*
33. cf. Ellis, *AM*, pp. 72–5.
34. Demades, *Twelve Years,* 17 (who adds sarcastically that Demosthenes and Lycurgus 'almost exhibited the body of Alexander on the platform for us to see'); Justin 11.2.7–8.
35. Diod. 17.8.2; Arrian 1.7.2–3; Aelian *VH* 12.47; Justin 11.2.9.
36. Arrian 1.7.1–3; cf. Plut. *Alex.* 11.3; Diod. 17.8.2.
37. For a useful summary of the facts see Mitchel, *GR*, pp. 189 ff.; also Ferguson, *Hellenistic Athens*, pp. 7–10.
38. Plut. *Demosth.* 23.2; Demades, *Twelve Years* 17; Diod. 17.8.6–7; Justin 11.3.3–5; cf. Arrian 1.7.4.
39. Plut. *Moral.* 327c.
40. References to this affair are numerous but (inevitably) biased. Demosthenes, for instance, was accused by his enemies of large-scale embezzlement. See in particular Deinarchus *In Demosth.* 10, 18–22; Hypereides, *In Demosth.* 4 (5) col. 17 [=*MAO* II, p. 513]; Plut. *Demosth.* 14.2, 20.4–5, 23.2–3; Aeschines *In Ctesiph.* 157, 160–1, 173, 209–10, and 239–40 (where he suggests that Demosthenes held back the money which would have delivered the Cadmea and brought Arcadia's mercenaries from the Isthmus).
41. Diod. 17.7.1–2, 9; cf. Badian, *Stud. Ehrenb.*, pp. 40–41.
42. Diod. 17.7.1–10; Polyaenus 5.44.5; [Arist.] *Oecon.* 1347a 7, 1351b 29. My interpretation differs substantially from the only other full-scale analysis I have seen, that by Badian (*ut supr.*), which seems somewhat cavalier with the order of events as recorded in our sources. The crux of the matter, clearly, is to explain why, when Memnon received orders to go to Cyzicus, his *shortest route* lay over Mt Ida.
43. Diod. 17.7.2.
44. Olmstead, pp. 491–4.
45. Arrian 1.17.9, 1.25.3 ff.; Diod. 17.48.2; Plut. *Alex.* 20.1. QC 3.11.18 probably refers to another Amyntas.
46. Justin 11.2.3, 12.6.14; QC 6.9.17.
47. Arrian 1.5.4.
48. Paus. 8.7.7; Justin 9.7.12; Plut. *Alex.* 10.4.

49. Arrian 1.7.5–7.
50. Diod. 17.9.2–4; Arrian 1.7.7–8; Justin 11.3.6; cf. Wilcken, p. 72.
51. Diod. 17.9.1, 5–6; Plut. *Alex.* 11.4–5; Arrian 1.7.11.
52. Diod. 17.11–13 *passim*; Arrian 1.8.1–7; Plut. *Alex.* 11.5–6; Justin 11.3.8. Arrian, following Ptolemy, suggests that Perdiccas 'jumped the gun' and started the attack without orders. This is extremely unlikely. Ptolemy, it is clear, wanted to minimize Alexander's responsibility in the matter: he further suggests that all atrocities were committed by allied troops, none by the Macedonians. Besides, Perdiccas was never a friend of his. For once Diodorus' account is fuller, more coherent, and intrinsically more plausible than Arrian's, and I have no hesitation in following it. cf. now Milns, pp. 40–41. For the figures of the dead and captured see also Aelian, *VH* 13.7; for the burning of the Thebaid, Paus. 9.25.10.
53. Plut. *Moral.* 260c; Paus. 9.10.1.
54. Diod. 17.14.1–4; Arrian 1.9.6–10; Plut. *Alex.* 11.5–6; Justin 11.3.8–11.4.8.
55. Arrian 1.9.9–10; Plut. *Alex.* 11–12, *Moral.* 259D–260D; Aelian *VH* 1.7.
56. Arrian 1.9.1–8; cf. Demades, *Twelve Years* fr. 65, where the orator declares, 'Greece has lost an eye in the destruction of the Thebans' city.'
57. It was formerly thought (e.g. by Tarn, *CAH*, vol. VI, p. 356 = *AG* I, p. 7 and n. 2; but then Tarn always minimized Alexander's faults when he could, quantitatively if not qualitatively) that the average price of a slave was between 3–400 drachmas, and that therefore the recorded number of persons enslaved at Thebes must be 'only a stereotyped figure'. We know now that such a price applied only to highly trained specialists, and that 88 drs. was not far off the average for an unskilled worker. See, e.g., W. K. Pritchett, 'The Attic Stelae', *Hesperia* 25 (1956), 276–81. In any case 30,000 slaves coming on the market at once was bound to create a glut and depress prices somewhat.
58. Arrian 1.10 *passim*; Plut. *Demosth.* 23, *Alex.* 13, *Phoc.* 17, *Moral.* 847c; Diod. 17.15 *passim*; Justin 11.3.3–5, 11.4.9–12; Deinarchus *In Demosth.* 101.
59. Deinarchus *In Demosth.* 32–4, with Burtt's notes *ad loc.*, *MAO* II, pp. 196–7. Cf. Plut. *Moral.* 847F, 848E; Arrian 1.10.6.

Chapter 5

1. Justin 11.5.1–2, 12.6.15; Diod. 17.16.1. Amongst those executed was Eurylochus (Berve, *APG*, II, no. 323, p. 159), who had carried out diplomatic missions for Philip and in 342/1 held the office of *hieromnemon* to Delphi.

2. Burn, pp. 65–6; *contra*, Bosworth, *CQ* ns21 (1971), 104 (arguing for calculation).
3. Cited from Barbara Tuchman, *The Guns of August* (Dell, 1963), p. 374.
4. Arrian 7.9.6.
5. Griffith, *GR*, p. 127, n. 4.
6. See Plut. *Alex.* 15.3, *Moral.* 342D–E; Justin 11.5.5; Dessau, *SIG*³ 332 (cf. Berve, *APG*, II, no. 672, p. 337).
7. On Alexander's debts see Plut. *Alex.* 15.1, *Moral.* 327D (both from Onesicritus); Arrian 7.9.6 (following Ptolemy). For his general shortage of money see the evidence assembled by Hamilton, *PA*, pp. 36–7, and add Aeschin. *In Ctesiph.* 163. For the cash and provisions which he had when he crossed into Asia add Plut. *Moral.* 342E. cf. Bellinger, pp. 36–8, for a (very conservative) analysis of the army's expenses. Yet even he reckons a month's outlay at 193⅓ talents, assuming the average daily pay for a foot-soldier to be 4 obols rather than 1 drachma. (However, he calculates the cavalry's wage at 2 drachmas, which is almost certainly correct.) This, we may note, was not the last occasion on which Alexander had recourse to his Companions for ready cash: see below, p. 431. Justin (11.5.9) emphasizes the troops' firm expectation of rich booty from the expedition.
8. Only Diodorus (17.17.3–4) gives a detailed breakdown. Totals in round figures are supplied by a number of sources, as under:

Infantry	Cavalry	Source
32,000	5,100	Diod. 17.17.3–4
32,000	4,500	Justin 11.6.2
30,000 [min.]	4,000 [min.]	Plut. *Alex.* 15.1 (Aristobulus)
43,000 [max.]	5,000 [max.]	Plut. *Alex.* 15.1 (? Onesicritus)
30,000+	5,000+	Arrian 1.11.3 (Ptolemy)
30,000	4,000	Plut. *Moral.* 327D–E (Aristobulus)
30,000	5,000	Plut. *Moral.* 327D–E (Ptolemy)
43,000	5,500	Plut. *Moral.* 327D–E (Anaximenes)
40,000	4,500	Polybius 12.19.1 (Callisthenes)

The best modern study is that by P. A. Brunt, *JHS* 83 (1963), 32–4. He explains the main discrepancy between these sets of figures by assuming that some include the expeditionary force that was already in Asia, and by postulating an omission of 600 cavalry in the final sum. This is confirmed by Diodorus, who adds up his own figures wrong to produce totals of 30,000 and 4,500 respectively. Brunt reaches an overall total of 42,000 foot (32,000 + 10,000: the latter is a round figure and should probably be emended to 11,000) and 6,100 horse (5,100 + 1,000), the second figure in each case being that of the advance expedition.

9. Diod. 17.9.3.
10. See Brunt, ibid., pp. 34 ff., and Griffith, *GR*, pp. 129 ff., who provides a clear and sensible summary of the available evidence.
11. Justin 11.5.3. For the Corps of Pages see Arrian 4.13.1; QC 5.1.42, 8.6.2–6; Val. Max. 3.3.
12. cf. Parke, p. 186. Some modern scholars (e.g. Milns, p. 49) challenge this figure and estimate that Alexander had at least 15,000 mercenaries with him at the outset of the expedition. I remain unconvinced by their arguments. For the numbers of mercenaries serving Darius see QC 5.11.5; Paus. 8.52.5. Their numbers rose sharply after Issus; before that battle the total force is put at 30,000 (QC 3.2.9). But see below, pp. 228–9 and note *ad loc.*; cf. pp. 499 ff.
13. For a good and up-to-date account of this unit see Milns, p. 48.
14. Milns, ibid.
15. Justin 11.6.4–7, a crucial passage, but not utilized in the only discussion of the problem I have seen, that by Griffith, *GR*, p. 132. For the allocation of key posts to Parmenio's relatives and supporters, see Badian, *TAPhA* 91 (1960), 327–8.
16. Tarn, vol. I, pp. 12–13.
17. Justin 12.6.17.
18. Diog. Laert. 5.5, citing Homer, *Iliad* 18.95; cf. T. S. Brown, in *MP*, pp. 36–7.
19. I am much indebted here to the brilliant and politically acute analysis of Callisthenes' position by J. E. Atkinson, 'Primary sources and the Alexanderreich', *Acta Class.* (Cape Town), 6 (1963), 125–37, esp. pp. 126–7. As a parallel, Atkinson adduces the employment by President Kennedy of two reputable American journalists, Bartlett and Alsop, to write up the development of Ex Comm policy after the Cuban missile crisis. For Aristotle's views on his nephew's lack of common sense see Plut. *Alex.* 54; Johannes Lydus *De Mens.* 4.77.
20. For these poetasters see QC 8.5.7–8; cf. Tarn, vol. II, pp. 55 ff., Brown, *MP*, pp. 38–9. Choerilus: Horace *Epp.* 2.1.232, Porphyry on Horace *AP* 357. Pyrrho: Sext. Emp. *Adv. Gramm.* 1.282.
21. Arrian 1.11.1–12; Diod. 17.16.3–4; Plut. *Moral.* 1096B; Athen. 12.538c, 539d.
22. Callisthenes ap. Arrian 4.10.2; Eratosthenes ap. Plut. *Alex.* 15.2; and for the story of Seleucus and Laodice, Justin 15.4.1–6. The anchor-mark was said to be hereditary in Seleucus' family (ibid., §9): a handy proof of legitimacy, one might suppose.
23. Olmstead, p. 496.
24. Arrian 1.11.3–6; cf. Wilcken, p. 84; Hamilton, *PA*, p. 38; Hogarth, p. 177; C. A. Robinson Jr *AHR* 62 (1957), 328–9 = *MP*, pp. 56–7.
25. The party needed sixty ships to cross the straits: see Diod. 17.17.1.
26. Arrian 1.11.5–7; Justin 11.5.4–10; Diod. 17.7.1–2; Hdt 7.54. For the

spear-throwing incident (only recorded by Justin, which does not necessarily invalidate it) see. W Schmitthenner, *Saeculum* 19 (1968), 31 ff., and H. U. Instinsky, *Alexander der Grosse am Hellespont* (Godesburg, 1949), who argues strongly that the conquest of the Great King was premeditated, and emphasizes Alexander's Panhellenic propaganda references to the Trojan and Persian Wars. *Contra*, F. W. Walbank, *JHS* 70 (1950), 80 (reviewing Instinsky), and Badian, *GR*, p. 166, n. 1 and *Stud. Ehrenb.*, p. 43, with n. 29.

27. Justin 11.5.11: '*precatus ne se regem illae terrae invitae accipiant*'. For Alexander's fundamental religiosity see now the excellent survey by Lowell Edmunds, *GRByS* 12 (1971), 363–91.

28. Strabo 13.1.25–6, C. 593, with Jones's notes *ad loc.*, Loeb edn, vol. VI, pp. 50–51.

29. Arrian 1.11.7–8, 1.12.1; Plut. *Alex.* 15.4, *Moral.* 331D; Diod. 17.7.3; Justin 11.5.12; Aelian *VH* 12.7, 9.38; cf. Olmstead, p. 496. For the murder of Priam by Neoptolemus see Paus. 4.17.3, 10.27; Virgil, *Aen.* 2.547. For Achilles' lyre-playing see, e.g., *Iliad* 9.185–91. Aelian's clear implication is that the relationship between Achilles and Patroclus (and therefore that between Alexander and Hephaestion) was homosexual. Evidence for such a view goes back as far as Aeschylus (see frs. 228–9 Mette, and cf. Plato, *Symp.* 179E–180B), though how Homer interpreted it, despite Plato's somewhat *parti pris* testimony, is anyone's guess.

30. Diod. 17.17.6–17.18.1, with Welles's note, p. 167; cf. 17.21.2; Plut. *Alex.* 15.4; Arrian 1.11.7–8, cf. 1.11.2, 6.9.3.

31. Arrian 1.12.6; Diod. 17.17.3, cf. Hdt 7.44; Justin 11.6.1; Polyaenus 4.3.15. Alexander here borrowed a trick used by the Spartans against Pericles (or to be more accurate, a trick which Pericles *anticipated* that they would employ to discredit him) at the beginning of the Peloponnesian War: see Plut. *Per.* 33.

32. Anaximenes himself, as paraphrased by Pausanias (6.18.2–4), claimed to have begged Lampsacus off by a well-known philosophical ruse; but the truth is hinted at in Pliny, *HN* 37.193, where the *quid pro quo* is identified as some highly valuable gems from the local mines. Memnon was well aware of Alexander's financial straits: see Diod. 17.18.2–4, and cf. Badian, *Stud. Ehrenb.*, p. 43 and n. 32.

33. Arrian 1.12.6–7.

34. Diod. 17.18.2. Milns, p. 56, suggests that the assassination of Philip in 336 still left them convinced as late as 334 that no invasion would take place. This seems scarcely less improbable than Justin's explanation (11.6.9) that Darius deliberately let the Macedonians cross his frontiers in order to win more glory by defeating them in pitched battle.

35. Arrian 1.12; Diod. 17.18.2–4. E. W. Davis (see Bibliography) sur-

veys most of the difficulties (his is the only detailed study devoted to the Granicus within recent years), but though he produces cogent criticisms of Tarn, Schachermeyr, and Beloch, he fails to produce any convincing suggestions of his own.

36. Plut. *Alex.* 16.1.3; Arrian 1.13.4; Strabo 13.1.11, C. 587; cf. Schreider, p. 15.

37. The Persians may also, as Tarn suggested (*CAH*, vol. VI, p. 361 = *AG*, vol. I, p. 16; cf. Fuller, pp. 148–9) have been determined to 'strangle the war at birth by killing Alexander', but this was a regular objective in all ancient battles and a good many modern ones (witness the Long Range Desert Group's commando raid on Rommel's H.Q. in 1942). On the present occasion it was, beyond any doubt, subsidiary to the Persians' main strategic plan.

38. cf. Fuller, p. 149.

39. For a full analysis of these figures see pp. 498 ff.

40. Arrian 1.13 *passim*; Diod. 17.19.1–2; Plut. *Alex.* 16.1–2.

41. cf. Hamilton, *PA*, p. 39, and reff. there cited.

42. Arrian 1.14.5–6, 15.1–5; Plut. *Alex.* 16.2–4; cf. Brunt, *JHS* 83 (1963), 27.

43. For examples of 'bad' advice see (besides the present instance) Arrian 1.18.6 ff., Plut. *Alex.* 29.3, 31.10 ff. The incident at Gaugamela: ibid., 33.10. For Callisthenes' role in smearing Parmenio generally see now Hamilton's excellent and informative note, *PA*, p. 89 – and for Alexander's characteristic desire to 'compensate at once for his few failures', Badian, *Stud. Ehrenb.*, p. 47.

44. It is surprising how often this simple ruse seems to have worked in antiquity: see, e.g., its employment by Nicias during the retreat to the Assinarus, Thuc. 7.80, and by Darius I in Scythia, Hdt. 4.134–5. It is not necessary to argue, from Arrian 5.9 ff. (see below, pp. 394 ff., on Alexander's tactics at the Jhelum), that such a move would have required days of elaborate preparation. In any case, after that afternoon's events, Arsites is unlikely to have expected any action on Alexander's part till the following day.

45. Diod. 17.19.3; Polyaenus 4.3.16; Justin 11.6.10–12; cf. Schreider, p. 15. For a full discussion of sources and tactics see pp. 489 ff. Arrian (1.14.4) places the Persian cavalry line parallel with the river, and makes the attack take place the previous afternoon. The account – a sentence merely – by Polyaenus makes it clear that he is describing neither the first assault (if it actually took place) nor the final battle; it therefore seems logical to assume that what we have here is a minor action at the time of the dawn crossing. It would, in fact, be surprising if an army as large as Alexander's had got across totally unobserved.

46. A similar helmet is portrayed on the silver decadrachm he struck (? in 324) to commemorate his victory over the Indian rajah Porus

(Paurava) at the Jhelum: see Hamilton, *PA*, p. 40, and reff. there cited.

47. Diod. 17.19.6, 20.2; cf. Arrian 1.14.7 (transferred by Ptolemy to the first assault), and see Fuller, pp. 151–2, who understands this manoeuvre very well, though he retains the Ptolemy–Aristobulus context.

48. Main sources for the details of the battle recorded here: Diod. 17.19. 6–21.5; Plut. *Alex*. 16.4–7; Arrian 1.15.6–16.3.

49. See Diod. 17.21.6; Plut. *Alex*. 16.6; Arrian 1.16.2–3, 5; and cf. pp. 497 ff. for a detailed discussion of the losses on both sides.

50. Arrian 1.16.4; Plut. *Alex*. 16.7 (on the authority of Aristobulus): Justin 11.6.12.

51. For the statues at Dium (executed by Lysippus) see Plut. *Alex*. 16.8; Arrian 1.16.4; Vell. Pat. 1.11.3–4.

52. Arrian 1.16.2–3, 6; Plut. *Alex*. 16.6–7.

53. Arrian 1.16.7; Plut. *Alex*. 16.8; cf. (e.g.) Wilcken, pp. 88–9, and my Appendix, pp. 508 ff.

54. Diod. 17.21.6; Arrian 1.16.5; Plut. *Alex*. 16.8; Justin 11.6.13.

Chapter 6

1. Badian, *Stud. Ehrenb.*, p. 46, cf. *GR*, p. 166.

2. Badian, *Stud. Ehrenb.*, ibid.

3. Arrian 1.17.1–2.

4. Arrian 1.17.8; Diod. 17.22.1.

5. Plut, *Alex*. 17.1; Diod. 17.21.7; Arrian 1.17.3–8. For the Persian Royal Roads from Sardis and Ephesus, see Cary, *The Geographic Background of Greek and Roman History* (Oxford, 1949), p. 151; cf. pp. 162–3.

6. cf. the illuminating discussion by Griffith, *Proc. Camb. Phil. Soc.* 10 (1964), 23–39, esp. pp. 24, 31–4, on which I have drawn heavily here. For Alexander's treatment of local mints see Bellinger, pp. 46–7; and for his dealings with the Lydians in general, the acute remarks of Badian, *Stud. Ehrenb.*, pp. 44–5.

7. Arrian 1.17.9–13, 18.2; Strabo 14.1.22–3, C. 641; cf. Badian, *Stud. Ehrenb.*, pp. 45–6; Ehrenberg, *Alexander and the Greeks*, p. 14; Tod, vol. II, p. 142; Milns, *Historia* 15 (1966), 256.

8. Aelian *VH* 2.3; Pliny *HN* 32.95, 35.16.12; cf. Bieber, pp. 37–8, 45 ff.; E. von Schwarzenberg, 'Der lysippische Alexander', *Bonner Jahrbücher*, 167 (1967), 58 ff.

9. Arrian 1.18.1–2; cf. Badian, *Stud. Ehrenb.*, pp. 45–6, 53, *GR*, pp. 167–8; Bellinger, p. 48; Ehrenberg, *Alexander and the Greeks*, ch. 1. For Alexander's shortage of money at this point see Arrian 1.20.1 and p. 156.

10. Paus. 2.1.5, 7.3.9, 7.5.1–3; cf. Hdt 1.16; Strabo 14.1.37, C. 646.
11. Arrian 1.18.4.
12. That the Greek fleet was at Ephesus can be deduced, with reasonable certainty, from the fact that it beat the Persians to Miletus by three days; Darius' squadrons are unlikely to have been sighted till they were well past Rhodes, and we still have to allow time for the news to reach the king.
13. The garrisons of Dascylium and Sardis accounted for 5,000 league troops; Parmenio's force had the remaining 2,500, plus 2,500 Macedonians; and Alcimachus' corps also totalled 5,000. See Arrian 1.17.7–8, 18.1. This does not take into account the cavalry and light-armed troops left with Asander.
14. Tod, vol. II, nos. 184, 185, pp. 241–4; cf. Badian, *Stud. Ehrenb.*, pp. 47–8.
15. Arrian 1.18.3–19.6; Diod. 17.22.1–5; Plut. *Alex.* 17.1, *Moral.* 180A 8; Val. Max. 1.1 ext. §5; Hdt 6.6; Strabo 14.1.7, C. 635; cf. Tarn, vol. I, pp. 18–19; Stark, *AP*, pp. 230–32; Milns, pp. 60–61.
16. Arrian 1.20.1; Diod. 17.22.5–23.1; QC 3.1.19.
17. Badian, *Stud. Ehrenb.*, p. 48 (by far the most realistic discussion of this problem); cf. Tarn, vol. I, pp. 18–19 (who takes Ptolemy's account at its face value); Stark, *AP*, pp. 231–2, and Milns, p. 61, who adds some useful points.
18. Diod. 15.90, 17.23.4–6; Arrian 1.20.2–3.
19. Arrian 1.23.7–8; Strabo 14.2.17. C. 656–7; Diod. 17.24.2–3; Plut. *Alex.* 22.4–5, *Moral.* 180A 9; cf. Badian, *GR*, pp. 170–71, Stark, *AP*, pp. 234–5.
20. Diod. 17.24.1–3, an extremely revealing account.
21. Stark (*AP*, pp. 232–4) suggests a route by way of Alabanda and Lagnia; but this does not take into account the evidence concerning Iasus (see n. 22 below).
22. Diod. 17.24.1.
23. Tod, vol. II, no. 190 and note *ad loc.*, pp. 252–3.
24. Pliny *HN* 9.8.27; cf. Athen. 13.606d–e. A different version of the story appears in Aelian, *HA* 6.15; here the boy is accidentally spiked on the dolphin's erect dorsal fin, and dies of his injuries.
25. For the siege of Halicarnassus in general see Arrian 1.20.2–23.6 *passim*; Diod. 17.24.4–27.6 *passim*; cf. Fuller, pp. 200–206. Over details of logistics I am much indebted to an unpublished paper, 'Some problems on the provisioning of Alexander's army', by Mr Don Engels of the University of Texas at Austin. See especially the material in n. 27 below.
26. So Fuller, p. 205.
27. F. Maurice, *JHS* 50 (1030), 221; Naval Intelligence Division, *Turkey*, vol. II (Naval Intelligence Division of Great Britain, 1943), pp. 36, 147; QC 3.5.6.

28. The story that this attack was initiated accidentally by two drunks from Perdiccas' battalion (Diod. 17.25.5; Arrian 1.21.1–2) is another instance of Ptolemy exculpating Alexander at the expense of his personal enemy Perdiccas: see above, p. 147 and n. 52, for a similar episode during the assault on Thebes. cf. Diod. 17.12.3, and Milns, p. 63.

29. Arrian 1.22.6. Diodorus (17.27.4) says the Macedonians forced their way through; but this makes Alexander's withdrawal less understandable.

30. Pliny, *HN* 5.31.134, records an anecdote according to which Alexander dumped all the homosexuals in Halicarnassus on this offshore island, renaming it Cinaedopolis.

31. Arrian 1.23.6–7, 1.24.1–2, 2.5.7; QC 3.1.1, 3.7.4.

32. Arrian 1.24.3–4, 1.29.3–4; Diod. 17.27.6–7; Plut. *Alex.* 17.2.

33. For the topography of Alexander's campaigns in Lycia, Pamphylia and Pisidia I have largely followed Freya Stark, *JHS* 78 (1958), 102–20, = *AP*, pp. 229 ff., and *Geog. Journ.* 122 (1956), 294–305.

34. Polyaenus 5.35; Arrian 3.6.6. A similar ruse had been employed by the democratic exiles who recaptured Thebes in 379: see Xen. *Hell.* 5.4.1–5.

35. Arrian 1.24.4–5; Strabo 14.3.9, C. 666; cf. Stark, *AP*, pp. 238–43.

36. Plut. *Alex.* 17.2–3; cf. Stark, *AP*, pp. 245–7.

37. Arrian 1.26.1; Plut. *Alex.* 17.4; cf. Stark, *AP*, pp. 86–7.

38. Arrian 1.25 *passim*; Justin 11.7.1–2; cf. Diod. 17.32.1–2, who gives the detail about Olympias' correspondence, but places the whole episode much later, when Alexander was at Tarsus.

39. Plut. *Alex.* 17.3–5; Arrian 1.26.1–2; Callisthenes ap. Schol. T. Eustath. Homer, *Iliad* 14.29. It has recently been argued, e.g. by Pearson, pp. 36 ff., cf. Badian *Gnomon* 33 (1961), 661, that Callisthenes did *not* say the sea made obeisance to Alexander, and that the remark may be due to the scholiast. This I find most improbable. Badian points out, correctly, that Callisthenes was a man of principle who died for his beliefs. But men who die for a principle do not invariably live by it, as every Catholic knows; and the split in Callisthenes' mind between verbal rhetoric and the harsh realities of life is absolutely characteristic of the mandarin element in fourth-century Greek intellectual training.

40. Menander ap. Plut. *Alex.* 17.4 (=Kock, vol. III, p. 240); Strabo 14.3.9, C. 666–7.

41. For the topography of the Pamphylian coast see Stark, *AP*, pp. 248 ff., and Snyder, pp. 51–2.

42. Diod. 17.28.1–5; Arrian 1.24.6; cf. Stark, *AP*, pp. 80–81, 250–51.

43. Arrian 1.26.2–27.4; cf. Badian, *GR*, p. 167, and *Stud. Ehrenb.*, p. 49, where he writes: 'The freedom of the Greek cities of Asia, at this time, was not unlike that of the satellite governments in the Stalin

era, or that of Victor Emmanuel III, who was popularly said to be free to do everything that Mussolini wanted.'

44. Arrian 1.27.6–28.1; cf. Stark, *AP*, pp. 253–5, to whom I am greatly indebted for this reconstruction of events.

45. Stark, *AP*, p. 103. For Sagalassus see Arrian 1.28.2–8.

46. Arrian 1.29.1–4; QC 3.1.1–13; Hdt 7.26; Xen. *Anab.* 1.2.7; Livy 38.13; cf. Cary, *Geographical Background*, pp. 154–5; Tarn, vol. II, pp. 177–8.

47. Diod. 17.29.1–3, 17.31.3–4; Arrian 2.1.1–3 (placing Memnon's death before the siege of Mytilene was complete). For the revolt of Cos and Samos see Arrian 1.19.8; Diod. 17.27.5–6. For Chios, cf. Tod, vol. II, no. 192, with commentary pp. 263–7. Miletus and Priene: Badian, *Stud. Ehrenb.*, pp. 48–50, with reff. *ad loc.*

48. For the episode of the Gordian Knot see Arrian 2.3 *passim*; QC 3.1.14–18; Plut. *Alex.* 18.1–2; Justin 11.7 *passim*; schol. Eur. *Hipp.* 671; cf. Schachermeyr, pp. 159–62, and especially E. A. Fredricksmeyer, *CPh* 56 (1961), 160–68.

49. QC 3.1.9–10, 19–20; Arrian 1.29.56, 2.2.3; Diod. 17.31.3–4.

50. Arrian 2.4.1–3; QC 3.1.22–4; Plut. *Alex.* 18.3; Diod. 17.29.4, 17.31.4. For the chronology of these vital summer months see Miltner, *Jahr. Oest. Arch. Inst.* 28 (1933), 71; Judeich, in Kromayer and Veith, *Antike Schlachtfelder* 4 (Berlin, 1929), 355–6; and, now, Murison, *Historia* 21 (1972), 404–6 with n. 21. I do not accept his (admittedly tentative) suggestion, following Beloch, *GG* III 2² 311–12, that Alexander lingered at Gordium to watch the situation in the Aegean. On the other hand, he may well have spent more time than is generally supposed on the 'pacification' of the area round Ancyra, since news of Darius' move to Babylon only reached him there in mid July (Murison 406), and he did not reach Tarsus till September.

51. Arrian 2.1.3–2.2.5; QC 3.2 *passim*, 3.3.1; Diod. 17.30 *passim*, 31.1–2.

52. Arrian 2.4.2–6; QC 3.1.24, 3.4.1–15; Justin 11.8.1–2; cf. Snyder, pp. 57–8. Alexander's practice of force-marching over ill-supplied stretches of terrain was first pointed out to me by Mr Don Engels (see above, n. 25), and I am much indebted to him for the observation.

53. The date of entry into Tarsus: Bellinger, pp. 10–11, cf. Judeich, op. cit., p. 355. Alexander's illness: Diod. 17.41.4–6; Arrian 2.4.7–11; QC 3.5–6 *passim*, 3.7.1; Justin 11.8.3–9; Plut. *Alex.* 19; Val. Max. 3.8 ext. §6; Pap. Oxyrh. 1798, fr. 44, col. 1; cf. Strabo 14.5.12, C. 673. I am informed by Mr David Kusin that many of Alexander's symptoms – including the sweetish odour of his breath and body (Plut. *Alex.* 4.2) and his three-day recovery-spells after extreme physical or emotional shock – are typical of borderline diabetics.

54. For Alexander's coining activities in Cilicia, Syria and Phoenicia see Bellinger, pp. 10–11, 34 ff., and especially pp. 54–5, quoted in the text. Parmenio's movements round the Gulf of Alexandretta: Diod. 17.32.2; Arrian 2.5.1; QC 3.7.6–7.

55. Arrian 3.6.7; Plut. *Alex.* 41.4; cf. (with reservations) Badian, *Historia* 9 (1960), 245–6. For Alexander of Epirus' campaign in S. Italy see Arist. fr. 614 (Rose); Justin 12.2.1–11; Livy 8.24; QC 8.1.37; Plut. *Moral.* 326B (cf. 818B–C for Cleopatra's reputedly lax sexual habits); Strabo 6.1.5, C. 256, 6.3.4, c. 280.

56. The story is related by numerous sources: see Arrian 2.5.2–4; Aristobulus ap. Athen. 12.530b–c; Plut. *Moral.* 336C, cf. 330F; Strabo 14.5.9, c. 672; Photius and the *Suda* s.v. Sardanapalos. That the tomb and inscription actually were what they were claimed to be is very unlikely: see Snyder, p. 60, who suggests a possible explanation. For Aristotle's use of the anecdote see *Eth. Eud.* 1216a 16 (cf. Cicero, *Tusc. Disp.* 5.35), and Jaeger, *Aristotle*, pp. 253–5.

57. The object of this operation was to safeguard the only good land-route into Anatolia west of the Cilician Gates: see Stark, *AP*, p. 16.

58. Arrian 2.5.6–2.6.2; Diod. 17.32.4; QC 3.7.2–15. The movements of Alexander and Parmenio before Issus are hard to reconstruct from our sources. Alexander made a major error of judgement, and Ptolemy in particular was anxious to obscure this unpalatable fact as far as possible. Arrian does not help by mixing up the Pillar of Jonah and the Syrian Gates. Between Mallus–Castabala–Myriandrus Alexander was certainly in a spectacular hurry, covering the distance (about 75 miles) in some 48 hours, timing which has provoked incredulity from scholars (see Murison, op. cit., p. 409, nn. 30, 32) but seems by no means impossible if we take it as the speed of the advance guard. Cf. above, p. 325 and note *ad loc.*

59. Identification of the R. Pinarus remains dubious: for a conspectus of conflicting views see Murison, op. cit., p. 403, n. 10. He himself follows Janke, who came down decisively in favour of the Deli; but Janke's autopsy has lately been challenged by another on-the-spot topographer, Freya Stark. See *AP* p. 6, note cited by Murison. Mr Don Engels similarly opts for the Payas.

60. Arrian 2.7.1–2.8.3, 2.11.9–10; QC 3.8.11–21; Diod. 17.32.3; Plut. *Alex.* 20.1–3; Polyb. 12.17.2–4, 12.19.4–9; Pap. Oxyrh. 1798, fr. 44, col. 2; cf. Tarn, vol. I, pp. 25–6 (quoted here).

61. On this important point see Marsden, *The Campaign of Gaugamela*, pp. 4–5.

62. For the battle of Issus see Diod. 17.33–35.4; Polyb. 12.17–23; QC 3. 8–11.5; Justin 11.9.1–9; Plut. *Alex.* 20.1–5, *Moral.* 341B–C; Arrian 2.8–11 *passim*; cf. Fuller, pp. 157–62, Marsden, pp. 1–6.

63. Diod. 17.35–37.4; Plut. *Alex.* 20.5–21.3; QC 3.11.16–12.12; Justin 11.9.12–16; cf. Tarn, vol. I, p. 28 (quoted here).

64. cf. Jaeger, *Aristotle*, pp. 132 ff.; Eddy, *The King Must Die*, pp. 62–3 and reff. there cited.

Chapter 7

1. QC 3.12.15–26; Diod. 17.37.5–38.7; Arrian 2.12.6–8; Val. Max* 4.7 ext. §2.
2. Arrian 2.12.1–2, 14.7, 3.6.4 ff.; Plut. *Alex.* 24.1–2; Ael. *VH* 9.3; cf. Wilcken, pp. 105–7, Milns, pp. 85–6. For Alexander's coining activities see the monographs by E. T. Newell (Bibl. I c), and Bellinger, pp. 10–11.
3. Arrian 2.13.8–14 *passim*; QC 4.1.6–14; Diod. 17.39.1–2; Justin 11.12.1–2; Isocr. *Phil.* 120, *Paneg.* 162; cf. F. M. Abel, *Rev. Bibl.* 43 (1934/5), 528–39 (on the topography of Alexander's march through Phoenicia); Hamilton, *PA*, pp. 76–7, with reff. there cited; Marsden, pp. 6–7. On the exchange of letters between Darius and Alexander see E. Mikrojannakis, *AM*, pp. 103–8, summarizing his earlier work in modern Greek (see Bibliography II), and in particular G. T. Griffith, *Proc. Camb. Phil. Soc.* 194 [ns14] (1968), 33–48.
4. Arrian 2.13.1–6; Diod. 17.39.1, 48.1–6; QC 4.1.1–3, 27, 29–40 *passim*, 4.8.15; Justin 9.5.3; cf. Marsden, pp. 6–7, Parke, p. 200, Badian, *Hermes*, 95 (1967), 176–9; Tarn, vol. II, p. 73 (on the communications bottleneck); Burn, *JHS*, 72 (1952), 81–3 (on Darius' western strategy).
5. Arrian 2.11.10, 15 *passim*; QC 3.13.1–17; Plut. *Alex.* 21.4–5, 22.2, 26.1, *Moral.* 85c; Athen. 11.781–2, 784a–b, 13.607f–608a; Justin 11.10.1–3; Cic. *Pro Arch.* 10; Plin., *HN* 7.29.108–9; Strabo 13.1.27, C. 594; cf. Bellinger, p. 56. Alexander's treatment of the ambassadors was splendidly illogical. He released the two Thebans because one was an Olympic victor and the other an aristocrat; he kept the Athenian with him as a favoured guest (though Athens was a member of the league), and placed the Spartan under open arrest (though Sparta had never signed the league treaty). The most sceptical treatment of the Barsine episode is (predictably) that by Tarn: see his excursus §20, 'Barsine and her son Heracles', vol. II, pp. 330–38. *Contra*, Berve, *APG*, II, nos. 206 and 353, pp. 102–4, 168. It is possible (see Arrian 7.4.4) that there was a confusion of identity here, and that 'Barsine' was also the name of Darius' elder daughter – in which case Parmenio would have good dynastic reason for urging the alliance. Darius himself offered no less in due course: see Arrian 2.25.1 ff., and pp. 264, 287, above, with nn. 56 and 76 *ad loc.*
6. Arrian 2.15.6; QC 4.1.15–26; Diod. 17.46.4–6; Justin 11.10.8–9;

Plut. *Moral.* 340D; Anaximenes ap. Athen. 12.531d–e; cf. Snyder, pp. 78–9; Bieber, pp. 48–52; Newell, *Sidon and Ake*, pp. 22–3, *Royal Greek Portrait Coins*, p. 13.

7. Arrian 2.15.6–7; QC 4.2.1–2; Justin 11.10.10.
8. Diod. 17.40.3.
9. QC 4.2.10.
10. Arrian 2.15.7, 16.7–8; QC 4.2.2–5; Diod. 17.40.2; Justin 11.10.11.
11. Diod. 17.40.3; QC 4.2.10–12; Justin 11.10.12.
12. QC 4.2.15.
13. Arrian 2.17 *passim*; cf. QC 4.2.18.
14. QC 4.2.6–9, 16; Arrian 2.18.1–2, 21.4; Diod. 17.40.4; Plut. *Alex.* 24.3.
15. QC 4.2.17; Arrian ibid.; Plut. ibid.
16. For the siege of Tyre in general see Diod. 17.40.2–46 *passim*; Arrian 2.15.7–24 *passim*; QC 4.2–4 *passim*; Plut. *Alex.* 24.3–25.2; Polyaenus 4.3.4; Justin 11.10.10–14; Zachariah ix, 1–8; cf. Fuller, pp. 206–16; Abel, pp. 543–4; K. Elliger, *Zeitschr. f. Alttest. Wiss.* 62 (1949/50), 63–115; M. Delcor, *Vet. Test.* 1 (1951), 110–24.
17. Diod. 17.40.5; QC 4.2.18.
18. QC 4.2.18 (timber brought from Mt Libanus); Josephus *Ant. Jud.* 11.317. Though most of Josephus' narrative (ibid., §§ 304–5, 313–45) concerning Alexander's relations with the Jews clearly depends on legend rather than historical fact, some genuine details can be salvaged from it, of which the present passage is probably one.
19. Arrian 2.18.3–4.
20. Diod. 17.41.1; QC 4.2.20.
21. Diod. 17.41.2; QC 4.3.20; Justin 11.10.14.
22. Diod. 17.41.3–4; QC 4.2.12.
23. Arrian 2.18.5; QC 4.2.21–2.
24. Arrian 2.18.4–6; QC 4.2.23–4.
25. QC 4.2.24.
26. Arrian 2.19.1–5; Diod. 17.42.1–2; QC 4.2.24, 3.2–5.
27. Arrian 2.19.6–20.2–3; QC 4.3.1; Plut. *Alex.* 24.2.
28. Arrian 2.20.4–5; Plut. *Alex.* 24.6–8; Polyaenus 4.3.4; cf. Snyder, pp. 85–6.
29. QC 4.3.11; Arrian 2.20.5.
30. Arrian 2.20.9–10; Diod. 17.43.3; QC 4.3–12.
31. Arrian ibid.; Diod. ibid.; QC 4.3.11.
32. Diod. 17.42.5.
33. QC 4.3.6–7, 9–10; Diod. 17.42.5–6.
34. Arrian 2.21.1 ff.; QC 4.3.13; Diod. 17.42.5–7.
35. Arrian ibid.; QC 4.3.14–15.
36. Arrian 2.21.3; Diod. 17.43.1–3; QC 4.3.13.
37. QC 4.3.16–18.

38. Arrian 2.21.4; Diod. 17.43.7–44 *passim.*
39. QC 4.3.19–20.
40. QC 4.3.21–2; Diod. 17.41.7–8, cf. 23; Plut. *Alex.* 24.3–4.
41. Arrian 2.21.5–7; cf. QC 4.3.10.
42. Diod. 17.43.5.
43. QC 4.3.24–6; Diod. 17.43–4 *passim.*
44. QC 4.4.1; Diod. 17.45.7.
45. Arrian 2.21.8–22.7 *passim*; QC 4.3.24, 4.4.6–9.
46. Arrian 2.22.7; Diod. 17.43.4–5.
47. Plut. *Alex.* 25.1–2; Arrian 2.23.1; QC 4.4.10.
48. Arrian 2.23.2–3.
49. Arrian 2.23.4–6, 24.1; Diod. 17.45–46 *passim*; QC 4.4.10–11.
50. Diod. 17.46.3–4; Arrian 2.24.2; QC 4.4.12–13.
51. Arrian 2.24.3–4; Diod. 17.46.4; QC 4.4.13.
52. QC 4.4.15–16.
53. QC 4.4.17–18; Arrian 2.24.5; Diod. 17.46.6; Plut. *Alex.* 4.4.
54. Arrian 2.24.5–6; Diod. 17.46.4; QC 4.4.16–18.
55. For these operations in the Aegean and Asia Minor see QC 4.1.35–6, 4.5.13–18, 22, cf. 3.1.24. Pharnabazus was captured by Hegelochus, but afterwards escaped (Arrian 2.3).
56. For Darius' second mission to Alexander see QC 4.5.1–8; Justin 11.12.3–4; Diod. 17.54.1. It is generally assumed by modern scholars – against the majority of our ancient sources – that there were only *two* embassies: see e.g. Hamilton, p. 77, and other reff. there cited, relying largely on Arrian 2.25.1–3. I cannot accept such a view. For the third mission, shortly before Gaugamela, see above, p. 287 and n. 76 *ad loc.* At the time of Tyre Darius would certainly not have conceded all territory west of the Euphrates. Neither Griffith nor Mikrojannis clarifies this point.
57. Darius' assembly of a new army at Babylon: Diod. 17.39.3–4; QC 4.6.1–4, 4.9.1–2.
58. Arrian 2.25.4–27; QC 4.5.9–12, 4.6.7–30; Diod. 17.48.6–7; Hegesias ap. Dion. Hal. *De Comp. Verb.* 18, pp. 123–6 R; cf. Abel, pp. 43 ff.; Fuller, pp. 216–18. On problems of logistics I must once again acknowledge my indebtedness to the work of Mr Don Engels. As regards mythical precedent for the killing of Batis, Alexander may have imitated Achilles more closely than Homer would suggest; both Sophocles (*Ajax* 1031) and Euripides (*Androm.* 399) know a tradition according to which Hector was still alive when Achilles slit his ankles and dragged him round the walls of Troy at his chariot-tail. There is no reason to suppose that Alexander, too, did not know this tradition – much less that he was incapable of emulating it.
59. Casualties and recruiting: Arrian 2.24.5–6; Diod. 17.49.1; QC 4.6.30–31; cf. Badian, *Hermes* 95 (1967), 187. The march into

Egypt: Diod. 17.49.1–2; QC 4.7.1–3; Arrian 3.1.1–4; cf. Bellinger, p. 66. Alexander's enthronement as Pharaoh: Beloch, *Griech. Gesch.* III, ii, p. 315; Wilcken, pp. 112–16. The selection of Alexander's future site: Diod. 17.52.1–3; Arrian 3.1.5; Strabo 17.1.78, C. 792–4; cf. Welles, *Historia* 11 (1962), 271 ff.; Borza ap. Wilcken, pp. 335–6. For the Homeric reference to Pharos see *Od.* 4.354–5, cited by Plut. *Alex.* 26.3.

60. Arrian 3.2.2–7; Diod. 18.48.2, cf. Plut. *Phoc.* 30.2; Aeschin. *In Ctesiph.* 3.163 ff.; Plut. *Moral.* 818E; Tod, II, no. 192 (pp. 263–7); [Dem.] *On the Treaty with Alexander*, esp. §§4–5, 7, 10–11, 12, 17, 20, 26; cf. G. L. Cawkwell, *Phoenix* 15 (1961), 74–8; *JHS* 81 (1961), 34; Ehrenberg, *Alex. and the Greeks*, p. 27.

61. On this episode see, in general, Diod. 17.49.2–51.4; QC 4.7.6–32; Justin 11.11.2–12; Plut. *Alex.* 26.6–27; Arrian 3.3–4; Strabo 17.1.43, C. 814; Ps-Call. 1.30; Jul. Val. 1.23; Plut. *Moral.* 180D 15; Tod, II, no. 196. The modern literature is vast and often jejune; I mention only those works which I have found particularly helpful: Olmstead, pp. 510–12 (with further reff.); Hamilton, *PA*, pp. 68–70; Tarn, vol. II, pp. 347–59; Wilcken, pp. 121–9; Welles, *Historia* 11 (1962), 275 ff. For further reff. see Bibliography.

62. Arrian 3.3.1–2; Strabo 17.1.43, C. 115; cf. Snyder, pp. 102–3.

63. Arrian 3.3.3; Diod. 17.49.2–3; QC 4.7.6–9; cf. Welles, ibid., pp. 280–81.

64. Arrian 3.3.3–6; Plut. *Alex.* 26.6–27.3; Diod. 17.49.3–6; QC 4.7.10–16.

65. Arrian 3.4.1–4; Diod. 17.50.1–5; QC 4.7.16–22.

66. Justin 11.11.6.

67. Diod. 17.50.6–51.4 *passim*; QC 4.7.23–8; Arrian 3.4.5; Plut. *Alex.* 27.3–5, 5–6; Justin 11.11.7–12. The traditional responses were: (1) Alexander hailed as son of Ammon (Just. 11.11.7; QC 4.7.25; Diod. 17.51.1; Plut. *Alex.* 27.3–4), (2) The punishment of Philip's murderers (Just. 11.11.9; QC 4.7.27; Diod. 17.51.2–3; Plut. *Alex.* ibid.), (3) Victory for Alexander in war and empire (Justin 11.11.10; Diod. 17.51.2; QC 4.7.26; Plut. *Alex.* ibid.), (4) Alexander to be honoured as a god (Justin 11.11.11; Plut. *Alex.* 27.5–6), (5) Site for foundation of new city approved (Welles, *Hist.* 11 (1962), 275–6), (6) Instructions on the gods to whom Alexander should sacrifice when he became Lord of Asia (Arrian 6.19.4).

68. Arrian 3.3.5, 3.4.5; QC 4.8.1; cf. Welles, ibid., pp. 278–9; Borza ap. Wilcken, p. 336.

69. Diod. 17.52.1–7; Arrian 3.1.5–3.2.2; Plut. *Alex.* 26.2–6; Strabo 17.1.6–10, C. 791–5; QC 4.8.1–2, 5–6; Justin 11.11.13; Val. Max. 1.4.7 ext. §1; Pliny *HN* 5.11.62–3; cf. Welles, ibid., p. 284 and n. 67 (for the date), 285–9.

70. Olmstead, p. 512 and reff. there cited; Strabo 17.1.43, C. 814.

71. Arrian 3.5.1–5, cf. 7.23.6 ff., *Succ.* 5; QC 4.8.4–6; [Arist.] *Oecon.* 1352a–1353b; cf. Badian, *GR*, pp. 171–2 and reff. there cited.
72. Arrian 3.6.1–5, 8; QC 4.8.7–15; Diod. 17.48.1–2; Plut. *Alex.* 29.1–3; cf. Badian, *Stud. Ehrenb.*, pp. 54–5, *Hist.* 9 (1960), 245–6; Griffith, *Proc. Camb. Phil. Soc.* 10 (1964), 23 ff.
73. For the account of Gaugamela which follows I am greatly indebted to E. W. Marsden's brilliant and incisive monograph *The Campaign of Gaugamela* (Liverpool, 1964), which should be consulted by anyone wishing to study the battle and its preliminaries in detail.
74. Arrian 3.6.4, 3.7.1–2, 3.8.3–6; QC 4.6.1–4, 4.9.1–6, 12, 14–15, 4.10.11–15; Diod. 17.53.3–4; cf. Marsden, pp. 15–23.
75. Diod. 17.55.3–6; Arrian 3.7.2–3.8.1; QC 4.9.14–4.10.17.
76. The death of Darius' wife: Diod. 17.54.7; Plut. *Alex.* 30; QC 4.10.18–34; Justin 11.12.6–7; Plut. *Moral.* 338E. The third embassy from Darius: Diod. 17.54.1–6 (with Welles', note, Loeb edn, vol. VIII, p. 228, n. 1); QC 4.11 *passim*; cf. Arrian 2.25; Justin 11.12.7–16; Plut. *Alex.* 29.4.
77. The reconnaissance patrol: Arrian 3.9.1–3. Alexander's night-work on tactics and logistics: QC 4.13.16–17; Plut. *Alex.* 31.2–8; Diod. 17.56.1; cf. Marsden, pp. 46–7. On the relative size of the armies, Marsden, ch. III *passim* and reff. there cited. For Alexander's oversleeping, and his remarks on the morning of the battle, see QC 4.13.23–4 (cf. Marsden, p. 9, whose translation I have borrowed here); Plut. *Alex.* 32.2; Diod. 17.56.1.
78. Marsden, p. 64.
79. The speeches before the battle: QC 4.13.12–14; cf. Eddy, p. 31; Hamilton, *PA*, pp. 80 ff. (Darius); Plut. *Alex.* 33.1–2; cf. Wilcken, pp. 138–9 (Alexander).
80. For the battle of Gaugamela in general see Diod. 17.56–61; Arrian 3.8.7–3.15.7 *passim*; QC 4.12.18–4.16.33 *passim*; Plut. *Alex.* 32–3; Justin 11.13–14.5 *passim*; Plut. *Moral.* 180C 13; Polyaenus 4.3.6, 4.3.17; Strabo 16.1.3–4, c. 737, cf. 15.1.29, c. 399. I accept Marsden's date for the battle, 30 September; other suggested dates include 1 October (the most common choice), and 27 September (Burn, *JHS* 72 (1952), 84–5). See also Hamilton, *PA*, pp. 83–90; Fuller, pp. 163–80; and Milns, pp. 122–6 (the best recent general account, embodying the most useful parts of Marsden's thesis).
81. QC 5.1.3–9; Diod. 17.64.1–2; Arrian 3.16.1–2, cf. 3.19.1–2.

Chapter 8

1. Plut. *Alex.* 34.1–2; QC 4.11.13; cf. Hamilton, *PA*, pp. 90–99, Wilcken, pp. 137–8. For the tyrannies in Greece see [Dem.] *On the Treaty with Alexander* (xvii), §§4, 7, 10, 16; cf. Badian, *JHS* 81 (1961), 28.

2. For Persian religious opposition to Alexander see Eddy, pp. 41–7, 58–63, on which I have largely drawn here; for Aristotle's knowledge of Magian lore cf. Jaeger, pp. 132–5.

3. Diod. 17.64.3; Arrian 3.16.3; QC 5.1.10–16; Plut. *Alex.* 35.1–7; Strabo 16.1.15, c. 743; cf. Hamilton, *PA*, p. 93. There is a story (told by Plutarch and Strabo *ad loc.*) that Alexander set a plain-faced young slave of his on fire in the bath to find out whether naphtha was, in fact, water-resistant when ignited. For another anecdote of Alexander concerning ordeal by fire (again with a young boy as victim) cf. Val. Max. 3.3 ext. §1.

4. QC 5.1.20–39; Diod. 17.64.3–4; Arrian 3.16.3–5; Justin 11.14.8; cf. Hdt 1.179 ff cf. Olmstead, pp. 237, 517–18; Badian, *Hermes* 95 (1967), 184–5; André Parrot, *Nineveh and Babylon* (1961), pp. 170–76; Eddy, p. 105.

5. Administrative changes: Arrian 3.16.4–5; cf. QC 5.1.43–4, Diod. 17.64.6, and the valuable discussions by Badian, *GR*, pp. 173–5, and *Hermes* 95 (1967), 185. The Babylon mint: Bellinger, pp. 60–63, cf. Tarn, vol. I, pp. 130–31. Callisthenes' astronomical researches: Aristotle *De Caelo* 2.12. Restoration of Esagila and Alexander's relations with the Chaldaeans: Arrian *ut supr.* and 7.17.1–4, 7.24.4; Strabo 16.1.5, C. 738; Plut. *Alex.* 57.3; cf. Nock *JHS* 48 (1928), 21 ff.; and P. Jouguet, *Homm. J. Bidez et F. Cumont, Coll. Latomus* II (Brussels, 1949), p. 162. Troop-leave: QC 5.1.36–9; Diod. 17.64.4. Back pay and bonuses: Diod. 17.64.5–6; Plut. *Alex.* 34, 39; and especially QC 5.1.45.

6. Diod. 17.65.1–66.7; Arrian 3.16.6–7; QC 5.1.39–5.2.15; Justin 11.14.9; Strabo 15.3.10, C. 731; Plut. *Alex.* 36; Esther 6–7; cf. Olmstead, pp. 164–5; Parrot, op. cit., 198–9; and especially R. Ghirshman, *Perse: Proto-iraniens, Medes, Achéménides* (Paris, 1963), pp. 139–45.

7. Diod. 17.66.3–7, with Welles's important note, pp. 306–7; QC 5.2.13–15; Plut. *Alex.* 37.4, cf. 56, *Moral.* 329D. For Alexander's *faux pas* with Sisygambis see QC 5.2.18–22, cf. Diod. 17.67.

8. The revolt in Thrace, and Zopyrion's Scythian expedition: Diod. 17.62; Plut. *Ages.* 15.4; Justin 12.1.4, 12.2.16–17, cf. QC 9.3.21; Tod, II, p. 272; Badian, *Hermes* 95 (1967), 178–81. Agis' defeat at Megalopolis: Diod. 17.62.6–63.4; QC 6.1; Justin 12.1.6–11; cf. Badian, ibid., 190; Parke, pp. 201–2. Borza, *CPh* 66 (1971), 230–35, argues convincingly that the rebellion was put down before Gaugamela, but that Antipater's full report on it and other matters (e.g. Zopyrion's ill-fated expedition against the Scythians and Alexander of Epirus's death in S. Italy, cf. above, pp. 308–9) only reached Alexander in the summer of 330, after Darius' death, the essential facts having been sent through by fast courier (a topic on which Borza has collected some very useful information) while the king

was still at Persepolis. Cf. now his further article, 'Fire from Heaven: Alexander at Persepolis', *CPh* 67 (1972), 233–45, esp. 239–40 (with n. 41) and 242, where Borza argues, persuasively, that news of Agis' defeat could have reached Alexander at any time from mid December, perhaps even as early as October. The tyrannicide group: Arrian 3.16.4–8. Bribes to Phocion and Xenocrates: Plut. *Phoc.* 18.1–4, *Moral.* 181E 30, 188C 9, 331E; Diog. Laert. 4.8–9. Alexander also sent back 800 talents to Aristotle for research on animal biology (Athen. 9.398e); Aeian, *VH* 4.19, suggests, interestingly, that this grant was originally made by Philip.

9. Diod. 17.67–69 *passim*; QC 5.2.7–5.5.4 *passim*; Arrian 3.17.1–3.18.9; Plut. *Alex.* 37; Polyaenus 4.3.27; cf. Stein, *Geogr. Journ.* 92 (1938), 314 ff., Fuller, pp. 226–34; Burn, *JHS* 72 (1952), 89–91. My account of the bridging of the Araxes follows Diodorus (17.69.1–2) and Curtius (5.5.2–4) rather than the more generally accepted, but less intrinsically plausible, version by Arrian (3.18.6,10). H. E. Del Medico, 'A propos du trésor de Panaguriŝte', *Persica* 3 (1967/8), 37–67, pls. II–IV, figs. 8–15, suggests that the great rhyton-amphora in this collection illustrates the bribing of a guide to show Alexander the mountain-path round the Susian Gates. For a different view see G. Roux, *Ant. Kunst* 7 (1964), 30–41. The mutilated Greek prisoners: Diod. 17.69; QC 5.5.5–24; Justin 11.14.11–12. Their numbers are variously given as 800 or 4,000.

10. For this analysis of Magian opposition to Alexander I am much indebted to Eddy, esp. pp. 12–19; I have also used his translation of *Orac. Sib.* 3.388 ff. For the New Year festival in Persepolis see Ghirshman, op. cit., esp. pp. 147 ff.; cf. Parrot, pp. 193 ff.; Olmstead, pp. 172–84, 519–22.

11. Diod. 17.70–71; Plut. *Alex.* 37.1–2; QC 5.6.1–10; Justin 11.14.10; Strabo 15.3.9, C. 731; Athen. 12.514e; cf. Olmstead, pp. 519–524; Eddy, p. 29 and reff. there cited; Borza, *CPh* 67 (1972), 239, 243.

12. QC 5.6.10; Plut. *Alex.* 39.6–41.2, Moral. 333A; Strabo 15.3.7, C. 730; cf. Ghirshman, pp. 130 ff.

13. Badian, *Hermes* 95 (1967), 186 ff.; for a different view see Borza-Wilcken, pp. 336–8. For the length of Alexander's delay at Persepolis see Plut. *Alex.* 37.3 (wrongly questioned by Robinson, *Ephemerides*, pp. 74 ff., and *AJPh* 5 (1930), 22 ff.); cf. T. B. Jones, *CW* 28 (1935), 124 ff., and the excellent note by Hamilton, *PA*, pp. 98–9. Ice and snowdrifts may also have hampered Alexander's advance.

14. QC 5.6.11–20; Diod. 17.73.1; cf. Hamilton, *PA*, pp. 98–100.

15. Diod. 17.72; Plut. *Alex.* 38; QC 5.7.1–11; Strabo 15.3.6, C. 730; Athen. 576e; cf. Ghirshman, pp. 154 ff.; Borza-Wilcken, pp. 336–8; Hamilton, *PA*, pp. 99–101, and Borza, *CPh* 67 (1972), 243–4.

16. Olmstead, p. 523; for excavations at Persepolis see E. F. Schmidt,

Persepolis, 2 vols. (Chicago, 1953, 1957), esp. vol. II, pp. 91–111.
17. Arrian 3.19.1–5; QC 5.6.11, 5.7.12–19 *passim*; Diod. 17.73.1–2.
18. Arrian 3.19.5–8; Plut. *Alex.* 42.3; Diod. 17.74.3–5; Justin 12.1.1; QC 6.2.10.
19. Tarn, vol. I, p. 55. For the position of Parmenio (and Harpalus) see Arrian 3.19.3, 7; Plut. *Alex.* 35; Justin 12.1.3; Diod. 17.108.4; cf. Griffith, *Proc. Camb. Phil. Soc.* 10 (1964), 24–7; Milns, pp. 143–5; Badian, *JHS* 81 (1961), 16–43, and *Hermes* 95 (1967), 188–90.
20. QC 5.12.18–20.
21. Diod. 17.74.1–2; QC 6.6.13; Arrian 3.25.3; cf. Hamilton, *PA*, pp. 114–15.
22. For the pursuit and death of Darius see Arrian 3.19.5, 3.20–22.1; QC 5.10–13.25 *passim*; Plut. *Alex.* 42–3, *Moral.* 332F; Justin 11.15; Diod. 17.73.2–4; Aelian *HA* 6.25 (Darius' dog); cf. Milns, *Historia* 15 (1966), 256 ff.; C. Neumann, *Historia* 20 (1971), 196–8; Hamilton, *PA*, pp. 113–14.
23. Wilcken, p. 150.
24. Plut. *Alex.* 43.2–3; QC 5.13.28; Diod. 17.73.3–4.
25. Diod. 17.74.3; QC 6.2.9, 6.3–4 *passim*; Plin. *HN* 6.17.44–5;. Plut. *Alex.* 47.1–2.
26. The advance to Zadracarta: Diod. 17.75; Arrian 3.23.1–9; QC 6.2.12, 6.4 *passim* (see §§8–14 for Nabarzanes' letter); Plut. *Alex.* 44. Surrender of Persians and mercenaries: Diod. 17.76.1–2; Arrian 3.23.4–5, 3.24.4–5; QC 6.4.23–6.5.10. Alexander's shortage of horses: Justin 12.1.2; Plin. *HN* 12.18.34. Expedition against the Mardi: Diod. 17.76.3–8; QC 6.5.11–21; Arrian 3.24.1–3, 5.19.4–6; Plut. *Alex.* 44.2–3, 45.3, *Moral.* 341B.
27. QC 6.5.23; Dicaearchus ap. Athen. 13.603b = Plut. *Alex.* 67; cf. Badian, *CQ* ns8 (1958), 144–57; *contra*, Tarn, vol. II, pp. 320–23, who does his disingenuous best to dismiss Bagoas altogether, as a fiction invented by the Peripatetics.
28. Diod. 17.77.4–78.1; Justin 12.3.8–12; QC 6.6.4–12; Plut. *Alex.* 45.2–3, 47.5–6, *Moral.* 329F–330A; cf. Hamilton, *PA*, pp. 120–22.
29. cf. Milns, p. 157.
30. Justin 12.3.11–12.4.6, a significant and generally neglected passage.
31. QC 6.6.12.
32. Plut. *Alex.* 47; Arrian 3.25.1–7; Diod. 17.78.1–3; QC 6.5.32–6.6.35; cf. Tarn, vol. I, pp. 60–61; Wilcken, pp. 152–7; Cary, *Geogr. Background*, p. 197. For the episode of the Queen of the Amazons see Diod. 17.77.1–3 (with Welles's notes 2–3, pp. 338–9); Plut. *Alex.* 46.
33. The main source for the 'Philotas affair' is Curtius (6.7–7.2.34 *passim*); cf. Diod. 17.79.1–80.4; Plut. *Alex.* 48–49.7; Arrian 3.26; Justin 12.5.1–3; cf. Badian, *TAPhA* 91 (1960), 324–38, also *JHS*

81 (1961), 21–3; and Hamilton, *PA*, pp. 132 ff. (with some extremely sensible comments).
34. Plut. *Alex.* 48–9.
35. QC 6.9.18, 6.10.26–8, 6.11.23–5.
36. Plut. *Alex.* 49.3–4; QC 6.7.18–21; Diod. 17.79.3–4. For Philotas' own interpretation of the affair as suggested here cf. QC 6.10.15–18 (based on the defence speech he made at his farce of a trial).
37. QC 6.7.22; Diod. 17.79.4.
38. QC 6.7.23–8; Diod. 17.79.5.
39. Diod. 17.79.6; QC 6.7.24.
40. Diod. 17.79.2; QC 6.7.15.
41. QC 6.7.29–30; Diod. 17.79.6; Plut. *Alex.* 49.4.
42. QC 6.7.31–5; Diod. 17.79.6.
43. QC 6.8.1–14.
44. QC 6.7.2–17; Diod. 17.79.2.
45. QC 6.8.15–22.
46. QC 6.9.14–15.
47. QC 6.8.23–6.11.40; Plut. *Alex.* 49.6–7; Diod. 17.80.2.
48. Diod. 17.80.2; QC 7.1.5–9.
49. QC 7.1.10–14; Arrian 3.27.1–3; Plut. *Alex.* 49.7.
50. Arrian 3.27.5.
51. Diod. 17.80.3; QC 7.2.11–34, cf. 10.1.1 f.; Arrian 3.26.3–4; Strabo 15.2.10, C. 724; cf. Badian (n. 33).
52. Diod. 17.80.4; Polyaenus 4.3.19; QC 7.2.35–8; Justin 12.5.4–8.
53. For Hephaestion's promotion see Arrian 3.27.4; cf. Hamilton, *PA*, pp. 131–2.
54. Put. *Moral.* 183F 1.
55. Plut. *Alex.* 49.1; cf. Badian, *TAPhA* 91 (1960), 331 and n. 18, with reff. there cited. On the other hand Tarn, vol. I, pp. 62–4, accepts Philotas' guilt without any detailed examination of the evidence – though elsewhere (vol. II, pp. 270 ff.) he leaves no stone unturned (vainly, as he himself perforce admits) in an effort to exculpate Alexander from the murder of Parmenio. As Lowell Edmunds remarks, *GRByS* 12 (1971), 367–8, 'the death of Parmenio epitomizes the end of the Macedonian phase of Alexander's career'.

Chapter 9

1. Our sources (Arrian 3.28.1; Diod. 17.82.1–8; QC 7.3.5–18; Strabo 15.2.10, C. 725), with their talk of houses totally covered by snow, etc., may exaggerate the hazards which Alexander had to face during this stage of his march. Mr Don Engels informs me that 'in Kandahar, at least, the snow melts as soon as it hits the ground, and by the time Alexander reached the passes between Kandahar and

Kābul (where the snow lies for only two or three months) the temperature would be moderating'.

2. For Alexander's campaigns up to the crossing of the Hindu Kush see Diod. 17.81–3 *passim*; Arrian 3.27.4–28.4; QC 7.3.3–19; Strabo 15.2.10, C. 725. The defeat of Satibarzanes: Diod. 17.81.3–6; QC 7.3.2, 7.4.33–40; Arrian 3.28.2–3. For the geography of Areia and Arachosia, cf. Cary, *GB*, pp. 196–7. Alexander may also have received the titular submission of Gedrosia at this time: see Diod. 17.81.2 (with Welles's note); Arrian 3.28.1. For the date of his arrival at the Hindu Kush see Strabo, loc. cit., and Jones (Bibl.), pp. 124–5. The crossing of the Hindu Kush: Diod. 17.83.1–3; Arrian 3.28.4, cf. 5.3.2–3; QC 7.3.19–23; cf. Milns, p. 168, Cary, *GB*, pp. 198–9. Bessus' scorched-earth policy and retreat beyond the Oxus: Arrian 3.28.8–10; QC 7.4.20–25.

3. Arrian 3.29.1, 5, cf. 5.27.5, 4.17.3; QC 7.4.32–7.5.12, cf. 7.5.27; C. A. Robinson Jr, *AHR* 62 (1957), 335 (=*MP* p. 63). The crossing of the Oxus: QC 7.5.13–18; Arrian 3.29.2–4; cf. Wilcken, pp. 155–6.

4. Milns, p. 169 (based on Arrian 3.29.7).

5. The surrender and execution of Bessus: Arrian 3.29.6–30.5, 4.7.3; QC 7.5.19–26, 36–43, 7.10.10; Diod. 17.83.8–9; Justin 12.5.10–11; cf. the very sound note by Hamilton, pp. 114–15, and reff. there cited. Ptolemy-Arrian tells the story of Bessus' arrest as I have given it here; Aristobulus and Curtius suggest that Spitamenes brought the prisoner to Alexander himself, which seems in the circumstances fundamentally improbable (but quite consistent with a source hostile to Ptolemy, who did not *invariably* tell lies to present himself in a courageous or generally favourable light, and on occasion – as here – did things his enemies would prefer forgotten, even if they were forced to produce a glaring improbability in the process).

6. The advance to Maracanda: Arrian 3.30.6–11; QC 7.6.1–10. Envoys from 'Scythians': Arrian 4.1.1–2; QC 7.6.11–12. Foundation of Alexandria-the-Farthest (Eschate): Arrian 4.1.3–4, 4.4.1; QC 7.6.13, 25–7. Revolt of Spitamenes: Arrian 4.1.4–4.3.6; QC 7.6.13–23; Plut. *Moral.* 341B. The raid across the Jaxartes: Arrian 4.4.2–9; QC 7.7.5–7.19.6; Plut. *Alex.* 45.5; cf. Fuller, pp. 237 ff. The destruction of Pharnuces' task force: Arrian 4.3.6–7, 4.5.2–4.6.2; QC 7.6.24, 7.7.31–9; cf. Hdt 1.201–13 (the destruction of Cyrus by the Massagetae). For Alexander's forced march on Maracanda see Arrian 4.6.3–7; cf. Borza-Wilcken, p. 338 (on the topography of the march).

7. Arrian 4.7.1–5, 4.15.1–6; QC 7.10.11–12; Strabo 11.7.4, C. 509. On Pharasmenes' visit cf. C. A. Robinson Jr, *MP*, pp. 63–4; and Hamilton, *CQ* ns21 (1971), 106–11. For Asander and Nearchus see Berve, *APG*, II, no. 165, p. 87, and no. 544, pp. 269–72.

8. Arrian 4.15.7–8; Plut. *Alex.* 57.4–5; QC 7.10.13–15; cf. Athen. 2.42 f.; Strabo 11.11.15, C. 518; Hamilton, *PA*, pp. 158–9.

9. Arrian 4.16.1–3; QC 7.10.15–16; Strabo 11.11.4, C. 517; Justin 12.5.13.

10. Arrian 4.16.4–4.17.2; QC 8.1.1–7; cf. Plut. *Moral.* 334F.

11. For the murder of Cleitus in general see QC 8.1.19–8.2.12; Arrian 4.8–9 *passim*; Plut. *Alex.* 50–52; Justin 12.6.1–17; cf. T. S. Brown, *MP*, pp. 40–44; Badian, *Stud. GR Hist.*, pp. 197–8 (extremely important). The passage from Euripides' *Andromache* (vv. 693–700) is, except for the first line, taken from the translation by J. F. Nims (*Compl. Gk. Trag.*, vol. VI, p. 184).

12. Province allotted to Cleitus: QC 8.1.20–21. The banquet before C's departure: Arrian 4.8.2; Plut. *Alex.* 50.2; QC 8.1.22; Justin 12.6.1. Arrian (4.8.1–2) and Plutarch (*Alex.* 50.3–4) both introduce a suspect 'prophetic' element which strongly suggests *ex post facto* tinkering by Aristander or Anaxarchus to relieve Alexander of responsibility for Cleitus' death by making that death predestined, and hence inevitable. Plutarch recounts a dream of Alexander's in which he saw Cleitus, dead and black-garbed, with the (similarly dead) sons of Parmenio – a gambit which the cynical might interpret as getting two absolutions for the price of one. He further recounts how Cleitus did not finish his sacrifice before accepting Alexander's invitation, but arrived for dinner with the sacrificial sheep trailing along behind him; whereupon Alexander (according to this tradition) consulted the seers, found the omens bad, and ordered sacrifices for Cleitus' safety. *Verb. sap.* Arrian, more restrainedly, but clearly drawing on a similar propaganda tradition, suggests that Alexander mistakenly sacrificed to the Dioscuri instead of Dionysus, thus presumably incurring the latter deity's wrath, with what results we know.

13. Arrian 4.8.2–3; QC 8.1.22.

14. Arrian 4.8.4–5.

15. Arrian 4.8.6; QC 8.1.23–6; Justin 12.6.2.

16. QC 8.1.30–37; Arrian 4.8.6; Justin 12.6.3.

17. Plut. *Alex.* 50.4–5.

18. Arrian 4.8.6–7; Plut. *Alex.* 50.6; QC 8.1.41–2.

19. According to Plutarch, *Alex.* 50.2, the original impulse for the feast came to Alexander from a consignment of Greek fruit, brought up by traders from the coast, which he wanted to share with Cleitus. The port in question must have been Harmozia (Hormuz) at the entrance to the Persian Gulf. It was probably on this occasion that a Sidonian merchant told Alexander of a shorter way to Egypt than the normal Susa–Babylon–Damascus route: that by way of Charax, Petra, and Rhinocolura (see Lucian, *Rhet. Praec.* 5–6, a most valuable but seldom quoted passage, with A. M. Harmon's useful note

ad loc., Loeb edn, vol. IV, pp. 140–41). Alexander – ill-advisedly – dismissed the merchant as a liar. His concern over the communications-problem had been sparked off by reports of disaffection in Egypt, perhaps as a result of Cleomenes' depredations (see above, pp. 278–9), which naturally made him anxious to get dispatches through to his officers on the spot as fast as possible. Lucian mentions in passing that 'postmen had to run to every quarter of the realm carrying Alexander's orders', one of the few allusions to this vital service which we possess.

20. Plut. *Alex.* 51.1–4; Arrian 4.8.7–8; QC 8.1.43–7.
21. Plut. *Alex.* 51.5–6; Arrian 4.8.8–9; Justin 12.6.3; cf. QC 8.1.28–9. Curtius presents a variant version of the actual killing of Cleitus, in which Alexander rushed into the lobby, snatched a spear, and waited there until Cleitus, the last guest out, passed him. Justin (12.6.4) has a passage of rather tawdry rhetoric in which Alexander heaps reproaches on his dead victim for praising Philip's military genius. I do not subscribe to T. S. Brown's belief (*MP*, pp. 40 ff.) that Plutarch's version is superior to all others and should if possible be followed against them; this is to apply in historical source-criticism the principle which A. E. Housman pilloried in editors, that 'of leaning on one manuscript like Hope on her anchor and trusting to heaven that no harm will come of it' (*D. Ivnii Ivvenalis Satvrae*, rev. edn, Cambridge, 1938, p. v: the whole preface is replete with advice which historians could well take to heart). For an episode such as this, where there must have been numerous original eyewitness accounts (with the inevitable complementary details and discrepancies), subsequently contaminated by various sorts of propaganda, exculpation, and special pleading, the historian can only sift every detail of each account on its intrinsic probability. There are no short cuts.
22. Arrian 4.9.1–2; QC 8.2.1–5; Plut. *Alex* 51.6; Justin 12.6.7–8, 10–14 (all describing his repentance and attempted suicide).
23. Arrian 4.9.3–5; Plut. *Alex.* 52.1; QC 8.2.6–7 (reporting the tradition that Alexander now remembered that he had forgotten to make sacrifice to Dionysus).
24. QC 8.2.8–10.
25. Three days: QC 8.2.11; Arrian 4.9.4. Four days without eating: Justin 12.6.15. One and a half days: Plut. *Alex.* 51.2.
26. Brown, loc. cit., places far too much reliance on Justin 12.6.17 to argue in favour of Callisthenes' continuing influence over Alexander at this point.
27. Plut. *Alex.* 52.1–4; Arrian 4.9.7–9; QC 8.2.11–12; Justin 12.6.17.
28. Further details in Berve, *APG*, II, pp. 206–8, no. 427.
29. Arrian 4.17.3–4.18.3; QC 8.2.13–8.3.17, cf. 8.1.20.
30. QC 8.4.1–17; Isocrates *Ep.* 3 (*Phil.* II) 5, cf. *Philippus* 113–14, 151.

31. Arrian 4.18.4–4.19.4; QC 7.11 *passim*; Strabo 11.11.4, C. 517; Polyaenus 4.3.29.
32. M. Renard, J. Servais, *Ant. Cl.* 24 (1955), 29–47; cf. G. F. Abbott, *Macedonian Folklore* (Cambridge, 1903), pp. 158 ff., 173. For Alexander's marriage to Roxane in general see Plut. *Alex.* 47.4, *Moral.* 332E, 338D; Arrian 4.19.5–6; QC 8.4.22–30; Diod. 18.3.3; Strabo 11.11.4, C. 517; Justin 12.15.9, 13.2.5, 9; cf. Robinson, *MP*, pp. 64–5; Hamilton, *PA*, pp. 129–30; Berve, *APG*, II, no. 688, pp. 346–7.
33. Arrian 4.21 *passim*, 4.22.1–2; Strabo 11.11.4, C. 517–18.
34. For Alexander's eastern foundations see Tarn, vol. II, pp. 234 ff. (a most exhaustive study). For the cities as a dumping-ground for malcontents see Justin 12.5.8, 13. The Greek mercenary revolts in Bactria: QC 9.7.1–11; Diod. 17.99.5–6, 18.4.8, 18.7.1–9.
35. Bactrian reinforcements: Arrian 4.22.3. For the 'Successors' see QC 8.5.1 (emphasizing their role as hostages); Arrian 7.6.1; Diod. 17.108.1–3; Plut. *Alex.* 47.3, 71.1.
36. QC 8.6.6; for a general account of the Corps, ibid., 2–5, and Arrian 4.13.1.
37. Balsdon, 'The "divinity" of Alexander', *Historia* 1 (1950), 375 (=*MP*, p. 191). The whole article is of the greatest interest and cogency. cf. Hdt 1.134; Athen. 10.434d; Arrian 4.10.5 ff.; Plut. *Alex.* 54–5.1; QC 8.5.9–24.
38. Balsdon, p. 376, and reff. there cited. For the incident involving Polyperchon see QC 8.5.22; cf. Plut. *Alex.* 74.2 and Arrian 4.12.2 for similar episodes.
39. Arrian 4.10.5 ff.; QC 8.5.5 ff. For a good analysis of the conflict between Anaxarchus and Callisthenes over *proskynesis*, see now Lowell Edmunds, *GRByS* 12 (1971), 386–90.
40. For this clique, and its deleterious effect on Alexander, see especially Plut. *Moral.* 65C–E; cf. QC 8.5.5–8.
41. See, e.g., Badian in his review of Lionel Pearson's *The Lost Histories of Alexander the Great*, *Gnomon* 33 (1961), 661–2.
42. Plut. *Alex.* 54.3–55.1; QC 8.5.9–24; Arrian 4.12.3–5; Justin 12.7.1–3; cf. Brown, *MP*, pp. 44 ff., and Balsdon, ibid.
43. The whispering campaign: Plut. *Alex.* 54.1–2, 55.1–2; Arrian 4.10.1–4; cf. Homer, *Iliad*, 21.107. The eristics challenge: Plut. *Alex.* 53.2–5; cf. Philip Merlan, *Historia* 3 (1954/5), 76–7. The translation from the *Bacchae* is that by William Arrowsmith, *Compl. Gk Trag.*, vol. VII, p. 369.
44. QC 8.8.15. For the Pages' conspiracy see Arrian 4.13–14; QC 8.6–8; Plut. *Alex.* 55.2–5. A convenient conspectus of sources for evidence on Callisthenes' death in Robinson, *HA*, pp. 45–54 (trs. of Jacoby *FGrH* II B 124 T); see esp. Arrian 4.14.3–4; QC 8.8.19–23; Strabo 11.11.4, C. 517.

45. Plut. *Alex.* 55.3–4.
46. Arist. *Met.* 1.13.15, 350a 21 f., cf. *Pol.* 7.14, 1332b, where he reveals acquaintance with the *Periplus* of Scylax; Hdt 3.94, 98–106, 4.40, 44; Ctesias (ed. R. Henry) *Indica, passim*, esp. chs. 7, 11, 22–4, 31. Post-Alexander testimony (e.g. Arrian 5.4–6; Diod. 17.90.1–3; QC 8.5.1–4, 8–9 *passim*; Strabo 15.1.5, C. 686) is useless in this context, being invariably contaminated with material collected during the expedition itself. cf. Wilcken, pp. 173–4 (also 184–6, where he oddly asserts that Alexander knew nothing of Scylax's voyage down the Indus); Woodcock, pp. 16 ff.; and esp. A. Dihle, 'The conception of India in Hellenistic and Roman literature', *Proc. Camb. Phil. Soc.* 10 (1964), 15–23.
47. Heracles in India: Arrian 8.8–9. Dionysus' exploits: Diod. 2.38. 3.63, 4.3; Arrian 8.5; cf. Strabo 11.5.5, C. 505. Semiramis: Diod. 2.1–20 *passim*. For Alexander's aspirations see, e.g. QC 8.8.15 – '*utinam Indi quoque deum esse me credant*' ('Would that the people of India too may believe me to be a god!').
48. Reforms in the cavalry: Brunt, *JHS* 83 (1963), 27–46, esp. 29–31; Griffith, ibid., 68–74. For the size of the invasion force see Tarn, vol. I, pp. 82–4, cf. vol. II, p. 169; Milns, pp. 186–7; and Fuller, p. 124 (quoted here).
49. Arrian 4.22.3–4.23.1, cf. 4.30.4; QC 8.10.1–4; Strabo 15.1.26, C. 697; cf. Narain, *MP*, pp. 156–7; Cary, *GB*, pp. 197–8.
50. The Swat campaign: Arrian 4.23–30 *passim*; QC 8.10.4–8.12.3; Diod. 17.84–6; Justin 12.7. For the massacre of the Indian mercenaries see Diod. 17.84; Plut. *Alex.* 59.3–4; Arrian 4.27.3–4; Polyaenus 4.3.20; cf. Narain, p. 157 and reff. there cited.
51. Plut. *Alex.* 28.3, *Moral.* 180E, 341B; Aristobulus ap. Athen. 251a; cf. Arrian 4.26.4; QC 8.10.28; Homer, *Iliad*, 5.340; Tarn, vol. II, p. 358, n. 5; Hamilton, *PA*, p. 74. Cf. Lowell Edmunds, *GRByS* 12 (1971), 363 ff.
52. The Nysa episode: Arrian 5.1–5.3.4; QC 8.10.7–18; Plut. *Alex.* 58.3–5; Justin 12.7.6–8. Philostratus (*Vit. Apoll. Tyan.* 2.9) says that the inhabitants of Nysa deny that Alexander ever went up the mountain ('in order to preserve the sobriety of his army – on water'). For an excellent first-hand modern account of the Kalash Kafirs see Fosco Maraini, *Where Four Worlds Meet* (London, 1964), pp. 242–71.
53. Milns, p. 205.
54. *On Alexander's Track to the Indus* (London, 1929), p. 154.
55. The capture of Aornus: Arrian 4.28–30.4; Diod. 17.85; QC 8.11; Justin 12.7.12–13; Plut. *Alex.* 58.3; Plut. *Moral.* 181C 25, D 27; Strabo 15.1.8, C. 688; cf. Fuller, pp. 248–54, and A. R. Anderson, *Harv. Stud. Cl. Phil.* 39 (1928), 12–25, esp. 18: 'The Greeks naturally believed their religion, that is, their mythology and its divinities, to be ecumenical and universal (hence their identifications), and as

their geographical horizon was extended, so likewise the sphere through which their gods exerted their power was enlarged.' Cf. Edmunds, op. cit., pp. 374–5.

56. An identical pontoon-bridge of boats – soon to be replaced by a more permanent structure – still spanned the Indus at Attock, as recently as 1967, during the winter season, being dismantled at the approach of the spring floods. See *Nat. Geogr. Mag.* 133, no. 1 (January 1968), p. 56.

57. Arrian 4.30.7–9, 5.3.5–5.7 *passim*; Diod. 17.86.3–7; QC 8.12.4–9; Plut. *Alex.* 59.1; Strabo 15.1.28, C. 698, 15.1.32, C. 700 (the breadth of the Indus). For the excavations of Taxila, cf. Sir John Marshall, *Taxila*, 3 vols., Cambridge, 1951. The city Alexander saw was Taxila I, the so-called Bhir Mound north-west of Sirkap.

58. QC 8.12.10–18; Arrian 5.8.1–2; Plut. *Alex.* 59.1–3.

59. Son of Neoptolemus, and a Companion: born *c.* 360. See Berve, *APG*, II, no. 494, pp. 249–50.

60. Arrian 5.8.2–3; QC 8.13.1–5. For estimates of Porus' forces see Arrian 5.15.4; Diod. 17.87.2; QC 8.13.6. The elephants have given rise to much controversy: Arrian estimates their number at 200, Diodorus at 130, Curtius (in a context which suggests others in reserve) at 85. Burn, *GR*, p. 151 n. 2, objects that 200 elephants at 100ft intervals would produce far too long a battle-line; this is very probably true. Diodorus' estimate seems the likeliest. The Macedonians (see pp. 399, 407) were badly scared by these great beasts, which would inevitably lead to an exaggeration of their numbers – just as the number of infantry which crossed the river with Alexander was later minimized to conceal their enormous losses: see Tarn, vol. II, pp. 192–3 and Hamilton, *JHS* 76 (1956), 26, though neither draws the inference as to motive, and Tarn describes the reduced figure as 'inexplicable'. The actual force which engaged Alexander was about 20,000 infantry, 2,000 cavalry: see Plut. *Alex.* 62.1. For the monsoon see Aristobulus ap. Strabo 15.1.17, C. 691–2.

61. Arrian 5.8.4–5.

62. Philostratus, *Vit. Apoll. Tyan.* 2.42; Pliny *HN* 6.21.62; cf. Fuller, p. 181.

63. QC 8.13.6, 8–9, 10–11; Arrian 5.9.1, 3–4.

64. Arrian 5.10.1–2.

65. Arrian 5.9.2–3; QC 8.13.12–16; Plut. *Alex.* 60.1–2.

66. Arrian 5.11.1–2; QC 8.13.17; Frontinus, *Strat.* 1.4.9.

67. Arrian 5.10.3–4; QC 8.13.17–19.

68. Diod. 17.87.3.

69. Arrian 5.11.1–2.

70. QC 8.13.20–21.

71. Arrian 5.12.1; cf. Fuller, pp. 186–7, Milns, p. 211.

72. Arrian 5.11.3–4.
73. See Fuller's excellent analysis, pp. 188–90, with fig. 14.
74. Fuller, ibid.
75. Arrian 5.12.2–13.3; QC 8.13.22–7; Plut. *Alex.* 60.2–4.
76. QC 8.14.1–2.
77. Plut. *Alex.* 60.4; Arrian 5.13.4.
78. Arrian 5.14.3–6; QC 8.14.1–2.
79. Arrian 5.14.1–2.
80. Arrian 5.14.4–5.15.1–2; QC 8.14.3–8; Plut. *Alex.* 60.5; Justin 12.7.4.
81. Arrian 5.15.3.
82. Arrian 5.15.4; Plut. *Alex.* 60.5.
83. Arrian 5.15.4–7; Diod. 17.87.4–5; QC 8.14.10–13; cf. Burn, *GR*, pp. 151–2.
84. Burn, ibid., p. 151.
85. cf. Milns, pp. 213–14.
86. Arrian 5.16.1–3; Plut. *Alex.* 60.5; QC 8.14.14–15.
87. Here I follow Hamilton, *JHS* 76 (1956), 26–31, against the majority of modern scholars, from Veith to Fuller, Burn, and Milns, who all assume that either the Indian cavalry, or Coenus' hipparchies, or both, moved *in front of* Porus' infantry line. But this (from Coenus' point of view) would be sheer tactical lunacy, involving him in a four-mile gallop during which his left flank was permanently exposed.
88. Arrian 5.16.3.
89. Arrian 5.16.4; Diod. 17.88.1; cf. Burn, *GR*, pp. 153–4.
90. Arrian 5.16.4.
91. Arrian 5.17.1–3; QC 8.14.18; cf. Fuller, pp. 196–7.
92. Arrian 5.17.3; cf. QC 8.14.19.
93. Arrian 5.17.3–5; Diod. 17.88.1–2.
94. Arrian 5.17.7.
95. Arrian 5.17.6–7; Diod. 17.88.2–6; QC 8.14.22–29; Plut. *Alex.* 60.6.
96. Arrian 5.18.1–3; Diod. 17.89.1–3.
97. Arrian 5.18.4–19.3, esp. 19.1 (quoted here).
98. Diod. 17.88.6–89.6; QC 8.14.31–46; Plut. *Alex.* 60.6–8; Justin 12.7.5–6.
99. Arrian 5.18.3; Diod. 17.89.3. The higher estimate would represent the difference between the total *figures* which Arrian (5.14.1) gives for the assault-group, and the strengths which can be deduced from a study of the actual *units* involved (given by Arrian, 5.12.2, and well analysed by Tarn, vol. II, pp. 192–3). cf. above, no. 60.
100. This point is well brought out by Milns, p. 215.
101. General sources for the battle of the Jhelum (Hydaspes): Arrian 5.9–19 *passim*; QC 8.13.7–8.14.46; Plut. *Alex.* 60; Diod. 17.87–89.3; Justin 12.8; Polyaenus 4.3.9, 22; Pliny *HN* 6.21.62; Philostratus, *Vit. Apoll. Tyan.* 2.42; cf. Fuller, pp. 180 ff.; Hamilton (cf. n. 87),

and *PA*, pp. 163 ff. For the effect of the battle on Macedonian morale see esp. Plut. *Alex.* 62.1; and for the army's general exhaustion because of long service, worn-out equipment, and the monsoon, cf. Arrian 5.25.2, QC 9.3.1, Diod. 17.94.1.

102. Diod. 17.89.6; Arrian 5.19.2–3, 5.20.2–4; Plut. *Alex.* 60.8, cf. *Moral.* 332E.

103. Narain, *GR*, pp. 158–9.

104. Arrian 5.19.4–6, 5.20.1–2, 7; Plut. *Alex.* 60.7–8, 61, *Moral.* 332E; Plin. *HN* 8.64.155; Diod. 17.89.6; QC 9.1.1–2, 6, 9.3.23; Strabo 15.1.29, C. 698–9; Aul. Gell. *NA* 5.2.

105. Arrian 5.20.5–6; Diod. 17.90.4; QC 9.1.7–8; Strabo 15.1.28, C. 698.

106. Diod. 17.89.4–5; Arrian 5.24.8.

107. I am not convinced by the arguments of Droysen (*Gesch. des Hellenismus*, repr. Basle, 1952, pp. 356–7), or Andreotti, *Saeculum* 8 (1957), 143, that Alexander knew of the existence of the Ganges while still at the Jhelum: there is nothing in our sources which warrants such an assumption.

108. Arist. *Met.* 2.5, 362b 20–29. Aristotle reckons that the distance from the Pillars of Hercules to India exceeds that from Aethiopia to Lake Maeotis and the farthest parts of Scythia by a ratio of more than 5:3. Hdt 3.98 and 4.40, describing a 'barren wilderness' to the east of India, probably refer to the Sind Desert.

109. By Mr Philip O. Spann, of the University of Texas at Austin, in an unpublished paper, 'Alexander at the Beas: Fox in a Lion's Skin', from which I have derived much useful information.

110. H. G. Rawlinson, *India: A Short History* (London, 1938), p. 60.

111. Arrian 6.1.2; local informants were not slow (6.1.5) to correct so preposterous a story.

112. For the construction of the fleet see Arrian 5.20.1–2; Diod. 17.89.4–6; QC 9.1.4; Strabo 15.1.29, C. 698.

113. Philostratus, *Vit. Apoll. Tyan.* 2.42; QC 9.1.6; Arrian 6.1.1–6; Diod. 17.89.5–6; Strabo 2.1.6, C. 69, 15.1.25, C. 696. For characteristic views on Alexander's geographical knowledge at this point see, e.g., Schachermeyr, *MP*, pp. 123 ff. ('Alexander und die Ganges-Länder'), with copious bibliography; Hampl, *Nouv. Clio* 6 (1954), 106; Radet, *AG* (Paris, 1931), 300; Tarn, vol. II, p. 281; Wilcken, pp. 184–5; Snyder, pp. 158–9. For a more realistic view cf. now Milns, pp. 220–21.

114. Arrian 5.20.8–5.24.8; Diod. 17.90–92 *passim*; QC 9.1.14–35; Strabo 15.1.30–31, C. 698–700.

115. Arrian 5.25.2; Diod. 17.94.1–2; QC 9.2.8–11, 9.3.1, 10; Plut. *Alex.* 62.1.

116. Arrian 5.24.5 (Macedonian losses); Diod. 17.93.1 (state of the Beas); for the various estimates of troops beyond the Sutlej see

Diod. 17.93.2 (20,000 cavalry, 200,000 infantry, 2,000 chariots, 4,000 elephants, cf. QC 9.2.3), and Plut. *Alex*. 62.2 (80,000 cavalry, 200,000 infantry, 8,000 chariots, 6,000 elephants). For reports on the lands beyond the Beas see, in general, QC 9.2.1–10; Diod. 17.93.1–2; Plut. *Alex*. 62.1–3; Arrian 5.25.1.

117. A. V. Williams-Jackson, *Cambridge History of India*, vol. I, p. 341; Tarn, vol. I, p. 98, vol. II, p. 284. Andreotti, *Saeculum* 8 (1957), 144, improbably asserts that no one either knew or cared where this frontier was.

118. QC 9.2.10–11; Diod. 17.94.1–4.

119. Diod. 17.94.4–5.

120. QC 9.3.1 (confusing two separate meetings).

121. Arrian 5.25–26 *passim*; Diod. 17.94.5; QC 9.2.12 ff.

122. Arrian 5.27.1–9; QC 9.2.31–9.3.15; Justin 12.8.10–15.

123. Arrian 5.28.1–3; Plut. *Alex*. 62.3; QC 9.3.16–18.

124. Arrian 5.28.4.

125. Arrian 5.29.1–2; Diod. 17.95.1–2; QC 9.3.19; Plut. *Alex*. 62.4; Justin 12.8.16–17.

126. *Vit. Apollon. Tyan*. 2.43.

127. Milns, p. 223.

128. General sources for the mutiny at the Beas: Arrian 5.24.8–5.29.2; Diod. 17.94–5.2; QC 9.2.1–9.3.19; Plut. *Alex*. 62.1–4; Justin 12.8.10–15; Strabo 3.5.5, C. 171, 15.1.32, C. 700; Philostratus, *Vit. Apollon. Tyan*. 2.42–3; cf. Schachermeyr, pp. 357–9, Hamilton, *PA*, pp. 170–73. On the whole question of the territories beyond the Beas see Tarn, vol. II, pp. 275–85, and Schachermeyr, *MP*, pp. 137–49. I accept Pliny, *HN* 6.62, as evidence for the altars having been erected on the *eastern* bank: cf. (with reservations), Hamilton, *PA*, p. 175.

Chapter 10

1. Plut. *Alex*. 47, *Moral*. 337A (cf. Hamilton, *PA*, pp. 130–31); QC 9.1.35; Arrian 5.29.2–5.

2. Arrian 6.1, 8.18; Diod. 17.89.4–5, 17.95.3; QC 9.3.20.

3. QC 9.3.21–2; Diod. 17.95.3–4.

4. Ephippus ap. Athen. 4.146c; Arrian 8.18.3–9, cf. Wilcken, p. 188; Plut. *Eum*. 2.2–3.

5. Plut. *Alex*. 35.8; Plin. *HN* 16.62.144 (exotic gardening); Theopompus ap. Athen. 13.586c, 595a–d; Python ap. Athen. 13.586d; Philemon ap. Athen. 13.595c; cf. Badian, *JHS* 81 (1961), 16 ff. = *MP*, pp. 206 ff.; Bellinger, pp. 78–9; Tarn, vol. I, p. 131; Diod. 17.108.5–6; Tod. II, no. 196 (pp. 273–6); Snyder, p. 160, with nn. 24–5.

6. Plut. *Alex.* 41.4; Python as above and ap. Athen. 13.595e–596b; for the *Agen* cf. (with reservations) Bruno Snell, *Scenes from Greek Drama* (Berkeley, 1964), pp. 99–138.

7. Arrian 6.2.1; QC 9.3.20–22.

8. Arrian 6.2.2–6.3.5, 8.18–19; Diod. 17.96.1; QC 9.3.24; Plut. *Alex.* 63.1; Plin. *HN* 19.5.22.

9. Lucian, *Quom. Hist. Conscrib.* 12. This anecdote – seldom quoted by modern historians – does not increase one's confidence in the writer who, with Ptolemy, was Arrian's main source. However, Aristobulus only began composing his final version of events at the age of eighty-four, by which time his views may have mellowed somewhat. Cf. Ps-Lucian, *Macrob.* 22.

10. The passage of the rapids: Arrian 6.4.4–6.5.4; Diod. 17.97; QC 9.4.8–14; cf. Plut. *Alex.* 58.4; Homer *Iliad* 21.228–382. The mobilization of the Malli and Oxydracae: Diod. 17.98.1–2; QC 9.4.15. The threat of mutiny: QC 9.4.16–23. Alexander's raid across the desert: Arrian 6.5.5–6.6.5. The campaign against the Malli: Arrian 6.6.6–6.7.6, cf. Tarn, vol. I, p. 103.

11. The incident of the soothsayer: QC 9.4.27–30. The storming of the Brahmin city, and Alexander's wounding: Arrian 6.9. 11; Diod. 17.98.3–99.4; QC 9.4.26–9.5.18; Plut. *Alex.* 63.1–4; Justin 12.9.5–11; Plut. *Moral.* 327B, 343D–344D.

12. QC 9.5.22–30; Plut. *Alex.* 63.5–6; Justin 12.9.12–13; Plut. *Moral.* 344F–345B.

13. Arrian 6.12–14.3; Diod. 17.99.5–6; QC 9.6.1, 9.7.12–15; Plut. *Alex.* 63.5–6. The revolt in Bactria: QC 9.7.1–11; Diod. 17.99.5–6, cf. Badian *JHS* 81 (1961), 25–7 = *MP*, pp. 216–17; Parke, pp.195–6.

14. QC 9.6.26–7.

15. Diod. 17.100–101; QC 9.7.15–26. Dioxippus (see above, p. 383) was the man who told Alexander that the blood flowing from his wound was divine ichor; he seems to have been born unlucky.

16. Arrian 6.14.4–6.17.2; Diod. 17.100–102; QC 9.8.3–16; Plut. *Alex.* 59.4, 64; cf. V. A. Smith, *Oxford Hist. of India*, pp. 88 ff.; Badian, *GR*, p. 179.

17. Arrian 6.15.5, 6.17.3–4; Justin 12.10.1; Strabo 15.2.4–5, C. 721, 15.2.11, c. 725. For the use of arrows poisoned with snake-venom, and Alexander's cure of Ptolemy, see Diod. 17.103.4–8; QC 9.9.17–28; Justin 12.10.2–3; Strabo 15.2.7, C. 723.

18. Arrian 6.17.1–6, 6.27.2; Diod. 17.104.2; QC 9.8.28–30, 10.1.20; cf. Narain, *GR*, pp. 161–3, and reff. there cited.

19. Arrian 7.1.4–7.2.1. For the literature on the *gymnosophistae* see esp. Arrian 7.3 *passim*; Plut. *Alex.* 59.4, 65; Strabo 15.1.61, 63–5, 68, C. 714–18; cf. Woodcock, pp. 26–7; Narain, *GR*, pp. 160–61. H. Van Thiel, *Hermes* 100 (1972), 343 ff.

20. Arrian 6.18.3–6.20.5; QC 9.8.30–9.10.4; Plut. *Alex.* 66.1–2; Diod.

17.104.1-3; Justin 12.10.4-8; cf. Fredricksmeyer, p. 167 n. 39.

21. Arrian 6.21-22.3, cf. 8.20.1-11, 8.32.11; Diod. 17.104.3-105.5; QC 9.10.5-11; Plut. *Alex.* 66.2; Strabo 15.1.5, C. 686, 15.2.1-3, C. 720-21, 15.2.5, C. 722; Plut. *Eum.* 2.2-3; for mint production in Asia Minor cf. Thompson and Bellinger, *Yale Class. Stud.* 14 (1955), 30 f.

22. General sources for the march through Gedrosia: Arrian 6.22.4-26.5 *passim*; Diod. 17.105.6-7; QC 9.10.11-18; Plut. *Alex.* 66.2-3; Strabo 15.2.3-7, C. 721-3; Pliny *HN* 12.18.34. The request for supplies in Carmania: Arrian 6.27.6; Diod. 17.105.7-8; QC 9.10.17; Plut. *Alex.* 66.3.

23. If 120,000 represents Alexander's original force in India (Plut. *Alex.* 66.2-3), and we subtract from this (a) Craterus' force of about 16,000 (Arrian 6.17.3-4; 7.12.1-2; Diod. 17.109.1-2), (b) Nearchus' complement of not more than 18,000 (Arrian 6.14.4, cf. 8.19.2-3), we get a figure of 86,000 for Alexander's force, assuming that losses and reinforcements more or less cancelled each other out. For the Companion Cavalry see Tarn, vol. II, pp. 162, 166 (who however refuses to accept the implication of this drop in numbers). On the march generally see H. Strasburger, *Hermes* 80 (1952), 456 ff., and 82 (1954), 251, cf. Brunt, *GR*, pp. 209-10 and n. 6. Alexander's route: Stein, *Geogr. Journ.* 102 (1943), 193-227 (against Strasburger).

24. Plut. *Alex.* 68.7; Arrian 7.4.2; cf. Badian *CQ* ns8 (1958), 147 f. *Contra*, Bosworth, ibid., ns21 (1971), 124 and n. 1, who argues against Apollophanes having been one of Alexander's victims on the grounds that he was cooperating with Leonnatus, and Leonnatus afterwards continued in favour: Ptolemy, Bosworth supposes, confused Apollophanes with Astaspes of Carmania. But Nearchus, whose dereliction of duty had arguably been at least as great (see above, p. 441), also retained the king's favour.

25. Athen. 13.595-6; cf. above, pp. 414 ff., and Diod. 17.108.5-8; Paus. 1.37.5; QC 10.2.1-3; Plut. *Dem.* 25.6.

26. Arrian 6.27.3-5, 6.29.3, 7.4.2 f.; Diod. 17.106.2-3; QC 9.10.19 f., 10.1.1-9; Plut. *Alex.* 68.2, 7; Badian *JHS* 81 (1961), 19-20 = *MP*, 209-10; Bosworth, *CQ* ns21 (1971), 124.

27. For the fragments of Nearchus see Jacoby *FGrH* 133F *passim* (=Robinson, *HA*, pp. 104 ff.) and especially Arrian's *Indica*, 8.17.6-8.42.10. It is just worth noting that Ps-Callisthenes 3.31.8 and the Metz Epitome, c. 97, name Nearchus among the final conspirators against Alexander. Badian, *JHS* 81 (1961), 20, suggests that Coenus' stand during the mutiny at the Beas 'suddenly presented the terrible threat of cooperation between the nobles and the men'. But this threat had in fact been present *ab initio*; it explains (for instance) Alexander's determination to purge Parmenio and all his supporters.

28. Diod. 17.105.8; Arrian 6.27.1, cf. 6.22.3, 7.5.5, 8.23.4–5; QC 9.10.19; cf. Badian *CQ* ns8 (1958), 148, cf. *MP*, p. 211.

29. Report from Craterus: QC 9.10.19–20; news of trouble in the satrapies: Arrian 6.27.3–5; Diod. 17.106.2–3; QC 10.1.1–9; Plut. *Alex.* 68; cf. Badian, *JHS* 81 (1961), 16 ff. = *MP*, 206 ff. The Dionysiac rout through Carmania: Arrian 6.28.1–4; Diod. 17.106.1; QC 9.10.22–28; Plut. *Alex.* 67. The arrest of Astaspes: QC 9.10.21, 30; the trial and execution of Cleander and Sitalces: Arrian 6.27.3 ff.; QC 10.1.1 ff., cf. Badian, ibid., and Bosworth, op. cit., p. 124. The flight of Harpalus: Diod. 17.108.5–8, cf. QC 10.2.1–3; Paus. 1.37.5; Plut. *Demosth.* 25. For Artaxerxes Ochus and the satraps' revolt see Olmstead, pp. 424–5 and reff. there cited. The order to disband mercenaries; Diod. 17.106.3, 17.111.1, cf. Badian, ibid., p. 211. Cleomenes and Philoxenus: Ps-Arist. *Oecon.* 1352a–b; Plut. *Alex.* 22, *Moral.* 333A, 1099D.

30. Craterus' arrival: Arrian 6.27.3; QC 10.1.9; Strabo 15.2.11, C. 725. The voyage of Nearchus: Arrian 8.21 ff. *passim*, cf. 6.28.5–6; Nearchus ap. Strabo 15.2.5, C. 721–2, 15.2.11–13, C. 725–6; Diod. 17.104.3, 106.6–7. The celebrations in Gulashkird: Plut. *Alex.* 67.3–4; Dicaearchus ap. Athen. 13.603a–b; Arrian 6.28.3, 8.36.3–4; Diod. 17.106.4–6; cf. Badian *CQ* ns8 (1958), 141 ff. The quarrel between Craterus and Hephaestion: Plut. *Alex.* 47.5–6, *Moral.* 337A. The length of Nearchus' voyage was convincingly calculated by Niese (see Welles's note 2 to Diod. 17.106.4, with ref.) as seventy-five days: Pliny, *HN* 6.100, gives its duration as six months, a patent impossibility.

31. Arrian 6.28.7–29.1, 8.36–37.1; Diod. 17.107.1.

32. Arrian 6.29–30.2; QC 10.1.22–38; Plut. *Alex.* 69; Strabo 15.3.7, C. 730; cf. Badian as above, n. 28. Arrian, Plutarch and Curtius all comment specifically on the degeneration of Alexander's character: Arrian 7.4.3; QC 10.1.39–42; Plut. *Alex.* 42.1–2.

33. Arrian 6.30.1–7.4.3; Plut. *Alex.* 68.1–4; Diod. 17.106.4; QC 10.1.17–19.

34. In particular W. W. Tarn, 'Alexander the Great and the Unity of Mankind', *Proc. Brit. Acad.* 19 (1933), 123–66, = *MP*, 243–86.

35. By E. Badian, in a crucially important article, 'Alexander the Great and the Unity of Mankind', *Historia* 7 (1958), 425–44, on which I have drawn heavily here.

36. Tarn, vol. II, pp. 296–7.

37. See in particular H. C. Baldry, *The Unity of Mankind in Greek Thought* (Cambridge, 1965), chs. I–III, and on Alexander's own attitude (a sceptical analysis of the Tarn theory), pp. 113 ff.

38. Arrian 7.6 *passim*; Diod. 17.108.1–3; Plut. *Alex.* 68.2–3, 71.1–2; Justin 12.11.4–5; QC 10.1.43–5; cf. Hammond, *Epirus*, p. 559; Milns, pp. 245–6.

39. The Susa marriages: Arrian 7.4.4–8; Diod. 17.107.6; Plut. *Alex.* 70.1, *Moral.* 329D–E; Justin 12.10.9–10; Chares of Mytilene ap. Athen. 12.538b–539a; cf. Tarn, vol. I, p. 117, vol. II, p. 166; Badian, *Stud. GRHist.* p. 201 (quoted here).

40. Arrian 7.5.1–3; Justin 12.11.1–4; Diod. 17.109.2; cf. Plut. *Alex.* 70.3–4, *Moral.* 339C.

41. On the Exiles' Decree see Hypereides *In Demosth.* 18; Deinarchus *In Demosth.* 81–2; Diod. 17.109.1–2, 17.111.1–2, 18.8.2–7; QC 10.2.4–7; Justin 13.5.2–5; Paus. 1.25.5, 8.52.5; cf. the masterly discussion by Badian, *JHS* 81 (1961), 25–31, = *MP*, pp. 215–21. Two inscriptions concerning Mytilene and Tegea (Tod, II, nos. 201–2) show just what sort of chaos the decree could produce. E. Bikerman, *REA* (1940), 25–35, suggests that Alexander's main motive may have been to plant supporters in the Greek cities.

42. As argued by Tarn, vol. II, pp. 370 ff.; well disposed of by Balsdon *MP*, pp. 202–4. Badian (ibid., p. 219) writes: 'This attempt to justify perjury by blasphemy is now (one may hope) worth citing chiefly as a curiosity of scholarship.'

43. Plut. *Moral.* 219E–F, cf. Aelian *VH* 2.19.

44. Badian, *Stud. GRHist.* p. 202.

45. On the Deification Decree a voluminous modern literature exists: see in particular Balsdon, *MP*, pp. 199 ff. (with reff. there cited) who denies that Alexander ever requested deification at all. I appreciate his arguments but cannot accept them. Cf. Plut. *Moral.* 219E and Aelian as above, n. 43. F. Taeger, *Studies in the History of Religions (Numen Supplements)* 4 (1959), 394 ff., suggests that Alexander's claims to divinity were largely his own idea, and not derived from sophisticated Greek notions (e.g. those of Aristotle or Isocrates). For Alexander's growing megalomania see J. R. Hamilton, *CQ* ns3 (1953), 156–7. See now in general Lowell Edmunds, *GRByS* 12 (1971), 363–91.

46. The voyage from Susa to Opis, and the weir-system: Arrian 7.7.1–7; Strabo 16.1.9, C. 739–40.

47. Arrian 7.8.1–2; Plut. *Alex.* 71.2; Justin 12.11.4.

48. General sources for the mutiny: Arrian 7.8–11.7; Plut. *Alex.* 71.2–4; Justin 12.11.4–12.12.7; Diod. 17.108.3, 109.2–3; QC 10.2.12–10.3.14; cf. Badian, *Stud.GRHist.*, p. 200, and *Historia* 7 (1958), 428 ff.

49. Arrian 7.8.2–3; Diod. 17.108.3, 109.2; Plut. *Alex.* 71.2; Justin 12.11.5; QC 10.2.12–13.

50. Arrian 7.8.3; Diod. 17.108.3; Justin 12.11.6.

51. Arrian 7.8.3; Justin 12.11.7.

52. Arrian 7.8.3; Diod. 17.109.2; Justin 12.11.8; QC 10.2.30, 10.4.2–3.

53. Arrian 7.9–10 *passim*; QC 10.2.15–30; cf. Plut. *Alex.* 71.3.

54. Arrian 7.11.2.

55. Arrian 7.11.1; QC 10.3.5.
56. Arrian 7.11.1–2; QC 10.3.7–14; Diod. 17.109.3; Plut. *Alex.* 71.3; Justin 12.12.1–4.
57. Arrian 7.11.2–3.
58. Arrian 7.11.4; Plut. *Alex.* 71.4; Justin 12.12.5–6.
59. Arrian 7.11.5–7; Diod. 17.109.3; Justin 12.12.7.
60. Arrian 7.11.8–9; cf. Plut. *Alex.* 71.4–5, *Moral.* 329A–D; Badian *Historia* 7 (1958), 428–32 = *MP*, pp. 290–94.
61. Tarn, *Proc. Brit. Acad.* 19 (1933), 123–66 = *MP*, pp. 243–86, cf. his *Alexander the Great*, vol. II, pp. 440 ff.
62. Arrian 7.8.1, 7.12.1–3; Plut. *Alex.* 71.1–3, 5; *Moral.* 339C–D, 180–81, 21; QC 10.2.8–11; Diod. 17.109.1–2; Justin 12.12.7–10.
63. Diod. 17.110.3; Arrian 7.12.1–2; Plut. *Alex.* 71.5.
64. Badian, *Stud. GRHist.*, p. 201.
65. Quoted by Arrian, 7.19.6; cf. Strabo 16.1.11, C. 741. The plans for conquest as far as the Atlantic: Diod. 18.4.4, cf. Schachermeyr, *MP*, pp. 324 ff; Badian, *Harv. Stud.* 72 (1967), 184–9; Bosworth, *CQ* ns21 (1971), 127 and n. 5.
66. QC 10.10.4; Arrian 7.12.6, cf. Plut. *Alex.* 39.11, Livy 8.24.17, Bosworth, op. cit., p. 126. For Alexander having been prompted to remove Antipater at the instigation of Olympias, see Ps-Call. 3.31.1, Metz Epitome 87, cf. Diod. 17.118.1, Justin 12.14.1–3.
67. Arrian 7.12.3–7; QC 10.10.15; Plut. *Phoc.* 18.4–5, 29, *Moral.* 472E (cf. 78D, 545A), 180E 17; Justin 12.12.8–9; Aelian *VH* 12.16 (on Alexander's jealousy of Antipater and others for their individual talents.– in Antipater's case leadership); *Suda* s.v. Antipatros.
68. cf. Bosworth, *CQ* ns21 (1971), 125–6.
69. For the poisoning theory see Justin 12.14; Plut. *Alex.* 77.1–3; Arrian 7.27; QC 10.10.14–17. The most persuasive modern advocate of this theory is Milns, pp. 255–8, cf. Hamilton, *PA*, pp. 213–14. See now also Bosworth, op. cit., pp. 113–16.
70. Bosworth, op. cit., esp. pp. 134–6; cf. Diod. 18.23.2; QC 10.6.9, 16–18, 21 ff.
71. For Antipater's secret negotiations with Athens and Aetolia, see Plut. *Alex.* 49.8; Diod. 18.8.6–7; Justin 13.5.1–8; QC 10.2.2; cf. Badian, *MP*, pp. 223–7, with reff. there cited; Bosworth, op. cit., p. 127.
72. The best modern investigation of Harpalus' return to Athens and the events which followed is that by Badian, *JHS* 81 (1961), 131–6 = *MP*, pp. 221 ff. See also Berve, *APG*, II, no. 143, pp. 75 ff. Sources: Plut. *Dem.* 25, *Phoc.* 21.3 [*Vit. X Orat.*] 846A–C, *Moral.* 531A, 845C; Diod. 17.108.7, 17.111.3; Paus. 2.33.3–4; Hypereides *In Demosth.* 3, cols. 8–13, 4(5) cols. 18–19, 7(8) col. 32, cf. fr. A13 (speech in defence of Harpalus, probably spurious); Deinarchus *In Demosth.* 68–71, 81–2, 89–90, 112–13, *In Philocl.* 1–2, cf. fr. B12

(speech on the refusal to surrender Harpalus to Alexander, probably spurious). All these passages from Hypereides and Deinarchus may be conveniently studied in J. O. Burtt, *Minor Attic Orators*, vol. II (Loeb, 1954). For the Samos affair see Plut. *Alex.* 28, and J. R. Hamilton, *CQ* ns3 (1953), 151 ff., =*MP*, pp. 235 ff.

73. Tod, II, nos. 201–2, pp. 289–301, cf. Hamilton, op. cit., p. 152 f.; Badian ibid., p. 227; Wilcken, pp. 217–18.

74. Plut. *Moral.* 187E, 804B, 842D; Aelian *VH* 2.19.5.12, cf. Athen. 6.58; Diog. Laert. 6.8, 6.63; Val. Max. 7.2, ext. §13; Timaeus ap. Polyb. 12.12b.3; Hypereides *In Demosth.* 31; Deinarchus *In Demosth.* 94; cf. Badian, *MP*, pp. 223–4; Balsdon, op. cit., pp. 199–200.

75. Arrian 7.13–14 *passim*, 23.6–8; Diod. 17.110.7–8, 115–25 *passim*; Ephippus ap. Athen. 12.538a–b; Aelian *VH* 7.8; Lucian *Cal.* 17; Justin 12.12.11–12; Plut. *Alex.* 47, 72, *Eum.* 1, 2.4–5, *Moral.* 181D 29, 180D 14; cf. Berve, *APG*, II, no. 357, pp. 169 ff., and Hamilton, *PA*, p. 129 with reff.

76. Diod. 17.108.7–8, 18.19.2; Paus. 2.33.4; Hypereides *In Demosth.* col. 38 (cf. *MAO* II, pp. 167–8); [*Vit. X Orat.*] 846c. Philostratus, *Vit. Soph.* 538, suggests that Alexander himself provided the evidence on which Demosthenes was condemned. For Demosthenes' link with Hephaestion see Marsyas of Pella, *FGrH*, nos. 135–6, fr. 2, cf. Aeschines 3.162, both cited by Hamilton, *PA*, p. 130.

77. Arrian 7.15.1–3; Diod. 17.111.4–6; Plut. *Alex.* 72.3; Strabo 11.13.6, C. 524, cf. 16.1.11 (the region was a good source of timber).

78. Arrian 7.15.4–7.17.6; Plut. *Alex.* 73; Strabo 16.1.5; C. 738; Diod. 17.112 *passim*; Justin 12.13.3–5; Appian *BC* 2.153.

79. The embassies: Arrian 7.15.4–6, 7.19.1–2; Diod. 17.113.1–4; Justin 12.13.1–2; cf. M. Sordi, Rend. Inst. Lomb, 99 (1965), 435–52. The plan for invading Arabia: Arrian 7.19.3–20 *passim*; Strabo 16.1.11, C. 741, 16.4.27, C. 785; Plin. *HN* 16.80.221, 12.42.86–7. Alexander's ambition to outdo Dionysus: Plut. *Moral.* 326B.

80. Hephaestion's funeral: Diod. 17.114–5 *passim*. Other events: Arrian 7.21–2 *passim*; Diod 17.116.5–7; Strabo 9.2.18, C. 407; Appian *Syr.* 9.56, cf. Strabo 16.1.11, C. 741; Eddy, pp. 108–9; Cary, *GB*, p. 179.

81. Arrian 7.18 *passim*, 7.23.1–24.3; Diod. 17.110.1–2, 116.1–4; Plut. *Alex.* 73.3–4, 75.1–2; Justin 12.13.3–5; Ps-Call. 3.30; cf. Eddy, ibid., Milns, p. 254, and (with reservations) P. J. Derchain and J. Hubaux, *Ant. Cl.* 19 (1950), 367 ff.

82. Bosworth, *CQ* ns21 (1971), 126–7, 134–6.

83. Arrian 7.23.2; Plut. *Alex.* 74 *passim*; cf. Badian, *MP*, pp. 226–7.

84. Arrian 7.23.5; Aelian *VH* 3.23; Plin. *HN* 14.5.58; Plut. *Moral.* 207D 8; cf. Brunt, *GR*, p. 213; and D. Kienast, *Gymnasium* 76 (1969), 430–56.

85. For the chronology of Alexander's last days see A. E. Samuel,

Historia 14 (1965), 8, citing A. J. Sachs, *Late Babylonian Astronomical and Related Texts* (Rhode Island, 1955), no. 209; Wells, Loeb Diodorus, vol. VIII, p. 467 n. 5, cf. Hamilton, *PA*, p. 210. For the events of this night, including Medius' party, see Arrian 7.24.4–25.1; Plut. *Alex.* 75.3; Diod. 17.117.1–3; Ps-Call. 3.31.8; Athen. 10.434a–c, 12.537d. The so-called 'Royal Ephemerides', purporting to give an account of the king's final illness and death (cf. Arrian 7.25–6, Plut. *Alex.* 76, Jacoby *FGrH* 117) have been much discussed, and until recently over-utilized, by scholars: see esp. C. A. Robinson, *The Ephemerides of Alexander's Expedition* (Providence, 1932: a fanciful if ingenious reconstruction). Corrective evaluation now provided by A. E. Samuel, 'Alexander's Royal Journals', *Historia* 14 (1965), 1–12; E. Badian, 'A King's Notebooks', *Harv. Stud. Class. Phil.* 72 (1967) 183–204, and, most recently, A. B. Bosworth, *CQ* ns21 (1971), 117 ff., who presents an excellent case for regarding the Ephemerides as a forged concoction put out as propaganda by Alexander's murderers.

86. For what is known of this person see Berve, *APG*, II, no. 521, pp. 261–2.

87. See in particular Arrian 7.27.2. The only list of conspirators (not *per se* an implausible one, though see Bosworth, op. cit., p. 116 and n. 3) is that given by Ps-Call. 3.31.8: Meleager, Leonnatus, Cassander, Peucestas, Philip the physician, and Nearchus.

88. Cleitarchus ap. Diod. 17.117.2, cf. 3–4, and Ephippus of Olynthus ap. Athen. 10.434, who suggests a syncope brought on by attempting to down the contents of a giant 12-pint cup.

89. Plut. *Alex.* 77.1–3; Arrian 7.27; QC 10.10.14–17; Justin 12.14; Paus. 8.18.4. For Apollodorus and Peithagoras cf. Berve, *APG*, II, nos. 101 and 618, pp. 55–6, 310.

90. Bosworth, op. cit., pp. 114 ff.

91. Badian, *JHS* 81 (1961), 36 (=*MP*, p. 226), n. 151.

92. *Alexander the Great*, pp. 256–8.

93. Theophr. *HP* 7.15.4, 9.11.5 ff.

94. Bosworth, op. cit., p. 136.

95. Demetr. *De Eloc.* §283; Plut. *Phoc.* 22.

96. Lucian, *Quom. Hist. Conscr.* 12.

97. On this see now Bosworth, op. cit., pp. 115 f.

98. See the useful article by E. N. Borza, 'Cleitarchus and Diodorus' Account of Alexander', *Proc. Afr. Class. Assoc.* 2 (1968), 25–45; and Hamilton, *PA*, pp. xlix ff.

99. vol. II, pp. 69 n. 1, 96–7, 131; *contra*, Badian, *CQ* ns8 (1958), 153–7 and Borza-Wilcken, pp. xxiv ff.

100. Borza-Wilcken, pp. xxvii–viii. Truesdell S. Brown, reviewing Schachermeyr's biography of Alexander, *AJPh* 72 (1951), 74–7, complained of Schachermeyr's 'contradictory' interpretation as a

'dangerous approach' because 'a contradictory Alexander can do anything, however noble or degrading, and we are left with no test for separating the true and false stories about him in our sources'. *Verb. sap.*

101. *Sat.* 10.168–172.
102. For an excellent brief notice of Droysen's position see Borza–Wilcken, pp. xii–xiii.
103. Ibid., p. xiii.
104. cf. Roberto Andreotti, *Historia* 1 (1950), 599: 'Il profilo più netto é quello del soldato'. Cf. Schachermeyr, pp. 91 ff., 220, 233.

Appendix

1. Our sources are Ptolemy and Aristobulus, who supplied most of the details reported by Arrian, 1.13–16 *passim*, and Plutarch, *Alex.* 16 – cf. Hamilton's commentary *(PA)* p. 38, citing Brunt, *JHS* 83 (1963), 27, n. 3 – together with whatever source, or sources, Diodorus (17.18.2–21.6) may have been following on this occasion: see Borza, 'Cleitarchus and Diodorus' account of Alexander', *Proc. Afr. Class. Assoc.* 2 (1968), 25–45. Justin, 11.6.10–13, provides a more than usually bald summary, while Polyaenus, 4.3.16, offers one tantalizingly ambiguous sentence (see above, p. 496).
2. 'The Persian Battle Plan at the Granicus', in *Laudatores Temporis Acti*: Studies in Memory of Wallace Everett Caldwell, Professor of History at the University of North Carolina, by his Friends and Students. Edited by Mary Frances Gyles and Eugene Wood Davis (Chapel Hill, Univ. of North Carolina Press, 1964, = vol. 46 of the *James Sprunt Studies in History and Political Science*), pp. 34–44. Hereafter cited as 'Davis'.
3. Davis, p. 42.
4. Davis, p. 44. Arrian 1.16.3 makes it quite clear that Arsites regarded himself as ultimately responsible, not only for Persian policy at the Granicus, but also for its implementation. It has been represented to me that Arsites (Arrian 1.12.10) cannot give orders to the Council: they agree with him. But *someone* has to command in a battle, if not at the council-table, and the Granicus lay in Arsites' satrapy. Nor would Persian autocracy take well to the kind of tripartite quasi-democratic command which so sadly hampered the Sicilian Expedition at its outset. Arsites' position may have been akin to that of Agamemnon, i.e. an uncomfortable *primus inter pares* – but *primus* nevertheless.
5. Davis, p. 34.
6. See above, chapter 5, n. 7, p. 530, with reff. there cited; also Badian, *Stud. Ehrenb.*, p. 43 and n. 32.
7. Arrian 1.12.9; Diod. 17.18.2–3. On the possibility of a Persian

advance into Greece see above, chapter 6, pp. 212 ff., with nn. 47, 50–51. Tarn, *CAH*, vol. VI, p. 361 = *AG*, vol. I, p. 16, argues that Memnon did not in fact advocate carrying the war into Greece because when, later, he had the chance he failed to take advantage of it. But as Davis correctly points out, 'Memnon had to show some successes before approaching the Greeks, and he was in the process of acquiring island bases in the Aegean when he died' (p. 35, n. 3). cf. above, pp. 212, 216.

8. See above, chapter 5, p. 169, with nn. 32–3, for the respective treatment meted out to Percote, Lampsacus, Colonae and Priapus.

9. Arrian 1.12.9–10, 13.2; Plut. *Alex.* 16.1; Diod. 17.18.3–4.

10. F. Schachermeyr, *Alexander der Grosse: Ingenium und Macht* (Vienna, 1949), pp. 141–2, cf. Diod. 17.18.3.

11. cf. A. R. Burn, *Persia and the Greeks* (London, 1962), pp. 62–3.

12. op. cit., pp. 35–6, with n. 4; cf. K. J. Beloch, *Griech. Gesch.*, 2nd edn (Berlin-Leipzig, 1922), vol. III, i, p. 624.

13. The Persians may well have underestimated the skill, experience, and determination of their opponents. It is also possible (see above, p. 170 n.) that Persian troops which might otherwise have been available were still tied up in Egypt: cf. Davis, p. 36; Olmstead, *Hist. of the Persian Empire* (Chicago, 1948), pp. 492–3, 496.

14. A. Janke, *Auf Alexanders des Grossen Pfaden*: Eine Reise durch Kleinasien (Berlin, 1904), pp. 136 ff. with pl. 5; J. F. C. Fuller, *The Generalship of Alexander the Great* (London, 1958), pp. 147–8; H. and F. Schreider, 'In the footsteps of Alexander the Great', *Nat. Geogr.* 133 (1968), 15.

15. op. cit., p. 148.

16. Arrian 1.14.4, cf. Diod. 17.19.1, 3.

17. op. cit., p. 37.

18. *CAH*, vol. VI, p. 361 = *AG*, vol. I, p. 16.

19. Wilcken-Borza, p. 84.

20. ibid.

21. loc. cit., n. 18 above.

22. *Hellenistic Military and Naval Developments* (Cambridge, 1930), p. 70.

23. Davis, p. 39.

24. Fuller, p. 149.

25. ibid., p. 148.

26. op. cit., p. 143.

27. ibid.

28. See esp. pp. 159 ff. and 170 ff.

29. Xen. *Anab.* 1.8.4 ff.; Plut. *Artax.* 8.

30. cf. Arrian 1.12.10; Diod. 17.18.2–3.

31. For a good account, and rebuttal, of the 'Cleitarchan theory' see E. N. Borza, 'Cleitarchus and Diodorus' account of Alexander', *Proc. Afr. Class. Assoc.* 2 (1968), 25–45.

32. Well refuted by Brunt, *CQ* 12 (1962), 141–55.
33. C. B. Welles, Diodorus Siculus, vol. VIII (Loeb edn), pp. 13–14; cf. Borza op. cit., p. 26. Justin (11.6.10) places the battle *in campis Adrasteis*, which does not suggest an attack across-river, and might thus support Welles's hypothesis of Trogus as a contributory source for Bk 17 of Diodorus – though as Ellis remarks, *JHS* 91 (1971), 21, Trogus' 'own relationship to his own sources is anybody's guess'.
34. Plut. *Alex.* 16.2; cf. Arrian 1.13.3–7; Diod. 17.19.3.
35. Arrian 1.14.5 ff.; Plut. *Alex.* 16.3 ff.; Diod. 17.19.3 ff.
36. cf. the remarks by Welles, op. cit., pp. 170–71, n. 1.
37. K. Lehmann, 'Die Schlacht am Granikos', *Klio* 11 (1911), 230–44 (not 340 as reported by Davis, p. 34 n. 2, who also misquotes Beloch's publication-date, and cites a page-title of Schachermeyr's as though it were an integral part of his text); J. Beloch, *Griech. Gesch.*, vol. III, i (Berlin-Leipzig, 1922), pp. 623–5; Berve, *APG*, II, no. 606, p. 300, and n. 1; Milns, *Alexander the Great* (1968), pp. 56–7.
38. op. cit., p. 625, n. 1.
39. Davis, p. 34; cf. pp. 40–41.
40. Arrian 1.5.5–1.6.9 *passim*; cf. above chapter 4, pp. 131 ff., with nn. 30–32.
41. Arrian 1.13.3–7; Plut. *Alex.* 16.1–3.
42. *Alex.* 16.3.
43. 4.3.16. Professor Badian argues that this passage of Polyaenus is in fact derived from the Ptolemy-Aristobulus vulgate; that ἐξ ὑπερδεξίων here, as in Arrian, means simply 'from above', and that διαβαίνων pegs Alexander's movements to an attack made *through* the river, so that Polyaenus' battle (outflanking movement included) takes place parallel with the Granicus rather than at right-angles to it. The former point cannot be proved either way: both usages exist. The latter phrase, I would argue, means no more than 'at the crossing' of the river, in a temporal sense – and whichever version we believe, it still remains true that the river *was* crossed.
44. L-S-J s.v. ὑπερδέξιος.
45. Diod. 17.19.6; cf. Arrian 1.14.1–3.
46. Fuller, p. 166.
47. cf. Brunt, *JHS* 83 (1963), 30–34.
48. But see Plut. *Eum.* 2.2.
49. Probably commanded by Petines and Niphates: see Arrian 1.14.4.
50. Arrian's figure of 1,000 seems to refer exclusively to Iranian losses.
51. So Tarn, vol. I, p. 16; Schachermeyr, pp. 140–41 with nn. 84–5; Hamilton, *PA*, p. 39.

52. Diod. 17.17.2; Polyaenus 5.44.4. For Memnon's appointment to the overall command see Diod. 17.29.1, cf. 23.5–6.
53. Arrian 2.2.2; QC 3.3.1.
54. Recruitment before Issus: Diod. 17.29.1; QC 3.2.9. The final total of 50,000: QC 5.11.5; Paus. 8.52.5. For arguments against these figures see above, p. 229, and footnote *ad loc.*
55. For the details see Plut. *Alex.* 16.6–7; Arrian 1.16.2, 6.
56. Diod. 17.14.1; Plut. *Alex.* 11.6; Aelian *VH* 13.7.
57. Diod. 13.19.2 (18,000 killed, 7,000 taken prisoners), cf. Thuc. 7.83–5.
58. See, e.g., besides the muster-lists already given, Diod. 17.19.5, 21.6; Plut. *Alex.* 16.6–7.
59. Arrian 1.14.1–3, cf. Diod. 17.19.6.
60. Arrian 1.15.1–2; Plut. *Alex.* 16.3–5.
61. Plut. *Alex.* 16.4–5, 7–8; cf. Diod. 17.20.3, 5, 6. Strabo, 15.3–18, C. 734, defines the σαυνίον as a hunting-spear, to be used for throwing from horseback (I owe this reference to Professor Badian).
62. Arrian 1.15.5 and elsewhere, e.g. Xen. *Cyrop.* 4.3.9, 6.2.16.
63. Arrian 1.15.1–3.
64. Some critics (e.g. Bryan) have actually suggested emending αἱ πεζαί here to αἱ Περσικαί, or adding Περσῶν after πεζαί: see Hamilton, *PA*, p. 41. His own comment is: 'Plutarch has failed to realize that the Persians had no foot-soldiers apart from the mercenaries'; this of course is question-begging. Aristobulus (cf. above, n. 58) says that they did (16.6). It all depends on the degree of one's faith in Ptolemy's consistent veracity.
65. Arrian 1.16.2; Diod. 17.21.5.
66. Diod. 17.21.1, with Welles' note *ad loc.*, pp. 176–7. This is the only example in the present context of the verb ἀκοντίζω being used in connection with the Persian cavalry. Even here Diodorus may be using it in the sense of throwing (undefined) missiles.
67. Davis, p. 41.
68. Hamilton, *PA*, p. 39, says that Alexander 'realized the propaganda value of forcing a crossing in the teeth of Persian opposition'. This may be true, but I am inclined to doubt it. The best propaganda of all is a crushing victory, however that victory may be won. Strategy which hazards an initial defeat may leave one with no propaganda whatsoever. On systematic bias in Ptolemy's work see now the excellent article by R. M. Errington, *CQ* ns19 (1969), 233–42.
69. A similar thesis was recently propounded with great (but in my opinion mistaken) ingenuity for the battle of Marathon: see J. H. Schreiner, 'The Battles of 490 B.C.', *Proc. Camb. Phil. Soc.* 196 (ns16) (1970), 97–112. It may be as well to say here that the first draft of this Appendix had been completed some time before Dr Schreiner's article came to my notice.

70. Plut. *Alex.* 14, cf. Diod. 17.93.4; Tarn, vol. II, pp. 338–46, and above, p. 124.
71. See above pp. 360 ff., and elsewhere.
72. e.g. at Miletus: Arrian 1.19.6, Plut. *Alex.* 17.1. The argument that Alexander could not afford their services until Miletus still does not explain the almost hysterical savagery with which he treated them after the Granicus. For a comparable incident we have to wait for his massacre of the Indian mercenaries at Massaga; see above, ch. 9, p. 383 and n. 50.
73. Arrian 1.16.6, cf. 2–3, with Plut. *Alex.* 16.6–7.
74. See above, chapter 4, pp. 147 ff., with nn. 54–7; for the use of the league as a justificatory instrument, Diod. 17.14.1–4, Arrian 1.9.6–10, Plut. *Alex.* 11.5–6, Justin 11.3.8–11.4.8.
75. Plut. *Alex.* 16.7.
76. Plut. *Alex.* 16.1–2; Arrian 1.13.3–5.
77. So Fuller, p. 149 (wrongly queried by Hamilton, *PA*, p. 39).
78. cf. Badian, *TAPhA* 91 (1960), 327–8.
79. *JHS* 91 (1971), 196.
80. There was nothing to stop such a scheme at this point. Alexander had not yet proved himself charismatically invincible; to the Macedonian barons he was simply a clever, dangerous, determined boy who had forced Parmenio's hand over the succession. cf. Badian, *Phoenix* 17 (1963), 249–50.
81. Plut. *Alex.* 16.3–4; cf. Arrian 1.14.6.
82. Nevertheless, the numerous occasions on which Callisthenes or sources dependent on him make a point of recording supposedly bad advice given by Parmenio to the king – advice which is invariably ignored, to the benefit of all concerned – is highly suggestive: see, e.g., Arrian 1.18.6 ff., Plut. *Alex.* 16.3, 29.8, 31.10 ff. We can hardly doubt that this was at Alexander's instructions: see now the excellent note by Hamilton, op. cit., p. 89, and for Alexander's characteristic desire to 'compensate at once for his few failures', Badian, *Stud. Ehrenb.* (1966), p. 47.
83. Arrian 1.14.6.
84. Arrian 1.16.4, cf. Plut. *Alex.* 16.8, Vell. Pat. 1.11.3–4.
85. It will hardly do simply to make Cleitarchus responsible for Diodorus' version, as Schachermeyr does (op. cit., pp. 504–5, n. 86) and thus discredit the latter at one stroke by the mere mention of an 'unsound' source, '*der von den damaligen Gegensätzen im Hauptquartier so wenig wusste wie von einem nachmittägigen Schlachttermin*'. Schachermeyr goes on to say: '*Vermutlich hatte sich Kallisthenes über derartiges überhaupt nicht ausgesprochen.*' Not *vermutlich* at all, I would have thought; this is pure speculative fiction.

Sources of Information

BIBLIOGRAPHY I: ANCIENT EVIDENCE

(a) *Literary*

Since this book is designed for the general reader, I have wherever possible listed the appropriate parallel-translation Loeb edition for each author: it should not be supposed that I invariably regard this as the best edition available, or indeed the best translation. If a better translation is known to me, and easily available, I list it. Minor writers not listed can be found in Jacoby or Robinson (see below s.v. MISCEL-LANEOUS). L = Loeb.

AELIAN Claudius Aelianus (*c*. A.D. 170–235). Roman-domiciled epitomist. *Varia Historia*, ed. R. Hercher (Teubner), 1864. No English translation available.

AESCHINES (*c*. 397–*c*. 322 B.C.). Athenian orator and politician. *Works*, ed. and tr. C. D. Adams, London, 1919 (L).

ARISTOTLE (384–322 B.C.). Philosopher and scientist. *Politics*, ed. and tr. H. Rackham, London, 1932 (L). *Eudemian Ethics*, ed. and tr. E. Rackham, London, 1935 (L).

ARRIAN Flavius Arrianus (second century A.D.). A Greek from Bithynia, who governed Cappadocia under Hadrian, saw military action during the Alan invasion of 134, and studied under Epictetus. His *History of Alexander*, based largely on Ptolemy and Aristobulus, is still the soundest study of Alexander (though by no means so sound as romantic enthusiasts sometimes like to pretend: he is a master of artful omission). *History of Alexander and Indica*, ed. and tr. E. I. Robson (L), 2 vols., London, 1929–33 (both text and translation are highly erratic). *Arrian's Campaign of Alexander*, tr. Aubrey de Selincourt, London (Penguin Classics), revised edition with introduction and notes by J. R. Hamilton, 1972.

ATHENAEUS of Naucratis in Egypt (*flor. c*. A.D. 200). His one surviving work, *The Deipnosophists*, ed. and tr. C. B. Gulick, 7 vols., London, 1927–41 (L), is chiefly valuable for the innumerable fragments it preserves from fifth and fourth century B.C. authors (playwrights in particular) whose work is otherwise lost. Relevant fragments collected by Jacoby and Robinson (see below s.v. MISCELLANEOUS).

CTESIAS of Cnidos (late fifth century B.C.). Greek physician at the Achaemenid court in Persia: wrote works on Persia and India.

J. Gilmore, *Fragments of the Persika of Ctesias*, London, 1888; R. Henry, *Ctesias: La Perse, L'Inde, les Sommaires de Photius*, Brussels, Office de Publicité S. C., 1947.

DEMADES, DEINARCHUS, HYPEREIDES, LYCURGUS. Statesmen and orators in Athens in the time of Philip and Alexander. Their surviving speeches and fragments are collected in *Minor Attic Orators*, vol. II, ed. and tr. J. O. Burtt, London, 1954 (L).

DEMOSTHENES (384–322 B.C.) of Paeania in Attica. Athenian orator and politician. *Olynthiacs, Philippics, &c.*, ed. and tr. J. H. Vince, London, 1930. *De Corona* and *De Falsa Legatione*, ed. and tr. C. A. and J. H. Vince, London, 1926 (L).

DIODORUS SICULUS (first century B.C.). A Sicilian from Agyrium, who wrote a *Universal History*, much of it preserved, in forty books. This is the earliest connected account of Alexander's reign which we possess: Diodorus devotes the whole of Book 17 to the period 336–323. The sources he uses are still a matter of fierce scholarly debate; despite his chronological confusion and scissors-and-paste methods he often presents extremely valuable material. Books 17 and 18 form vols. VIII and IX of the Loeb edition, edited respectively by C. B. Welles (vol. VIII, 1963: a brilliant piece of scholarship) and R. M. Geer (vol. IX, 1947).

DIOGENES LAERTIUS (? early third century A.D.). Biographical epitomist. *Lives of Eminent Philosophers*, ed. and tr. R. D. Hicks, London, 1925 (L).

HERODOTUS (*c.* 485–*c.* 425 B.C.) of Halicarnassus. *The Histories*, ed. and tr. A. D. Godley, 4 vols., London, 1920–25 (L); tr. A. de Selincourt, London (Penguin Classics), 1954.

HESYCHIUS (? fifth century A.D.) of Alexandria, lexicographer. Ed. M. Schmidt, Jena 1858–68. Kurt Latte's superb edition (Hauniae, Munksgaard: vol. I, 1953; vol. II, 1966) had reached the letter O at the time of his death.

ISOCRATES (436–338 B.C.). Athenian pamphleteer, rhetorician and orator. *Works*, ed. and tr. G. Norlin and LaRue Van Hook, London, 1928–45 (L).

JULIUS VALERIUS (? third–fourth century A.D.). Wrote a Latin version of the Alexander-Romance by Pseudo-Callisthenes. Ed. B. Kuebler, Leipzig, 1888. No English translation available.

JUSTIN (? third century A.D.). Marcus Junianus Justinus, epitomizer; made a digest of Trogus Pompeius' *Historiae Philippicae*, written during the reign of Augustus. *Abrégé des Histoires Philippiques de Trogue Pompée*, ed. and tr. E. and L. T. Chambry, 2 vols., Paris, 1936. No English translation available.

MISCELLANEOUS. W. W. Boer (ed.), *Epistola Alexandri ad Aristotelem*, The Hague, 1953. F. Jacoby (ed.), *Die Fragmente der griechischen Historiker* (FGrHist), Pt II (Zeitgeschichte) B, pp. 618–828 (Alexandergeschichte) with Commentary (pp. 403–502, nos. 117–53), Berlin, 1929.

C. A. Robinson (ed.), *The History of Alexander the Great*, vol. I (Brown University Studies XVI), Providence R.I. (1953) translates all the fragments in Jacoby, including those of Callisthenes, Nearchus, Chares of Mytilene, Ptolemy, Cleitarchus, and others.

PAUSANIAS (second century A.D.). Travel-writer and geographer, best known for his *Description of Greece*: tr. and ed. W. H. S. Jones, H. A. Ormerod, R. E. Wycherley, 5 vols., London, 1918–35 (L). Now also available in a new translation by Father Peter Levi, S.J., Penguin Classics, 2 vols., London, 1971.

PLINY Gaius Plinius Secundus (A.D. 23/4–79). Military officer and polymath, whose scientific curiosity led to his death during the eruption of Vesuvius which destroyed Pompeii. *Natural History*, ed. and tr. H. Rackham, W. H. S. Jones, 10 vols., London, 1938–62 (L).

PLUTARCH of Chaeronea (*c.* A.D. 46–120). Biographer, dilettante scholar, Delphic priest; procurator of Achaea under Hadrian. His *Life* of Alexander is based on a number of authors now known only from fragments, including Callisthenes, Aristobulus, Chares and Onesicritus: tr. and ed. B. Perrin, *Plutarch's Lives*, vol. VII, London, 1919 (L). See also his *Lives* of Demosthenes (ibid.) and Phocion and Eumenes (vol. VIII). Plutarch wrote two early essays on Alexander, *On the Fortune or the Virtue of Alexander*, *Moral.* 326D–345B (Loeb *Moralia*, vol. IV, tr. and ed. F. C. Babbitt, London, 1936), and there are numerous other references scattered through the *Moralia* (see especially 179D–181F, 219E, 221A9, 522A, 557B, 781A–B, 804B, 970D, 1043D). For a first-class discussion and commentary see J. R. Hamilton's edition of the Alexander *Life* (Oxford, 1968).

POLYAENUS (*flor. c.* A.D. 150). A Macedonian rhetorician and excerptor, now remembered only for his volume of tactical anecdotes, *Strategemeta* (ed. J. Melber, Leipzig, 1887). No English translation available.

POLYBIUS (?203–?120 B.C.). Greek statesman and historian; later moved to Rome under the patronage of the Scipionic circle. His main value for this period is his detailed criticism (20.17–22) of Callisthenes as a military historian, especially as regards Issus. *The Histories*, ed. and tr. W. R. Paton, London, 1925 (L).

PSEUDO-CALLISTHENES. Name given to the unknown author of the so-called 'Alexander-Romance', extant in many versions (including three Greek ones) of which the earliest is perhaps late second century A.D., though probably based on a romance in circulation not long after Alexander's death. Text: W. Kroll, *Historia Alexandri Magni*, second edition, Berlin, 1958; tr. E. H. Haight, *The Life of Alexander of Macedon*, New York, 1955. See also P. H. Thomas, *Incerti Auctoris Epitoma rerum gestarum Alexandri Magni cum libro de morte testamentoque Alexandri*, Leipzig (Teubner), 1960.

QUINTUS CURTIUS (? first century A.D.). His *History of Alexander* (ed. and tr. J. C. Rolfe, 2 vols., London, 1946 (L)) lacks Books 1 and 2, and has gaps between Books 5 and 6 and in Book 10. As a source Curtius' stock has risen somewhat in the last few years: he is frequently uncritical and given to overblown rhetoric, but careful analysis reveals highly valuable material (e.g. in relation to geography).

STRABO (64/3 B.C.–A.D. 21 +). A Greek from Amaseia in Pontus, who spent long periods of his life at Rome and in Egypt. His *Geography*, ed. and tr. H. L. Jones, 8 vols., London, 1917–32 (L), is a vast storehouse of useful facts and anecdotes, historical as well as geographical, concerning every area through which Alexander passed.

SUDA. Not a personal name, but the title of a lexicon ('The Suda' = 'Fortress' or 'Stronghold') compiled in its present form about the tenth century A.D., mostly based on other digests and epitomes. Yet much material in it derives, ultimately, from first-class sources now lost.

VALERIUS MAXIMUS (first century A.D.). Rhetorician and excerptor: his *Factorum ac dictorum memorabilium libri IX* (ed. C. Kempf, Leipzig, Teubner, 1888) was dedicated to Tiberius, and, though entirely uncritical, contains one or two illuminating anecdotes.

(b) *Epigraphic*

Inscriptions from Philip's and Alexander's reign of historical significance are collected, with a full commentary, by M. N. Tod in *Greek Historical Inscriptions*, vol. II, from 403 to 323 B.C., Oxford, 1948.

(c) *Numismatic*

AULOCK, H. von. 'Die Prägung des Balakros in Kilikien', *JNG* 14 (1964), 79–82.

BABELON, J. *Le Portrait dans l'antiquité d'après les monnaies*, Paris, 1942.

BELLINGER, A. R. *Essays on the Coinage of Alexander the Great* (Numismatic Studies II), New York, 1963.

HILL, G. F. 'Alexander the Great and the Persian lion-gryphon', *JHS* 43 (1923), 156–61.

KLEINER, G. *Alexanders Reichsmünzen* (Abhandlungen der deutschen Akademie der Wissenschaften zu Berlin, Klasse für Sprachen, Literatur und Kunst, Akademie-Verlag, no. 5), Berlin, 1949.

KRAAY, C. M. *Greek Coins*, London, 1967.

NEWELL, E. T. *The dated Alexander coinage of Sidon and Ake*, Oxford University Press, 1916. *Myriandros kat'Isson*, New York, 1920. *Tarsos under Alexander*, New York, 1919.

NOE, S. P. 'The Corinth Hoard of 1938', *ANSMusN* 10 (1962), 9–41.

SELTMAN, C. *Greek Coins*, second edition, London, 1955.

(d) *Iconographic and miscellaneous*

ANDREAE, B. *Das Alexandermosaik (Opus nobile XIV)*, Bremen, 1959.

BANDINELLI, G. 'Cassandro di Macedonia nella Vita plutarchea di Alessandro Magno', *RFIC* 93 (1965), 150–64. 'Un ignorato gruppo statuario di Alessandro e Bucefalo', *SE* 18 (1944), 29–43, with plates V–VII.

BERNOULLI, J. J. *Die erhaltenen Darstellungen Alexanders des Grossen; Ein Nachtrag zur griechischen Ikonographie*, Munich, 1905.

BIEBER, M. *Alexander the Great in Greek and Roman Art*, Chicago, 1964.

BIJVANCK, A. W. 'La bataille d'Alexandre', *BVAB* 30 (1955), 28–34.

DAUX, G. 'Chroniques des Fouilles en 1961', *BCH* 86 (1962), 805–13. 'Chroniques des Fouilles en 1957', *BCH* 82 (1958), 761–5 with figs. 14–16.

DELLA CORTE, M. 'L'educazione di Alessandro Magno nell'enciclopedia Aristotelica in un trittico megalografico di Pompei del II stile', *MDAI(R)* 57 (1942), 31–77.

DEL MEDICO, H. E. 'A propos du trésor de Panaguriste: un portrait d'Alexandre par Lysippe', *Persica* 3 (1967/8), 37–67, plates II–IV, figs. 8–15.

GEBAUER, K. Alexanderbildnis und Alexandertypus. *MDAI(R)* (1938/9), 1–106.

JOHNSON, F. P. *Lysippos*, Durham, N. Carolina, 1927.

JONGKEES, J. H. 'A portrait of Alexander the Great', *BVAB* 29 (1954), 32–3.

LUNSINGH-SCHEURLEER, R. A. 'Alexander in faience', ibid. 40 (1965), 80–83.

MINGAZZINI, P. 'Una copia dell'Alex. Keraunophoros di Apelle', *JBerlM* 3 (1961), 7–17.

NEWELL, E. T. *Royal Greek Portrait Coins*, New York, 1937.

PFISTER, F. 'Alexander der Grosse in der bildenden Kunst', *F und F* 35 (1961), 330–34, 375–9.

PICARD, C. 'Le mosaïste grec Gnôsis et les nouvelles chasses de Pella', *RA* 1 (1963), 205–9.

RICHTER, G. M. A. *The Portraits of the Greeks*, 3 vols., London, Phaidon, 1965.

ROBERTSON, M. 'The Boscoreale figure-paintings', *JHS* 45 (1955), 58–67, plates XI–XIII.

RUMPF, A. 'Zum Alexander-Mosaik', *MDAI(A)* 77 (1962), 229–41.

SCHREIBER, T. *Studien über das Bildniss Alexanders des Grossen*, Leipzig, 1903.

SJÖQVIST, E. 'Alexander-Heracles. A preliminary note', *BMusB* (Boston) 51 (1953), 30–33, figs. 1–5.

SUHR, E. G. *Sculptured Portraits of Greek Statesmen, with a special study of Alexander the Great*, Baltimore, 1931.

UJFALVY, C. de. *Le Type Physique d'Alexandre le Grand*, Paris, 1902.

BIBLIOGRAPHY II: MODERN STUDIES

This bibliography does not claim to be exhaustive (the literature on Alexander is so vast that to list it all would fill a fair-sized volume); I only include here items I have found of special use or interest – often through differing radically from the views which they express. For further study the following guide may be profitably consulted:

BADIAN, E. 'Alexander the Great, 1948–67', *CW* 65 (1971), 37–56, 77–83.

ABEL, F. M. 'Alexandre le Grand en Syrie et en Palestine', *Rev. Bibl.* 43 (1934), 528–45; 44 (1935), 42–61.

ADCOCK, F. E. *The Greek and Macedonian Art of War*, Berkeley, 1962. 'Greek and Macedonian Kingship', *Proc. Brit. Acad.* 39 (1954), 163–80.

ALTHEIM, F. *Alexander und Asien: Geschichte eines geistiges Erbes*, Tübingen, 1953.
Zarathustra und Alexander, Frankfurt a.M., 1960.

ANDERSON, A. R. 'Alexander's Horns', *TAPhA* 58 (1927), 100–122. 'Bucephalas and his legend', *AJPh* (1930), 1–21.

ANDREOTTI, R. 'Die Weltmonarchie Alexanders des Grossen', *Saeculum* 8 (1957), 120–66.
'Per un critica dell'ideologia di Alessandro Magno', *Historia* 5 (1956), 257–302.
'Il problema di Alessandro Magno nella storiografia dell'ultimo decennio', *Historia* 1 (1950), 583 ff.
Il problema politico di Alessandro Magno, Parma, 1933.

ATKINSON, J. E. 'Primary sources and the Alexanderreich', *Act. Class.* (Cape Town), 6 (1963), 125–37.

AYMARD, A. 'Le protocole royal grec et son évolution', *REA* (1948), 232–63.
'Sur quelques vers d'Euripide qui poussèrent Alexandre au meurtre', *Ann. Inst. Phil. Hist. Or.* (Brussels) 9 (1949), 43–74 (= Mélanges Grégoire I).
'Un ordre d'Alexandre', *REA* (1937), 5–28.

BADIAN, E. 'Agis III', *Hermes* 95 (1967), 170–92.
'The Administration of the Empire', *GR* 12 (1965), 166–82.
'Alexander the Great and the Creation of an Empire', *Hist. Today* 8 (1958), 369–76, 494–502.
'Alexander the Great and the Greeks of Asia', *Ancient Societies and Institutions: Studies presented to Victor Ehrenberg on his 75th birthday* (Oxford, 1966), 37–69.
'Alexander the Great and the Loneliness of Power', *Journ. Austral. Univ. Lang. Assoc.* 17 (1962), 80–91; repr. in *Studies in Greek and Roman History* (Oxford, 1964), 192–205.

'Alexander the Great and the Unity of Mankind', *Historia* 7 (1958), 425–44; repr. in Griffith, *Main Problems* (*MP*), q.v., pp. 287–306.
'Ancient Alexandria', *Stud. Gr. Rom. Hist.*, pp. 179–191.
'The death of Parmenio', *TAPhA* 91 (1960), 324–38.
'The death of Philip II', *Phoenix* 17 (1963), 244–50.
'The Eunuch Bagoas', *CQ* ns8 (1958), 144–57.
'The first flight of Harpalus', *Historia* 9 (1960), 245–6.
'Harpalus', *JHS* 81 (1961), 16–43.
'A King's Notebooks', *Harv. Stud. Class. Phil.* 72 (1967), 183–204.
'Orientals in Alexander's army', *JHS* 85 (1965), 160–61.
BALDRY, H. C. *The Unity of Mankind in Greek Thought*, Cambridge, 1965.
BALSDON, J. P. V. D. 'The "Divinity" of Alexander the Great', *Historia* 1 (1950), 383–8.
BELOCH, K. J. *Griechische Geschichte*, 2nd edn, vols. III, i–ii; IV, i, Leipzig-Berlin, 1922–5.
BERVE, H. *Das Alexanderreich auf prosopographischer Grundlage*, 2 vols., Munich, 1926.
'Die Verschmelzungspolitik Alexanders des Grossen', *Klio* 31 (1938), 135–68. Repr. Griffith, *MP* pp. 103–36.
BEVAN, E. R. Chapter XV of *The Cambridge History of India* (ed. E. J. Rapson), vol. I (1922), pp. 345–86.
BICKERMANN, E. 'Alexandre le Grand et les villes d'Asie', *REG* 47 (1934), 346–74.
'La Lettre d'Alexandre le Grand aux bannis grecs', *REA* 53 (1940), 25–35.
'A propos d'un passage de Chares de Mytilène', *Parola del Passato* 18 (1963), 241–55.
BIDEZ, J. 'Hermias d'Atarnée', *Bull. Class. Lett. Sc. Mor. Pol. Acad. R. Belg.* 29 (1943), 133–46.
BORZA, E. N. 'Alexander and the return from Siwah', *Historia* 16 (1967), 369.
'Cleitarchus and Diodorus' account of Alexander', *Proc. Afr. Class. Assoc.* 2 (1968), 25–45.
'The End of Agis's Revolt', *CPh* 66 (1971), 230–35.
'Fire from Heaven: Alexander at Persepolis', *CPh* 67 (1972), 233–45.
'Some notes on Arrian's name', *Athens Annals of Archaeology* 5 (1972), 99–192.
See also s.v. WILCKEN, U.
BOSWORTH, A. B. 'Philip II and Upper Macedonia', *CQ* 21ns (1971), 93–105.
'The Death of Alexander the Great: Rumour and Propaganda', ibid., 112–36.
'Arrian's Literary Development', *CQ* ns 22 (1972), 163–85.
BRELOAR, B. *Alexanders Kampf gegen Poros*, Stuttgart, 1933.

BROWN, T. S. 'Alexander's Book Order (Plut. *Alex.* 8)', *Historia* 16 (1967), 359–68.

'Callisthenes and Alexander', *AJPh* 70 (1949), 225–48; repr. Griffiths, *MP*, pp. 53–72.

Onesicritus, Berkeley/Los Angeles, 1949.

BRUNT, P. A. 'The Aims of Alexander', *GR* 12 (1965), 205–15.

'Alexander's Macedonian Cavalry', *JHS* 83 (1963), 27–46.

'Persian accounts of Alexander's campaigns', *CQ* 12 (1962), 141–55.

BUCHNER, E. 'Zwei Gutachten für die Behandlung der Barbaren durch Alexander den Grossen?', *Hermes* 82 (1954), 378–84.

BURN, A. R. *Alexander the Great and the Hellenistic World*, 2nd rev. edn, New York, 1962.

'The generalship of Alexander', *GR* 12 (1965), 140–54.

'Notes on Alexander's campaigns, 332–330 B.C.', *JHS* 72 (1952), 81–91.

CAROE, O. *The Pathans, 550 B.C.–A.D. 1957*, London, 1958.

CARY, G. *The Mediaeval Alexander*, Cambridge, 1956.

CASSON, L. 'The grain trade of the Hellenistic world', *TAPhA* 85 (1954), 168–87.

CASSON, S. *Macedonia, Thrace and Illyria*, Oxford, 1926.

CHROUST, A. H. 'Aristotle and Callisthenes of Olynthus', *Classical Folia* 20 (1966), 32–41.

'Aristotle's sojourn in Assas', *Historia* 21 (1972) 170–176.

'Aristotle leaves the Academy', *GR* 14 (1967) 39–44.

CLOCHE, P. *Alexandre le Grand*, Neuchatel, 1953.

Histoire de la Macédoine jusqu'à l'avènement d'Alexandre le Grand (336 av. J.-C.), Paris, 1960.

Un fondateur d'empire: Philippe II, Roi de Macédoine (382/2–336/5 avant J.C.), St-Etienne, 1955.

COLOMBINI, A. 'Per una valutazione dei rapporti delfico-macedoni dalle origini del regno Argeade ad Alessandro Magno', *Stud. Class. e Orient.* 12 (1963), 183–206.

CROSS, G. N. *Epirus: A Study in Greek Constitutional Development*, Cambridge, 1932.

CULICAN, W. *The Medes and Persians*, London, 1965.

DASKALAKIS, A. *Alexander the Great and Hellenism*, Thessaloniki, 1966.

'L'origine de la maison royale de Macédoine et les légendes relatives de l'antiquité', *AM*, pp. 155–61.

DAVIS, E. W. 'The Persian battle plan at the Granicus', *Stud. Caldwell* (*Laudatores temporis acti*, ed. M. F. Gyles and E. W. Davis), 34–44 (Univ. N. Carolina, 1964).

DELCOR, M. 'Les allusions à Alexandre le Grand dans Zach. IX 1–8', *Vet. Test.* 1 (1951), 110–24.

DELL, H. J. 'The western frontier of the Macedonian monarchy', *AM*, 115–26.

DERCHAIN, P. J., and HUBAUX, J. 'Le fantôme de Babylone', *AC* (1950), 367–82.

DE SANCTIS, G. 'Gli ultimi messaggi di Alessandro ai Greci, I: La richiesta degli onori divini', *Riv. fil.* (1940), 1–21.

DIHLE, A. 'The conception of India in Hellenistic and Roman literature', *Proc. Camb. Phil. Soc.* 10 (1964), 15–23.

DILLER, A. *Race Mixture among the Greeks before Alexander*, Univ. Illinois, 1937.

DROYSEN, J. G. *Geschichte Alexanders des Grossen*, 1833; rev. edn (H. Berve), 1931.

EDDY, S. K. *The King is Dead. Studies in the Near Eastern resistance to Hellenism, 334–331 b.c.*, Lincoln Univ., Nebraska, 1961.

EDMUNDS, L. 'The religiosity of Alexander', *GRByS* 12 (1971), 363–91.

EDSON, C. F. 'Early Macedonia', *AM*, 2–44.

EHRENBERG, V. *Alexander and the Greeks*, tr. R. Fraenkel van Velsen, Oxford, 1938: ch. II, 'Pothos', repr. in Griffith, *MP*, pp. 73–83.

Alexander und Aegypten, Leipzig, 1926.

EHRHARDT, C. 'Two notes on Philip of Macedon's first interventions in Thessaly', *CQ* 17 (1967), 296.

ELLIGER, K. 'Ein Zeugnis aus der jüdischen Gemeinde, 332 v. Chr.', *Zeitschr. f. Alttest. Wiss.* 62 (1949/50), 63–115.

ELLIS, J. R. 'The security of the Macedonian throne under Philip II', *AM*, 68–75.

'Amyntas Perdikka, Philip II and Alexander the Great', *JHS* 91 (1971), 15–24.

ERRINGTON, R. M. 'Bias in Ptolemy's History of Alexander', *CQ* ns63 (1969), 233–42.

FAKHRY, A. 'A temple of Alexander the Great at Bahria Oasis', *Ann. Serv. Ant. Egypt.* 40 (1940/41), 823–8.

FERGUSON, W. S. *Hellenistic Athens*, New York, 1911.

FORTINA, M. *Cassandro, re di Macedonia*, Torino, 1965.

FOUCHER, A. 'Les satrapies orientales de l'empire achéménide', *Compt. Rend. Acad. Inscr.* (1938), 336–52.

FOUCHER, A., and E. B. 'La vieille route de Bactre à Taxila', *MéM. Délég. française en Afghanistan* II (1942).

FRASER, A. D. 'The "breaking" of Bucephalas', *CW* 47 (1953), 22–3.

FRASER, P. M. 'Alexander and the Rhodian Constitution', *Parola del Passato* 7 (1952), 192–206.

'Current problems concerning the early history of the cult of Sarapis', *Opuscula Archaeologica* 7 (1967), 23 ff.

FREDRICKSMEYER, E. A. 'Alexander, Midas, and the oracle at Gordium', *CPh* 56 (1961), 160–68.

'The ancestral rites of Alexander the Great', *CPh* 61 (1966), 179–81.

The Religion of Alexander the Great, Diss. Univ. Wisconsin, 1958, Résumé: *Diss. Abstract.* 19 (1959), 1747.

FRYE, R. N. *The Heritage of Persia*, London, 1962.
FULLER, J. F. C. *The Generalship of Alexander the Great*, London, 1958.
GALLET DE SANTERRE, H. 'Alexandre le Grand et Kymé d'Eolide', *Bull. Corr. Hell.* 71.2 (1947/8), 302–6.
GEYER, F. 'Philippos' (7) in Pauly-Wissowa-Kroll (PWK) *Real. Enc.* (*RE*), vol. XIX, cols. 2266–303.
'Makedonien bis zur Thronbesteigung Philipps II' (Beiheft 19, *Hist. Zeitschrift*), München/Berlin, 1930.
GHIRSHMAN, R. *Iran: Parthians and Sassanians*, London, 1962.
Perse: Proto-iraniens, Mèdes, Achéménides, Paris, 1963. (English tr. by S. Gilbert and J. Emmons, London, 1964.)
GITTI, A. *Alessandro Magno all'Oasi di Siwah. Il problema delle fonti*, Bari, 1951.
'Alessandro Magno e il responso di Ammone', *Riv. stor. ital.* 64 (1952), 531–47.
'L'unitarietà della tradizione su Alessandro Magno nella ricerca moderna', *Athenaeum* 34 (1956), 39–57.
GLOTZ, G., ROUSSEL, P., and COHEN, R. *Histoire grecque*, vol. IV: *Alexandre et l'Hellénisation du monde antique*, pt i, 'Alexandre et le démembrement de son empire', Paris, 1938.
GRIFFITH, G. T. 'Alexander and Antipater in 323 B.C.', *Proc. Afric. Class. Assoc.* 8 (1965), 12–17.
'Alexander's generalship at Gaugamela', *JHS* 67 (1947), 77–89.
'Alexander the Great and an experiment in government', *Proc. Camb. Phil. Soc.* 10 (1964), 23–39.
'The letter of Darius at Arrian 2.14', *Proc. Camb. Phil. Soc.* 14 (1968), 33–48.
'The Macedonian Background', *GR* 12 (1965), 125–39.
'*Makedonika*. Notes on the Macedonians of Philip and Alexander', *Proc. Camb. Phil. Soc.* 4 (1956/7), 3–10.
The Mercenaries of the Hellenistic World, Cambridge, 1935.
'A note on the Hipparchies of Alexander', *JHS* 83 (1963), 68–74.
'Philip of Macedon's early interventions in Thessaly (358–352 B.C.)', *CQ* ns20 (1970), 67–80.
(ed.) *Alexander the Great: The Main Problems*, Cambridge, 1966.
GROTE, G. *A History of Greece*; rev. ed. 12 vols., London, 1888.
GUNDERSON, L. L. 'Early elements in the Alexander Romance', *AM* 353–75.
HADAS, M. *Hellenistic Culture: Fusion and Diffusion*, New York, 1959.
HADLEY, R. A. 'Deified Kingship and propaganda coinage in the early Hellenistic Age', Diss. Univ. Pennsylvania, 1964. Résumé in *Diss. Abstracts* 25 (1965), 5881–2.
HAMILTON, J. R. 'Alexander's early life', *GR* 12 (1965), 117–24.
'Alexander and his so-called father', *CQ* ns3 (1953), 151–7; repr. in Griffith, *MP*, pp. 235–42.

'Alexander and the Aral', *CQ* ns21 (1971), 106–11.
'The cavalry battle at the Hydaspes', *JHS* 76 (1956), 26–31.
'Cleitarchus and Aristobulus', *Historia* 10 (1961), 448–58.
Plutarch: Alexander. A Commentary, Oxford, 1968.
'Three passages in Arrian', *CQ* ns5 (1955), 217–21.
HAMMOND, N. G. L. 'The archaeological background to the Macedonian Kingdom', *AM* 53–67.
A History of Greece, 2nd edn, Oxford, 1967.
Epirus: The geography, the ancient remains, the history and topography of Epirus and adjacent areas. Oxford, 1967.
'The two battles of Chaeronea (338 B.C. and 86 B.C.)', *Klio* 31 (1938), 186–218.
HAMPL, F. *Alexander der Grosse*, Göttingen, 1958.
'Alexander der Grosse und die Beurteilung geschichtlicher Persönlichkeiten in der modernen Historiographie', *Nouv. Clio* 6 (1954), 91–136.
'Alexanders des Grossen *Hypomnemata* und letzte Pläne', *Stud. pres. to D. M. Robinson* II, Washington U.P., 1953, 816–29. Repr. in Griffith, *MP*, pp. 307–21.
Der König der Makedonen, Weida in Thuringen, 1934.
HARMAND, L. 'Les rapports entre la Grèce et l'Orient du début du VIIe siècle à la mort de Philippe de Macédoine (336)', *Inform. Hist.* (1952), 51–6.
HARRIS, R. I. 'The dilemma of Alexander the Great', *Proc. Afric. Class. Assoc.* 2 (1968), 46–54.
HARTMAN, S. S. 'Dionysus and Heracles in India', *Temenos* 1 (1965), 55–64.
HEUSS, A. 'Alexander der Grosse und die politische Ideologie des Altertums', *Antike und Abendl.* 4 (1954), 65–104.
HOGARTH, D. G. *Philip and Alexander of Macedon*, New York, 1897.
INSTINSKY, H. U. *Alexander der Grosse am Hellespont*, Godesburg, 1950.
'Alexander, Pindar, Euripides', *Historia* 10 (1961), 248–55.
JACOBY, F. 'Kallisthenes', PWK, vol. X, ii, cols. 1674–1707.
'Kleitarchos', PWK, vol. XI, i, cols. 622–54.
JAEGER, W. *Aristotle*, tr. Richard Robinson, 2nd edn, Oxford, 1948.
JANKE, A. *Auf Alexanders des Grossen Pfaden*. Berlin, 1904.
'Die Schlacht bei Issus', *Klio* 10 (1910), 137–77.
JONES, A. H. M. *The Greek City from Alexander to Constantine*, Oxford, 1940.
JONES, T. B. 'Alexander and the winter of 330–326 B.C.', *CW* 28 (1935), 124–5.
JOUGUET, P. 'Alexandre à l'oasis d'Ammon et le témoignage de Callisthène', *Bull. Inst. Egypt.* 26 (1943/3), 91–107.
'Apropos d'un livre de H. Berve . . .', *Rev. Phil.* 54 (1928), 361–74.
L'Impérialisme macédonien et l'hellénisation de l'Orient, Paris, 1926.

KAERST, J. 'Alexandros' (10), PWK, vol. I, cols. 1412–34.
Geschichte des Hellenismus, 2 vols., 2nd edn, Leipzig, 1926–7.
KAHRSTEDT, U. 'Das athenische Kontingent zum Alexanderzuge', *Hermes* 71 (1936), 120–24.
KALLERIS, J. N. *Les anciens Macédoniens. Etude linguistique et historique,* vol. I, Athens, 1954.
KANATSOULIS, D. 'Antipatros als Feldherr und Staatsmann in der Zeit Philipps und Alexanders des Grossen', *Hellenica* 16 (1958/9), 14–64.
KEIL, J. 'Der Kampf um den Granikos-Uebergang und das strategische Problem der Issosschlacht', *Mitt. d. Vereins klass. Phil. in Wien* 1 (1924), 13 ff.
KERN, O. 'Der Glaube Alexanders des Grossen', *Forsch. und Fortschr.* (1938), 405–7.
KIENAST, D. 'Augustus und Alexander', *Gymnasium* 76 (1969), 430–56.
'Alexander und der Ganges', *Historia* 14 (1965), 180–88.
LAMOTTE, E. 'Les premières relations entre l'Inde et l'Occident', *Nouv. Clio* 5 (1953), 83–118.
LARSEN, J. A. O. 'Alexander at the Oracle of Ammon', *CPh* 27 (1932), 70–75, cf. 274–5.
Representative Government in Greek and Roman History, Berkeley, 1955.
LECLANT, J. 'Per Africae sitientia. Témoignages des sources classiques sur les pistes menant à l'oasis d'Ammon', *Bull. Inst. franç. d'Arch. Orient.* 49 (1950), 193–253.
LEHMANN, K. 'Die Schlacht am Granikos', *Klio* 11 (1911), 230–44.
LENSCHAU, T. 'Alexander der Grosse und Chios', *Klio* 15 (1940), 201–24.
LEWIS, D. M. 'Two days: (1) Epicurus' Birthday (2) Alexander's Death-day', *CR* ns19 (1969), 271–2.
MACURDY, G. *Hellenistic Queens,* Johns Hopkins Studies in Archaeology no. 14, 1932.
'The refusal of Callisthenes to drink the health of Alexander', *JHS* 50 (1930), 294–7.
MARAINI, F. *Where Four Worlds Meet,* tr. P. Green, London, 1964.
MARINATOS, S. 'Mycenaean elements within the royal houses of Macedonia', *AM* 45–52.
MARSDEN, E. W. *The Campaign of Gaugamela,* Liverpool U.P., 1964.
Greek and Roman Artillery: Technical Treatises, Oxford.
MARSHALL, J. *Taxila,* 3 vols., Cambridge, 1951.
MCEWEN, C. W. *The Oriental Origins of Hellenistic Kingship,* Chicago, 1934.
MERKELBACH, R. *Die Quellen des griechischen Alexanderromans,* München, 1954.
MERLAN, P. 'Alexander the Great or Antiphon the Sophist?', *CPh* 45 (1950), 161–6.

'Isocrates, Aristotle, and Alexander the Great', *Historia* 3 (1954), 60–81.

MIHAILOV, G. 'La Thrace aux IVe et IIIe siècles avant notre ère', *Athenaeum* 39 (1961), 33–44.
'La Thrace et la Macédoine jusqu'à l'invasion des Celtes', *AM*, 76–85.

MIKROJANNAKIS, E. 'The diplomatic contacts between Alexander III and Darius, III', *AM*, 103–8.
Αἱ μεταξὺ 'Αλεξάνδρου Γ' καὶ Δαρείου Γ' διπλωματικαὶ ἐπαφαί, Athens, 1964.

MILNS, R. D. 'Alexander's pursuit of Darius through Iran', *Historia* 15 (1966), 256.
'Alexander's seventh phalanx battalion', *GRByS* 7 (1966), 159 ff.
'The Hypaspists of Alexander III – some problems', *Historia* 20 (1971), 186–95.
'Philip II and the Hypaspists', *Historia* 16 (1967), 509–12.
Alexander the Great, London, 1968.

MILTNER, F. 'Alexanders Strategie bei Issus', *Jahr. Oest. Arch. Inst.* 28 (1933), 69–78.
'Der Okeanos in der persischen Weltreichidee', *Saeculum* 3 (1952), 522–55.

MITCHEL, F. 'Athens in the Age of Alexander', *GR* 12 (1965), 189–294.

MITSAKIS, K. 'The tradition of the Alexander Romance in modern Greek literature', *AM*, 376–86.

MOMIGLIANO, A. *Filippo il Macedone*, Firenze, 1934.

MOSSÉ, C. *La fin de la démocratie athénienne* ..., Paris, 1962.

MURISON, C. L. 'Darius III and the Battle of Issus', *Historia* 21 (1972), 399–423.

NADELL, J. *Alexander and the Romans*, Ann Arbor, 1959.

NARAIN, A. K. 'Alexander and India', *GR* 12·(1965), 155–65.

NEUFFER, E. *Das Kostüm Alexanders des Grossen*, Giessen, 1929.

NEUMANN, C. 'A note on Alexander's march-rates', *Historia* 20 (1971), 196–8.

NOCK, A. D. *Conversion. The old and the new in religion from Alexander the Great to Augustine of Hippo*, Oxford, 1933.
'Notes on Ruler-Cult, I–IV', *JHS* 48 (1928), 21–43.

OLMSTEAD, A. T. *A History of the Persian Empire*, Chicago, 1948.

PARIBENI, R. *La Macedonia sino ad Alessandro Magno*, Milan, 1947.

PARKE, H. W. *Greek Mercenaries*, Oxford, 1933.

PEARSON, L. 'The Diaries and Letters of Alexander the Great', *Historia* 3 (1955), 429–55; repr. Griffith, *MP*, 1–28.
The Lost Histories of Alexander the Great (Philol. Monogr. 20), New York, 1960.

PERLMAN, S. 'Isocrates' "Philippus" and Panhellenism', *Historia* 18 (1969), 370–74.

PETSAS, P. 'New discoveries at Pella, birthplace and capital of Alexander', *Archaeology* 11 (1958), 246–54.

PFISTER, F. 'Alexander der Grosse. Die Geschichte seines Ruhms im Lichte seiner Beinamen', *Historia* 13 (1964), 37–79.

Alexander der Grosse in den Offenbarungen der Griechen, Juden, Mohammedaner und Christen, Berlin, 1956.

'Studien zur Sagengeographie', *Symb. Osl.* 35 (1959), 5–39.

'Dareios von Alexander getötet', *Rhein. Mus.* 101 (1958), 97–106.

'Das Nachleben der Ueberlieferung von Alexander und den Brahmanen', *Hermes* (1941), 143–69.

PICARD, C. 'Les marins de Néarque et le relais de l'expédition d'Alexandre dans le Golfe persique', *Rev. Arch.* 1 (1961), 60–65.

PICKARD-CAMBRIDGE, A. W. 'The Rise of Macedonia' and 'Macedonian Supremacy in Greece', chs. VIII and IX of *The Cambridge Ancient History*, vol. VI (1927), pp. 200–270.

PRENTICE, W. K. 'Callisthenes, the original historian of Alexander', *TAPhA* 54 (1923), 74–85.

PRIDIK, E. *De Alexandri Magni epistularum commercio*, Berlin, 1893.

PRITCHETT, W. K. 'Observations on Chaeronea', *AJA* 62 (1958), 307–11, with pls. 80–81.

RADET, G. *Alexandre le Grand*, 2nd edn, Paris, 1950.

'Alexandre en Syrie. Les offres de paix que lui fit Darius', *Mélanges syriens offerts à R. Dussaud* (Paris, 1939), vol. 1, pp. 235–47.

'Notes sur l'histoire d'Alexandre, IX', *REA* 43 (1941), 33–40.

RAMSAY, W. M. *Historical Geography of Asia Minor*, London, 1890.

REHORK, J. 'Homer, Herodot und Alexander', *Festschr. F. Altheim* (Berlin, 1969), 251–60.

RENARD, M., and SERVAIS, J. 'Apropos du mariage d'Alexandre et de Roxane', *AC* 24 (1955), 29–50.

ROBINSON, C. A. *Alexander the Great*, New York, 1947.

'Alexander's brutality', *AJA* 56 (1952), 169–70.

'Alexander's deification', *AJPh* 64 (1943), 286–301.

'Alexander's descent of the Indus', *TAPhA* 60 (1929), xviii–xix.

'Alexander the Great and the Barbarians', *Class. Studies pres. to E. Capps on his seventieth birthday*, Princeton U.P., 1936, 298–305.

'Alexander the Great and the Oecumene', *Hesperia* Suppl. 8 (1949), 299–304.

'Alexander the Great and Parmenio', *AJA* 49 (1945), 422–4.

'Alexander's Plans', *AJPh* 61 (1940), 402–12.

The Ephemerides of Alexander's Expedition. Providence, Brown University, 1932.

'The extraordinary ideas of Alexander the Great', *AHR* 62 (1957), 326–44; repr. Griffith, *MP*, pp. 53–72.

ROBINSON, D. M. 'Olynthus – the Greek Pompeii', *Archaeology* 5 (1952), 228–35.

ROEBUCK, C. 'The settlements of Philip II with the Greek states in 338 B.C.', *CPh* 43 (1948), 73–92.

ROSTOVTZEFF, M. *Social and Economic History of the Hellenistic World*, 2 vols., Oxford, 1941.

SALAČ, A. 'Alexander of Macedon and Al Iskander Dhu-I-carneiu', *Eunomia* 4 (1960), 41–3.

SAMUEL, A. E. 'Alexander's Royal Journals', *Historia* 14 (1965), 1–12.

SCHACHERMEYR, F. *Alexander der Grosse: Ingenium und Macht*, Wien, 1949.

'Alexander und die Ganges-Länder', *Innsbrucker Beiträge zur Kulturgeschichte* 3 (1955), 123–35; repr. in Griffith, *MP*, pp. 137–50.

'Die letzten Pläne Alexanders des Grossen', *Jahr. Oest. Arch. Inst.* 41 (1954), 118–140; repr. in Griffith, *MP*, pp. 322–44.

SCHIWEK, H. 'Der persische Golfals Schiffahrts- und See-handelsroute in Achämenidischer Zeit und in d. Zeit Alexanders des Grossen', *Bonner Jahrb.* 162 (1962), 4–97.

SCHMIDT, E. F. *Persepolis*, 2 vols., Chicago, 1953, 1957.

SCHMITTHENNER, W. 'Ueber eine Formveränderung der Monarchie seit Alexander dem Grossen', *Saeculum* 19 (1968), 31–46.

SCHREIDER, H. and F. 'In the footsteps of Alexander the Great', *Nat. Geogr.* 133 (1968), 1–65.

SCHWARTZ, E. 'Aristoboulos', PWK, vol. II, cols. 911–18.

'Arrianus', PWK, vol. II, cols. 1230–47.

'Curtius Rufus', PWK, vol. IV, cols. 1870–91.

SNELL, B. *Scenes from Greek Drama*, Berkeley, 1964.

SNODGRASS, A. M. *Arms and Armour of the Greeks*, New York, 1967.

SNYDER, J. W. *Alexander the Great*, New York, 1966.

SORDI, M. 'Alessandro e i Romani', *Rend. Inst. Lombard.* 99 (1965), 435–52.

STAGAKIS, G. S. 'Observations on the ἑταῖροι of Alexander the Great', *AM*, 86–102.

STANDISH, J. F. 'The Caspian Gates', *GR* 17 (1970), 17–24.

STARK, F. *Alexander's Path*, London, 1958.

'Alexander's march from Miletus to Phrygia', *JHS* 78 (1958), 102 ff.

'Alexander's Minor Campaigns in Turkey', *Geogr. Journ.* 122 (1956), 294–305.

STEIN, A. *On Alexander's Track to the Indus*, London, 1929.

'An archaeological journey in W. Iran', *Geogr. Journ.* 92 (1938), 313–42.

'Notes on Alexander's crossing of the Tigris and the battle of Arbela', *Geogr. Journ.* 100 (1942), 155–64.

'On Alexander's route into Gedrosia', *Geogr. Journ.* 102 (1943), 193–227.

'Alexander's campaign on the Indian north-west frontier', *Geogr. Journ.* 70 (1927), 417–540.

'The site of Alexander's passage of the Hydaspes and the battle with Porus', *Geogr. Journ.* 80 (1932), 31–46.

STIEHL, R. 'The origin of the cult of Sarapis', *Hist. Rel.* 3 (1963/4), 21 ff.

STRASBURGER, H. 'Alexanders Zug durch die gedrosische Wüste', *Hermes* 80 (1952), 456–93.

'Zur Route Alexanders durch Gedrosien', *Hermes* 82 (1954), 251.

Ptolemaios und Alexander, Leipzig, 1934.

TAEGER, F. 'Alexander der Grosse und die Anfänge des hellenistischen Herrscherkults', *Hist. Zeitschr.* 172 (1951), 225–44.

'Alexanders Gottkönigsgedanke und die Bewusstseinlage der Griechen und Makedonen', *Studies in the Hist. of Religions* (Numen Suppl.) 4 (1959), 394 ff.

TARN, W. W. *Alexander the Great*, 2 vols., Cambridge, 1948.

'Alexander the Great and the Unity of Mankind', *Proc. Brit. Acad.* 19 (1933), 123–66; repr. Griffith, *MP*, pp. 243–86.

The Greeks in Bactria and India, 2nd edn, Cambridge, 1951.

'Persia from Xerxes to Alexander', *Cambridge Ancient History*, vol. VI (1927), pp. 1–24.

TARN, W. W., and GRIFFITH, G. T. *Hellenistic Civilization*, 3rd rev. edn, London, 1952.

THOMAS, C. G. 'Alexander the Great and the Unity of Mankind', *CJ* 63 (1968), 258–60.

THOMES, F. C. *Il problema degli eteri nella monarchia di Alessandro Magno*, Torino, 1955.

TIBILETTI, G. 'Alessandro e la liberazione delle città d'Asia minore', *Athenaeum* ns32 (1954), 3–22.

TODD, R. 'W. W. Tarn and the Alexander Ideal', *The Historian* 27 (1964), 48–55.

TRITSCH, W. *Olympias, die Mutter Alexanders des Grossen. Das Schicksal eines Weltreiches*, Frankfurt a.M., 1936.

VARIOUS. *Grecs et Barbares: Entretiens sur l'antiquité classique* 8, Geneva, 1962.

WALSER, G. 'Zur neueren Forschung über Alexander den Grossen', *Schweiz. Beitr. z. allgem. Gesch.* 14 (1956), 156–89; repr. in Griffith, *MP*, pp. 345–88.

WARDMAN, A. E. 'Plutarch and Alexander', *CQ* 49 (1955), 96–107.

WEINSTOCK, S. 'Victor and Invictus', *Harv. Theol. Rev.* 50 (1957), 211–47.

WELLES, C. B. 'Alexander's historical accomplishment', *GR* 12 (1965), 216–28.

'The discovery of Sarapis and the foundation of Alexandria', *Historia* 11 (1962), 271–98.

'The reliability of Ptolemy as an historian', *Misc. di studi alessandri in mem. A. Rostagni* (Torino, 1963), 101–16.

Royal Correspondence in the Hellenistic Period, New Haven, 1934.

WILBER, D. N. *Persepolis. The archaeology of Parsa, seat of the Persian Kings*, New York, 1969.

WILCKEN, U. *Alexander the Great*, tr. G. C. Richards; new edn with introduction, notes and bibliography by E. N. Borza (q.v.), New York, 1967.

'Die letzten Pläne Alexanders des Grossen', *Sitzungsb. d. preuss. Akad. d. Wiss. Ph-hist. kl.* (Berlin, 1937), 192–207.

'Philipp II von Makedonien und die Panhellenische Idee', ibid. (Berlin, 1929), 18 ff.

WOODCOCK, G. *The Greeks in India*, London, 1966.

WORMELL, D. E. W. 'The literary tradition concerning Hermias of Atarneus', *Yale Class. Stud. Phil.* 5 (1935), 55–92.

WUEST, F. R. *Philipp II von Makedonien und Griechenland in den Jahren von 346 bis 338*, München, 1938.

Note: This seems an appropriate place to express my deep gratitude to all those scholars who have so generously sent me copies of their books or offprints of their articles concerning Alexander, as well as corresponding with me on various related topics. Since the present study is very far from exhausting either my concern with, or my investigations into, fourth-century Greek history in general, and Philip and Alexander in particular, I would take it as an especial favour if students in this field would continue to keep me abreast of their researches and future projects. (There are, too, many titles in my bibliography to which access remains difficult, and where, again, I would be more than grateful for an offprint if any remain available.) As Professor W. K. C. Guthrie said when making a similar plea apropos a far more ambitious undertaking,* 'I cannot promise any adequate *quid pro quo*; I can only say that I shall be sincerely grateful.'

P. M. G.

* *A History of Greek Philosophy*, Cambridge, 1962, vol. I, p. xii.

Genealogical Table

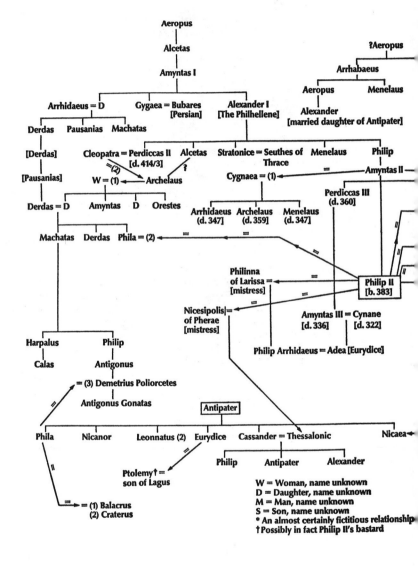

Aeropus

Alcetas

Amyntas I

Arrhidaeus = D   Gygaea = Bubares   Alexander I
                  [Persian]   [The Philhellene]

Derdas   Pausanias   Machatas

[Derdas]

[Pausanias]   Cleopatra = Perdiccas II   Alcetas   Stratonice = Seuthes of   Menelaus   Philip
                         [d. 414/3]   Thrace
               =(2)   Cygnaea = (1)
               W = (1)   Archelaus

Derdas = D   Amyntas   D   Orestes   Arrhidaeus   Archelaus   Menelaus
                                         (d. 347]   (d. 359]   (d. 347]

Machatas   Derdas   Phila = (2)

?Aeropus

Arrhabaeus

Aeropus   Menelaus

Alexander
[married daughter of Antipater]

Amyntas II

Perdiccas III
(d. 360)

Philip II
[b. 383]

Philinna
of Larissa =
[mistress]

Nicesipolis| =
of Pherae
[mistress]

Amyntas III = Cynane
[d. 336]   [d. 322]

Philip Arrhidaeus = Adea [Eurydice]

Harpalus   Philip

Calas   Antigonus

= (3) Demetrius Poliorcetes

Antigonus Gonatas

Antipater

Phila   Nicanor   Leonnatus (2)   Eurydice   Cassander = Thessalonic   Nicaea

                                     Ptolemy† =   Philip   Antipater   Alexander
                                     son of Lagus

= (1) Balacrus
(2) Craterus

W = Woman, name unknown
D = Daughter, name unknown
M = Man, name unknown
S = Son, name unknown
* An almost certainly fictitious relationship
† Possibly in fact Philip II's bastard

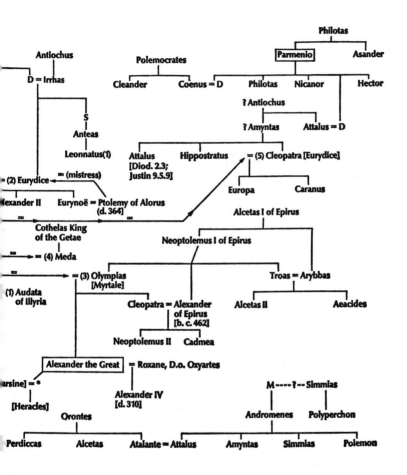

THE ARGEAD ROYAL HOUSE OF MACEDONIA
AND RELATED FAMILIES, FIFTH TO
FOURTH CENTURIES BC

General Index

Abdalonymus: 246
Abisares: 388, 389, 392, 403, 412
Abreas: 420
Abu Wajnam: 285
Abulites: 306, 444
Abydos: 64, 140, 168, 172, 214
Academy, Academics: 61–2
Acarnania: 42, 220
Achaea: 121
'Achaean harbour': 166
Achaemenid dynasty: 18, 50, 52,
    95, 167, 235, 240, 275, 295, 299,
    300, 304, 307, 308, 314, 315,
    319, 321, 326, 329, 355, 448,
    455, 468
Achilles: 5, 14, 17, 40, 41, 42, 55,
    60, 92, 118, 153, 161, 163, 165,
    167, 168, 175, 177, 267, 289,
    418, 452, 455, 465, 488, 508,
    532n.29, 541n.58
Ada of Caria, Queen: 41, 99, 193,
    194, 199–200, 223, 270
Adler, A.: 56, 487
Admana I.: 391, 393, 394
Admetus: 261
Adramyttium, Gulf of: 98
Adrasteian Plain, the: 176, 502,
    510, 566n.33
Adriatic: 130
Aeacids, the: 40
Aegae: 4, 23, 97, 102, 108, 113,
    163, 513n.13
Aegean, the: 29, 48, 72, 79, 191,
    192, 211, 216, 238, 239, 242,
    243, 254, 263, 271, 277, 280,
    440, 454, 520n.9, 537n.50,
    565n.7
Aegina, Aeginetan: 351n., 467

Aelian (cited): 167
Aeolid, Aeolis: 139, 187
Aeropus (I): 11
Aeropus (II), 111, 112
Aeschines: 21, 45, 46, 79, 116,
    118n.
Aeschylus: 32, 104
Aetolia: 461, 463
Afghanistan: 338, 350
Africa: 274, 351, 444, 469
Agamemnon: 6, 77, 166, 520n.8,
    564n.4
Agathon: 10
Agen, the: 415
Agenor, shrine of (Tyre): 261
Agesilaus (b.o. Agis III, q.v.):
    280, 491
Agis III, King of Sparta: 242,
    271, 277 and n., 280, 281, 308,
    309, 315, 317, 458, 544–5n.8
Agrianians, the: 90, 130, 131,
    133, 230
Ajax: 167
Ake: 266
Alabanda: 535n.21
Albania, Albanians: 2, 131, 142
Alcimachus: 83, 187, 188, 189,
    535n.13
Aleppo: 222, 282n.
Aleuadae, the: 27, 28
Alexander of Epirus (the
    Molossian): 38, 64, 97, 103,
    105, 117, 223 and n., 309,
    383n., 544–5n.8
Alexander of Lyncestis (s.o.
    Aeropus, q.v.): 111, 112, 115,
    141, 143, 184, 202–4, 220, 345,
    347, 349, 459, 524n.65,